Competency	Chapter
Professional Identity	
Practice Behavior Examples ...	
Serve as representatives of the profession, its mission, and its core values	1, 2, 14, 15
Know the profession's history	2, 7, 8, 9, 10, 11, 12, 13, 14, 15
Commit themselves to the profession's enhancement and to their own professional conduct and growth	2, 14, 15
Advocate for client access to the services of social work	2, 14, 15
Practice personal reflection and self-correction to assure continual professional development	2, 14, 15
Attend to professional roles and boundaries	14, 15
Demonstrate professional demeanor in behavior, appearance, and communication	
Engage in career-long learning	1, 14, 15
Use supervision and consultation	
Ethical Practice	
Practice Behavior Examples ...	
Obligation to conduct themselves ethically and engage in ethical decision-making	1, 14, 15
Know about the value base of the profession, its ethical standards, and relevant law	1, 7, 8, 14, 15
Recognize and manage personal values in a way that allows professional values to guide practice	1, 14, 15
Make ethical decisions by applying standards of the National Association of Social Workers Code of Ethics and, as applicable, of the International Federation of Social Workers/International Association of Schools of Social Work Ethics in Social Work, Statement of Principles	2, 12, 13, 14, 15
Tolerate ambiguity in resolving ethical conflicts	2, 13, 14, 15
Apply strategies of ethical reasoning to arrive at principled decisions	2, 13, 14
Critical Thinking	
Practice Behavior Examples ...	
Know about the principles of logic, scientific inquiry, and reasoned discernment	7, 8
Use critical thinking augmented by creativity and curiosity	3, 8, 12, 14, 15
Requires the synthesis and communication of relevant information	2, 5, 7, 8, 12, 13, 14, 15
Distinguish, appraise, and integrate multiple sources of knowledge, including research-based knowledge, and practice wisdom	12, 14, 15
Analyze models of assessment, prevention, intervention, and evaluation	
Demonstrate effective oral and written communication in working with individuals, families, groups, organizations, communities, and colleagues	

CSWE's Core Competencies and Practice Behaviors in this Text

Competency	Chapter
Diversity in Practice	
Practice Behavior Examples ...	
Understand how diversity characterizes and shapes the human experience and is critical to the formation of identity	3, 4, 5, 6, 14, 15
Understand the dimensions of diversity as the intersectionality of multiple factors including age, class, color, culture, disability, ethnicity, gender, gender identity and expression, immigration status, political ideology, race, religion, sex, and sexual orientation	1, 3, 4, 5, 6, 7, 8, 9, 10, 11, 12, 13, 14, 15
Appreciate that, as a consequence of difference, a person's life experiences may include oppression, poverty, marginalization, and alienation as well as privilege, power, and acclaim	1, 3, 4, 5, 6, 7, 8, 9, 10, 11, 12, 13, 14, 15
Recognize the extent to which a culture's structures and values may oppress, marginalize, alienate, or create or enhance privilege and power	1, 2, 3, 4, 5, 6, 7, 8, 9, 10, 11, 12, 13, 14, 15
Gain sufficient self-awareness to eliminate the influence of personal biases and values in working with diverse groups	1, 2, 9, 10, 13, 14, 15
Recognize and communicate their understanding of the importance of difference in shaping life experiences	3, 4, 7, 6, 10, 12, 13, 14, 15
View themselves as learners and engage those with whom they work as informants	1, 2, 14, 15
Human Rights & Justice	
Practice Behavior Examples ...	
Understand that each person, regardless of position in society, has basic human rights, such as freedom, safety, privacy, an adequate standard of living, health care, and education	2, 3, 4, 5, 6, 7, 8, 9, 10, 11, 12, 13, 14, 15
Recognize the global interconnections of oppression and be knowledgeable about theories of justice and strategies to promote human and civil rights	3, 6, 7, 8, 9, 10, 11, 12, 13, 14, 15
Incorporate social justice practices in organizations, institutions, and society to ensure that these basic human rights are distributed equitably and without prejudice	8, 9, 10, 11, 12, 13, 14, 15
Understand the forms and mechanisms of oppression and discrimination	1, 2, 3, 4, 5, 6, 7, 8, 9, 10, 11, 12, 13, 14, 15
Advocate for human rights and social and economic justice	2, 9, 10, 11, 12, 13, 14, 15
Engage in practices that advance social and economic justice	1, 12, 13, 14, 15
Research-Based Practice	
Practice Behavior Examples ...	
Use practice experience to inform research, employ evidence-based interventions, evaluate their own practice, and use research findings to improve practice, policy, and social service delivery	12, 13, 14, 15
Comprehend quantitative and qualitative research and understand scientific and ethical approaches to building knowledge	7

CSWE's Core Competencies and Practice Behaviors in this Text

Competency	Chapter
Use practice experience to inform scientific inquiry	7, 8, 9, 10
Use research evidence to inform practice	6, 9

Human Behavior

Practice Behavior Examples ...

Know about human behavior across the life course; the range of social systems in which people live; and the ways social systems promote or deter people in maintaining or achieving health and well-being	3, 4, 5, 6, 7, 8, 9, 10, 11, 12, 13, 14, 15
Apply theories and knowledge from the liberal arts to understand biological, social, cultural, psychological, and spiritual development	3, 4, 5, 6, 7, 8, 9, 10, 11, 12, 13, 14, 15
Utilize conceptual frameworks to guide the processes of assessment, intervention, and evaluation	
Critique and apply knowledge to understand person and environment	1, 7, 8, 9, 10, 11, 12, 13, 14, 15

Policy Practice

Practice Behavior Examples ...

Understand that policy affects service delivery and they actively engage in policy practice	2, 6, 9, 10, 11, 12, 13, 14, 15
Know the history and current structures of social policies and services; the role of policy in service delivery; and the role of practice in policy development	3, 4, 5, 6, 7, 8, 9, 10, 11, 12, 13, 14, 15
Analyze, formulate, and advocate for policies that advance social well-being	1, 2, 7, 8, 9, 10, 11, 12, 13, 14, 15
Collaborate with colleagues and clients for effective policy action	

Practice Contexts

Practice Behavior Examples ...

Keep informed, resourceful, and proactive in responding to evolving organizational, community, and societal contexts at all levels of practice	2, 8, 9, 10, 11, 12, 13, 14, 15
Recognize that the context of practice is dynamic, and use knowledge and skill to respond proactively	2, 14, 15
Continuously discover, appraise, and attend to changing locales, populations, scientific and technological developments, and emerging societal trends to provide relevant services	2, 13, 14, 15
Provide leadership in promoting sustainable changes in service delivery and practice to improve the quality of social services	14, 15

CSWE's Core Competencies and Practice Behaviors in this Text

Competency	Chapter
Engage, Assess, Intervene, Evaluate	
Practice Behavior Examples ...	
Identify, analyze, and implement evidence-based interventions designed to achieve client goals	
Use research and technological advances	
Evaluate program outcomes and practice effectiveness	2, 3, 12, 14, 15
Develop, analyze, advocate, and provide leadership for policies and services	14, 15
Promote social and economic justice	1, 2, 10, 11, 12, 13, 14, 15
A) Engagement	
Substantively and effectively prepare for action with individuals, families, groups, organizations, and communities	
Use empathy and other interpersonal skills	
Develop a mutually agreed-on focus of work and desired outcomes	
B) Assessment	
Collect, organize, and interpret client data	
Assess client strengths and limitations	
Develop mutually agreed-on intervention goals and objectives	
Select appropriate intervention strategies	
C) Intervention	
Initiate actions to achieve organizational goals	
Implement prevention interventions that enhance client capacities	
Help clients resolve problems	
Negotiate, mediate, and advocate for clients	
Facilitate transitions and endings	
D) Evaluation	
Critically analyze, monitor, and evaluate interventions	6, 7

MySearchLab Connections in this Text

In addition to the outstanding research and writing tools and a complete e-text in **MySearchLab**, this site contains a wealth of resources for social work students.

Below is a listing of the videos and readings found in **MySearchLab**, keyed to each chapter in this text.

In addition, a wealth of assessment questions (including those based on CSWE's core competencies) and useful online resources can be found under the appropriate chapters in **MySearchLab**.

VIDEOS

Working Mothers (1)

The Great Contradictions of the Twentieth Century (1)

* Social and Economic Justice: Understanding Forms of Oppression and Discrimination (2)

* Advocating for Human Rights and Justice (2)

* Professional Roles and Boundaries (2)

The Slave Trade (3)

Working Poor (3)

Atlantic Connections: Sugar, Smallpox, and Slavery (4)

The American Revolution as different Americans saw it (5)

Slavery and the Constitution (5)

Women in the Workplace 1904 (6)

The Great Migration (6)

Ellis Island Immigrants 1903 (6)

African-American Women and the Struggle for Civil Rights (7)

Punching the Clock (7)

Trials of Racial Identity in Nineteenth-Century America (8)

The Lives of Southern Women (8)

The Women's Rights Movement in Nineteenth-Century America (8)

Responding to the Great Depression: Whose New Deal? (9)

Rosie The Riveter (10)

Rev. Dr. Martin Luther King (10)

Creating Apartheid in South Africa (10)

English—Who Needs it (11)

Abortion Wars (11)

* Understanding Forms of Oppression and Discrimination (11)

* Engaging the Client to Share Their Experiences (12)

* Learning From the Client to Co-create an Action Plan (13)

* Developing an Action Plan (13)

The Great Contradictions of the Twentieth Century (13)

The Historical Significance of the 2008 Presidential Election (13)

Marrying Kind (14)

* Keeping Up With Shifting Contexts (14)

* Attending to Changes and Relevant Services (14)

* Providing Leadership to Promote Change (14)

MS-13 Gang Life (15)

Intersex (15)

Questioning Islamic Traditions (15)

The In-Crowd and Social Cruelty (15)

---

* = CSWE Core Competency Asset

Δ = Case Study

MySearchLab Connections in this Text

READINGS

* Diversity in Practice (1)
* Human Rights and Justice (1)
  Richard Wright, "Are We Solving America's Race Problem?" (1945) (1)
* Policy Practice (2)
* Professional Identity (2)
  Women on the Breadlines (1932) (3)
  Andrew Carnegie, "Wealth," North American Review (1889) (4)
  Anne Bradstreet, Before the Birth of One of Her Children (c. 1650) (5)
  Helen Hunt Jackson, from A Century of Dishonor (6)
  Susan B. Anthony, The "New Departure" for Women (1873) (6)
  Jane Addams, "Ballots Necessary for Women" (1906) (7)
  Caroline Manning, The Immigrant Woman and Her Job (1930) (7)
  Abraham Lincoln, The Emancipation Proclamation (7)
  Secretary of Interior's Congressional Report on Indian Affairs (1887) (7)
  Jane Addams, from Twenty Years at Hull House (1910) (7)
  Keating-Owen Child Labor Act of 1916 (8)
  Upton Sinclair, from The Jungle (1905) (8)
  Herbert Croly, from Progressive Democracy (1914) (8)
  Negro Workers and Recovery (1934) (9)
  Flint Sit-Down Strike (1936) (9)
  John Lewis, Address at the March on Washington (1963) (10)
  Fannie Lou Hammer, Voting Rights in Mississippi (1962-1964) (10)
  Stokely Carmichael and "Black Power" (1966) (10)
  Student Nonviolent Coordinating Committee, Statement of Purpose (1960) (10)
  Southern Manifesto on Integration (1956) (10)
  Cesar Chavez, from "He Showed Us the Way" (April 1978) (11)
  The Gay Liberation Front, Come Out (1970) (11)
  Lyndon B. Johnson, The War on Poverty, (1964) (11)
  Tori Derricotte, Black in a White Neighborhood (1977–1978) (11)
  Jesse Jackson, Common Ground (1988) (12)
Δ Ethical Dilemmas (13)
Δ Frank (13)
Δ A Narrative in New Masculinity (14)
Δ Community to Community: A Unique Response to Long Term Disaster Relief (14)
Δ Volunteer Experiences with the Neighbors Helping Neighbors Program (14)
Δ Annie (14)
Δ Social Workers Involved in Political Action (15)
Δ Dylan James: A Case in School Social Work (15)
Δ Chelsea Green Space and the Power Plant (15)

---

* = CSWE Core Competency Asset

Δ = Case Study

SEVENTH EDITION

A New History of Social Welfare

Phyllis J. Day

with

Jerome H. Schiele
University of Georgia

PEARSON

Boston   Columbus   Indianapolis   New York   San Francisco   Upper Saddle River
Amsterdam   Cape Town   Dubai   London   Madrid   Milan   Munich   Paris   Montreal   Toronto
Delhi   Mexico City   Sao Paulo   Sydney   Hong Kong   Seoul   Singapore   Taipei   Tokyo

Editorial Director: Craig Campanella
Executive Editor: Ashley Dodge
Editorial Product Manager: Carly Czech
Editorial Assistant: Nicole Suddeth
VP/Director of Marketing: Brandy Dawson
Executive Marketing Manager: Wendy Albert
Marketing Assistant: Frank Alarcon
Senior Digital Media Editor: Paul Deluca
Production Manager: Meghan DeMaio

Creative Director: Jayne Conte
Cover Designer: Karen Salzbach
Cover Image: ©Nito/Fotolia
Editorial Production and Composition Service:
  Sneha Pant/PreMediaGlobal
Interior Design: Joyce Weston Design
Printer/Binder: Edwards Brothers
Cover Printer: Lehigh-Phoenix Color

Credits appear on Page 511, which constitutes an extension of the copyright page.

Library of Congress Cataloging-in-Publication Data
Day, Phyllis J.
  A new history of social welfare / Phyllis J. Day; with Jerome H. Schiele. — 7th ed.
    p. cm.
  Includes index.
  ISBN-13: 978-0-205-05273-8
  ISBN-10: 0-205-05273-8
 1. United States—Social policy.   2. Social policy.   3. Public welfare—United States—History.
 4. Public welfare—History.   I. Schiele, Jerome H.   II. Title.
  HN57.D33 2013
  361.6'10973—dc23
                                                                    2012012779

8   17

Student Edition
ISBN-10: 0-205-05273-8
ISBN-13: 978-0-205-05273-8

Instructor Edition
ISBN-10: 0-205-05365-3
ISBN-13: 978-0-205-05365-0

à la Carte Edition
ISBN-10: 0-205-05311-4
ISBN-13: 978-0-205-05311-7

Contents

3. The Beginnings of Social Welfare   58

4. Feudalism and the Welfare State   83

6. America to the Civil War   151

7. The American Welfare State Begins   189

8. The Progressive Era, War, and Recovery   225

9. The Great Depression and Social Security for Americans   260

10. Civil and Welfare Rights in the New Reform Era 295

Preface

Traditionally, a preface is the place to thank those who have contributed to the accomplishment that is a book. Throughout my life, people have touched me with their feelings, thoughts, and knowledge, and this book is, in a very true sense, a part of me that was part of them. My teachers, my colleagues, my students, my friends, my family of origin and of marriage—all who participated in my life have contributed.

The book tries to answer the "why" of social welfare. In great part, it is a history of those involved in the social welfare institution not as wielders but as subjects, victims, recipients, and clients. It seeks to redress in part the loss of history for women, nonwhite people, and other groups oppressed by social institutions, and to relate intimately the place of the labor force and working people with the social welfare institution. The breadth of the book ensures its failure to adequately cover its aspirations. I am well aware of much left undone, through lack of either space/time or knowledge. However, it is a beginning from which students and others can seek more deeply and, hopefully, fill in its blanks.

A New History of Social Welfare looks at the earliest forces for both aspects of social welfare: social treatment and social control. These themes are carried forward from a perspective that considers the synergistic relationships of economy, polity, religion, and social welfare and asks the "why" of treatment and/or control. To this end, I view the ways people related to each other from early history within their societal contexts and the needs of society either to provide care for valued members or to ensure enough members for social tasks.

Because social welfare is so deeply affected by institutional racism, sexism, classism, and "otherism," the historical and evolutionary sources of these "isms" are given a great deal of attention. One of the results of institutional discrimination has been an "elimination" of history, or a selective compilation of a series of achievements of men who are generally Caucasian or Aryan and of the elite and/or warrior classes. That reading of history ignores or belittles the contributions of women, nonwhite people, and the poor laborers on whose backs history occurred. *A New History* hopefully provides new or reinterpreted historical information to set a less biased social context.

Of particular import in this perspective is the analysis of humankind's relationships with deity—religions—both in providing charity and in elaborating on or perpetuating social control. This dichotomy of religiously legitimated charity and control underlies the development of social welfare in all its ramifications, the values that provide the push to helping or controlling "others" and the ways in which the profession of social work itself came into being and grew. Religions are synergistically related to other major institutions of society, whether we speak of European feudalism, the European invasions of the Western Hemisphere, colonial America, the Progressive movement of the early 1900s, the conservative backlash of the Reagan era, the power of the Far Right and the Religious Right to destroy the safety net of the poor or the makings of an imperialist president in the new millennium. This synergism, then, is the key to the historical analysis of social welfare and the social work profession.

When I wrote the first edition of the book in the Reagan years, the conservative backlash occurring seemed to be just a glitch to be overcome. By the 1990s, I saw that the Reagan years were probably a permanent trend to ultimately reverse the social morality we had over the past 300 years. Under policies endorsed by the presidential administrations of George H. W. Bush, Bill Clinton, and George W. Bush, we destroyed programs that underlaid our social responsibility. Rather than replacing them, we now simply refuse to look at the consequences. Social responsibility and morality have taken a back seat to greed at both national and international levels. Our world has narrowed, but worse, we as individuals and as a nation have narrowed, condensed, and encapsulated ourselves. We have no space, no heart, for others, and this plays itself out in our social policies.

While social policies continue to be made every day, only time will tell if the lessons learned from history will have impact on future social work practice and the evolution of the social welfare institution. I hope, at the very least, that events, values, and perspectives presented here will serve social work students well in their attempts to find social justice for their future clients. The many fine policy analysis texts now extant can provide frameworks for analyzing the "what" and "how" of social welfare, and perhaps *A New History* can help define the "why."

And now to thank those who helped me with this project. The greatest influence on the book and on my life was my mother, Nora Seymour Phelps, dead these many years. She gave me, from the beginning of my life, the courage to follow my convictions and search for reality no matter where the path led. Although her heart finally failed her, her spirit never did. Also, my sisters contributed more than they knew with strength, endurance, and courage throughout their hard lives and harder deaths: Avah, who always knew that "things will be better tomorrow"; Evah, with her gentle courage; and Lois, who never gave up and always faced the world with valor. Thanks also to my mentors, Rosemary C. Sarri, who serves as a model, however unattainable, for more women than she knows; and John E. Tropman, who always believed in me. My gratitude to dear friends Joan Bowker, Keetjie Ramo, Harry Macy, and Mary Ann Foley, all of whom have saved my life in ways they will never know; and to my former husband, Jerald R. Day, and my children—Jerry II, Nora Gaye, Merry Rose, Sean, and Joy Alyssa.

For the first edition, I continue to thank the editors and personnel at Prentice Hall/ over the past more than 25 years: Nancy Roberts, Marianne Peters, Judy Fifer, Julie Cancio, Jennifer Miller, Jacqueline Aaron, Michael Granger, Patricia Quinlin, and Annemarie Kennedy.

Also, many thanks to my reviewers of all editions of this text, including Albert Roberts, Indiana University; George Siefert, Jr., Daemen College; Jack Otis, University of Texas–Austin; Patricia K. Cianciolo, Northern Michigan University; Paul H. Stuart, University of Alabama; Marcia B. Cohen, University of New England; Nancy L. Mary, California State University–San Bernadino; James D. Stafford, University of Mississippi; Marina Barnett, Temple University; Karen A. Ford, James Madison University; Walter Pierce, Barry University; and Beverly Stadum, St. Cloud State University. Thanks for the seventh edition go to Ashley Dodge, Carly Czech, Nicole Suddeth, Greg Johnson, Meghan DeMaio, and Sneha Pant.

Special thanks also to my colleague, Professor Jerome H. Schiele of the University of Georgia, for his help in developing the Afrocentric perspective, defining White Privilege as a social value, and collaborating with me in preparing this seventh edition of *A New History* of Social Welfare for publication.

Thanks also to all my colleagues in social work education who have taken *A New History* to heart for their classes, and to students who have read it and found it useful in their lives. I hope you enjoy the new edition.

PHYLLIS J. DAY, MSW, MA, PH.D.
WITH
JEROME H. SCHIELE, D.S.W.

Dedicated to my mother, Nora Isabel Seymour Phelps 1892–1957, who loved unconditionally and taught me unconditional love, and to all women for their wisdom, strength, courage, and endurance.

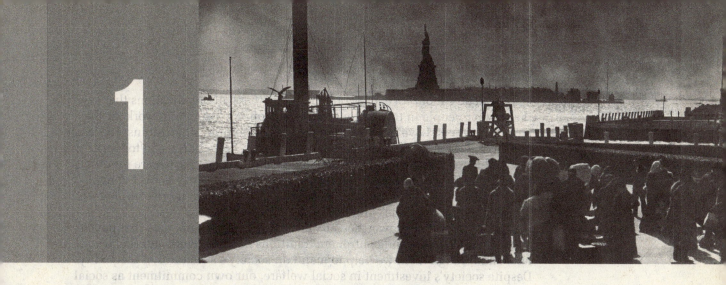

1

Values In Social Welfare

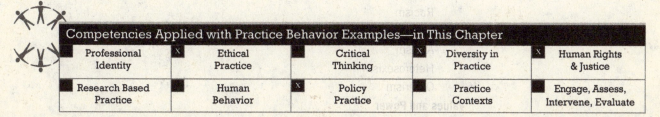

Competencies Applied with Practice Behavior Examples—in This Chapter				
Professional Identity	X Ethical Practice	Critical Thinking	X Diversity in Practice	X Human Rights & Justice
Research Based Practice	Human Behavior	X Policy Practice	Practice Contexts	Engage, Assess, Intervene, Evaluate

Once upon a time . . .

... love is not enough. Social welfare and the profession of social work are much more complex, and we must not let fairy tales blind us.

This is a book about love: of people helping others, of organizations that ease the way for people in trouble, and of people joining together to work for the benefit of others. Love is not simply the idea of helping others; it inspires each of us to enter the field of human services, to share our efforts, and to work for the well-being of humanity. Our first and best intentions are to care for others, to help the disadvantaged "live happily ever after." But love is not enough. Social welfare and the profession of social work are much more complex, and we must not let fairy tales blind us.

Love's dark side is power; society, through social welfare, uses that power to control. Both help and control are traditions of social work and social welfare, and through them we help to maintain society's structures of inequality. Despite society's investment in social welfare, our own commitment as social workers, or the willingness or ability of our clients, we will not be able to change those structures unless we understand both sides of social welfare. As it is, our targets for blame and change are misplaced. We blame our clients when they fail despite our efforts, they blame themselves for failure, and society blames both clients and social workers for wasted money and lost effort

Times and Events

Welfare based on the synergistic evolution of values . . . resulting from interplay of politics, economics, and religion, and based on society's deliberate decisions concerning full personhood in a society.

The "whys" of discrimination against the poor, the elderly, gays, or ethnic minorities

Social Treatment and Social Control

American Social Values

- Judaeo-Christian Charity
- Democratic Egalitarianism and Individualism
- Work Ethic and Capitalism
- Social Darwinism
- New Puritanism
- Patriarchy
- White Privilege
- Marriage and the Nuclear Family
- The American Ideal

Issues of Discrimination: Prejudice with

- Power
- Classism and poverty
- Racism
- Sexism
- Ageism
- Heterosexism
- Otherism

Values and Power

when poverty continues, deviant behaviors rise, and clients remain ungrateful and unrepentant. To understand this, we must begin to question the *why* of social welfare and social work.

Why is a good question, one we should ask more often. Why have our welfare rolls grown, and why is there hunger in America? Why is there more crime and delinquency? Why are so many people homeless? Why are mental health clinics doing a booming business? Why are there so many people with problems, and why are our prisons overflowing? Why do the costs of all forms of social welfare continue to rise? The answers lie in understanding the values that created society's institutions, how social welfare evolves from the interactions among these institutions, and what purposes social welfare really serves.

A New History will help us answer these questions. First, we must understand that social welfare does not stand alone in any society. Across human evolution, across societies, and across time, the dynamic, ever-changing interactions of any society's polity, economy, and dominant religion create societal values. These, in turn, determine concepts of social problems and construct a society's social welfare institution to deal with them. In our society, social welfare is comprised of and vies with aspects of religion, polity, and economy, and may be carried out by social work, its action arm, or a variety of other agents such as bureaucrats, clerks, religious bodies, and so on (Figure 1.1).

A New History considers the trends and choices that have shaped attitudes toward those involved in social welfare—women with dependent children, the poor, the aged; people of ethnic, cultural, or religious minorities; those with physical, emotional, or mental disabilities; and anyone not somehow in accord with current standards of behavior, such as people who are gay, who are unmarried with children, who do not work. The book's purpose is descriptive rather than analytical and is not meant to provide policy analysis guidelines, *except* that our major values and their pursuant ideologies always underlie present and emergent policies. Looking at values, we can discover the "why" of refusing financial aid to dependent children after two years in the Temporary Assistance to Needy Families (TANF) program; the "why" of denying marriage privileges to people of nontraditional sexual orientations; the "why" of over-representation in prisons of people of ethnic minorities; the "why" of denying adequate prescription financing for the elderly.

We lay the groundwork for answering questions by looking at the place of social work and social welfare in society. First, we look at American social values; second, at issues of poverty and classism; and finally, at institutional discrimination in American society. In the process, we will discover the synergistic sources and meanings of our values and their impact on perceptions and practices of social welfare. To do this, we must place some of our own beliefs

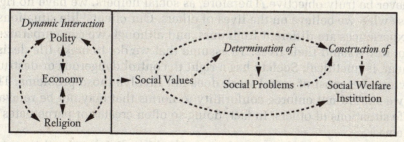

Figure 1.1
Society's Creation of the Social Welfare Institution

and values in abeyance, for much of what we "know" is, in fact, value. This is not an easy task, but it is essential.

VALUES IN SOCIAL WELFARE

Social welfare in any society has two major purposes: social treatment (helping) and social control. We easily agree with the helping purpose but are generally unaware of the social control function of social welfare hidden in ideas about equality and what we consider our "right" to change our clients. Society needs certain social controls, for some behaviors must be regulated so that interdependent people can live and work together. However, not all such control is positive, especially when aimed at our most vulnerable citizens. Because our clients need our help, they must meet our (and society's) demands. Seldom do they participate in social welfare decisions that affect their lives, and the price they pay for our help is often their personal freedom.

Our personal, societal, and social work values, therefore, are perhaps the most important factors in the practice of social work. Naomi Brill pointed out that

> We hold that all people are equal, but that those who do not work are less equal. . . . We hold that individual life has worth, but that only the fit should survive. We believe that we are responsible for each other, but that those who are dependent upon others for their living are of less worth.

She said further that human service workers are walking value systems, and that they must become aware of those values, evaluate them rationally, and change the irrational ones.[1] Paternalism, or the idea that we know what is good for others, is another problem. Because *we* have succeeded, we think we have the right to impose our values and decisions on those who have not. It implies that our clients lack something, that they are less than whole people who

> need to be brought up to our . . . levels. . . . [W]e, as experts and whole persons, have the ability, knowledge and the right to round out, remake, fulfill, or "pull [them] up" . . . there is a "right way" which the expert knows, and a "wrong way" which the client does that underlies and colors the whole intervention process.[2]

Values permeate social welfare, whatever the perspective, culture, or period of history: what we "ought to" provide or how we "ought to" deal with deviants. Every perception or reaction is value-laden and value-based, and we can never be truly objective. Therefore, as social helpers, we have no right to impose what we believe on the lives of others. Our clients' life situations and life experiences are different from ours, and although we can empathize, we cannot understand their lives. To assume that we do, to make life decisions for them, is unethical. Society has a right to control dangerous or destructive behaviors, but most of social work does not involve those problems. Therefore, we should not enforce conformity to norms that may not be relevant to the life situations of others. In fact, doing so often creates or perpetuates their problems.

Our attitudes and values are often couched in religious, moral, or patriotic terms, and these attitudes and values are so much a part of our lives that we

Our clients' life situations and life experiences are different from ours, and although we can empathize, we cannot understand their lives.

think they are facts rather than beliefs. A fact is the quality of being actual or having objective reality,[3] whereas a value is something intrinsically desirable.[4] In more practical terms, a fact is the way things are, and a value is how we wish they were.[5] We "know" both facts and values, but we may confuse them and base important judgments on what we wish rather than on what is. We should always test what we "know" by remembering that fact is something that has existed throughout history and in every culture. Everything else is value.

What Are Values?

In addition to being the way we wish things were, values have four identifiable characteristics, according to Hunter and Saleeby.[6]

- Values are *conceptual abstractions* drawn from immediate experience—from what we ourselves have learned about the world. Our unique experiences make each value unique to each of us (and to our clients).
- Values are *affectively charged for emotional mobilization*; that is, they make us want to take action or make us feel emotionally positive or negative about a situation. Racism, for example, makes us angry when we see it in others, and perhaps embarrassed or unhappy when we see it in ourselves, and we want to do something about the problem.
- Values are *criteria by which our goals are chosen*. For example, abortion is a tremendously charged value in our society. Almost every one of us takes a stand on abortion, based on whether we believe in the right of every fetus to survive or the right of every woman to control her own body. We set goals about abortion for ourselves and often work to set abortion standards for others.
- Values are *important rather than trivial concerns*. We may prefer the color blue, or to go to one university rather than another, but these issues do not stir us to emotionally charged action. Rather, issues that involve basic questions of life, death, freedom, our rights as citizens or as workers, the concern we have for others—these are concerns that move us to anger, pride, fear, hope, or love and to actions to attain or resolve these emotions.

Miringoff and Opdycke say that values

are always in a state of change; sometimes they merge to form coherent systems, sometimes they have vague relationships, often they are in conflict. . . . [They] may be influenced by occupation, race, age, class position, or by external factors such as changing economic conditions and new norms of social behavior.[7]

Foundations of Charity and Control

According to *Webster's New Collegiate Dictionary*, 1980, "a society is an enduring and cooperating social group whose members have developed organized patterns of relationships through interaction with one another."[8] To find where dominant American values come from, or the reasons for the way we treat others, we must trace our way to two human characteristics so important that they are doctrines basic to

Ethical Practice

Practice Behavior Example: Recognize and manage personal values in a way that allows professional values to guide practice.

Critical Thinking Question: Reflect upon your own values and identify where they align and differ from the NASW code of ethics. How will you manage your own personal values while maintaining the code of ethics?

society. The first is *mutual aid*; the second is *protection from others and otherness*. These characteristics are, respectively, the bases of values concerning social treatment and social control. Often contradictory, they have caused major dilemmas in the way our social welfare institution works.

For early humankind, protection and aid included actions against predators (animal or human) and care for dependents (at first probably a mother–child bond). The need for defense resulted in fears of outsiders and otherness, whereas bonding was extrapolated into mutual aid in the wider society. As families bonded together to share food and protection, mutual aid expanded to include other cooperative efforts such as building, hunting, and farming. Care of children expanded to include caring for the helpless or valued members of the tribe, often the elders who had been instrumental in leadership or religious activities. In tandem with mutual aid, the abhorrence of otherness and defense against it meant protection of herds and homes from predators and, later, aggression to win more land and wealth from others. Eventually, fear and hatred of those outside the kin group were extended to in-group people who were "different" or posed a threat to tribal solidarity. A reluctance to share with others became firmly based, and today it is a reluctance to help those who do not "fit in."

The results of fear of otherness and a reluctance to share are not universal cultural themes. Considerable variation exists in how human beings have interacted with each other in relation to otherness and the distribution of material resources. To explain this human diversity, historian Cheikh Anta Diop offers a two cradle thesis of human societies.[9] Diop suggests that in antiquity, there were two distinct cultures or cradles: the northern and southern cradles. The northern cradle was associated with what we now know is Europe, including the middle east, and the southern cradle was associated with what we now call Africa. Diop contends that the northern cradle was characterized by a patrilineal and patriarchal social order, and an individualistic and xenophobic cultural milieu. In contrast, the southern cradle was characterized by a matrilineal and matriarchal social order and a collectivistic and xenophilic cultural environment. We posit that the American cultural value thrust appears to affirm more of the northern than southern cradle and that these attributes significantly shape dominant social welfare values in the United States.

DOMINANT AMERICAN SOCIAL VALUES

Many values affect the human services, and all seem so positive that we rarely question them even when they contradict one another. However positive they may be for society in general, they can be intensely negative for certain groups in our society, such as women, children, the unemployed, and people of minority groups.

Values, of course, are the major premises by which we formulate our ideologies and are the bases for social welfare policies and practices. They are the motivations for our plans and create the blueprints for action. At the same time, they circumscribe our willingness to act. For example, our Judaeo-Christian values demand help for those in need, yet work ethic, marriage, and Puritan morality values determine that certain people—for example, women who have children out of wedlock or homeless men without jobs—are not worthy of aid. This limits financial aid except in combination with work-related programs, even when there are no jobs. Underlying every social welfare problem or program is this progression from values to ideology to policy, plan, and action. In addition, at each step (policy, plan, and action) more values and their derivative ideologies come into play.

The term *dominant American social values* is used to connote that although the United States is a multicultural society, there are values that tend to permeate the American social landscape. These values reflect the history, experiences, and worldviews of those who control the major political, economic, and religious institutions in the United States. We contend that those in power not only control the material resources of a society, but they also regulate our symbolic and internal lives that influence the values we endorse.

Among the most basic of these values are

- Judaeo-Christian charity values
- Democratic egalitarianism and individualism
- The Protestant work ethic and capitalism
- Social Darwinism
- The New Puritanism
- Patriarchy
- White Privilege
- Marriage and the nuclear family
- The "American Ideal."

Judaeo-Christian Charity Values

Judaeo-Christian charity values are based, first, on Judaic teachings of social justice and, second, on the teachings of Jesus as practiced in the early centuries of Christianity. They are *nonsectarian and social* rather than *religious*, and their major thrust is that those in need have a right to help and society has an obligation to provide for them. As society's primary social ethics, they are the bases for social altruism. Their prescriptions of love and charity are probably the reasons that people enter the human services.

Judaic prophets as early as Amos, in the eighth century B.C.E., enjoined people to charity as social justice and religious obligation. They believed that human relationships mirror those between deity and humanity, and that people must care for one another as God cares for them. Every person has intrinsic worth, and charity should be given without thought of self. Early Christian traditions reiterated and strengthened the prophetic Judaic teachings, adding ideas of equality for women. Jesus advocated for the poor and helpless, calling for justice for women, the poor, children, and other unfortunates. However, as time wore on, most of this advocacy position was lost.

If Judaeo-Christian values still underlaid social welfare, we would see a far different America. No one would be without enough food, clothing, or shelter. Every child would be assured of equal opportunity in the system, and society would take responsibility for the disadvantaged. Although work for self-support would still be encouraged, a person in need could seek help without stigma. Failure would not be blamed on the individual but on the social structures that prevented success. Oppression and exploitation would not exist, and success would be to invest in the lives of others rather than in personal wealth for oneself.

Social work *ethics* reflect Judaeo-Christian values, but social work *practice* owes more to other, more individualistic values. These distinctions help us to understand why our social programs are not always socially just and why our clients cannot succeed despite our "good works." Although we may have chosen social work as our profession because of its ethical Judaeo-Christian values, society's goals for social welfare are more accurately based on more restrictive values.

In the first decade of the twenty-first century, charity values continue to evolve in at least three ways, though their finished forms will be difficult to assess. First is a clear attempt to release the national government from the burden of social welfare, moving it to local levels by "guilting" religions to take up welfare responsibilities. President George H. W. Bush conceptualized this as becoming a "thousand points of light." "Faith-based initiatives" was the rallying cry, with government support going to religious agencies rather than social welfare or social work programs. Second is the movement of social welfare tasks, such as public assistance, food stamp allotments, prisons, and hospitals, to private enterprise, a trend championed by President George W. Bush. To date, neither move has been as effective as government programs, since massive problems require much more than stop-gap local measures by religious groups or profit-oriented corporations. The third is perhaps more interesting. Not particularly religion-oriented, its genesis arises from the nascent global society and has been conceptualized by individuals made spectacularly wealthy by extra-national business, such as Bill and Melinda Gates or Warren Buffett. This incipient movement, almost grass roots in nature, is oriented to globally-inspired needs such as hunger or HIV/AIDS, where problems are recognized and attacked with all weapons at hand, usually involving great sums of money.

Democratic Egalitarianism and Individualism

Democratic egalitarianism was a primary tenet in the founding of the United States: All citizens are equal before the law, and no one has privileges based on class, heritage, wealth, or other factors irrelevant to citizenship. No citizen is better than any other, and all can share equally in societal decision making through either direct vote or representation. Although an equal share of resources is not guaranteed, the right to opportunities such as education and employment is.

Despite the ideal, in practice we do not have equality in America. Originally, the Constitution gave citizenship only to male property-holders, denying it to women, the propertyless, white ethnic immigrants, and people of color—primarily Native Americans, people of African descent, Hispanics, and Asians. Although all native-born men (except for Native Americans) became full citizens after the Civil War, women could not vote until 1918, and Native Americans gained citizenship even later. The rights of African Americans were denied by *fiat* until the Civil Rights Act of 1964, and women are still denied explicit equal rights under national law. In addition, custom restricts achievement opportunities for people of color, women, and other minority groups. Moreover, choice of candidates and policies often depends on wealth and power. Poor people have little power to choose and middle-class people choose among those selected by the elite. Still, our persistent belief in American equal opportunity has major impact on our assessment of client motivations and capability.

Related closely to egalitarianism is individualism: the ideal of individual effort and personal motivation by which any American can achieve success. It is a frontier ideology, coming from early days in America when anyone could win success in the new world of free land. Today, the value persists in the ideas that there are frontiers of the mind and that education, technology, and hard work can win wealth and success if only we try hard enough. We must be self-reliant—in control of and responsible for our own lives—and sheer effort will bring success. To ask for help from others is an admission of weakness, and failure to achieve—money, happiness, status, whatever—is the fault of the individual rather than society.

From this comes our tendency to blame the victim, to place the burden of failure on personal lack of effort. We believe that people are poor because they will not work rather than because of high unemployment. A person who is robbed or raped should not have been where such crimes could happen, or in some way "asked for it." The aged poor should have planned better for retirement, and poor children are hungry because their parents fail rather than because society does not provide social insurance. Our "blanket value" of individual responsibility exonerates society and confirms personal failure for those who cannot or do not reach "success."

Success has many meanings. Our responsibility is to help clients to achieve their own successes, not ours. Moreover, because American society is neither fully egalitarian nor democratic, we realize that institutional discrimination and class stratification keep some people from achieving success regardless of their efforts. Opportunities do not accrue automatically with citizenship, and blaming the victim does not overcome structural barriers to success.

The Protestant Work Ethic and Capitalism

The Protestant work ethic is the moral basis for American capitalism: an economic system in which profit through business enterprise is mostly uncontrolled by governments. Bonacich says,

> Capitalism . . . depends . . . on exploiting the labor of the [poor]. . . .
> For this reason, [the wealthy] have an interest in [poverty], since if there
> were no have-nots, there could be no one to work for them, no one to rent
> their buildings, no one from whom wealth could be derived. This . . .
> means that capitalist societies . . . can never rid [themselves] of poverty.
> Poverty is the basis of wealth. The dependency of the rich on the poor is
> the fundamental hidden reality of this system.[10]

A social rather than an economic or religious creed, the Protestant ethic is a value accepted by most Americans regardless of religion. Its complex of values includes individualism, personal achievement and worth, the morality of wealth, and, for America, patriotism. Work for economic gain is the way to success, a sign of personal morality, and a moral obligation. Conversely, poverty and public dependency demonstrate immorality.

The work ethic springs from the mercantilist movement of the early Middle Ages and the Protestant Reformation. Martin Luther's belief in work as a calling and John Calvin's teachings on predestination came to mean that those predestined to salvation were identifiable by their wealth. If wealth showed morality, then surely poverty demonstrated immorality. With this line of reasoning, the wealthy justified both their wealth and their exploitation of workers to accumulate it; the rich felt they had a moral obligation to save the poor by making them work. Surplus production could then be sold and profits reinvested to make more profits—the "just rewards" of the wealthy.

Our definitions of *worthy* and *unworthy poor* come from that definition of the Protestant work ethic. The worthy poor are those who cannot work—the aged or disabled, for example. However, people who can work should, even if there is no work—they "can work if they want to" or "can support their families if they work hard enough." The doctrine of personal fault, then as now, relieved the wealthy of the economic burden of supporting the poor and gave them "religious credit" for not furthering the immorality of pauperism. We still believe that poverty is the result of laziness or degeneracy. The work ethic is so important a value in American society that we do not see who the poor are: young children, mothers who care for them, the aged, and the disabled. Although changing technologies and government programs create new unemployment and underemployment, because of the work ethic we insist that anyone who wants to work can earn enough to live on.

Social Darwinism

Darwinism, a biological theory never intended to become economic, says that organisms unable to survive in an ecological niche will die out. In the nineteenth century, Malthus extrapolated the theory into a social and economic one: Population trends predicted, to him, a future teeming with poor people supported by "worthy" hard workers. This theory became known as social Darwinism, which said that state support of the poor was against the laws of "economic nature" and that the lives of people who were "economically unfit" should not be saved by giving them public assistance. Moreover, it claimed they were poor by choice because of moral degeneracy, and so *should* perish. Any society continuing to aid them would be destroyed by their immorality.

Today, social Darwinist attitudes infect all of society's institutions. Founded on the economic issue of support for the poor, stigma spreads insidiously to groups *likely* to be poor, legitimating discrimination and exploitation against them *regardless* of their economic situations. Politically speaking, this maintains the status quo for the power elite. The idea that "they are not as good as us" permeates society's institutions and is directed against, among others, people of color; those of "different" religions; homosexuals denied equal family or job benefits; people differently abled physically, mentally, or emotionally; elders neglected in nursing homes or abused by their caretakers; and, of course, the poor, particularly mothers and their dependent children. Sadly, the TANF program classes children in their parents' economic status, and after two years of public assistance, they too become "unfit" to receive society's help.

Although rarely espoused openly today, social Darwinism exists covertly in many welfare policies and programs and in the public idiom. Along with the Protestant work ethic, it opposes Judaeo-Christian charity values and helps to explain our society's loathing of "reliefers." Public assistance programs demonstrate the value clearly in low grants, stigmatization of recipients, insensitive and irrelevant eligibility testing, and attempts to put recipients to work regardless of wage or personal situations. We still believe that supporting the poor contributes to their immorality, although we are blind to the support we give to the wealthy through tax breaks and government support of and investment in corporations.

The New Puritanism

Arising from political, economic, and religious changes in the fourteenth century, New Puritanism now permeates American society. It is an essential political thrust of the Religious Right, a powerful lobby group for legislation to enforce compliance to the patriarchal and Puritan values of the past. Puritan values include chastity, particularly for women; honesty in dealing with others; abstinence from things defined by religion and custom as immoral, such as promiscuity, gambling, and the use of alcohol or drugs to excess; and "proper" behavior (that is, behavior that will not offend others). Puritan morality also emphasizes the sanctity of marriage and family and patriarchal authority in the home and condemns lifestyles such as communal living and homosexuality.

The New Puritanism is somewhat analogous to what David Wagner calls the "New Temperance," a peculiarly American ideology that obsesses on sin and vice. It particularly concerns substance abuse, sexual behaviors, food and fitness, and suspect freedom of speech issues such as pornography, lewd language, and the content of music, movies, and so forth.[11] He contends that this constitutes a culturally normative "consensus war . . . primarily against the working class, ethnic and racial minorities, and poor people. . . ."[12] The result of this is to further the "otherization" of such groups and make them more subject to political control.

The Religious Right, made up primarily of Protestants with a sprinkling of Catholics and Jews, uses modern technology in its battles: Television brings the moral campaign into our homes and computer technology enables immediate contact with adherents on action issues. This New Puritanism has catapulted people from the radical Right into office, removed liberal incumbents, and sponsored laws and movements that reinforce religious beliefs on women's career and reproductive choices, prayer in school, and other moral issues. Militant on the side of domestic law and order, it advocates national insularity and military force to maintain it despite the interdependence of the world's nations.

Patriarchy

Patriarchy is a system in which power and authority are vested in men, whereas women and other powerless groups, such as children, workers, and slaves, are oppressed and often owned. More than the domination of women by men, it arose early in history when patriarchs (male heads of families) took absolute power over families and clans and began to conquer weaker groups. Religious legitimation of conquest bonded with patriarchy to produce a new kind of society, one based on male authority rights. Today, it is a worldwide system of exploitation of women (sexism), the poor (classism), nonwhite people (racism), and people and governments of developing countries (neocolonialism or imperialism).

In a patriarchal society, male authority permeates every institution: In the polity, men hold most appointed and elected offices and make laws, decisions, and policies; in the economy, men have control of capital, resources, and the production and distribution of goods and services; in religion, men hold the highest offices, dictating moral standards of society; and in the family, men make major decisions as "heads of the house." Under patriarchy, women suffer dual oppression: as women in male societies and as workers in patriarchal systems. They have been bought, sold, or married for political liaisons, and laws control their sexuality, including reproduction, which is geared to produce children as workers or to carry on men's inheritances. In marriage, in the labor force, and in systems of public assistance, they and their children are economically dependent, and ultimately their subsistence and well-being depends on the largesse (or lack thereof) of men.

Because of sex-role socialization in the patriarchal model, men and women are believed to have natural or God-given "spheres of competence." Men are believed to be stronger, more capable in politics and economics, more logical, and more independent, and so should control all social institutions. Their primary role is to support their families through paid employment. Women are believed to excel in caring for and loving others, in homemaking tasks, and in helping the dependent. They are presumed to be more emotional, more intuitive and less logical, less able to deal with stress, more dependent, and more given to unruly or flighty reactions. In the home, women's proper role is wife, bearer and rearer of children, and homemaker for a nuclear family. Outside the home, they should be caregivers—social workers, nurses, housekeepers, secretaries, and teachers, especially elementary school teachers.

Patriarchy controls the dependency of women and the work roles of men. For women, questions of whether, where, and when they will be employed, the kind of work they are hired for, and their income depend on men who control the job market. They usually work in lower-paying, stereotyped jobs, or with lower incomes than men for equal or comparable work. Married women, even if they work, depend primarily on their husbands for economic support and share their economic status. Women are ultimately responsible for their children and depend on man-controlled systems at all levels for support: husbands, the courts to ensure support if they are without husbands, social insurance, the employment market, or public assistance.

Men also are dependent on patriarchal structures but have more freedom because they are more "legitimate." Nevertheless, most men are workers, and they are constrained to the single role of family support. To lose their jobs is devastating, for their self-concepts are usually based on their work roles. Patriarchy can be brutal for men as well as for women.

White Privilege[13]

Despite the election of African-American president Barack Obama in 2008, White Privilege is a value so pervasive and so insidious in our culture that we are still nearly blind to its existence. Along with patriarchy's oppression of women (sexism) and the values that oppress the poor (classism), it is a key element in the development and support of many other values, such as social Darwinism, the work ethic, and capitalism. Endowed with an almost religious fervor, this elusive/unrecognized value is the adamant belief in the superiority of whiteness. According to Jerome Schiele, White Privilege is

> . . . the belief that European American norms and mores are universal and supreme to other cultural prescriptions and interpretations[14]

and that it

> . . . characterizes the power advantages that people of European descent collectively have over people of color.[15]

Joe E. Feagin calls White Privilege a "racialized hierarchy of power"[16] and says it is

> . . . the set of benefits and advantages inherited by . . . those defined as "white" in the social process and structure of U.S. society. The actual

privileges and the sense that one is entitled to them are inseparable parts of a greater whole [and can be] material, symbolic, or psychological. . . . Whiteness is so ubiquitous, so habitual, so imbedded that it exists even where and when most whites cannot see it. Stated or unstated, it is a fundamental given of this society. . . . [17]

White Privilege cuts across class lines, for even though higher economic classes have most obviously benefitted from it, all white people generally have access to better education, employment, housing, neighborhoods, health care, and so on than do people of color. Because White Privilege and its converse, racial oppression, are so entrenched in our societal institutions, we all, regardless of ethnicity, participate in and perpetuate them, perhaps unawares. The simple acceptance of white privileges, advantages, and beliefs in the moral and intellectual superiority of whiteness leads to Eurocentric standards by which we judge even the selfhood of nonwhite people. As Feagin says, "Whiteness is the national norm, and thus the white majority's views, practices, and culture are generally seen as normal."[18]

Marriage and the Nuclear Family

Normatively, marriage is a social, sexual, and economic relationship in which a man and a woman are legally joined to found and maintain a family. In America, we believe strongly in the nuclear family—husband, wife, and a few children—within the marriage system. Even with the explosive divorce rate—about half of all marriages end in divorce—the goals and customs of courtship, marriage, and family persist, and "happily ever after" is still the ideal.

Patriarchy underlies our expectations for marriage and family. Both men and women should be married, but we stigmatize singleness for women, particularly older women, whereas single men have a certain glamour. Despite the fact that, at present more women than men seek higher education, young women still expect to marry and their goals, both in high school and college, are generally speaking, not oriented to higher income fields. Young men, knowing they will support families, aim their educational goals at employment. Women who work after marriage often are considered to be "supplementing" their husbands' incomes, even though today both marriage partners usually work to support their families. Monogamy is both law and custom, and although serial monogamy is usual today (as people marry, divorce, and remarry), fidelity within marriage is demanded for women but often overlooked for men. Sexuality outside marriage is frowned upon, considered promiscuity for women but "sowing wild oats" for men. If pregnancy results, generally the woman is blamed, and before marriage, within marriage, or after marriage, custom demands that women take life responsibility for children. Heterosexual married couples are expected to have children, and those who do not are criticized. "A man's home is his castle," and men are the final authority in their homes. They are the major liaisons to the outside world (in fulfilling work roles, building credit ratings, and making major purchases, for example).

If marriages fail, although the emotional consequences may be terrible for both men and women, the financial consequences are usually more severe for women. Even in the best cases, where men pay support conscientiously, there now may be two families and two dwellings on a single income. Working women can rarely support their children alone if they have sex-stereotyped, low-paying jobs. Single women are more likely than any other group to sink into poverty, and woman-headed households—single mothers with children—are the fastest-growing type of family.

There are equally strong negative values based on marriage. Anti-singleness is one, particularly for women. Divorced and never-married women, with a few exceptions, also are stigmatized, and even widows undergo some social ostracism. Heterosexuality is required, and the fear and hatred of homosexual people (homophobia or heterosexism) is one of our strongest prejudices, even though homosexual marriages are now legal in some states. Also, new family patterns, such as communes or extended families, homosexual couples, or nonmarried heterosexual couples living together without marriage, are generally stigmatized by society.

However, a decade into the new millennium several new trends are emerging: an increasing acceptance of premarital sexuality with lone or serial partners—hooking up, or dating with sex as the expected outcome, being friends with (sexual) benefits, and co-habitation as an acceptable alternative to marriage. Additionally, child-bearing before marriage no longer seems to hold much stigma either for the mother or child, and a trend toward marriage after children are born is emerging. For many young people these trends appear not only acceptable but as proper steps in independence and life.

The "American Ideal": "Looksism" and "Otherism"

Values about personal appearance, although they may at first seem trivial, interact with other attitudes in society and underlie our self-concepts. In a society that values the white Anglo-Saxon Protestant ideal, to be or look different is no small thing. We are socialized early in life to admire the white middle-class look: clothes we should wear and television-clean homes. Our early readers are of the "Dick and Jane" variety, and children's books and games favor pretty white children. Our history books tell us of intrepid Protestant white men who built a new world and their own fortunes; they tell us also of Native American *savages* and black *slaves*. "Looksist" advertisements in books and on television show how we "ought to" look, and there are hundreds of books and health centers that promise to help us achieve that look.

This set of values includes individualism, racism (in that white people are preferred), and male work ethic and female dependency stereotypes. Generally speaking, men are supposed to be white, tall, dark (though sometimes blond), and handsome. They are heroes—strong, young, virile, and independent. They are assertive and intelligent, able to overcome all odds in the pursuit of excellence. The ideal woman is young, slender but buxom, blonde, and blue-eyed, with delicate, beautiful features. She is dependent on men and is loving, caring, and devoted to attaining a storybook home and family. Both men and women radiate health, youth, and vitality.

An often not-so-subtle discrimination against those who look different works against people who are not "handsome" or "pretty," against short men and tall women, obese people, older people, those who are not fair-skinned, and differently abled people who, defined by society as "handicapped" or "disabled," do not reach our standards of physical perfection. We also see it in schools, where poor children may not be "clean enough," or their clothes may be too shabby or unironed. It is particularly tied to racism: For example, African-American children prefer to play with white dolls, and may only "discover" that they themselves are not white when they come up against prejudice in schools.

Besides not liking others who are different, we dislike ourselves if we are different. We are not thin enough, not tall enough, not short enough, too fat, too old, too dark, too clumsy, or too ugly. Moreover, people prefer proximity to the American Ideal among those they work with, their love partners, their friends, and their significant others, for it reflects well on people if they can attract beautiful others to their lives. Although this kind of value should have no bearing on our attitudes to self or others, in fact it does, and we need to understand that some negative reactions come not from what people are but how they look.

A more pernicious ingredient of this value is "otherism," which uses stereotypes to objectify those who are different from "us." Hence, if the American Ideal is normal and good and we belong to it, those who are different are somehow abnormal or bad, and they become "them." This objectification enables us to manipulate, control, and label "others." Having done this, we define their actions, indeed their lives, by labels, such as obese, old, ugly, stupid, deviant, physically or mentally disabled, poor, unmarried mother, on public assistance, African American, Jewish, Hispanic, homosexual, and so on.[19]

ISSUES OF DISCRIMINATION

Our complex value systems legitimate social welfare as a helping process but also set up expectations that can be negative and controlling. These negative and controlling expectations dominate both economic life and social welfare services, creating classism/poverty and institutional discrimination in the United States.

Classism and Poverty

Stratification and Wealth

Despite our belief in egalitarianism, the United States is basically a stratified society. *Social* stratification considers issues of position in society, education, employment, income, and even social aspirations as indicators of social position. *Class* stratification is the division of society into strata based on economic resources and assumes that other social indicators depend on income. *Classism* is prejudice against the presumed immorality of those in lower economic classes, based on beliefs that they are lazy, unmotivated, immoral, promiscuous, stupid, or incompetent.

A major value that underlies stratification is the work ethic, which equates success with wealth and assumes the superior morality of those who attain it. Conversely, people who are unsuccessful are believed to have little work morality. The values of patriarchy, marriage and family, and Puritan morality compound the work ethic for women, particularly single women with children, with assumptions of sexual promiscuity. For people of ethnic or cultural minorities, the above values fuse with social Darwinism to form a wide basis for classism. Further, White Privilege and the American Ideal—distaste or even hatred for those who are different—round out the values that validate class stratification and classism in American society.

All societies have some system of stratification, and some argue that society *needs* to give rewards such as money, prestige, and status to ensure that necessary leadership positions are filled. "Higher" people are motivated toward

A major value that underlies stratification is the work ethic, which equates success with wealth and assumes the superior morality of those who attain it.

leadership and power,[20] whereas the unmotivated take on the less pleasant tasks at lower positions. This "theory of social positions"[21] blames the poor personally for their lack of success, for their

> low motivation, alienation, pathology, low incentive, authoritarianism, inability to defer gratification, dependence, inferiority feelings, illegitimacy, fatalism, weak ego, matriarchal family structure, social organization, deep-seated distortion, marital instability, inability to interact with community institutions, superficial interpersonal relationships, suspicion of people outside the family structure, poorly developed voluntary associations, low levels of participation.[22]

Others believe that society constructs barriers to achievement for some people based on class, race, religion, and sex, and that social stratification is repressive and limiting.[23] These concepts posit that government and the economic elite maintain the status quo through legislative and administrative agreements on production such as unemployment levels, minimum wages, public assistance levels, training and education grants and opportunities, restricted housing, and school systems. This gives employers a constant pool of laborers seeking work, and they can pay them minimum wages, hire and fire them more or less at will, and deny them fringe benefits available for long-term employment.

The proportions of wealth and income for economic classes in the United States remained fairly stable until the 1970s, with the richest 5 percent of the population holding 21 percent of wealth and income. However, from the 1980s on, a growing polarization occurred as the rich got richer and the middle class became poorer. Looking at income only, by 1990 the top 20 percent of families earned 44 percent of all income, increasing to 55 percent by 1995.[24] By 2009, the top 20 percent of the population earned 50.3 percent of the nation's aggregate income, while the lowest quintile earned only 3.4 percent.[25] Households with married couples comprised 22.1 percent of the lowest two quintiles; households headed by single women with children were 57.7 percent of these same quintiles. Nearly 73 percent of the lowest two quintiles were single women living alone.[26]

Household income inequality is a good measure of class stratification, but household net worth is a better one. Household net worth is the sum total of a household's assets minus its financial liabilities. In 2000, for example, the median net worth of U.S. households in the lowest quintile was $7,396.00, whereas the median net worth of households in the highest quintile was $185,500.[27] In 2007, the wealthiest one percent of households had one-third of total net worth, and the 95th to 99th percentile held more than one fourth. Thus the top 5 percent of wealth owners had about 60 percent of all household wealth. Wealth of the 50th to 90th percentile fell from 30 percent in 1989 to 26 percent in 2007.[28] It is important to keep in mind, however, that most of America's capital is owned not by individuals but by corporations, banks, insurance companies, and pension trusts.

Poverty and Welfare

Life for earliest humankind was surely hard and meager, and subsistence depended on cooperation. Poverty, a social definition of relative differences in resources, was based on availability of food, prowess in gathering it, and ideals of mutual aid. Today, poverty is the result of uneven distribution based on inegalitarian economics rather than scarcity of resources.

Poverty and the poor have been continually redefined over time, but before medieval times social and economic conditions were thought to cause poverty and there was no personal blame in being poor. With the end of feudalism (to be discussed in Chapter 4), poverty became first immoral and then criminal, and poor people were categorized into those whom society should or should not help (worthy versus unworthy poor). In the United States, women with children are the most stigmatized of public dependents, whether they are single, divorced, separated, or deserted. Their status—detachment from male authority—violates values of patriarchy, marriage and family, individualism, social Darwinism, and, because of their dependency, the Protestant work ethic.

Social welfare is based partly on the need to control the poor and keep workers available for low-wage work. Fortified by our value systems, in our society poverty is

- An *economic* issue, both to keep people working and to provide them with subsistence
- A *political* issue based on the power to command production of resources
- A *class* issue entailing the division of society in economic strata
- A *religious* issue, because religion legitimates differential accumulation of wealth and defines charity as a religious duty
- A *women's* issue because of women's vulnerability to poverty, their life responsibility for children, and their caretaking of the needy
- A racial issue because people of color relative to non-Hispanic white people disproportionately experience poverty and find it more difficult to escape
- An issue of *social control*, because the poor are considered a social liability rather than a social obligation.

A modern redefinition of poverty is the "underclass": people, usually African Americans, in inner-city areas beset by poverty and crime.[29] Regardless of the sociological intent of this appellation, it is now a derogatory catch-all, grouping and typing people in inner cities not on their characteristics or needs, but on demographic factors of institutional poverty, deteriorating houses and neighborhoods, homelessness, joblessness, and crime. In fact, the definition itself creates a ghettoizing, or blocking off, and the aim of police power in such neighborhoods seems more often to be containment and subjection rather than service or protection.

The poor are not a homogeneous group; they differ in as many ways as any segment of our population. However, their differences are stigmatized by society and often compounded: They are poor *and* unemployed *and* public dependents *and* women, or discriminated against because of race or ethnicity, or age, or being differently abled, and so forth. Multiple differences make for an increasing need for social control, and women have been more vulnerable because of the overlapping of sex and class discrimination. *Who* is poor is determined according to "poverty thresholds," which were first formulated in 1964 by Mollie Orshansky. Her budget cost was figured on number of family members multiplied by three, because at that time poor people generally spent about one-third of their income on food. Although her figures were only for a short-term emergency diet that experts believed inadequate for ongoing nourishment, this "market basket" diet became the nation's standard for measuring the poverty threshold. In 2011, the poverty threshold for a family of four was $22,350.[30]

Institutional racism, sexism, and ageism are reflected in poverty statistics. For 2010, poverty guidelines were, for one person alone, $11,369; for a person over age 65, $10,481; for a family of four, $22,541; and varying increments to a household of nine or more, in which the guideline was $48,400.[31] In 2009, when the U.S. median income was $49,777, the poverty rate was 14.3 percent, or 43.6 million people.[32] In 2008, real median income declined 3.6 percent, the largest single year decline on record.[33] Pavetti notes that "In July 2009, 35.9 million people, or 1 in 9 Americans, were enrolled in SNAP [Food Stamps, now called Supplemental Nutrition Assistance Program], including an estimated 17.4 million children, or 1 in 4 children. . . ."[34] This constitutes an increase of 6.8 million people in one year (since July 2008), or 23 percent.[35] In 2007, Hispanic families had a poverty rate of 21.0 percent; African Americans, 24.9 percent; Asians, 10.2 percent;[36] and Native Americans, 25.3 percent.[37] Poverty rates for older people remained steady at 9.7 percent.[38] Poverty in the United States is approximately equal to the total combined population of the nation's four largest cities, is larger than the population of Canada (by about 10 million), and is twice the combined populations of the seven nations of Central America. There are four times more poor people than there are college students, six times more poor people than Jewish people, twenty times more poor people than there are writers, artists, entertainers, and athletes combined. There are more poor people in the United States than there are seconds in a year.[39] Table 1.1 provides a summary of distribution of poverty by selected characteristics.

We know from the past that every year of child poverty at current levels will cost the economy between $36 and $177 billion in lower future productivity and employment, to say nothing of remedial costs such as hospitalization and long-term care for the disabled. Poor children are two or more times more likely than nonpoor children to suffer a variety of health problems, including stunted growth, severe physical or mental disabilities, anemia, and fatal accidental injuries. They are three times more likely to die than nonpoor children from birth defects or because of low-weight births, four times as likely to die in fires, and five to six times as likely to die of infectious diseases and parasites. In addition, they are nearly three times more likely to be diagnosed with learning disabilities and are diagnosed with extreme behavior problems in school more

Table 1.1   People Below the Poverty Level, 2007 and 2008 (Number in Thousands)

	2007 Number	Percent	2008 Number	Percent
Total	37,276	12.5%	38,829	13.2%
White	25,120	10.5	26,990	11.2
White, non-Hispanic	16,032	8.2	17,024	8.6
Black	9,237	24.5	9,379	24.7
Asian	1,349	10.2	1,576	11.8
Children under 18	13,324	18.0	14,068	19.0
Age 65 up	3,556	9.7	3,656	9.7

Source: U.S. Census Bureau, Current Population Survey, 2008 and 2009 Annual Social and Economic Supplements, Table 4: People and Families in Poverty by Selected Characteristics: 2007 and 2008 (see www.census.gov/apsd/techdoc/cps/cssmaart09.pdf).

than six times as often as nonpoor children. The U.S. Department of Education reports that the risk of a student falling behind in school increases by 2 percentage points for every year he or she spends growing up in poverty. Poverty's effects are separate from—and stronger than—those of race, region, having a teen parent, or living in a one-parent home.[40] In the 1990s, the United States had the highest child poverty rate of most industrialized nations, falling behind Australia, Canada, Great Britain, Norway, Sweden, and Switzerland.

Quoting statistics enables us to make comparisons among figures. Understanding the despair of people who cannot feed their children, or scavenge in garbage cans for their food, or live over heat grates in the streets is more difficult. Most of us believe that poverty does not exist in the United States, or that if it does, it is the fault of the poor. These are easy rationalizations, ways that permit us to maintain our own sense of well-being and keep our values about hard work and individualism intact. However, poverty does not "just happen." It comes from our social values and the systems they maintain, and it is the result of a class-stratified society. The gap is maintained through economic practices enforced by legislation that is deliberately intended to preserve the status quo.

With legislation and administrative decisions developed by people who confuse social values with facts, our system protects the wealthy and jeopardizes the rest of us. Altruism exists in such forms as grants and foundations, but only within the context of systems that perpetuate poverty and class stratification. As a society, we need major changes in social structures to end the disgrace of poverty, changes that require values oriented to the well-being of all rather than to the money privileges of the very few.

Institutional Discrimination

Institutional discrimination permeates American systems so deeply that we may not recognize it. Based on hostile attitudes reified in rules, regulations, and procedures, its forms—racism, sexism, ageism, homophobia or heterosexism, and "otherism"—deny equal rights and opportunities to groups even when no individual prejudice may be involved. Moreover, types of institutional discrimination interact with each other and with classism, enforcing the status quo of our society: People discriminated against are more likely to be poor, and if more than one discrimination is present, the likelihood of poverty is even greater. For example, an aged African-American woman is in triple jeopardy of being poor because of her age, race, and gender.

A United Nations decree in 1969 defines discrimination as

> . . . any distinction, exclusion, restriction or preference based on race, colour, descent of national or ethnic origin which has the purpose of effect of nullifying or impairing the recognition, enjoyment of exercise, on an equal footing, of human rights and fundamental freedoms.[41]

While some scholars protest that America's perception of discrimination should be widened to include people of other ethnic backgrounds, Feagin argues that white-on-black oppression is

> . . . a comprehensive system of exploitation and oppression originally designed by white Americans for Black Americans, a system of racism that for centuries has penetrated every major area of American society and thus shaped the lives of every American, black and non-black.[42]

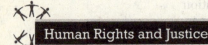

Human Rights and Justice

Practice Behavior Example: Understand the forms and mechanisms of oppression and discrimination.

Critical Thinking Question: What gaps exist in your own understanding of oppression and difference? What knowledge do you need to seek out in order to better understand the structures of American society?

Institutional Racism Racism is prejudice with power against people of color: African Americans, Hispanics, Asian Americans, and Native Americans. Our American values make us assume that race determines human traits and capacities and that white people are inherently superior to people of color. This is directly related to our hatred of "outsiders," or people who are different, to White Privilege, and to the Protestant work ethic. The Protestant religion of our forebears legitimated their pursuit of wealth, and the idea that people of color were not as "human" as Caucasians allowed their exploitation.

Native Americans Estimates of Native American population at the time of conquest range to nearly 10 million in North America and tens of millions in Central and South America. As a result of decimation by European weapons and disease, the number of North American natives fell to approximately 200,000–300,000 by 1850.[43] Today, Native Americans[44] number 4.4 million and are the most impoverished people in America. Their unemployment is more than double that of whites, and employment is heavily concentrated in lower-paying jobs: farm labor for men and service work for women. Twenty-four percent live in poverty, and housing and health care conditions are still worse for rural Native Americans than for any other group. Death rates are high, and people die young because of poor nutrition and lack of health care. Infant mortality is comparable to rates in poor developing nations.[45]

Asian Americans Both Japanese and Chinese immigrants lived in the severest poverty when immigration began in the middle 1800s. However, some managed to climb the economic ladder in America despite racism. Most are now in white-collar jobs, although in larger cities women are likely to hold low-status, low-income service jobs. Asian American women have less income than do white women, but median income for Japanese American families is slightly higher than that for whites. Chinese Americans have not been quite so fortunate, nor have the most recent immigrants from Thailand or Korea, who are still being harassed by white workers afraid of losing their jobs.[46]

Hispanic Americans Approximately 58 percent of Hispanic Americans are of Mexican origin, and 10 percent are of Puerto Rican heritage. Although the poverty rate of Mexican Americans is high, Puerto Rican Americans are the poorest ethnic group in the United States except for Native Americans. Most Hispanic workers are concentrated at lower job levels, and white households had incomes 40 percent higher than Hispanics in 2006.[47]

African Americans Even after 400 years in North America, African Americans continue to experience exclusion and marginalization because of racial discrimination. Their early slave status is not the determining factor; rather, unrelenting racism has kept them from education, jobs with good incomes, decent housing, and the many benefits available to most citizens. The unemployment rate for African Americans has remained twice that of whites. With underemployment—no jobs, part-time jobs, and jobs at poverty wages—their median income has remained at 55 to 67 percent of white income since the 1950s through 2006.[48] Intact African-American families are twice as likely as intact white American families to be poor, and woman-headed African-American families are nine times as likely to be poor as families headed by white men.[49]

Racism and Poverty Institutional racism has a circular relationship with poverty. For example, many African Americans are poor and, therefore, must live in rental units owned by white people not living in the area. Their homes have a low property tax base, leading to poorly funded and equipped schools. Given a choice, better or more experienced teachers will not work there. The lack of high-quality education and a high dropout rate limit future employment and income, which means they are trapped in high-poverty areas with poor schools. Even those who succeed may not be able to move because realtors and homeowners will not sell to them. In 1994, banks, savings institutions, and credit unions refused loans to 33 percent of African Americans who applied, 31.6 percent of Native Americans, 24.6 percent of Hispanics, 16.4 percent of whites, and 12 percent of Asian Americans.[50] As of 2005, three-fourths of white households owned their homes, but only 46 percent of African Americans and 48 percent of Hispanics were homeowners.[51]

African-American children continue to face discrimination and *de facto* segregation in education. They are one and a half times more likely to drop out of school than are white children, limiting their futures both socially and economically. Schools in poverty-stricken areas with high percentages of minority students have limited access to quality education. Such schools are more likely to employ beginning teachers, have substandard facilities and

equipment because of a limited tax base, and be overcrowded. Forty-seven percent of African-American children (and 51 percent of Hispanic children) attend schools where 75 percent of the students are poor, as compared to 5 percent of white children.[52] African-American college graduates are more likely to be unemployed than white people with only high school educations. African-American males in public schools are two times more likely than white males to be placed in special education as retarded (1 of every 34), 1.5 times as likely to be placed in programs for serious emotional disturbances (1 in 62), and 2.7 times as likely to be corporally punished.[53] In 2009, 90 percent of all young adults 18 to 24 were high school or GED graduates. The rate of African-American graduates increased from 75 to 87 percent between 1980 and 2009.[54]

Institutional Sexism   Sexism, probably our oldest prejudice with power, is gender privilege for men. Based on patriarchal values, it assumes the political, economic, intellectual, and spiritual inferiority of women based solely on sex and without regard to individual capabilities and has resulted in oppression and exploitation throughout history. It permeates all institutions of society: family, economy, polity, religion, and social welfare. At home, men have control of women, sometimes even to physical abuse or death. In the economic arena, women more than men are subject to low wages, part-time employment, and limited benefits. In the courts, male gender privilege often means low and often uncollectible grants for child support. Low public assistance grants when there is no other help completes women's povertization. Laws and religions continually challenge women's right to control reproduction. In juvenile justice systems, young women are incarcerated for "status offenses," or noncriminal morality charges, whereas young men usually answer only for crimes against persons or property. Mental health programs often base treatment on needs of families rather than women clients. The number of women in public office remains small compared with men in those offices. Most religions continue to restrict high positions to men and to teach the "proper" roles for women: submissive and secondary to men.

Customs of education and training keep women ghettoized in low-paying, sex-stereotyped jobs. They hold 80 percent of clerical jobs, 78 percent of service jobs, and 43 percent of professional jobs (mostly teachers and nurses). Even professional jobs, if they are "women's work," pay less than do men's lower skilled work, and often women are paid less for the same professional job. More women than men graduated from college in 1994, and a year later these women were earning 80 percent of their male colleagues' salaries. Yet by 2010, these same women earned only 77.4 percent of what their male counterparts earned.[55] Married women make up 55 percent of working women, and a family headed by a woman is four-and-a-half times more likely to be poor than an intact or man-headed family.

The myths of Cinderella and "the women's sphere" are so deeply ingrained in our society that women themselves help maintain them by not training for better jobs, accepting their secondary roles as natural, and relieving men of responsibility for their impoverishment. This is not to blame women for believing what society has taught them, but to indicate the power of social values to inculcate oppressive attitudes even in the oppressed. Women will continue to be oppressed and exploited until our society clarifies sexist values and overcomes sexist myths.

Institutional Ageism   Ageism is a preference for youth over the aging and manifests itself not only in disrespect and the shunting aside of older people, but in job discrimination against people over the age of about forty. Youth fits the American Ideal of active, assertive, future-oriented, and beautiful, and we see older people as ugly, doddering, unproductive, senile, or living in the past. Perhaps we fear our own aging, for we do not respect the wisdom and experience of our elders. Ageism is institutional in that, especially in economic issues but also in the family, older people are prevented from sharing in society. Many are poor despite Social Security, and we do little to ensure that they will be secure in their old age. Also, America's nuclear family system and dedication to individualism move our elders out of the center of family life and into loneliness. By 2008, people over age sixty-five represented 12.6 percent of Americans, of whom 9.7 percent lived below the poverty level.[56]

Age is a stereotype. Some people chronologically in their sixties may be as active, productive, and capable as much younger people. Others as young as thirty often have stopped learning and become resigned and rigid in thought and deed. *Old* is an artificial designation that, in America, coincides with the retirement age of about sixty-five. However, retiring people from work is relatively recent, beginning in about the last half of the twentieth century, resulting from longer life spans and the demands that younger people be employed. When the Social Security Acts of 1935 were passed, the United States was in the middle of its greatest depression. Giving pensions to older men not only gave them minimal support, but also took them out of the job market so that younger workers with growing families could be employed in what jobs there were. Women's retirement was not really an issue: They were discouraged from taking jobs away from men, but a great number were employed outside the home anyway. With labor demands and Social Security, they were retired from the labor market along with men but continued their usual jobs working in the home.

Aging is another complication for women vis à vis poverty. If they lose their husbands during their middle years, they are unlikely to find sufficient employment for family support because they lack current job training and experience. Social insurance payments end when their children reach age eighteen, and if they have no dependent children they cannot receive TANF (to be discussed in Chapter 14). If they have dependent children, they may receive TANF, but the grants are inadequate. Women's average earnings decrease compared to men's as they grow older. Because of lower overall wages during their employment years, they will receive lower social insurance and fewer pension benefits.

Our societal emphasis on youth borders on geriatricide, in practice if not in intent. If Medicare funds are exhausted by lengthy illnesses, Medicaid, the public assistance program, is an option only if patients divest themselves of most of their assets to become eligible. Life expectancy today is about seventy-one years (for white women 77.7 years), and over three-fourths of the aged have at least one chronic health problem. Moreover, the elderly face personal and emotional stress—loneliness, loss of loved ones, lack of purpose in life, retirement, and change of living arrangements—and these compound and often cause physical problems.

Institutional ageism is not confined to the elderly. Prejudice against aging begins around the age of forty. Many businesses are unwilling to hire workers over this age, even though age discrimination is prohibited by law. Employers fear that older people will take too long to train and that their productivity will therefore be limited. Also, experienced workers must be paid more than new workers. Finally, medical insurance and fringe benefit costs paid by the company rise with the number of older workers. For these reasons, hiring at a later age and keeping people on after the age of fifty or so is discouraged, even though older workers

> have lower turnover rates, produce at a steadier rate, make fewer mistakes, have a more positive attitude toward their work, and exceed younger employees in health and low-on-the-job-injury rates.[57]

This was one of the most painful problems of the recessions of 1981–1983 and 2007–2009, during which millions of blue-collar workers, young and old, lost their jobs. Unemployment for many became permanent, and, after unemployment benefits were exhausted, they found they could not get jobs because of company policies not to hire people over age fifty. Initially, this meant a lower standard of life when they had been used to better. In the long run, lower or no income in years when highest levels of earnings were expected meant lower Social Security and pension benefits at retirement. Some found work in marginal industries, but not before their lifetime savings were lost. Those unable to find work were reduced, after having lived all their lives in "the American Way," to living on public assistance and food stamps.

Homophobia or Heterosexism   This prejudice against or hatred of homosexuals—gay men and women along with others of nontraditional sexual or gender orientation and expression—is a product of Puritan morality and patriarchal values. Because their sexual orientation is toward people of the same sex, homosexuals fall outside the pale of "normal" value systems: patriarchy, morality, and marriage and nuclear family. Aside from sexual preference and gender expression, the actions of homosexual people are no different from those of other members of the population. Homosexuality has existed throughout human history and was often considered preferable to heterosexuality. Benford argues that it is an evolutionary strategy that helped preserve at least early societies. He notes that in kinship societies

> a gay man or woman [worked] for the betterment of his or her relations, laboring in the tribe as specialized labor, free of the burden of childrearing. . . . [Because] the gay brother or sister labors on, the tribe as a whole has a better chance of surviving. . . . It is preferred as a minority strategy by evolution of the hunter–gatherer hominids we once were . . . and still are.[58]

Some of our finest scholars, authors, and other highly productive people have been homosexual. However, in American society they have been forced out of jobs and personally persecuted. The profession of teaching is particularly forbidden because of the fear that children might be "seduced into homosexuality." Some denominations of religions have only recently allowed homosexuals among their clergy; most do not acknowledge homosexual love relationships. Foster care or adoption is very difficult for even the most stable homosexual couple, and homosexuals divorcing heterosexuals have great difficulty in maintaining custody of their children. Defamation, blackmail against those who keep their sexual preference secret, and even physical injury are part of the expectations of homosexuals, transsexuals, cross-dressers, and other people with nonheterosexual behaviors in our society. Discrimination forbids them the protection of many laws that most of us take for granted.

Otherism   This catch-all category refers to people who, because of physical or social differences, do not fit the American Ideal. They may be differently abled, unsighted, obese, unattractive, or "different" in innumerable other ways. Discrimination against them varies: Those whom society calls physically, emotionally, or mentally "disabled" are subject to more prejudice than are the obese or the unattractive. Those with physical disabilities, nearly 50 million people,[59] are probably the most discriminated against among the "different" in our society. Although they are guaranteed civil rights, especially with the enactment of the Americans with Disabilities Act in 1990, these rights often are denied in ways as simple as access to buildings. Of the disabled, estimated at 50 million, fewer than 6 million receive SSI.[60]

Although in 1843 Dorothea Dix testified about the horrendous treatment accorded people who were "different," treatment today is, in some cases, as brutal: Foster care operators abuse and sometimes kill their charges, homeless people scavenge in garbage cans to eat, defenseless people are murdered on the streets, and others freeze to death when their newspapers or cardboard homes cannot keep them warm enough.

The pervasive distaste toward "different" people in our culture adds an edge to those discriminated against in other ways. For example, nonwhite people can never reach the standards set for American appearance: They are not white. Most women can never meet the American Ideal of beauty, nor men of handsomeness. Obese people are constantly railed at, not only for health's sake, but because fat is "ugly." These stereotypes of what people "should" look like may seem trivial in the face of more serious disadvantages. However, they are another part of a value system that honors certain people and demonstrates a social dislike of others.

Although some individuals overcome the barriers of institutional discrimination, many cannot. This has very little to do with their capabilities, will to succeed, or hard work but is institutional in nature—part of the value systems with which Americans are indoctrinated. Whatever the discriminatory situation, we must look critically at why certain groups in our society cannot succeed, work to change our own discriminatory values, and develop programs to overcome centuries of institutional discrimination.

CONCLUSION: VALUES AND POWER

When people seek the help of social workers, they admit they have lost control of part of their lives. However, they are *not* asking us to take over; rather, they need us to help them regain their own control. We must be careful not to impose our own values on them or to exercise our power over them. There are times, of course, when we must assert power—when people are a danger to themselves or others or when society imposes social treatment/control upon them—but this is the exception rather than the rule. In most cases, the use of power is an abuse of people. Our most precious values may encourage this abuse.

In general, social workers come from middle-class backgrounds, where hard work is the way to success. We believe in and reflect values of work, education, and perceptions of family life and define deviance by those lights. These values are not "wrong" or "bad" for us, and we can use them in our own lives as we please. However, these values are not realities common to all societies and cultures but derive from the history and cultural belief systems that

> When people seek the help of social workers, they admit they have lost control of part of their lives. However, they are not asking us to take over; rather, they need us to help them regain their own control.

Practice Behavior Example: Gain sufficient self-awareness to eliminate the influence of personal biases and values in working with diverse groups.

Critical Thinking Question: Discuss ways that a social worker can avoid imposing their own personal value biases on their clients.

have dominated U.S. society. Most of our clients probably share these values, but because all people are unique, so are their value interpretations; some differences are sure to occur because reality is different for each of us. Furthermore, we live in an increasingly diverse society that includes values that diverge from the ones that currently prevail. Also, the life situations of our clients require that they make different choices from those we might. We can never be in "the same situation" and must learn to respect their rights to make the decisions best for them.

The provision of social services can be undermined by values in many ways. Although our primary mandate is to enable others, we may find ourselves placing unreasonable demands on their lives or seeking to control them. We become society's way of enforcing conformity to norms that may not be relevant to the problem at hand. Norman Goroff has called social workers "soft cops"[61] because our work often hides values that society, the agency, or we ourselves want to impose on clients. However, they quickly discover our hidden agendas and value biases, a discovery that may hurt them deeply or cause them justifiable anger.

We began this chapter speaking about love, but we have discussed values that seem anything but loving. Probably some of your deepest beliefs have been touched in ways you never expected. We may feel that because our work is inspired by love, it can have only good effects, but wisdom, not emotion, is the essence of the helping relationship. To help people to "fit in," if that is what they want, may be an appropriate task of social work. However, to aid them in understanding the institutions of society and to help them to use that knowledge in gaining their goals is probably the real gift of love to others.

The following questions will test your knowledge and understanding of t
this chapter. For additional assessment, including licensing-exam type
chapter content to practice behaviors, visit **MySearc**

1. What criteria are used to choose our goals?
   a. beliefs
   b. values
   c. desires
   d. needs

2. The most impoverished people in America are:
   a. Hispanic Americans
   b. African Americans
   c. Native Americans
   d. Asian Americans

3. Which belief system argues that society has an obligation to help those in need?
   a. Judaeo-Christian
   b. Social Darwinism
   c. Democratic Egalitarianism
   d. Capitalism

4. Which belief system argues that w and unmotivated?
   a. Democratic Egalitarianism
   b. The American Ideal
   c. Judaeo-Christian
   d. Individualism

5. Societies that embrace Social Darwinism would likely regard unemployment insurance as:
   a. a reasonable short-term solution to help workers transition back to new jobs.
   b. an ideal way to support unemployed workers during an economic downturn.
   c. an ineffective solution; they tend to favor government support in job retraining for high demand jobs.
   d. contrary to their beliefs against "saving" the poor by providing public aid assistance.

6. You are helping a family in poverty with public aid assistance and learn that they have a very strong Protestant Work Ethic. Keeping their value system in mind, which of these should you consider as you offer assistance?
   a. People are encouraged to seek public assistance when they fall on hard times
   b. Dependence on any kind of public assistance is a shameful stigma
   c. Poverty is met with compassion and community support
   d. Poverty is the result of systems that failed the citizens

7. Describe "Otherism" and the "American Ideal" and how they jointly contribute to discrimination.

Reinforce what you learned in this chapter by studying videos, cases, documents, and more available at **www.MySearchLab.com**.

Watch and Review

Watch these Videos

Working Mothers

The Great Contradictions of the Twentieth Century

Read and Review

Read these Cases/Documents

* Diversity in Practice

* Human Rights and Justice

Richard Wright, "Are We Solving America's Race Problem?" (1945)

Assess Your Knowledge

Go to **MySearchLab** to test your knowledge of key topics in this chapter with topic-specific quizzes. Conclude your assessment by completing the chapter exam.

* = CSWE Core Competency Asset

2

The Institution of Social Welfare: An Overview

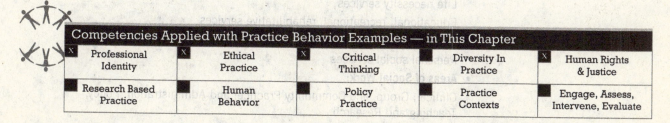

Competencies Applied with Practice Behavior Examples — in This Chapter				
x Professional Identity	x Ethical Practice	x Critical Thinking	Diversity In Practice	x Human Rights & Justice
Research Based Practice	Human Behavior	Policy Practice	Practice Contexts	Engage, Assess, Intervene, Evaluate

THE MEANING OF SOCIAL INSTITUTION

A social institution is a set of interrelated and interlocking concepts, structures, and activities enduring over time that carry out the necessary functions of a society, such as socialization, childrearing, education, and commerce.[1] The five major institutions of society are (see Figure 2.1):

- The economy
- The polity
- The family
- Religion
- Social welfare (which in our definition includes education).

The polity and the economy are the major underlying macrosystems by which our government is separated from other nations and by which people in our nation relate to society. Family, religion, and social welfare, although they also have wider applications, are usually more oriented to the internal systems (microsystems) of the society. Although social welfare has existed in some form since human society began, it became a social institution only when responsibility for particular groups of people became a function of society itself. In early societies the extended family fulfilled all functions: economic and political needs, social control, and social integration. However, as families became communities and nations, and as work became divided and specialized, societal functions diversified into social institutions. Today, in most societies, they overlap one another, and social welfare overlaps them all.

The major functions of religion and the family are socialization and social integration. Socialization teaches us the norms, values, and ways of behaving

Times and Events

- **Five major institutions of society:**
  Polity, Economy, Family, Religion, Social welfare
- **Social welfare as social control**
  Manifest and latent functions
  Social treatment and social control
  Residual and institutional social welfare
- **Perspectives in Social Welfare**
  Functionalist
  Conflict, including Feminist welfarist, Afrocentric paradigm, Black feminist thought
- **Fields of Social Services**
  Life necessity services
  Educational, recreational, rehabilitative services
  Protective social services
  Personal social services
- **Areas of Social Work:**
  Clinical, Group, and Community Practice; and Administration, Policy, Teaching and Research

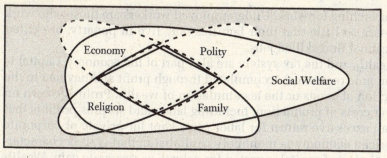

Figure 2.1
Social Institutions

in our society, and social integration helps us to fit in or be brought back into the fold after deviating in some way. Gilbert and Specht say that social integration

> has to do with the relationships among units in a social system. Members of a particular institution or of the system-as-a-whole must be loyal to one another and the system must achieve some level of solidarity and morale in order to function.[2]

Social integration makes us aware that we have stepped outside the bounds of the normal and points out how we can "change for the better." In addition, conformity to one's family, group, and society is taught more formally than is the case in socialization.

The Economy

The economy is all aspects of a society that relate to the production (making), distribution (meting out), and consumption (using) of goods and services. Production includes all outputs, from farm to manufactured goods, and capital (wealth accumulated in goods and profits and stored in stocks, bonds, sunk costs of manufacturing, savings, investments, and so on). Distribution is the marketing or meting out of products (goods and services). In America, we generally think that the market economy—what people buy and sell—is the major source of distribution. However, tax transfers are another major distributive factor. They are monies taken from taxes and given directly, in cash, goods, and services, to select groups in society outside the labor market. For example, the poor receive money, food stamps, or subsidized housing, and the wealthy get tax breaks and subsidies such as farm price supports and land-bank monies or bailouts for industries or corporations in trouble. Consumption, which keeps production and distribution moving, is the using up of consumer goods and services, whether through the market or through tax transfers.

The economy also includes the organization of the workforce, employment, and planned unemployment to ensure sufficient production and consumption of consumer goods. In the United States, the Council of Economic Advisors suggests an unemployment rate of about 5 percent to ensure workforce availability. The actual number of unemployed varies with the economy and with reporting because discouraged workers and the underemployed are generally not counted in unemployment statistics. Discouraged workers are those who have never been able to find work, those whose unemployment benefits have run out, and those who have been unemployed for so long that they have stopped searching for work. Underemployed workers are those who work full-time but earn so little that their families may live in poverty, or skilled workers who cannot find skilled jobs.

Capital, wealth, and the tax system are also part of the economy. Capital is money (or economic resources) accumulated through profit and devoted to the further production of goods or the accumulation of wealth. Profit is return on investment over costs of production, including labor, and surplus profit is that amount plus an excessive return for labor costs kept for private or corporate use. The American economy is monopoly capitalistic; that is, it is character- ized by accumulation of capital invested for private or corporate gain. Wealth is the result of profit making and the retiring of resources from the market economy. Although wealth is generally less available for investment than is capital, if need arises it can be sold and transformed into capital.

The tax system is the assessment of and levy on income, production, and wealth by the government. Poor and middle-class people are taxed propor- tionately more than corporations and the wealthy because of tax write-offs, loopholes, and the ability of the wealthy to influence tax legislation. This results in an increasing class stratification as the wealthy reinvest saved tax dollars in new profit making while the poorer classes have decreasing amounts to invest even in their own well-being. There are several direct taxes, including property, sales, and income tax. Property and sales taxes are regressive, or taxed at a set rate regardless of the economic status of the taxpayer. Poorer classes, then, spend relatively more of their assets on these taxes than do the wealthy. Income tax is progressive; that is, those who earn more generally pay a higher rate on their taxable income. Taxes on corporate wealth depend on both the amount of wealth and its form: Wealth held in trusts or foundations may be virtually untaxable despite its benefits to those who control it. Indirect taxes are taxes imposed on manu- facturers who pass them on to consumers in form of higher prices. Tax monies go to support the vast bureaucracies of the government; to provide for protection against other na- tions and negotiation with them; for public works such as roads, parks, and bridges; and for public well-being in pro- grams for the public good, such as education, health care, and welfare programs.

Human Rights and Justice

Practice Behavior Example: Advocate for human rights and social and economic justice.

Critical Thinking Question: What responsibility do social workers have in challenging eco- nomic inequalities like the disproportionate taxation of the poor?

The Polity

The polity is the exercise of power in a society. Any system—person, group, agency, organization, or wider system—that has legal or normative power, or in some instances nonlegal but coercive or customary power over other sys- tems, is a part of the polity.[3] Among systems constituting America's polity are national, state, and local governments based on national and state constitu- tions, laws, legislative and judicial decisions; the political system and political parties, including elections and appointments to office; the criminal and civil justice systems; and administrative rules, regulations, and customs at all levels of government and in all government bureaucracies.

Polities can enforce behaviors or impose or prevent change, whether or not people or systems agree with their actions. On the international level, polities engage in wars or other demonstrations of strength to the point of conquests of other nations or people, taking political prisoners or slaves, and enforcing their own laws and policies on unwilling countries by use of embargoes or occupation. Examples include the near-genocide of Native Americans and the enslavement of African-born people and their descendants in our own country; imperialism and colonialism in developing countries today; the spread of transnational corporations throughout the world; and the imitation of American capitalism in Eastern European nations.

In the United States, the polity and the economy are so closely tied that it is difficult to see them as separate, for laws and regulations are based on the ideals of capitalism and the free market and much of the economy is politically supported. Higher socioeconomic classes often determine what legislation will be passed (through lobbying), who will be elected to office (through financial contributions), and what contracts (such as for defense) will be developed and awarded. The close link between the polity and the economy is often captured in the term political economy.

The Family and Religion

Though each has clear boundaries, the institutions of family and religion are closely related. The major functions of religion and the family are socialization and social integration. Socialization teaches us the norms, values, and ways of behaving in our society, and social integration helps us to fit in or be brought back into the fold after deviating in some way. Gilbert and Specht say that social integration

> has to do with the relationships among units in a social system. Members of a particular institution or of the system-as-a-whole must be loyal to one another and the system must achieve some level of solidarity and morale in order to function.[4]

Social integration makes us aware that we have stepped outside the bounds of the normal and points out how we can "change for the better."

The family is an economic and social unit in which people live within a society and within which socially legitimated sexual relationships occur. In present-day America, the nuclear family—husband, wife, and children—is the normative ideal. In preindustrial times, the family was more clearly an economic unit, with members who worked at home farming, producing craft items, marketing, giving child care, and educating and training family members in all aspects of life. Today, the meaning of family is markedly different from what it was even two decades ago because of new kinds of extended and nuclear families. Examples include heterosexual or homosexual couples, married or unmarried, living as a social and economic unit sometimes with children and often with a contract specifying the rights and obligations of each partner; and, very common today, the single-parent household, often woman-headed and with dependent children. These and other families exist today with varying degrees of legitimacy.

Religion is the complex of systems, organized or unorganized, by which people relate to a deity and to their own existence with spiritual and moral values concerning personal life, work, and other people. Because of the interrelationships of the Protestant work ethic and Puritan morality with polity and economy, the United States has been called a Christian nation. However, although Christian religions are numerically predominant, other religions, such as Judaism, Islam, the Baha'i Faith, Buddhism, Unitarianism, and forms of paganism, also exist. Atheism and agnosticism, which either deny a deity or allow for the possibility of one, also are ways in which people relate to existence. Humanism, centered on a philosophy of the dignity and worth of people aside from consideration of deity, is another legitimate spiritual focus. Freedom of belief and the doctrine of separation of church and state are protected by the Constitution. Nevertheless, present-day conservative trends threaten this freedom as religious groups attempt to insert sectarian beliefs into the American legal system.

Social Welfare

Many definitions of social welfare have been offered. Macarov tells us, for example, that in Poland social welfare is compensation for injuries suffered in great risks, such as war, that lead to inability to work. In Australia it is a public right that benefits both individuals and society as a whole, and Sweden's social welfare goal is to redistribute income more evenly.[5] To most Americans, social welfare means giving money to the poor—to people who cannot or will not work to support themselves and their families. However, that benefit, more properly called public assistance, is not the whole of social welfare, which encompasses almost every kind of service provided to members of society. Friedlander says that social welfare is

> [an organized] system of laws, programs, benefits, and services which strengthen or assure provisions for meeting social needs ... basic for the welfare of the population and ... the social order ... to aid individuals and groups to attain satisfying standards of life and health, and personal and social relationships which permit them to develop their full capacities and to promote their well-being in harmony with the needs of their families and the community.[6]

The *Encyclopedia of Social Work* adds that social welfare is for the purpose of ensuring a basic standard of physical and mental well-being and providing universal access to the mainstream of society.[7] Others add that it provides for those who cannot cope by themselves, creates social change and the modification of social institutions, strengthens society while it helps individuals, and provides services outside the market economy for those unable to succeed within it.[8]

Two additional areas should be included in the definition of social welfare. First, social welfare now includes such new areas as *for-profit* services, including some nursing homes, day care centers, and increasingly, privatized services such as administration of food stamps (now called the SNAP program), Medicaid, and so on; social services in business organizations, such as substance abuse counseling and day care for employees' children; and "natural" networks, the neighbors or parish priests who refer people to professional systems.[9] Second is the *welfare model* of deviance, which, Peter Day says, presents welfare problems as

> public [social problems] for which some remedial, correctional, or therapeutic intervention is required to alter, modify, or control the deviant and his [sic] behavior ... [as] a public responsibility.... First, it sees deviant behavior as a public problem existing outside the framework of normal social life; second, it considers this behavior to be an expression of a deviant self different from that of the normal person; third, it promotes efforts to account for and correct this difference.[10]

This area of social welfare entails work with the delinquent, emotionally disturbed, or poor, among others. Although such social control has been a legitimate part of American social welfare since its beginnings, some social work

interesting how social welfare is different all over the world (never thought of that)

professionals have denied its existence as antithetical to individual freedom. However, more recent perspectives clearly indicate that social welfare is, in many ways, social control.

For our purposes, <u>American social welfare is the social institution that provides society's sum total of all goods and services</u>

- to enhance the social and economic well-being of society's members or
- to ensure their conformity to current societal norms, standards, and ideologies.

It is based on society's values, whether altruistic, economic, or political; is legitimated by legislation or custom; and is carried out by public agencies, private not-for-profit agencies, or agencies whose major goal is to enhance profit making for their owner-investors. Social welfare has two kinds of functions:

- *Social treatment*: the provision of goods and services for the enhancement of human life
- *Social control*: generally, the provision of services to ensure conformity from deviants.

These functions determine the activities of human service professionals in carrying out society's mandates (laws and policies) regarding social services.

<u>Most social welfare activities take place outside the market system as people do not individually purchase or pay for services that may or may not be altruistic.</u> For example, criminal justice programs require control of those we fear, businesses provide counseling or child care services as much to ensure optimum productivity as to help their workers, and for-profit care homes, although they give care, are obviously run for money. Some services cross the line between social treatment and social control; for example, education or recreational programs such as Girl Scouts are aimed essentially at socialization and conformity but also are life-enhancing. In any case, <u>social welfare goods and services are provided both for the benefit of individuals, families, and groups and to maintain order in society.</u>

Ethical Practice

Practice Behavior Example: Make ethical decisions by applying standards of …

Critical Thinking Question: While social control is contrary to much of the National Association of Social Work Code of Ethics, it is nonetheless part of agency, state, and federal policies. How should social workers negotiate the tensions between social control and social treatment in the delivery of services?

Social welfare's tremendously broad scope includes provision of sustenance (cash, food stamps, housing, and medical care); parts of the legal system, as in juvenile and criminal justice; education and educational services aimed at counseling or rehabilitation; mental health care; child, family, and marital counseling; programs for special groups such as the aged or those who are developmentally disabled; substance abuse programs; and rehabilitative programs. <u>Whenever other social institutions such as family, church, and economy do not provide a service, social welfare fills in the gaps.</u> For example, public programs such as Social Security pensions now care for aged people who were once supported by the extended family.

Perspectives on Social Welfare

A perspective is a viewpoint based on values from which to look at a phenomenon. Our perspectives on social welfare come from diverse values that determine what we think social welfare should do and what its causes, purposes, functions, and results ought to be. Although we traditionally believe social welfare's causes to be altruistic, they are in fact interplays between altruism, the needs of the disadvantaged, and the desires of those in control. The purposes of social welfare are both to aid those in need and to maintain other structures and institutions of society, and these dual purposes reflect ambivalent goals and, hence, ambivalent programs, effects, and results. Their outcomes must be dually assessed on how well they serve clients and how effective they are for society's need to control. If assessed only on client benefit, most would be considered failures, for the lives of clients are not changed much by most social welfare programs. Looked at from the viewpoint of control, however, they may be very effective.

Our key to understanding this is *functionalism*, which is the usefulness of social welfare in maintaining society's structures. For example, public assistance programs are functional in a number of ways. The low levels of support give some subsistence, but they also save tax money and provide a "work incentive" to get people off welfare. They relieve society of the burden of adequate support and provide employers with sufficient workers at low wages and minimum benefits. Public assistance programs also control sex-role behaviors by requiring that men work at almost any job and that women maintain "moral" sexual, economic, and childrearing behaviors (upon threat of losing their grants and sometimes their children). Other programs have other functions: For example, mental hospitals warehouse the unwanted, emotionally ill, or aged; low assistance grants maintain markets for substandard or used goods; and social welfare programs provide jobs in social work and human service fields. If programs are not functional, they will cease to exist, and the fact that they continue despite public outcry and lack of service effectiveness indicates their functionalism for society. There will always be a need for social work.

A program may have both manifest and latent functions. A *manifest function* is one that is evident, usually written into the laws, mandates, or organizational constitutions and bylaws of a program. *Latent functions* are unstated and either assumed or hidden. Because a function is latent does not necessarily mean it is bad, but it does mean that workers, clients, and relevant others may be unaware of its real purposes. For example, socialization to conformity in Girl or Boy Scouts is not written into the bylaws, nor is it particularly a bad thing, but it is a latent, or unadvertised, function. A more insidious example is that the control of women, through public assistance programs or mental health systems, functions to maintain a patriarchal society.

The Residual Perspective

The traditional American perspective of social welfare is that, although society should help in emergencies, people in need are responsible for their own problems and should solve them with minimal societal intervention. This is called the *residual perspective*[11] and prescribes short-term, stopgap social welfare measures that last only until the social institutions normally providing help can resume their functions (the family or employment in the economy, for example). A major criterion is whether people are above a set level of money and assets, determined by *means testing* to ensure that applicants get no more help than they "should." Organizations and agencies have different eligibility levels or standards of need, but they are usually based on some relationship to the federal poverty level. Residual programs may also involve severe restriction of personal freedom (jail, long-term commitment to mental hospitals), short-term emergency care such as that offered by hospital emergency rooms, or twenty-four-hour holds for people with acute or life-threatening psychiatric disturbances. In cases of emergency or personal detainment, danger to self or others, rather than financial resources, is the general criterion for eligibility.

To discourage the use of social welfare programs, services often are the least or smallest possible, aid is given grudgingly, and people who seek help are stigmatized by society. Control rather than treatment often is the goal. Means testing is used particularly in subsistence programs (those offering food, shelter, and clothing), but also in such programs as mental health or family planning and health facilities to determine a sliding fee, based on how much clients can afford. Closely related to means testing is "less eligibility," a concept arising with the Elizabethan Poor Laws of 1601 (to be discussed in Chapter 4). In this concept, no person receiving public aid should get a grant higher than the lowest wage in the locality. Even today "less eligibility" may be considered when setting maximum amounts for public assistance grants.

The residual perspective is the basis for the *medical model* of social work treatment, in which social services are intended to "treat and cure" people who deviate from "healthy society." This complex of ideas leads to blaming victims[12] as responsible for their problems and does not consider structural problems—such as lack of employment opportunities or special problems—as relevant. The most common example of a program in which the residual perspective dominates is public assistance. This perspective has kept public assistance limited in both eligibility and amounts of grants, often too little to maintain health and welfare. Few programs are so residual in nature, but many have residual elements.

To recapitulate, a residual perspective mandates that social welfare programs should give aid to people

- In emergency situations, when other social institutions fail
- On a short-term basis
- As a stopgap measure, until "normal" social institutions come back into play
- With eligibility usually determined by means testing
- In a way that encourages recipients to find other means of help, usually by stigmatizing them
- Begrudgingly, especially in assistance programs, where minimal aid is given.

Let us consider a concrete example of a mother applying for Temporary Assistance to Needy Families (TANF):

- *Emergency.* She will be considered only if her income falls below state eligibility limits. It is assumed that as soon as possible she will become employed or find some other means of support (such as marriage or other family resources) and will leave the program.
- *Short-term.* The specified time limit to TANF is twenty-four consecutive months or sixty months lifetime limit.
- *Stopgap.* She will be allowed to receive TANF only as long as she has no other means of support. A major program goal is to move people off the rolls as soon as possible.

The residual perspective is the basis for the medical model of social work treatment, in which social services are intended to "treat and cure" people who deviate from "healthy society."

- *Means testing.* Her income and assets are assessed to ensure that they fall below the already low eligibility limits of TANF.
- *Stigmatizing.* Applying for TANF is demeaning because our American value system is so strongly opposed to public assistance. Also, the application process often entails speaking of intimate and personal details of one's life to a stranger, and permanent public records, though confidential, are made on the application.
- *Grudging and minimal.* Not only will she be subjected to the embarrassment of asking for public money, but the dollar amounts given are so minimal that they are known to be insufficient to maintain healthy subsistence on more than an emergency basis.[13]

The Institutional Perspective

The institutional perspective is at the opposite end of the continuum from the residual perspective. Its major criterion is membership in the society: Every person has a right to its services, without means testing or stigma. Programs are universal, that is, they cover every person within their designated mandate, whereas residual programs are selective in nature and apply only to a selected few or selected groups. The institutional perspective leads to the *structural or social model* of social work: Social problems are believed to come from oppressive or inegalitarian structures in society. Social problems are not based on personal fault, so solutions do not lie in controlling, punishing, or stigmatizing the individual; rather, they lie in root problems—such as classism, racism, and sexism—and their elimination.

Many programs of social welfare approach the institutional end of the residual–institutional continuum (see Figure 2.2). Public education, for example, is the right of all children in the United States, and Social Security ensures a retirement income for almost every person in the United States and supports surviving children of deceased workers. Mental health has evolved from residual to institutional in the past fifty years. Before the 1960s, the term used for people with emotional difficulties was *mentally ill*, and they were usually stigmatized for and ashamed of their problems. Now *mental health* is a social right. Although there is a sliding fee scale, private or public funds pay for services for those unable to pay, and no one is denied treatment because he or she is poor.

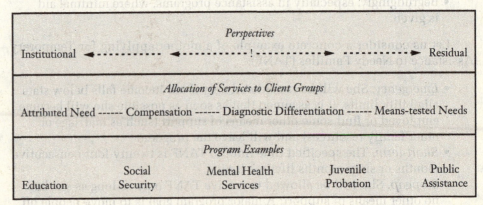

Figure 2.2

Continuum of Perspectives, Allocation of Services, and Program Examples

To recapitulate, then, the institutional perspective is a belief that

- social welfare services should be available to all members of society who fit a program's mandates;
- there is no time limit for services, although there may be a time at which services can begin (such as school attendance or eligibility for Social Security pensions);
- if there is any means testing, it is to determine the amount people can pay rather than to deny services;
- there is no stigma for either applying for or receiving services; and
- there is no societal pressure to leave the program.

The allocation of services or resources also lies on the institutional to residual continuum. Axinn and Levin[14] discuss the development of social welfare as a schematical which may be overlaid on the institutional to residual continuum: services allocated because recipients are members of society (institutionally attributed need); services in return for recipients' contributions to society (compensation); diagnoses given to those deviating from society's norms (diagnostic); and needs-based services. Looking at the continuum, its overlay, and examples of programs, we see Figure 2.2:

We can place programs along a continuum from residual to institutional as long as we remember that few programs are either wholly residual or wholly institutional. Some programs have both residual and institutional elements. For example, juvenile probation has residual elements because of the emergency nature of problems of children in trouble. However, institutional elements make protection under the system available to all children, including those who have suffered neglect and abuse. In contrast, even though education is one of our most institutional programs, services of truant officers and some administrators in schools deal with emergency problems that are residual in nature.

Although both functional and conflict theories are descriptive in nature, functional theories imply keeping a "status quo" in the social order whereas conflict theories incite toward prescriptions to attain change in power statuses. At times such change may lead to an increase in social justice, which may, within national, societal, or (today) international limits and capabilities, ensure that each member of every relevant group has unrestricted access, by virtue of being a member of society, to certain basic amenities of life. Among those are food, shelter, clothing, education, and health care adequate to the resources of the relevant society; and the ability to attain such rights through, for example, employment, legislation, court decisions, and so on; equitable treatment under law; and basic freedoms, including speech and self-expression.

Newer Perspectives in Social Welfare

Although the perspectives discussed so far provide some prescriptions for social work practice, they are basically static and descriptive, dealing only minimally with policy analysis or problem causation. Newer perspectives based on sociological, economic, Afrocentric, and feminist theories are now being applied to social welfare to assess its social history, and they suggest proactive and often radical models for human service work. More or less related to the institutional perspective and to structural models of practice, these perspectives view recalcitrant societal structures, rather than individual fault, as causes of social problems. They criticize these structures and prescribe social action and social change to a much greater degree than do present structural models.

Generally, the newer perspectives are based on *conflict theory*: They posit a conflict between those who control society's structures and those who are controlled and exploited by them. Piven and Cloward were among the first to develop these theories for social welfare, which remain controversial today. They noted in their 1971 book *Regulating the Poor* that throughout history, whenever the disadvantaged rebelled against exploitation, welfare programs and benefits expanded until the rebellion ceased.[15] Then benefits shrank, although it was seldom to prerebellion levels, and they were sufficient to keep people quiet for a time. Thus, expansion of welfare programs was not altruistic but political and economic: It quelled rebellions and, because benefits were always meager, kept a quiescent workforce eager to take jobs with low wages and few benefits. This made labor costs cheap and profitable to producers.

James Rule says that redefining social conflicts as social problems changes their nature and enables people to believe that solutions can be found.[16] The redefinition places the burden for change on "deviants" and those hired to change them—social workers—and relieves society of the burden of changing its status quo. For example, if poverty is class conflict, the higher class must fight to keep its privileged position from those who would take away its benefits. If it is redefined as a social problem, powerless social workers "own" and must solve the "problem" of poverty. The upper class is satisfied because society remains stratified, the poor believe that solutions will be found, and social workers find solutions that usually do not work because the conflict elements remain. In the same way, if high unemployment among African Americans is defined as racism because of job discrimination, action to end racism is implied, along with high risks and few rewards. However, if high unemployment among African Americans is defined as a social problem, the solution is job training programs, which are much easier to create than racial equality, even though they will not work because no jobs are available.

Seeing racism, sexism, and classism as social problems implies that solutions can be found in changing the victims rather than in changing society's exploitative structures. Because victims of society are not generally to blame for their victimization, only remedial, Band-Aid work can be done because the damage-causing structures remain. However, seeing the "isms" as conflicts implies action against society, though such action may never occur. In the first place, most Americans believe our society is egalitarian and democratic, and action against it means action against those principles. Second, although seeing "isms" as conflict issues might provide the right mind-set to work for change, restructuring of the system is too much for most of us to undertake.

To reiterate, conflict theory says that social problems

- lie in the structures of society rather than the fault of the individual;
- are the result of attempts of an elite group to maintain the privileges they have accumulated through exploitation of other classes and groups; and
- will endure until the structures themselves are changed.

Paradigms pertaining to social welfare which reflect conflict theory include Marxian, socialist, socialist feminist, radical feminist, feminist welfarist, the Afrocentric paradigm as discussed by Jerome Schiele,[17] and Black Feminist thought as developed by Patricia Hill Collins.[18] *Marxian and socialist perspectives* look at class stratification and exploitative behavior and perceive social welfare as helping to maintain inegalitarian structures. Rather than remedial treatment for the disadvantaged, eradication of the oppressive economic and political structures is advocated. Class advantages would be eliminated and profit sharing and a government based on worker control would redistribute wealth. Disadvantaged people would receive sufficient resources from the government to satisfy their needs. To a great extent, these perspectives ignore gender issues except to note that a different economic structure would eliminate gender stratification because it is based on worker oppression.

Socialist feminism's primary concern is the economic oppression of women, which began with the onset of private property and the loss of women's economic value to the family. In this view, women are doubly oppressed: first as workers in a capitalist economy and second as wives dependent on husbands who are in turn exploited workers. Women are involved directly in production at work, and at home in two kinds of reproduction that serve the capitalist economy: biological reproduction to supply a new generation of workers and maintenance of a home that offers surcease to the weary laborer and renews him for more productive work. A restructuring of class stratification and a redefinition of marriage and family roles—perhaps their elimination—would prevent both primary and secondary oppression. An altered economic system would provide new access for all kinds of social care, and social welfare's concerns should be social action and social change to give economic and political empowerment to women.

Radical feminism is concerned with political exploitation of women under a patriarchal system enforcing gender privilege throughout history. In this view, both class and gender exploitation began with the onset of private property and the loss of women's co-equal status. Patriarchal sex-role socialization keeps women in subordinate and powerless roles and increases their dependency on men and male systems (such as public assistance and mental health systems), so that women themselves believe in the "rightness" of male control and cooperate in their own subordination. Models for action include consciousness raising; values awareness; a reassessment of female roles in marriage, family, and society; and social action for empowerment even to the point of separatism, as in women's communities.

The *feminist welfarist perspective* is a critical analysis of American social history that incorporates conflict theory, socialist and radical feminist perspectives, and the synergistic evolution of social welfare, as described in Chapter 1. It pays particular attention to economy, polity, and spiritual motivations concerning social treatment and social control. According to this perspective, value systems create a morally legitimate oppression for women and for the poor, and race privilege is superimposed on these. Its arguments are predicated on sex-role socialization to a patriarchal society's expectations: women as dependent, incompetent in money management, less mature, and given to emotionality. Men also are victims of patriarchal sex-role stereotyping and exploitation. Although they have more power than women, their most important sex-role identification is as worker, making them very exploitable in a capitalistic society.

A major issue from this perspective is the povertization of women. Public dependency for women arises from different causes than for men, yet public assistance programs are based on male models of need; that is, the idea that adults who can work should work (male-pauper model). However, women are not simply capable workers, although they may be. They are socialized to family roles and away from lucrative employment by school and family systems, they have primary emotional and economic responsibility for dependent children, and the structures of society that deal with their dependence (courts and public assistance systems) do not provide adequate grants to lift them above poverty levels. Work itself is marginal and low-paying for most women, and few receive equal pay for equal or comparable work. To insist that work is their way out of poverty is a denial of the differential treatment accorded them throughout society's institutions.[19]

In addition, the needs of women, as well as care by women, create special problems for social welfare. Women are the majority of workers as well as the majority of clients in social welfare systems. They have little power or recognition, they cannot command resources because they are inadequately represented in welfare policy bodies, and their charity work is derogated by society's antipoverty values. Men in social welfare have more legitimation because they traditionally have worked with employment programs (such as unions, job training, and social insurance). From this differential association with "undeserving" and "deserving" groups, neither women, social work, nor clients gain society's respect. Finally, social welfare itself contributes to the patriarchal control of women, the poor, and people of color. Established, financed, and directed by a white male political system, although women do much of its work, it is in general a male system, and it is oriented to maintaining the status quo of society.

The *Afrocentric paradigm* provides a further step in the analysis of social welfare. While feminist models consider androcentrism, or male-centeredness, as engendering, influencing, and maintaining oppressive social structures, Afrocentrism looks at Eurocentricity, or white male domination. Eurocentricity derived from European invasions and colonialism beginning in the 1400s, spurred by new world travel and the search for wealth. Consequently, conquerors enforced their own cultural values on colonized and enslaved people; values that undermined their traditions and rights. Jerome Schiele says that

> Eurocentric political/economic oppression implies that people of Eurocentric descent have more material power than people of color ... [and its ensuing] cultural oppression implies that the values, experiences, and interpretations of people of European descent are imposed as "universal norms" of human culture and consciousness. This cultural imposition suppresses and denies the cultural integrity and particularity of people of color, especially people of African descent.[20]

Most, if not all, American social values are in fact Eurocentric, and, in the Afrocentric perspective "... engender and reproduce 'spiritual alienation'" which

> ... generates an unequal distribution of power and resources and diminishes the quality of interpersonal and intergroup relations.... [This] ... has adverse social, psychological, and economic implications for all people, not just African Americans ... [and arises] from core values of the Eurocentric worldview.[21]

Patricia Hill Collins' work on Black Feminist thought provides another dimension to our analysis. Looking primarily at African-American women and the problems they face today, she posits a construct of "intersectionality," where sex, race, gender, and class intersect to create a nexus of social

injustice. She defines intersectionality as "particular forms of intersecting oppressions,"[22] providing

> ... a fundamental paradigmatic shift in how we think about unjust power
> relations. By embracing a paradigm of intersecting oppressions of race,
> class, gender, sexuality, and nation ... [it] reconceptualizes the social re-
> lations of domination and resistance....[23]

Further, she notes that "Intersectional paradigms remind us that oppression cannot be reduced to one fundamental type, and that oppressions work
together in producing injustice."[24] She reminds us that "objectifying" those at
the margins of society—the "others"—is essential to oppression. Although she
speaks of Black womanhood, her analysis is applicable to all "others."

Because the authority to define societal values is a major instrument of
power, elite groups, in exercising power, manipulate ideas by exploiting
already existing symbols, or creating new ones. Hazel Carby suggests that
the objective of stereotypes is "not to reflect or represent a reality but to
function as a disguise, or mystification, of objective social relations." These
controlling images are designed to make racism, sexism, poverty, and other
forms of social injustice appear to be natural, normal, and inevitable parts of
everyday life.[25]

As we observed earlier, the institution of social welfare evolved to deal
with society's "others," those whose needs exceeded the obligations or capabilities of the institutions of polity, economy, family, or religion. Conflict theory and its paradigms clearly point out that, at least in the United States, any
such services, if they do not produce a profit, are objectified along with their
clients as "others" and stigmatized by society. Utilizing Marxist and socialist
perspectives, feminist welfarism, the Afrocentric paradigm, and the paradigm
of intersectional oppression help us analyze how social welfare in the United
States is inherently racist, sexist, classist, and "otherist." Only by acknowledging this can we achieve social justice.

To recap, conflict theory is a critical historical analysis that

- incorporates Marxist, socialist, and radical feminist perspectives and the Afrocentric and intersectionality paradigms;
- reconstructs social history to include perspectives of the poor, women, and races (and religions) other than the dominant white male system;
- sees social problems as the results of historical convergences of class privilege, race privilege, and patriarchal power;
- traces most social problems to structured inequalities primarily based on class, race, and gender; and
- indicts social welfare as causative in great part of the maintenance of structured inequalities.

THE SCOPE OF SOCIAL WELFARE

Social welfare ranges across all aspects of life, from birth to death, providing social services where other institutions fail or are inadequate.[26] Social services are activities that help or control, performed by people in the public (government) or private sectors, usually in social agencies formed around a particular social need, such as hunger, delinquency, or substance abuse. People who provide social services may be professional social workers with master's or bachelor's degrees; paraprofessionals (people indigenous to the client population who are trained by professional social workers but do not have professional degrees); laypeople, such as church volunteers; or people having little or no professional social work training but working in social agencies, such as departments of public welfare, the juvenile division of the court system, and Social Security offices. Also, nonsocial-work professionals, such as psychologists, psychiatrists, and members of the clergy, provide counseling services. Finally, self-help groups with or without professional association and staffing provide emotional support and help to members; examples include Alcoholics Anonymous or women's consciousness-raising groups.

Social welfare ranges across all aspects of life, from birth to death, providing social services where other institutions fail or are inadequate.

Public agencies are established by law on local (city or county), state, or federal levels and are administered by public officials according to legal mandates. Some have local representative boards, but power resides in the legislation. Private agencies are nongovernmental, although they may have government charters and often receive some funding from government bodies. They are often called voluntary agencies because they are established by voluntary groups, usually around a local need, and are funded substantially through private contributions. Some are developed by religious groups to provide social services specific to a religion's beliefs. Members of the community on volunteer boards make agency policy decisions, but staff and administration are often paid professionals. Although some still have individual fund drives, many are now part of United Way agencies, which run annual fund drives and apportion out contributions by locally established criteria to member agencies.

Some organizations offering social services are not social agencies but provide help to enhance their primary goals. For example, schools may provide counseling for children and their parents around the issues of absenteeism or lack of motivation, hospitals give social services to the families of dying patients or arrange extended care for aged patients, and churches carry out their religious mandates to care for the poor with food baskets and soup kitchens.

Some social agencies provide a wide variety of services, some target only a few, and often services or clientele overlap.

The following are certain generally identifiable fields of social services:

- Life necessity services
- Educational, recreational, or rehabilitative services
- Protective or custodial services
- Personal social services

Life Necessity Services: Overview

Life necessity services supply food, clothing, shelter, and medical assistance. Public agencies provide the bulk of such services, although churches and such private agencies as the Salvation Army, Goodwill Industries, Volunteers of America, and Catholic Charities supplement such programs with grants or donations or give temporary shelter. Food programs—lunch and breakfast or home-delivered meals—may be publicly or privately funded and are carried out in schools, churches, and senior citizens' centers.

By far the largest public programs are those of the federal Social Security Acts of 1935 and their amendments. The three major areas are Social Insurance, Public Assistance, and Maternal and Child Health (see Table 2.1). The largest program of social insurance is Old Age, Survivors, Disability and Health Insurance (OASDHI). Other social insurances include Unemployment Insurance and Workers' Compensation, both state programs with varying degrees of federal input. *Public assistance* programs include TANF, Supplemental Security Income (SSI), Medicaid, and general assistance or poor relief at state and county levels. The Food Stamp program, now called *Supplemental Nutrition Assistance Program* (SNAP), is also considered public assistance, although it is a program of the Department of Agriculture. Among maternal and child health programs are the Crippled Children's program, school lunches, family planning programs, and Women's, Infants', and Children's Nutrition (WIC).

Social insurance programs are work related and directed to the "worthy poor." Originally the Social Security Acts established retirement pensions for aged workers and their spouses and pensions for the children of deceased workers (Old Age and Survivors Insurance, or OASI). Health insurance (Medicare) was added in 1964, and Medicare Rx in 2006. Old Age Assistance, Aid to the Blind, and Aid to the Permanently and Totally Disabled (which had been public assistance programs) were added in 1972. OASDHI is funded through the FICA tax. Workers' Compensation pays pensions or settlements for disabilities or death suffered by workers, and Unemployment Insurance provides

Table 2.1 Selected Government Programs for the Poor

Social Insurance	Public Assistance	Maternal and Child Health
OASDHI	TANF	Family Planning
Medicare (the H in OASDHI)	Medicaid	WIC
Medicare Rx	SSI	Crippled Children
Unemployment Insurance	General Assistance	Child Nutrition
Workers' Compensation	Poor Relief	
	Food Stamps (SNAP)	

Critical Thinking

Practice Behavior Example: Requires the synthesis and communication of relevant information.

Critical Thinking Question: Should all social welfare programs be means tested? What advantages and disadvantages might accompany this type of policy change?

benefits to workers laid off from regular employment for a limited time period. Both the latter programs are federally mandated but financed by employers (through taxes or private carriers) and are administered by the states.

Although social insurance is not means tested, *public assistance* programs are, and applicants are not accepted if they have income and assets over state-set levels. The Aid to Families of Dependent Children (AFDC) program was federally mandated but administered by states, with 50–75 percent federal financing and the remainder paid by the state. Before 1988, the program was specifically for one-parent families with children, although states could choose to fund intact families where the wage earner was incapacitated (AFDC-I) or unemployed (AFDC-UP). However, the Family Support Act of 1988 mandated AFDC-UP for all states, depending on the willingness of wage earners to engage in job training, "workfare," or job search. The SSI program was financed by the federal government with state supplementation and administered by county departments of public welfare.

Most public assistance at the federal level was eliminated by the Personal Responsibility and Work Opportunity Reconciliation Act of 1996, specifically the TANF program, which replaced AFDC, SSI, WIC, school breakfast and lunch programs, and other benefit programs. Money formerly used for such programs was placed in block grants and given to states to administer at state and local levels, and states might opt to have TANF administered by private companies. Federal requirements and standards, generally, no longer applied. Work and work training were TANF goals, and with some exceptions recipients who fail to find work within twenty-four months are removed from TANF rolls. There is also a lifetime recipient cap of sixty months on TANF, and the program was reauthorized in 2006 and again in the 2008 Recover Act, adding an Emergency Contingency Fund (ECF) for additional resources.[27]

Medicaid is a federal/state program providing health subsidies for most people, depending on the state, whose incomes fall below state-determined standards of need; it is administered by state and county welfare departments. Whereas the social insurance program Medicare pays for hospitalization and some extended care in nursing facilities (along with a few other benefits) for the aged or permanently and totally disabled, Medicaid—a public assistance program that varies on options from state to state—can pay many medical costs, including hospitalization, surgery, physicians' office calls, and prescription drugs. Depending on the state, it can also pay for hearing aids, prosthetics, eyeglasses, and the like. Medicare Rx requires copays for prescription drugs through private health insurance programs.

Under the *maternal and child health* system, state public health departments can provide tuberculosis testing, immunization clinics, well-baby clinics, family planning programs, sexually transmitted disease testing and treatment, school health nurses, and control of communicable diseases, public health hazards, and epidemics. Other federal life necessity programs include *subsidized housing* in the form of loans, grants, or partial rent subsidies; railroad workers' and federal employee pensions; and medical costs for veterans (Veterans Administration). On the county and state levels, *general assistance* (GA) and *poor-relief programs* aid people who are not eligible for federal programs. Counties decide on the level of aid and administer the programs, with state matching funds (usually 60 percent state). Counties often have medical assistance programs for hospital care and burial subsidies for county indigents who are not covered by other programs.

A variety of private organizations and brotherhoods (such as the Elks and Lions) work to cure or control particular diseases or problems. Among them are the American Cancer Association, Crippled Children's Association, Muscular Dystrophy Association, March of Dimes Foundation, Epilepsy Foundation, Planned Parenthood clinics, and myriad others. They provide money for services, information, and education to the public; research; and prosthetics, eyeglasses, wheelchairs, and other equipment. The American Red Cross maintains a blood bank and provides a variety of health services to veterans and other citizens in times of emergency.

Educational, Recreational, or Rehabilitative Services: Overview

Educational, recreational, or rehabilitative services include job training, remedial education services, day care for children (custodial or educational), recreational programs and facilities, disability rehabilitation services, and educational and rehabilitative services for people in custodial care in prisons, mental hospitals, and juvenile detention facilities.

In addition to basic education, school districts often provide technical job training, such as auto mechanics or typing. For young people no longer in regular school, "alternative schools" may offer basic education, training, personal or employment counseling, or remedial programs for literacy. General education degrees (GEDs) or technical certificates may be awarded. School social workers ("visiting teachers") counsel students, visit their homes to solve non-academic problems, or undertake individual or group therapy with students or their families. Some may be "truant officers" or juvenile probation officers making sure that children attend school, stay out of trouble with the law, and are protected from neglect or abuse.

Several public programs offer job training and educational services for adults. TANF requires all public assistance recipients with children over age one to participate in work, job training, or public or private subsidized work in return for their grants. After two years in any one application, their public assistance ends, as do any kind of subsidized work or work training programs. After five years in the TANF program, they are ineligible for public assistance except under special waivers. Most War on Poverty job programs (such as the Manpower Development and Training Act of 1962, the Economic Opportunity Act of 1964, Job Corps for youth no longer in school, and the Neighborhood Youth Corps) were dismantled or severely cut by Reagan, Bush, and the 104th Congress. Programs previously written into public assistance also were cut (such as the Comprehensive Education and Training Act, the Job Partnership Training Act of 1981, and Job Opportunities and Basic Skills). However, state employment commissions still provide registration, testing, and counseling for jobs in addition to administering the unemployment compensation program.

Vocational Rehabilitation is a Department of Education program administered by state education departments (amendments of 1954 and 1973). It provides a full range of services to disabled people to train them for employment: medical testing to assess the extent of disability; medical and surgical services to lessen the extent of impairment; personal and rehabilitation counseling; education including college, depending on ability; vocational training in private or public schools; such special equipment as hearing aids, guide dogs, wheel-chairs, canes, and prosthetics; special training in sign language or social adjustment; sheltered workshops; money for transportation and living expenses while training; and assistance in finding a job and essential equipment, such as licenses, tools, or stock.[28] Private agencies such as Goodwill Industries and Volunteers of America also give training and rehabilitation in sheltered workshops, where people unable to work in the general marketplace receive minimal pay for the work they are able to do.

Prisons, mental hospitals, and other custodial care facilities also have rehabilitation and educational programs intended to provide released people with job skills that will enable them to earn a living once out of custody. In addition, private security companies are now more fully involved in custodial care. Day care and juvenile facilities run by private for-profit associations and individuals have existed for more than a century, and private nursing home care has skyrocketed since the beginning of the Medicare and Medicaid programs in the 1960s. With new legislation on drugs, including the "three strikes" law, prisons have filled to overflowing, causing some states to opt for privately owned and managed correctional facilities.

Day care facilities for children may be financed privately or through TANF (to encourage mothers to enter the job force). Public welfare departments license and monitor private (approved) homes and private or public day care centers. Head Start, a War on Poverty program, provides educational care for children and other services to parents. Nursery schools offer early education and socialization skills to children in addition to day care. For adults with emotional, physical, or developmental problems, departments of education, mental health clinics, and private entrepreneurs provide day care, nursing home care, halfway houses, or extended care. These may also give social opportunities, counseling, or a variety of other services, as do programs and centers for senior citizens.

Recreational agencies give opportunities for recreation, training, education, social experiences, and socialization to normative beliefs and standards in America. They include day camps, summer camps, programs of the Young Women's and Young Men's Christian Association or Hebrew Association (YWCA, YMCA, YWHA, YMHA), Boy Scouts, Girl Scouts, and their counterparts. Kahn says,

> In a major sense, social services exist to protect, to change, or to innovate with respect to many of the educational, child-rearing, value-imparting, and social induction activities once assumed by the extended family, the neighborhood, and relatives. The goal is socialization into communal values, transmittal of goals and motivation, and enhancement of personal development. Cognitive and emotional aspects of learning are encompassed.[29]

Protective or Custodial Services: Overview

Protective or custodial services include group homes and institutions for disturbed or delinquent children, programs for neglected or abused children and their parents, child guidance programs and school social work for troubled or troublesome children, foster care and adoption, homes for unwed mothers, mental hospitals or short-term group or custodial homes for emotionally disturbed people, and protective services and nursing homes for the aged or developmentally disabled. Rehabilitative work in prisons and juvenile institutions is included in this category, as are jails, prisons, and juvenile and adult parole and probation work. Public agencies offering such care are usually connected with either departments of public welfare or the juvenile or adult justice systems, but may include private for-profit institutions, such as nursing homes, or not-for-profit organizations, such as Crittenton Services and Salvation Army homes.

Protection for abused and neglected children and adults (particularly aged or developmentally disabled adults) was authorized by the Social Service Amendments to the Social Security Acts of 1935 (Title XX). Under this act, social workers from public welfare departments grant licenses to nursing homes, foster homes, and private care homes and deal with complaints of abuse by parents or other caretakers, including public or private institutions. At the local level, governments offer help for family violence through police department social workers, and private organizations are opening shelters for battered women and exploited children and runaways.

Personal Social Services: Overview

Personal social services offer

> brief, or intensive, personal help with environmental, situational, interpersonal, or intrapsychic programs. Frequently the goal is restoration of as much normal functioning as possible ... [assuming control over] ... dangerous or unacceptable deviance while help is rendered.[30]

It includes therapy for individuals or groups in such areas as child or marriage problems, substance abuse, and emotional difficulties related to divorce, death, and so on; psychological testing and psychiatric services; counseling on budgeting, credit, family planning, or employment; and access and advocacy services.

Although therapy and counseling are offered in some public settings—mental hospitals, for example—this has generally been the province of private social agencies. People intensively trained in clinical skills practice intervention techniques based on work by a number of theorists, including Freud, Adler, Jung, Rogers, Perls, Ellis, and Glasser. The techniques range across psychosocial casework, problem solving, task-centered therapy, psychoanalysis, client-centered therapy, Gestalt therapy, and behavior modification. Mental health clinics or family service agencies are among the primary providers of such care, but other organizations offer it as part of their services (Planned Parenthood, shelters for battered women, schools, group homes, probation offices, and juvenile and adult detention centers, for example). The relationship with the counselor and client motivation are essential elements in the counseling process.

Access services are a part of personal social services. They enable clients to find, understand, and use social services. Through information giving, referral, and follow-up, they help clients through the maze of bureaucracies and regulations that might preclude help. In addition, access services may help to locate gaps in service and coordinate agencies or develop new services to fill them. Advocacy services enable and empower clients to gain rights and services to which they are eligible or entitled under the law. Legal action, along with lobbying and influence, secures needed services, and clients are encouraged to undertake social action on their own behalf. Community action agencies, developed during the War on Poverty, were the forerunners in advocacy, but now most social agencies offer limited advocacy.

THE PROFESSION OF SOCIAL WORK[31]

Some would argue that social work is not a profession. Although it is theoretically based, other professions share both theory and skills used in social work, and those skills are neither exclusive nor (in many areas) highly technical. Its professional culture includes undergraduate and graduate schools, apprenticeships, and professional associations (National Association of Social Workers and Council for Social Work Education). However, other schools and programs teach human services, especially on the interpersonal level. Nevertheless, society recognizes the expertise of social work as a profession, even though its ethical stance is often in conflict with major American values. In addition, social work has another problem: respect. Most of its practitioners are women and its clients are "deviants." Therefore, many view the profession as a "socially contaminated" occupation with little credibility. Finally, because its scope is broad and its targets many, it has no exclusive domain for practice, with the possible exception of child protective services.

On the continuum of occupations, social work falls near the professional end. Its general definition as a profession is

> the professional activity of helping individuals, groups, or communities enhance or restore their capacity for social functioning and creating societal conditions favorable to this goal ... the professional application of social work values, principles, and techniques to one or more of the following ends: helping people obtain tangible services; counseling and psychotherapy with individuals, families, and groups; helping communities or groups provide or improve social and health services; and participating in relevant legislative processes.[32]

Social work is different from other helping professions in specific ways. Included in these are the overarching mission; the client system; the focus on client-in-situation; the target of practice; and the complex of values, knowledge, and skills that makes up the ethical stance of social work practice.

Social work intervention, although it may include intrapsychic therapy, goes far beyond personal problems of emotional or mental health. Social work's original mission was not personal but social intervention—reform of poverty and its causes. Although this has changed in many ways, the mission is still social in nature, dealing with elements beyond the individual client. These elements include not only mental health but financial security, employment satisfaction, marital health, elimination of inequality, and the attainment of civil and human rights for clients. Optimal social functioning in problematic areas of life is the goal of practice.

Unlike clients in other helping professions, the social work client may be an individual, a group, a family, an organization, a neighborhood group, or a political body. Moreover, the focus of practice is the client-in-situation (see Figure 2.3). The importance of the social environment in the helping process is a stated and formal criterion unique to social work, although other helping professionals surely deal with these relationships less formally. Social work considers the complex of systems that affect clients, influence their behavior, and may create and maintain their problems. Unlike such disciplines as medicine and

Social work's original mission was not personal but social intervention—reform of poverty and its causes.

Social work considers the complex of systems that affect clients, influence their behavior, and may create and maintain their problems.

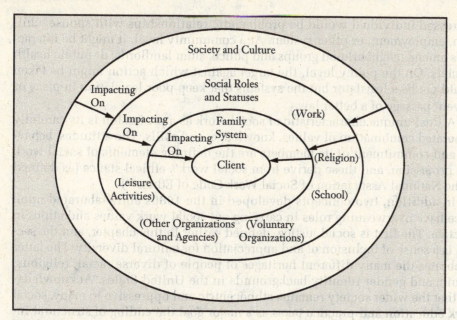

Figure 2.3
Client-in-Situation

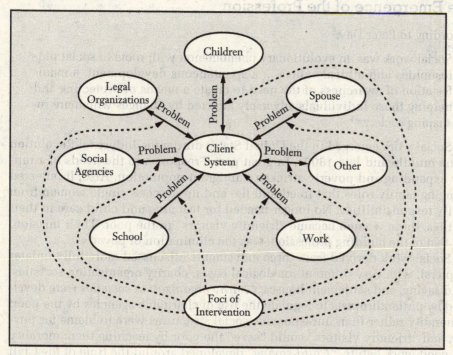

Figure 2.4
Targets of Practice

psychology, which generally separate clients from the contexts of their lives, social work recognizes that individual change is based on the context of lives.

In addition, the target of social work practice is not the client but the relationships and reciprocal interactions that instigate or perpetuate the problem situation (see Figure 2.4). To elaborate, the target of intervention for a depressed individual would be problematic relationships with spouse, children, employment, or other system. At a community level, it might be interactions among neighborhood groups and police, slum landlords, or public health officials. On the policy level, the target against which action might be taken would not be a legislator but the systems that keep poor legislation in place or prevent passage of a better law.

A final unique characteristic of social work as a profession is its carefully elaborated combination of values, knowledge, and skills. The attitudes, behavior, and commitment of its members are the defining elements of social work as a profession, and these derive from social work's ethical stance (as defined in the National Association of Social Work Code of Ethics[33]).

In addition, two concepts developed in the 1980s and elaborated upon since have overweening roles in carrying out social work values and ethics in practice. The first is social justice, defined earlier in this chapter, and the second is a sense of inclusion of and appreciation for cultural diversity. The latter celebrates the many different heritages of people of diverse racial, religious, ethnic, and gender identity backgrounds in the United States. Acknowledging that the wider society remains ethnocentric and oppressive to many, social work education and practice takes as a major goal the ending of structural inequalities that limit or deny social justice for all.

The Emergence of the Profession

According to Peter Day,

> Social work was an evolutionary phenomenon with roots in social philosophies and ethical values … a spontaneous development, a manifestation of awareness of the need to create a means of protecting and helping those individuals adversely affected by changes which are reshaping society.[34]

Social work emerged in the United States during the Industrial Revolution in the middle and late 1800s, in great part a response to the needs of a rapidly expanding and poverty-stricken immigrant population. Also, it reflected changing family roles that freed middle- and upper-class single women from family responsibilities. No longer needed for teaching and child care in their families, these women became "friendly visitors" to the poor. Their mission, and that of the budding profession, was the elimination of poverty.

Social work derived from three movements (discussed more fully in later chapters), with very different ideological bases: charity organization societies, child-saving, and settlement houses. *Charity organization societies* were developed by philanthropists to regulate the use of charitable agencies by the poor. Immorality rather than unresponsive social structures were to blame for poverty, and "friendly visitors" could "save" the poor by teaching them morality and good work habits. "*Child-saving*" developed around the time of the Civil War, when thousands of unsupervised children roamed city streets begging, stealing, and taking men's jobs at lower wages. Although early on child-saving acted more to rid the streets of young nuisances than to help children, it brought a new concept—childhood—that young people be viewed not as small adults but as needing special care because of their youth. *Settlement houses*, often developed by women, were based on the concept that people could work together for a common goal and change society to make it more relevant to the needs of the poor. In this view, the cause of poverty was not personal fault or immorality but unresponsive social structures, such as the economy and the polity. Grassroots organization, education, and training, provided in supportive group settings and without moral stigma, were the means to success. New immigrants were the targeted clientele, but other people needing help were also welcome.

Professional Identity

Practice Behavior Example: Know the profession's histoy.

Critical Thinking Question: How do the early social welfare movements of the charity organization societies, child saving, and settlement houses inform modern social work?

Early social workers soon realized that social structures were responsible for poverty, and they gathered data used to create social reforms. However, blaming the victim and the medical model remained in the public idiom. The medical model sees problems in the individual and seeks cures for the person rather than the society. The clinical model of practice, emphasizing personal attention and individual work with clients, is a direct result of the charity organization societies' friendly visiting. Group work, community action, and social action methods of social work developed from the settlement house movement; and adoption, foster care, and child guidance movements began with child-saving.

By the end of the nineteenth century, social work was no longer voluntary but paid employment and was given public recognition as an occupation. Still a women's job, the public looked on it as an extension of "women's sphere": home and family roles moved into the community. Formal training began in the early 1900s as the first step in professionalization, and social workers began to be acknowledged authorities on the needs of disadvantaged or deviant people. However, many practitioners have turned away from the mission of equality in order to accrue some of the benefits of a profession: status, better pay, and more authority in the community. A majority now enter middle-class, more status-laden mental health fields. Therefore, work with the poor or stigmatized disadvantaged is often left to people untrained in the knowledge, skills, and values of social work. Concern with social action and social change has, in great part, fallen by the wayside of professionalization, undercutting the historic mission of the profession itself.

The idea of a combination of skills, values, and knowledge is the underlying theme of practice at any level or in any style. We have already discussed the value base of social work; the knowledge base derives from many disciplines. For example, from psychology we obtain information on human development, mental health, and primary and secondary relationships; from sociology we learn of behavior in groups, societal values and norms, the place of person in organization, and the uses of power, status, class, race, and sex; from learning theory comes information on how people assimilate new ideas and their stages of mental development; and from history we become aware of the broad sweeps of economics, the polity, and religion in creating and changing the institution of social welfare.

Types of intervention techniques depend first on the purpose of the intervention—social treatment or social control—and are related to the needs of both the client system and society. Second, they depend on the client system type (individual, group, organization, or other). Third, the kind of technique depends on the theoretical base the worker is using. Therapists may use any of a variety of techniques, such as Freudian psychoanalysis, Gestalt therapy, confrontive techniques, principles of learning theory, and problem-solving models.

Professional social workers are trained and educated in colleges and universities with baccalaureate or graduate social work programs accredited by the Council on Social Work Education (CSWE). Baccalaureate education provides a generalist education, including orientation to social welfare and knowledge of direct and indirect practice. Master's level education trains graduates at an advanced specialist level that might include clinical counseling, work with special needs people (such as the aged or physically disabled), community practice, research, administration, and policy analysis and evaluation. Doctoral education produces new social work knowledge through research, consultants, and teachers for new social workers. Doctoral social work programs are not accredited by the CSWE. Unifying principles of social work education and practice include:

- Values, knowledge, and skills as practice bases
- A systems framework of person in environment
- Levels of practice, as noted above
- Relational and cognitive skills used simultaneously in practice
- A social justice perspective
- Social Work Code of Ethics.

In 2008, the CSWE converted its educational standards from an objective-based model to a competency-based one. Now, BSW and MSW social work students must be trained to demonstrate ten competencies with associated practice behaviors. The practice behaviors are operational indicators of the competencies that provide more concrete ways to demonstrate student learning. Additionally, the 2008 standards conceive field education as the *signature pedagogy*, which "represents the central form of instructional and learning in which a profession socializes its students to perform the role of practitioner."[35] Field education, or practicum as it is commonly called, requires BSW and MSW students to have internships in a community agency or organization. This experience is central because it requires students to integrate and apply what they learn in the classroom to real life client situations.

Traditionally, social work practice is direct practice on a personal level through clinical or group work, or indirect practice at the organizational or institutional level, such as community practice, administration, and policy.

- *Clinical Practice.* Personal counseling or intervention to help overcome personal, intrapsychic, or systemic problems (e.g., mental health or child guidance counseling).
- *Group work.* Intervention in groups or families to enhance the group process or give personal aid (e.g., groups in residential treatment centers, voluntary help groups such as Alcoholics Anonymous).
- *Community practice.* Work with indigenous groups, neighborhoods, areas, or communities to change recalcitrant or oppressive systems (i.e., slum housing) or create better systems (i.e., better police protection). This may involve direct work with client groups as a resource person or facilitator or indirect work with other systems to ensure clients' rights.
- *Administration.* Directing organizations, supervision of staff, budget development, organizational planning, creating and operationalizing programs, maintaining organizational goals and relationships with other community organizations.
- *Policy practice.* Professional program planning, evaluation and analysis of programs, processes, and policies; legislation development and enactment; lobbying; long-term planning.
- *Research and teaching.* Investigate social problems to find new ways of service, add to social work's knowledge base, teach new social workers.

CONCLUSION: SOCIAL WORK AND SOCIAL CONTROL

This overview of social welfare and social work particularly noted definitions of social institution, social welfare, and social work to provide common concepts. The perspective of social welfare as both social treatment and social control gave new insights into the political and economic purposes that maintain social problems and prevent disadvantaged people from attaining equality in our society. Social work is more than concern and care. It is also a political activity aimed at control. Peter Day says that

> social work acts have political implications ... about the way that an organization or group is run, and therefore about who has the power to get things done.[36]

and

> [c]are and control can be seen as complementary aspects of public policy towards the poor and deviant ... these two elements, originally separately institutionalized, have converged in the role of ... social workers.[37]

Our discussion of perspectives demonstrated that social conflict may be the basis for social problems, and that redefining social conflicts as social problems is functional for continuing inequality and the status quo in our society. Newer perspectives arising from the conflict model give us useful ways to understand this. The Marxist and socialist frameworks, the feminist welfarist perspective, the Afrocentric paradigm, and intersectionalism further illuminate the social welfare institution and the status of social workers as often unaware tools of forces not oriented to benevolence: We may have become middle persons of social control for those we wished to help. As Hannah Arendt once stated,

> Compassion may itself be a substitute for justice ... compassion always already signifies inequality. The compassionate intend no justice, for justice might corrupt current power relationships.[38]

The following questions will test your knowledge and understanding of the content found within this chapter. For additional assessment, including licensing-exam type questions on applying chapter content to practice behaviors, visit **MySearchLab**.

1. Which statement best defines discouraged workers?
   a. Workers who are paid at least 50% less than their skill set warrants.
   b. Unemployed people who have been actively looking for work for over six months.
   c. People who have been unemployed for so long that they finally stopped searching for work.
   d. Workers who are chronically dissatisfied in their current job

2. What is the role of means testing?
   a. To ensure that applicants get at least what they should.
   b. To ensure that applicants get no more than what they should.
   c. To control against any discriminatory practices in distributing assistance.
   d. To prevent applicants from abusing the system.

3. Which of the following programs is employer financed and state administered?
   a. Social Security
   b. TANF
   c. Unemployment Insurance
   d. Supplemental Security Income

4. Which school of thought advocates the creation of women's communities?
   a. Socialist Feminism
   b. Radical Feminism
   c. Feminist Welfare Perspective
   d. Marxism

5. An employee is injured at on the job and is unable to work. Which state-administered program would provide assistance to this employee?
   a. Unemployment Insurance
   b. Workers' Compensation
   c. TANF
   d. Medicaid

6. You are a social worker assisting a client who has just become homeless. Which statement best describes the target of intervention?
   a. Help the client come to terms with being homeless.
   b. Focus on what resulted in the client becoming homeless.
   c. Guide the client on how to create logical solutions and viable next steps.
   d. Provide counseling and therapy.

7. What are the main differences between the residual and institutional perspectives in granting social welfare programs to people?

Reinforce what you learned in this chapter by studying videos, cases, d
and more available at www.MySearchLab.com.

Watch and Review

Watch These Videos

✦ Social and Economic Justice: Understanding Forms of Oppression and Discrimination

✦ Advocating for Human Rights and Justice

* Professional Roles and Boundaries

Read and Review

Read these Cases/Documents

* Policy Practice
* Professional Identity

Assess Your Knowledge

Go to **MySearchLab** to test your knowledge of key topics in this chapter with topic-specific quizzes. Conclude your assessment by completing the chapter exam.

* = CSWE Core Competency Asset

3

The Beginnings of Social Welfare

Political Economy and Early Societies

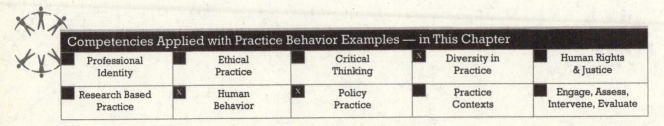

Competencies Applied with Practice Behavior Examples — in This Chapter				
Professional Identity	Ethical Practice	Critical Thinking	X Diversity in Practice	Human Rights & Justice
Research Based Practice	X Human Behavior	X Policy Practice	Practice Contexts	Engage, Assess, Intervene, Evaluate

Times and Events

6000–3000 B.C.E.

- African cultures united by Menes
- Africa leader in world trade, invention, science, arts
- Pictographic (hieroglyphic) writing in Egypt and Sumer, stone masonry, copper smelting
- Riverine societies in Africa, China
- Monotheism develops
- Importance of private property

3000–1200 B.C.E.

- Desiccation of Sahara increases
- Invasion of African kingdoms by Hyksos (Middle/Near East)
- 1567: African kings expel Hyksos, inaugurate New Kingdom
- Tribal warfare in Near East overwhelms pastoral cultures, ends matriarchal rule

1200–300 B.C.E.

- Code of Hammurabi
- Judaic social welfare, institutional perspective
- Assyrian conquest of Egypt, introduction of ironworking
- Development of feudal society in China
- Period of Greek classical culture
- India and the caste system
- Roman Empire begins

300 B.C.E.–400 C.E.

- Roman Society, status of women as chattel, the dole
- Birth of Christianity, Jesus, Isis religion
- Greek philanthropy, democracy, solutions to poverty

Tracing social welfare throughout history, we can see the interrelationships among the polity, economy, and religion that determine the ways in which social welfare is carried out in every society. In addition to the usefulness of this knowledge, the trip back in time clarifies the evolution of attitudes and processes toward women, workers, the poor, and the "other" which permeate and pattern social welfare today.

THE BEGINNINGS OF HISTORY: 6000–1200 B.C.E.

During the centuries between 6000 and 3000 B.C.E., wave after wave of migration—some peaceful and some based on conquest—surged across the world. Freedom from constant nomadism brought permanent settlements in areas most conducive to agriculture—around the Mediterranean, in the fertile basins of the Tigris and Euphrates Rivers, in the still-verdant stretches of Africa and all along the Nile River, in the high plateaus of India, and along the valleys of the Yellow and Yangtze Rivers of China. To the north, in the colder mountainous regions of the Caucasus, settlements were later in coming, and nomadic and warlike tribes presented a constant threat to the established societies of the warmer south.

Sharing was no longer the only means of personal and tribal survival, for as some people sank into poverty, new forms of social care were established. Altruism played a part, but a more pressing purpose was the coordination of work and protection under the political control of patriarchs: flooding and irrigation, adequate pasturing for herds, and control of marauding nomads. Patriarchal religions based on the needs to control workers and women (to ensure their legitimacy) evolved. Massive efforts to ensure an orderly system of flood control, irrigation, and crop distribution were undertaken in China and Egypt, and dynasties also arose in pastoral areas around the Mediterranean and in the valleys of the Tigris and Euphrates Rivers. The patterns of patriarchal classist societies developed among all the peoples of the known world except in the early dynasties in Africa.

Africa: Birthplace of Humankind

A curious hiatus exists in our thinking and knowledge about Africa based on a Eurocentric racism so pervasive that it has blanked out at least seven millennia of history.

A curious hiatus exists in our thinking and knowledge about Africa based on a Eurocentric racism so pervasive that it has blanked out at least seven millennia of history. Although most archeological experts agree that humankind (homo sapiens) as we know it originated around the Olduvai Gap in East Africa's Tanzania, the centrality of Caucasian cultural myths has erased and Caucasianized the color of Africa's people. Indeed, when we think of the great early kingdoms, especially in Egypt, despite pictographic and sculptural evidence to the contrary, we assume their leaders were bronze or white in color. Yet black Africans led the world in civilization. They built mighty reservoirs to tame the Upper and Lower Nile River for agriculture, used iron tools and mathematics, cultivated grain, painted pictures, and created pottery of great beauty. For a thousand years, beginning under King Menes (about 3500 B.C.E.), Africa's Egyptian or Kemetic (Kemet was the original name of the region) dynasties traded throughout the known world, inspiring and promoting

> . . . progress on all fronts. Agriculture, industrial development, science, the arts, engineering, massive building programs, mining and shipbuilding. . . . [Here] stone was first used in building [massive structures such as reservoirs], hieroglyphic writing was first invented, the great pyramids were built, stone quarrying [was] perfected and expanded....[1]

There were many great Egyptian or Kemetic dynasties, especially the 18th and 19th, that spanned many years and produced many great people and contributions. One such person was Imhotep, who was noted for his multitalented skills in philosophy, medicine, religion, and architecture.[2] After a period of decentralization and invasion, the African king Mentuhoteps II regained sovereignty in Egypt in 2040 B.C.E., driving Caucasian invaders from Egypt. Yet later dynasties could not quell the mighty influx from the north, and by 1786 B.C.E. this new age of greatness had fallen. It arose again about 720 B.C.E., when the Ethiopian kings Kashta and Piankhy reconquered Egypt, and Ethiopians ruled benevolently for more than a century, extending their empire well into the Middle East. Throughout the world Ethiopians were honored for their intelligence, their beauty, and the extent of their civilization, as "the most powerful, the most just, and the most beautiful of the human race."[3]

For early African societies, generally ruled by a group of elders with a designated leader, kinship and clan were major factors in religious life. Societies financed temples through a central treasury, and these were places of worship, education, and public relief for any clan member in need. To these temples foreign scholars came to study, and from here religious, scientific, and cultural ideas spread. Ancient Greek scholars through the time of Herodotus spoke with pride of their educations in Ethiopia.

In ancient Egypt before 5500 B.C.E., a strongly matriarchal system existed, and the royal successor was probably female. As patriarchy gained power, there arose a strong inducement for sister–brother marriage, and the ruler of the First Dynasty was expressly said to be male.[4] From then on, the ruling houses, called "pharaohs," slowly shifted to male rule until even the word *pharaoh* came to mean *male ruler.* "Poor laws" developed to provide for a reasonably healthy and constant workforce, with administrative channels for the poor to take their complaints directly to the pharaoh. It was believed that God gave the poor the power to curse their oppressors throughout eternity, and those in power feared the curse. Therefore, Egyptian social welfare was based on both the economic need for workers and the religious need for life after death.[5] Egyptian or Kemetic social welfare was also predicated on the ethical principles and practices of *Maat.* Maatian ethics affirmed truth, justice, and righteousness in shaping social relationships and laid the foundation for what many contemporary progressives now call social justice.[6] The need to build dikes against the ever-threatening floods caused the development of the *corvée,* in which every adult man owed the pharaoh one year's work out of every seven. This was not slavery (although there were slaves in Egypt), but for that year the person belonged to the pharaoh and could be used to the death in his service. After systems of irrigation and flood control were well established, corvée labor built tombs and shrines. A bureaucratic system directed by a grand vizier was responsible for labor projects, for harvesting, storing, and distributing grain, and for charity oriented to maintaining the strength of laborers for work.

From the Fourth through Sixth Dynasties (2700–2200 B.C.E.), peasants were owned by mid-level lords. Dutiful work was among the strongest ethics, as was the accumulation of personal wealth through trade. Supplies were centrally controlled, and when uprisings occurred or when food was limited, frontiers were closed so that

> the available harvest and supplies would suffice for the local population.... Thus centralized planning and coordination are not inventions of the modern age and, specifically, careful provision of food supplies was a fundamental social welfare effort directly tied to national intentions and needs.[7]

Mesopotamia in the Bronze Age: To 1200 B.C.E.

In the fertile valleys of the Tigris and Euphrates Rivers, a more pastoral, more diverse, and more egalitarian set of societies evolved. Not dependent on mass labor as in Egypt, they were smaller and less monolithic. Wave after wave of migrants settled with and assimilated into the Semitic tribes of the region. By about 3000 B.C.E., most cities were walled against aggression and came under the protection of individual warlords, and private ownership in herds of sheep and goats had begun. Shrines still provided for the needy, and those especially designated for care were widows, orphans, disabled people, and "strangers at the gate," or foreigners.

The creation of accounting methods and the rudiments of written languages developed among the Sumerians who moved into Mesopotamia in about 3000 B.C.E. Driven from their homes in central Asia by drought, they settled peaceably among the indigenous Semites in the area that is now Iraq and some parts of Turkey and Syria. At first, Sumerian leaders were elected by vote based on strength and popularity, as occurred in most prehistoric tribes, and this evolved into a system of rulers and ruled. Gradually the Sumerians took over the land until their families and clans collectively owned about seven-eighths of it, the rest belonging to shrines where as early as 2000 B.C.E., widows, orphans, and the poor were protected by the goddess Nanshe.[8] Land could be sold only if all the prominent members of the family or clan agreed, and the new owners became the ruling class or nobility. The land was worked for them by poor, landless freemen.

Three principal classes developed: the noble (*awilum*), or full citizen; the ordinary freeman, or second-class citizen (*mushkenum*); and dependent freemen, generally called *clients*. Slaves were a fourth class, mainly prisoners of war, and were not citizens but chattel. Only the wealthy were given education, possibly daughters as well as sons. Aside from officials, about one-fifth of the population were craftsmen and the remainder were laborers. Men, women, and children worked at herding and irrigating, and they were paid in corn, wool, clothing, wine, and oil, or they might be paid in part or in full in silver.[9]

Around this time, Semitic tribes began conquests resulting in a series of short-lived dynasties: The Akkadian dynasty, established in 2750 B.C.E., ruled for 500 years. The dynasty of Ur, characterized as an efficient bureaucracy, lasted from 2100 to 2000 B.C.E. Amorite warriors formed a third dynasty, and then Babylon ruled. The sixth ruler, from 1792 to 1750 B.C.E., was Hammurabi, a benign ruler noted for social justice. He codified current laws and practices in the Stele of Hammurabi, developed several centuries before Moses, whose laws were similar.[10] The Stele demonstrated the general way of life until Babylon fell to Persia in 539 B.C.E. and set down laws particularly to protect widows, orphans, and the weak. Kingdoms in Mesopotamia depended mostly on agricultural production and flocks of sheep and goats and, for a time, their kings dealt peaceably with one another to pasture or irrigate lands. When conditions were particularly bad, arrangements might be made with a neighboring ruler to allow the flocks to cross into better-provided territory. At times, kings joined together in armies to prevent raids on their cultivated lands by the nomadic people of the desert.[11]

Until about 2000 B.C.E., shrines continued to serve the poor, distributing food in times of need. However, as societies evolved, the shrines began to lend at interest rather than give aid. Free peasants who had no resources in hard times gave themselves and their children into temple ownership, and by 1000 B.C.E. the shrines owned many prisoners of war, slaves donated or bequeathed, and formerly free people. However, temples remained an important source of care. Dolgoff and Feldstein say,

> There are three noteworthy points to observe about this ancient culture: temples were important economic forces; governmental action was taken to relieve economic burdens and pressures, probably to avoid serious conflicts; and temples served as "social welfare" agencies, anticipating major religious institutional functions to follow in later centuries.[12]

The synergy of economy, polity, religion, and social welfare is obvious.

Invasion, Conquest, and Patriarchal Religion

Pomeroy says,

> Patriarchal religion . . . appeared in recognizable form in about 3000
> B.C. and is clearly associated with invasion—the Cretes by the Greeks,
> the Mediterranean by people from beyond the Caucasus, and so on.
> This . . . [shows] the connection of a powerful male deity with invasion
> and war.[13]

The association of patriarchal religion with aggression reified economic stratification and the accumulation of private property. Where once strangers and
foreigners had been treated benevolently and aided, they were now "out-
groups," people who worshipped other gods. It became a religious obligation
to conquer or destroy them.

In about 2000 B.C.E., warlike tribes swarmed across the Caucasus and
Transoceana and invaded the Persian highlands south of the Caspian Sea. Of
greater size and strength than the indigenous people, they mowed through
them from Greece to India with a deadly new war technology: horse-drawn
war chariots with sickles on their wheels. So devastating were these invasions
that, after more than twelve centuries of written records, a complete interruption occurred:

> Egyptian inscriptions virtually disappear between 1730 B.C. and 1580
> B.C.; after the fall of Babylon around 1530 B.C. inscriptions in Babylonia
> also disappear . . . and are not resumed until 1400 B.C. Assyrian records
> vanish between 1720 B.C. and 1400 B.C. Hittite inscriptions suffer the
> same fate for more than a century. In short, a catastrophic hiatus occurred
> throughout the Middle East, a sort of Dark Ages brought about by multiple
> invasions of iron-bearing, horse-drawn chariot-riding barbarians . . .
> these great invasions . . . wrecked countless states, kingdoms, and even
> empires, and destroyed more than one rudimentary civilization.[14]

The invaders settled, intermarried, and assimilated into the indigenous Semitic
tribes of the areas (see Figure 3.1). Their male war gods became predominant
and tribal warfare became a way of life. Communally oriented societies
became stratified by class and gender.

The Israelite Influence

In the fourteenth century B.C.E., a few Semitic tribes formed the Twelve Tribes
of Israel, a coalition based on spreading monotheism across the known world.
Their method, in common with like societies of the era, was conquest. Early
Israelite society laid the foundations of Western civilization: looking at monotheism alone we see that pattern of human/deity relationship as a cornerstone
of belief through the ages, and the concept of coalition is mirrored at every
societal level today. As with others on journeys through social evolution, they
committed terrible acts and wonderful acts. That they were Israelite does not
lessen either the horrendous or wondrous nature of those acts: Social evolution is social evolution.

Inspired by a male war god to spread monotheism, they ravaged Assyria
and much of the Middle East for three centuries. Perhaps more deadly than
their enemies because they believed that worshipers of other gods should be
killed, they often slew every person and every living creature and burned

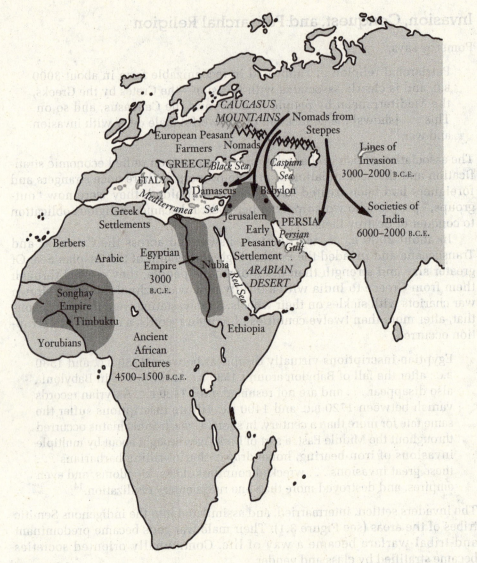

Figure 3.1

Peoples of Africa, Europe, and the Middle East, 6000–1500 B.C.E.

every field in the kingdoms they conquered. (This pattern was not invented by the Israelites and persists in warfare today.) Because their enemies were polytheistic and did not worship the Israelite god, their deaths were perceived as inconsequential. Conquest and assumption of the land, wealth, and people of "out-groups" was a religious obligation. Their new wealth and power demonstrated again the synergism among economy, power, and religion.

The Israelites laid the religious bases of Western Judaeo-Christian society, influencing social welfare in many unrecognized ways. Both the positive elements of dealing with the poor and the negative reasons for their dependency are clear in the Old Testament of the Bible, which demonstrates that, *like all other tribes emerging from the Bronze Age*, our Israelite ancestors were warriors. Although many prescriptions exist for care of widows, orphans, strangers, and the poor, these occurred three centuries after the period of conquest and may have been necessary reactions to aggression and restrictive patriarchy as the society matured. Before this happened, the oppression of women, the poor, and "outsiders from the faith" had been *set into society as religious precepts* for Western civilization.

The outstanding characteristics of ancient tribes were aggressive and warlike behaviors, differentiation into classes of ruling elite and dependent vassals, and male-dominant or patriarchal authoritarianism. Caring for others, as it had arisen from an interdependent desert existence, no longer existed as part of the natural order except within the tribes. Rather, aid became a necessary addition to a stratified society, to maintain allegiance and a workforce. Warlords and priests became the elite upper classes. The lower classes were artisans and laborers (*gerim*, who belonged to the tribe, and *metics*, or foreigners). *Gerim* were personally free but ritually impure, had no political rights, and could not own property, although they were given shelter and grazing rights. After the Exile, they were allowed intermarriage and conversion to Judaism, yet class stratification and, often, debt slavery, continued. *Metics* had no protection or personal rights under law unless they bonded themselves to a warlord.[15]

In addition, allegiance to a male deity reified the secondary status of women. Pagan women could be killed out of hand or forcibly "married" to their conquerors. However, the social and legal position of Israelite women also suffered.

> The Decalogue ranked a wife among her husband's possessions, and while he could repudiate her she could not ask for divorce, and she remained legally a minor all her life. Wives and daughters did not inherit, except in the absence of male heirs.[16]

Wives called their husbands *ba'al* (master) or lord, as slaves addressed their masters. Although wives in Egypt and Babylon at that time were heads of families and could acquire property, take legal action, and inherit, Israelite women had no legal status. If husbands died, women were remarried to the husbands' brothers or put under guardianship of a male relative. This protected them in the society, but the society itself made the protection necessary.

Matrilineal inheritance was the pattern in surrounding polytheistic religions, but in patriarchal Israelite tribes, male line inheritance required celibacy for unmarried women and monogamy for married women. Stone says,

> [T]he lack of concern for the paternity of children among people of the Old Religion, which allowed matrilineal descent patterns to continue . . . was the crux of the persecution of ancient beliefs. [If] a religion existed alongside their own, a religion in which women owned property, were endowed with a legal identity, and were allowed to relate sexually to various men, it would be difficult for the Israelites to convince their women that they must be property. . . . Each woman must be retained as possession of one man for the purposes of legitimizing their children.[17]

The admonitions against women written into the Deuteronomic revisions of the Jewish Book of Law clearly delineate the fate of Israelite women who disobeyed sexual prohibitions. Unmarried women had to remain virgin and were stoned or burned if they did not.[18] Unmarried women, if raped, were married to the rapist. After marriage, women had to be monogamous, although men might acquire any number of wives and concubines. Adultery was an offense against the husband's property, so both men and women taken in adultery could be put to death.[19] Women could be divorced at will by their husbands,[20] and daughters, like slaves, could be sold by fathers. Non-Israelite women could be killed outright or, if virgins, could be taken as wives or slaves.

Although later Judaic teachings redressed ancient Israel's aggressive behavior, three particular groups became more vulnerable. One group was the poor, as class stratification occurred; the second was women, whose fate became dependent on the goodwill of men; and the third was "out-group people"—those who, because they served other gods, were considered expendable and exploitable.

MOVING INTO THE IRON AGE: 1200–400 B.C.E.

A thousand years before Christ, the legendary black African Queen of Sheba made her visit to Solomon, and the riches of the earth seemed assured to Israel. It was the era of Zoroaster's revelation and the Magi of Persia,

> the age of Confucius, Lao-Tzu, and the great Chinese schools of philosophy, the age of the Upanishads and the Buddha in India, of Socrates, Plato, and Periclean Athens; of the great Hebrew prophets in Palestine— Elijah, Isaiah, and Jeremiah.[21]

The skill of writing became common and oral traditions fell into disuse. In Greece, Homer began to write his epic poetry. During the Archaic period (700–400 B.C.E.), both Greek and Roman civilizations grew to prominence. In Africa, the Ethiopian pharaoh Taharka steadfastly resisted the attacks of Assyrians, became a hero in Greek poetry, and ensured Ethiopia's sovereignty for centuries.[22]

Early Judaic Social Welfare

After its period of conquest, Israel's powers began to decline from about the eleventh century B.C.E. Eventually, the Israeli people were captured and enslaved in Babylon and the prophets began to exhort the Jewish people to altruism. New laws began to address the grievances of the poor and the problems of women. Judaic charity rested on a priestly-influenced community of free peasants and herdsmen,[23] and was based on humankind's relationship with God and a God-ordered responsibility for self and others. Because all belonged to God, charity and giving without thought of self or salvation was one's responsibility to God.[24] Need was the only requirement for aid, and help was a duty and a human right. Responsibility for self meant to work for one's own support but, when necessary, to receive help without shame (Jeremiah). Charity, prayer, and repentance were the three pillars of the world.[25]

Policy Practice

Practice Behavior Example: Know the history and current structures of social policies and services; the role of policy in service delivery; and the role of practice in policy development.

Critical Thinking Question: Compare and contrast the Israelite's provision of services to the poor with current practices in the United States. Which values and practices remain stable and which change over time?

Dolgoff and Feldstein say that "Judaism bases its requirements for altruism on essentially two concepts: *tzedakah* (or *tzaddakah*), a mixture of charity and justice; and *chesed*, loving kindness." The word for charity means righteousness or justice, and so giving charity meant being just or righteous, or as God required one to be. No special effort or conscious behavior was denoted as being charitable: Honor to the poor was honor to God, and oppression was blasphemy. These concepts became law around the eleventh century B.C.E. and were codified in the Talmud after the Persian king Cyrus freed Israel from Babylonian captivity (600 B.C.E.). The Talmud is a collection of laws and traditions completed between 500 and 400 B.C.E. when, with imperial Persian approval, it became law for the Israelite people. Even today, it constitutes authority on social welfare among most Jews.[26]

The Talmud and the Old Testament laid out laws for the treatment of the poor, widows, children, the sick, the old, and strangers. The hungry were to be fed, the naked clothed, and the stranger sheltered.[27] Farmers were forbidden to glean the corners of their fields or to pick up fallen fruit, so that those in need might have them.[28] The hungry were allowed to eat from the crops of others, but could not carry food away with them.[29] Harvests every seventh year were dedicated to the poor, and in every fiftieth year—the Jubilee—slaves were emancipated and property outside the walled cities was returned to its original owners. (This has been seen as an attempt to lessen the importance of private property but might have continued class stratification because of the earlier unequal distribution of land.) In fact, there was no record of starvation in peaceful times in Judaic culture.

The universal and institutional perspectives of Judaic social welfare are among its most notable characteristics, for charity was without stigma. For example, in early times people reached into the community charity box either to deposit money or take it out without others knowing which they did. Dolgoff and Feldstein say charity was institutionalized in two important respects: expected behavior of the donor and nonstigmatization and entitlement of the poor.

> Essentially, a culture developed that valued enterprise but without categorizing the poor as evil or idle . . . the society and individuals in it would be judged on the degree to which they provided for the poor without demeaning them.[30]

In later centuries, Hebrew philosopher Maimonides refined charity into eight degrees, ranging from giving grudgingly to preventing poverty. These refinements and earlier Judaic laws concerning social welfare have been carried out for centuries in the daily lives of the Jewish people. They constitute a major basis for the institutional perspective on social welfare in society today: that members of society have a right to receive help.

In the theory and practice of present-day Jewish religion, many of the problems of class stratification legitimated by the religion of their early ancestors have been redressed by what Miringoff and Opdycke call temporizing values—those that place humanistic charity before such overriding values as individualism and the work ethic.[31] However, in early societies, *all* Western tribal societies, including the Judaic, were warrior societies in which male deities legitimated oppression. This was coincidental to the era but is a fact of Western history, and the religious values that legitimate oppression still underlie our society.

> The universal and institutional perspectives of Judaic social welfare are among its most notable characteristics, for charity was without stigma.

The Dynasties of China

China's history parallels that of Egypt, though at a later date. In early years, leaders were elected, but by about 1500 B.C.E., short-lived dynasties had developed. By 1000 C.E., the patriarchal Chou dynasty had overthrown the matriarchal Shangs,[32] and male rule became hereditary. Although clans and families owned property in common, the patriarch's decisions were absolute. Development of a feudal society coincided with patriarchy, and in about 800 B.C.E.

monarchy developed. Serfs were taxed as property, so many were emancipated because of major tax assessments between 600 and 400 B.C.E. Left to fend for themselves, many turned to the state for help.[33] Buddhism, founded in 500 B.C.E., inspired its priests, such as Mencius in the fourth century B.C.E., to exhort China's rulers to care for the poor, and poverty was redefined as a holy state. A meager system of welfare developed, providing only food and shelter.

As feudalism collapsed, the ruling elite instituted the first unified Chinese empire in 221 B.C.E.[34] The emperor, as Son of Heaven, was owed obedience and loyalty but was obligated by God to provide for his subjects.[35] Local patriarchs became an intermediary level of privileged bureaucrats over common people, who had few rights and were conscripted for armies and the government workforce on coordinated systems of irrigation and flood control. The bureaucracy was hierarchical, with two senior officials roughly corresponding to prime minister and head of civil service. Below them were offices of astrology, records, court and imperial household superintendent, security, crime and punishment, foreign affairs, treasury, and taxes and work projects. Next were forty-two civil service posts. The officials had their own social welfare system: one day of rest in five, sick leave, education for their children (the next generation of civil servants), and often retirement pensions of money or textiles.[36]

The bulk of the population was working-class commoners. In return for service to the emperor, they received a subsistence level of support. Each adult man served one month per year on state building projects, and each spent two years in the army.[37] By the first century B.C.E., in times of natural disaster the government's relief policy enabled the poor to buy food from its granaries or, if they could not pay, to receive free grain. In addition, the poor were taken from ravaged areas and resettled on new lands. We know little about poor women, but the patriarchal precepts of Confucius, teaching the traditional roles of wife and mother, came to prevail completely during the Han dynasty (200 B.C.E.–200 C.E.),[38] so we can assume few benefits for women apart from those of their men.

Noncitizens or substandard people were without rights to citizenship or social welfare. Slaves, less than one percent of the population, had been prisoners of war or children sold into slavery by their parents in times of hardship. Their masters had rights to their labor, but not power of life and death. Those owned by the wealthy fared far better than did free peasants, who were subject to drought, famine, and pestilence. Concubines of the wealthy—sisters or female servants of their wives—were another group of the substandard, and were usually released from concubinage into marriage. Convicts in the well-developed system of criminal justice also were substandard people. Punishment included head shaving (signifying loss of life after death), a maximum sentence of five years at hard labor, beheading, or cutting in two at the waist. Relatives of convicts also became noncitizens and were confiscated along with other goods. In extreme cases, family members also were exterminated.[39]

India and the Caste System

Great civilizations developed in India well before 2000 B.C.E. but collapsed during the great patriarchal invasions. Indian society rebuilt, reifying the Hindu caste system and immutably setting inequalities in social position. The caste system had different effects for social welfare than did Western class systems. Poverty was not a condition for personal blame, nor was it traceable to unjust structures of society; rather, it was the effect of *karma*, a spiritual belief in reincarnation that placed people in life positions so that they might atone for past lives or prepare for future ones. Because one's position in the next life (reincarnation) was determined by actions in the present life, an obligation prevailed to care even for the lowest caste, the "untouchables," along with a fatalism about the inevitability of poverty.

Rulers were enjoined to care for the poor by religious beliefs, but as in all societies, social aid was modified by economic and political elements. Nevertheless, as early as 300 B.C.E., hospitals and shelters for both people and animals were endowed by Prince Asoka of India. Much interpersonal helping was carried out by clans and kin within castes. For women, the caste system produced a rigid structure of inequalities within inequality, although women seemed to have far greater freedom in early Vedic times, when female deities held sway and before social and political patriarchy triumphed.[40] However, although in both China and India Tantric Buddhism emphasized the basic metaphysical equality between the sexes, neither granted women real equality. The freedom of Indian women was increasingly curtailed. They were not allowed education, and widows could not remarry, thus forcing them into poverty or prostitution if no male guardian would protect them. In fact, the problem of widows was solved by the practice of *suttee*, where widows were burned with their deceased husbands (along with other possessions). Although it is commonly believed that they went willingly to death because of their sorrow, if they refused they were bound and thrown on the pyre anyway.[41] Islamic invasions dating from about 700 C.E. exacerbated the position of Indian women, and until only recently, historically speaking, India lay under severely misogynist governments.[42]

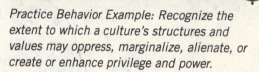

Diversity in Practice

Practice Behavior Example: Recognize the extent to which a culture's structures and values may oppress, marginalize, alienate, or create or enhance privilege and power.

Critical Thinking Question: Discuss how different ancient societies used religion to define the scope and justification for charitable work.

GREECE, CHRISTIANITY, AND THE ROMAN EMPIRE

Greece and the City–States

At about the time ancient Judaism triumphed in the Middle East, the societies of Greece and Rome began to develop. In Greece, during the Bronze Age raids and forays to gain slaves and booty were the way of life. Military preparedness was vital, and men served as warriors while women served as bearers of future warriors. Still, because upper-class wives maintained homes and businesses for husbands away at war, they acquired some wealth and power and had higher status at the close of this period (about 700 B.C.E.) than at any other time until the Hellenic period, about the time of Christ (see Figure 3.2).

From 700 B.C.E. until about 400 B.C.E., colonization was the goal of conquest. Population pressure was one reason: There was a rise in fecundity and a decrease in infant and juvenile mortality, although there were twice as many men as women because of female infanticide. The Greek city–states were established by about 500 B.C.E., and many farmers left the land to become a new poor working class, exacerbating the already-present class stratification. To the early Greeks, work was a curse that brutalized the mind and made it unfit for thinking about truth or practicing virtue, and because work was despised, so was the worker. The wealthy became an elite class based on the labor of slaves and poor citizens. Slaves, whether men or women, did much of the work of ancient Greece. However, their status could actually be higher than that of freedpersons,

Figure 3.2
European Peoples and the Persian Empire, 500 B.C.E.–300 C.E.

> To the early Greeks, work was a curse that brutalized the mind and made it unfit for thinking about truth or practicing virtue, and because work was despised, so was the worker.

depending on the wealth of their owners, and many when freed stayed with their old masters rather than become part of the poverty-stricken underclass.

Upper-class women in Athens were at first confined to the home. As their activities became more visible they became less valued, particularly because they worked at tasks deemed appropriate only to slaves. There was a steady erosion of their legal status and matrilineal inheritance, and they could not inherit their husband's property or incur debt, nor were their legal actions binding. Although they were citizens, they were under the guardianship of men (fathers, husbands, or male next-of-kin). Fathers arranged marriages to secure political liaisons and material bonds among families, retaining the right to revoke marriages. Girls were first married at about age fourteen to men twice that age, and many died young in childbirth. Dying or divorcing husbands arranged new marriages for their wives. A wife's rape or adultery required divorce, and such women became outcasts, although the only penalty for rapists was a monetary fine.[43]

Women in the city–states of Sparta and Gortyn, though under the same general laws, had more status than did Athenian women because they could inherit from their husbands, too often killed at war. In time, women owned half the wealth of the cities. In Sparta, both men and women belonged to the state, and marriages were arranged eugenically. Children could be killed at birth because of physical weakness or deformity, for the goal was to produce superior people. However, once breeding obligations were fulfilled, sexual freedom—heterosexual or homosexual—was permitted. Homosexuality flourished in Greece, for the love of men for men was considered sacred. The women of Sparta and Lesbos were particularly valued among both men and women, and both homoerotic and heterosexual relationships were formed with the approval of society.[44]

For *poor* women in all the city–states, life was more difficult, although their status as virtual possessions of men by 500 B.C.E. gave them some protection. Pomeroy says that the lives of women lacking such protection were truly pitiful, especially if they had children, for most of the work they could do was done by slaves. Their work was essentially an extension of women's work in the home; they were washerwomen, workers in the clothing industry, vendors in the market, midwives, or nurses for children. Some became prostitutes, and some of these, the *hetairai*, even acquired transitory wealth and influence (though denied civil rights). Few Greek women became rich, but some foreign women who engaged in large-scale financial transactions did.[45]

The ideals of philanthropy and democracy, both important to Western social welfare, arose with the Greek city–states. Democracy was only for the free citizen, man or woman. Slaves and foreigners were excluded. The concept of *democracy*, though limited, entered into Western political thought to influence ideas about human rights.[46] It exists today in our value of individualism, in ideas of equality, and in the representative structure of American government. *Philanthropy* meant, in that era, the benevolence of gods toward humankind, but by the fourth century B.C.E. its meaning had evolved to refer to the obligation of the powerful to help their subjects or dependents. Greeks sought honor by giving donations of food, money, or oil to the city treasury for emergencies and food shortages, to citizen mutual aid societies, or to people of elite status in financial difficulty. Volunteer service in public offices was another road to honor, as was help to the "worthy poor"—generally nobles or merchants—who were well reared and educated but had fallen on hard times. The "unworthy poor" were people at the bottom of society—workers and the unemployed—and philanthropic gifts were denied them; they were not "worth" help because their gratitude did not bestow "honor." The unemployed were considered lazy and were expected to get along any way they could. Slaves were not eligible for citizenship and could not receive help. Needy foreigners were expected to return to their homelands. Beggars were rounded up and sent away, for aiding them was thought to encourage their pauperism. Poor, landless, or unemployed citizens were recruited as mercenary soldiers or given shares of land to colonize in far-off lands.

Caring for the poor in Greek city–states was self-seeking rather than altruistic. Still, hostels and medical centers, the remnants of older religious shrines, were scattered throughout the country, and the Athenian state distributed grain during food shortages—but only to citizens. There were also allowances and pensions for the crippled, public distribution of grain in bad times, and institutions for the custodial care of various unfortunates.[47] Orphanages and pensions were provided for children of fathers killed in war, and other orphans were supported until their eighteenth birthdays. However, attitudes toward the poor were harsh. Contraception, abortion, and infanticide were encouraged, and Plato urged euthanasia for the disabled or aged. Slavery, concubinage, and enforced colonization were also considered welfare, for the well-being of state rather than individual was the primary goal. Macarov believes that, despite the fact that the concept of philanthropy originated in Greece, the *spirit* of philanthropy never existed there, for

> the nature of the society was such that the citizens *were* the state. . . . [This] may have arisen from a lack of religious commandments concerning charity. A concept of gods who competed with people, manipulated people, and behaved like people did not lend itself to divine commandments concerning people's actions. . . . Indeed, according to Plato's *Republic*, the aged and the handicapped were to be done away with.[48]

In 359 B.C.E., Macedonian conquerors under Alexander the Great brought an end to the Greek city–states. This gradually ushered in new laws for women in all social classes. Earlier antifeminist legislation was rejected, and women were no longer confined to their houses. Polygamy, especially in royal families, became common, and divorce was often anticipated in marriage contracts. Queens ruled jointly with kings, and although women in Greece might need a male guardian, those in Hellenized areas away from the Greek mainland and in Egypt did not. The birthrate declined drastically, exacerbated by the practice of putting unwanted children out to die and the lack of interest in maintaining family lineage.

In response to the need for a growing population, new doctrines glorifying wife and mother roles for women arose, promulgated by the Stoics. Marriage and child-rearing were elevated to the level of moral, religious, and patriotic duty. The straight-line, rational thinking and logic so loved by the Greeks were carried over into Roman society, and the dualistic reasoning of man as mind versus woman as body was reemphasized, particularly in the period of Christianization.

Human Behavior

Practice Behavior Example: Know about human behavior across the life course; the range of social systems in which people live; and the ways social systems promote or deter people in maintaining or achieving health and well-being.

Critical Thinking Question: What positions did children and the elderly hold in ancient societies?

Early Roman Society and the Beginning of Christianity

Social welfare in Roman society was political. Whereas in Judaism it was given from kinship and caring and in Greece for honor, in Rome in the early Republic it was given in the form of doles—irregular gifts, especially to free men and boys—to gain votes. Therefore, only minimal help (if any) was given women and girls. Even wealthy women gave to men, for men held the power.

> The doles were motivated not so much by humanitarian reasons as by political desires to keep men pacified and curry favor with the crowds. . . . Since women, although citizens, could not vote, and their hunger was not likely to drive them to revolution, there was little point in including

them in the largesse. Moreover, including women would have meant reducing the portions of men, and the benefactor would not have won the good will of those he courted.[49]

The dole was only enough for one, so wives and children of poor men might starve. However, eligibility depended not on need but on voting power, so even if they received a dole men could work to support their families.

In the late Republic (450–150 B.C.E.), there were a number of assistance programs in addition to the dole: occasional distributions of food by rich Roman citizens, private food programs, and public feasts established by private benefactors. In addition, trade and craft groups organized as *collegia*, giving monthly contributions to a common fund for mutual aid.[50] Patronage by the wealthy supported dependent workers with food, clothing, shelter, and other necessities. Some children's assistance programs were set up in the early Empire (100 B.C.E.–100 C.E.) specifically for future recruitment of soldiers. Boys received more money than girls and were supported until age seventeen or eighteen. Girls were not supported as often—in one town, of 300 recipients, only thirty-six were girls—and their doles were at a lower level and stopped at age fourteen, when they were expected to marry. Female infanticide and neglect meant a higher death rate for girls, and if they lived, their life span was shorter by five to ten years than that of males because of poor health resulting from malnutrition and childbearing at an early age.[51] Life expectancy in general was short, about forty or fifty years for the elite class. Over half the wives of the poor died before age thirty, most between twenty and twenty-five.

Patriarchy was a major characteristic of both the late Republic and early Empire. The *paterfamilias*, or father of the family, had absolute authority (*manus*) over women and children, even to slavery and death. Only men had legal rights; women could not appear in court, buy or sell property, or inherit their husbands' estates. Husbands judged their wives for crimes and could sentence them to death even for misdemeanors, and certainly for infidelity. Priestesses and wealthy courtesans had some autonomy, as did freedwomen of guilds and crafts, who were not supervised by their husbands and seemed really to be free.[52] Most poor freedwomen, however, were working-class shopkeepers, artisans, domestics, woolworkers, or clothes makers. Slaves, men or women, could buy their freedom (manumission), but many stayed with their former owners rather than being released into the ranks of the poor to starve.

At the turn of the millennium, Greek, Roman, Jewish, Egyptian, and Eastern societies converged and blended, and Rome moved fully into the Empire to become ruler of the Western world (see Figure 3.3). Its territories expanded as far as the British Isles, and conquests amassed riches for the ruling class. Great wealth led to increasing corruption and even wider disparities between the rich and the poor. The need for defense garrisons in far-flung lands and profligate spending by those in power led to huge tax assessments. Unbelievable poverty existed: By the second century C.E., despite dole and patronage systems, "of 1.2 million people, all but 150,000 heads of families in Rome needed to draw on public foods, and in Constantinople another 80,000 were receiving free food."[53]

The financial structure was based on a tax system in which the poor were assessed proportionately more, significantly increasing poverty and bringing even less money into the central treasury as former workers fell into bankruptcy. For centuries Rome had hired mercenaries to man troops, but now wealth was concentrated in individual estates rather than in the central government, and mercenaries could no longer be paid.

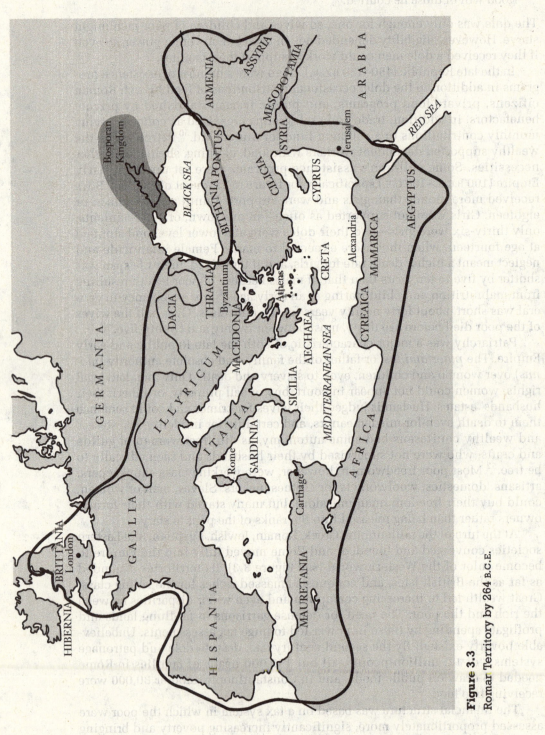

Figure 3.3
Roman Territory by 264 B.C.E.

This destructive economic stratification was only one of the internal problems besetting the Roman Empire. Internal revolt arose on all fronts: slaves under Spartacus, for example, or the revolt of Palestine in 66 C.E., where, in retaliation four years later, Titus razed Jerusalem. Jews, whose laws and customs differed from Roman laws, sought new political power, and radical Jewish zealots agitated for religious freedom. Among non-Jews, the religion of Isis, spreading from Egypt, brought new hope to the poor and enslaved, inspiring revolt. Its primary converts were the disenfranchised—women and the poor—who gained little from the male dominant and class-stratified state religion of Rome (under the war god Mithras). Roman religion denied religious office to most women and all slaves and freedpersons, but the cult of Isis allowed women as well as men, slave as well as freedperson, and poor as well as rich into its hierarchy. Each insurrection increased demands on the Empire's strained economy.

From the time of the late Republic, women were increasingly emancipated. New marriage laws took away the rights of the *paterfamilias* and set limits on the legal subjection of wives. Common-law marriages were usual, and a wife could retain her legal position by bearing three children or spending three nights a year away from her husband's home. After 195 B.C.E., women could administer their own dowries and divorce their husbands at will. By the end of the Republic, upper-class women were equal with men and owned much of Rome's wealth. In 18 B.C.E. Augustus brought marriage under control of the state because, as upper-class women refused to have children, Rome had increasingly fewer men to become controllers, officers, and bureaucrats in Rome's far-flung Empire. However, the birthrate among the lower class remained stable, producing ever more children born into poverty and more fuel for rebellion. At the same time, Teutonic barbarians began a series of increasingly successful border wars and raids against the Empire. Rome was beset from both within and without.

Jesus and the New Religion

Into this time Jesus was born, a revolutionary who opposed both class and gender oppression. He reminded Jewish society of its prophetic past and spiritual teachings regarding the poor and oppressed and decried the personal accumulation of wealth, emphasizing that unless their bounty was shared, rich men could not attain salvation.[54] Although Jesus and many of his associates were of the middle class, his appeal to the poor was immense. For a time, egalitarianism and communal sharing of resources and work were attempted, and leaders of the new religion encouraged the wealthy to take responsibility for the poor.

Jesus came from a patriarchal society (Judaism) that was very aware of class stratification but blind to the oppression of women. His awareness of gender oppression probably came from ideals of gender equality in Greek society and from the religion of Isis. Both women and men became his disciples, and one of his closest disciples was Mary Magdalene.[55] He overturned inequalities of punishment for sexual offenses,[56] revised marriage laws to give women protection against divorce,[57] enforced monogamy on men as well as women, and recognized women's spiritual status.[58] Although patriarchy reasserted itself in the new religion within three centuries of his death, Jesus' teachings on women's spirituality and equality were clear.

Two perspectives on women fought for primacy in Christianity in the following centuries. The Byzantine Church and movements such as Gnosticism and Montanism regarded both men and women as spiritual beings. Gregory of Nyssa, for example, postulated that both sexes have a spiritual and a bodily nature[59] and all have access to God through redemption. Rome's Paulist doctrines, advocated by Augustine (354–430 C.E.) and Tertullian (c. 130 C.E.), posited that men were beings of spirit and intellect whereas women represented earthliness and sin. Their ideas were based on women's (Eve's) original sin and on Paulist letters about women's proper place in home and church, that is, as secondary to husband in all matters sacred and secular.[60] Such teachings reconfirmed the patriarchy of Jewish and early Roman and Greek societies. By 300 C.E., the Roman Church had decreed Gnosticism heresy, disallowed teachings of the spiritual equality of women, and decreed that women, because of their deficient natures, could be redeemed only by their husbands or by renouncing their womanhood to enter convents. These doctrines became dominant in Western society and are transmuted today into societal sex roles, including women's dependency.

> **Christianity was a blending of Greek thought, Jewish teachings, and the resurgence of ideas on class and gender equality from the religion of Isis.**

Christianity was a blending of Greek thought, Jewish teachings, and the resurgence of ideas on class and gender equality from the religion of Isis. Although we generally think of its center as Rome, in the early days the Roman Church was basically a small illegal enclave of Hellenized Jews and Greeks. Jesus was a Jew from Semitic Asia Minor, and his teachings were first and more enduringly accepted there. Until the fourth century C.E., when Christianity became Rome's state religion, most of the Roman clergy were recruited from the Eastern Church centered in Constantinople. The Latin Church did not have time to grow, for all Rome's energies, including those of the church, went to protect the city, the greatest prize of the Empire for invading barbarians.

> [T]he Latin Church was soon engulfed by the barbarian invasions and, with little time for pointless theological disputations, had to take over the main burden of preserving what was left of civilization during the Dark Ages.[61]

In the Eastern Church, an extensive system of relief developed. Christians pooled their possessions to provide a daily distribution of food. Both men and women were teachers and leaders, and women of wealth were instrumental in financing Christianity's growth and activities, establishing hospitals and monasteries, and working with the poor:

> [T]he Byzantines [were] a nation . . . characterized by . . . many works of practical philanthropy . . . a virtue not only of the rich and prominent, but of all organizations and classes of people.[62]

In both Eastern and Roman Churches, care for the needy became a major activity. In a sense, poverty was sanctified by Jesus, and early Christians based an "ethic of poverty" on his teachings.[63] To aid the poor was like having aided Jesus himself. Poverty, not wealth, was the way to salvation. The poor, slaves, widows, orphans, and those imprisoned, exiled, or working in mines as punishment for their Christian beliefs were aided. From the first, women were actively engaged in charitable works, opening the first hospitals and even the first monastic communities. Because Christians met in each other's homes, the concept of hospitality was elevated to religion.[64]

Ideas of work, private property, and wealth changed. Work was no longer degrading, as Christians worked to support themselves, to demonstrate their worth to nonbelievers, and to serve the needy. Private wealth was considered immoral by early Christians because it created class disparities, but the religion's leaders soon realized it was a permanent characteristic of society and developed a new doctrine on wealth. Now the wealthy "owed" the needy the excess products of their wealth. By the fourth century, the good that wealth could do and the salvation it would provide for the rich were major tenets of the religion. Salvation depended on how one treated the needy: the hungry, thirsty, strangers, those needing clothes, the sick, and prisoners.[65]

By the middle of the second century, Christian charity was organized, with each church member expected to give a regular donation, often weekly, to the poor box. In addition, contributions of bread and wine were collected at the Eucharist and a chosen officer, often a bishop, distributed the excess to the poor of the congregation.[66] Although at first this care was restricted to Christians, it was later extended to the poor regardless of religion. Christianity became legal in 313 C.E. and was declared the state religion of the Empire under Constantine in 361 C.E., with his personal conversion. He believed that religion should be responsible for the needy, and Christianity became the state agency for charity. State, church, and voluntary social welfare functions thereafter overlapped and the state was relieved of some of its burden regarding the poor. Privately endowed foundations, especially in Italy, invested capital in real estate mortgages, and interest was given to towns or state administrators for charitable uses. In Byzantium, clergy distributed assistance, and in Rome, a private voluntary group administered a state-supported social welfare system.[67]

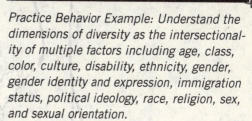

Diversity in Practice

Practice Behavior Example: Understand the dimensions of diversity as the intersectionality of multiple factors including age, class, color, culture, disability, ethnicity, gender, gender identity and expression, immigration status, political ideology, race, religion, sex, and sexual orientation.

Critical Thinking Question: How did class and gender intersect to define the roles and opportunities avalible to women in ancient societites?

State and Church in Rome

Chastising the rich in the third century C.E., St. Cyprian said, "[They] add properties to properties and chase the poor from their borders. Their lands extend without limit or measure."[68] Although feudalism—in which serfs are hereditarily bound to the land and service to its lord—did not develop for centuries elsewhere in Europe, it began in Rome even before the fall of the Empire (about 476 C.E.) as Rome disintegrated under internal forces and repeated Teutonic barbarian attacks. Many of the poor traded their freedom to wealthy landowners for protection in walled "manors." Small freeholders placed their land under the lord's control and became tenant farmers. The urban poor, competing with slaves for scarce jobs, also bonded themselves into serfdom, along with runaway slaves, army deserters, vagabonds, tax-ruined farmers, and peaceful immigrants from barbarian tribes. Accustomed to hereditary service, by the fourth century these serfs were officially tied to the land.[69] Large Roman estates expanded considerably, and the lords were relieved of labor worries while their wealth was ensured.

Rome's ability to support itself and the Empire was dealt a fatal blow in 410 C.E. when Visigoths, under Alaric the Great, destroyed the city and pillaged nearly its entire wealth.[70] In such a weakened state, the Empire was easy prey for waves of Teutonic invaders eager for its fabled opulence. The whole central ruling structure collapsed and Western Europe was left in disarray, reverting to localized tribes. Cities shrank and trade and communications diminished. Although several kingdoms followed the Roman Empire, none were able to hold the vast area together. Intermarriage between the invaders and the Roman senatorial and landowning classes took place in Gaul, Spain, and Italy, and from this sprang the feudal nobility that was to rule Europe. Angles and Saxons invaded Britain to be overthrown in turn by Danes and Normans. The process of barbarization became irreversible, plunging Western Europe into the Dark Ages (see Figure 3.4).

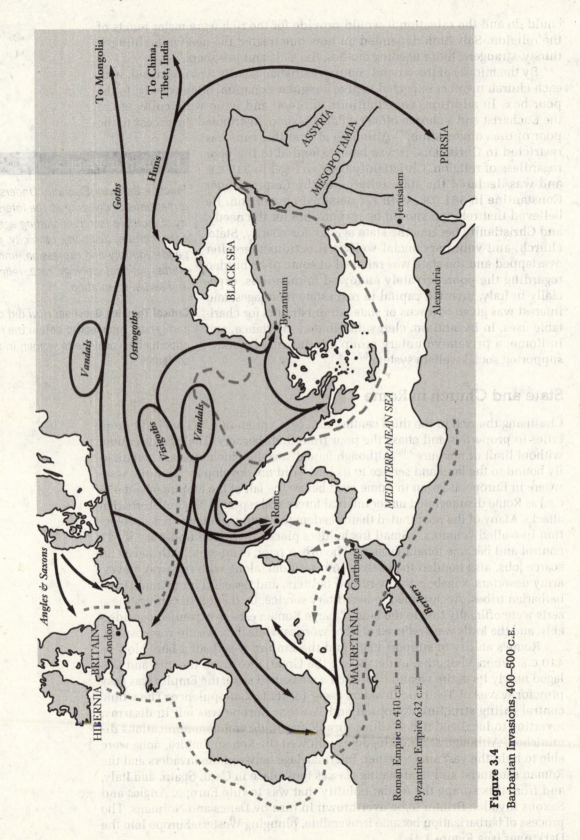

Figure 3.4
Barbarian Invasions, 400–500 C.E.

As the Roman Empire fell, the power of the Holy Roman Church rose. It attracted the best administrative and political talents that the Western classical world had to offer and substituted its own bureaucracy for that of the collapsing imperial machinery. Roman civilization and culture now rested in the hands of the Church. The invading kings, respecting that culture, converted to Christianity. This legitimized the new royalty with the Catholic people of the conquered regions and demonstrated the power of the Church at king making. Whereas the Church had been a creature of the state, now many states owed the Church fealty and its spiritual bond held the Western world together.

A synergistic spiral of power occurred: The conversion of conquerors to Christianity gave them power over the local populaces, whereas the right to crown kings bestowed political power on the Roman Church. Now political rulers could claim they ruled by divine right, and because Rome conferred this right on the many kings, uniting them in spirit, the Holy Roman Empire became the center of power throughout Europe. For example, in the fifth

Saint Adélard (St Allard) distribuant des Aumônes.
Gravure de Hans Burgkmaier (École allemande fin du XV siècle.
À gauche Lépreux avec taches rétractions; à droite un autre, la ambe mutilée.
Collection du Dʳ HENRY MEIGE (Paris)

century, Clovis, the victorious king of the Salic Franks in Gaul, was baptized a Christian along with 3,000 Frankish warriors. He then allied with other Christians and defeated his Visigoth and Burgundian enemies. With his Christian wife, Clothilde, he subsequently turned Roman Gaul into what would become France.[71]

CONCLUSION: BEGINNINGS OF CHARITY AND CONTROL

In this chapter, we have considered the history of humankind and mutual aid, traveling across cultures, across time, and across religions, culminating with the beginnings of Christianity. Through all this, the synergistic relationships of religion, economics, and politics that evolved class and gender stratification have been demonstrated, and we have seen social welfare change from communal mutual aid to a complex system that not only helped the poor but controlled their work behavior. Women's loss of economic and sacred power made them possessions of men, and class differentiation put the mass of workers under the control of a small male-dominated ruling elite. In societies where humankind moved toward patriarchy and private property, a new political economy based on class stratification and gender oppression evolved, and religiously legitimated exploitation became commonplace.

The history of social welfare is also a history of societies and cannot be considered apart from them. Jewish, Greek, Roman, barbarian, and Christian societies reified gender and class stratification even though their religions ostensibly relieved oppression. Within each, social welfare took on new meanings with new times. In Judaism, social justice and human need were the keynotes, providing an institutional perspective that underlies some aspects of our social welfare today. Greek society developed ideals of both democracy and philanthropy, although the meanings of those ideals were far different in those times than today. Roman society, a blending of many trends from the past, gave us political structures and processes that continue to affect our legal and social systems. Christian altruism as taught by Jesus is still part of social welfare today. In the following centuries, patriarchal church leaders continued patterns of oppression as well as aid. The Holy Roman Empire became a religio-political system of diverse kingdoms under the spiritual leadership of Rome, and a spiral of power between kings and church ensured the success of Christianity in the Western world and the success of royal lineages in the many kingdoms of feudal Europe.

Social welfare came full circle, for again religion was responsible for the poor, although its tenor had changed. Poverty was still considered the result of social and economic conditions (rather than personal fault) and was redefined as a holy state. Although the Holy Roman Church worked ceaselessly to alleviate the misery of the poor, through its benisons to kings and the ruling elite it also helped to maintain structures that perpetuated oppression. The poor remained subject to the whims and desires of ruling elites in their pursuit of wealth and power, and social welfare became a means by which such goals were achieved. In all, synergistic relationships created forces that, a few centuries after the birth of Christianity, would set the economic, political, and religious overtones for social welfare in much of our world today.

The following questions will test your knowledge and understanding of the content found with.. this chapter. For additional assessment, including licensing-exam type questions on applying chapter content to practice behaviors, visit **MySearchLab**.

1. Which of the following describes tzedakah, the basis of the Judaism principle of altruism?

   a. charity and justice

   b. loving-kindness

   c. karma

   d. giving freely

2. The belief that reincarnation places people in life positions allowing them to atone for past lives or prepare for future ones is called:

   a. karma

   b. chesed

   c. suttee

   d. hetairai

3. Which statement best describes the ancient Judaic beliefs toward charity?

   a. Everything belonged to God and God's will was to give to anyone in need.

   b. People do not have an obligation to help those in need if they deem them immoral.

   c. People must ask for charity only in times of desperation.

   d. God's will did not include charity, only prayer and repentance.

4. In ancient China, what led to the beginnings of the first welfare system?

   a. the introduction of Buddhism, which urged rulers to care for the poor

   b. a string of violent riots from the poor insisting for help

   c. the collapse of Feudalism

   d. an epidemic of disease that rendered many citizens too sick to work or care for themselves

5. What insight might you give a poor female citizen of ancient Rome regarding doles?

   a. One dole would provide enough for two people.

   b. Women receive doles only until age 18.

   c. Every child in poverty under age 15 receives a dole.

   d. Boys receive larger doles than girls do.

6. How would an early Christian have responded to a citizen in poverty?

   a. With disdain; being in poverty was a sign of immorality.

   b. With charity; helping the poor was like helping Jesus himself.

   c. With discreetness; there was a stigma attached, but people wanted to help.

   d. With resentment; people in poverty should take whatever work they could get without relying on the resources of the hardworking citizens.

7. Discuss how Christian charity provided for the poor and needy.

Reinforce what you learned in this chapter by studying videos, cases, documents, and more available at **www.MySearchLab.com.**

Watch and Review

Watch these Videos

The Slave Trade

Working Poor

Read and Review

Read these Cases/Documents

Women on the Breadlines

Assess Your Knowledge

Go to **MySearchLab** to test your knowledge of key topics in this chapter with topic-specific quizzes. Conclude your assessment by completing the chapter exam.

4

Feudalism and the Welfare State

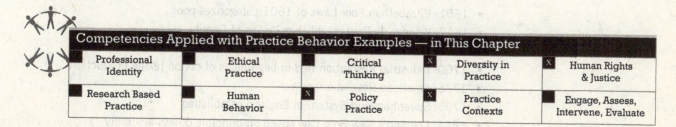

Competencies Applied with Practice Behavior Examples — in This Chapter				
■ Professional Identity	■ Ethical Practice	■ Critical Thinking	X Diversity in Practice	X Human Rights & Justice
■ Research Based Practice	■ Human Behavior	X Policy Practice	X Practice Contexts	■ Engage, Assess, Intervene, Evaluate

Times and Events

The Dark Ages in Europe: Circa 400–1200 C.E.

- Fall of the Roman Empire, Holy Roman Empire anoints kings in Europe, rise of feudalism
- 527–565: Rule of Justinian and Theodora, Justinian Code of Laws
- Establishment of Christian hospitals giving all social welfare services
- Seventh century: Islam begins, sweeps across Northern Africa, the Middle East, and into Europe
- 800: Charlemagne's laws forbid begging, classify worthy and unworthy poor
- Scientific Revolution brings new inventions to agriculture, travel, and trade; crafts and guilds begin
- 1066: Battle of Hastings; William the Conqueror brings feudalism to England
- 1140: Gratian compiles *Decretum*, supporting social justice for the poor
- 1215: Magna Carta signed
- By 1200, the Holy Roman Church condemned homosexuals, sorcerers, witches, and Jews punishable by death. Inquisition and Knights Templar established, massacres begin

1200–1500 C.E.

- 1235 and 1285 laws in England establish Enclosure Movement, which closes common land, streams, and forests from common people
- 1348: first onslaught of bubonic plague decimates England and Europe
- 1349: Statute of Laborers passed
- 1337–1600: Witchcraze
- 1388: England's Statute of Artificers requires letters patent for travelers
- Labor riots in Europe, 1358, 1378, 1381, 1382 fail: mercantilism replaces feudalism
- 1421–1423: Discovery of America by Chinese
- 1431: Jeanne d'Arc burned as a witch
- 1492: Discovery of America by Columbus

1500–1800 C.E.

- 1513: Henry VII requires all beggars to be licensed
- 1517: Martin Luther begins Protestant Reformation
- 1535: Juan Luis Vives develops parish model for care of poor
- 1536: Henry VIII establishes Church of England, confiscates Catholic Church lands; responsibility for poor moved from church to state
- 1536: England's Act for Punishment of Sturdy Beggars makes poverty a crime
- 1583: Statute of Artificers regulates workforce by wage and hour laws
- 1601: Elizabethan Poor Laws of 1601 categorizes poor
- 1617: Vincent de Paul establishes Ladies of Charity
- 1722: Workhouse Act sets workhouse test
- 1760: Industrial Revolution tied to beginnings of cotton textile production
- 1776: American Revolutionary War
- 1795: Speenhamland System in England established
- 1834: England's New Poor Law based on principle of less eligibility

Many forces changed Western society, first to a feudal society and then to states in which laws regulated the treatment of laborers and the poor. Religion was one such force: The Roman Church completed the conversion of all barbarian peoples in Europe around 1000 C.E., legitimating kings and legitimated in turn by the new European rulers who appointed priests, bishops, and even popes. The Scientific Revolution and its growing agricultural technology was another, moving humankind from its organic relationship with nature and placing the power of production in the hands of an elite. Feudalism and church power changed as the Commercial Revolution brought the onset of capitalism and the Protestant Reformation. Social welfare became control rather than aid for the poor.

THE DARK AND MIDDLE AGES

Between the fall of the Roman Empire and the creation of the Magna Carta in 1215, the Dark Ages descended on Europe. Without a unifying government, cities shrank and communication and travel were disrupted. But the world was far from "dark" in the sense of stagnant. New forms of polity, economy, and religion were fomenting to create the framework for Western society. Throughout Europe, would-be kings fought to maintain new territories, and the common people suffered as wars raged across their lands. The Christian religion continued its rise in the Byzantine and Holy Roman Empires, and Islam rose and conquered great swaths of the Middle East, Africa, and Europe, bringing with it new concepts of government and scholarship (see Figure 4.1).

In the Byzantine world, Constantinople remained the center of civilization until the thirteenth century (see Figure 4.2). More influenced than Rome

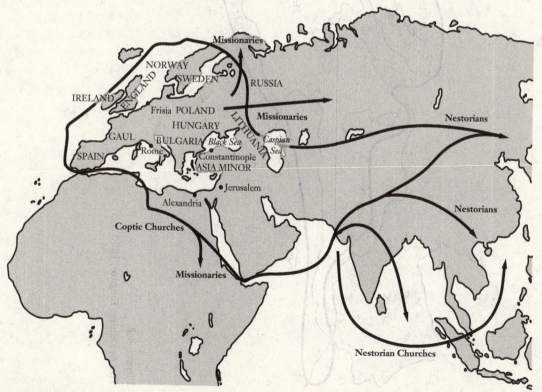

Figure 4.1
Christianity, 600–1500 C.E.

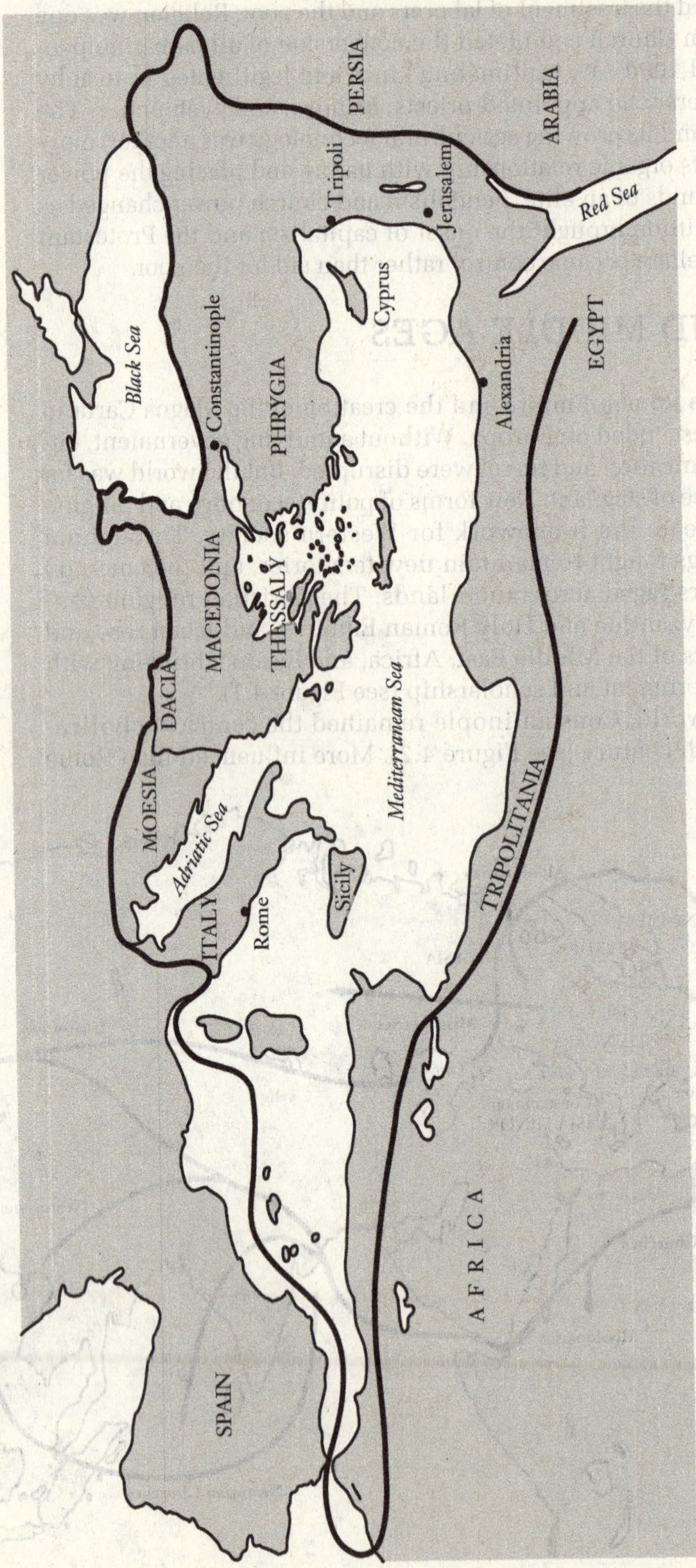

PERSIA

ARABIA

Red Sea

Tripoli

Jerusalem

Cyprus

EGYPT

Alexandria

Black Sea

Constantinople

PHRYGIA

THESSALY

MACEDONIA

DACIA

MOESIA

Adriatic Sea

ITALY

Rome

Sicily

Mediterranean Sea

TRIPOLITANIA

AFRICA

SPAIN

Figure 4.2
The Byzantine Empire, 1200 C.E.

by egalitarian philosophies and traditions, the Eastern church discouraged both class and gender stratification. In Asia Minor, Syria, and Egypt, peasants settled into small farms and villages as free farmers. Taxes were reasonable, and in hard times the government and church collaborated to buy products and ensure employment in the monasteries.[1] Whereas women in the Roman Church remained under the hard hand of patriarchy, Byzantine women were free under the famed Justinian Code of Laws (Justinian and Theodora, 527–565 C.E.). In the East, inheritance through women was retained, the penalty for adultery was reduced from death to life in a convent (although men were still subject to capital punishment), and rape became punishable by death, with the rapist's property given to the injured woman.[2] Women and men often reigned together, and by the seventh century a church-supported welfare state had developed in Alexandria, with maternity hospitals, medical facilities, and food rationing.[3]

In the seventh century, the new religion of Islam swept across Arabia and the Middle East, into Africa to the south, and to the Pyrenees Mountains in Europe. By the eleventh century, it had seized Hungary, Poland, and Prussia from the Byzantine Empire. An aggressive and militant monotheism, it followed earlier monotheistic traditions by wiping out old religions and eradicating the rights of women.[4] Although a few royal women retained power, most were totally subjugated and veiling, once a mark of honor, became required as women were isolated in homes and harems. Moral living and right conduct were at the core of Islamic belief, and it promoted an ethic of individual work and commercialism not unlike later Calvinist and Puritan beliefs. New sciences, including architecture and engineering, and new concepts of mathematics with Arabic numerals were developed by its scholars, and the concept of nation–state was instituted. By the twelfth century, Islamic hospitals were magnificently built and equipped and Islamic universities were the centers of scholarship and culture.

Islam's basic tenets were belief in God and Muhammad as His Apostle; obligatory rituals such as prayer at appointed times, fasting, and pilgrimage; and almsgiving, whether as a poor tax (*zakat*) or voluntarily (*sadaqah*). In Islam's first century (622–722 C.E.), almost a thousand years before the punitive Christian Elizabethan Poor Laws (1601), charity was both a social ideal and a national program among Muslims, with national welfare taxes and paid full-time welfare workers to collect and distribute them.[5] According to the noted scholar Maulana Muhammad Ali, "Prayer is primary, but charity toward men, in the widest sense, is ... the second great pillar on which the structure of Islam stands."[6] The tax rate was one-fortieth (2.5 percent) of all saved or accumulated wealth, including most kinds of property.[7] Religiously speaking, charity was a means of showing faithfulness and stewardship to God and would be rewarded in the afterlife.[8]

In Africa, the Sudanese kingdoms of Ghana, Mali, and Songhay, newly influenced by Islam, rivaled those of Rome. The University of Sankore in Songhay's Timbuktu was the world center of learning for law, surgery, and history. Ghana reached its peak early in the eleventh century, and Songhay apexed in the fifteenth century under the brilliant King Askia (1493–1512 C.E.). He was said to be the equal of and superior to many European monarchs of the time,[9] and his realm, larger than all Europe, encompassed most of West Africa. The great Sudan empires ended in the seventeenth century, although states in East and South Africa, the East Coast, and Southern Rhodesia and Zimbabwe were centers of trade and culture into the eighteenth and nineteenth centuries.

In Europe, a hectic transition to a new kind of civilization began with the fall of the Roman Empire. Teutons, Franks, Visigoths, Angles, Saxons, and Celts warred across the continent, and about the time Justinian ruled the Byzantine Empire (527–565 C.E.), feudalism began its rise in France and Italy. Saxon kingdoms were established in England in the years 490–530, and in the eighth century the Viking Danes invaded England, to be defeated by Alfred the Great. In 800, Charlemagne was crowned by the pope as King of Italy, Germany, and France, founding the new Western empire, and two centuries later Macbeth murdered Duncan and usurped the throne of Scotland.

Normans and Saxons fought for control of England until, at the Battle of Hastings, William the Conqueror became king (1066). A short-lived feudalism came to England, ending in the thirteenth century with the signing of the Magna Carta by King John in 1215. The document granted civil rights to the people of England, but because it challenged the "divine right of kings," it was immediately annulled by the pope. Thereafter, it was reissued three times in modified form by Henry III (1216–1272). Toward the end of the Dark Ages, Huns and Poles repeatedly invaded Russia, and Genghis Khan subdued the north of China in 1216. By 1236, Mongolians and Tartars under Batu Khan were invading Russia and Europe, burning Moscow in 1236 and ending Russian independence. By 1259, Kublai Khan had united China and built Peking as his capital.

Women had little status in Europe, except among the liberal Visigoths, under whose laws they jointly administered community property with their husbands and could claim a share of the land if the husband died first. In general, however, women were perpetual minors and possessions, to be bought and sold in marriage. Rape was a property crime against the husband, polygamy was common, and divorce or renunciation of wives and concubines was easy. Although there were queens and female warriors, most women were adjuncts to the male household and under feudalism belonged as well to the liege-lord and the estate. Marriage of feudal serfs involved a "bride price" to be paid to the lord. If the bride were comely, the price could be increased beyond the groom's means. By *droit de seigneur*, when the new price was defaulted, the husband could be thrown out and the wife raped by the lord, his knights, squires, pages, and possibly the chaplain. This was considered an honor for a mere peasant woman.[10]

Christianity enforced monogamy and decried divorce, and in this way brought a somewhat better life for women. By the eighth century, adult Frankish women were free of male guardianship, and by the tenth century Anglo-Saxon women had considerable power over property. Upon the husband's death, if there was no male heir, widows could inherit lands and title even if remarried, for the land belonged to family rather than individual. Also, in the rapidly growing cities, working women were freed from male domination of their earned property. Toward the end of the Dark Ages, married or single women could hold land, sell it, give it away, own goods, make a will or a contract, sue and be sued, and plead in the law courts in England and in Europe.[11] However, not until the eleventh century was a law written to forbid the selling of women.

The Feudal Society

Prefeudal Europe was a rural free-peasant economy counterpointed by great medieval cities in which the church and the rich held sway. Family and community constituted the fundamental economic units, although each farm family shared the natural resources of the territorial commons (forests, pastures, and water). Communal resources were regulated by elected or appointed officers. Women and men worked their freeholds and resisted the would-be kings warring across their lands. The European population between the Baltic and the Mediterranean, estimated to have been 27 million in 700 C.E., reached 60 or 70 million by 1200. The creation of a bourgeois class brought with it the emancipation of the rural masses.[12]

In the best of times the lives of peasants were in constant jeopardy; life expectancy for all people was no more than forty years or so. Harsh living conditions, poor health care, and poor nutrition made people weak, small in stature, prone to illness, and decimated by the plagues that periodically swept across Europe. Death by war was common for men, and childbirth a mortal hazard for women, rich or poor. Strayer and Munro say,

> While … there was much inequality in normal times … all [were] equally helpless in periods of misfortune. They all lived in unsanitary conditions; they had no doctors, and at times pestilence swept away whole communities. Few families could store grain; a year of flood or drought created terrible famines. The peasants could not defend themselves against heavy-armed feudal cavalry, and if their lord became involved in a war they were almost sure to see their fields ravaged and their houses burned.[13]

Feudalism did not come easily to Europe, for peasants dreaded the near slavery of serfdom, which was

> a degrading thing.… What men feared and resented … was not its subordination but its arbitrariness. The hatred of that which was governed not by rule, but by will, went very deep in the Middle Ages.[14]

Finally, however, force and the need for military security made peasants give up their lands and freedom and swear allegiance to local strongmen. They bonded themselves to a lord in return for protection and rights to land use (as tenants or in "commons"). Every person had an ascribed status: Roles were predetermined, inherited, and immutable (as opposed to being achieved through work or effort). According to Handel,

> Feudal society was the quintessence of hereditary aristocracy, privilege by birth instead of proved merit. A virtually impassable gulf separated the ruling class of lords and their fief-holders from the masses of peasants. Whatever their virtues or their vices, the rulers monopolized wealth, power, and prestige.[15]

Feudalism tied landhold with military service, and there was an "embeddedness" in the relationships among serfs, lords, and sovereigns. Nonfree peasants owed their lives and work to the lord, and he owed them protection and good management of the community so that, in hard times, they might survive. Lords had land, power, a stable workforce, the right to military conscription for their own battles and those of their sovereigns, and taxing power without redress. In time, the care of serfs by liege-lords became a kind of trust, a *noblesse oblige*, or obligation of honor, and in theory all were provided for. However, the lord's right took precedence over every right, need, facet of life, or desire of the serfs. Every man and woman was bound

Human Rights and Justice

Practice Behavior Example: Understand the forms and mechanisms of oppression and discrimination.

Critical Thinking Question: Can noblesse oblige be construed as a mechanism of oppression or a form of social justice?

to the lord, and brutal treatment, up to and including rape and murder, was not uncommon.

As the centuries passed, the serfs won some concessions. Many "owned" their property and their heirs could "inherit" if each swore fealty to the lord. As population increased and agricultural technology changed, serfdom became economically infeasible for lords. They began to charge rents and fees for use of the land and a new money economy emerged. Ascribed status obligations vanished and poverty became rampant under contract labor. A new era of individualism and alienation began as lords were no longer obligated to support their serfs.

The Scientific Revolution

During the thousand or so years of the Dark and Middle Ages, new technologies changed industry, architecture, and agriculture, alleviated suffering, and enhanced life. Inventions included the spinning wheel, water mill, windmill, wheelbarrow, crank, cam, flywheel, rudder, compass, stirrup, gunpowder, lateen sail, padded horse collar, and nailed horseshoe.[16] The invention of new farming equipment was of primary importance: In particular, the padded horse collar could enormously increase the amount of land under plow. Because of the wars flying back and forth across Europe, the invention of new weapons such as the longbow and later the crossbow made conquest easier. In addition, the newly invented stirrup was the key to new armored warfare for lords and knights.

For women, cloth making took on added importance in commerce with the invention of the spinning wheel, and "piecing out" became a way of life for poor women (although nonpoor women continued in their cloth-making work, through guilds and crafts often owned by their husbands). Gies and Gies say,

> As in Roman times, linen and wool remained the principal textiles. The manufacture of cotton cloth, a Roman luxury import, was carried by the Arab conquest to Spain, Sicily, and Southern Italy as early as the tenth century, but it was not mastered by Christian Europe until the twelfth.[17]

Spinning never ceased, and the skill was universal, especially for women of the lower classes, who always had a spindle in hand. Spinning was so identified with women that the female side of the family was known as the "distaff side," or the "spindle side."[18]

As mechanization changed the way of life, the church developed a doctrine that intermingled religion and science and mandated stewardship of the earth by men. Nature, already equated with the female, now took on characteristics assigned to women, seen as passive, submissive, and controllable. This gynomorphic relationship was exacerbated as such church scholars as Thomas Aquinas posited a dual spirit/body approach to religion, in which mind and spirit were equated with men, and women (and the earth) were equated with body, earthiness, and evil. The persecution of women during the time of the Inquisition and Europe's ecological devastation during the Middle Ages were results of this equation.[19]

Until early feudal times, hand-hoeing and the three-field system, where land was allowed to lie fallow to increase its productivity, were the basic agricultural technologies. The invention of the oxen-drawn plow, although it put more land into production, kept an ecological relationship in which the number of acres needing manure and the number of animals supported on the manor were integrated. In times of good harvests, more oxen could be purchased to keep the land rich and to raise the subsistence level. However, as feudalism encroached, the new technologies and the demands of the lords altered the economy in significant ways. The invention of the horse collar began ecologically unsound production as more land was brought under cultivation in a shorter time (including fallow land), and fewer animals meant less manure. The commandeering of horses and oxen for war and taxes exacerbated this practice and prevented reinvestment in animals to keep the ground fertile.

The Roman water wheel and handmills slowly spread northward from Italy, reaching the British Isles by the eighth century and Scandinavia by the twelfth. Lords took a monopoly on them, requiring payment for grinding grain, making cloth and paper, and sawing timber. People who kept illegal mills faced retribution in the form of higher taxes, higher mill costs, or destruction of property. The draining of swamps, fens, and waterways for agriculture ruined local water and forest ecologies. By the thirteenth century, common use of woodlands was outlawed so that the elite could use wood as fuel in their homes and factories and for the building of the great sailing ships of the new international trade.[20]

The Enclosure Movement, from the twelfth century onward, was part of the social evolution that changed relationships between landowners and workers from an ascribed to a money economy. "Enclosure" meant the process of fencing, ditching, hedging, or barricading land formerly held "in common" by local villagers and peasants. In England, its legal basis began in statutes in 1235 and 1285 permitting landlords to enclose "wastelands," though this was conditional on leaving sufficient land for tenants. Most peasants and marginal people lived in villages having "common areas"—meadows, fields, forests, and water areas. There they planted small gardens, pastured their pigs and chickens, hunted and fished, and gathered firewood, reeds, fruits, and nuts to eke out their existence.

However, with the move to wage labor and the use of money as the preferred medium of exchange, high rent and taxes pushed peasants from their land. Those who had held the land by custom had no legally documented claim, and even those with legal rights could not afford the costs of enclosure, so many sold out and left.[21] Commons were declared "wastelands" and were seized for enclosure. Some were bought by wealthy farmers in need of larger tracts of land to support new agricultural technologies, but more often landowning lords made them part of their manorial holdings. Outside the jurisdiction of both city and guild regulations, the former common land was given over to the raising of sheep for wool for the international trade in cloth.

The Enclosure Movement reflected the continued growth of the textile industry in the fifteenth century, with improved spinning and weaving instruments and a proto-industrialization of the organization of work.[22] The "putting out" piecework system in Western Europe was gradually replaced by the factory system. In both home and workshop, "bells rang for the beginning and end of the working day as well as for meals, and inspectors regularly monitored all the workers."[23] It also reflected a loss of self-sufficient communities and an ever-widening international trade and economic system. Some have noted that the Enclosure Movement led to the creation of the wage-earning class by separating the workers from their land.[24] In any case, it was the end of an ascribed economic system and changed the face of land ownership, tenantship, and power. Although, people fought enclosure, with land revolts in England in 1536, 1569, and 1607, it was a losing battle for the common person.

The Church and Social Welfare

The Roman Church was immersed in the politics of feudalism, a law unto itself, with governance, taxes, courts, and punishments. At its highest levels, corruption—the use of power for economic gain—was rampant. Any dissatisfaction or uprising to gain better treatment, such as the Magna Carta, was considered heresy. During the later Dark Ages, the Church established its own army, the Knights Templar, and its judicial arm, the Inquisition, to enforce its power both on foreign fronts (during the Crusades) and in Europe. Muslims and Jews were persecuted, as were non-Catholic Christians. For example, in 1209 a forty-year Crusade began against the Albigensian Christians in southern France. The whole of Languedoc was ravaged, crops destroyed, towns and cities razed, and the entire population put to death. In Béziers, at least 15,000 people were killed, many in the church sanctuary:

> When an officer inquired of the Pope's representative how he might distinguish heretics from true believers, the reply was "Kill them all. God will recognize his own."[25]

Lack of salvation and damnation to hell were overriding fears in the general populace, and to think or behave outside church mandates was nearly inconceivable. Coulton says,

> Medieval [thought] is characterized ... by the convictions that each man has a soul to save, and that therefore, salvation is the main end of every human being, not a distant ideal but the most practical duty that is set before all ... the last moment of life marked the man for an eternity of unspeakable bliss or of torment beyond all conception.[26]

Because both body and soul were charges of the Church, rulers did not need to give charity to control the populace. What little was given was, generally, either from whim or for salvation, often occurring on the ruler's deathbed and usually to relatives, immediate retainers, military leaders, or the Church.

Many manor lords were also Church bishops, receiving taxes as well as tithes, donations, and legacies. Many used these for their own purposes rather than to help their parishioners. Although Rome had central authority in the distribution of charity, local Church authorities established their own regulations, and the lower levels of the Church remained dedicated to serving the poor. Priests collected money and distributed food and help throughout their parishes. Need was still considered the result of social, political, and economic forces rather than personal fault, although some Church fathers believed that indiscriminate giving was morally harmful to recipients. Generally, though, help was given anyone seeking it, even Muslims and Jews. The able-bodied were expected to work for their keep after a few days.

By the sixth century, both women and men had established religious orders whose primary duty was to care for the unfortunate. Their monasteries and abbeys evolved into the medieval hospital, which provided medical assistance but also housed and cared for travelers, widows, orphans, the aged, and the destitute.[27] By the eighth century, all Church members were required to tithe, at first to support diocese and bishop. In time, Church revenues supported four areas equally: the bishop; the parish clergy; church upkeep; and the poor, widowed, disabled, orphaned, and aged. In England in the tenth century under King Ethelred, support of the poor became a state law rather than a religious custom. As early as 800 C.E., Charlemagne's laws prohibited begging and fined those who gave alms to the able-bodied.[28]

Women were increasingly involved in services to the poor under Church auspices, and some conventual orders pioneered in nursing elderly and indigent patients.[29] Abbeys and convents also served as refuges to unmarried women, nonconformists, and female intellectuals, and most learned women of the Middle Ages were nuns (although the majority were barely literate).[30] Nuns came primarily from the nobility, although some were from gentry and merchant classes. Peasant girls, craftsmen's daughters, and serfs almost never became nuns, because the Church required dowries of lands, rents, or cash, and sometimes even clothes and furniture. The Church's view of the spiritual inadequacy of women limited nuns' activities and restricted them to convents, but some, under the direction of a few powerful and wealthy abbesses, served in communities. Semiconventual orders, such as the twelfth-century Beguines, took temporary vows and served the poor, ill, disabled, aged, and prisoners in both cities and rural areas.

In about 1140, the Italian monk Gratian compiled the *Decretum*, a set of laws made up of papal decrees, canons of church councils, and commentaries of church lawyers. It eliminated inconsistencies in canon law and distinguished between "voluntary poverty"—poverty for clerics, monks, or nuns—and the involuntary poverty of widows and orphans. It decreed that poverty was not a crime and that need alone obligated the Church to help the poor. Social justice was again the keynote, and the Church became increasingly critical of private wealth. By the beginning of the thirteenth century, the rich had to support the poor by law. These two interpretations of canon law—social justice and the obligations of the wealthy to the poor—set the institutional perspective on social welfare into Christian doctrine.

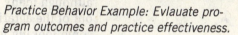

Practice Contexts

Practice Behavior Example: Evlauate program outcomes and practice effectiveness.

Critical Thinking Question: What were the latent and manifest functions of the Catholic Church during the Middle Ages?

Forms of Private Welfare

Besides the overall responsibility of church and feudal manor for the poor, private welfare continued throughout this era. Care for fathers who turned over their trades to their sons in return for support in their older years was court-enforceable, as were deceased husbands' provisions for widows. Although in most places such women were encouraged to remarry, they also could continue to work their husbands' lands or receive a portion of the land until their deaths, when it reverted to the eldest son. Sons might also take their mothers into their households or purchase *corrodies* from local monasteries. A corrody was a daily ration of bread and ale and a dish of pottage from the monastery kitchen; a room, a servant, and firewood; and a new robe, shoes, and under-linen once a year. Candles and fodder and stalling for horses, or sometimes a house and garden, might also be included.[31]

In the cities, crafts and guilds—voluntary societies for the protection and mutual aid of their members—aided disabled workers or those unable to earn a living and gave pensions to survivors of deceased workers. Dowries for craftsmen's daughters might also be a part of the benefits. In addition,

> [Guilds] maintained hospitals, fed the needy on feast days, distributed
> corn and barley annually, provided free lodgings for poor travelers, and
> gave other incidental help.[32]

Women could become guild members, but often not as equals. Usually craftsmen could employ only their own wives or daughters, and women were paid less for the same work. Many eked out their income with prostitution or thievery, for which they were punished in stocks and pillory.

Finally, some kings, dukes, merchants, and lords provided alms or established hospitals or almshouses. Every major city in Europe and many of the smaller ones had hospitals. Between the twelfth and sixteenth centuries more than eight hundred were built in England alone (including those built by towns and craft and religious guilds). Private benefactors also underwrote almshouses for particular groups of people such as retired and disabled soldiers and sailors, old merchants, and fishmongers.[33] Funeral feasts or doles were given, often specifically to the working poor, at donors' funerals and on anniversaries of their deaths. The amount of donation was not as important as wide disbursement, for the purpose was to ensure the deceased's salvation. Charity demonstrated to all that the pursuit of wealth was justified and pleasing to God. Although they misrepresented their wares, gave short measure, or charged high interest, by giving charity they could "achieve" the best of both worlds: maximum financial gain on earth and salvation in the afterlife.[34]

THE DISSOLUTION OF FEUDALISM

Agricultural production increased phenomenally with new technologies, but although many peasants became small landholders, the majority were pushed out of the agrarian economy. Increasing numbers of vagrants roamed the land, some looking for work, some on religious pilgrimage (during the Crusades), some as itinerant peddlers. Church provision for able-bodied beggars and travelers caused friction between the Church and the lords: lords wanted to keep serfs bound to the land, but Church policies supported them as they looked for better work. This threatened the lords' labor supply and increased the numbers of "rogues and vagabonds" who preyed on other travelers and townsfolk and poached on lords' lands and forests. Begging also became a problem and laws were established to control the poor. Increasingly, voluntary charity and the Church were blamed for supporting beggary and undercutting profits.

As crafts such as cloth making moved from home industry to organized production, people of all ages, including children, were hired as pieceworkers in their homes. The entrepreneur, a profit-making businessman,

> purchased wool in England, shipped it home, parceled it out to a family to clean, spin, card, and weave, took it back and gave it to another to full, then to another to dye, and to another to stretch, tease ... and shear. Retrieving it for the last time, he gave it to an agent to sell.[35]

Work was from dawn to dusk, six days a week, with entrepreneurs controlling the lives of pieceworkers. They owned the houses in which workers lived and the stores where they bought goods and sat on city councils to make their laws. Workers could work only for their own entrepreneurs, and this protected entrepreneurs from market fluctuations, war, or other calamity, for they could simply leave workers with unsellable cloth. Workers often bankrupted themselves to avoid debtor's prison. Conflict often resulted—the first strike in the industry occurred in 1245, among the weavers of Douai—but strikes were put down with the force of law. Punishments ranged from cutting out tongues and banishing especially vocal protesters to seizing their goods.[36]

During this era, the booming textile industry brought enormous social changes. Lopez says,

> Perhaps most significant ... was the advance toward modern business methods and organization. Unstinting credit was the great lubricant of

the Commercial Revolution. The formation of large trading companies dealing extensively in credit transactions gave rise ... to commercial banking dominated by such swiftly growing family-based institutions as the House of Medici.[37]

Cloth making was the only work that achieved the status of a large-scale commercial industry. Although its workers benefited little, the social changes it created were enormous. Cloth sails made travel for merchanting one of the most important means of achieving wealth and broadened the horizons of international travel. Large trading companies emerged that dealt extensively in credit transactions, with interest hidden in shipping fees to circumvent the admonitions of the Church against usury. These businesses were the precedents for transnational corporations that today rule the economic world.

Population increased slowly, held down by infant mortality, late marriages, early adult deaths, and abortion, infanticide, and available contraception. By the fourteenth century, the growth rate halted and began to decline. In 1315, because of the massive displacement of people from agriculture, food shortages became acute and waves of famine swept over Europe. The famines, exacerbated by ever-mounting war taxes, meant ever-higher prices. Thousands died of starvation.

The Black Death and the Witchcraze

An already weakened population was then devastated by recurring waves of the Black Death—bubonic plague—probably carried from India on flea-infested rats riding the great sailing ships of the new international trade. In 1348, plagues swept over Europe and England and 90 percent of those infected died. In some places, half the population succumbed.[38] A frantic populace demanded scapegoats for God's curse on the land, and they were found in "socially indigestible" people—those unwanted by society. Among these were Jews, Muslims, lepers, the disabled, homosexuals, and women.

In the late 1200s, hatred of "different" people began to rise, partly because of massive economic upheavals and the reification of Christian doctrine. Jews, for example, had to wear yellow stars or other distinctive dress. There was missionary fervor against Jews, Muslims, and Christian heretics such as the Albigensians. Homosexuality, which was apparently widely accepted and practiced in twelfth-century Europe, was condemned by the Church by 1200, grouping homosexuals with arsonists, sorcerers, and Jews as criminals deserving execution. Women, always under the surveillance of the Church because of their sexuality, exceeded the population of men by 1300 and were persecuted particularly during the witchcraze, which began about that time. Accused women were often described as homosexuals or as practicing aberrant sexuality.[39]

Jews were accused of poisoning public wells, and in the hysteria that followed some estimate that 90 percent were massacred,[40] their wealth confiscated by Christians. Often, they were herded into wooden buildings that were torched or walled up in houses and left to suffocate or starve. Muslims were expelled in growing numbers, and their culture in Europe began to fall into ruin. In France, King Philip ordered every leper burned to death, and throughout Europe people who were "different"—diseased and mentally or physically disabled, for example—were accused of witchcraft and burned. Most massacres, except those of women, waned with the plague, ending by 1351.[41] The slaughter, along with the massive plague mortality, caused a great shift in wealth as survivors usurped the resources of the dead, becoming a macabre *nouveau riche*.

Beginning around the time of the first bubonic plague, women became more vulnerable to charges of witchcraft, and their treatment as witches became much more horrifying. Until this time, *malifice*, the belief that some people could cause sickness or kill cattle by curses, had been dealt with by local vendettas or vigilantes. Clergy were urged to counsel women out of the belief that they could curse. However, the belief in witches, often women who were healers or midwives, became conflated with fear of Satanism to become a virulent misogyny.[42] Over the next 300 years, hundreds of thousands of women were accused of witchcraft and killed. Only about 20 percent of the accused witches were men, but they do not seem to have been accused of deviant sexual relationships with the devil, as were women.[43]

At first the poor and old were accused of witchcraft, tried, and burned. However, as the witchcraze rose, women of every age, status, and class, and some men, were killed. The first description of sorcery appeared in 1337, when a woman was sentenced to burn by the famous legal authority Judge Bartolo.[44] Soon ordinary conjurers' tricks and women's work at healing were metamorphosed into witchcraft. A papal bull by Innocent VIII put the Inquisition in charge of witch hunting, and new and marvelous tests were created to try witches. If they died, they were innocent, but if they survived they were witches and had to be burned in the cleansing fire to save their souls.[45]

Accused women were often stripped, raped, and tortured before their trials, and estimates of the numbers killed range as high as 9 million.[46] Some towns were completely depopulated of women, and many women committed suicide rather than undergo the Inquisition. Women were burned before their children's eyes as examples, and often the children were then thrown in the fire as well. No woman was safe: Even the saintly Jeanne d'Arc, warrior woman and leader of the king's forces in France, was accused and burned at the stake in 1431, at the age of nineteen.

In most cases, women accused of witchcraft were single beggar women between the ages of fifty-five and sixty-five who had asked their neighbors for charity and had been denied. Klaits says,

> To exist by the charity of their neighbors was the only recourse of the propertyless and enfeebled. Giving alms to the poor was an everyday reality, not simply an abstract religious injunction. The beggar was the typical welfare case…. Her knock on the door to ask for a bit of bread, butter, or beer was entirely ordinary in a society that relied heavily on individual acts of charity to assist the needy.[47]

According to Thomas and MacFarlane,

> saying no to a request for neighborly charity may have inspired a considerable sense of guilt … the emerging ethic of individualism may have been powerful enough to cause the denial of charity … but the old medieval ideal of communal responsibility could still provoke guilt feelings over the refusal. A justified curse was thought always to work, and … the ambivalent householder, later regretting his failure to give charity and thereby to forestall the domestic disaster that had subsequently occurred, suffered under a heavy burden of guilt…. Instead of blaming himself, the householder could project his guilt onto the charity seeker: she was the wrongdoer.[48]

Many witch accusations originated in charges against a quarrelsome neighbor, and midwives were often accused if the mother or infant died at childbirth, which was all too common. Poor widows lived on the margin of society, outsiders and newcomers aroused suspicion, and prostitutes, procurers, and tavern keepers, all of whom threatened family and community stability, were also among the extremely vulnerable groups.[49]

Politically, economically, and religiously the paranoia was reasonable. According to religious thought of the time, women without husbands were unqualified for salvation, were potential temptresses to sin, and often were consorts of Satan. Their life span had increased so that they outnumbered men, so many could not marry, and widows often outlived their husbands. Thus, they became economic burdens to families and society, although there was some meager support for widows and children. Many became prostitutes to survive, reaffirming the Church's condemnation of women's sexuality. Those who supported themselves by healing—typical women's work in this era—were in growing danger as healing was redefined as a science. Because scientific education was available primarily to men through the Church, the skills of women who practiced it were believed to have come from Satan. There was often an economic incentive to an accusation of witchcraft: Canon law divided a witch's property between accuser and judge.

There were independently wealthy women in that era, such as those who had worked in guilds or developed their own businesses. Dowry law also returned women's marriage dowries to them on the deaths of their husbands, and this money could not be touched by others. Some used the money to begin commercial enterprises such as money changing, loans, surety in commercial activities for others, and speculations. Many gifted their daughters and other women so that they might be independent. This threatened patriarchal control of the economy, and where no other legal means could gain control of their wealth, the accusation of witchcraft immediately forfeited that wealth into the hands of men.[50]

The religious legitimation for gynocide allowed men to reaffirm religious and political power over women. In a social sense, the witchcraze rid society of an unwanted, perhaps threatening population: independent women. In the economic sphere, society no longer had to support excess women and their never-to-be-born children who might have added to unemployment and dependency.

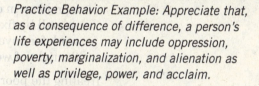

Diversity in Practice

Practice Behavior Example: Appreciate that, as a consequence of difference, a person's life experiences may include oppression, poverty, marginalization, and alienation as well as privilege, power, and acclaim.

Critical Thinking Question: The witchcrazes of the Middle Ages effectively demonized difference while simultaneously benefiting those in power. Can you think of and name other historical events that have had a similar effect on a society?

POVERTY BECOMES A CRIME

The Statute of Laborers

After the Black Death, a new "little Dark Age" descended on Europe. The devastation was so great that society seemed to stop, take a breath, and refocus on emerging needs and practices. The still agrarian-based economy was shattered by the phenomenal loss of labor, and in the cities the developing mercantile economy faltered without a needy and exploitable workforce. The diminished population created severe labor shortages and, as peasants' work became scarce and valued, their status increased. In places such as Germany, some reclaimed control of the land.

Until the fourteenth century, rulers had not been required to deal with issues of employment. Now, however, both nobility and the middle class

The Statute of Laborers was the first significant law on a national level aimed at the poor, and it was not for their benefit but to protect the interests of a commercially oriented government.

(bourgeoisie) began to clamor for laws to control labor and vagrancy. Laws governing the right of people to come into cities, restrictive guild regulations, and city wage ordinances were enacted; in Paris, for example, wage raises could not exceed one-third of the former level, prices were fixed, and profits of merchants were regulated. Workers were forbidden to organize for their own benefit.[51] England under Edward III gave Western society's most important response to the labor problem: the Statute of Laborers, enacted in 1349 and revised within two years for harsher enforcement and to ensure worker availability. Its intent was to bring employment under government control and to quell social unrest.[52]

The Statute of Laborers was the *first significant law on a national level aimed at the poor*, and it was not for their benefit but *to protect the interests of a commercially oriented government*. The statute regulated the movement of laborers to keep them where they were needed for production. Those found away from their own parishes were whipped, branded, sent to toil in the royal galleys, put into stocks, or given to anyone who claimed them. Able-bodied men and women under age sixty with no means of support were forced to work for any employer in need of their services, at no more than the prevailing wage, or be jailed. People who gave alms to the able-bodied or hired them away from their own parishes could themselves be fined and punished. During the 1350s and 1360s, fugitive laborers were declared outlaws and branded on the forehead with an *F*. Compton says,

the essential notions ... were that begging, movement, vagrancy, and the labor shortage ... were essentially the same problem ... begging was not a problem in destitution but a threat to the labor supply ... [and could be solved] by fixing a maximum wage, by forcing any unattached person to work for anyone who needed labor, by forbidding alms, and by limiting the right of workers to movement.[53]

Treating the poor as criminals meant that poverty had become a crime in society's eyes.

The Statute of Laborers reified Charlemagne's eighth- and ninth-century legal codes, classifying the poor as "worthy" and "unworthy," and ushered in the belief in personal rather than societal failure for poverty. It also began a gradual shift from church care for the poor to state control of labor by welding the nobility into an interest group in a *national* effort—for the first time—to dictate the future of labor. State and the elite classes would, from this time on, collaborate for their mutual good; labor was at the mercy of both, through state control of the movements, wages, and subsistence of workers and the unemployed. The statute did not completely reject the idea of charity: Those unable to work—the impotent poor—might still receive alms in their own communities. However, not until the end of the 1400s were such groups as pregnant women, the severely ill, or people over age sixty allowed charity.

As government control became more repressive, social unrest increased. Riots occurred throughout Europe: in France in 1358 and 1382, in Italy in 1378, and in England in 1381. To stem the tide in England, in 1388 Parliament enacted the Statute of Artificers. It required all people leaving their place of birth to have a *letter patent* telling their reasons for traveling, destinations, and date of return. Travelers without such documents might be returned home and indentured. Sturdy beggars—the able-bodied unemployed—transients, and those seeking higher wages were all treated the same, but the disabled or incapacitated were licensed to beg in their original home places.

Over the next century, the European population increased—by 60 percent during the 1500s and another 30 percent between 1600 and 1640—causing a massive glut in labor.[54] Small farms were enclosed by the nobility, pushing farmers from the land and causing vast unemployment and poverty. Because of fluctuating markets, an intermittent supply of raw materials, seasonal demands, rising prices and inflation, and the failure of wages to keep up with needs, about a third of England's population could not find work. The number of rogues and vagabonds in the 1500s was larger in proportion to the population than ever before or since, and fear of crime and disorder was rampant.[55]

The Commercial Revolution

Mercantilism, or a trade economy, became the predominant political economy of Western society during the Middle Ages. Laborers were pressed into service to produce trade goods for the new international markets. This, in turn, took them away from the production of their own food, especially with the enclosure movement, and turned them into a workforce dependent on the largesse of the mercantile class. Moreover, it ended the organic interrelationships of the old feudal society and moved people into cities and under labor contracts that could be broken at will by the upper classes. A new money economy began in which wealth was no longer in land and goods but in cash, a fluid asset enabling the accumulation of profits beyond the reasonable costs of materials, labor, and investment. This created interest-gathering investments where wealth could be stored rather than distributed, opening the era of capitalism.

In the early days of mercantilism, a paternalistic elite provided for the poor, much as had feudalism. Over time, however, mercantilist and national labor policies were influenced by foreign trade, in which cheap labor played the critical role. This created a new ideology about the poor: Low wages would make them work longer and harder, and low wages would also keep them from buying foreign products, thus keeping money within the nation and aiding the favorable balance of trade. Following this ideology, social welfare became an adjunct to labor policy rather than protection for the poor. Its purpose was to keep a viable labor force for mercantilists and the state. Increasingly, new ideas of "work morality" placed responsibility for the livelihood of the poor solely on their own shoulders, in a political and economic climate over which they had no control. By state policy, they were now merely units of production in the great national economy, dispensable commodities to be bought and sold or warehoused according to the economic decisions of others. Unemployment became a problem for employers only if workers became so debilitated by starvation that they could not work, and for the state only if poverty created social unrest that lowered production and upset the international balance of trade.

THE PROTESTANT REFORMATION: NEW MEANINGS FOR WORK AND WELFARE

According to Gies and Gies,

> The fourteenth century ended on a somber note, the Black Death paying its return visits to a Europe that had not yet recovered from its earlier devastations. Population, urban and rural, was still below its pre-plague level, the Hundred Years War smoldered in a precarious

truce, and the Church was riven by the Great Schism, which enthroned
rival popes in Rome and Avignon. Yet ... Europe had advanced to a
point where it at last rivalled Asia as a center of civilization ... [in]
power sources, industrial organization, architecture, shipbuilding, and
weaponry.[56]

Under mercantilism, both church and state became supported by the mon-
eyed middle class. New religions arose: In Germany Martin Luther began his
Protestant Reformation in 1517, and England's Henry VIII instituted the
Church of England in 1536. Klaits says,

> With the Reformation came the dissolution of the Catholic welfare or-
> ganization ... and the state assumed the burden of welfare.... As for the
> poor, in this capitalistic world they were losers, to whom winners need
> no longer feel any special obligation.[57]

Now landowners and merchants paid taxes to support welfare, making charity
less incumbent on them and placing it into a governmental bureaucracy.

Lutheranism, Calvinism, and the Work Ethic

By far the most important event for the growth of mercantilism, capitalism,
and ultimately social welfare was Martin Luther's break with the Catholic
Church in 1517. Luther (1483–1546), a priest, protested Church corruption
and deplored the selling of "indulgences" to ensure salvation after death. He
taught that salvation could be attained only through the grace of God and that
"right living" was the only means to salvation. One's vocation or work was a
calling from God. Although Luther did not end poor relief and called for community chests to aid the needy, the implications of nonwork were clear. Those
who accepted their calling through hard work obviously were more acceptable
to God. John Calvin, one of Luther's followers, made these implications even
clearer with new definitions of work and wealth. He taught that salvation was
predestined—decided by God before one's birth—and that wealth in this life
was the evidence of the grace of God. Therefore, the purpose of all human
activity was not to attain salvation but to glorify God. Industry, thrift, frugality, and asceticism were the marks of true Christians, and frivolity, sentiment,
and interest in comfort and luxury were deplored. Work was more than a requirement imposed by nature or as punishment, it was a spiritual discipline.
Calvin's influence gave Protestantism an international appeal from which both
capitalism and modern Western society developed. Its creed was essentially
hard, stoical, and uncompromising in its demands.

> **A small ideological leap by Calvin's followers gave mercantilists religious affirmation both for their new wealth and for the exploitation of their workers to produce it.**

A small ideological leap by Calvin's followers gave mercantilists religious
affirmation both for their new wealth and for the exploitation of their workers
to produce it. If wealth demonstrated morality, then surely poverty demonstrated immorality. Work as the means to wealth became the standard of the
Protestant Reformation. Weber says,

> The pursuit of riches, which once had been feared as the enemy of reli-
> gion, was now welcomed as its ally. The habits and institutions in which
> that philosophy found expression survived long after the creed which
> was their parent had expired ... it ends as an orgy of materialism.[58]

The encouragement of work in others became a holy task and the financial
benefit to those who reaped profits was a just reward for ensuring morality.

Meanwhile, the poor were doubly damned by the necessity of making a living in an exploitative economy and by their newly defined immorality. The Protestant ethic became the keynote of Western society's policies in social welfare. Its psychological impact was phenomenal, for it fostered alienation from family and community, justified social stratification by income, became the model for self-concept, and made work the definition of spirituality. Poverty became moral degeneracy, and fault became centered in the self rather than in the structures of society.

Until this time, work had been considered at worst a punishment from God and, at best, a responsibility toward God and others. Before new technologies of storage and shipment, producing more than could be used was only wasteful. Ancient Jews had considered work a necessity by which, in partnership with God, they would advance civilization. For early Greeks and Romans, work was a degrading activity that took the mind away from its essential tasks of thinking and spirituality. Early Christians considered work a penance for original sin and admired the nobility of poverty, encouraging work not for its own sake but to support self and the needy and gain salvation. However, the needs of the mercantile society and the Protestant Reformation changed our attitudes completely. Weber says,

> this philosophy of avarice appears to be ... the idea of the duty of the individual toward the increase of his capital, which is assumed as an end in itself. Truly what is here preached is not simply a means of making one's way in the world but a peculiar ethic. The infraction of its rules is treated not as foolishness but as forgetfulness of duty.[59]

Puritans joined businessmen in emphasizing the danger of pampering poverty, and giving charity meant abetting the immorality of the poor.

Women Under Protestantism

Protestantism also reified religion's harsh patriarchy. Luther did not believe in celibacy for the religious and closed down monasteries and convents, putting an end to their widespread charitable work. Although he married a former nun, his attitudes toward women were oppressive. Women's calling, and their proper role, was "church, kitchen, and children." He said,

> Take women from their housewifery and they are good for nothing.... If women get tired and die of bearing, there is no harm in that; let them die as long as they bear; they are made for that.[60]

Under Luther, marriage lost its status as a sacrament, for he agreed with some of his wealthy supporters that polygyny was not forbidden by the Old Testament. In fact, he recommended it to Henry VIII as a way out of his marriage difficulties. When Philip of Hesse requested a second wife, Luther married them secretly in 1540, in the presence of two eminent Protestant theologians. The scandal leaked out and although Luther withdrew from the position of bigamy, he would not condemn it.[61] The early Anabaptists, following this lead, set up a system of "companion wives."

No less misogynistic were Calvin and the Scottish minister John Knox. The latter was eloquent in his condemnation of women rulers such as Mary Tudor, Mary Stuart, Elizabeth I, and Catherine de Medici. In 1558 he said their rule was

> contumely to God.... For who can deny that it is repugnant to Nature that the blind shall be appointed to lead and conduct such as do see ...

that the foolish, mad, and phrenetic shall govern the discreet and give counsel to such as be of sober mind.... Woman in her greatest perfection was made to serve and obey man.[62]

Social Welfare and Work Morality

Protestantism and the work ethic swept over the world and, as the new standard of an emerging society, was reflected in all society's institutions, including social welfare. Mencher says,

> modern social welfare policy may be conceived of as commencing with the shift in the sixteenth century from the economic assistance programs of a declining feudal society to those of a rising commercial and secular world.[63]

Poverty as a crime was inextricable from vagrancy and begging, and work relief became a major innovation, setting people to work off their "criminal dependency" by such tasks as building roads and farming.

In 1525, Juan Luis Vives developed a prototype of present-day social welfare. A noted scientist, teacher of the daughters of Catherine of Aragon (a wife of Henry VIII), and a philosopher, he stressed individual and local investigation of the morality of the poor, dividing cities into parish quarters for a census of poverty. He advocated vocational training, employment, and rehabilitation for the able-bodied poor. Children were indentured for work training. Those incapable of work or the genteel poor were given piecework in return either for outdoor relief—support in their homes—or care in almshouses, for although outdoor relief was far less expensive, he believed it supported immorality. Parallel programs arose in Germany, Venice, France, Spain, and the Netherlands within the next twenty years. All centralized the distribution of voluntary charity in neighborhoods and communities and encouraged community chests and community responsibility.

Another prototype of service began with the Ladies of Charity, founded in 1617 by Vincent de Paul in France. A Catholic priest, he had been captured and sold as a galley slave. Upon his escape, he devoted his life to care for the poor and for prisoners, founding the Lazarites in 1618, an "association of priests organized to work among the outcasts of society and in the aid of prisoners."[64] The royal court of France helped to support his efforts, and the ladies of the court initially began to work with the poor. However, they lost interest and in 1663 the Sisters of Charity, a holy order with temporary vows, was founded. They did not wear habits or live in cloisters and tended to the aged, poor, sick, wounded, dying, and prisoners in the community. Following St. Vincent de Paul's ideals, the Conference of St. Vincent de Paul was organized in the 1700s by students Frederick Ozanam and Sylvain Bailly. They lived among the poor, visited them, and collected necessities for distribution. The pattern of anonymous giving, as well as the Society of St. Vincent de Paul, still exists.

Throughout Europe, social welfare activities of church and state were merging and the governmentalization of social welfare began. Early in the 1700s, Syndic Sillen devised a plan for Hamburg, Germany, in which public officials (burgomasters) were appointed to personally investigate the city's poor, so that "the deserving might be discovered and the undeserving rebuked." All charitable institutions were placed under a central bureau, and to prevent anyone from receiving unearned money the able-bodied were compelled to work and the unemployed were given public work.[65] People were placed in "work training"—given flax and yarn and taught to spin, and released after three months with a spinning wheel and a pound of flax.

The lack of good public health, which caused unemployment and poverty, was a major concern of the Hamburg plan. To combat illness and increase capability for employment, Hamburg built a hospital for incurables, free schools for children ages six to sixteen, and free day care centers for children of working parents. The programs were financed from a combination of public taxes, one-half of church poorbox collections, and weekly or annual citizen collections. Even children and servants had their own poorboxes at home, in which they put their pennies for the poor. Such programs became common in all of the European nations. In Bavaria, Count Rumford, a native Bostonian, recommended food and employment for every man, woman, and child and established a House of Industry that provided piecework and dinner. In Glasgow, Reverend Thomas Chalmers encouraged the formation of charity societies by districts and proclaimed that every boy be taught to read and every girl to sew.

However, it was soon apparent that normal channels of employment, private training, or state-created jobs could not solve the massive problems of poverty. Neither state nor employer took personal interest in laborers except to ensure that they would work, and employment and its converse, poverty, depended on the needs of the employer rather than the worker. According to Handel, idleness became a triple threat: to the order of the state, the productivity of capitalism, and the carrying out of God's will.[66]

SOCIAL WELFARE IN ENGLAND: THE TUDOR PERIOD

When Columbus voyaged into the New World, his first trip was delayed for a day by ships carrying Jews and Muslims away from Spain in their final exile. At the same time in England, the Tudors began their reign under Henry VII (1485). A contemporary of Luther and Calvin, he responded to the problems of the poor by putting beggars and idlers in the stocks, flogging them, and returning them to their place of origin. By the time of Henry VIII (1509–1547), social unrest, labor problems, and vagrancy were rampant, and in 1531 he required that all beggars be licensed. In 1536, angered by the pope's refusal to let him divorce, he founded the Church of England and confiscated most Catholic Church and monastery property. As had happened in Germany, the back of the church's care for the poor was broken, and great numbers of monks, nuns, and monastery workers were released to unemployment. Thereafter, major responsibility for poor relief fell on the state, and although private foundations, guilds, and donors continued to support some charities, state welfare was the new rule.

Also in 1536, the Act for Punishment of Sturdy Vagabonds and Beggars prohibited begging and casual almsgiving, with such severe penalties as branding, enslavement, and execution. Idle children from ages five to fourteen were taken from their parents and indentured. The English government charged church wardens and mayors to collect funds on Sundays, holidays, and festivals, for the first time paying them for their relief work and requiring accurate accounting. Although giving was still voluntary, the government was now involved in securing contributions. Funds from rich parishes were redistributed to poorer ones, instituting a kind of equity in poor relief throughout the kingdom, but poverty was so great that large-scale riots continued to occur.

In succeeding legislation under Henry VIII and Elizabeth I, the government moved from encouraged volunteerism to the imposition of taxes (compulsory giving) based on property and income. Refusal to pay or to serve as overseer of the poor if appointed by justices of the peace (for one-year terms) could mean imprisonment. The hoax of "voluntary giving" ended in 1572 with a general tax to provide poor relief. A community registration of the poor who had lived in the parish for three years was taken, and justices of the peace assigned them to private homes, paying their upkeep with the general tax. Over the next five years, a national system of welfare emerged in which, in one way or another, all people could have been provided for.

A new Statute of Artificers that regulated wages and hours was passed in 1583. Intended to control and stabilize the labor market, it forced vagrants, vagabonds, and beggars between ages twelve and sixty to work at hard labor or be indentured. Indenture lasted a minimum of one year, and release required approval of local justices of the peace. Both employer and employee had to give three months' notice, and workers could not leave without a certificate of lawful departure. Apprenticeship lasted seven years, with the minimum age at completion twenty-one or twenty-four. This served other functions besides learning a trade: It gave the master skilled labor, prevented young men from setting up competitive businesses, delayed marriage, and ensured control of the young and support of the old.

The Elizabethan Poor Laws of 1601

In the 1590s, between one-fourth and one-third of the populations of most English towns could not find work, and many starved or froze to death. Bread riots broke out in some parts of the country; and rioting, thievery, and social disorder were common. To maintain civil order, the English poor laws were recodified in 1597, authorizing every county to build civil (rather than religious) almshouses for the impotent poor and workhouses for the able-bodied poor. Responsibility for relatives became law: Parents were required to support their own parents and their children, grandparents their children and grandchildren, and capable children their parents and grandparents. Handel says,

> requiring family members to support one another involves a recognition of social change on the part of the Parliament ... an awareness that the traditional feudal relationships, which assured the aged or disabled serf a livelihood, had substantially passed out of existence. The traditional manorial village was being replaced by ... independent household units ... a concept of the family as distinct and separable from the community.[67]

The famous Elizabethan Poor Laws of 1601, a recodification whose power has existed for nearly three centuries, legalized and formalized England's responsibility for the poor. The importance of these laws lies not in the amount spent for care of the poor, for public relief supplied less than 7 percent of the total spent.[68] Rather, their importance is in *defining social welfare as part of the national labor policy*, placing it under the authority of the Privy Council. Never has the connection of social welfare to labor maintenance been so clear, setting the patterns of public assistance not only for England, but also for the United States. They included local investigation and administration of relief, work as a component of all assistance, and categorization of the poor into three groups: the able-bodied poor, or "sturdy beggars"; the impotent poor, those incapable of self-support; and dependent children (a new category). That same Parliament passed

the Law of Charitable Trusts to keep trusts and endowments under government surveillance and control. Private donors, churches, monasteries, foundations, and guilds continued to support the charities of their choice under this umbrella, but they were restricted from giving so indiscriminately that the poor could leave local employment. The law resulted in a great outpouring of private money for education, outdoor relief, and the building of almshouses,[69] functions that abetted rather than contradicted national policies toward the poor; almshouses became the placement of choice.

The Privy Council's labor policy discouraged the mobility of laborers and encouraged permanent employment. Employers were exhorted to create new jobs, to employ workers even

Policy Practice

Practice Behavior Example: Know the history and current structures of social policies and services; the role of policy in service delivery; and the role of practice in policy development.

Critical Thinking Question: Are modern social welfare programs for the poor a form of de facto labor policy?

in hard times, and to purchase raw materials and produce goods for sale even when no market existed. Rents, prices, and wages were controlled, labor competition restricted, and marriage and the establishment of new households among the poor discouraged by the burning of available housing. Finally, the "normal" heavy punishments were given the unemployed or those who would not work for the "common wage": whipping and returning to place of residence, commitment to prison (or houses of correction), and in extreme cases banishment and death.[70]

At the local level, under the jurisdiction of the Privy Council, justices of the peace authorized the building of almshouses and workhouses, assessed taxes, and appointed tax collectors. They also appointed public overseers of the poor to ensure accountability for expenditures, to place more emphasis on labor than was common with church charities, and to be more efficient in the use of tax money. (Service was compulsory and refusal meant fines or imprisonment.) They set the amount of poor relief; made disposition of the poor to private homes, almshouses, or workhouses; and decided on removal of children from parents judged unable to care for them (for economic or moral reasons). Imprisonment was the punishment for both those who would not work and those who would not pay poor taxes.

New mechanisms for the differential treatment of categories of the poor were also clarified under the Elizabethan Poor Laws. Institutionalization was preferred because people believed that levels of support could better be set; costs for food, clothing, and shelter clearly determined; and "immoral" work behavior monitored. All institutional arrangements—orphanages, almshouses, workhouses, and prisons—had conditions in common. Many were little more than sheds divided into warrens of rooms with little heat or insulation. They had few, if any, sanitation facilities, and food was inadequate and often little more than watery gruel. Health and medical care were virtually nonexistent, and in most cases, well people were expected to care for those who could not care for themselves. Disease and infection ran rampant, and the bedridden or those chained in their places because of their behavior (the "insane," perhaps), were often left to live or die in their own excrement. House overseers or managers were usually given a flat fee for the support of their inmates and to buy materials for work, and they were allowed to keep what was not spent. If they could skimp on the amount of food, heat, clothing, and shelter allowed the inmates, they could make profits for themselves, and this was a common practice. Work done by the inmates was sold to private entrepreneurs or contractors, and the profits went to the overseer or the state rather than to the workers. Although some institutions were well run, most were not, and most eventually became undifferentiated dumping grounds for the unwanted.

Almshouses for the Impotent Poor

The impotent poor were those unable to support themselves (the aged, ill, disabled, and the genteel poor), those unequipped to work because of their upbringing, and sometimes pregnant women. Some outdoor relief was authorized for people able to stay in their homes, but this was always controversial because of the belief that it encouraged laziness and beggary. People were also assigned to live in private homes, and homeowners were paid at the "lowest bid" for their keep. All the poor had to do piecework to the extent of their capabilities. Women pregnant out of wedlock, however, were treated brutally, not only because of their sexual "immorality," but because their families, their communities, and the state feared the future dependency of their children.

Almshouses were usually mean buildings with little heat or insulation. Disease, lack of food, the cold of English winters, and lack of health care led to a high mortality rate, particularly among the aged and the sickly. The houses were usually out of the way, state supervision was rare, and being sent to an almshouse was often a sentence of death—again, an easy way for society to get rid of those who were no longer productive in the labor market.

Dependent Children

As social welfare became labor policy, *all its beneficiaries were considered past, potential, or present labor force.* Social welfare efforts were bent on ensuring that each category of the poor would fit into its proper "work niche." Therefore, dependent children—orphans, foundlings, unwanted children, or those removed from their parents—were considered either future laborers or, more often, future dependents, and their assigned treatment was often so uncaring as to be murderous. Often they were simply left by their mothers on the roadside to die. When the government assumed responsibility, their treatment was little better. They could be placed in foster homes, sold to the lowest bidder (the family that would require the least public support for them), placed into indenture, or put in state orphanages, where social reformer Jonas Hathaway estimated that 82 percent died in their first year.[71] Infants were also placed with paid wet nurses, but because nobody really wanted these children, few follow-up checks were made. Killing them or allowing their deaths was not uncommon and was, in a way, a service to the state, because they would not grow up dependent. Pay for their keep would continue until the officials discovered they were dead, often several months later. Fostering of older children or indenturing them to families was usually a means of getting work from them, and they were often worked to death. Those who survived were indentured to learn a trade (girls until eighteen or married and boys until twenty-four).

With the rise of the factory system, dependent children were contracted out to work in textile mills as early as age three or four, for their small fingers were nimble at looms and spinning jennies. They worked from daybreak until dusk, with a half hour for breakfast and an hour for lunch. If they fell asleep during their fourteen- to sixteen-hour workday, or if they had to relieve themselves, they were slapped or whipped back to work. A great number died before they reached their teen years, but neither their deaths nor their lives were important in the scheme of labor policy. Not until 1802 did the law limit children's working hours to twelve a day, also forbidding night work; however, this did not apply to children hired directly from their parents, for they could be worked without limitation. Under the Factory Act of 1833, children under age nine were prevented from work; by 1847, women and children under eighteen could work only ten hours a day in England.

Sturdy Beggars: The Able-Bodied Poor

Workhouses were another major aspect of the labor policy. The forerunners of the later factory system, they were modeled on the combination almshouse, workhouse, and penal institution of Amsterdam (1596), where inmates worked in fine textiles and lace. Going into the 1600s, England was in fierce competition with the Dutch in the textile business, and by 1650 workhouses were widespread. The goal was to make a profit for the state, and inmates were often contracted out to private merchants and entrepreneurs. Some workhouses were run fairly, with artisans in charge of production and fair wages paid to the inmates, but most were forced labor prisons. The Workhouse Act of 1696 put inmates to work at spinning, knitting, linen weaving, lacework, and the manufacture of nets and sails, but they could not compete with trained workers, and workhouses continued to lose money.

Any able-bodied man seeking public aid was required to leave his family and live in the workhouse. This was called the "workhouse test," for it was believed that only the "truly needy" would agree to it. Work tests were devised to demonstrate willingness to work—chopping wood or moving rocks, for example (and later, sewing tests for women)—even if the work itself was unnecessary, unimportant, or inefficient. Workhouses were considered essential both to maintain work behavior and to punish those who did not want to work. Tied to morality, they were maintained despite their high costs.

Although workhouses were first designed only for men, a revised Workhouse Act in 1722 put both men and women in workhouses, along with their children, adding a new category of the poor, able-bodied women, to the poor laws. Women were allowed to care for their children only at specified times during the day, and of the children forced to enter workhouses with their parents, only seven of one hundred survived the first three years.[72] Relief was refused to those who would not enter workhouses. Reformers Jonas Hathaway and Thomas Gilbert bitterly opposed workhouses, and Hathaway was able to push through a bill in 1767 that ruled that foster homes must be found for children under age six, rather than have them in workhouses. In 1782, Gilbert introduced a statute directing overseers either to find work for the poor in the community (rather than contracting them out to private entrepreneurs) or to maintain them on poor relief. This began a revival of outdoor relief, made national policy in 1795 as the poor were given the right to receive relief in their own homes.[73]

Prisons

Prisons were the final solution to the problem of unwanted people. They can be considered a part of social welfare because of the nature of the crimes for which people could be sentenced and the categories of people incarcerated. Poverty, nonwork, and even the inability to pay small debts might mean imprisonment. People were as likely to be imprisoned or hanged for stealing bread as for murder or highway robbery. Prisoners were forced to pay fees to their jailers for their upkeep, and they would not be released until they could; money was also extorted from their families. Men and women of all ages, criminals, debtors, the poor, the "insane," people with such diseases as epilepsy, prostitutes, pregnant women—all were thrown, willy-nilly, without segregation, into prisons. Conditions were worse than any other kind of institution, for the only law was that proclaimed by the jailer. People suffered from filth, cold, disease, attacks by other inmates, or the brutality of the jailers. Feeding, clothing, and caring for the ill was farmed out to the lowest bidder, and liquor was always available. Clubs and whipping were used freely, and excrement was left to accumulate in the sleeping cells.

Prison reform began in 1681, when philanthropist Thomas Firmin began to pay debtors' costs and fees to free prisoners of good character. (He also put the greater part of his fortune into building a model self-supporting workhouse.) Reformer John Howard, who had been himself imprisoned by a privateer and later became the sheriff of Bedford (1733), demanded that jailers guilty of extortion be dismissed. However, real reform did not begin until the Prison Act of 1877 transferred prison administration to a central authority.

Overview of Social Welfare in England

During the 1600s and 1700s, social welfare in England wavered from harsh enforcement of work and settlement laws to supporting workers in hard times. Police measures to control labor and prevent riots and revolutions were social welfare functions, and they favored employers and the entrepreneurial middle class. A new Settlement Act in 1662 kept laborers from seeking better jobs and could fine both worker and employer if higher wages than those set by the central authority were paid. Class interests continued to influence legislation, often in the guise of charitable intent. For example, in 1675 Parliament enacted a law providing poor relief from the public treasury

> to eke out the wages of the poor who received it—thus acting as a bounty upon the oppression of their employers ... in weekly installments proportional to the number of children in the families ... this acting directly as a bounty upon the increase of population.[74]

This enabled employers to pay low wages and refer their workers to poor relief for supplement while it paid a bounty for increasing the labor force. The 1675 act also gave authorities the ability to predict the future: It allowed them to eject people and families from the locality if they *might* become dependent. This was never well enforced because poor relief was cheaper than the ejection process, but it did give poor relief agents the power to declare certain people unwanted in advance. Those who could pay advance rent or put up a bond could stay, but by 1691 newcomers had to acquire a certificate to guarantee that they would not become dependent.

Policies in England continued to seesaw between restrictiveness and charity. One major revision was the Speenhamland System (1795), a wage supplementation program based on the cost of living. Justices of the peace paid subsidies to poor employed families and relief to dependent families in their homes, according to family size, when the cost of bread rose to one shilling, a kind of early consumer price index. As with the earlier law, however, the government thereby subsidized low wages. On the other hand, Speenhamland allowed the poor to work in sheltered workshops rather than being incarcerated in workhouses, urged employers to raise wages, and requested counties to set aside land on which the poor could grow food.

THE INDUSTRIAL REVOLUTION AND THE EMERGENCE OF CAPITALISM

The Industrial Revolution is tied to the beginnings of cotton textile production (about 1760), when capitalism emerged, legitimated by the Protestant work ethic and tied to international trade and the new money economy. Government laissez-faire policies offered legal protection to employers in their exploitation of workers, a collaboration that benefited both employers and government. A new middle class of artisans, professionals, and managers arose from the undifferentiated laboring class. Social reformers addressed themselves to altruism in the sense of supporting the poor so that they might better labor and

Government laissez-faire policies offered legal protection to employers in their exploitation of workers, a collaboration that benefited both employers and government.

to the new ideals of socialism: the right of workers to share in the decisions and the profits of their labor. Capitalism was an outgrowth of political and economic mercantilist policies.

The Emergence of Capitalism

Keeping wages low increased the margin of profit, so low wages were necessary to the nation's political economy. So was poverty. The mercantilist society that had overrun feudalism was transmuted, at least by the 1700s, into a capitalist society where

> the primary motivation ... is the drive for profit. Each capitalist enterprise must try to grow and to expand its profits. If it does not do so, then another, more aggressive capitalist enterprise will take that company's share of the market.... [It is] an economic system organized on the basis of competitiveness and competition ... a value system and human behaviors which define a meaningful and successful life in the same terms.[75]

This had certain direct results for the poor. First, poverty was the most appropriate means, it was believed, to ensure a ready workforce and maintain profits, so wages were deliberately kept low. Second, poverty increased because wages either were kept too low for survival or, in times of economic depression, were nonexistent. Third, poverty's result for society was starvation, criminal activity, or social unrest. To control this and to maintain the economy, the government collaborated with the elite in controlling the poor.

Fourth, although the government ostensibly maintained a laissez-faire attitude—noninterference in business affairs—in reality it kept the workforce available through restrictive social welfare policies that took police action against workers or subsidized low wages. Thus, government actually rewarded its successful businesses with protection for such rapacious business practices as underselling, monopolization, and worker exploitation. Finally, capitalism led to a society highly stratified by economics: a wealthy elite primarily interested in maintaining wealth; an emerging middle class of artisans, professionals, and managers; and a vast majority of the poor—those in and out of unemployment whose labor was perceived as a commodity for the good of business and the nation.

A great many theorists appeared out of this Age of Enlightenment to analyze and rationalize the movement toward capitalism and industrialization. The first to precisely address the laissez-faire principle was Adam Smith, whose treatise *The Wealth of Nations* was published in 1776. He said,

> it is in vain ... to expect ... benevolence only. [Men] will be more likely to prevail if [they] can interest their self-love ... and shew them that it is for their own advantage.... Give me that which I want, and you shall have this which you want, is the meaning of every such offer.... We address ourselves, not to their humanity but to their self-love, and never talk to them of their own necessities but of their advantages.[76]

Describing men's relationships in competition, he further said,

> men ... feel so little for another with whom they have no particular connection, in comparison of what they feel for themselves; the misery of one ... is of so little importance to them in comparison even of a small convenience of their own ... they would, like wild beasts, be at all times

ready to fly upon him; and a man would enter an assembly of men as he enters a den of lions.[77]

Philosopher John Locke supported capitalism and held that the most important human right was the right to hold property. Utilitarians Jeremy Bentham, John Stuart Mill, and Joseph Townsend supported the idea of laissez-faire because they believed that wealth was the primary source of happiness. The Utilitarian philosophy propounded the greatest good for the greatest number and espoused the equality of all members of society and their right to compete for their happiness. Education of the poor would help them safeguard their own interests rather than having the government do it for them. Although they believed that the unhappiness of some diminished the happiness of all, they felt that the government's efforts to redistribute wealth through poor relief would threaten the national economy. Therefore, they suggested a gradual elimination of poor relief.

Thomas Malthus's theories on population (1798) gave scientific support to the elimination of poor relief and the protection of wealth. He believed that population would outrun the world's ability to produce food and that poor relief encouraged paupers to have more children, thus prolonging the misery of their ultimate starvation. Moreover, because poverty and immorality were equated, Malthus and later social Darwinists believed that helping the poor would result in a population of moronic and immoral people because the poor reproduced more rapidly than did the wealthy "moral" and intellectual elite. Malthus and economist David Ricardo (1772–1823) believed that unfettered self-interest was the only way society could progress. Direct concern for the welfare of others, then, defeated the progress of society and was sure to result in failure.[78]

Karl Marx, Friedrich Engels, and their followers took the opposite view, criticizing capitalism for its exploitation of the poor and warning of the coming revolution of workers. Marx formulated the ideas of a class society or political economy in which the government was economically allied with and supported the elite, resulting in the constant oppression of the working force. This posited an ongoing class struggle that in time would cause the workers to overthrow the oppressive government. Then all would give according to their ability and be helped according to their need. Neither Marx nor Engels dealt in any depth with the problems of women in a capitalist society but recognized their double exploitation as both workers and "reproducers of labor." Although economic history has not demonstrated Marxist theories to be correct in all areas, the ideas illuminated both social reform and social welfare activism in that age and into the next century. Among such reformers was Robert Owen, a textile mill owner, who set up an ideal self-supporting industrial community and devised plans for cooperative agrarian organizations. His work became the model for English socialism.

The Industrial Revolution and the New Poor Law

In England and on the Continent, agricultural and industrial production revolutionized the social and economic bases of Western society as it moved into the 1800s. An extraordinary dislocation of people from their homes and employment occurred. People had moved to the cities for jobs, but now one machine could do the job of ten workers at less cost. Hundreds of new five- and six-story factories were built to use new labor-saving technologies, putting vast numbers of workers out of jobs. In many towns, workers destroyed and burned hundreds of machines and factories, as in the Luddite movement of 1811. Police power put down all such conspiracies, protecting the employers' interests. Fear of revolution, spurred by the American and French revolts, inspired antiworker legislation such as the Combination Acts of 1799 and 1800, which considered trade unionism to be conspiracy and treason.

The trend away from home industry was complete, and the family ceased to exist as an integrated economic unit. Now, each wage earner—man, woman, or child—went out of the home to work hard in distant factories. The home became divorced from the workplace, for producing, selling, and consuming were relocated in different areas. Men could not support their families on such meager wages, so wives had to work at any kind of wage labor or in weeding and hoeing gangs on farms. Their competition with men for work kept wages for both sexes low. In the higher classes, women became "work useless," consumers of the goods others produced. It became "unladylike" to work, and idle wives were badges of social success for their prosperous husbands. Contract labor removed workers from the production of their own food and necessities, and they became parts of the work machine itself—often replaceable parts.

Among the rich, altruism toward the poor continued under new social philosophies whose leaders included Thomas Bernard, Hannah More, and John Wesley, the founder of Methodism. Bernard established a society for "bettering the conditions and increasing the comfort of the poor" in 1796, in which the rich were enjoined to serve the poor. More established charity schools (1801) so that poor children could be educated; and Wesley spoke out for just wages and fair prices based on social justice rather than the free market.

During the period between 1760 and 1820, real wages decreased by one-third[79] because of wars, rapid industrial change, poor agricultural years, and heavy taxes. Rents rose precipitously and governments destroyed homes to limit the increase in new families. By now, the Enclosure Movement begun so long before was complete, and poor people had no rights to common lands, pastures, or water. By 1830, widespread revolt had created a demand for new, harsher poor laws on one hand and a cry for social reform for the poor on the other. Middle-class professionals and artisans began to organize to provide mutual aid benefits, but poor workers had little protection. Capitalism, industrialization, and the restrictive social welfare that supported them were the clear victors in the battle for workers' rights.

In 1832, every county in England underwent a study by the Royal Commission on Poor Relief. Its conclusions, on completion in 1834, were that poor relief was responsible for "permanent paupery" and that poor taxes were used as subsidies for profit making by employers. The study resulted in the New Poor Law of 1834, which blamed the poor for their own poverty and declared public assistance no longer a right. In 1868, Benjamin Disraeli, one of the most eminent of Britain's prime ministers (1874–1880), said that it "announced to the world that in England poverty is a crime."[80]

According to the New Poor Law, the government would no longer take the responsibility for providing work. There would be no more outdoor relief except for the impotent poor and widows with small children. Two hundred new workhouses were built to house pauper families, where conditions were purposely so terrible that people went into them as an alternative only to starvation. Counties were coordinated into poor relief regions under a central board appointed by the king, and the principle of *less eligibility* (no public dependent can be given more aid than the lowest-paid local worker) was the guiding factor in meting out poor relief. From a work ethic and labor control point of view this made good sense, for it provided an incentive to work. However, it enforced work at any wage, punished those who could not work or could not find employment (and their dependents), and did not consider special needs such as illness or other emergencies that arose. Nevertheless, the idea of *less eligibility* is so popular it is still the standard of public assistance in the United States today.

In 1852, some outdoor relief, or aid outside institutions, was granted, and by 1854, 84 percent of paupers were on poor relief. By 1898, 216,000 people in England were in workhouses.[81] Reform in England continued, resulting in a more socialistic system than in the United States. Studies to determine the causes of poverty revealed that widespread illness and disease were major problems among the poor. Malnutrition and unsanitary living conditions were to blame:

> [P]eople lived in overcrowded quarters, and often adolescents and children of both sexes slept in one bed. This led to promiscuity, quarrels, delinquency, immorality, and rapid spread of contagious diseases. Many workingmen-boarders lived with families in the same room. Often seven to ten used one sleeping room, or lived in damp, dark cellars, without any ventilation. All over England the poorer quarters were without water supply and drainage; drinking water was often polluted in rivers or deficient pipelines. There were usually no outside toilets and no sewers.... Refuse was thrown into the public gutter, and the dead were left unburied.[82]

In the late 1800s, Edwin Chadwick, a Poor Law Board commissioner, appalled by the living conditions of the poor, developed plans for water systems, sewage, drainage, and free public vaccination for cholera, typhus, and smallpox. However, he was bitterly opposed and lost his position. Within a decade, and with better results, Florence Nightingale (1820–1910), a nurse in the Crimean Wars, began reforms of nursing, hospitals, and medical practice that would revolutionize England's public health system. Octavia Hill was also influential in the fight for the poor. With the help of philanthropist John Ruskin, she started rebuilding slums in London in 1864:

> She rented sanitary decent living quarters at low prices to working families who could not afford to pay higher rents ... enlisted ... volunteers who collected the monthly rents ... and advised the families in economical home management.[83]

She was also one of the founders of the Commons Society, which built parks, gardens, and recreational facilities for the poor in London.

Among the most influential groups of this time was the Fabian Society, an English socialist group among whose leading members were Sidney and Beatrice Webb. They were primarily interested in practical reforms such as women's suffrage, wage and working hours legislation, housing projects, and education. Charity organization societies and the settlement house movements began in England about the same time. Edward Denison, a philanthropist, moved into a slum district to teach the Bible, history, and economics. He counseled the poor and became an advocate for them. Canon Samuel Barnett, a teacher, brought his students to his home in the slums at Whitechapel to serve the poor. Among his students was Arnold Toynbee, in honor of whom the first settlement house in the world, Toynbee Hall, was built. Its basic purpose was to bring educated men and women into contact with the poor, so that by common work and studies they might both learn.

Following that period, care for the poor took a different turn in England than in the United States. It is important to discuss English social welfare here because welfare in the United States was modeled on that of England, particularly in terms of the Elizabethan Poor Laws of 1601 and the New Poor Law of 1834. However, although English social welfare was softened by its exposure to the ideas of socialism and the activities of socialist reformers, welfare in the United States remained uninfluenced by, and perhaps adamantly opposed to, socialist influence. Without historical traditions of care for the poor, cut off from pre-Protestant Christian traditions, and influenced at a vulnerable state of development by a strict capitalist political economy, social welfare in the United States became "stuck" in its harsh antipoor, worker-exploitative past.

CONCLUSION: REIFYING THE VALUES OF THE PAST

> Whereas England and Europe progressed into new beliefs about social welfare despite primarily capitalist philosophies, the ideals of Protestantism and Puritanism as civil or state religion and capitalism as the morally appropriate economic system became a basic tenet of the United States.

From the fall of the Roman Empire until the Industrial Revolution, the very basis of human existence was altered. Politically, small warring tribes became feudal estates and then nations, and social relationships changed from organic interconnections with family and community to alienated individuals whose primary concern had to be survival. Economically, a wealthy elite grew to control governments and to deal with the poor as cost units in production.

Vast changes in technology created the beginnings of mercantilism, and such ecological catastrophes as the Black Death and the destruction of balances of nature increased the difficulties of survival for the poor. Religion reified the secondary status of women and certain "out-groups"—Jews, homosexuals, and handicapped people—even to the point of killing them, and mutated in response to both polity and economy from supporting the poor in difficult times to justifying their exploitation.

Social welfare changed from ideals of social justice and charity as a right to redefinition of poverty as a crime, and its administration became civil rather than religious. It now controlled labor for the purpose of personal profit making by the new moneyed class. Although kind hearts and good deeds continued, the Protestant work ethic became the moral basis underlying the new political economy, and people of all religions picked up its secular ideas of work and wealth. With governments justifying exploitation based on the laissez-faire philosophy, capitalism became the major economic tenet of both Old and New Worlds. Whereas England and Europe progressed into new beliefs about social welfare despite primarily capitalist philosophies, the ideals of Protestantism and Puritanism as civil or state religion and capitalism as the morally appropriate economic system became a basic tenet of the United States.

The following questions will test your knowledge and understanding of the content found within this chapter. For additional assessment, including licensing-exam type questions on applying chapter content to practice behaviors, visit **MySearchLab**.

1. What was significant about The Statute of Laborers?
   a. It was the first major law on a state level designed to assist the poor.
   b. It was enacted to bring employment under government control.
   c. It forbade workers from organizing for their own benefit.
   d. It's primary focus was on granting assistance to the unemployed.

2. Able-bodied men seeking public assistance were required to leave their families to live and work in a/an:
   a. workhouse
   b. prison
   c. government institution
   d. almshouse

3. After the Black Death (bubonic plague) took the lives of 90 percent of those infected, Europeans responded by:
   a. seeking a scapegoat to blame it on—Jews, Muslims, the disabled, women.
   b. implementing public assistance programs for the surviving members who had no one to care for them.
   c. developing public health centers for the poor so they wouldn't spread disease to other "worthier" citizens.
   d. removing the stigma attached to poverty since most survivors were left poor.

4. What became the main political economy of Western society during the Middle Ages?
   a. Capitalism
   b. Mercantilism
   c. Feudalism
   d. Calvinism

5. You are an advocate of Lutherism counseling a church member about his or her desire for wealth. Which best describes what you may say?
   a. Money is the root of all evil and will lead to immorality.
   b. Karma determines whether you shall have wealth or not in this lifetime.
   c. Wealth is proof of the grace of God and should be welcomed with joy.
   d. Wealth can come only by righteous prayer.

6. Which statement best describes how business owners successfully ran a company under a capitalist society in the 1700s?
   a. Keep wages low in order to increase the margin of profit.
   b. Pay workers reasonable rates which allowed companies to attract the best workers available.
   c. To protect their interests, donate generously to public assistance efforts because poverty had detrimental impacts on business.
   d. Employ only the wealthy, elite, and educated.

7. Describe the changes implemented in England after the Elizabethan Poor Laws of 1601 were implemented.

Reinforce what you learned in this chapter by studying videos, cases, documents, and more available at **www.MySearchLab.com**.

Watch and Review

Watch these Videos

Atlantic Connections: Sugar, Smallpox, and Slavery

Read and Review

Read these Cases/Documents

Andrew Carnegie, "Wealth," North American Review (1889)

Assess Your Knowledge

Go to **MySearchLab** to test your knowledge of key topics in this chapter with topic-specific quizzes. Conclude your assessment by completing the chapter exam.

5

Social Welfare Moves to the Americas

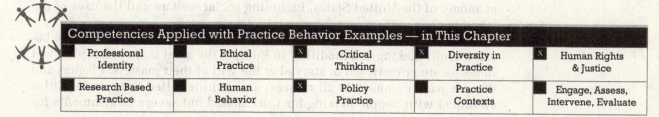

Competencies Applied with Practice Behavior Examples — in This Chapter				
■ Professional Identity	■ Ethical Practice	X Critical Thinking	X Diversity in Practice	X Human Rights & Justice
■ Research Based Practice	■ Human Behavior	X Policy Practice	■ Practice Contexts	■ Engage, Assess, Intervene, Evaluate

Times and Events

- **1421:** China discovers America
- **1455:** Papal bull authorizes Portugal to enslave all infidels
- **1492:** Columbus travels to Caribbean Islands
- **1524:** Cortez conquers Aztecs
- **1526:** African slaves abandoned by Europeans in South Carolina
- **1536:** Pizarro conquers Incas in Peru
- **1565:** First Spanish settlement at St. Augustine, Florida
- **1607:** Jamestown colony founded by England
- **1619:** First African slaves brought to Jamestown
- **1636:** First American pensions for veterans of Indian wars
- **1638:** Slave trade begins in Boston
- **1639:** "Warning out" of the poor begins in colonies
- **1650:** Apache nations of Great Plains conquered
- **1660:** First "House of Correction" built in Boston
- **1664:** Virginia Black Codes define slaves as property
- **1676:** English win King Philip's War over Wampanoag in Massachusetts
- **1680:** Pueblo rebellion, led by Popé, drives Spanish from New Mexico
- **1689:** First public school established in Philadelphia
- **1692:** Witchcraft trials in Salem, Massachusetts
- **1700s:** Indentured servants brought to North America
- **1776:** American Revolutionary War begins
- **1777:** All states except Connecticut have special provisions for veterans

Turning now to the New World, the conquest of the Americas demonstrates decisively Western society's obsession with wealth. Although some early explorers were priests who came to convert Native Americans, most came for fortunes for themselves and the governments that supported them. Their religions, moreover, legitimated conquest and exploitation of others in the name of the now-moral quest for wealth. Protestantism, with its dour philosophies of labor and profit, changed the social, spiritual, and economic consciousness of the world, and Catholicism, responding to the economic imperatives of emergent mercantilism, did not seriously object. Persecution of women, Jews, and non-Christian people was common, and a papal bull issued in 1455 authorized Portugal to enslave all infidel people,[1] legitimating slavery even before the discovery of the New World. Such attitudes and behaviors in the colonization centuries (1500–1800) provided the basis for the political economy of the United States, including social welfare and the uses of the laboring poor.

Life in this era was bitter, exploitable, and cheap, and poor people became profit-making commodities. In Europe, the great mass of people lived in desperate poverty, fed or starved at the will of their masters. Plagues and disease were common to all classes, and famine killed thousands. Cities swamped with people looking for work meted out severe punishments for large or small transgressions as the poor eked out their meager living with crime and prostitution. They lived in hovels, under bridges, or in the streets, or were confined in almshouses or jails. Concern for the poor was almost always directed to increasing their ability to work or keeping them from rebelling, and their treatment depended not on humanitarianism but on the business decisions of others.

Europeans who came to the Americas found a new land ripe for economic plunder. Whether in the high cultures of Meso-America or the democratic societies of North America, gold, silver, land, and the greater commodity, human labor, were available for the taking. At first contact, there were more than five hundred distinct and competing tribal and language Native American groups, with a population estimated at ten million in North America and tens of millions in the rest of the hemisphere.[2] In North America, anthropologists divide these societies into nine geographic and language groups:

- Southeast: Gulf of Mexico and north into the Carolinas, including the Natchez, Choctaw, Cherokee, Muskogee
- Southwest: New Mexico and the Yucatan peninsula (Mohave, Hopi, Apache, Navaho, Yaqui)
- Plains: Great Plains from Texas into Canada (Crow, Blackfeet, Sioux, Cheyenne, Pawnee, Arapaho, Comanche)
- Plateau and Basin: East of the Rockies to the Great Plains (Yakima, Spokane, Nez Perce, Paiute, Shoshoni)
- California (Shasta, Hopi, Miwok, Cahuilla)
- Northwest Coast: California to the Bering Straits (Tinglet, Kwakiutl, Chinookans)
- Subarctic: Societies as diverse as the Kolchan and Taniana to the west and Beaver, Cree, Ojibwa in the east
- Arctic Zone (Inuit, Aleut)
- Northeast (Ojibwa, Menominee, Winnebago, Fox, Sauk, Potawatami, Miami, Huron)[3]

Within each of these geographic groups were multitudes of distinct societies, some numbering from a few hundred people to tens of thousands (see Figure 5.1).

These many societies were at greatly differing stages of development, some with highly diversified social and economic systems. In North America, most of those along the Eastern Coast and in the Midwest were agrarian, and most had national boundaries within which they farmed, fished, and hunted. Some Southwestern societies were nomadic; others were farming and herding societies. In Meso-America, the Inca, Maya, and Aztec peoples had hierarchical priest-king societies that rivaled those of Egypt, Greece, or Rome. These existed alongside slash-and-burn agricultural societies in the lowlands.

Although every society was different, they were unilaterally treated as one by the invaders; that is, they were forced to submit or die. Disease, forced labor, and the technologies of gunpowder, muskets, and cannon devastated the Native American population. Of the millions of Native Americans living in the Americas at first contact, by about 1850 only about 200,000 remained in North America and the high cultures of Meso-America had been wiped from the earth.

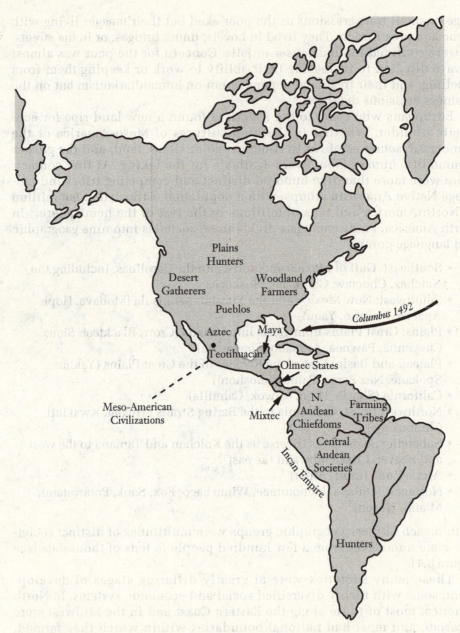

Plains
Hunters

Desert
Gatherers

Woodland
Farmers

Pueblos

Aztec   Maya

Columbus 1492

Teotihuacán

Olmec States

Meso-American
Civilizations

Mixtec

N. Andean
Chiefdoms

Farming
Tribes

Central
Andean
Societies

Incan Empire

Hunters

Figure 5.1
The People of the Western Hemisphere at the Time of Columbus

THE INDIGENOUS PEOPLES OF AMERICA

As early as 25,000 B.C.E., immigrants from the Far East crossed the Siberian
land bridge to range downward and outward through the Americas (see
Figure 5.2). By about 9000 B.C.E., Paleo-Indian big-game hunting societies
stretched from the grasslands of the Pacific coast to the Rockies. Archaic
cultures flourished, and after several millennia Woodland societies, with
their invention of horticulture, emerged in the Ohio and Illinois valleys.
Their stages of social development closely paralleled those of early Europe.

Mongoloid Peoples

10,000 B.C.E.

(Ice Age 10,000 B.C.E.)

GREENLAND

Bering Strait

9000 B.C.E.

9000 B.C.E.

8900 B.C.E.

Throughout South America by 8500 B.C.E.

Figure 5.2

The First Immigration to the Western Hemisphere

They lived in dispersed villages, built huge burial mounds and earthworks, and demonstrated a highly developed religion and a system of social stratification with their grave goods. The Hopewell culture began about 300 B.C.E. and reached its peak in the early centuries after Christ, enduring until about 850 C.E. An extensive trading network developed among societies from the Rockies to the Great Lakes regions.

The democratic societies of North America counterpointed the hierarchical systems of the Incas, Mayans, and Aztecs in South and Central America. Here priests and kings, with their bureaucracies, ruled peasants and artisans through labor conscription, tribute, and taxation. *Corvées* farmed, worked in the royal mines, herded royal alpaca and llama, built roads, monuments, and temples, and warred and colonized; whole populations were moved to new territories to ensure common language and ethnic groups. Intensive agricultural systems, in which two-thirds of the population labored to provide food for the national granaries from which the people were fed, included both permanent and floodwater irrigation, permanent crop rotation, and fertilization. Great pyramids, statuary, and colonnaded temples graced cities that spread over hundreds of acres,[4] and vast engineering projects brought water to Peru's coastal valleys as early as 500 C.E. Ceramic crafts and textile manufacturing compared in excellence with those of Europe, and metallurgical techniques for bronze, silver, and gold were widespread.[5] The Mayan calendar was more accurate than that used in contemporary Europe, and long before the concept of the zero had become part of European mathematics, the ancient Maya used it in their calculations.

In architecture, metallurgy, astronomy, and statecraft, the most highly developed of the Native American states were fully comparable with Old World civilizations. For example, the supreme Inca controlled the lives of as many as six million people. Teotihuacán, the largest city in the New World, covered an area of some 2,000 acres by 800 C.E. Ten thousand people labored over a period of ten years to build its Pyramid of the Sun, and probably as many as 30,000 constructed the Incan Sacsahuaman fortress, where 300-ton megaliths were fitted together to form 30-foot-high walls. A vast network of roads and suspension bridges across ravines and rivers connected the Incan empire.[6] For all practical purposes, the Americas remained in the Stone Age because of the lack of large animals suitable for riding and traction:

> In the absence of traction animals, the wheel was not invented (except as a toy); consequently, the wheeled vehicle, the potter's wheel, the spinning wheel, and the waterwheel all remained unknown. The discrepancy in technological levels conditioned much of the relationship between the European discoverer–adventurers and the Native Americans.[7]

The Stone Age technology of the Americas was no match for medieval firepower and horse-warfare.

THE EUROPEAN INVASION OF NORTH AMERICA

... exploitative colonization of the New World began when European nations, spurred by the Middle Ages' social and technological innovations and the push for international markets, began their incursions.

Although we are usually told that Columbus discovered the Western Hemisphere in 1492, in fact we have knowledge of two explorations that preceded him. First came Norsemen led by Erik the Red, sailing the Atlantic to explore North America's northeastern areas, settling in Greenland until the Little Ice Age destroyed their colonies. Then, in 1421, China's third Ming Emperor, Zhu Di, appointed his close advisor, the Grand Eunuch Zheng He, as China's Admiral. Having ordered the construction of the largest fleet ever built—more than 3,600 vessels—Zheng He and his subadmirals sailed across the Pacific Ocean and down the western shores of North America as well as around Africa and up its western coast. They also crossed the Atlantic and explored the coasts of both North and South America (see Figure 5.3). The voyages left in their wake settlers, artifacts, parasites, and new species of plants and animals, including rice, taro, yams, pigs, and chickens.[8]

However, exploitative colonization of the New World began when European nations, spurred by the Middle Ages' social and technological innovations and the push for international markets, began their incursions. Within a few decades after Columbus's first voyage, Dutch, English, French, Spanish, and Portuguese began the expansion that would create European-controlled nations on the bones of indigenous New World societies (see Figure 5.3).

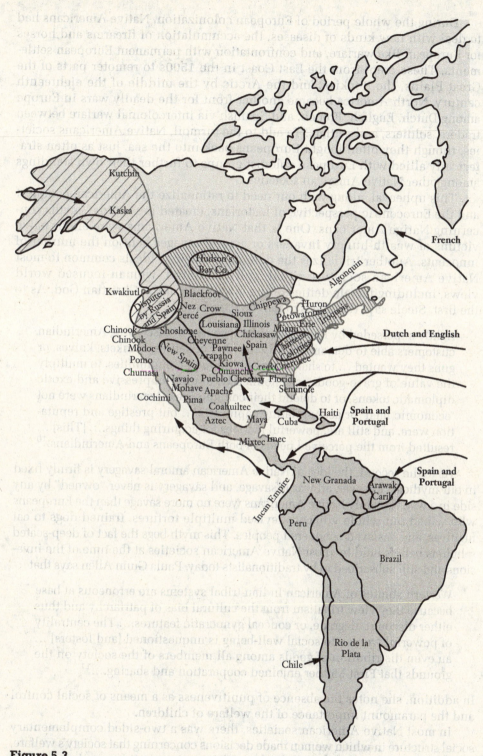

Figure 5.3
European Invasions in the New World

During the whole period of European colonization, Native Americans had to deal with new kinds of diseases, the accumulation of firearms and horses for European-like warfare, and confrontation with permanent European settlements. These crept from the East Coast in the 1500s to remoter parts of the Great Plains, the Rockies, and the Arctic by the middle of the eighteenth century. North America became another front for the deadly wars in Europe among Dutch, English, French, and Spanish via intercolonial warfare between traders, soldiers, and settlers. To add to the turmoil, Native Americans societies, though they often fought Europeans back into the sea, just as often strategically allied with European colonist groups to further their own standings among other Native American societies.[9]

This upheaval, along with our need to rationalize the American conquest and the Eurocentric perspective of historians, created present-day myths concerning Native Americans. One is that Native Americans were either naive victims of wealth-hungry invaders or amoral savages bent on the murder of innocents. Another trivializes the dominant religious ideals common to most Native American societies: ritual, spirit-centered, woman-focused world views, including female deities of the magnitude of the Christian God. As to the first, Steele says that ideas of naive victims are

> rightly superseded by more plausible accounts of discerning Amerindian customers able to demand exactly the kind of kettles, blankets, knives, or guns they wanted … to share them within their communities, to multiply the value of grave-goods astronomically, to offer impressive and exotic diplomatic tokens, or to defend their communities. Amerindians were not 'economic men' or accumulating capitalists … but prestige and reputation were, and still are, powerful motives for acquiring things…. [This] … resulted from the perceived needs of both Europeans and Amerindians.[10]

As to the second, the idea of Native American amoral savagery is firmly fixed in our mythos. However, all war is savage, and savagery is never "owned" by any side in a war. Certainly Native Americans were no more savage than the Europeans who wiped out whole villages, devised multiple tortures, trained dogs to eat fugitives, and enslaved conquered peoples. This myth begs the fact of deep-seated religious beliefs held by most Native American societies at the time of the invasions and still subscribed to by traditionalists today. Paula Gunn Allen says that

> Western studies of American Indian tribal systems are erroneous at base because they view tribalism from the cultural bias of patriarchy and thus either discount, degrade, or conceal gynocratic features…. The centrality of powerful women to social well-being is unquestioned [and fosters] … an even distribution of goods among all members of the society on the grounds that First Mother enjoined cooperation and sharing….[11]

In addition, she notes the absence of punitiveness as a means of social control and the paramount importance of the welfare of children.

In most Native American societies, there was a two-sided complementary social structure in which women made decisions concerning that society's welfare, both internally and externally, while men were the out-riders and protectors. Although war was not uncommon, women generally made the war decisions and men fought, for trade, territory, or prestige. Patriarchal history tells us that men ruled these native societies while women submitted to them. In fact,

> there is reason to believe that many American Indian tribes thought that the primary potency in the universe was female, and that

understanding ... authorizes all tribal activities, religious, or social. That power inevitably carries with it the requirement that the people live in cooperative harmony with each other and with the beings and powers that surround them.[12]

In addition, the idea of "owning" land made no sense to Native Americans because "land" was a spiritual concept closely akin to the "First Mother."

In sum, our Eurocentric perspective has mythed away much of the truth of the colonial years when Native American cultures were mutilated, societies decimated, and gynocentric religions and cultures nearly exterminated. We have blanked out the rivalries and alliances among Native Americans, settlers, traders, and diverse groups of European invaders who extended their wars into the Americas. But the greatest evils visited on North America during the 500 years of colonization were, first, the diseases that wiped out half its population (and a multitude of the colonist population) and, second, the unending number of colonists from Europe's grossly overpopulated nations. The religion of these settlers legitimized their rights to ownership of the new continent and, unwilling to assimilate with indigenous peoples, they drove them out with force, false treaties, and murder. And they never stopped coming.

The French in the New World

The French in early America were perhaps the least exploitative of the European invaders, for they assimilated with rather than tried to change Native American cultures. Voyageurs and priests, looking for adventure, trade, and souls to convert, sailed the Atlantic Coast and the St. Lawrence Seaway. France's Verrazano explored the Atlantic shores to Nova Scotia in 1524, and in 1534 Cartier found the Iroquois in the St. Lawrence Valley. Marquette and Joliet, followed by LaSalle, journeyed across the Great Lakes, down the Mississippi to Louisville, and finally into the Gulf of Mexico in 1682. The French first settled, unsuccessfully, in Canada in 1541 and did not attempt settlement again until the founding of Quebec in 1608. France's occupation of Florida and part of the Gulf Coast began in 1562, and Jesuit missions were on the Great Lakes by 1633, ministering to the Five Nations—Mohawk, Oneida, Onondaga, Cayuga, and Seneca—who inhabited the area north of Lake Ontario. However, "as they spread the gospel they also spread disease.... Half the Hurons in Georgia Bay died between 1634 and 1640."[13]

The primary interest of the French was to "harvest" beaver, and Native Americans responded by overkilling beaver, unraveling the fabric of their rituals of the hunt. The introduction of alcohol

amounted to an additional epidemic.... They believed that liquor produced a welcome transformation of the personality and that they were not responsible for what they did when in an altered state ... [including] men killing each other, husbands burning wives, wives dishonoring husbands, and fathers putting their children in cauldrons.[14]

In 1663, King Louis XIV took an interest in colonization. The French settlers lived on scattered farms, and the King sent troops to protect them. He also encouraged them to marry Iroquois women. Jean Talon was appointed first governor of new France in 1665, and he began colonization in earnest.

The same year Talon arrived ... the first shipment of "daughters of the king," from orphanages in France, also docked.... In fifteen days, all were married and in 1666 New France had a population of 3,215, of whom 204 were men.[15]

The Spanish in the New World

Before the marriage of Ferdinand and Isabella (1469) united Aragon and Castile, a warrior class—the *hidalgos*—ruled the dukedoms that became Spain. Soldiers good with weapons and horses, they had fought the Moors for seven centuries and considered ordinary work beneath them. These were the *conquistadores* who came to America for riches for themselves and their monarchs. Catholic priests accompanied them to convert Native Americans to Christianity, and together they mapped the Caribbean, the Gulf of Mexico, Meso-America, much of South America, and the Southwest from the Rio Grande to California and Oregon. The first nonindigenous permanent settlers in what would become the United States were a group of African slaves abandoned by their Spanish owners in the area of South Carolina, in 1526.[16] The first permanent city in the New World was settled not at Plymouth Rock but by the Spanish at St. Augustine, Florida, in 1565.

Although the Spanish were not interested in colonization, Columbus wanted a governorship as his reward. On his second voyage, in 1493, he founded the town of La Isabela on the northern shore of the Dominican Republic and set up a system of forced labor to help settlers work the land. To "pacify" the rebellious Taino Native Americans, he sent 500 to Spain to be sold as slaves, and then began to raid other settlements to make up for labor shortages. Those who resisted being sent into underground mines had their arms cut off and were sent back to their villages as warnings.[17] A new governor, Nicolas de Ovando, was appointed in 1502. He regulated forced labor into a system called the *encomienda*, in which workers mined in return for wages, protection, and Christian instruction. If the Tainos ran, the *hidalgos* chased them with greyhounds fed on human flesh to make them better man-hunters. Within fifty years of Columbus's first voyage, the Tainos had been exterminated.[18]

Slaving expeditions and disease stripped the Greater Antilles and the Bahamas of its indigenous inhabitants by 1513, when Ponce de León raided Florida. Many who were enslaved committed suicide, others ran away, and a great number were simply worked to death. The decimation of Caribbean societies was abetted by the native peoples' lack of resistance to European diseases such as smallpox, measles, bubonic plague, and respiratory infections. Epidemics of monstrous proportions occurred all through the first centuries of contact: One-third of the population of the Tupinanba in Brazil was wiped out by smallpox in 1562, and Borinquén (Puerto Rico), which had a native population of 50,000 in 1493, was so reduced by 1530 that newly imported black slaves were the majority.[19] By the end of the 1600s, when sugar from the West Indies became the major import to Europe, most of the Caribbean's native populations had vanished.

De Soto landed in Tampa Bay in 1539, where Native Americans lived in large villages called *chiefdoms*. Following his arrival,

> [t]he enslavement of men and women, the many pitched battles, the destruction of villages, the psychological shock of defeat, the looting, and the epidemics destroyed a social system.... Fifty years later, the world of the chiefdoms—Apalachee, Ocute, Coose, Pacacha, and others—had vanished.[20]

The Spanish also plundered Meso-America, beginning with the Aztec nation's subjugation in 1519 by Hernando Cortés. Reigning rulers and bureaucracies were reduced to puppet governments, and the people were enslaved to work in gold and silver mines. By 1550, the fabulous silver mines of New Mexico had been discovered, giving Spain wealth untold in Europe, and within a century the indigenous population had been so drastically reduced that society could not be sustained, and blooming cultures rivaling those of Europe ceased to exist. Recent demographic studies of central Mexico during the sixteenth century reveal an astonishing decline in population, from some twenty million to one million in less than one hundred years.[21]

Coronado's expedition up the Rio Grande (1540–1542) found villages of whitewashed and frescoed three- to five-story buildings with thousands of hospitable Pueblo Indian inhabitants. They had cultivated fields of maize, beans, squash, and cotton, had domesticated turkeys and dogs,[22] and had stores of grain for the winter and seeds for future plantings. Within a few years, tributes demanded by the Spanish had wiped out their stores and mass starvation began. A particularly despotic crown-appointed governor, Oñate, ravaged the tribes to such an extent that his removal was demanded by Franciscan missionaries, who were then given control. By the 1600s there were 3,000 missionaries in the area, with a European Catholic system of welfare for now poverty-stricken people who, before the invasion, had fully supported themselves.

The Apache nations of the Great Plains, whose societies surrounded the Pueblos, were conquered by 1650. Spanish farms began to enclose their land, and disease and crop failures added to the distress already caused by massive tributes, leading to mass starvation and, finally, rebellion by both Apache and Pueblo Indians. Apache raids were common all during the 1600s and more frequent after 1650. In 1675, Juan de Treviño, the Spanish-appointed governor in what is now New Mexico, decided to stamp out native religious practices and arrested forty-seven shamans. Three were hanged, one hanged himself, and the others were whipped and released. In response, a Tewa shaman named Popé organized the Hopis in the Rio Grande valley, the Jemez valley, and the Zuni Basin in 1680. He developed a network of 6,000 warriors among the 25,000 Native Americans, outnumbering the Spanish almost three to one, and led a siege on Santa Fe. A predawn attack killed 300 of the besiegers but Santa Fe was abandoned:

> It was a triumph for Popé.... For the first and last time in North America, the native people had defeated and thrown out the colonizer, and the land was returned to its original settlers.[23]

Shortly thereafter, a massive retaliation ensued in which the Hopis, disheartened, surrendered without a fight, leaving the Spanish once more in control.

The Spanish Church maintained an essentially hands-off policy on slavery because it was profitable for both church and monarchy. Even priests owned both Native American and African slaves. However, Native Americans were considered subjects of the crown and church, and one of the express purposes of sending priests and missionaries to the Americas was to save their souls. This moral paradox resulted in Spanish laws in 1542 to protect Native Americans from exploitation. The church maintained that slaves had human and spiritual rights, and slavery in South America was looked on as a contract in which masters owned the slaves' labor but not their humanity.[24] The sanctity of marriage and family was upheld and spouses and children were unlikely to be sold away from each other, they could earn money for themselves after work for their masters was done, and they could buy freedom for themselves and their families. The possibility of freedom meant the development of a class of workers and artisans, which over time became a stable and free middle class. Moreover, the invading Spanish took wives among the Native Americans and the African slaves, beginning a unique Hispanic heritage in which priests and missionaries took an important leading role.[25] In the northern colonies, where not only the work but the lives of slaves belonged to the master, these possibilities did not exist.

The Dutch in North America

Northern Europeans came to America from about 1522 and found Native Americans in permanent homes in palisaded villages, cultivating fields of corn, squash, and cucurbits. Eager for furs and for the fish abounding in the Atlantic waters, both Dutch and English set up joint-stock businesses, partly financed by merchants in Europe, and by 1632 the indigenous peoples had iron kettles, axes, arrowheads, and knives, although few had firearms.

The Dutch East India Company sought to expand its profitable international trade with resources from the New World by giving colonists patroonships (absolute ownership of huge tracts of land) in return for establishing a colony of fifty adults. Although Dutch settlers were at first scrupulous in their dealings with the Native Americans, land had a different meaning for Dutch and Native Americans, and before long the Dutch took advantage of this difference. According to Native Americans, Mother Earth could not be sold, so in return for insignificant amounts, the Dutch "bought" their lands from them. When Native Americans refused to move, the Dutch began to kill them, often wiping out whole villages. In 1642, the brutal Dutch governor William Kieft launched a five-year war against the Native Americans living in his "territory." Settlers noted that after a raid on Staten Island killed eighty Native Americans, some survivors "came … with their hands or legs cut off … and some holding their entrails in their arms."[26] Kieft also began the practice of bounties on scalps: The going rate was ten fathoms of *wampum*.[27]

The initial purpose of the Dutch invasion of North America was profit from the fur trade to finance the Dutch war for independence from Spain (1569–1648). To this end, the Dutch under Kieft allied with the Five Nations of the Iroquois, arming them so well in the 1640s that they became a military and economic power on the Eastern seaboard. In addition to wiping out societies bothersome to Kieft's New Amsterdam, the Five Nations obliterated the Huron Confederacy which, in alliance with the French, dominated the northern fur trade.[28] When the English conquered the Dutch in New York, the Five Nations became English allies against the French. This alliance led to the division of North America into Canada for the French and most of the rest of the continent for the English.

From 1623 to 1626, New York, New Jersey, and part of Delaware were settled by Dutch Protestants. Their charter required that each settlement provide preachers, schoolmasters, and comforters of the sick and required pastors' assistants to give help and solace to the unhappy, ill, or disabled. These systems of welfare were undertaken from both religious and business perspectives. Vagabonds and beggars

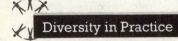

Diversity in Practice

Practice Behavior Example: Recognize the extent to which a culture's structures and values may oppress, marginalize, alienate, or create or enhance privilege and power.

Critical Thinking Question: Discuss the treatment of Native American peoples under English, French, Dutch, and Spanish colonization.

were "bonded" to patroons in return for their board and clothing, often for life. Deacons supervised by clergy gave outdoor relief gleaned from church collections and fines to the impotent, ill, and disabled. The church was the community conscience, encouraging neighborhoods to care for their own poor and to establish mutual aid associations. By 1664, ten of the twelve Dutch settlements had established schools controlled by church and court and supported by taxation, tuition, the Dutch East India Company, and the church. When the Dutch lost New Amsterdam to the English, English poor laws were substituted for Dutch community care.

The English in New England

English colonists came for many reasons: to escape the poverty of peasant life in Europe, to find fortunes or adventure, or, in the case of Pilgrims and Puritans, to escape retaliation by the newly restored monarchy: Under Oliver Cromwell they had beheaded King Charles I in 1649. The depletion of England's own natural resources, especially its forests, made the New World a bonanza for materials increasingly scarce in England, such as potash, timber, pitch, tar, resin, iron, and copper. In addition, production of New World goods, particularly sugar, tobacco, coffee, and chocolate, made new fortunes. Adventurers, many of them second (or later) sons who could not inherit in England because of laws of primogeniture, came seeking legal or illegal fortunes and became pirates, lawbreakers, highwaymen, businessmen, and a new mercantilist elite. Some came not so freely, transported to America as an alternative to prison, kidnapped by ship captains or "Newlanders" who received a bonus for every man, woman, or child arriving alive in the New World, or enslaved by traders seeking free labor in the sugar plantations of the Caribbean or the cotton plantations of the South.

The first English colony was established at Roanoke, Virginia, in 1564, by Sir Walter Raleigh. It survived only three years, and the next colony, founded at Jamestown in 1607, was a commercial venture financed by the joint-stock Virginia Company and expected to produce a profit. The Massachusetts Bay Colony was settled in 1629 by Puritan businessmen. Pennsylvania was settled by Quakers who followed William Penn into exile from England. Georgia was the only New England colony not established as a religious haven or a business: England transported free people and gave them land and tools in return for a promise of military service should it be needed. Georgia also was the only colony to accept Jews as equals, and slavery was not permitted under its earliest charter.

At first the companies and colonists followed the Dutch lead in land purchase and relied on friendly natives to help them through severe winters. Soon, however, colonists simply took the land, killing or enslaving its inhabitants: During the mid-1700s, 5 to 10 percent of slaves were Native Americans, and as late as 1790, 200 of the 6,000 slaves in Massachusetts were Native Americans.[29] The colonists' brutality precipitated such wars as that against the Wampanoag in 1675, where the leader, King Philip, was drawn and quartered and his skull displayed on a pole until the 1700s. Quakers were the major exception to such genocide, continuing to deal scrupulously with the Native Americans, although they, too, had both Native American and African slaves.

Although resources were plentiful in the New World, labor was scarce, and a concerted effort to populate the colonies began. By 1640, there were thousands of English colonists in New England. Spanish immigration to the entire New World between 1509 and 1790 was only about 150,000 people, but between 1600 and 1700, half a million English moved to North America[30] to begin the hard life of subsistence farming. In the early days, caves or houses covered with bark served as homes because colonists had no tools for turning logs into lumber. All members of the family worked, both in domestics (cleaning house, making yarn, grinding and milling flour, sewing, and spinning) and in the fields as they were needed. Men, when their labor in the fields was completed, worked with their wives at spinning and weaving. Religion as well as necessity prompted the work, for idleness was, according to religion, a sign that Satan was at work. In Massachusetts, a wife's refusal to serve her husband by laboring obediently and frugally was considered grounds for divorce. Both boys and girls were taught household work, and both spent as much time in the workshop as in home or field. Many colonists, wealthy or poor, bound out their children as domestic help to others so that they might learn the value of work.

Whereas New England and Pennsylvania were settled by immigrant family groups, setting the stage for community democracies, the South was settled by people who transported the English manor system to the New World. They accepted the burden of *noblesse oblige*, taking on government and public responsibility, becoming justices of the peace and overseers of the poor. The ideal of lord and serfs was also imported, making the concept of slavery easy. Tobacco was the staple crop and was often used as currency, selling for three shillings a pound as early as 1614. Virginia became a one-crop colony, exporting 2,500 pounds in 1616 and more than one million pounds in 1628.[31]

The cultivation of this crop required a large workforce for planting, transplanting, topping, suckering, weeding, worming, cutting, curing, binding, and packing. At first, indentured servants were used, but they soon paid off their bonds and became landowners themselves. The first slaves were brought by the Dutch to Jamestown in 1619, and landowners began to acquire an all-slave

labor force. There were several reasons for this, including an incipient racism: White workers disliked working with the slaves. Slaves were also more docile and cheaper to keep because they could not make demands for better food, shelter, and clothing. Moreover, they reproduced themselves and, because they had nowhere to go, did not run away.[32] For some time, small farmers remained in the tobacco industry, but large plantations soon took over. In the 1600s in Virginia, small farmers were about one-twentieth of the population, but by 1730 one-fourth of them had been squeezed out.[33]

WORK IN NORTH AMERICA

The Practice of Indenture

Because labor was scarce and the cost of passage high, the practice of *indenture* arose, whereby the price of passage was advanced to settlers who agreed to work it off, usually in five to eight years. The first indentured servants to arrive in the New World were probably a group of twenty Africans, brought to Jamestown a year before the *Mayflower*,[34] and between 1619 and 1660 some Africans continued to enter the country as indentured servants. In addition, a quarter of a million people—probably one-half of all white immigrants, a third of them women—came as indentured servants.[35] For almost one hundred years, white indentured servants were the principal source of labor in the New England colonies. In 1683, white servants represented one-sixth of Virginia's population. Two-thirds of the immigrants to Pennsylvania during the 1700s were indentured, and in four years 25,000 came to Philadelphia alone. In 1624 there were only twenty-two people of African descent in Virginia, at a time when several thousand a year were being brought into South America. After 1680, slaves began to arrive in increasing numbers, but not until the 1750s did they exceed 25 percent of the population.

A regular and profitable traffic developed in indentured servants, and between 1654 and 1685, 10,000 sailed from Bristol alone, chiefly for the West Indies and Virginia. To control this traffic, a Colonial Board was created in 1661. People of all statuses were involved in the trade, and kidnapping and "recruitment" by "Newlanders" were common, with a commission gained on each person delivered alive to the New World. The punishment for "man selling" was the pillory, a mild punishment considering the profit gained. In 1654, burgomasters of Amsterdam sent a cargo of nearly thirty poor children to Peter Stuyvesant at New Amsterdam; under English laws, any dependent children could be deported to the colonies. London took from its almshouses 300–400 boys and girls ages ten to fifteen to ship to the colonies.[36]

Convicts could opt for indenture in the New World or Australia rather than British imprisonment and so provided another steady source of white indentured labor. Three hundred capital crimes were recognized for which the choice of punishment was hanging or indenture, including pickpocketing more than a shilling or shoplifting five shillings, stealing a horse or sheep, or poaching rabbits on a gentleman's estate. In 1717, a law gave indenture of fourteen years to those sentenced to death. Lesser offenses meant seven years of indenture: stealing clothing, burning corn, maiming or killing cattle; engaging in trade union activity, or being a vagrant, rogue, idler, petty thief, gypsy, or frequenter of brothels.[37] Ship captains also bought indentures for the danger-fraught three-month trip across the Atlantic, giving each person a space of six feet by two feet. Food was very scarce because captains overbooked by double, and people fought with each other for the dead bodies of mice and rats. No one could leave the ships until their indenture was bought, and those without a buyer were put on the auction block. Parents were forced to watch as their children were sold, and husbands and wives were separated. Children under five could not be sold but were given away to serve until the age of twenty-one.[38] Male indentured servants were more valuable, so ships' masters were paid twice as much for men as for women.

Bonds were usually for five to seven years, but they often lasted longer because of debts to the master. Wages were room and board plus fare to America and "freedom dues"—a little extra to start off—at the end of indenture. These included clothing, food, a gun, and sometimes fifty acres. Lucky servants might get an additional wage, perhaps three pounds a year, or a suit of clothing at the end of service. Cash payments were rare; payment was often given in tobacco or other produce. Although the master controlled all personal affairs, indentured servants had legal rights and could sue. Usually marriage was forbidden, and childbearing was considered an interruption in work and an impairment of health and stamina. Nevertheless, about one in five women did have children, and both mother and father had to pay a fine to reimburse the master for loss of services during pregnancy or submit to another two years of indenture.

Political dissent was another cause for indenture. For example, when Ireland was conquered by England early in the 1600s, Irish peasants were pushed off their lands and were often shipped to the colonies to work for English colonials. About half were indentured at double the passage rate of others and for double the time—about twenty years, with extra years for debts to the master. Before the massive trade in Africans began, many Irish indentured servants were shipped to Caribbean plantations to replace Native Americans in the burgeoning sugar industry. In Barbados, they were used for

> grinding at the mills and attending the furnaces, or digging ... having nothing to feed on ... but potatoe roots, nor to drink, but water with such roots washed in it, besides the bread and tears of their own afflictions; being bought and sold still from one planter to another, or attached as horses and beasts for the debts of their masters, being whipt at the whipping post ... for their masters' pleasure, and sleeping in sties worse than hogs in England.[39]

Some say that colonization of America was the largest and most successful welfare program in history.

White servants and black slaves worked together in the West Indies for some time. Indentured servants, because they were not long-term property investments, were often more cruelly treated than were African slaves.[40] Africans were the better bargain because the same money that could buy a white laborer for ten years could buy an African for life.[41] However, indentured servants had some right to personal property, and their children were free, whereas children of slaves became the slavemaster's property.

By the 1700s, English migration had slowed considerably because overpopulation was no longer a problem and political dissent had lessened. Although indenture continued for some time, the vast numbers of migrants coming in by this means also declined, and kidnapping and illegal recruitment were no longer so common. Some say that colonization of America was the largest and most successful welfare program in history.[42] Certainly for England this was true. It removed from the country its overpopulation, the poor, criminals, and undesirables, and at the same time returned a vast profit to the mother country. According to Handel,

The colonizing efforts ... combined philanthropic motives with political motives.... James Oglethorpe, an activist in the English movement to free debtors from prison, had the idea of helping such men get a new start in a New World. The project was financed with money raised by Oglethorpe and a large contribution from the English government, which hoped that [the] project would help solve the problems of vagrancy in England.[43]

Women in the Colonies

Women constituted a third of the early immigrants to North America. Many were kidnapped to provide the new country with wives and laborers, and male colonists paid for wives from Europe; for example, the settlers at Jamestown ordered two boatloads of women in 1619, paying 120 pounds of tobacco each for their passage.[44] Once they arrived in the colonies, regardless of their status, women's scarcity made their lot better than that of their European counterparts; there were six men for every woman in seventeenth-century Virginia, for example. Most could marry if they wanted or had the leverage to refuse an unsuitable proposal.[45] To increase the population, young people had much freedom in choice of mate. Women married and died young in the colonies. According to Jacobs,

> [P]erhaps as many as four of every five of the first groups of women [died] ... within five years.... [W]omen married early, sometimes at twelve or thirteen.... [There was] the common phenomenon of a man's outliving three or four of his wives.[46]

Childbirth was one of the most common causes of death, and women feared pregnancy because they knew they might have less than nine months to live. The average number of children was nine, but it was not uncommon for a woman to have twelve or fifteen, not many of whom lived to adulthood.

Marriage was considered the natural and desirable life for women; although they contributed equally to the economy, they were secondary to men both politically and religiously. Most sexual behavior was not disapproved if the couple planned to marry, but if not, sexual activity was taken very seriously. Women who bore children outside marriage could be taken to court and sentenced to public whipping, branding, and fines. Their children, if they could not support them or could not or would not name the father, could be taken and apprenticed to a tradesperson.[47] Moreover, ministers cautioned women to remain under husbands' control, and those who objected could be punished by both the husband and the town. Adultery was the worst crime a woman could commit, for it was an offense against men's property rights. Divorce and legal separation were possible for women, but grounds were very difficult, and there were no laws forcing a man to support a wife from whom he was separated. In a separation, the woman usually lost everything, even her children. A 1748 law allowed husbands to appoint guardians for their children and to apprentice them out to learn a trade, specifying that mothers were entitled only to their love and respect.[48] For most women, legal and religious ties could not be broken by men's adultery, abuse, or even desertion—only by death—and women alone seldom could find work that would free them from economic dependence on their husbands or the government.

Early in colonization, women had more rights than in later times, especially on the frontier, where their labor was so desperately needed. There, even married women could own property and sue in courts, and they were generally favored by judges who defended them against personal abuse, enforced conjugal rights, and recalled runaway husbands.[49] They could also receive land grants as heads of families. For example, Pennsylvania offered seventy-five acres to female settlers, and if they brought servants and children the grants were larger. Women also could develop their own lands: Margaret Brent, the colonies' first female lawyer, arrived in Maryland in 1638 and built a fortune in real estate. However, because land enabled women to remain single, most colonies soon refused to grant them land and denied them the right to inherit it.

Women and their daughters spun cotton, flax, and wool, looked after livestock, made butter and cheese, baked bread, cleaned and cooked, and bore and raised children. They doctored and nursed their families and prepared their own medicines (salves, balms, ointments, potions, and cordials).[50] Some women operated sawmills, distilleries, and slaughterhouses and were newspaper publishers or printers and teachers. They opened schools for women and achieved status as midwives, physicians, and apothecaries at least until the mid-1700s, when men entered the field of obstetrics. Women with a little capital opened small shops, selling anything from pastries and dry goods to hardware and liquor. Women could more easily take on unconventional roles in the South than in Puritan areas, for Puritans attached particular importance to regulating female behavior.[51]

Under common law, never-married women had the same rights as men and could buy and sell property, own businesses, and sue in court (*femme sole*). Once married, however, women entered the state of *femme couverte*, their rights "covered" by those of their husbands. Husband and wife were one person, and that person was the husband.[52] Married women had no property and no money of their own. Even their clothing, jewels, household goods, livestock, and furniture belonged to their husbands, along with dowries and inheritances. In most instances, husbands could sell wives' property without consent or take all their wives' earnings and allow them to starve.[53] Spaeth says,

> The husband's absolute authority over his wife included the legal privilege of beating her ... [to be interfered with] only if the husband was unduly brutal. At the beginning of the eighteenth century Elizabeth Wildy complained ... that her husband not only whipped and maimed her but also held her in the fire until her clothes burned. The justices felt that in this case the husband had exceeded his right of "reasonable chastisement" and ordered him to appear in court and explain.[54]

Most American colonies granted three exceptions to these practices of common law. They upheld the wife's right to share her husband's home and bed, the right to be supported by him even if he abandoned her, and the right to be protected from his violence. However, if these happened there was not much recourse because married women could not sue in court.

Widows had the same status as *femmes soles* in business affairs, although eldest sons got the bulk of deceased fathers' real estate, and personal property was divided among all the children. In common law, when a man died without a will, his widow inherited one-third of her husband's real estate and a third interest in slaves and personal property; the real estate reverted to the eldest son at the mother's death. If a man left less than his "third" to his wife, the woman could sue; courts upheld the thirds custom because this reduced the chances that widows could become public dependents. Custom was more generous than law, and often husbands left more to widows than their thirds, especially if there were minor children. Also, they rarely deprived their widows of minor children by appointing a legal guardian. Poor widows, however, had to depend on poor relief or hiring out, often to churches, and many took on the jobs of their husbands—farming, running shops, and smithing—to support themselves and their children.

Because of their secondary spiritual status (a legacy from western religion as early as 3000 B.C.E.), women were generally forbidden to speak out on such important topics as religion. The dozens of Quaker women who came to the colonies seeking religious freedom in the 1600s were considered heretics and were fined, whipped, jailed, pilloried, and, in a few instances, hanged.[55] Because government and religion were so closely related, especially in the Puritan colonies, those who argued religion might be considered traitors. An example was Anne Hutchinson, the charismatic and intellectual wife of a prosperous businessman, who came to Massachusetts Bay Colony in 1634. She taught that people could approach God through prayer rather than solely through the mediation of a minister (antinomianism). Brought to trial as a heretic before Governor John Winthrop, who was both judge and prosecutor, she was declared guilty before the trial and exiled from the colony. She then helped found Portsmouth, Rhode Island, on the basis of religious freedom. When her husband died in 1642, leaving her without protection, she fled to the wilderness and was killed, along with several of her children, in an Indian raid.

As in Europe, the colonies had a morbid preoccupation with women's devilish powers. Accusations of witchcraft were used to eliminate bothersome women, and leaders popularized the idea that intellectual women were influenced by Satan. A clear example was Mary Dyer, one of Anne Hutchinson's followers. Accused of being in league with the devil, she was hanged in Boston Commons.[56] In another instance, in 1640 Ann Hibbens was excommunicated for complaining about poor work done in her home by carpenters. The magistrates said her complaints were really against godly authority, and sixteen years later, after her respected husband died, she was executed as a witch.[57] In Salem, 150 (mostly women) of the 200 people accused in 1692 were imprisoned. Fifty confessed and twenty-eight were condemned to die. Fourteen women and six men, one an ordained minister, were actually executed.[58]

By the late 1600s, there was an increasing market for textiles, and town councils saw home piecework for women and their children as a way to reduce public relief.[59] Merchants paid high prices for yarn, and by 1675 towns were providing the capital to set up woolen mills where poor women and their children were put to work at spinning. In Boston, where dependent women were very numerous, the town collected 900 pounds to build a workhouse. This was the first attempt to organize female labor under one roof:

> The widows for whom it was designed refused to go there, objecting to the indignity, to the rigidity of its rules, and to being cut off from friends and community.[60]

The town fathers finally opened it as a factory in 1750.

Home manufacture waned as factories were built in response to the cotton revolution. Soon there were hundreds of cotton mills throughout New England, and factory owners, citing philanthropy as well as economics, petitioned towns to send them poor women and children to work in their mills. By the late 1700s, many towns required overseers of the poor to bind out indigent women and children to the factories.

SOCIAL WELFARE IN THE COLONIES

Although the colonists adopted England's poor laws almost whole cloth, there were fundamental differences in their ideologies of poor-relief practice. First, in England, there was an overabundance of workers in cities, the result of people being pushed off the land. Vast unemployment, pools of workers waiting to be hired, poverty, vagrancy, and crime were the issues social welfare addressed. In a subsistence economy of extreme scarcity, money was not available for the poor, even those obviously dependent because of disability. In contrast, in the early days of colonial America labor was scarce and, theoretically, everyone could work. In fact, wages in New England were 30 to 100 percent higher than in England.

Second, whereas in New England upward mobility was limited only by effort (at least in theory), class stratification was firmly set in England and *noblesse oblige* provided a system of private charity, including legacies, endowments, and bequests to provide substantial funds for hospitals, asylums, and orphanages. In the colonies, private charities played an insignificant role until the end of the eighteenth century.[61] Finally, religion, historically the bastion of last resort for the poor, now insisted on individual effort and decried poor relief as contributing to the spiritual degradation of the poor. (These influences came from early Christian religion, added to the Protestant Reformation's Work Ethic.) People who did not abide by the idea of the work ethic were punished, driven out, deported, or even hanged.

Early American Poor Laws

As in European Protestant countries, there was a belief that wealth and condition were divinely ordained. Paupers were treated as morally deficient and were required to take paupers' oaths and have their names exhibited in the city hall or marketplace or published in newspapers. In some places they were required to wear the letter *P* on their sleeves. The numbers of "worthy poor" were very slim; because everyone started with an "equal chance," few were considered worthy of government help. One group considered worthy from the first was veterans, along with their families or survivors, because of their service to the colonies in the Indian wars. As early as 1636, they received pensions—outdoor relief—as a right.[62] By 1777, all states except Connecticut had special provisions for veterans. People injured in Indian raids were also worthy, at least of short-term help, as disaster victims.

Keynotes in care of the poor were local responsibility, relative and community responsibility, and categorization. Even in earliest colonial times there were many public dependents. Essentially, they were the unemployable (the aged, disabled, orphans, unwanted children, and widows with children). Another group needing public relief was children of mixed races and old slaves who were freed so their masters would not have to support them when they could no longer work. More public dependents came from the frequent wars with Native Americans; recurring epidemics of smallpox, dysentery, measles, yellow fever; poor harvests or bad weather in times when production of food depended on nature and natural disasters could mean starvation; uncontrollable fires; high childbirth mortality; and the hazards of life in a new country.

Local Responsibility

By 1642, colonial towns had given township or parish supervisors authority to collect poor taxes, to investigate applicants for poor relief to determine their worthiness for aid, and to dispense poor relief. In addition to poor taxes, money for relief came from fines for refusing to work at harvest time, selling at short weight, not attending church, and illegally bringing a pauper into town. If a town would not collect poor taxes, local county courts were empowered to assess and dispense funds. By 1636, Plymouth and Massachusetts courts were placing out the poor in homes, and in 1642 Plymouth's first official poor law directed that every case of poor relief be discussed at town meeting. By 1662, the colonies had adopted the English Law of Settlement and Removal, and all colonial towns had to supply food, firewood, clothing, and household essentials for their own poor.

To qualify for poor relief, people had to own property or have lived in a town for a prescribed time (one year was established by 1700). In England, the unemployed had to stay in their home areas, but in the colonies the unemployed and undesirables had to move on. As early as 1639, eight years after Boston was settled, the courts there had the power to send the poor to towns where they could be employed[63] or to deport them from the country. Strangers were not welcome: Newcomers or "foreigners," even if they came from other colonies, were given three years' probation in some communities. If they could not support themselves and their families within that time, they were sent back to their former places of residence or banished. By 1725, strangers could stay no more than twenty days in many towns without the council being officially informed, and by 1767 no one could move into a town without the council's permission. In 1789, residency laws required that people be in a town for two years or be age twenty-one and have paid taxes for five years. They could also become residents by town vote. By 1793, five years without being warned out was required for residency.[64] *Warning out* had two meanings. First, it warned outsiders that they were not welcome in the towns, were not eligible for poor relief, and might be subject to punishments that ranged from stocks and pillory, flogging, or tarring and feathering, to hanging. Second, residents themselves could be warned out, serving notice that if they stayed they could not expect poor relief and might be indentured if they were in danger of becoming public dependents.

Family Responsibility

Families had a unique importance in colonial poor laws because they provided social control for the religio-political governments. Their role was to ensure that their members would not become dependent on the government. Every person under age twenty-one had to live with a family, and county courts or administrators had the power to place any child or dependent person with a family. Families that could not maintain independence for their members were considered dangerous to the community both economically and morally. Axinn and Levin say,

> Despite the family's usefulness, the impetus to maximize individual and family well-being did not center on the individual as family member or on the individual family as a unit. When a family was in trouble, the concern was to save its potentially productive members.[65]

By 1675, relative responsibility was established by law: People had to be bonded by their families to move in, and diseased or poor people had to be cared for by relatives.

People were expected to care for their own as a matter of course, but when this was not possible the needy were placed with families with the understanding that they would work to pay their keep. The aged, disabled, ill, and infants were placed house-to-house for their care, with the town paying the family to tend to them. The poor—unemployed men and women, widows and their dependent children, and children who were orphaned, unwanted, born out of wedlock, or removed from their parents by order of the court—were auctioned off to the person who would charge the town the least for their care; indentured, so that their bonds were held by the family where they were placed; or apprenticed. Apprenticeship was usually reserved for children of the higher classes so that they might learn a trade.

Some outdoor relief was given to those who were more or less worthy, such as the aged and the ill, so that they could stay in their own homes. Guardians might be appointed for them to make sure they were properly cared for. However, the general rule was to place them. Some families made it a business to provide places for the needy and set up what today would be called private care homes to take in several people in return for pay from the town. These differed from the town poorhouses, which were built, supported, and administered by the courts or towns. Although almshouses and workhouses were growing in popularity in larger towns, most small towns could not support them.

Classification of the Poor

Most people who were poor, regardless of their situations, were assumed to be morally unworthy and were classified as follows:

- *Impotent poor* were aged or disabled long-term residents who could no longer work or people with severe physical or mental handicaps.
- *Able-bodied poor*, both men and women, were employable in some capacity but still solicited aid from the community.
- *Dependent children*, for whom the goal of towns and courts was to ensure that they did not follow in the degenerate footsteps of their pauper parents.

The Impotent Poor   The *impotent poor* were considered burdens on family and community and were expected to work to their limits. If not, the family had control of their lives up to but not including murder, and care ranged from the loving care of relatives to being chained or locked in unheated sheds, at the mercy of the elements until they died. Dependent children were under the care of local governments rather than parents from the first; they could be taken from parents considered unworthy. Also, they included orphans and abandoned, unwanted, or out-of-wedlock children. Widows were unlikely to be considered worthy poor and were urged to remarry, but a significant number, those whose husbands had been poor or indentured, were left destitute and could not find new husbands. Single women were seen as a threat to the morality and economic security of the town. Both they and widows were often banished from the community if they could not eke out a living as servants or seamstresses and family or neighbors would not provide bond.[66]

The Able-Bodied Poor   Men and women who were employable in some capacity were considered to be going against God's law when they asked for relief. Punishments for poverty were the same as those for offenses against the community: bonding, warning out, selling to the lowest bidder (auctioning off), flogging, branding, or jailing. By the early 1700s, New England had a surplus of unwed and widowed women. Inability to marry or find work meant that many women were homeless and near starvation, and towns were unwilling to support public dependents. Warned out of towns, along with their children, they wandered the country seeking work, and many disappeared into the forests forever. Often, the able-bodied were put to work on public projects, but usually they were auctioned off. Because this led to brutal treatment, inadequate care, hunger, and exploitation, reformers demanded they be placed in almshouses, workhouses, or houses of correction.

In 1660, Boston built a house of correction in which all indigents were herded together, and in 1739 the city built a workhouse that was a combination penal institution and poorhouse for vagabonds, rogues, idlers, criminals, the poor, and the mentally ill. Grob describes almshouses:

> [C]leanliness is an unknown luxury, all is filth and misery and the most degrading, unrelieved suffering. The inmates, sane and insane, were found in many instances huddled together without discrimination of age, sex, or condition; conmingling in unrestrained licentiousness and with results shocking to all sense of decency and humanity.[67]

Children ranging in age from one month to fourteen years could be found in many such almshouses.

Idlers and vagabonds constituted threats to colonial self-sufficiency and safety, but *any* objectionable people—for religious, political, or moral reasons—could be brought before the local courts and judged "rogues." Punishment for both men and women was public whipping and deportation to their former residences or confinement in jail. Demented or maimed people were deported or sold into indenture and criminals and delinquents were driven from town. For lesser crimes they were flogged or mutilated, and for more severe crimes they could be executed. Debtors were imprisoned for owing as little as two cents, and they had to provide their own necessities while in prison or go without.

Policy Practice

Practice Behavior Example: Know the history and current structures of social policies and services; the role of policy in service delivery; and the role of practice in policy development.

Critical Thinking Question: Discuss the institutions in Colonial America that provided social assistance. How effective were they at responding to need?

Dependent Children Colonial laws were particularly concerned that children should not follow the road into idleness and poverty. Poor families were requested to bind out their children to service, and as early as 1641 the courts had the right to take the children of the poor and indenture them to guard against the "contagion of parental failure."[68] A statute in Virginia in 1646 accused the poor of obstinacy in not binding out their children and ordered county commissioners to take two children from every poor family and bind them out to flax houses. The county also placed orphans, children born out of wedlock, and unwanted children. White children born out of wedlock "belonged" to the parish if fathers failed to support them, and they were bound out by church wardens until fathers reimbursed the parish. Children of slaves and indentured servants also were bound out.

According to parish records, one-third of all those bound out were orphans. The remainder were children whose parents apprenticed them to learn a trade. They then lived with the master and rarely saw their families, and masters were responsible by law not only for material welfare but for spiritual guidance. Apprentice masters, along with guardians of wealthy orphans and orphanage matrons, were required to teach boys reading and writing and give all children Christian training. Most boys were apprenticed to carpenters, shoemakers, blacksmiths, or planters, whereas girls became domestics, although some learned to knit, spin, and sew. Apprenticeship contracts were registered by the courts, and the practice ensured an ongoing supply of artisans and craftspeople for the colony.

Child labor was viewed as beneficial to both child and society, teaching the sanctity of work and the evils of idleness. Boston spinning schools opened in 1656, and children and other poor were placed in them and paid by the piece. This gave the town income at minimum expense and provided employment for society's potentially rebellious elements. Unlike apprentice masters, employers were not responsible for children's well-being or education, although often they had contracts supposedly to protect them. To promote the work ethic among the poor, in 1759 Boston opened a spinning school for girls, and in 1751 the Society for Encouraging Industry and Employing the Poor was established to promote the manufacture of woolen cloth and to employ indigent women and children.

The importance of education in America led to both public and private school systems. In 1647, Massachusetts required towns of over fifty households to have a teacher for elementary school, and if there were more than a hundred families in a town a high school was mandated. This system, paid for by fees and taxes, was not compulsory; however, town selectmen could investigate any home to see that children were adequately taught there. In New York and New Jersey, Dutch Reformed parochial schools allowed poor children to attend free and charged fees to those who could afford them.[69] New Jersey had the first land-grant schools, in which certain lands were set aside for support of schools, and in 1704 New York and New Jersey established private catechism schools for people of African descent. In 1787, New York City created the first free school for such children, and a New Jersey law in 1788 required that they be taught to read. In the South, education lagged because farms and plantations were scattered. White families had tutors for children or educated them in England, but children of African descent were, on the whole, denied education because it was thought to make them unruly.

Private Philanthropy

Despite the lack of money available for social welfare in the early colonies, there was some private philanthropy based on either mutual aid or the desire to provide work as a solution to pauperism. Quakers, for example, asked the needy—even non-Quakers—to present their problems to the group, and the meeting voted food, clothing, shelter, and coal. "Friendly visitors" called on those needing help. Voluntary giving rather than taxes supplied necessities, which often included employment or materials for home handicrafts.[70] Quakers also established almshouses, workhouses, and later penitentiaries, where the immoral could reflect on their misdeeds.

There were many craft or religious welfare societies, such as the Friends Almshouse in Philadelphia for poor Quakers, established in 1713, or the Boston Episcopal Society (1724). In New York, the Society of the House of Carpenters was established in 1767. Like many ethnic groups, free African Americans founded mutual aid societies to help both the free and slaves; for example, in Boston, a Masonic Lodge was founded by free African Americans in 1784, and in 1787 the Philadelphia Free African Society was founded to provide mutual aid for the sick and for widows and orphans, along with schooling and apprenticeship for children.[71]

Benjamin Franklin was a strong proponent of voluntary associations and self-help. He preached the gospel of industry, frugality, and sobriety as the way to individual freedom, and he believed in personal, social, and civic responsibility. To these ends, he established a library and a volunteer fire company, worked to ensure the paving of roads and the cleaning and lighting of Philadelphia, helped establish a police force, and founded a hospital and an academy that became the University of Pennsylvania. As a founding father of our country, he epitomized the meaning of social welfare of the time.[72]

Religion, particularly the Evangelical movement, brought new concern for the poor, along with ethics of individual responsibility and social order. It claimed that the rich had a responsibility toward the poor, and that the poor owed gratitude and work to them. Another religious movement, the Great Awakening, brought two great preachers, George Whitefield and Johnathan Edwards, who led a series of religious revivals between 1730 and 1750. They preached a humanitarian ethic that transformed philanthropy from the province of the upper classes to a shared activity of all classes, appealing to both conscience and altruism.

In the century before the Revolution, great depressions created a need for social welfare that neither public nor private funding alone could handle. Joint funding, therefore, became the pattern, one that continued until 1935. Rather than giving money for explicit causes, private donors gave money to the government for charitable purposes, and government officials, such as overseers of the poor, asked churches to take up collections to be used for support of public dependents.

SLAVERY IN THE AMERICAS

Many Africans were in the New World before the importation of slaves to the colonies. They were explorers, servants, and slaves who accompanied French, Spanish, and Portuguese in expeditions in both North and South America. One of these was Pedro Alonso Niño, who piloted one of Columbus's ships. Free African immigrants were not considered racially inferior in early days. They could accumulate property and testify in court, and they toiled in the fields and fraternized with white indentured servants.[73] However, with slavery came racism.

Racism, slavery, and jurisprudence were intimately entwined in slave laws,[74] even though in 1619, when Africans captured from a Spanish ship were brought to the colonies, there were no legal precedents concerning slavery. Within twenty years, in Virginia legislation based on presumptions of black people's inferiority appeared, "uniquely excluding blacks from the normal protections [of] ... the government."[75] Legal decisions after that time were consistent with the inferiority assumption. According to Judge A. Leon Higginbotham, Jr., "The inferiority of African Americans was given the standing of a natural principle embodied through the existing moral and social climate of the time...."[76]

Higginbotham writes that the interrelationship of race and the American legal process had two bases: the profitability of slave ownership and the fear of slave revolts. In 1659, statutes reduced import duties on slave ships from Africa, thus encouraging the slave trade's profitability. By 1660, statutory enslavement had begun.[77] The first major slave codes, from 1680 to 1683, prohibited slaves from carrying arms or leaving the owners' plantations without "certificates"; limited time slaves could be absent; and mandated lashing for slaves who "lifted their hands" against any white person. Runaway slaves were put to death because they deprived owners of their "rightful property."[78]

Other legal mechanisms of control included bounties for bringing in scalps and ears of runaway slaves and the right to threaten, beat, lash, and even kill slaves without retaliation. A Virginia court in 1669 decided that, because slaves could not be punished by extending their terms of servitude, threatening and beating them would increase their productivity. Harder beatings meant a greater chance of killing them, so courts passed legislation that slave owners would not be criminally prosecuted for the "casual" killing of slaves.[79] Legislation in 1699 made manumission impossible unless the freed slave was deported from the country within six months, on penalty of reenslavement. In 1705, Virginia statutes led the way in reclassifying black people from human status to "real property," such as land or houses. In South Carolina, they were declared chattel or personal property similar to sheep, horses, or belongings.[80] Higginbotham says that

> … the purpose of the legal system was to convince each slave he had no will of his own … [and that] the power of the master must be absolute to render the submission of the slave perfect.[81]

To ensure the understanding of black people's inferiority, interracial sexual relationships were carefully codified. By 1662, it was legally decided that the mother's slave condition (slave or free) determined the child's slave status. White women who had children by slaves could be punished by fining or putting them into indenture, whereas white men received no punishment and often profited by selling their own progeny as slaves. In interracial marriages, the white partner could be imprisoned for six months.[82] Even free blacks were controlled: In Pennsylvania in 1725–1726, statutes required that all children of free blacks be bound out for service until age twenty-one for women and twenty-four for men. If the parents were married, the black partner was to be sold into slavery and their children were put out to service until they were thirty-one years old. The white partner was not punished.[83]

Higginbotham cites the *Dred Scott* decision (*Scott v. Sandford*, 1857) as embodying these precepts of slavery jurisprudence. In it, Chief Justice Taney wrote that people of African-American descent are a subordinate and inferior class that, whether slave or free, remains subject to the authority of the dominant and superior white race. Higginbotham states, "In effect, the Supreme Court's majority opinion in *Dred Scott* codified into law, at the highest level of the American legal process, the precept of black inferiority."[84]

Slavery as practiced in North America was a response to the Protestant religio-economic dictum that wealth demonstrates morality and to the even older dictum of fear and hatred of "outsiders." Because Africans did not worship the Christian God, their lives were insignificant compared to the mandate of wealth for their masters. Whereas South American slaves had human rights because of the intercession of the Catholic Church, North American slaves were considered less than human and were bred as livestock. Masters owned not only their work but their lives, and Protestantism did not forbid their use (or that of white workers), even to death.

Critical Thinking

Practice Behavior Example: Requires the synthesis and communication of relevant information.

Critical Thinking Question: What factors impacted the construction of the "worthy" and "unworthy" poor in Colonial America?

Wealth-producing work was an end in itself, dictated by God to the faithful, and therefore religiously legitimate. Although certainly some people detested slavery, the protests of the few were drowned in the approval of the many. For the most part, slavery was not seen as evil at all but almost a moral imperative because it "protected" slaves from destitution, put them to work, and led to wealth for God's chosen. These beliefs created a system of slavery unequaled in brutality and gave rise to the American brand of racism.

The Golden Triangle and the Triangular Trade

The slave trade was called the *triangular trade*, with Europe, Africa, and North America as the corners of the triangle. Beginning in Europe, ships and exports supplied by the English and French went to Africa to purchase slaves. From Africa, the ships went to North America via the West Indies, where slaves produced sugar. The triangle was completed when raw materials—lumber, iron, sugar, and so on—were shipped to England for manufacture (with a stopoff in New England to make rum of the sugar).

In the early 1600s, many Caribbean farmers produced sugar themselves because the cost of passage for slaves from Africa was too high to be expedient. However, as coffee and chocolate became popular in Europe, sugar consumption skyrocketed, so that by 1700 it was the most valuable agricultural commodity in international trade. This had two results. The first was an economic dispossession of small farmers in the Caribbean as the wealthy plantation owners took over:

> Barbados in 1645 had 11,200 small white farmers and 5,680 Negro slaves.
> In 1667, there were 745 large plantation owners and 82,023 slaves....
> The price of land skyrocketed. A plantation of 500 acres which sold for
> 400 pounds in 1640 fetched 700 pounds for a half share in 1648.[85]

Because of the sugar trade, Barbados, with its 166 square miles, was worth more to England in the 1700s and 1800s than the whole of New England, New York, and Pennsylvania combined. Second, African slavery became economically profitable.[86] White indenture in the Caribbean was dying down and Native American workers were dying out. One African was said to be worth five Native Americans because of resistance to European diseases and experiences as slaves in Africa. African slavery was the wave of the future, first with sugar plantations and then for cotton plantations in the South.

Most African slaves came from an area bordering the West Coast of Africa—they were Hausas, Mindinagos, Yorubas, Ibos, Efiks, Krus, Fontins, Ashantis, Dahomeans, Binis, and Sengalies.[87] First the Portuguese, then the Dutch, French, and English (under Elizabeth I) seized leadership in the slave trade. Slave raids throughout Africa, especially the West Coast, robbed the continent of as many as 40 million people, most in the prime of their lives.[88] The strongest and healthiest men and women survived the passage to the Americas; many of the rest either died in Africa during and after their capture, walking hundreds of miles to the coast to be picked over, branded, and chained, or died on slave ships. During this Middle Passage, they were packed into holds and chained at the neck and feet, often with no more than 18 inches of head room each for the six to ten weeks of the passage. They died of suffocation, starvation, and epidemics of smallpox and dysentery. Some committed suicide or killed those they loved or those who had food. Those who died were thrown overboard, and sharks followed slave ships regularly. Some gave birth to children while still in chains. Young women and girls were often taken for the pleasure of the crew.

Occasionally, when a ship was seriously damaged or disease ran rampant, slaves were thrown overboard to make the ship lighter, or ships were deserted in mid-ocean, their cargo of men and women chained helplessly together below the decks,[89] for they were considered animal cargo. In 1783, short of water, the captain of the slave ship *Zong* threw 132 slaves overboard (they often did this with livestock such as horses). Damages were awarded the owners for property, and the idea that this was mass murder never occurred.[90] One African recorded his voyage:

> I was soon put down under the decks and ... with the loathesomeness of the stench and crying together, I became so sick and low that I was not able to eat.... On my refusal to eat, one of them held me fast by the hands and laid me across, I think the windlass, and tied my feet, while the other flogged me severely.... One day, when we had a smooth sea and a moderate wind, two of my wearied countrymen who were chained together ... preferring death to such a life of misery, somehow made through the nettings and jumped into the sea.[91]

There were 155 recorded slave uprisings on ships between 1699 and 1845. When they reached America, diseased slaves were left to die and the remaining sold either to dealers or directly to plantation owners. The price of slaves fluctuated with the market: George Washington bought a man in 1754 for $250 but ten years later had to pay $285. Slaves were available either for cash or for a small down payment with small monthly payments.

During the slave trade from 1502 to 1860, 9.6 million Africans were brought to the New World, 6 million of them in the 1700s, at a rate of 50,000 to 100,000 a year. Of the nearly ten million taken, about three-fourths died in capture or transit. Most were sold in the West Indies and South America, with about half a million (6 to 7 percent) sold in North America. Of these, an estimated 345,000 were sold before 1800.[92] Aside from the disruption of cultures of those brought to the Americas, the societies of Africa, large and small, advanced or more primitive, were ruined as millions of the strongest and youngest were taken from their homes. Estimates on the total killed in the attempt to enslave, or those actually enslaved, range to at least the twenty-eight million mark.[93] Undoubtedly, this mass deportation of native Africans led to the ease with which colonialism was soon enforced on Africa itself.

In England after the 1700s, slave owners dominated Parliament, and the founding of banks based on the triangular trade began in the late 1700s and early 1800s. England and Scotland also developed insurance houses—such as Lloyds of London, originally a coffee house that listed runaway slaves— to insure both slaves and slave ships, and thus began the property insurance system of the world.[94] The slave trade, of course, was not seen as inhumane. In a time when life was so cheap and poverty was so much looked on as personal sin, slavery was merely another very lucrative business. Indeed, many English humanitarians were included in those who ran the slave trade. Edmund Burke was one such humanitarian, as was John Cary, who in England founded the Society for the Incorporation of the Poor. Bryan Blundell, a noted slave trader, was trustee, treasurer, chief patron, and most active supporter of a charity school. Slave traders, because of their wealth from the trade, often held high offices in the government of England.

By the time George Washington became president in 1789, there were four million people in the North American colonies. Approximately one of every four of them was a slave, of whom about one-third were women.

TOWARD THE REVOLUTION

Economics was at the base of the rebellion against King George and England. English law forbade the colonies to manufacture goods from the raw materials they produced, and only English-built ships could be used to transport raw materials to England and the finished products colonists were required to buy back from England. To aid England's wool business, laws required that all slaves and servants wear wool, even in the Caribbean, and that the dead be buried in suits of wool. Colonists were required to eat fish caught from English ships on Fridays and Saturdays, and as early as 1615 England had a monopoly on refining sugar produced in the West Indies. Such laws galled the colonists, many of whom had come to America to find freedom and financial success, and they began to fight against forced purchase of goods more efficiently produced in America. In addition, English treaties with Native Americans kept them from legally exploring and settling the land beyond the Appalachians.

The northern colonies produced food for sugar workers because planters did not want to take the land out of sugar production. By supplying food, however, they were taking trade from England in return for sugar supplies. England therefore imposed the Stamp Act, which required a tax on sugar imports to the northern colonies, and Americans refused to pay or to ship food to the sugar islands. Because of this, 15,000 Jamaican slaves died of famine between 1780 and 1787.[95] Moreover, colonials began to manufacture and process the raw materials of America despite English bans. They especially began to trade in rum from Caribbean sugar, textiles from southern cotton, and iron from northern mines. American rum production competed with English spirits made from corn and gave Americans an edge in the slave trade. In 1770, New England's exports of rum to Africa represented over four-fifths of the total colonial exports of the time. Metallurgy and mining also became important for making fetters, chains, padlocks, irons for branding, axes for clearing the colonial land, and guns.

Women in the Revolution

Because of the general status of women at the time of the Revolution, their participation in developing the new country was limited. For example, although in North Carolina fifty-one women proclaimed their right to participate in political activities, no women attended the Continental Congress or state congresses convened to argue the question of Revolution. Abigail Adams, wife of John Adams, was nearly alone in her outspoken insistence that men misused their political power when they denied women equal rights. She continually tried to encourage the inclusion of women's legal and civil rights in the new government, writing to her husband to

> remember the ladies ... if particular care and attention is not paid to [us] we are determined to foment a rebellion, and will not hold ourselves bound by any laws in which we have no voice or representation.[96]

Mercy Otis Warren, sister of patriot James Otis, was among the major intellectual writers of the Revolution. An antifederalist, she wrote plays and published under a male name, corresponding on public questions with both Samuel and John Adams, John Hancock, and George Washington. John Adams and many other men were concerned with women's rights, for a spirit of equality permeated liberal thought. Thomas Paine wrote an impassioned plea for their inclusion in the Constitution, and Benjamin Franklin said the women were unequal only because of the limits placed on them by education and tradition.[97]

As many as 20,000 women went to war in the Revolution, on both the British and American sides.

As many as 20,000 women went to war in the Revolution, on both the British and American sides. They were cooks, nurses, doctors, laundresses, guides, seamstresses, and porters. British women were paid, while American soldiers could rely on volunteer patriots to care for their needs. Women were not simply observers, as this account of the British entering Cambridge illustrates:

> Poor dirty emaciated men, great numbers of women, who seemed to be the beasts of burden having a bushel basket on their back by which they were bent double, the contents seemed to be pots and kettles, various sorts of furniture, children peeping through gridirons and other utensils, some very young infants who were born on the road, the women bare feet, clothed in dirty rags.[98]

Hundreds of women participated in Benedict Arnold's disastrous assault on Montreal, which began in late fall. Led by ill-informed guides, ill-equipped for the bitter winter, and unaware that game would not be available, many starved, died of pneumonia and typhoid, or became lost and froze to death.

The Daughters of Liberty formed to boycott British products, especially tea, and many women supplied the Revolutionary army with clothes, food, and other provisions. Some women fought as soldiers and were rewarded with army pensions for themselves and their families. For example, Deborah Sampson Gannett dressed as a man and became an infantry soldier at age eighteen. After the war she married, and when she died at age sixty-seven, her husband applied for and received a pension based on her military service. (Not until the 1970s was there another ruling, by the Social Security Administration, that the spouse of a working woman was entitled to a pension.) Other well-known women heroes were Mary Ludwig Hayes, who went with her husband and replaced him at the cannon when he was wounded, and Molly Pitcher, who carried water to the wounded men.

THE NEW NATION AND ITS CONSTITUTION

The Constitution ... was an elitist document; that is, it was written by white male property owners and ensured their rights without due consideration of the rights of women, people without property, and nonwhites.

It is ironic that one goal for which the Revolutionary War was fought was equality when in America women still had the status of children and idiots and the slave trade was still active. Both free and slave people of African descent fought during the Revolution, many for the English, for they were not welcomed in the Revolutionary army. However, after the winter at Valley Forge, Washington was willing to accept any fighting man, and approximately 100,000 runaway slaves joined the Revolutionary army and were freed.

In 1773, slaves in Massachusetts petitioned the legislature for freedom, and this petition was followed by eight others during the Revolutionary War. Slavery was effectively terminated in the North by 1777. Five of the original thirteen states emancipated their slaves before the federal Constitutional

Convention met in New York in 1788. Partial antislavery measures were enacted by New York in 1788, with total emancipation in 1799, and New Jersey began to pass antislavery legislation in 1786.[99] Vermont was first to abolish slavery in 1777, followed by Massachusetts and New Hampshire in 1783 and Connecticut and Rhode Island in 1784.

Despite the new freedoms the Constitution guaranteed, it was a creation of its time. As such, it was an elitist document; that is, it was written by white male property owners and ensured their rights without due consideration of the rights of women, people without property, and nonwhites. Although there was some agitation to ensure the abolition of slavery, this was dropped to gain ratification by southern slaveholders. Slavery was given formal recognition by the Constitution in the determination that slaves were three-fifths of a white man for purposes of determining voter representation and taxation; in the fugitive slave section, which ensured that slaves would be returned to their masters; the exemption from export duties of goods made by slaves; and in the permission to continue the slave trade until 1808.

According to Joe R. Feagin, *systemic racism* was established by the writers of the Constitution as a foundation of American society to reinforce and legitimate "... a system of racist oppression that they thought would ensure that whites, especially white men of means, would rule for centuries to come."[100] He says that systemic racism includes

the complex array of antiblack practices, the unjustly gained political-economic power of whites, the continuing economic and other resource inequalities along racial lines, and the white racist ideologies and attitudes created to maintain and rationalize white privilege and power ... manifested in each of society's major parts.[101]

Feagin further notes that many of the Constitution's framers favored a permanent slave society.

[T]he majority of white Americans, in spite of the professed ethic of liberty, saw nothing wrong with the brutal subordination of black Americans or the driving away or killing of Native Americans.... Religious leaders like Cotton Mather, the famous Puritan, and William Penn, a Quaker ... owned black Americans. The founder of American psychiatry and perhaps the leading intellectual of his day, Dr. Benjamin Rush, owned a black American. Men of politics like Thomas Jefferson, George Washington, Alexander Hamilton, Patrick Henry, Benjamin Franklin, John Hancock, and Sam Houston enslaved Black Americans. Ten U.S. presidents (Washington, Jefferson, James Madison, James Monroe, Andrew Jackson, John Tyler, James Polk, Zachary Taylor, Andrew Johnson, and Ulysses S. Grant) at some point in their lives enslaved African Americans.[102]

In addition, the Constitution gave the vote only to property owners and men with certain levels of education, ensuring an elitist and mercantilist bent. For example, James Madison believed that the establishment of a national government was the most important protection for the elites against mass movements that might threaten property. Dye and Zeigler say,

Men like Patrick Henry and Richard Henry Lee of Virginia vigorously attacked the Constitution as a "counter-revolutionary document" ... the new government would be "aristocratic," "all-powerful," and a threat to the "spirit of republicanism" and the "genius of democracy."...

[It sets up] … an aristocratic upper house and an almost monarchial presidency.[103]

In fact, the leaders of the Revolution had asked George Washington to be permanent president, and had even prepared a throne for him, but he refused. To counteract accusations of aristocracy, Congress provided a Bill of Rights at its first meeting.

Although four decision-making bodies were established by the Constitution, only one, the House of Representatives, was to be elected by the people. The Senate was to be elected by state legislators and the president by an Electoral College. The powers of government were almost unilaterally based on the protection of property rights. Congress was given power to tax, to regulate interstate commerce, to protect money and property, to regulate communication and transportation, to conduct military affairs, and to protect the rights of slave owners to their slaves.

The Constitution did not deal with the problems of the poor, although popular workers' movements demanded a federally controlled monetary system (rather than factory scrip), the abolition of debts, and an equal distribution of property. Congress was given the authority to provide for the common welfare, but common welfare was not social welfare. The theme of individual responsibility and individual achievement permeated the new government, and the upsurge of liberalism did not change the nation's perspective on the causes of poverty or the needs of the poor. Because the political economy of the times was elitist, so was the Constitution: Those who wrote it were involved in profit making through the labor of the poor. Factions seeking equality were either ignored or defeated in the battle, and the class stratification that had been custom in the New World became a legal part of American government. Those who had no voice before the Revolution were denied voice in the new nation.

Human Rights and Justice

Practice Behavior Example: Understand the forms and mechanisms of oppression and discrimination.

Critical Thinking Question: Is the Constitution a tool for social justice or a document that codifies oppression?

CONCLUSION: REVOLUTION TO STATUS QUO

The Constitution does guarantee citizens certain freedoms and civil rights, whether or not its authors intended. Many such rights have been fought through courts of the land; the Constitution and its amendments, particularly as interpreted by the Supreme Court, have made it possible for these fights to be won. Since the Constitution was written over two hundred years ago, although the basic protection of property rights has been maintained, civil rights probably not believed possible at the Revolution have come to pass. The abolition of slavery was the first of many civil rights to be granted, with women's suffrage and equal opportunity in employment, education, and other areas of life to come later. Despite its elitist beginning, and despite the roadblocks put in the way of equality, the basic underpinnings of the Constitution and the democratic orientation of the people of the United States have slowly made inroads into our racist, sexist, and classist society. Although we may be impatient that the promises of equality have not been fulfilled, patterns of equality were set into law, traditions, and customs as the United States became a nation.

The following questions will test your knowledge and understanding of the content found within this chapter. For additional assessment, including licensing-exam type questions on applying chapter content to practice behaviors, visit **MySearchLab**.

1. Roughly one-half of all white immigrants came to the New World as indentured servants, which meant:

   a. they had to pay for their passage by providing free work service for five to eight years.

   b. they served a lifetime of free work service in order to gain passage.

   c. their children were also treated as indentured servants until they reached age eighteen.

   d. they were treated significantly better than slaves were treated.

2. Which statement best describes the impotent poor?

   a. Citizens who were able to work and chose not to.

   b. Citizens with severe physical and mental disabilities.

   c. Citizens who were unable to find or maintain a job to support themselves.

   d. Citizens who engaged in immoral activities that left them poor, such as gambling.

3. Which statement best describes the Native American perspective on land ownership?

   a. Land cannot be "owned" because land is a spiritual concept.

   b. Land is automatically "owned" by those who live upon it and make it their space.

   c. Seeking to own land is a misguided principle and leads to greed and immorality.

   d. The wildlife are the only true "owners" of land and must be respected.

4. Preventing nonwhite citizens from owning property was an example of:

   a. systemic racism

   b. internalized racism

   c. structural racism

   d. institutionalized racism

5. What advice would you give a citizen in New England who had just received a "warning out" notice?

   a. He needs to find a new place to live because public assistance housing shelters for the poor are closing.

   b. If he does not leave town, he risks becoming an indentured servant.

   c. He is eligible for poor relief but since funds are running out, he should not wait before requesting assistance.

   d. He is about to become unemployed and should begin looking for a new job.

6. What advice would you give to a woman living in colonial America in the 1600s who is miserable in her marriage?

   a. Women do not have the right to divorce or separate from their husbands.

   b. If a woman chose to separate or divorce, she could expect financial support from her husband.

   c. If she separated, she would lose everything except for her children.

   d. For most women, the grounds for divorce were extremely difficult; only death of the husband would break the legal tie.

7. Describe the main differences between slaves and indentured servents in the New World.

Reinforce what you learned in this chapter by studying videos, cases, documents, and more available at **www.MySearchLab.com.**

Watch and Review

Watch these Videos

The American Revolution as different
Americans Saw It

Slavery and the Constitution

Read and Review

Read these Cases/Documents

Anne Bradstreet, Before the Birth of One of Her
Children (c. 1650)

Assess Your Knowledge

Go to MySearchLab to test your knowledge of key topics in this chapter with topic-specific quizzes.
Conclude your assessment by completing the chapter exam.

6

America to the Civil War

Competencies Applied with Practice Behavior Examples — in This Chapter									
■	Professional Identity	■	Ethical Practice	■	Critical Thinking	X	Diversity in Practice	X	Human Rights & Justice
■	Research Based Practice	■	Human Behavior	X	Policy Practice	■	Practice Contexts	X	Engage, Assess, Intervene, Evaluate

Times and Events

- **1770–1800:** Revolution and the New Nation: British Tea Act precipitates Boston Tea Party; Cherokee leader Molly Brant convinces Six Nations of the Iroquois to join the British; First Continental Congress meets; United States fights British at Lexington, Concord; Second Continental Congress meets

- **1776:** Jefferson drafts Declaration of Independence

- **1779:** New York militia destroys forty Iroquois villages

- **1781:** Articles of Confederation, developed in 1777, ratified by eleven colonies

- **1783:** Revolutionary War ends; Chief Joseph Brandt organizes alliance of Northwest tribes to protect native rights; Benjamin Rush begins "moral treatment" for the mentally ill

- **1787:** Northwest Ordinance passed

- **1788:** Eleven states ratify Constitution; First Congress convenes; Washington elected first President in 1789

- **1791:** Bill of Rights unanimously passed

- **1793:** First Fugitive Slave Law passed

- **1794:** Anthony Wayne wins decisive victory over Native Americans in Ohio

- **1800:** Gabriel Prosser's slave rebellion fails in Virginia

- **1802:** Toussaint de L'Ouverture leads successful Haitian rebellion

- **1808:** United States ends legal slave trade

- **1809:** Shawnee Chief Tecumseh unites Native Americans against white army, his followers massacred at Tippecanoe River; Elizabeth Bayley Seton founds Sisters of Charity of St. Joseph

- **1812–1814:** War of 1812 to end British impressment of U.S. sailors; Tecumseh joins British and is killed; Treaty of Ghent ends war and secures Great Lakes region to United States

- **1817:** First Seminole War begins as United States invades Florida in pursuit of fugitive slaves; first institute for the deaf is established by Thomas Gallaudet and Laurent Clerc

- **1818:** Report by Society for Prevention of Pauperism blames poverty on drunkenness

- **1820:** Missouri Compromise sets Mason–Dixon line between slave and free states

- **1821:** Emma Willard opens Troy Female Seminary in New York to provide college education for women

- **1822:** Denmark Vesey leads slave rebellion in South Carolina

- **1823:** Monroe Doctrine affirms U.S. right to expand across North America

- **1825:** Creek Treaty cedes most native lands in Georgia to United States; mammalian ovum discovered

- **1830:** Indian Removal Act issued, Trail of Tears begins

- **1831:** Nat Turner leads slave rebellion in Virginia; Seminoles cede remaining territory in Florida to United States

- **1833:** Lucretia Mott founds Philadelphia Female Anti-Slavery Society, Angelina and Sarah Grimke join in 1835; New York opens poorhouses

- **1834:** Department of Indian Affairs established; Lowell Mills women workers strike

- **1843:** Association for the Improvement of the Poor forms
- **1846:** Dr. Samuel Howe opens Perkins Institute for the Blind, expands to include mentally retarded persons
- **1848:** Dorothea Dix submits Ten Million Acre Bill to Congress, vetoed by President Franklin Pierce in 1851; Elizabeth Cady Stanton and Lucretia Mott hold First Women's Rights Convention in Seneca Falls, New York
- **1849:** Harriet Tubman escapes slavery and begins rescuing other slaves
- **1850:** Compromise of 1850 strengthens Fugitive Slave Law
- **1851:** First YMCA founded in Boston; Sojourner Truth speaks at second Women's Rights Convention in Akron, Ohio
- **1854:** Kansas–Nebraska Act repeals Missouri Compromise; Elizabeth Cady Stanton founds New York Suffrage Society
- **1857:** Drs. Elizabeth and Emily Blackwell and Marie Zakrzewska open New York Infirmary for Women and Children; Dred Scott decision declares slaves property, not citizens
- **1859:** John Brown leads antislavery raid at Harper's Ferry
- **1860:** Southern States secede from Union and organize Confederate States of America

THE FIRST CIVIL RIGHTS MOVEMENT

After the Revolution, egalitarian ideals took second place to laissez-faire capitalism, industrialization, and expansionism. The Constitution and new state governments ensured elitist control: Only white male Christians had suffrage in most states, and some states had minimum property requirements (some as high as $5,000) for eligibility to vote or run for office. Not until 1856 could all white men vote in the New England states, regardless of property ownership, although frontier states usually gave suffrage to all white men.[1] Some territories came into the Union with suffrage for women; for example, Wyoming would not enter the Union unless it was allowed to continue women's suffrage, and Utah insisted on women's suffrage in order to maintain polygamy for the Mormon Church against the voting power of newcomers.

Jacksonian democracy declared that every (white male) person could succeed with individual hard work. This was, according to Dye and Zeigler, "by no means a philosophy of leveling egalitarianism. The ideal of the frontier [was] wealth and power won by competitive skill ... [creating] a *natural aristocracy*."[2] Laissez-faire capitalism expanded to the West, where a new elite developed. Money was federalized: Rather than state or company scrip, federal money was put in state banks, thus breaking the Eastern monopoly of economic and political power.[3] Uncontrolled industrialization moved work from agrarian households to the cities.

The proportion of wage laborers increased (from 5.5 percent in 1796 to 27 percent in 1855 in New York City, for example), enabling employers to lower wages and increase their profits. Men were hired from the crowds of unemployed on the streets for day or seasonal work, and irregular employment, vast unemployment, labor uprisings, and the growth of labor movements resulted.[4] The powerful Protestant orientation to work remained. Macarov says,

> Factories needed workers, and workers need jobs, not just to make money but also to be moral, religious, law-abiding people. Factory owners thus did people a favor by allowing them to work, and workers were expected to be grateful to the point of not ... asking for higher wages or better working conditions. This was not only ingratitude but almost blasphemy.[5]

Mobility and industrialization weakened family structure and community ties. Churches, neighbors, friends, and relatives could no longer be depended on for help in need. As the family and the economy changed, surplus unmarried women became teachers and social reformers. The idle wife became a mark of status for wealthier men, who hired (or bought) lower-class women to do household chores. The latter, considered sexually available and usable by upper-class men, were thought of as the "sexual sewer" of the rich.

The 1800s brought massive social experimentation, with money, time, and energy available to indulge in such issues as the franchise for women, ending exploitation of children, emancipation of slaves, temperance, and moral reform of the poor. The altruism of the times was based on the ideals of the poor's immorality, work as the only moral source of income, and almsgiving as the path to immorality. Social responsibility for poverty was rejected even though social data convinced such eminent philosophers as John Stuart Mill and John Marshall that poverty was the result of social exploitation.[6]

Slave labor and the cotton gin, invented in 1791, made cotton easy and cheap to produce. By the 1820s, cotton textiles constituted more than half of American exports, and Southern plantation owners refused to relinquish their new near-aristocracy by ending slavery. In the North, the new industrial elite made fortunes from the labor of immigrants—men, women, and children as young as five years old—who produced textiles, made clothes, mined iron and coal, and built transportation and communication links across the nation and around the world.

Immigration and Migration

Shortly before the Revolution, America had some 2.25 million white settlers, and only five cities had populations of 8,000 or more. Within fifty years, the population had reached 10 million,[7] a quarter of whom, by 1820, settled beyond the Alleghenies on Native American lands. Coll says the tide of immigrants

> rose steadily from only 129,000 in the 1820s to 540,000 in the following decade ... to a pre-Civil War peak of more than 1.75 million in the 1850s. Altogether, about 6 million immigrants crossed to the "land of opportunity" between 1820 and 1860—roughly half of them from Great Britain and Ireland, about 2 million from Germany, and about 50,000 from the Scandinavian countries.[8]

For a short time, the move West averted a labor flood and maintained reasonable wages in the Eastern cities. Soon, however, destitute immigrants "were like an army encamped in the midst of New York,"[9] stranded, with little help either to move inland or to establish new lives.

Almshouses, which cared for the poor and ill, were often the first stop of immigrants sick from infections and the deprivations of the Atlantic crossing.

By 1796, almshouse commissioners were complaining of the enormous expense from foreign-born immigrants, and not until 1847 did immigration authorities decide that immigrants were entitled to aid based on their payment for passage. The Board of Commissioners of Immigration collected taxes and imposed indemnity bonds on immigrants, crews, and ships arriving at New York ports. These funds supported arriving immigrants or reimbursed local communities for outdoor relief, medical help, education, transportation, and job placements. Ward's Island in New York City's East River became a hospital and refuge for unemployable people and a nursery and school for orphans and children born out of wedlock. By 1855, there was a central landing for immigrant processing at Ellis Island.[10]

While immigration exploded, migration from rural areas increased dramatically as people moved to the cities for work. The urban population grew at the rate of about 40 to 50 percent per decade, and cities became squalid warrens of people living in acute poverty, beset by plagues and death-dealing illnesses, unemployment, and starvation. Even minimal sanitation and safety were lacking: Garbage and refuse flowed through the streets in open drains. There were no bathing facilities and almost no indoor plumbing, and water was drawn from street pumps or hydrants:

> [S]ewage disposal and police and fire protection were often left to chance.... Water supplies became polluted, and epidemics, gang wars, and street crime raged unchecked. Saloons, brothels, and gambling houses flourished in ethnic neighborhoods, confined there by authorities who would not tolerate their existence in "better" neighborhoods, and patronized by people from all over the city.[11]

The slums were breeding grounds for tuberculosis, pneumonia, and diphtheria, and children often died of "some unknown disease"—starvation:

> Periodically ... the United States was ravaged by deadly plagues—yellow fever, cholera, typhoid, to name the most virulent—caused by filth, impure water, and other unsanitary conditions. The plagues struck with most force in the cities ... and here sickness and death claimed first—and in greatest numbers—the poor.[12]

The supply of housing and services never caught up with the need, and people lived in sheds, garrets, and dark and poorly ventilated tenements. One row of tenements could house 500 people, with up to 200 in a single building—almost a thousand an acre.[13] Rooms were divided and redivided, and when there were no more rooms, people lived in cellars. In 1843 in Boston there were nearly 8,000 people in cellars, and in 1846, just three years later, there were 29,000. By 1850 one of every twenty lived in a cellar, the average number per room was six and the maximum twenty. Begging was widespread, and an estimated 10,000 abandoned, orphaned, or runaway children roamed the streets. Life expectancy after moving into the Boston slums was fourteen years.[14] Hymowitz and Weissman write,

> Though most immigrants were in the prime of life, between the ages of fourteen and forty-five, they died more readily than the native-born. Their children, and especially their babies, died even more frequently.... In Chicago, before 1900, three of every five babies died before age five.[15]

Employment and Unionization

For a short while after the Revolution, most people did not depend solely on wages: They were artisans, small landowners, tenants, traders, and urban mechanics. Even in New England, where large textile mills had developed by the beginning of the 1800s, factories were considered temporary places of employment for the poor or for young women putting away savings for marriage.[16] Men found farm work and the ownership of land more profitable than factory labor, so unmarried women, children, older married immigrant men and women, and people who otherwise would have been on welfare became the logical factory labor force.[17] According to Hymowitz and Weissman,

> The ten- to twelve-hour work day of women and children was spent in factories and mills that were dirty, noisy, dark, smelly, and dangerous. Hundreds of workers were jammed together in dimly lit rooms that were stifling hot in summer, cold and drafty in winter. The moist, lint-filled air in the cotton mills bred tuberculosis. In other industries women breathed dangerous fumes of paint and naphtha, tobacco, and glass and brass dust. Materials were flammable, and factory buildings were firetraps. Machines were cleaned and adjusted while they were running ... workers often lost fingers and even hands in accidents.[18]

Wars with France (1807–1809) and England (1812) depleted the economy and caused a severe depression (1815–1821). By the end of the War of 1812, approximately two-thirds of all factory workers were women[19] and children, who got about a fourth of the wages earned by men for the same work. Their average week's pay was $1.50, the same as for women who did piecework at home. The factory day began at 4:30 A.M., even for small children, and ended at sundown,[20] a day of hard physical labor in dangerous settings. Children were "sold out" to labor, with parents and employers colluding, lying about their ages so they could work:

> Here is a little child, not more than five years old.... She has on one garment, if a tattered sacking dress can be so termed! Her bones are nearly through her skin, but her stomach is an unhealthy pouch, abnormal. She has dropsy.
>
> It is eight o'clock when children reach their homes—later if the mill work is behind and they are kept over hours. They are usually beyond speech. They fall asleep at the table, on the stairs.[21]

By 1819, 500,000 people were unemployed, and at times a third of the labor force was idle. According to Mencher, "In Philadelphia alone, of 9,700 employed in thirty businesses, 7,500 were fired. Properties of farmers and small businesses were taken over by creditors."[22]

Before the Revolution, mill work for women was socially acceptable and often closely supervised. Some mills, such as that established by Francis Cabot Lowell in Massachusetts, were model communities with limited hours, schools, and chaperoned dormitories. However, conditions deteriorated even here, and in both 1834 and 1845 women struck for the ten-hour workday and higher pay. In response, the state legislature upheld the employer, conducting hearings and then visiting

> for an on-the-scene investigation. The committee report rejected the workers' demands for a ten-hour day, noting the *special responsibilities that laborers owed to their employers.*[23]

By 1831, mills employed nearly 19,000 men and 39,000 women; by 1850 women were 24 percent of the total number of workers; and by 1900, 19 percent.[24]

Families were often paid in liquor, tobacco, or company scrip, usable only in company stores or for company-owned housing. Company credit, necessary in layoffs, increased their indebtedness and dependency on the company and limited their job mobility. This was common in mines, construction, factories of all sorts, and handwork industries such as sewing. There were

> almost no pensions; few men left much in the way of savings when they died; and life insurance spread slowly, especially among the working class.... [F]actory production replaced the putting out system, and ... contrary to popular stereotypes (which are based on the minority of young women who worked in mills), there was very little industrial work open to any women in towns and cities before the late 19th century and almost none to married women.[25]

Wages fell 30 to 50 percent, most New England factories closed, and whole families starved or froze to death.[26] The unemployed formed citizens' committees and marched on the government, and fighting, looting, violence, and employment riots were common. Few social programs could cope with the mass distress, and soup kitchens opened and newspapers ran ads calling for food, money, clothing, and shelter for the poor.[27]

Trade unions formed as early as 1790, demanding a family wage for men, that is, enough pay to support a family; free education for children and the curbing of child labor and apprenticeship abuses (both to help children and to keep them out of the labor market); free public lands for settlement; restriction on private use of prison labor, as when prisoners were contracted out for work, undercutting wages; the establishment of a ten-hour day; control of currency by the government (rather than scrip issued by employers); the right to organize; and public work programs to protect the unemployed.

By 1837 there were at least five national unions: cordwainers (shoemakers and leather workers), combmakers, carpenters, weavers, and printers; and two-thirds of New York's workers were organized, with women taking the lead in organizing the mills. Strikes became common, even though the police were brought in and workers were brutalized and killed. However, by the beginning of the Civil War the labor movement had collapsed. In part, this was because of the adamant opposition of businesses and the courts, because the Civil War made soldiers out of unemployed boys and men, and, finally, because the Homestead Act of 1862 made free lands available for Western settlement.

PRIVATE PHILANTHROPY

Private philanthropy, as meager as it was, provided primarily for white people. Others were of no concern to most charities.

Despite mass unemployment and wages so low that saving was impossible and illness or accident devastating, the rich continued their diatribe against the laziness and intemperance of workers. There was little separation of public and private interests: Private groups formed associations and worked for legislation, often later inspecting or administering agencies set up and funded by government. Private philanthropy, as meager as it was, provided primarily for white people. Others were of no concern to most charities. This remained true at least until the 1950s.

Religious Answers to Poverty

Protestant religious groups led the way in social reform with dual goals: to help the unfortunate and to win newly arrived, supposedly un-Christian immigrants to Protestantism. Such organizations as the New York City Mission Society and the New York Female Moral Reform Society distributed food and clothing along with religious tracts and advocated better housing and sanitation along with moral improvement.[28] The Protestant reform movement led to

> reform schools, mental hospitals, and new kinds of prisons. In cities, experiments with mass education began under private auspices ... by the middle decades ... public educational systems had started to appear ... private philanthropists created YMCAs for young rural migrants to cities, other reformers founded specialized institutions for the deaf and dumb, blind, feeble-minded, and idiots ... [and began] campaigns to alter the treatment of criminals, delinquents, the mentally ill, and school children.[29]

Jewish immigrants brought with them their heritage of charity and mutual aid. Although Sephardic Jews came to America as early as the 1600s, by 1800 there were still only 5,000 Jews in the United States. Although they contributed substantial monies to the Revolution, they were denied voting rights except in South Carolina. By 1790 they could vote in five states, but restrictions remained as late as 1869 (North Carolina) and 1876 (New Hampshire). Excluded, by and large, from American social welfare, they shared their resources with new immigrants through mutual aid societies, especially for education and work.

Catholicism supplied its traditional forms of charity both in the Hispanic Southwest and with the new immigrants from Ireland and Italy in the East. Despite the poverty of Eastern immigrants in the 1850s and 1860s, Catholics began a highly effective program of outdoor relief. Catholic Charities, St. Vincent de Paul Societies (1850), and Little Sisters of the Poor groups (1840) sprang up and, on the model set by Sisters of Charity as early as 1809, began to build orphanages, schools, hospitals, and other facilities for those in need. Katz says,

> Catholic spokesmen distrusted the [Protestant] ... often militantly anti-Catholic bias. They viewed [for example] the Children's Aid Society ... as an agency designed to place Catholic children in Protestant homes.[30]

Especially after 1860, the Catholic Church made heroic efforts to alleviate urban suffering, dependence, and sickness. For example, Catholics probably provided half the money for children's institutions in Buffalo near the end of the 1800s and probably spent more of their incomes on charity than did Protestants.[31] The Catholic Church also gave more attention to needs of African and Native Americans, particularly those of children, than did Protestant charity.

Social Reform Ideals

Coinciding with the great depressions of the 1800s, eminent philanthropists began to issue reports on poverty, blaming it on the poor: their idleness, ignorance, spendthriftiness, hasty marriages; their use of pawnbrokers, lotteries, and houses of prostitution; and their gambling.[32] The most intense criticism was aimed at intemperance (despite the fact that the poor were often paid in liquor): A report in 1817 estimated that of the 15,000 people on charity, seven-eighths were pauperized by liquor;[33] John V. N. Yates, New York's secretary of state, stated in his famous report in 1824 that intemperance was the cause of two-thirds of permanent dependency.

Yates also found that poor laws were inadequate, ripe for misuse, and inhumane, and that a ninth of poor relief funds were used in court suits to deny clients' eligibility rather than for the benefit of the poor. He noted the barbarity of farming out or selling the poor, particularly children, and deplored their treatment and lack of education in the local almshouses. People he called "idiots" and "lunatics," also placed in almshouses, had no adequate care and were often brutally mistreated. Along with other philanthropists, Yates called for poor relief to be turned over to private charities, both to provide more humane treatment and to save money. He also claimed that present laws encouraged beggary and vagrancy, and he called for provision of employment for the able-bodied poor in almshouses, where they could both support themselves and provide for other inmates unable to do so.[34]

Yet the Yates report concluded that only 27 percent of the poor could actually work. The rest were aged, blind, or ill, had mental or physical handicaps (35 percent), or were under the age of fourteen (38 percent). He recommended that every county have a poorhouse with education for children, farms for producing food, and facilities for hard labor for able-bodied inmates. In addition, he asked that no healthy male age eighteen to fifty be given outdoor relief, that street begging be punished, that attempts to return paupers to earlier places of residence be abolished as too costly, and that an excise tax be levied on distilleries to combat drunkenness.[35]

Plans for rehabilitation of the poor and poor relief administration were similar to those in Europe in the 1500s. The 1818 Report by the Society for the Prevention of Pauperism recommended the prevention of beggary and the restriction of saloons, the establishment of employment bureaus and savings banks, mutual aid and life insurance to deal with employment hazards, supplies for home industry, and cooperation among charitable agencies. It also recommended division of cities into districts, with poor relief administered by friendly visitors to give moral support on living without temptation to drink and other vices.[36]

Reform advocate Matthew Carey summed up the prevailing reform viewpoint, saying that

- every man, woman, and grown child able and willing to work should be given employment;
- the poor should be able to support themselves by industry, prudence, and economy, without depending on aid;
- their sufferings arise from their idleness, dissipation, and extravagance; and
- to support the poor through taxes, charitable individuals, or benevolent societies leads to the fostering of their idleness and improvidences, producing or increasing the distress it is intended to relieve.[37]

Unitarian minister Joseph Tuckerman was among the most socially aware reformists. He argued against wages too low

to supply even the bare necessities of life, and the frequent occurrence of periods, even of months together, during which numbers ... find it impossible to procure any employment whatever by which to keep themselves from destitution and suffering.[38]

In 1832, Tuckerman began a "ministry at large" that anticipated almost every aspect of the later charity organization societies and the profession of social work. He found inadequate housing and urban problems instrumental in other problems and noted the radical importance of the "child problem" as a special charity issue:

[H]is most detailed report, written as agent of a State Commission ... advocates ... tests of work for the able-bodied, houses of industry worthy of the name for the more capable, and the refer[ral] of all temporary poverty [relief] to private relief.... [He] was the first American not only to distinguish between pauperism and poverty but to advocate consistently the abolition of outdoor relief, the cooperation of all forces working on charitable problems, the principle of the registration bureau, and personal visitation or friendly visitation.[39]

The Association for Improving the Condition of the Poor

A bitter winter from 1837 to 1838, in the middle of a massive depression, broke the back of private charity, and starvation and death by freezing were once more common. By 1840, there were over thirty relief-giving agencies, and in 1843 the most notable was developed: the Association for Improving the Condition of the Poor (AICP), founded by philanthropist Robert Hartley in New York. His plan was the European model: division of cities into wards with local residents as advisory committees; planned rather than haphazard giving; trained friendly visitors to investigate poverty, distribute relief, and give counsel, encouragement, and advice; and the cooperation of all charities, including reciprocal referral. Casework—personal attention—was believed helpful in itself even without providing relief, and paid staff and volunteers should both be used.

The AICP's friendly visitors—usually women—were told:

> You become an important instrument of good to your suffering fellow-creatures when you aid them to attain this good from resources within themselves ... when [their] sufferings are the result of improvidence, extravagance, idleness, intemperance, or other moral causes which are within their own control; and endeavor ... to awaken their self-respect, to direct their exertions, and to strengthen their capacities for self-support.... Avoid all appearance of harshness, and every manifestation of an obtrusive and censorious spirit.[40]

Less eligibility remained the primary tenet, and the AICP would not, at first, distribute alms, giving only a little money and small quantities of food and clothing.[41] Recipients were required to abstain from alcohol, send young children to school, and apprentice children of a suitable age for vocational training. Though based on Protestant ideals, the AICP did not limit its help to Protestants.

Soon the AICP became involved in social reform, acting against lotteries, Sabbath desecration, gambling dens, and intemperance. As it accumulated data on social conditions, its leaders became convinced that alcoholism, promiscuity, and child neglect came from the filth and overcrowding of the slums rather than personal fault. On this basis, it opened a model tenement and petitioned for the appointment of the first state legislative commission to investigate tenements. Concern for public health and personal hygiene led it to open two dispensaries for the indigent sick (1846), establish a hospital for crippled children, open a public bathhouse, and campaign for a law forbidding the adulteration of milk. For children, it demanded compulsory school attendance laws and was instrumental in passing legislation to provide for the care and instruction of idle truants and for the arrest and detention of vagrant children. In 1851, under AICP auspices, New York opened a juvenile asylum for such children.[42]

AICPs spread throughout the country, and by 1877 they had reversed their stand on almsgiving, which then became their major function. Although the AICP movement provided innumerable services to the poor, perhaps in the long run its most valuable contribution was in the compilation of data: the beginnings of social research about poverty and deviance and the framework for the profession of social work.

Special-Interest Charities

A number of other charities based on special needs or particular populations developed over the decades before and around the Civil War. Among them were the American Female Guardian Society, Homes for the Friendless, the Mission to Children of the Destitute, the Society for the Relief of the Ruptured and Crippled, the Association for the Relief of Respectable Aged and Indigent Females, the Home for Little Wanderers, and the American Temperance Society. Youth agencies and missions became common, the most noted of which was the Young Men's Christian Association, established in America in 1851 to protect young men coming to the city from the dangers of irreligion, intemperance, and immorality. It provided inexpensive living quarters with sanitary facilities, gave relief to poor families in the neighborhood, coordinated local welfare services, and surveyed needs. Jewish centers for both boys and girls were established in the 1840s. The first Young Women's Christian Associations opened in Boston in 1866 and New York in 1867. Boys' Clubs began about 1860 to give boys opportunities to participate in sports and activities in a Christian atmosphere. The Salvation Army, known for its charitable work with the urban poor, was organized by William Booth in 1865; Volunteers of America, providing shelter and some work for indigent male vagrants, was founded later by his son and daughter-in-law.[43]

Ethnic groups also formed mutual aid societies. By the 1830s there were more than a hundred for people of African descent. Chinese immigrants brought mutual aid societies based on family, territories in China, trade and guild associations, and mutual political groups. Immigrant women organized local and national mutual aid clubs such as the Finnish Cooperative Home and the Polish Women's Alliance. The latter was one of the largest women's groups to develop in the late 1800s, with ties both to Polish nationalism and the international feminist movement. Such groups raised money for ethnic churches and lodges, built orphanages and hospitals, formed health insurance and death benefit companies, and gave outdoor relief. Their leaders championed the rights of workers, especially women and children employed in the mines and mills, and supported women's strikes with food and money. The Polish Women's Alliance gave health insurance to women workers' families and death benefits to husbands and orphaned children.[44]

Government Responses

The American Revolution scarcely changed poor laws: Categorization into worthy and unworthy poor, local and relative responsibility, harsh treatment, and the work component remained virtually the same as in colonial times. The four basic treatment methods continued to be:

- Workhouses or poorhouses (almshouses)
- Outdoor relief (alms to people in their own homes)
- Auctioning off the able-bodied
- "Selling" those unable to work to the lowest bidder

However, two new trends began to influence social welfare. First was a gradual shift from local to state power, with states demanding that every county build a poorhouse. Whereas local authority and responsibility had been the keynote of care in colonial times, increasingly the states set policy and standards for poor relief in the 1800s. Second, both private and public charities came to believe that poorhouses were less expensive, more efficient, and more humane than outdoor relief, and institutionalization became a major goal in social welfare.

Institutionalization gathered momentum during the 1820s as increasing restrictions were placed on outdoor relief. In 1821, the general court of Massachusetts ordered Josiah Quincy (later governor) to lead a committee to investigate poverty. The committee concluded that

- Outdoor relief was wasteful, expensive, and destructive to morals.
- Almshouses were most economical because the poor could be forced to work in them.
- The poor should be employed in agricultural work.

- A citizen's board should supervise the almshouses, rather than leaving them to local contractors.
- Intemperance was the most powerful cause of pauperism.

Quincy said,

[t]hat of all modes of providing for the poor, the most wasteful, the most injurious to their morals and destructive to their industrious habits is that of supply in their own families.... [T]he most economical mode is that of Alms Houses; having the character of Work Houses or Houses of Industry, in which work is provided for every degree of ability in the pauper; and thus the able poor made to provide, partially, at least, for their own support; and also to the support, or at least the comfort of the impotent poor.[45]

Such men as Yates, Quincy, Hartley, and others remarked on the inhumanity of auctioning off workers or selling the dependent poor, acknowledging that they were often tortured, forced to live in filth, ignorance, and disease, and literally worked to death. Children, the aged, and the ill were taken in only for the pittance paid by poor relief officials, and the money was used not for their support but as income for the caregivers. Infants given out for care (babyfarming) died early from starvation and neglect. Coll says,

Whatever their shortcomings, almshouses were humanitarian as compared with the irresponsible, cruel systems of auctioning the poor or contracting for their care with persons who were often on the edge of dependency themselves.[46]

However, the real purpose of almshouses (poorhouses) was always to save taxpayers money. Katz says,

Stripped of rhetoric, the goals of much nineteenth-century reform can be reduced to a desire to lower property taxes and to keep the streets safe. Although some reform advocates claimed lofty social goals, by and large prosaic fears of crime and rising expenses for poor relief fueled the moral–social control tradition.[47]

Almshouses were forerunners of penitentiaries, for poverty was considered petty criminality except in times of epidemics or severe depressions.

By 1832, fifty-one of New York's fifty-five counties had poorhouses, and soon they were everywhere. Supervisors were political appointees whose pay came from inmates' work, either on the workfarm or contracted out to private businesses. "Savings" were accrued by holding down the costs of food, clothing, and heat. Supplies for poorhouses were also contracted out privately. A report on county poorhouses says,

In two counties, the committee found that the poorhouses were supplied by contract, the contractor being allowed to profit by all the labor which he could extract from the paupers. In both counties, the contractor was a *superintendent of the poor*; in one, he was also *keeper of the poor house*. In one, the keeper received his compensation from the contractor; and in this case the food supplied was not only insufficient in quantity but consisted partly of tainted meat and fish. The inmates were consequently almost starved. They were also deprived of a sufficiency of fuel and bedding, and suffered severely from the cold. So gross and inhuman was the conduct of the contractor for this poor house that two female inmates (lunatics) were frozen in their cells (or rather sheds) during the last winter, and are now cripples for life.[48]

The committee spoke out against almshouses and for outdoor relief, saying that "half the sum requisite for their maintenance in the poorhouse would often save them from destitution" and that

> Common domestic animals are usually more humanely provided for than the paupers in some of these institutions; where the misfortune of poverty is visited with greater deprivations of comfortable food, lodging, clothing, warmth and ventilation than constitute the usual penalty of crime. The evidence taken by the committee exhibits such a record of filth, nakedness, licentiousness, general bad morals, and disregard of religion ... as well as of gross neglect of the most ordinary comforts and decencies of life, as if published in detail would disgrace the State and shock humanity.[49]

With each year poorhouse conditions deteriorated as overcrowding waxed and supervision waned. People with all kinds of problems were put in them together, without sanitation or privacy: orphans, foundlings, unmarried mothers, prostitutes, and criminals. Even the deserving poor—the aged, ill, or disabled—were confined in poorhouses,

> the lunatic suffering ... in a dark and suffocating cell in summer, and almost freezing in the winter ... a score of children ... poorly fed, poorly clothed, and quite untaught ... the poor idiot ... half-starved and beaten with rods because he is too dull to do his master's bidding ... the aged mother ... lying in perhaps her last sickness, unattended by a physician, and with no one to minister to her wants ... a [mentally ill] woman ... is made to feel the lash in the hands of a brutal underkeeper.[50]

In 1858, the Massachusetts State Charities Board appointed a special committee to investigate public charitable institutions. Its report found that

> [i]n the month of May, 1858, there were in the State almshouses ... a total of 2425; and of these 1176 were little boys and girls, 483 were on the sick list, 200 were insane or demented, and only 70 were able to do any kind of outdoor labor.... The entire proceeds for the labor is only $1.50 per head ... [and] the average weekly support is 83 cents per person.[51]

Poorhouse inmates had little medical care and died quickly, often from malnutrition. According to that same report, in a poorhouse that accommodated 800 people, from May through October, thirty-nine adults and twenty-one children died, and in the previous six months, in the winter, forty-eight adults and forty-six children died. No more than 3 percent of children under the age of one lived.[52] The deaths were of "natural" causes—starvation—rather than contagion. The committee recommended that

- a permanent State Board of Charities be created;
- the board be given the power of examination, the power to transfer inmates from one institution to another, and the power to pardon;
- the local trustee/investigator system be maintained;
- trustees be appointed by the State Board to hold office for five years; and
- harmless, mentally ill inmates be transferred to almshouses, where they could be kept more cheaply.

The committee also recommended that children placed in reform schools be given work or education, placed in foster homes where feasible, given privileges for good behavior, and that their parents be forced to pay for their keep. Finally, they spoke out against the administration of almshouses, saying that

> in fact, it has seemed to us … that the great problem to be resolved in regard to these institutions was not how the unhappy inmates can be made to pay their way, but how the swarms of officials we found in them could be made to earn their own salaries.… [T]he salaries of the overseers and officials absorb so much that no kind of labor, agricultural or mechanical, can be made profitable to the State when carried on in governmental institutions.[53]

One result of such studies was that churches and benevolent associations began to found institutions for specific groups. Another was that states rather than local counties began to take responsibility for certain classes of the distressed or deviant, such as the mentally ill and people with mental retardation.

In the early 1800s, women made up about 30 percent of all poorhouse inmates, rising to 40 percent by the Civil War and 47 percent during the Civil War. Short-term residency for all people was high: in the period between 1853 and 1886, 29 percent were there less than a week and 44 percent less than three weeks. About 20 to 25 percent remained about fifteen months, and the elderly and children remained for years. Until about 1850, whole families were incarcerated. Poorhouses were used more heavily during depressions, especially by young men who remained only until they found work. After 1875, children were no longer placed in poorhouses; the poorhouses became homes for the aged poor and for single mothers with infants. By 1900, 85 percent of the inmates were aged.[54]

Various institutions and organizations grew out of the poorhouse experience, including penitentiaries, the juvenile justice system, schools for people who are deaf or blind, general hospitals, and mental hospitals. It is ironic that the poorhouse idea—care in nursing homes, orphanages, and day care centers—arose again nearly two hundred years later as "privatization" under the Reagan and Bush administrations and the 104th Congress in 1995.

Outdoor Relief

Although institutionalization was intellectually a more popular solution for caring for the distressed and deviant, outdoor relief was more manageable, less expensive, and less likely to cause labor rebellions or the breakup of families. In the South, where *noblesse oblige* still existed, outdoor relief was both common and acceptable for poor white families.[55] Still, in the North, it was increasingly discouraged (only Baltimore prevented it entirely). In New York, for example, between 1830 and 1860 temporary outdoor relief accounted for 34 to 50 percent of all expenditures for relief; in Boston in 1832, while 4,500 people were in almshouses, more than 1,500 families and nearly 400 individuals were on outdoor relief.[56]

As politicians took over poor relief, graft and corruption became rampant. Administration was careless, extravagant, and corrupt. To combat this, stricter rules of eligibility were

Engage, Assess, Intervene, Evaluate

Practice Behavior Example: Critically analyze, monitor, and evaluate interventions.

Critical Thinking Question: Discuss the effectiveness of private philanthropy and public programs in early America. Were public or private interventions successful in ameliorating poverty?

instituted and paid personnel were hired to administer aid. Private charities demanded that poor relief be returned to them, arguing that public charity was degrading to its recipients and that politicians could not be trusted with it.[57]

SOCIAL TREATMENT IN THE 1800s

Medical Care and General Hospitals

The first general hospital, for both the mentally and physically ill, was begun in 1755 by Thomas Bond and Benjamin Franklin, who solicited public monies matched by private funding. In Philadelphia a decade later, Dr. John Morgan established the first medical school at King's College (Columbia University). Marine Hospitals Service, the first federal program in public health, was set up in 1789 to care for seamen. However, the first public hospitals were really the county poorhouses, for every county was required to care for the medically indigent. In rural poorhouses, care, if given at all, depended on the other inmates, which is one reason so many died. However, by the end of the 1700s larger almshouses set aside special medical wards where inmates occasionally saw a doctor. Urban poorhouses became teaching hospitals, where treatment was a combination of old remedies, guesses, and experimental treatment or surgery, for little was really known about the human body. Few healing medicines existed, and smallpox, yellow fever, diphtheria, malaria, tuberculosis, and dysentery resulted in high death rates.

The dangers of childbearing had changed little over history, except that the use of forceps presented new dangers from infection and injury. For poor women, without adequate nutrition and forced to work during their pregnancies, the dangers were worse. Employers gave no time off for pregnancy or recovery from childbirth, and a day's absence from work could mean loss of the job.[58] For the poor,

> only those too far gone to protest would make the trip to a public hospital where inadequate nursing and unsanitary conditions actually diminished one's chance of survival.[59]

Those who could not avoid hospitals often paid for it in the coin of experimentation. This was especially true for women, as male doctors developed an interest in gynecology and reproduction after the discovery of the ovum in 1827. Although poor women and slaves rarely had the kind of "women's problems" that incapacitated upper-class women, their organs could be explored to determine why such problems occurred. If the experiments were successful, the treatment was extended to middle-class clients. By 1830, thirteen states had laws establishing that only "regular" doctors could practice, and in 1848 the American Medical Association was established.

During this era, women were increasingly being constrained to idleness or invalidism. An upper-class wife

> was the social ornament that proved a man's success: her idleness, her delicacy, her childlike ignorance of "reality" gave a man the "class" that money alone could not provide.[60]

A host of mysterious ailments rose, among them sick headaches, nerves, and hysteria; and doctors related them all to women's reproductive organs. "Ladies" were sickly and sickly was feminine: Normal female processes such as puberty, menstruation, pregnancy, childbirth, and menopause (the "death of the woman in the woman") were considered pathological. Possibly the fees paid by wealthy women increased the diagnoses of ill health. Perceptions of beauty for "ladies" also caused such illnesses:

> The fainting and swooning attributed to many nineteenth-century ladies was often caused not by an innate delicacy but by their constrictive underwear. The corset caused more than discomfort, when laced too tightly it could actually dislocate a woman's kidneys, liver, and other organs.[61]

The new gynecological specialists controlled women in many ways. Often female castration (ovariotomy) was prescribed for "taming" unruly women, education was discouraged, and women were told to cultivate their maternal feelings, because "good" women had no sexual feelings.

Medical treatments were often worse than the problem. According to the earliest available records (circa 1912), patients had a fifty–fifty chance of coming away from treatment worse than when it began. Standard therapeutic approaches were bleeding, violent purges, heavy doses of mercury-based drugs, and use of opium. Treatments for "women's ailments" could be bizarre indeed: bleeding by leeches applied to the genitals or breasts to provoke menstruation, and

> in some cases leeches were even applied to the cervix despite the danger of their occasional loss in the uterus.[62]

Men generally controlled the medical field during the decades of the 1800s, but a few women were able to make inroads on their monopoly through alternative medical schools, which graduated women as well as men. Harriet Hunt, denied admission to Harvard twice, went to such a school and practiced medicine and her own brand of psychiatry with mostly women clients. Elizabeth Blackwell (1821–1910) was admitted to Geneva Medical College where, despite being ostracized and harassed, she graduated first in her class in 1849. Denied employment by hospitals, she opened a small dispensary in a slum district. Her patients were mostly women and children.

She was joined in 1858 by her sister Emily (1826–1910), who had graduated from the medical college at Western Reserve in 1854, and Dr. Marie Zakrzewska (1829–1902), a Polish immigrant who had received her medical certificate in Europe in 1856. The younger Blackwell began medical social work for patients in their homes, and she and Zakrzewska raised funds for the dispensary, incorporated in May 1857 as the New York Infirmary for Women and Children:

> Perhaps nobody, nowadays, can understand the willingness and devotion of the women who assisted me in … this primitive little hospital: who were willing to work hard, in and out of hours; who fared extremely plainly and lodged almost to uncomfortableness, yet who felt that a good work was being accomplished for all womankind. And this was true of all—students, nurses, and domestic help…. We had constant applications from students to share in the experience of practice.[63]

During the Civil War, Elizabeth Blackwell organized the Women's Central Association of Relief and the United States Sanitary Commission, selecting and training nurses. Later, she opened the Woman's Medical College within her infirmary. Emily Blackwell took over operation of both medical college and infirmary when her sister retired, and Zakrzewska, after having accepted a professorship of obstetrics in Boston, went on to found the New England Hospital for Women and Children in July 1862.

Mental Hospitals and Psychiatry

The first law for the treatment of the mentally ill was passed in Massachusetts in 1676, ordering selectmen to provide care and protect the community from them. In North Carolina in the early 1700s, church wardens were ordered to confine the "insane" in almshouses. Generally, however, the mentally ill and people with retardation were left with their families. Those who were violent were thought possessed by the devil, and they were often whipped, shackled in the marketplace, or kept in outdoor pens despite the weather. Many were locked in basements, attics, or outhouses, put in straitjackets, chained to walls, or jailed. The first colony-wide mental hospital was built in 1769 in Virginia, but most communities simply sectioned off rooms from other institutions; for example, in 1791 New York General Hospital appropriated its cellar for the mentally ill. In 1821, Bloomingdale Asylum was created in the New York General Hospital, but not until 1870 did Willard, the first state hospital for the mentally ill, open.

Benjamin Rush—statesman, physician, and educator—is considered the father of American psychiatry. Physician-general for Washington's forces in the Revolution, he opened the first free medical clinic in America during the early 1800s. Becoming interested in the treatment of the mentally ill, he studied under Phillippe Pinel of France, who advocated "moral treatment": paternal kindness, guidance, occupational therapy, and humaneness. Rush introduced "moral treatment" in a Pennsylvania hospital in 1783. His methods included cold and hot baths, heated and ventilated rooms, simple tasks for the patients, and training the staff for kindness. He also separated the sexes and separated the violent from quiet patients. His methods certainly surpassed earlier treatment for the mentally ill, yet by today's standards the techniques were inhumane: "scientific" experiments on patients who were perceived as objects and oddities rather than as human beings.

In the early 1800s, private asylums were established on Rush's model. The mentally ill were often treated in their own communities, where they could be visited by friends and family. The asylums became training centers for the new science of psychiatry and charged the public fees to see patients exhibited once or twice a week. People were committed easily and informally, with an application from a relevant other signed by a physician. It was particularly easy for husbands to commit troublesome wives.

While private care progressed, public care remained intolerable. A report from Maryland says,

> As you enter, the crash of bolts and clank of chairs are scarcely distinguishable amid the wild chorus of shrieks and sobs which issue from every department. The passages are narrow, dark, damp, and exude a noxious effluvia. The first common room you examine ... is perhaps for females. Ten of these, with no other clothing than a rag around their waists, are chained to a wall, loathesome and hideous, but when addressed evidently retaining some of the intelligence and much of the feeling which in other days ennobled their nature. In shame or in sorrow one of them perhaps utters a cry; a blow which brings blood to temple and a tear from the eye, and additional chain, a gag, an indecent or contemptuous expression compels silence. If you ask where these unfortunate creatures sleep, you are led to a kennel eight feet square with an unglazed airhole eight inches in diameter [where] ... five persons sleep. The floor is covered and walls bedaubed with filth and excrement; no bedding but wet decayed straw, and the stench so insupportable that you turn away and hasten from the scene.[64]

The push toward state care of the mentally ill began with the Boston Prison Discipline Society's study of conditions in public jails. This led to other investigations, including that by Dorothea Dix (1802–1887). Born in 1802 to a moderately wealthy family, Dix became interested in the mentally ill when she volunteered to teach Sunday School to women in a Cambridge, Massachusetts, jail in 1841. There she found a group of mentally ill women locked in unheated cells and suffering from gross neglect. Bettering the treatment of people with retardation and the mentally ill became her life's work. She visited every almshouse, workhouse, prison, and jail in Massachusetts, finding inmates in bare, filthy, and often unheated cells. Often the straw and chaff from their beds, cemented with their own excrement, was their only covering. Men and women were kept together, nude, with only male attendants. Whippings and beatings were common.

Dix maintained that the state had moral and legal obligations to the mentally ill and called on influential friends Horace Mann and Samuel Gridley Howe to help her mobilize the press and the public. Together they secured passage of a bill to enlarge Worcester Asylum (1843). Following this success, Dix investigated other states, but most were either unwilling or unable to fund adequate care for the mentally ill. She concluded that the federal government must take the responsibility and in 1848 submitted a proposal to Congress to reserve 5 million acres of land, its income to be used for the care of the indigent mentally ill. The Ten-Million-Acre Bill noted that precedents existed in land grants for public schools, schools for people who are deaf, and support for the private railroad industry. It was passed with more than she had hoped for: 10 million acres for the indigent mentally ill and 2.5 million for facilities for indigent people who were deaf and mute.

However, President Franklin Pierce vetoed the bill in 1851, saying that to support the indigent mentally ill would open the doors to federal care for any indigent. He was probably right: For the first time, aside from a few veterans' benefits, comprehensive federal legislation would have provided an incipient welfare state nearly a century before the Social Security Acts of 1935. Although Pierce is portrayed as the villain who delayed social welfare for eighty years, he was acting within the political economy of his time: strict adherence to precedent, prohibition of use of federal lands for big business and special interest groups, and states' rights.

Dix could not muster enough support to resubmit the bill after Pierce's four-year tenure, even though federal land was subsequently disbursed for such worthy causes as the Morrill Act, which established land-grant colleges, and the Homestead Act. Nevertheless, she continued her work for the mentally ill until the end of her life.[65]

> **Dix maintained that the state had moral and legal obligations to the mentally ill.**

Education

Education as a way to individual achievement is a persistent American ideal. After the Revolution, particularly when industrialization produced a glut of workers, education grew from a desirable to a mandatory goal. Because agriculture no longer needed child workers, cities were flooded with them, unwanted, orphaned, abandoned, and neglected. To educate them would serve a multitude of purposes: help them get ahead, keep them from public dependency and crime, and preserve jobs for men whose wages their labor undercut. By 1802, overseers of the poor were required to provide education in Pennsylvania and in Washington, D.C., and had established schools for poor children by 1804. In 1812, New York required schools to stay open three months of the year to qualify for state funds. Although by 1831 education for children of African descent, even those who were free, was outlawed, the push for white education went on. In 1852, Massachusetts was the first state to require school attendance for children ages eight to fourteen, for nine months each year.

The first American educators included Anthony Benizet, who came to Pennsylvania in 1731 to teach both white children and those of African descent and to work for the rights of Native Americans and against racism and slavery, and Benjamin Franklin, who called for public education to combat poverty. However, women were the most instrumental in education, both for children and for themselves. Although high schools required college-educated male teachers, women with high school educations could teach in elementary schools (although they were paid two or three dollars a week compared to men who were paid ten or fifteen).[66] Frances Wright (1795–1852), a Scottish immigrant, traveled the country to gain support for free public schools. She opened an interracial school at Nashoba, Tennessee, but it failed. In 1833–1834, Prudence Crandall opened another school for girls of African descent in Canterbury, Connecticut, but after pupils and teachers were stoned, the well poisoned with excrement, the school doors smashed and broken, and the building set afire, she admitted defeat.[67]

Women leaders in education included Emma Hart Willard (1787–1870), Elizabeth and Emily Blackwell, Catharine Beecher, and Lucretia Mott (1793–1880). Their problems were many. For example, Willard was refused admission to Vermont's Middlebury College but later established the Academy for Female Education and, in 1821, the Troy Female Seminary, which offered a full high school education to girls: solid geometry, philosophy, science, and history. She wrote her own history and geography textbooks and became wealthy from their sale. In 1823, Catharine Beecher, sister of Harriet Beecher Stowe, established a teachers' seminary and unsuccessfully tried to start a chain of teachers' colleges. Oberlin College in Ohio, founded in 1833, was the first to set up a rigorous educational program for both women and men. Its original goal for women was to train them to become ministers' wives or intelligent mothers and homemakers, but it later became a center for antislavery and feminism.

Elizabeth Ann Bayley Seton (Mother Seton, 1774–1821) began parochial education in the United States. A convert to Catholicism after her husband died, she opened a Catholic free school in 1809 at Emmetsburg, Maryland, and later founded St. Joseph's College for Women.[68] In addition to her work in education, she established the American congregation of the Sisters of Charity and what would become the Gray Ladies in hospitals and orphanages. By the time of her death, the Sisters of Charity of St. Vincent de Paul had twenty communities of volunteers. Seton was beatified in 1963 and, in 1975, became the first native-born American to be canonized.

Care of Blind, Deaf, and Developmentally Disabled People

Children who were blind, deaf, or otherwise disabled were usually placed in almshouses. In 1810, Dr. John Stanford, a minister, became interested in teaching them. Later, Dr. Thomas Gallaudet traveled to Europe to learn how to teach deaf people and returned with a teacher, Laurent Clerc, to found America's first institute for people who are deaf in 1817. As state subsidies began, private asylums were built in Massachusetts and Connecticut in 1819, New Hampshire in 1821, Vermont and Maine in 1825, and Kentucky in 1826. Essentially, the treatment used rewards and punishments to develop internal control.

Drs. John Fisher and Samuel Howe traveled to France and Switzerland to observe how children who were blind or mentally retarded were taught. Returning to the United States, they established a facility for the blind: Perkins Institute, which became the Massachusetts School for the Blind (Thomas Perkins donated his mansion for the school). In 1846, Dr. Howe was given state funds to establish the Massachusetts School for Idiotic and Feeble-Minded Youth at Perkins.[69] By the time of the Civil War, schools for people with mental retardation had been established in New York, Pennsylvania, Ohio, and Connecticut, under state, rather than local, auspices.

SOCIAL CONTROL

Juvenile Justice Systems

In the cities, thousands of children of working parents were abandoned, orphaned, or left home alone with latchkeys. They committed petty crimes but were judged as adults, sentenced to adult jails and prisons without hope of probation or pardon, and whipped, mutilated, or hanged for stealing bread or shoes. Their age was not grounds for mercy, for there was no concept of childhood—children were simply small adults. However, the growing sciences of sociology and psychology, the lessened need for their labor because of new factory technologies, and the growing altruism of the times led to new concern for them. In 1823, philanthropists Thomas Eddy and John Griscom established the Society for Reformation of Juvenile Delinquents and, with an initial subscription of $418,000 from private donors, developed the New York City House of Refuge in 1825. It was a prison, factory, and school until 1932, when it merged with the New York State Vocational Institution. Boston opened a House of Reformation in 1836, Philadelphia in 1828. In 1847, a public state reform school for boys opened in Westboro, Massachusetts, and one in Lancaster for girls in 1854. The latter had small group cottages, no fences, and no barred windows. Courts had the right to commit children over the objections of parents on charges of vagrancy or incorrigibility. Not until 1869 were children given legal representation, and the first Juvenile Court was not established until 1899, in both Illinois and Colorado.

The reformatory movement was part of the burgeoning child-saving concern, and it went hand in hand with the development of new forms of penology. Reformatories were based on indeterminate sentencing—at the discretion of either the judge or reformatory administrator—and "organized persuasion" rather than "coercive restraint." The idea was to give the inmate control over his or her progress toward freedom through "industry and good conduct" and to keep delinquents safe from exposure to temptation. Zebulon Brockway recommended a series of graduated reformatory institutions. The first was a House of Reception, where the prison authorities took information on prisoners' ancestry, constitutional "propensities" (toward crime or poverty—part of social Darwinism), and early "socialization" to formulate a plan of treatment. The second was an Industrial Reformatory to train inmates for work; the last was an Intermediate Reformatory, where they worked and learned to live in society.[70]

Frederick Wines was appointed a special commissioner to the second International Penitentiary Congress in Stockholm in 1878 and returned to advise Congress on child legislation. Among his proposals were that children should not be punished but rather educated for work through moral training, religion, and labor; that reformatories should be segregated according to religious preferences; and that the number in each should be small enough for personal attention. The lives of the inmates were to include primary education and be characterized by simplicity in diet, dress, and surroundings. Reformatories were built away from the cities so children would not be distracted from their moral education. Manual labor was favored over intellectual education, to maintain a class bias, and children of African descent were taught to cook, wait on tables, and launder whereas white children were taught agriculture and factory work, maintaining racist bias.

The Elmira Reformatory in New York, for male first offenders ages sixteen to thirty, was founded in 1870 and opened six years later. Intended as a model system to rehabilitate young people through education and training, it was soon so overcrowded that reform took second place to control. With only 500 cells, by 1899 it held 1,500 inmates. Discipline was an integral part of the "treatment" program: Military drill, "training of the will," and long hours of tedious labor were the essence of the reformatory plan.[71] Zebulon Brockway, its director, required inmates to

> observe regular army tactics, drill, and daily dress parade.... By means of the military organization ... the general tone ... changed from that of a convict prison to the tone of a conscript fortress ... a convict community under martial law.[72]

In the 1890s, charges of brutality by Brockway prompted investigation, but Brockway's political influence cleared him and within a year divested the accusing Board of Charities of its authority to monitor prisons.[73]

Beginning with Elmira, reformatories were built across the nation. Despite the reformers' enlightened ideas, the reality was repressive: steel cages, maximum-security cell blocks, inmate feuds, and corporal punishment, often vicious. Many child-savers and reformers, including Homer Folks, began to advocate a "cottage system," where inmates were placed in small group homes on the reformatory grounds, presided over by a "Christian gentleman and lady who ... hold the relation of father and mother toward the youth."[74] These medium-security cottage reformatories gradually replaced the jaillike large reformatories.

Adult Criminals and Penitentiaries

The adult criminal justice system rose from almshouses, jails, and prisons. In 1776, Quakers established the Philadelphia Society for Alleviating the Miseries of Public Prisons, on the principle that the best treatment was isolation and meditation in country settings, away from the temptations of city life. In 1823, they established the first penitentiary for the able-bodied poor, where prisoners—including debtors and vagrants—were confined only at night and worked in silence during the day in prison workshops. Older people were put in solitary cells and deprived of communication, whereas younger offenders were placed in dormitories. All were expected to work, meditate on their deviance, and pray for forgiveness, with the expectation that this would teach them the error of their ways. Penitentiaries were the beginning of the idea that criminals could be rehabilitated by treatment rather than punishment.

Other prisons not based on the penitent model but using some of their ideas were built: one at Auburn, New York, in 1816, followed by Sing Sing in 1825 and San Quentin in California in 1852. The two major systems of the reform era were the Auburn, or "silent," system characterized by enforced silence and group activities, and the Pennsylvania, or Eastern, system of solitary confinement. This latter "star model" had a central rotunda and seven cell blocks starring out like the spokes of a wheel, enabling guards at the center to observe inmate activities in all the cell blocks.[75] Although methods were more humane than the previous floggings, physical abuse, and incarceration without work or recreation, rehabilitation was rare. The inmate power system—a hierarchy among the prisoners based on force—taught criminality much more effectively than prison officials taught rehabilitation. Prisoners were neither penitent nor rehabilitated when released, yet the innovations remained because of the political power of the reformists. Officials also liked the rehabilitative methods for they gave them more power over inmates.[76]

Probation began with Isaac Hopper, a man who informally helped discharged prisoners find homes and jobs. In Boston in 1841, John Augustus agreed to supervise people who had committed minor offenses, to post their bail, and to report back to the court rather than have them put in prison. He used his own money for their rehabilitation, and his method was both more conducive to rehabilitation and much less expensive than prison. Thereafter, the practice grew throughout the criminal and juvenile justice systems. From this time forward, social workers were involved in probation work, surveilling probationers and helping clients stay away from criminal activity.

NONWHITE MINORITIES: EXPENDABLE COMMODITIES IN THE NEW NATION

Galper writes,

> The genesis of racism in the United States is deeply rooted in capitalism.... Racial oppression, as the basis for generating an unpaid labor force, enabled this country to move from a relatively primitive agricultural state of economic development to a more mature, heavily industrialized state. It provided a speedy way to accumulate the surplus that industrialization requires.[77]

Although white workers were also exploited, the effects were greater for people of color: genocide for Native Americans, the destruction of cultures and societies of Africans brought to America, and imperialism in the lands of Hispanics.

Native Americans: A Case of Genocide

Under English rule, Native Americans had the rights of independent sovereign nations, and this *ideal* continued after the Revolution. However, American independence was a catastrophe for Native Americans:

> When France, Spain, and England vied for the North American continent, the tribes could play the Europeans off against one another. After [1783] ... America was dominant and the tribes were losers.[78]

Washington declared a policy of peaceful adjustment, and Supreme Court decisions and the Northwest Ordinance of 1787 upheld the rights of Native Americans to hold their lands. Under the ordinance,

> The utmost good faith shall always be observed towards the Indians; their land and property shall never be taken from them without their consent; and in their property, rights, and liberty, they shall never be invaded or disturbed, unless in justified and lawful wars authorized by Congress; but laws founded in justice and humanity shall from time to time be made, for preventing wrongs being done to them, and for preserving peace and friendship with them.[79]

Indian traders were licensed, and in 1796 government stores opened to give supplies on credit to Native Americans.

However, it was never suggested that Native Americans become citizens, for they were considered "incompatible" as

> pagan, preliterate, and nomadic. [White society] was Christian, literate, and agricultural.... There was no need to go to war to take Indian land when it could be bought for a pittance [after the whites had impoverished the Native Americans]. But the question remained of what to do with the Indians once their land had been acquired.[80]

The Northwest Ordinance applied to Native American lands and included the germ of *manifest destiny*—the belief that white people should own all of North America. It was, in fact, a political declaration of war:

> [T]he Indians shall never be invaded or disturbed, *unless in just and lawful wars authorized by Congress.* [Italics added.][81]

It warned the tribes that if they did not cede their lands by purchase, they would be forced off. All presidents after Adams gave tacit approval, and white people began to invade Native American lands. As Native Americans defended their territories, the invaders retaliated with murders, planned raids, and action by state and federal militias. Their rationalization was that the Native Americans had been British allies. Wars followed treaties followed wars, but no treaty made by whites with Native Americans was ever honored.

The diversity of the Native American nations generally prevented organized resistance against the invaders. Even so, the great Shawnee Chief Tecumseh, along with his prophet brother, Tenskwatawa, began to organize the diverse societies. However, when Tecumseh went south to recruit for his Shawnee Confederacy, Indiana Territory Governor William Henry Harrison marched against his Tippecanoe encampment with 800 militiamen. The Prophet led the defending Shawnees, promising that bullets would not hurt them, and most were slaughtered. That defeat, while Tecumseh was only days from bringing 50,000 men against the United States, ended organized resistance by the Shawnee Confederacy. Tecumseh joined the British in the War of 1812 and was killed in 1813.[82]

Under Presidents Monroe (1824) and Adams (1825), the Bureau of Indian Affairs was organized in the War Department (moving to the Department of Interior in 1849). Pressures to remove Native Americans beyond the Alleghenies increased as twelve states gained enough white population to be admitted to the Union between 1816 and 1848. Treaties were negotiated, honored, and broken as Native Americans were forced out of their lands east of the Mississippi.[83] Andrew Jackson, inaugurated in 1828, encouraged states to defy Supreme Court rulings that protected Native American rights, and their militias wiped out Native American protest or retaliation. Jackson's Indian Removal Act of 1830 authorized $500,000 to aid Native Americans in their "adjustment" to new territories and moved all but a handful of Eastern Native Americans west of the Mississippi along the infamous Trail of Tears.

About half the Creek nation died during the migration and the first years in the West. Oklahoma, already the home of the Five Nations of the Southeast, became "a vast concentration camp."[84] During the next ten years, more than 70,000 people were moved. Among them were the Sauk and the Fox, who made a desperate but doomed stand in Illinois, and the Ottawas, Potawatomies, Wyandots, Shawnees, Kickapoos, Winnebagos, Delawares, Peories, and Miamis. Only a few remnant groups were left, in New York, Florida, Maine, and Virginia, along with a large group of Cherokees in the Great Smoky Mountains who had resisted so strongly they were allowed to remain:

> Forced migration at gunpoint was the lot of some native groups after they had been defeated. Among the famous forced marches was the one imposed on thousands of Cherokees, Creeks, Chicasaws, Choctaws, and Seminoles, who ... were forced to move to the Oklahoma Territory.... Other tribes in the West, such as the Navahos, were rounded up after military engagements and forced to migrate to barren reservations.[85]

The Indian Trade and Intercourse Act (1834) was supposedly intended to strengthen the federal government's aid to Native Americans, but white intrusion continued, ranging from honest treaty making to genocidal forays aimed at exterminating the "Indian menace." The discovery of gold in California in 1849 sent thousands of whites westward, and the Kansas–Nebraska Act of 1854 and the Homestead Act in 1862, which gave 160 acres of unoccupied government land to anyone (not Native American) who lived on it for five years, authorized white settlement of Iowa, Kansas, and Nebraska. Between 1840 and 1860, an estimated 250,000 white settlers migrated across the Plains to the West Coast.[86] In 1869, the transcontinental railroad brought white hunters, who destroyed the bison-based economy of the Plains tribes.

Despite present-day media glamorization of the battles of white settlers against "savage" Native Americans,

> a total of only 362 white settlers and 426 Native Americans died in all the recorded battles between the two groups along wagon train routes. There is only one documented attack by Native Americans on a wagon train, in which there were two dozen casualties for the white settlers.[87]

White settlers, seen as victims of Native Americans and glorified as pioneers, in fact succeeded in massive territorial aggression.

White settlers, seen as victims of Native Americans and glorified as pioneers, in fact succeeded in massive territorial aggression. Their conquest refuted most religious and political doctrines of equality and personal freedom. Ironically, some of the democratic traditions of the United States probably arose from Native American cultures; for example, the statement that "all men are created equal, that they are endowed by their creator with certain inalienable rights" comes from the laws of the League of the Iroquois. These laws were also the model for state–federal relations, where the sovereignty of each nation balanced with that of the League; the processes for referendum and recall; and suffrage for both men and women.

The conquest reinforced two major doctrines: that of profit and that "outsiders," or the "different in beliefs," are less than human. Though legitimated in the names of progress and Christianization, it was genocide: the trickery and deceit with which the conquest began; the murder and enslavement of Native American peoples; their removal person by person and nation by nation until the continent "belonged" to the white government; attempts to wipe out Native American culture by taking away their children, placing them on reservations, and denying them such essentials as food, clothing, and shelter; and the savage decimation of their remaining population by war and murder. It is a tribute to the persistence of their cultures and religious beliefs that they still survive.

Chinese in America

Chinese were among the first immigrants to North America after its rediscovery in 1492, when Spanish explorers moving up the coast toward Oregon before the 1600s hired them to build ships. However, few Chinese came to settle permanently because of strong family ties and religious needs to tend the spirits of their ancestors in their homelands. In fact, emigration from China was a capital offense. China had remained a self-sufficient feudal economy from the onset of the dynasties in 221 B.C.E. and did not take up world trade until European invasions in the middle 1800s. European demands caught China in its last dynasty (which lasted until 1917) with an emperor more interested in building monuments than in defense. In 1840, the British, Spanish, and Portuguese waged the first Opium War against China, opening it for trade. The second Opium War, from 1856 to 1860, ended China's unity and self-sufficiency.

Although Americans did not make war on China, they took advantage of the new China trade, including the trade in men. "Shanghaiing" became common, and the Portuguese based in Macao were the biggest traders in kidnapped Chinese. This "pig trade" sold Chinese men to Americans for the price of passage to work in mines and on railroads. Though nominally free, the Chinese began life in America in debt slavery to those who bought their passage. They were shipped in conditions similar to those of African slaves: chained, in 18-inch spaces, with minimal food, water, and health care. A high death rate during passage was common.[88]

According to Feagin, *systemic racism* is one of the foundations of American society, reinforced and legitimated to ensure white supremacy.[89] Though applied originally to people of African descent, systemic racism and white supremacy defined all non-Caucasians as inferior, especially when competition for work was at stake. When white enterprise began to import Chinese laborers—some two hundred thousand between 1848 and 1882—to work on the railroads, in the mines, and in personal service jobs, antiblack racism was well in place. As white people moved West, this racism expanded to include any people of color. The Chinese were "Africanized" and seen as another threat to white racial purity.[90] This led to immigration laws banning "undesirable" Chinese immigrants in 1882 and

> between 1878 and 1923 a series of federal court cases decided that the following Americans were *not* white and thus were ineligible for citizenship: Chinese Americans, native Hawaiians, those half-Asian, those half-Indian, Burmese Americans, Japanese Americans.[91]

The Contributions of People of African Descent

As the worldwide demand for cotton became insatiable, the price of slaves increased until it became cheaper to breed than to buy them. There were premiums on good breeders, and female slaves, because they could reproduce, became more valuable than male slaves. A breeding woman was worth one-sixth to one-fourth more than one who did not breed.[92] Infants could be sold away like calves from cows, and white men, who had free access to slave women, sold their own children. Virginia, which did not depend on the cotton industry, became a primary slave-raising state and Washington, D.C., was among the top slave markets until the 1850s.

> The price of a good slave for the fields increased from $300 in 1820 to over $1000 in 1860 ... [and] the slave population grew from about a million and a half to nearly 4 million during this period.[93]

The Constitution authorized slavery by saying that a person of African descent was three-fifths of a white for representation purposes, requiring the return of fugitive slaves to their masters, and delaying the ban on slave trading until 1808, although slave trading continued into the 1850s. Though the slave trade was officially banned in 1808, the last slave ship landed at Mobile Bay, Alabama, in 1859 (the same year that John Brown attacked Harper's Ferry, where thirteen white men and men of African descent were captured and hanged by Robert E. Lee). Nor were free African Americans in the North considered people: They could not vote except in a very few cases where they owned property, their children could not be educated in schools with white children, and they were segregated in housing, employment, transportation, and medical services. Employment was mostly limited to domestic service at extremely low pay for women, with little work available for men.

Slave Owner and Cotton Culture

Fewer than one in four Southern families owned slaves, and nearly half the slaves lived on small farms worked by twenty or fewer. However, about seven thousand families owned fifty or more slaves, and these were the families who set the goals of the South. Slaves on small farms were sold away less often than were those of larger plantations, and those in the coastal South—Virginia, Maryland, Georgia, and the Carolinas—worked under better conditions than did those in Alabama, Mississippi, Arkansas, Texas, and Louisiana.[94]

The *cotton culture* existed from the Carolinas and Georgia into the Mississippi Valley, and every state had its own *slave code*. Slaves could not assemble in groups of more than five or so when away from their plantations and could not leave plantations without passes. Even free African Americans had to carry passports to prove their status. At first, religion was not allowed, but after a time, slaves were allowed to believe in the parts of the Christian religion that taught unquestioning obedience to their masters in return for happiness in heaven. Preachers could preach only what they were told, and religious meetings had to be witnessed by white people. Every white person had police power over every person of African descent, free or slave:

> [T]he slave, if slavery were to be successful, had to believe he was a slave.... Each slave was taught ... that he was totally helpless and that his master was absolutely powerful ... that he was inferior to the meanest white man and that he had to obey every white man without thinking, without questioning. Finally, if these lessons were learned, the slave looked at himself through the eyes of his master and accepted the values of the master.[95]

Although some slave owners earned a reputation for kindness and others for cruelty, most fell in between, taking some care of slaves as property but willing to resort to cruel punishments:

> Masters who were psychotic [or] sadistic ... devised ingenious methods of punishment. And "kind" masters whipped the skin off slaves' backs and washed them down with brine.[96]

Plantation owners' wives were an integral part of slave life. They supervised work in the home, sewed clothes for slaves, and doctored them. These white women often treated the female slaves and their children with vicious cruelty if they knew of or suspected their husbands' sexual involvement with the slaves. The census of 1860 testified to the frequency at which masters exercised their sexual "privileges" on slave women: By that year there were nearly 600,000 children of mixed racial background.[97] Husbands of women slaves could take no action against white rapists on pain of death. According to Jacobs,

> The rape of black women was an attack on black men as well as on black women, who were warned not to call on their men for protection unless they wanted to see them lynched and raped. Rape was used to reinforce a sense of powerlessness in black men.[98]

Rape was one tool in the dehumanization of people of African descent, justifying their use as commodities. Deborah Gray White says that

> Slave owners controlled Black women's labor and commodities.... [and their] bodies as units of capital.... Efforts to control Black women's sexuality were tied directly to slave owners' efforts to increase the number of children their female slaves produced.[99]

As Feagin reminds us, "Under the American system of racism, the children resulting from the coerced sexual relation were automatically classified as black, even though they had substantial European ancestry ... "[100] and could be, and usually were, sold as slaves. Collins says that

> While the sexual and racial dimensions of being treated like an animal are important, the economic foundation underlying this treatment is critical. Under capitalist class relations, animals can be worked, sold, killed, and consumed, all for profit....[101]

She further states that exhibiting black women on the auction block was not a "benign intellectual exercise," but defended real material and political interests. Beyond the plantation and personal, such objectification meant profit for the Eurocentric world.

Slave Families

Slaves were encouraged to marry and have families and could often pick their own mates because their owners felt that families and love relationships stabilized the slaves and kept them from running away. Monogamy was enforced, with adultery a major offense. If slaves married outside their plantations, the man was generally given a pass to visit on Wednesday and Saturday nights and all day Sunday. Children took their fathers' names and adoptions were permitted. However, family life depended on the grace of the master, and there was the constant threat of selling away children or spouses. In fact, rebellions often occurred because of this, and often whole families escaped together to avoid it.

Children usually were cared for in a communal arrangement, mothered and fathered by anyone who was near, because of the constant labor demanded of both men and women. Old women tended them in "children's houses," with older children helping until the age of eight or so, when they were given shoes and clothing other than gunny sacks and were set to work:

> Feeding slave children out of a common pot as though they were animals and ignoring their desire for modesty ... was part of the attempt to condition slave children to view themselves as less human than whites and perhaps not human at all.[102]

There was sexual equality among men and women slaves, with both taking over the chores of the family after their work for the master was completed. Food was issued once a week, clothes twice a year.

Although slave owners often lightened the work of pregnant women, the cumulative effect of malnutrition, hard work, and many babies was devastating. There were many miscarriages, babies were often sickly, and infant mortality was high. Some say that mothers often smothered their children to keep them from slavery, but more recent evidence indicates that the term *smothering* was used to record unexplained deaths. The incidence and timing of the deaths indicates a striking resemblance to sudden infant death syndrome, a reflection of extreme poverty, low birth weights, and poor post- and prenatal care. After emancipation, when women resisted gang labor and took lighter tasks through their pregnancies, the rate of "smothered infants" was only one-fifth of that before the Civil War.[103]

A key factor in slave families, and one which many feel impacts on the lives of African Americans today, was the practice of extended kinship. Schiele says that, in traditional Africa, people's identity was embedded in their social groups, and this fostered an extended concept and practice of family called "fictive kinship."[104] As the Triangular Trade decimated African societies, American slaves transferred these concepts to include their slave communities as extended families. Collins notes that

> one way that many resisted the dehumanizing effects of slavery was by re-creating African notions of "blood" whereby enslaved Africans drew upon notions of family to redefine themselves as part of a Black community consisting of their enslaved "brothers" and "sisters."[105]

According to many African-American scholars, these kinship bonds, forged in slave families, remain the societal and spiritual foundations of African-American lives today.[106]

The Work of Slavery

The plantation was a combination factory, village, and police precinct, complete with totalitarian regimentation. On large farms, work was organized either by tasks or by gangs. On the task system, when a job was done the slaves had free time for themselves, for gardening and the like. In the gang systems, field hands were worked by overseers paid for immediate production and "drivers" with whips given rewards for fast pace.[107] There were rewards for hard work, such as bonuses, prizes, and the opportunity for occupational mobility into skilled trades or manager positions. This was effective to the extent that, at the end of the Civil War, 83 percent of mechanics and artisans in the South were people of African descent.[108]

Seven out of eight slaves were field workers. Women were expected to work as hard as men in the fields and then do women's work in the slave quarters. Their third job was to reproduce. Davis says,

> Where work was concerned, strength and productivity under threat of the whip outweighed considerations of sex. In this sense, the oppression of women was identical to the oppression of men.... Expediency governed the slaveholder's posture toward female slaves. When it was profitable to exploit them as if they were men, they were regarded, in effect, as genderless; but when they could be exploited, punished, and repressed in ways suited only for women, they were locked into their exclusively female roles.[109]

Slave women were also used for hauling ore in Southern mines. House slaves in the South were treated as nonexistent, often sleeping in the same rooms as their masters. Urban slaves could be hired out a year at a time and had more freedom than did plantation slaves.

Benefits of the work of slavery—Feagin calls it "plantation capitalism"—depended on slave-grown cotton and textiles made from it. Cotton accounted for about half of all exports from the United States from the early 1700s to the mid-1800s, and the textiles industry powered America's commercial and industrial revolutions. "Cotton-related activities were perhaps the most important source of economic expansion in the United States before the Civil War, and most of the cotton was grown by enslaved Black Americans."[110]

Moreover, the slave trade and trade in slave-produced products financed large-scale investments in new technologies of industrial production across western Europe, and were a main cause of wealth and luxury in France and England:

> These investments also spurred a rapid buildup of the financial and insurance industries.... It seems unlikely that British and other European economic development would have occurred when it did without the very substantial capital generated by the slavery system.[111]

In fact, slave labor was the backbone of the Industrial Revolution in both Europe and America, financing new technologies and circulating through banks and lending enterprises, and changing work, family, and community systems forever.

Slave Rebellions

Slavery did not continue without resistance, which included nonviolent resistance, slowed working pace, feigned illness, and strikes. Violent resistance and rebellion were constant fears among plantation families, and at least 250 slave revolts were recorded. Southern families feared their slaves would copy the revolt in Haiti in 1791, where more than 100,000 of its half-million slaves joined with a voodoo priest named Boukman and for three weeks ravaged the white plantations:

> In an instant ... 1200 coffee and 200 sugar plantations were in flames; the buildings, the machinery, the farmhouses, were reduced to ashes; and the unfortunate proprietors were hunted down, murdered, or thrown into the flames.[112]

Toussaint L'Ouverture took over leadership as governor of Haiti in 1801 but, betrayed by Napoleon on a state visit to France, he died in prison. His successor, Jean-Jacques Dessalines, continued to fight so persistently that in 1803 Napoleon gave up his dream of making Haiti the foothold of his western empire and ceded the Louisiana Territory to America for four cents an acre.

Slave rebellions in the South followed. In the early 1800s, Gabriel Prosser gathered weapons and a force of a thousand slaves to march on Richmond. When heavy rains cut them off from the city, they were captured and at least thirty-five, including Prosser, were hanged. In 1811, near New Orleans, several hundred slaves attacked whites on plantations. Dozens were killed and the leaders executed, their heads displayed along the route to New Orleans. An 1822 conspiracy of several thousand armed slaves, led by Denmark Vesey against Charleston, South Carolina, was betrayed, and Vesey and thirty-six others were hanged.[113] The most famous rebellion was led by Nat Turner in 1831. It spread throughout Virginia and North Carolina, and entire white families died on their plantations. The Turner rebellion ended when the militia was called out, and although Turner escaped, he was executed several months later.

Harriet Tubman (1820?–1913) led another kind of resistance. Called the Moses of Her People, she escaped slavery in 1849, then returned time after time to lead others—more than 300—to freedom. Rewards for her capture reached $40,000. During the Civil War she served as scout, spy, and nurse for the Union forces in South Carolina, and after emancipation she settled in Auburn, New York, taking orphans and old people into her home. The Harriet Tubman Home for Indigent Aged Negroes was supported by former abolitionists and the citizens of Auburn. When she applied for a federal pension for her war service, she was awarded $20.00 per month (half that of white pensioners).

Free People of African Descent

From the time of the Revolution, abolitionists of both races worked together. One such movement was the American Colonization Society (1817), which sought to settle freed slaves in Liberia. The American Anti-Slavery Society, formed in 1833 under the leadership of William Lloyd Garrison and Arthur Lewis Tappan, tried to educate free African Americans to gain U.S. citizenship. The most famous abolitionist was Frederick Douglass, a powerful orator and ex-slave, who spoke out for both abolition and women's rights.

In 1826, John Russwurm became the first man of African descent in America to graduate from college, at Bowdoin, Maine and joined with Samuel E. Cornish to found the first newspaper for people of African descent, *Freedom's Journal*, in 1827. Their first national convention, chaired by Richard Allen, was held in 1830. In 1838, David Ruggles founded the first magazine for people of African descent, the *Mirror of Liberty*. Two colleges for men of African descent opened: Lincoln University in Pennsylvania and Wilberforce University in Ohio, founded by the African Methodist Episcopal Church. In 1855, John Mercer Langston became the first elected public official of African descent, a township clerk in Ohio.

The Missouri Compromise of 1829 divided the Louisiana Purchase along the Mason–Dixon line, ensuring that Southern states could continue slavery: Maine was admitted a free state and Missouri a slave state. In 1850, a new compromise admitted California as a free state, created two new territories in New Mexico, and added a drastic fugitive slave law to soothe Southern plantation owners. It also prohibited slave trade in Washington, D.C. However, the compromises began to give way: In 1857, a Southern-dominated Supreme Court handed down the *Dred Scott* decision, claiming that slaves were personal property, to be protected for their owners. It also declared the

Practice Behavior Example: Understand the forms and mechanisms of oppression and discrimination.

Critical Thinking Question: Discuss the different mechanism used to oppress people of color in nineteenth-century America.

Missouri Compromise unconstitutional because the federal government did not have the power to forbid slavery in any territory (the states' rights issue).

Before the Civil War, there were half a million free people of African descent in the United States (11 percent of the total population), half in the South. Many were well-to-do. They had churches, literary debating societies, fraternal organizations, and societies for mutual aid. Among the freed slaves, indigent or helpless people were supported by relatives, friends, neighbors, and relief associations, and free African Americans established schools and orphanages to aid children of African descent.[114]

Hispanic Americans

Hispanic Americans have a history divergent from that of Native Americans because, having been conquered by Spain, they became Spanish citizens. Their settlement of the Southwest dates from about 1530, when land grants were given to them by the Spanish crown. Mexico won independence from Spain in 1821, and Anglo-Americans almost immediately began infiltrating, at first by trying to purchase Mexico's northern border along the Rio Grande. There, several thousand Hispanics had a self-sufficient economy, with almost no poverty because the church and landowners found work for the indigent.

An estimated 4,000 white settlers were in the Texas area in 1821, but by the 1830s there were 20,000 Anglo immigrants.[115] In 1845, the United States simply annexed Texas, precipitating the Mexican War of 1846. In 1848, the Mexican government was forced to cede Texas for $15 million under the Treaty of Guadalupe Hidalgo, giving the United States most of northwest Mexico, including California where, before the Gold Rush, there were 7,500 Hispanic settlers. The Treaty guaranteed protection for Mexican land rights, along with personal property rights and religious freedom. However, white settlers moving into the Southwest ignored the guarantees. Anglo settlers sued against Spanish land grants and typically won in Anglo courts, for many Hispanics had lost evidences of title and had little money to fight the court decrees. The 1853 Gadsden Purchase gave white settlers even more Mexican land. Taxes were used to disinherit the Hispanics: The United States levied property tax rates at levels only the largest of Spanish landholders could afford, forcing small Hispanic entrepreneurs off their land and into low-wage labor.[116] Violence was common: In the 1850s, 2,000 white miners attacked Mexicans in Sonora, killing dozens and wiping out a community.

Lawlessness against Mexicans had a semiofficial status with the Texas Rangers, a kind of vigilante force created to terrorize and subordinate Mexicans. Numerous lynchings were recorded, and white settlers often became rich with the help of the Texas Rangers. An estimated 2.0 million acres of private land and 1.7 million of communal land were lost between 1854 and 1930 in New Mexico alone. A study in Texas found that from 1850 to 1860, one-third of Hispanic Americans were ranch- and farmowners, one-third skilled artisans or professionals, and one-third manual laborers. However, by 1900 the number of ranch- and farmowners had dropped to 16 percent, and two-thirds of the Mexican population had become manual laborers.[117]

As with Native American resistance, there are persistent myths about heroic battles of white settlers against Hispanics. The most popular is the myth of the Alamo, where 180 principled, presumably native-born Texans fought against Mexican bandits led by Santa Ana. However, the Mexican troops were a legal army and most of the "defenders" of the Alamo were ne'er-do-well newcomers and adventurers, brawlers such as James Bowie, William Travis, and Davy Crockett. The Alamo, in addition, was one of the best fortified sites in the West, with twice as many cannons, better rifles, and better training than the Mexican forces had. Many whites at the Alamo chose to surrender rather than be killed, and the Hispanics were winning until General Sam Houston made a surprise attack from the north, wiping out most of the Mexican army.

The same myths persist about Mexican bandits attacking white settlers. However, these fighters were actually guerrillas resisting the takeover of Mexican land and wealth. There were numerous raids during the 1830s and 1840s, and Juan Cortina, a Mexican hero, fought for the poor in the Texas borderlands, clashing with local militia and Texas Rangers in the 1850s and 1860s. Far from being an uneducated and uncouth criminal, he issued formal statements of grievances detailing the stealing of lands and the bias of Texan legal systems. Colonel Robert E. Lee was sent to Texas to put down Cortina, but succeeded only in limiting his activities.

By the 1880s, Hispanic manual labor was being used extensively on the railroad, and by 1900 American capital—railroads, agribusiness, and the federal government—owned the Southwest. In 1902, the National Reclamation Act brought irrigation to Southwest farms, and the Homestead Act was extended into that area. White farming population was insufficient to meet labor demands, and Mexican workers became the agrarian labor class.

THE WOMEN'S MOVEMENT IN THE 1800s

Although the image of the strong and hardy pioneer woman persisted into the 1800s, new theories of human behavior placed women in a sphere that limited them to home, family, and economic control by husbands. "Feminine traits" became desirable and necessary for middle-class women. Poor women, of course, were not included in this image; they continued to labor in domestic and factory work and often took in sewing or laundry or kept boarders in their homes for extra money.

The two major issues of this era were abolition and suffrage. Suffragists recognized the economic ties among slavery in the South, economic exploitation of workers in the North, and the suppression of women. Although women were not owned in the sense that slaves were, they were

> almost treated like Negro slaves, inside and outside the home. Both were expected to behave with deference and obedience towards owner or husband; both did not exist officially under the law; both had few rights and little education; both found it difficult to run away; both worked for their masters without pay; both had to breed on command and to nurse the results.[118]

Women could not vote; could not practice law, theology, or medicine; could not sign wills or contracts without their husbands' consent; and could not serve on juries. All wages they earned belonged to their husbands, as did real estate and other property; laws of divorce favored the husband and husbands were awarded custody of children.

Among the first to note the connections between abolition and women's rights were Sarah and Angelina Grimke. The daughters of an aristocratic

Women could not vote; could not practice law, theology, or medicine; could not sign wills or contracts without their husbands' consent; and could not serve on juries.

slave-holding family in the South, Sarah joined the Quakers and moved to Philadelphia in 1822, and Angelina joined her seven years later. They became active abolitionists, and Angelina became the first "respectable" American woman to speak in public, presenting the Massachusetts legislature with a petition signed by 20,000 women demanding an end to slavery. Her pamphlets were burned in the South, and both sisters were condemned by the clergy, who saw their public lobbying as an un-Christian assault on the social order and the sanctity of home and family.[119] (The 1837 pastoral letter of the Congregationist Churches, using the New Testament as a base, implied that feminists were antiscripturalists whom God would punish with the loss of ability to have children, degeneracy, and ruin for "taking the place of men.")

Other women also were active in the movement. Lucy Stone was an ardent feminist who worked with William Lloyd Garrison against slavery. She married Henry Blackwell (brother of Drs. Emily and Elizabeth), and both she and her husband agreed that she would be called by her maiden name. (Others who adopted the style were called "Lucy Stoners.") Ernestine Potowski Rose (1810–1892), a Polish immigrant in 1836, was a fearless abolitionist, speaking against slavery even in the South. She campaigned for property rights for women, women's suffrage, and easier divorce laws.[120] Lucretia Mott (1793–1880), a teacher and social reformer, helped to organize the Philadelphia Anti-Slavery Society. She and her husband, James, gave up a profitable cotton business because it was the product of slavery. In 1840, she attended the World Anti-Slavery Convention but was refused seating as a delegate because she was a woman. At the convention she met Elizabeth Cady Stanton, and the Motts and Stantons became close friends.

Elizabeth Cady Stanton married abolitionist Henry B. Stanton over her father's objections and became an ardent worker for women's suffrage. Along with Susan B. Anthony and others, including Frederick Douglass, she organized the Seneca Convention on women's issues in 1848, where the audience of 300 included forty men (but no people of color). The convention called for equal educational rights; fairer laws for marriage, divorce, and property ownership; the end of a double moral standard; the right to write, speak, and teach on a basis equal with men; and equal participation in the trades, professions, and commerce. All the resolutions passed immediately except Cady Stanton's demand for women's suffrage. Even her husband opposed it, but Frederick Douglass lectured in its favor and the resolution survived a close vote on the floor.[121]

Well before the Seneca Falls Convention, Susan B. Anthony (1820–1906) had joined Cady Stanton in working for women's suffrage. Cady Stanton did the theoretical work, including the ideals and language of the campaign for women's rights, and Anthony built the organizational machinery. The daughter of a prosperous mill owner, Cady Stanton took a job teaching when her father suffered reverses in his business. Astonished at the low pay she received as a teacher, she became a radical feminist. She arranged state and regional women's conventions, organized a petition campaign for women's property laws that passed in 1860, and became a leader for Garrison's American Anti-Slavery Society.

Sojourner Truth, born as a slave around 1797, was as concerned about women's rights as with abolition. All twelve of her brothers and sisters and two of her children were sold before her eyes. One of her first acts when freed by New York's emancipation law (1827) was to sue, successfully, for the return of a son who had been sold away from her. She felt she had been touched by

God to work for abolition and women's rights and became an evangelist and an abolitionist, walking and preaching throughout New York and Connecticut and later Ohio, Indiana, Missouri, and Kansas. She became known as a moving speaker on both topics, rivaling in eloquence Frederick Douglass, with whom she often shared the speaker's platform.

Between the Seneca Falls Convention and the beginning of the Civil War, there were some changes in the status of women. In 1848, New York enacted a law guaranteeing that women could keep the property they had before marriage, along with new bequests and gifts. Pennsylvania, California, and Wisconsin soon followed suit. (However, the intention was not completely altruistic—it protected the land of wealthy property owners who resented seeing land and riches pass out of the family through marriage.) In 1860, another bill in New York granted married women rights to wages, allowed wives to make contracts without the husband's approval if he were incompetent, and guaranteed inheritance rights after a husband's death. In addition, the Homestead Acts of 1860 and 1890 gave free land to both men and women: Husbands and wives together were given 640 acres, whereas single men and women received only half that amount.

The common interests between women and slaves bound them together until after the Civil War, when the Fourteenth Amendment specifically gave the right to vote to men, including men of African descent, but not to women. Even faithful supporters of women's rights such as Horace Greeley and Wendell Phillips would not support women's protests against the amendments. Frederick Douglass told women to be patient, for this was the Negro's hour, and race, not sex, was the issue because people of African descent were still being killed. The women's movement split bitterly: Lucy Stone and Julia Ward Howe led the American Women Suffrage Association, supporting freedmen's suffrage and seeking to work within the system and avoid "peripheral" women's issues. Cady Stanton and Anthony formed the more radical National Women's Suffrage Association and aligned themselves with all kinds of women's causes: the double standard in marriage, free love, labor unions, and the civil rights of prostitutes.[122] Anthony approached the issue in very racist terms, suggesting a trade-off in suffrage: educational but not sexual qualifications for voting. "Educated suffrage" meant gaining the votes of middle-class educated white women for politicians and writing off those of lower-class people of African descent and immigrants.

Diversity in Practice

Practice Behavior Example: Recognize the extent to which a culture's structures and values may oppress, marginalize, alienate, or create or enhance privilege and power.

Critical Thinking Question: Why were upper-class women prominent in the reform movements of the nineteenth century?

The National Suffrage movement probably had no more than ten thousand members at any one time and faced its greatest opposition in the South, whose people remembered suffragists as abolitionists. Western states very often offered state suffrage to women, for women were a scarce commodity, often outnumbered by men by twenty to one. Wyoming, Utah, Colorado, and Idaho all granted women's suffrage.

CONCLUSION: WORKING TOWARD FREEDOM

Between the Revolutionary and Civil wars, the United States fomented with social reform and social change. The economy changed from colonial agrarian to massive industrialization, and because of the demand for cotton, America took its place in international trade. On both international and continental fronts, the United States became a power to reckon with: Both France and Spain gave up their rights to American territories; England ceded rights to the sea while America sprawled and brawled across the continent, taking by force what it could not buy or gain by trickery. The structure of families changed, from extended to nuclear, isolated, and alienated. Fortunes were made in both the North and the South on the exploitation of workers—immigrants, freedpersons, and slaves—who were helpless against the political, economic, and social control of the wealthy elite.

In social welfare, Protestant ideas of poverty and the morality of work continued to direct the treatment of the distressed and deviant. Both private charity and public agencies called for institutionalization of those who could not care for themselves. This created almshouse and poorhouse conditions so horrendous that, with the growing social awareness of the century, new treatment was devised for special groups, such as the mentally ill, children, those who were blind or deaf, those with mental retardation or other disabilities, and juvenile and adult offenders. New methods of treatment and rehabilitation grew, some succeeding while others failed.

Finally, in the major social movements of the century, white women of all economic classes and all people of the laboring classes (slave or free) were the driving forces for change. Their formidable foes were the white male elite, bolstered by church and government and determined to maintain the status quo of power and profit—the battle was slow. Incremental changes were inevitable, but even such a revolutionary change as the Civil War brought few increments in practice. The equality won for slaves, if only in the abstract, was not mirrored in new rights for women, Native Americans, Hispanics, or Asians. Those freedoms, and true freedom for African Americans, were to be delayed for decades more.

The following questions will test your knowledge and understanding of the content found within this chapter. For additional assessment, including licensing-exam type questions on applying chapter content to practice behaviors, visit **MySearchLab**.

1. Manifest destiny described which belief?
   a. All citizens should have rights to adequate health care.
   b. Native Americans should never be invaded or disturbed.
   c. White people should own all of North America.
   d. No citizen should be without proper shelter, food or clothing.

2. The term used to record unexplained deaths of children was:
   a. infanticide
   b. smothering
   c. dousing
   d. Sudden Death Syndrome

3. Which of the following was a common practice during the American Revolution?
   a. Selling people who were unable to work to the lowest bidder.
   b. Exiling the dependent poor to other towns that would take care of them.
   c. Falsely imprisoning those in poverty in order to get them off of the streets.
   d. Snuffing out the poor by donating poisoned food to them.

4. Poorhouse inmates usually died from:
   a. disease
   b. malnutrition
   c. lack of medical care
   d. severe abuse

5. During the movement for institutionalization, you worked on a committee with Josiah Quincy to improve poverty. Which of the following actions would you have recommended?
   a. Increase outdoor relief efforts because they are the most cost-effective solution.
   b. Utilize the poor for agricultural work.
   c. Shut down almshouses because they are too expensive to maintain.
   d. Require religious groups to supervise almshouses in order to protect the poor from being abused and mistreated.

6. During the early American Revolution era, you are advising a juvenile who has just committed a petty crime. What warning would you give him?
   a. If found guilty, he will go to an adult prison and suffer the same punishment an adult would receive (i.e., hanging or mutilation).
   b. He will be tried as an adult only if he is over 18.
   c. He will be let free, but his parents will pay the cost of his crime by being sentenced to prison.
   d. He has a right to legal representation and should seek counsel.

7. The father of American Psychiatry, Benjamin Rush, advocated moral treatment. Describe the methods he used with patients.

Reinforce what you learned in this chapter by studying videos, cases, documents, and more available at **www.MySearchLab.com.**

Watch and Review

Watch these Videos

Women in the Workplace 1904

The Great Migration

Ellis Island Immigrants 1903

Read and Review

Read these Cases/Documents

Helen Hunt Jackson, from A Century of Dishonor

Susan B. Anthony, The "New Departure" for Women (1873)

Assess Your Knowledge

Go to **MySearchLab** to test your knowledge of key topics in this chapter with topic-specific quizzes. Conclude your assessment by completing the chapter exam.

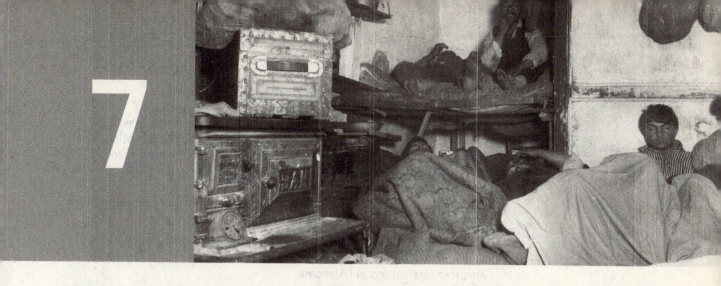

The American Welfare State Begins

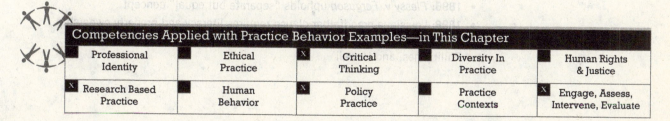

Competencies Applied with Practice Behavior Examples—in This Chapter				
■ Professional Identity	■ Ethical Practice	X Critical Thinking	■ Diversity In Practice	■ Human Rights & Justice
X Research Based Practice	■ Human Behavior	X Policy Practice	■ Practice Contexts	X Engage, Assess, Intervene, Evaluate

Times and Events

- **1864:** Homestead Act
- **1865:** Civil War ends; Freedman's Bureau established as first U.S. welfare agency; thirteenth amendment passed; Union military and Naval national veterans' asylums established; Lincoln assassinated and Johnson becomes President; last slaves emancipated on June 19th, or "Juneteenth"; Mississippi established first system of Black Codes
- **1866:** Veterans' pensions established; Civil Rights Act of 1866 gives full citizenship and civil rights to African Americans
- **1867:** United States purchases Alaska from Russia (Seward's Folly); Ku Klux Klan founded in Tennessee; Medicine Lodge Treaty establishes Native American reservations in Oklahoma
- **1868:** Fourteenth amendment grants citizenship to African Americans; Custer kills Cheyenne in Washita Massacre
- **1869:** Knights of Labor Union begins
- **1870:** Pensions setup for Union veterans; Fifteenth amendment gives voting rights to African-American men
- **1871:** Indian Appropriations Act makes all Native Americans wards of the U.S. government
- **1873–1878:** Massive depressions throw thousands out of work
- **1873:** Comstock Act makes it illegal to give or transport contraceptive advice
- **1874:** Jim Crow laws upheld
- **1875:** Women's Christian Temperance Union forms (WCTU)
- **1876:** Sitting Bull and Crazy Horse win Battle of Big Horn; Anti-Chinese labor unions established
- **1877:** Hayes-Tilden Compromise awards presidency to Hayes in exchange for removal of federal troops from South; Nez Perce removed to Kansas reservation; Charity Organization Societies begin in Buffalo
- **1878:** Susan B. Anthony's woman's suffrage amendment defeated
- **1880:** Salvation Army begins in United States
- **1881:** Federation of Organized Trades and Labor Union, forerunner of American Federation of Labor (1886), forms
- **1882:** Chinese Exclusion Acts ban Chinese immigrants for 10 years
- **1887:** Jane Addams founds Hull House; Dawes Act denies Native American tribal rites
- **1890:** Massacre at Wounded Knee; Oklahoma Territory established
- **1892:** Dawes Act opens 2 million acres of Crow lands to white settlement
- **1894:** Pullman Strike led by Eugene Debs; Coxey's Army marches on Washington
- **1896:** *Plessy v. Ferguson* upholds "separate but equal" concept
- **1898:** Louisiana grandfather clause requires literacy and property ownership for African-American voters; United States annexes Guam, Puerto Rico, Philippines, and Hawaii

The Civil War affirmed federal responsibility over states' rights and laid the groundwork for the United States to become a welfare state. The first evidence came in the Freedmen's Bureau, a federally legislated program that cut across state lines to care for people displaced by the Civil War. Massive economic problems, including major depressions, pushed responsibility for social welfare upward from local overseers of the poor, first to city or county welfare departments, then to states, and finally, with the Social Security Acts of 1935, to the federal government.

Three social welfare movements attained importance during the period from 1865 to 1900: the Charity Organization Society (COS) movement, the settlement house movement, and the child-saving movement. The first two led the developing profession of social work down two different paths, the COS toward individual casework and settlements toward grass-roots organizing for social action and social reform. Child-saving overlapped the others: It took children from their parents and placed them where they might learn the values of hard work, following COS beliefs in overcoming the genetic elements of pauperism, whereas settlement house movements worked on child labor laws, grass-roots aid, and education for children. The labor movement also became a social welfare issue, as COS workers tried to hold down social unrest and settlement house workers fought for reforms.

Both the COS and the settlement house movements were based on socio-religious ideals: the morality of work and wealth, the personal fault of the poor, and ideas of social justice. In addition, burgeoning new sciences—genetics, sociology, and psychology—had growing influence in both. Whereas COSs sought to contain change brought by immigrants from Southern and Eastern Europe, settlement work was a part of the wider reform movements that included socialism, populism, and the social gospel movement.

Although history looks on the emerging social work profession as a caring society's response to need, this was not wholly true:

> Welfare reform ... served industrial capitalism in three ways: ... it made relief increasingly humiliating and unpleasant and so provided an incentive to labor; ... emphasized the parasitic and degraded qualities of the very poor, thereby reducing popular sympathy and justifying retrenchment and repression; and ... divided the working class against itself ... when labor militancy was growing.[1]

The class backgrounds of social welfarists and the political dynamics of the times demonstrated the presence of elite ideals in the developing profession. They quite intended

> to pacify an unruly, exploited urban proletariat through encouraging them to accept their class position as morally just.[2]

According to Saville, the welfare state is a result of the interaction of three main factors:

- the struggle of the working class against exploitation;
- the requirements of industrial capitalism for a more efficient environment in which to operate and the need for a highly productive workforce; and
- the recognition of the price of political security.[3]

Piven and Cloward state the case more succinctly, saying that the provision of welfare arises from the need to quell rebellion among the poorer classes and maintain a low-wage workforce through provision of some, but not all the demands.[4]

Fundamentally, although the developing welfare state aimed at helping the disadvantaged, the definition of "disadvantaged" was Eurocentric, Androcentric, and Protestant in nature. Therefore, whatever the need, aid usually was predicated on moral reform, especially of work habits, which often strengthened oppressive policies toward women and minority persons. The fact that women often founded and staffed welfare programs did not prevent white male-directed structures and processes. Moreover, people of minority groups—African Americans, Native Americans, Chinese Americans and so on—usually were excluded from services. They often developed social programs based on their own traditions; however, these efforts were not supported by mainstream agencies or the government, which often sought to eradicate them (for example, care of Native American children by their own societies).

THE CIVIL WAR: A NEW NATION EMERGES

For 150 years from the beginning of the Civil War, Americans have finessed that war's real genesis. We have insisted that states' rights, secession, economic issues in both North and South, the opening of the West to settlement, and a myriad other reasons culminated in this war that, counting both North and South, killed more than 600,000. The right to secession provided both political and economic rationales, for if one state could secede so could any state, for any reason. Underlying all this, however, was the issue of slavery. According to Orville V. Burton, all rationales

> ... came together to portray the Civil War as a collision of two noble civilizations from which black slaves had been airbrushed out.[5]

Though African-American historians such as W.E.B. Du Bois insisted on looking at slavery, white historians ignored its importance for secession and supported this half-fantasy for at least a century.

The number of slaves in the United States grew from about 900,000 in 1800 to 4 million by 1860. As early as 1819, the South threatened secession to protect slavery, but the Missouri Compromise (1820), which admitted Missouri as a slave state in return for Maine as free, and the Fugitive Slave Law (1850) in return for California as free soothed the Southern states for a time.[6] However, the election of Lincoln brought the issue to a head, and in December of 1860, South Carolina held a secessionist convention calling on Southern states to join a "great Slaveholding Confederacy." As ten other states seceded one by one, Lincoln made the decision to hold Fort Sumter as Union territory. On April 12 secessionist troops fired on it and the Civil War began.[7]

Looking at the political economy at the time of the war, the Southern states were trying to maintain economic control over their own production. Foreign manufactured imports boosted the South's agricultural economy, undercutting prices of Northern factories. The North, in international competition with England, sought high tariffs against foreign goods, but the South insisted on lower tariffs and adopted a *doctrine of nullification* in which they simply would not charge taxes they opposed. To fight this, Northerners and Westerners created the Republican party, and in the four-way presidential race in 1860, their conservative candidate, Lincoln, won 40 percent of the vote (98.6 percent of the Northern vote).[8]

Lincoln was not an abolitionist. In fact, he opposed civil and social equality for slaves, saying in 1858

> I am not, nor ever have been, in favor of bringing about the social and political equality of the white and black races ... of making voters or jurors of Negroes, nor qualifying them to hold office nor to intermarry with white people ... there must be a position of superior and inferior; and I as much as any other man am in favor of having the superior position assigned to the white race.[9]

However, he was a pragmatist who did not want to destroy the Southern elite on whom the manufacturing North depended. His goals were to restore orderly government, establish federal over states' rights, and prevent the disruption of the Northern manufacturing monopoly.

His election moved the nation toward secession and conflict. Unable to tolerate the loss of economic control secession threatened, and pressured by liberals to abolish slavery, Lincoln declared war. Southern politicians left the government and Northern industrial capitalists took their place, changing the political emphasis of the nation from agrarian to industrial and plunging the South into economic depression. The North's economic diversification enabled it to profit immensely from the sale of armaments and provisions for soldiers and to continue its profitable international trade. Meanwhile, the South faced devastation and famine as it sought to produce food on cotton plantations and to buy arms for the war. Working people in the North feared that an influx of freed slaves would take their jobs, and after the Draft Law of 1863, rioted in the streets of New York. The riot left hundreds of people of African descent dead and caused a million dollars' worth of damage.[10] At the onset of the Civil War, more than 500,000 free people of African descent lived in the United States, half in the South.

For the North, the Civil War was a poor man's war. The Draft Law gave upper-class men the legal right to buy their way out of the army for $300 or hire others to take their places. Poor men had no such escape, and their families became destitute, for soldiers' pay was about $13.00 per month, with no allotments provided for the families they left behind. Although in 1862 the government established a pension fund for disabled veterans and for the dependents of those killed in the war, along with orphanages and homes for the disabled, dependents of living soldiers, particularly women and children, went without help. They took jobs in textile mills and munitions factories in greater numbers than ever but were paid a fraction of what men had earned.

Most Civil War battles were fought in the South. Formerly pampered Southern white wives tried desperately to produce food for themselves, their families, and the Confederate troops and to supervise now unruly and rebellious slaves. Union soldiers storming through the country burned the fields and killed livestock so that Confederate soldiers could not be provisioned, and the meager supplies grown or hoarded by Southern women were destroyed. To survive, they looted stores and stole, and some few—Rose O'Neal Greenhow and Belle Boyd, for example—joined the Confederate forces as spies and saboteurs, blowing up bridges and communication lines used by Union forces.

The many slaves who sought to enlist in the Union forces were an embarrassment to Lincoln, who maintained that the war was a disagreement among white gentlemen that had nothing to do with slavery. When Northern freedmen tried to volunteer, he thanked them and sent them home, although liberals, abolitionists, and leaders of African-American descent asked Lincoln to "hit the South where it would hurt the most: free the slaves and give them guns."[11]

He insisted that his policy on slaves was to have no policy and for almost two years appeased slave-holding border states by allowing Union commanders to return fugitive slaves to their owners. Although the Emancipation Proclamation went into effect January 1, 1863, it did not apply to slaves in loyal border states or in sections under Union control in the South. Finally, Congress emancipated the District of Columbia and declared that escaped slaves were contraband rather than property and generals stopped returning them.

Soldiers of African descent were paid only half the salary of white soldiers, and many fought without pay. Overall, there were at least 186,017 of these troopers in the Union army, with losses of 68,l78.[12] Their rallying cry was "Forty acres and a mule"—the same chances given white settlers. When captured by Southern forces, they were routinely killed. For example, when Fort Pillow, Tennessee, was captured by Southern Major General Nathan Forrest, 300 people of African descent, including women and children, were slaughtered—shot, nailed to logs and burned, and buried alive.[13] Nevertheless, people of African descent fought bravely against their former owners and for freedom and the Union.

CHARITY IN THE CIVIL WAR

Of the 300,000 Union soldiers who died in the Civil War, two-thirds died from infections—typhoid, malaria, and dysentery—rather than battle wounds. The casualty rate on both sides was about 50 percent. The Army Medical Corps was unprepared for such carnage and had fewer than 150 surgeons, some of whom joined the Confederacy. Women stepped into the breech, at first with an interest in "moral regeneration" or "medical charity." Soon, however, at least 3,200 women were tending the wounded alongside doctors. Early in the war, such women, who actually handled men's bodies, were considered little more than prostitutes, but this changed because of the value of their work to the armies. Dr. Elizabeth Blackwell began to train women for combat work, and later Dorothea Dix supervised them as superintendent of nurses of the Army Medical Corps.[14] Clara Barton, who founded the American Red Cross after the Civil War (1881), organized a facility that secured medicine and supplies, searched for the missing, and nursed the wounded. In 1864, she was formally appointed superintendent of nurses for the Army of the James (River).

Middle-class Northern women concerned about the destitute dependents of soldiers established more than 20,000 female aid societies to relieve the poor and sew clothes for soldiers. Then, looking at conditions on the battle-field, a group of women from the wealthiest families in New York—Blackwell, Schuyler/Hamilton, Roosevelt, Astor, and Stuyvesant—formed the Women's Central Association of Relief to improve conditions on the battlefield. The group gained official Union recognition and evolved into the U.S. Sanitary Commission, a private agency. Schools, newspapers, theaters, private donors, and a series of "sanitary fairs" contributed $50 million to support it. The commission inspected camps and hospitals, transported the wounded, provided food and clothing on the battlefront, and arranged special relief for dependents. It constructed new buildings to provide accommodations for bathing, washing, and the sanitary disposal of wastes, and developed new techniques to evacuate the wounded, including railroad cars with swinging bunks, operating rooms, and quarters for nurses and surgeons.[15]

It also set up an entire fleet of floating hospitals for coastal and river work and developed a massive campaign against scurvy by asking women to collect lemons, potatoes, dried fruit, onions, and pickled vegetables. Special projects helped the "walking wounded" by distributing paper and envelopes to write home, collecting vital statistics, obtaining back pay and removing false charges of desertion from records, and establishing soldiers' homes where transient soldiers could find food and lodging. Over the period of the war, the Commission served more than 4.5 million meals and furnished more than 1 million men with places to sleep.[16] It aided both Union and Confederate soldiers in prison camps.

Critical Thinking

Practice Behavior Example: Requires the synthesis and communication of relevant information.

Critical Thinking Question: Why did the Civil War spur the growth of state and federal social welfare programs?

AFTER THE CIVIL WAR

The Freedmen's Bureau

In 1862, 10,000 slaves were left to fend for themselves when the Union defeated Confederate forces at Port Royal. To aid them, Lincoln authorized two volunteer organizations—the National Freedman's Relief Association of New York and the Boston Education Commission—to distribute food and clothing, rehabilitate abandoned and pillaged homes, establish schools for children of African descent, and use free labor in cotton cultivation. After the war, the Freedmen's Bureau was established on the Port Royal model. Located in the War Department from which it drew food, clothing, and medical supplies, it was the first federal welfare agency in the United States. In 1866, it was renewed for two years over President Johnson's veto, with an allotment of $6.9 million. Extended until 1872, it helped repair the damages of the Civil War for all the needy in the South, regardless of race or wartime loyalties.

Thousands of white southerners and freed slaves relied on the Freedmen's Bureau for relief, for need was the only criterion for eligibility. There were no residence requirements because of the great displacement caused by the war. A comprehensive family agency, it provided food, shelter, and clothing; counseling to restore family relationships; advocacy for children; and free medical care and employment services, including training. It also distributed land and building materials at minimal cost, established institutions for the orphaned and elderly, and opened more than four thousand schools for children of both races. Furthermore, it became an agency for civil rights advice and advocacy.

In its first three years, the bureau distributed 18.3 million rations, of which about 5.2 million went to white people. By the end of its fourth year, 21 million rations had been distributed, with 6 million going to white people. The bureau either helped found or supported Howard, Atlanta, and Fisk universities, Hampton Institute, and Talladega College.[17] Its most important impacts for social welfare, aside from its overarching federal nature, were that it was a model for private and public cooperation and that it required high standards of accountability from its cooperating agencies.

In its first three years, the [Freedmen's] bureau distributed 18.3 million rations, of which about 5.2 million went to white people.

Services for Veterans

Over 2 million men served in the Union forces, with a casualty rate of 43 percent. For them, but not for survivors of the Confederate army of 781,000 men (casualty rate 52 percent), the government undertook a wide range of services. In March 1865, Lincoln nationalized military and naval asylums for totally disabled officers and voluntary servicemen. Later, the government built and operated a group of national homes for veterans in economic distress because of wartime disabilities. Veterans' homes in the South served only Union veterans, whereas Southern states provided pensions, outdoor relief, and institutions for the disabled and for orphaned children of Confederate veterans.

Over the next twenty-five years, the federal government liberalized eligibility for veterans' services and increased the level of benefits. In 1866, it spent $15 million for veterans' pensions, increasing in 1882 to $30 million and in 1889 to $86 million. In 1890, Congress passed the Dependent Pension Act to keep Union veterans who had served at least ninety days (and their wives) from going to poorhouses or becoming public dependents. By 1898, expenditures for veterans had tripled, covering over 745,000 people, with federal and state governments providing cash payments, medical services, and homes.[18]

POSTWAR POLITICAL ECONOMY

Before the war, states were almost independent nations, but the Civil War made each a unit of the Union. The victory reinforced economic domination by the industrial North, which now dictated its terms of production and blocked industrialization in the South. The loyal were rewarded: Union veterans got pensions, Northern manufacturers got tariffs, and the people of both West and North got free lands in the West (under the Homestead Act of 1864). Railroad promoters received land grants that tied West and North together and ensured that the flow of commerce would bypass the South.[19] Finally, the Constitution's Thirteenth Amendment freed people of African descent from slavery, and the Fourteenth Amendment granted them due process and equal protection under the law and rescinded the three-fifths clause to certify that they were fully equal to white persons. The Fifteenth Amendment granted universal suffrage to men of African descent, though not to women, but did not prohibit mechanisms to prevent voting such as poll taxes, literacy tests, and laws that forbade voting by men whose fathers or mothers were slaves. Not until the Civil Rights movement of the 1960s did questions arise about the implementation, not only in the South but also in the North, of these amendments.

The war brought wealth and power to Northern industrialists. New markets opened in the expanding West and the rebuilding South, and Eastern banks and stock markets established credit to aid in the accumulation of capital. Corporate pools, trusts, holding companies, and monopolies appeared, and free-market competition declined. V.O. Key says,

> ... as business became increasingly national in scope, only the strongest or the most unscrupulous survived. Total output and total capital investment increased while ownership became concentrated and small competitors disappeared. Monopolies merged, and great family fortunes developed.[20]

Industrial workers, including women and children, worked a six-day week, twelve to fourteen hours a day, for one or two dollars per week.

Capital investment in manufacturing nearly quadrupled in the twenty years following 1879 (at $2.5 billion), to reach $11.5 billion in 1904.[21] Whereas in 1860 there were 140,000 factories and 1 million laborers in the workforce, by 1900 factories increased to 208,000 with a workforce of 4.7 million laborers. Manufactured products increased in value from $1.8 billion to $11 billion, and the gross national product nearly tripled ($6.7 billion in 1869 to $17.0 billion in 1900).[22] Taxes and tariffs protected the small wealthy elite of the nation.

The federal government tried to limit monopoly building by passing the Interstate Commerce Act (1887) in an effort to control railroad barons. By 1890, fourteen states and territories had antimonopoly laws and thirteen had antitrust laws. However, these laws and the Sherman Anti-Trust Act of 1890 were mostly ineffective. In 1884, the Bureau of Labor Statistics was formed to collect information on the subject of labor and its relationship to capital and earnings, and in 1889 problems of farmers led to the Department of Agriculture being upgraded to cabinet status. The large low-wage labor force—immigrants, African Americans, women, widows, and children—aided national growth, although they profited little from it. Industrial workers, including women and children, worked a six-day week, twelve to fourteen hours a day, for one or two dollars per week. Periods of unemployment were common in cities, and agricultural workers faced floods, blizzards, and droughts. Two major depressions, in 1873–1878 and 1893–1898, threw hundreds of thousands of people out of work.[23] In the 1893–1894 depression, 40 percent of the factories in the country shut down. Fifty to 66 percent of working families were poor and 33 percent lived in abject poverty. Labor armies (such as Kelly's, 1894) marched on Washington to demand jobs.

Labor and Unionization

Women

During the war, women entered the labor market in great numbers—almost 300,000 of them, earning about one-third the wages of men. The government hired many in post office and clerk jobs, where they earned an average of $300 a year less than men for the same jobs. They also sewed for the government, obtaining cut fabric from government warehouses and returning finished clothes for a fixed price.[24] By 1879, 70 percent of all women workers were domestics, and one-fourth of all nonfarm workers were women. By 1890, 4 million women ages fourteen and up were employed—18 percent of the female population and 17 percent of the labor force. A decade later, 5 million were working, especially women of color and the foreign-born. Many were married. When the typewriter came into general use in the 1890s, women who had refused to work alongside immigrant women or in factories took jobs in offices, earning as much as $7.00 a week.[25]

Women were subject to many kinds of exploitation but seldom complained for fear of losing their jobs. In the garment industry, for example, bosses made "mistakes" in computing piecework; fined them for singing, talking, laughing, or washing; and charged for everything they used: machinery, electricity, needles, thread, drinking water, and washrooms. The price for needles was 25 percent more than bosses paid, and for electricity 20 percent more. They were charged 325 to 400 percent above the cost of materials, and often had to give sexual favors in return for the job, a raise, or a better position.[26]

Tramps

One of the most problematic issues of the period was that of "tramps." Men out of work began traveling the country looking for jobs, asking for handouts, and staying temporarily in poorhouses. The Civil War had taught them that tramping was no worse than bivouac duty, where they had camped out and lived off the land. Although American generosity dictated that refusing food to a wanderer was the worst form of meanness, a massive fear of tramps began to shake the nation:

> It was the context as well as the quantity of population movement—increased labor, militancy, and the unmistakable emergence of an industrial proletariat—that prompted respectable citizens to transform unemployed, wandering, hungry, and perhaps often angry men into a new and menacing class called tramps.[27]

Professor Francis Wayland of Yale helped to legitimate public hatred of tramps by writing that tramping was not the inability to find employment, but the unwillingness to work, and that tramps were labor agitators who stirred up discontent, preached revolution, and threatened the political and social stability of America. He called tramps "a disease, a virus of demoralization infecting the will of the working class."[28] In fact, working people were joining together in what might have become a revolution against the great corporations and monopolies. The abolition of outdoor relief and the call for imprisonment of tramps was related to the control of this union.

> Nineteenth century discussions of pauperism either omitted or rejected the impact of depressions, economic cycles, seasonal unemployment, and technological change on the ability of men to find work ... [and] refused to acknowledge that most tramps were men on the road only a short time seeking work, not a permanent and dangerous class.[29]

Labor Unions

Although labor unions had been agitating for labor reform from the early 1820s, the war and free land in the West had all but ended their activity. After the war, they began again to gain strength. The first National Labor Council was called by craft unions in 1866, and in 1878 the International Labor Union was formed (it ended in 1882). Farmers organized to prevent railroad robber barons from taking their lands, and by 1875 there were 30,000 local granges with a membership of 2.5 million. More than 1 million African-American farmers organized the Colored Farmer's Alliance in union with the populist grange movement.

The Knights of Labor formed in 1869, gaining 50,000 members by 1883 and 700,000 by 1886.[30] It demanded an eight-hour day, equal pay for equal work, an end to child labor, and cooperation among workers. Teachers, farmers, and even housewives formed their own women's locals and sent delegates to the general assembly. Women were welcomed in the Knights of Labor, which accepted everyone but bankers, lawyers, gamblers, and owners of stock. In 1886, women constituted 10 percent of its 500,000 members, with 200 separate locals ranging from housewives and washerwomen to farmers and factory workers. However, the Knights of Labor became identified with radicalism and, beset by internal turmoil, its membership dropped to 100,000 by 1890.

One of the most important unions for women was the Working Women's Protective Union, joined by women of all classes. Until 1894, it provided legal services for victimized women, built boarding houses and protective shelters for women, placed nearly 2,000 women in jobs each year, and collected unpaid wages for them.[31] African-American women formed their own unions, which were welcomed into the National Colored Labor Union at its founding in 1869.

The American Federation of Labor (AFL), created in 1881, was a federation of craftsmen and artisans and welcomed neither laborers nor women. Although its national policy admitted women, locals generally did not, and the few that did would not seek equal pay. In fact, the AFL sought to get women out of the labor force through protective legislation, proposed in both 1892 and 1894. The AFL claimed that the eight-hour workday and the prohibition of female employment on foot-powered machinery were aimed at "protecting" weak women, but these rules actually were aimed at taking women out of better-paying jobs. Berch says,

> The leading figure in AFL's anti-women worker campaign was ... president Samuel Gompers ... [who contended] that "the wife as a wage-earner is a disadvantage economically considered, and socially is unnecessary."[32]

POPULATION, IMMIGRATION, AND THE PEOPLE

White Immigration, African-American Migration

During the Civil War, immigration was encouraged and immigrants were excused from military service to staff the factories or secure the West. From 1870 to 1900, the U.S. population more than doubled, from 31.5 million to 76 million. Nearly 14 million of this increase—a third of population growth—was from immigration.[33] Migration to the cities increased: In 1860, 20 percent of the population was in the cities, but forty years later 40 percent was urban. By 1900, nonfarm employment was substantially greater than farm employment: In a labor force of 29 million workers, 18 million were nonfarm workers.[34] The percentage of African Americans in the population remained stable: 13 percent in 1865 and 12 percent in 1900. Their in-migration to the North was limited during this period: In 1860 there were 156,000 in the East, 184,000 in the North Central states, and 4 million in the South. By 1900, there were only 385,000 in the East and 175,000 in the North Central states, but the southern African-American population reached 8 million.[35]

The presence of new ethnic and religious groups, along with freed slaves, brought new dilemmas of racism, religious discrimination, and ethnocentrism or nativism. Immigrant Italian Catholics refused to adopt the new (Protestant) ways of America, keeping their language, religion, and native customs intact. Often, immigrants saved enough money to bring kin and even entire villages to America, where they developed their own churches and schools. Political exiles, such as Jews forced from their German, Russian, and Austro-Hungarian homelands, brought new and disturbing ideas of political freedom with them: socialism and the right of workers to share in profits.

Asian Immigrants

Chinese men began to immigrate to America in 1820, but women were rarely allowed in. Nearly all these immigrants came from seven districts in southern China, in the province of Kwangtung near Canton. The Chinese knew little about current wages and so were easy to exploit, but they were unwilling to return to China because poverty there was so desperate. Their immigration continued to be encouraged for a short time after the Civil War when the Central Pacific Railroad, finding itself behind the Union Pacific, began to hire them from Western mines and directly from China. During the 1870s, Chinese men were almost one-quarter of the wage laborers in California.[36]

However, the United States was in the midst of a great economic depression in these decades, and the Chinese were perceived as taking jobs from white men. They were forced out of mining by whites and, after the intercontinental railroad was completed, lost construction jobs also. In a time of unionization, "anticoolie" unions were formed: the United Brothers of California and the Anti-Chinese Union of San Francisco in 1876 and the California Workingmen's Party in 1877. Samuel Gompers of the AFL declared that the Chinese worked for depressed wages and were beyond the pale of labor organization, and the International Workingmen's Association and the Knights of Labor advocated an end to their immigration. Republican candidate Rutherford B. Hayes put an anti-Chinese plank in his platform.

Violence marked anti-Chinese activities throughout the Civil War decade, but after 1870 it became sustained and coordinated. Laws were passed regulating Chinese shrimp catches, prohibiting the hiring of Chinese by corporations and municipal works, authorizing the removal of Chinese residents from city boundaries, prohibiting them from engaging in fishing, denying them licenses for businesses or occupations, prohibiting attendance at public schools, and finally stopping all Chinese immigration via the Exclusion Acts of 1882. In 1871, a massacre took place in Los Angeles in which twenty-two Chinese were killed and hundreds were driven from their homes. "Riot Night" in San Francisco on July 23, 1877, began when a crowd listening to labor organizers erupted into violence against the Chinese, and over the next three days burned Chinese laundries and homes, attacked a steamship company that brought Chinese to America, and did half a million dollars' worth of damage before police, army troops, the navy, and about five thousand citizens ended the riot.[37]

Between 1879 and 1882, Congress passed two bills suspending Chinese immigration, but both were vetoed because they violated international treaties with China. In 1882, the first Chinese Exclusion Act was passed, suspending immigration for ten years and barring Chinese aliens from citizenship. Renewed in 1892 and made permanent in 1904, it was not repealed until 1943, when the Chinese were America's allies in World War II. The Geary Act of 1892 and the McCreary Amendment of 1893 required all Chinese to carry certificates of residence with identifying photographs or be subject to arrest and deportation.[38] The Immigration Acts of 1924 virtually ended Chinese and other Asian immigration until 1968.

Social Darwinism, racism, and economic motivation made Chinese the targets of discrimination and violence from their first immigration. Local ordinances prohibited them from working in some areas, taxed them discriminately, and controlled them with mob violence: They were beaten, burned, shot, and lynched. By 1900, 57 percent of Asians in the United States, primarily Chinese, were in domestic service.[39] They became a middleman minority in the West, working in trade and commerce as agents, labor contractors, rent collectors, money lenders, and brokers—people with easily liquidated assets. Many invested in laundries, for there they owned businesses rather than having to sell their labor. Few white protectors or social reformers took their part, probably because reformers, if they cared, were in the East, and the frontier West had few laws to control violence.

The Chinese brought with them traditions of mutual aid: trade guilds that were both work and birthright associations giving fraternal welfare; Hui Kuans, or linguistic divisions; class or lineage clubs and organizations; and "tongs," voluntary associations based on mutual interests, primarily protection and the provision of illegal goods such as drugs and prostitutes.

In great part, the welfare efforts were aimed at financing education for the young. Another Chinese welfare device was the Rotating Credit Association, where a core of participants each made a contribution and then each contributor got all or a part of the amount.

Native Americans After the War

Railroads were at the heart of American expansionism and created new elites of robber barons who took land from farmers and decimated the resources of Native Americans. By 1865, there were 35,000 miles of railroads, four years later the transcontinental railroad was completed, and by 1900 there were 175,000 miles of railroad across the United States. For Native Americans, the railroads often meant starvation as the great herds of bison were killed off for sport.

In 1871, the federal government in effect eliminated the political rights of Native Americans by declaring them wards of the federal government and refusing to recognize them as independent nations. It was cheaper to feed them than to kill them: A study in 1870 estimated that the cost per dead Native American was about $1 million. The Allotment Act of 1887, called the Dawes Act, further destroyed their cultures by dividing the land—approximately 140 million acres—among individual freehold farmers. Many quickly sold or were cheated out of their allotments, and some 90 million acres of the best land was transferred to whites, while 90,000 Native Americans were left landless.

The Bureau of Indian Affairs was responsible, through Indian agents, for supplies, education, instruction in farming, and supervision of lands. They were also to distribute food when times were hard. However, by the 1880s Indian agents were notoriously corrupt and incompetent, withholding supplies to sell for profit. In some agency towns, agents were near-dictators, helping white settlers to take over Native American land. A member of the Assiniboine testified before a Congressional Committee:

> They gave us rations once a week, just enough to last one day, and the Indians they started to eat their pet dogs. After they ate all their dogs up they started to eat their ponies. All this time the Indian Bureau had a warehouse full of grub…. Early that spring in 1884 I saw the dead bodies of the Indians wrapped in blankets and piled up like cordwood … the other Indians were so weak they could not bury their dead; what were left were nothing but skeletons.[40]

Well-wishing reformers won government support to open boarding schools for Native American children, taking them from their parents and interrupting the child-rearing process to "Americanize" them. In 1887, the government appropriated $1.2 million to the Bureau of Indian Affairs and to missionary groups for 227 boarding schools to enroll 14,300 children.[41] Placed there for four to eight years, the children were subjected to strict "moral" discipline, their hair cut to end their "heathen" ways, and not allowed to see their parents for months.

One result of the oppression and decimation of Native American societies was the rise of a new religion: the Ghost Dance. It was developed by a Paiute Messiah named Wovoka, also called Jack Wilson, who was possibly a descendant of Tecumseh's brother, the Prophet. It taught that white men would disappear and that living and dead Native Americans would be reunited. In 1889, there was a resurgence of the Ghost Dance, and it became more militant as the injustices of the white man were counted: the extermination of the bison, the removal West of the many Eastern societies, confinement on reservations where the people were at the mercy of Indian agents, and the theft of their land. Some Ghost Dance followers began to preach active resistance to the whites, and apprehensive white authorities alerted the military to stop their assemblies.[42]

In 1890, the U.S. Cavalry mistook a gathering of Sioux Ghost Dancers at Wounded Knee, South Dakota, for an Indian uprising. Nearly three hundred Sioux, including women and children, were massacred. The soldiers continued to kill until almost everyone was murdered. A survivor, Black Elk, said,

> Men and women and children were heaped and scattered all over the flat
> at the bottom of the little hill where the soldiers had their wagon-guns,
> and westward up the dry gulch all the way to the high ridge, the dead
> women and children and babies were scattered.... The snow drifted deep
> in the crooked gulch, and it was one long grave of butchered women and
> children and babies, who were only trying to run away.[43]

This was only one massacre. Abetted by the new technology of the Gatling (machine) gun, federal soldiers, vigilantes, and settlers set about genocide. Not until after World War I was any real thought given to the rights of Native Americans, and by this time, their lives, societies, and cultures were all but lost.

Emancipation and the Plight of the Freedmen

In the South, cities were in ruin, transportation lines destroyed, and fields barren. There was no money for seeds, machinery, or livestock, and near-famine occurred because of drought and the lack of organized workers. The first concern of Southern states was to get artificial limbs and cash payments to veterans so they could work, and the second was to provide for war orphans. States established central public welfare offices to distribute food and clothes to poor whites but gave nothing to the impoverished freedmen. As in fourteenth-century Europe as feudalism fell, former slaves were left without even the small protections of food and shelter in the winter.

Poor white laborers returned to the South to find themselves in competition for work with 4 million freedmen. Cotton mills came to the South, and a populist alliance of freed slaves and white laborers was in the making. However, because this threatened white elite political and economic control, Southern capitalists encouraged race hatred and pitted white worker against black. Many white laborers believed that emancipation itself was a plot of Northern capital to lower wages and enlarge its labor pool.[44] Entrepreneurs—carpetbaggers—coming from the North to help the freed slaves or to cheat them aggravated the situation.

For freedpersons, the change from slavery to wage-earning status meant that tens of thousands of people died from starvation, disease, and privation. For example, in the years immediately following the war one-fourth of all infants in some communities died in their first year and life expectancy declined by 10 percent.[45] Before the war, the plantation had ensured stability; after the war, tenant farming, sharecropping, and the independent ownership of small farms became a tenuous way of life. African Americans from 1860 to 1900 never owned more than 6 percent of the land of the rural South.[46]

During Reconstruction (1867–1877) in the South, Senator Charles Sumner and House Representative Thaddeus Stevens were the strongest supporters of freedpersons. Bennett says, in fact, that slaves owed their freedom more to these two than to Lincoln.[47] Lincoln's plan for Reconstruction included giving free land to freedpersons, but his assassination left Reconstruction in the hands of easily influenced Andrew Johnson, who set out to appease plantation owners, first by pardoning them and then demanding that former slaves turn over their land to former owners. He refused to break up plantations and turned ex-slaves over to former masters with no protections against reprisals. Appalled, Stevens gained the support of Congress to put the South under military control until free elections could be held. Congress enacted the Fourteenth and Fifteenth Amendments, which granted citizenship and the right to vote to people of African descent and guaranteed their rights to life, liberty, and the pursuit of happiness. Because African Americans outnumbered whites in Mississippi, South Carolina, Louisiana, and Florida, they were elected as governors and lieutenant governors, secretaries of state, supreme court judges, and state treasurers. In their new positions they helped to formulate new state constitutions for the Southern states. Before long, however, their leaders were accused of corruption and of being led by Northern carpetbaggers and scalawags. At least five thousand leaders were killed. Bennett maintains that their greatest crime was the violation of the American caste system, saying "If there was anything Southern whites feared more than a bad Negro government, it was a good Negro government."[48]

Revenge became the keynote of the South. Retaliation against African-American Union veterans was common. In Memphis in 1866, forty-six veterans were killed and seventy-five were wounded, five women were raped, and twelve schools and four churches were burned. In New Orleans, thirty-five veterans were killed and more than one hundred wounded. The Ku Klux Klan held its first national meeting in Nashville in April 1867, under the leadership of Nathan Bedford Forrest, of the Fort Pillow massacre. Soon the South was honeycombed with chapters: the Knights of the White Camellia, Red Shirts, White League, Mother's Little Helpers, and the Baseball Club of the First Baptist Church.[49] Many Ku Klux Klan members were well-known politicians and landowners in the community.

Any atrocity against African Americans was permitted, from raiding their holdings to raping the women, from castrating men to lynching and burning them. There was no protection from the Ku Klux Klan except submission, and often that was not enough. Members of the Klan legitimated their actions by swearing devotion to the Flag, to "racial purity" (particularly of white women), and to Christianity. One lynching took place every two days or so, approximately one hundred per year in the 1880s and 1890s.[50] Newspapers advertised lynchings in advance, and crowds came on chartered trains to see them. People were also roasted alive over slow fires and otherwise mutilated. Although there was some opposition to lynching, the violence and horror of this reign of terror left most people in too much fear to protest or even to flee.

According to Feagin, the barbarity of white terrorism against African Americans had "a strongly ritualized character" and that

> ... at the heart of this ritualized barbarism is concern that white supremacy must be maintained against all challenges, real or imaginary.... In many cases... the black victims were brutally tortured, and pieces of their bodies were taken by white as souvenirs.... Such brutality underscores die deeply rooted, emotional character of much white-on-black oppression. This level of internalized racist thinking and emotion coupled with grisly rituals of extreme inhumanity is distinctive in the history of antiblack racism.[51]

The presidential race between Rutherford B. Hayes and Democrat Samuel J. Tilden was crucial in the treatment of freedpersons. Elections were disputed in South Carolina, Florida, and Louisiana. Although the Electoral Commission upheld Hayes's claim to the presidency, Democrats threatened to hold up election results past the day of inauguration, leaving the country presidentless, unless Hayes agreed to the South's demands for "home rule": the right to deal with freedpersons as they chose. Upon this agreement, he was elected. Federal troops were withdrawn from the South in 1877, and the racial caste system was established, excluding African Americans from nearly all trades except agrarian labor and domestic service, from education (Plessy *v.* Ferguson, 1896), and from the political process.

Soon new laws—Black Codes—were passed in all former Confederate states except Tennessee. They denied African Americans property rights, specified the work they could do, and forbade work as artisans and mechanics. Orphans or children whose parents were judged unable to care for them were apprenticed, often to their former masters, with no guarantees of food, clothing, or shelter, such as white apprenticed children had. Every freedperson needed to carry a written labor contract or a license from the police. Whereas white unemployed workers were "unemployed," unemployed freedpersons were "vagrants" who could be tried and sent to prison. Other charges for which they could be imprisoned were idleness, quitting a job or making too much money, insulting gestures, or "disrespect" (women who resisted sexual attacks by white men were "disrespectful.") Although victims of these laws could appeal, in white courts they seldom won. Black codes were ignored by a federal government eager to pacify the Southern gentry.

Once convicted, African-American men or women were likely to be sentenced to chain gangs, their labor sold to employers or factories or given for local government projects for leases of ten to twenty years. The convict lease system, first established in Georgia, was profitable to both employers and the state, and there came to be a "compelling economic reason for increasing the prison population."[52] Chain gangs were often used as "schools" for "undisciplined" young African Americans who had grown up since slavery. Chains welded to their bodies, men and women together (there was no sex discrimination in prison), they lived in unbelievable conditions, and 30 percent of those given over to state overseers died. Davis says,

> Whereas the slaveholders had recognized limits to the cruelty with which they exploited their "valuable" human property, no such cautions were necessary for the postwar planters who rented black convicts for relatively short terms. In many cases sick convicts are made to toil until they drop dead in their tracks.[53]

Bennett adds:

> After a study of Southern chain gangs, Fletcher Green, a modern scholar, concluded that they had no parallel except in the persecutions of the Middle Ages and the concentration camps of Nazi Germany.[54]

Those who learned to live under the Black Codes were, in a short time, once more subservient tenant farmers on land they had briefly owned. Seventy-five percent of African-American farmers became tenant farmers, and although they were paid for the food or cotton they produced, the cost of seed, equipment, housing, and food purchased from the landowner kept them in debt, often for life. This indebtedness produced a new form of quasi-slavery.

Seeing the continued retribution against freedpersons and hoping to lessen it, Booker T. Washington, president of Tuskegee Institute (which he built), declared there must be some kinds of segregation. He used the parable of the open hand with separate but equal fingers, one that could close in a fist for common causes, and said that questions of social equality were extremist folly. This speech, called the Atlanta Compromise, asked for support for education, an end to killing, and economic opportunity for African Americans. Although his hoped-for benefits did not appear, his "separate but equal" appeal helped to justify enactment of Jim Crow laws throughout the South.[55] Upheld by the Supreme Court in 1875, such laws asserted that individuals, but not states, could legally discriminate against African Americans.

Jim Crow laws limited areas in which African Americans could live, and Jim Crow sections appeared in both Northern and Southern towns. In addition, housing, facilities, education, medical treatment, and burial became segregated. Literacy, property, and poll tax tests kept African Americans from voting, as did the *grandfather clause*, which denied the vote to people whose grandfathers had not voted. This ended the political power of African Americans; for example, in 1896 there were 130,344 African-American voters in Louisiana, but in 1900, two years after the grandfather clause was passed, only 5,320 voted.

"True Womanhood"

After the Civil War, white middle- and upper-class career women formed a new generation of educated women. Seventy-five percent of college women who graduated before 1900 remained single, many moving into settlement work or casework. Freed by new homemaking technologies (washing machines, non-fire cookers, and vacuum cleaners) and new amenities that freed them from food preparation (canned food, bread cheaper to buy than to bake), middle-class women aspired to paid work, social reform, and college. Married women began to enter the labor force in great numbers, and by 1890 women made up 18 percent of the labor force.[56]

Puritan upbringings and Protestant beliefs still dominated American thought, and a moral outcry was raised against women who, by working outside the home, flouted the "natural order." Part of this was economic, for women now controlled their own money and undercut men's wages in the marketplace. However, a great deal had to do with the new definitions of the "virtuous" woman. The result was the "Cult of True Womanhood," which taught that women were more highly evolved spiritually than were men, as evidenced by their obvious lack of sexual desire,[57] that their unique attributes—compassion, nurturance, and morality—"unfitted them for competitive economic struggle."[58] Therefore, although their natural place was in the home, women—especially unmarried women—could move into the outside world, making it purer and more moral by attacking uncleanness and immorality. Moral issues such as prohibition, prostitution, criminality, prison improvement, pure food and drug laws, child labor, public sewers, corruption in government, and peace were the new province of "true womanhood."[59]

Across the nation, professional women, ethnic minority women, African-American women, and working women began to form thousands of clubs, and by the late 1880s coalesced into national organizations such as the National Council of Clubs and the General Federation of Women's Clubs. By 1920, the latter had nearly a million members active in improving the social environment by investigating sanitation and government corruption; raising money for worthy causes such as hospitals, schools, and homes for the aged; and becoming involved in the labor struggles of wage-earning women. Wealthy women, free to use their money as they wished, often sponsored meetings and speeches and donated their money profusely to good causes, especially those involved in health care. (For example, between 1885 and 1889, five new nursing schools were created in Chicago, founded and funded by women.)

African-American women's clubs supported the new class of working women by giving them places to live, a community of safety, and emotional and spiritual help. Of the 2.7 million African-American women over the age of ten, a million worked for wages: nearly 39 percent in agriculture, 30.8 percent in domestic service, 15.6 percent as laundresses, and 2.8 percent in manufacturing.[60] Despite discrimination, they still managed to enter some professions. Charlotte E. Ray (1850–1911) became the first African-American woman lawyer to practice in the United States, receiving her law degree from Howard University. When prejudice forced her from the practice, she turned to teaching. Caroline V. Still became a doctor, and Anna J. Cooper became a teacher in Washington, D.C. Fannie Barrier Williams founded the first school for African-American nurses.

In 1874, the first truly national women's organization was born: the Women's Christian Temperance Union (WCTU). The union considered alcohol not only the downfall of families but the support of powerful political machines, because saloons were the meeting places of political bosses. Its major purposes were to protect women from drunken husbands and fathers and to protect the sanctity of the home. In twenty years the WCTU gained more than 200,000 members and rose to prominence under the leadership of chief organizer Frances Willard (1839–1898), its president for twenty years (beginning in 1879). Called from the presidency of the Women's College of Northwestern University, Willard challenged WCTU's conservative leadership and linked suffrage and temperance, saying that women could stop the liquor traffic if they had the vote. She also fought the national drug trade from 1883 on, and any reform that would help women and children interested her. She lobbied for women's suffrage, recovery homes for alcoholic women, and reform schools for juvenile offenders. She helped to organize the General Federation of Women's Clubs in 1889 and laid the groundwork for the National Council of Women. By her death in 1898, WCTU had a membership of nearly a quarter million adults, with almost as many in youth groups.[61] At that time, a serious split developed between suffrage forces and antiliquor forces, and WCTU divorced itself from the suffrage issue.

Most women's issues were in some way connected with women's sexuality and men's attempt to control it. The Cult of True Womanhood, the arguments against women's suffrage, the extension of women's sphere into public service, and the fight against immorality—particularly sexual immorality—were both sexist and sexual in nature. Important influences at issue were the moral outrage against contraception and the spread of sexually transmitted diseases throughout the middle-class population.

Wives of the upper classes were "pure women," sexually passionless and dependent. They were proper wives, mothers, and moral social reformers. If they had to have careers, only those that spread their "womanliness" into society—charity work, teaching, and nursing—were acceptable. Even obvious signs of their sexuality—pregnancy and childbirth—were finessed away as "duty." In contrast, lower-class women were considered passionate and sexual, and therefore immoral. Their sexual or economic exploitation was, therefore, legitimate.[62]

Although research by Dr. Clelia Duel Mosher (1863–1940), a pioneer in the study of women's sexuality, indicated that the perception of women as passionless was a male fantasy,[63] this belief was common and strong. For example, Dr. Theophilus Parvin said in 1883,

> I do not believe one bride in a hundred ... accepts matrimony from any desire for sexual gratification ... it is with shrinking or even with horror, rather than with desire.[64]

Nathan Hale, Jr., summed up his review of the sexual advice literature at the turn of the century with a similar conclusion:

> Many women came to regard marriage as little better than legalized prostitution. Sexual passion became associated almost exclusively with the male, with prostitutes, and women of the lower classes.[65]

Male doctors in this era were so convinced that "normal" women had no sexual interest that, if it occurred, they took drastic measures against it, such as clitoridectomy, ovariectomy, and incarceration in insane asylums. Gynecologists sought to alleviate all kinds of physical and mental conditions through ovariectomies: incurable or obscure pelvic pains, hysteria, weakness, and "temperamentalism." Wives who did not "behave" or submit to the control of their husbands were often subjected to such operations and, given that little anesthesia was available, became docile at even the threat of ovariectomy. When antisepsis and anesthesia made abdominal operations safer and surgeons became more skillful at their tasks, operations to rid women of their "hysteria" became even more common.

Before the discovery of the ovum in 1824, abortion was considered contraception, and there were few restrictions. By 1840, there was an upsurge of abortions, and until the Civil War, one-third of the states had no abortion laws. In states where abortion was against the law, doctors rather than women were punished. At the end of the Civil War, when the population of men was decimated, physicians instigated and carried out a campaign against abortion. Forty statutes were passed in the period 1860–1890 declaring any interruption of gestation a crime, with the woman considered at fault and acting against God and nature.[66] The severely declining birthrate among white upper classes was another reason for the campaign: Between 1860 and 1910, live births decreased by nearly one-third. The birthrate among African Americans remained high but still declined, and the birthrate decreased by 26 percent among immigrant women. This inspired more outcries based on social Darwinism and the duty of white women to produce children so that the United States would not be taken over by the "degenerate classes."

Contraception also was condemned, and women who practiced it were called immoral. As early as 1821, Dr. Charles Knowlton of Boston was prosecuted for writing a book on mechanical and chemical means of contraception,[67] but it did not really become a legal issue until after the Civil War. There was, in fact, a great deal of contraceptive information available—the rhythm method, use of condoms or sponges soaked in antiseptic solutions, and intrauterine stem pessaries—but doctors generally refused to discuss it with women. The advice to women who wanted to avoid having children without a good reason was

> Get a divorce and vacate the position for some other woman, who is able and willing to fulfill all a wife's duties as well as to enjoy her privileges.[68]

The Comstock Act in 1873 made it illegal to give contraceptive advice, and some physicians were prosecuted under the new law.

The declining birthrate was not solely because of contraception. Rather, much of the decline, as well as infant mortality and blindness and maternal morbidity and mortality, was caused by sexually transmitted diseases. Barren marriages and "one-child sterility" were often the results of gonorrheal infection, most often in wives infected by their husbands (because doctors colluded with husbands in hiding the infection). One physician, writing in 1910, argued,

> ... prior to 1850, just 2 percent of our native-born white women were sterile, whereas by 1900 the ratio had increased to one in five. Venereal disease ... was behind this.... Other physicians presented figures purporting to show that from 20 to 75 percent of childless marriages were the result of venereal disease-induced sterility.[69]

German physician Emil Noeggerath stated in 1879 that most reproductive diseases were caused by gonorrhea. Others estimated that up to 75 percent of all major gynecological surgery was because of gonorrhea.[70]

Unfortunately, the attack against sexually transmitted disease became an attack against prostitutes. Prostitution was one way women could survive: It paid better than most low-wage jobs they could find, even though a prostitute's life expectancy was only four years. Many immigrant women, unable to find jobs, engaged in "casual prostitution" until they could find work. Many other women became unwilling prostitutes under the hard hands of their former lovers or white slavers who sold them in cities around the world. Seldom, if ever, were the men who frequented prostitutes blamed for carrying disease back to their wives; in fact, men were often encouraged to take sexual satisfaction elsewhere rather than to "bother" their "pure" wives. In 1874, Dr. Marion Sims, president of the American Medical Association, recommended national regulation and licensure of prostitution to control sexually transmitted disease. However, this was opposed by people who believed regulation would legitimate prostitution and open up legal red-light districts and by feminists who argued that women would be prosecuted for proliferation of disease rather than the men who used them.

EMERGING PHILOSOPHIES AND SOCIAL WELFARE

Two ideals influenced the development of social welfare after the Civil War. The first was social Darwinism, which defined the worthy and moral as those who succeeded economically. Charity Organization Societies followed this "scientific" ideal, relying also on the emerging sciences of genetics, sociology, administrative management, and psychology. The second ideal was the populist democratic/socialist movement influenced by the economic philosophy of Karl Marx and Friedrich Engels, the British Fabian socialist movement, and the social gospel movement. Marxism posited that the government was a tool of the economic elite in exploiting workers and the Fabians sought collective ownership of the means of production. The social gospel movement, led by Protestants, wanted social reform through a return to the basics of Christianity. From 1870 on, populism challenged capitalism, calling it "the science of extortion, the gentle art of grinding the faces of the poor."[71] Populism was one inspiration for labor unions, the grange movement, women's clubs, and, in social welfare, the settlement house movement.

Social Darwinism and the Charity Organization Society

Research-Based Practice

Practice Behavior Example: Comprehend quantitative and qualitative research and understand scientific and ethical approaches to building knowledge.

Critical Thinking Question: Discuss the flaws in the psudoscientific research behind social Darwinism.

Throughout the 1800s, some social reformers argued that poverty was caused not by personal deviance but by social and economic structures arising from industrialization. However, conservatism and work morality continued to have a greater impact than did social reform on employment practices and social welfare. New scientific knowledge about genetics and psychology provided "proofs" that, indeed, the causes of deviance (including poverty) lay in the individual. Social Darwinism taught that white Anglo-Saxons (preferably Protestants from northern Europe) were genetically better than people of other ethnicities. Moreover, a better world could be created by "containing" people afflicted with problems such as poverty, nonwhiteness, or mental, emotional, or physical disabilities. Nature should be allowed to take its course in ridding society of such defective people and to help them was against God's law. Therefore, science and religion joined in legitimating institutionalization, inadequate poor relief, taking children from families, and in the case of people of color, murder.

> ... science and religion joined in legitimating institutionalization, inadequate poor relief, taking children from families, and in the case of people of color, murder.

Herbert Spencer, an English philosopher with great influence in America between 1870 and 1890, became the spokesman for social Darwinism, saying

> If they are not sufficiently competent to live, they die, and it is best they should die.... The whole effort of nature is to get rid of such, to clear the world of them, and make room for better.[72]

He argued that poor laws provided for the

> ... artificial preservation of those least able to take care of themselves. The poverty of the incapable, the distresses that come from the imprudent, the starvation of the idle, and those shoulderings aside of the weak by the strong were "the decrees of a large far-seeing benevolence."[73]

The class bias is clear: Social aid takes people out of the labor market, makes them unavailable for work, and thereby undermines the God-given reward—wealth—of nature's fittest. The poor and needy,

> ... [u]nfit to survive ... were nevertheless kept alive by humanitarian charity. Far from contributing to the development of mankind and society, they were dead weight—a drag on the movement to ultimate perfection. Consequently, pity for those afflicted with problems was replaced with blame, leading to the creation of an outcast class viewed and treated not with indifference but with contempt.[74]

Helping the poor or deviant went against the efficient operation of the "invisible hand" of the market. Not only were the poor to blame—so were those who helped them. This guilt-by-association works against the social work profession even today.

Social Darwinism became a major creed of the Charity Organization Societies, which began in London in 1869 and in Buffalo in 1877 under the leadership of the Reverend S. Humphreys Gurteen. By 1894, there were ninety-two COSs in the United States, and at the close of 1904, approximately 150. The vast majority were in large cities in the East and North—over fifty were in cities with populations of more than 60,000.[75]

The purpose of COSs was to organize all charities in an area so that needy people could be served but would not be able to get help from more than one charity. To do this, they developed central case registries and forums in which all agencies, including the police, could work closely together on cases. Paid staff investigated applications for charity, and volunteer *friendly visitors* personally interviewed applicants in what would become casework practice. Volunteer boards determined eligibility and set grants on a case-by-case basis. Systems of accountability' were bureaucratized and COSs kept case records to collect social statistics on poverty, unemployment, wages, family expenditures, disease, and working conditions. Wealthy volunteers became difficult to find, and soon paid workers administered COSs in all major cities. By 1892, women workers far outnumbered men and thereafter dominated the leadership and development of the emerging profession of social work.

An explicit goal of the COS movement was to restore the "natural order" of class stratification. It was no coincidence that the movement began at a time of economic turmoil, with massive unemployment, low wages, and people displaced by the war. The burgeoning wealth of the upper classes was salt in the wounds of those without enough to eat, and social disruption was everywhere. The end of the Civil War brought war production layoffs at the same time the labor market was flooded with returning soldiers, new immigrants, war widows, and freed slaves. For the first time in history, unemployment was a national problem. COSs, developed and maintained by the elite classes, had more than altruism at stake.

Although heredity could not be changed, "moral" environments and treatment could alleviate some of the results of bad heredity. Casework consisted primarily of moral advice, although workers were told not to make moral judgments. Outdoor relief was given only as a last resort because it was material rather than spiritual and "demoralized the poor." Josephine Shaw Lowell (1843–1905), founder of the New York Charity Organization Society and of many custodial institutions for the retarded, said,

> … relief-giving … seeks material ends by material means, and therefore must fail…. For man is a spiritual being, and, if he is to be helped, it must be by spiritual means.[76]

People were encouraged to work even when no work could be found, and severe work tests were given the able-bodied, although at fair wages. Gambling, intemperance, and vice were attacked as routes to the disease of pauperism.

COSs helped women and children only if the breadwinner died, and then only if the friendly visitor felt it better to keep the family together. Institutionalization was preferred: Mothers were sent to poorhouses and children to orphanages, to "train them away" from the heritage of pauperism. Drunkards' families were not helped unless the drunkard left; their wives were then considered widows. Deserted families, however, got no help for fear that it would encourage other men to desert. The aged were helped only if they were not to blame for their own destitution. If families were eligible for support, the COS first asked relatives, friends, churches, former employers, and fraternal societies to support them. If that did not work, private donors and charities were approached.

COSs also cooperated with police, directing their actions toward beggars, vagrants, and wayward husbands. Plainclothes officers often reported daily to the COS. On COS advice, vagrants were sent to houses of correction for two to six months, and then to state farms on indeterminate sentences with a maximum of two years.[77] In addition, COSs worked with public relief agencies, investigating applicants and at times handling the entire public outdoor relief system. Early COSs lobbied for housing reform and worked to bring disease-prevention techniques, such as vaccinations, into the community. They built tuberculosis sanitariums and fresh air camps for slum children; provided day nurseries and sewing rooms; taught mothers thrift, better health care, and home economics; found employment for men; and lobbied for legislation to discourage vagrancy and vice.[78]

Josephine Shaw Lowell was a major force in the COS movement. She believed the almshouse or workhouse would become the agency for moral regeneration and training and was instrumental in setting up COS eligibility guidelines.[79] She soon adopted a structural view of poverty and became an advocate for labor and for the poor. During the Civil War, she had worked in the U.S. Sanitary Commission, later becoming chief fund-raiser for the National Freedmen's Relief Association of New York. A member of the New York Charities Aid Association, she did research in 1875 on able-bodied beggars, and in 1876 became the first woman member of the New York State Board of Charities. There she reported on the conditions in and administration of jails, almshouses, hospitals, orphanages, and other public institutions. Her call for reform led to the nation's first custodial asylum for mentally retarded women (Newark, New York, in 1885) and a state training school for girls in 1886. She was one of the founders of the New York Charity Organization Society in 1882 and led in organizing the Consumers' League of New York in 1890. She also founded the Woman's Municipal League to mobilize politically conscious women to lobby for reform legislation and, in later days, became a strong supporter of organized labor and a frequent organizer for striker relief. Lowell set the standards for the COS movement.

The most advanced thinking of the time on charity came from Amos G. Warner, a political economist who in 1894 wrote the book *American Charities*. Warner headed the Baltimore Charity Organization Society and the Public Charities of Washington, D.C. According to his analysis, poverty came not from personal willfulness, but from the complex interrelationships of personal and economic factors. The most common causes for relief applications were bad health, illness, industrial accidents, and industrial diseases. Most dependents, he found, were not capable of work. Despite the fact that unemployment and illness caused almost half the poverty in cases he studied, he concluded with a list of causes of poverty that included "evil associations and unwise philanthropy—which caused indolence and a variety of unhealthy appetites."[80]

By 1900, COS goals and delivery of services had changed significantly. Although in 1895 a majority of COSs in principle had no general fund for material relief, by 1901, of seventy-five societies, all but six provided outdoor relief in urgent cases from either emergency or general funds. By 1904, about half of all COSs maintained funds for relief.[81] The careful data workers had collected demonstrated clearly

Engage, Assess, Intervene, Evaluate

Practice Behavior Example: Critically analyze, monitor, and evaluate interventions.

Critical Thinking Question: What direct practice skills, origionally pioneered by the COSs, are still in use today?

that the causes of poverty were societal rather than personal in nature. Social work was becoming a profession, with casework practice and both personal and social diagnoses—the beginning of the person-in-situation focus of today's profession. Both United Funds and the Family Service Association came directly from the Charity Organization Society.

PRIVATE INTEREST AGENCIES

A multitude of other private agencies aimed at moral regeneration of the poor got their start or grew during the decades after the Civil War. By 1880, there were at least thirty nondenominational missions in city slums, along with orphanages, hospitals, homes for the aged, and homes or institutions to take in mothers or immigrants. Some aimed at religious conversion or help for tramps, among them the Salvation Army and Volunteers of America. Others, such as Crittenton Services, focused on the problems of women: unwanted pregnancy and prostitution.

William Booth founded the Salvation Army in London shortly after the Civil War. His daughter, Evangeline Cory Booth (1865–1950), grew up in Salvation Army work and in England became known as the White Angel of the Slums. In 1889, at the age of twenty-three, she took command of all Salvation Army forces in London and surrounding areas. Her older brother, Ballington, and his wife, Maud, commanded the Salvation Army in the United States. When they broke away to found the Volunteers of America, Evangeline took temporary leadership until her sister Emma Booth-Tucker and brother-in-law took charge. Evangeline took over the organization in Canada until Emma died (in 1904) and then returned to lead the U.S. forces, where she proved herself a fine administrator and efficient money raiser. She set up a disaster relief service following the San Francisco earthquake and later instituted hospitals for unwed mothers, a chain of residences for working women, and homes for the aged. During World War I, she set up canteens for soldiers, earning the Distinguished Service Medal for her work.[82]

Evangeline's sister-in-law, Maud Ballington Booth, joined the Salvation Army in 1882. After pioneering work in the London slums, she and her husband, Ballington Booth, moved to the United States and successfully established the U.S. Salvation Army. After being ordered by William Booth to another post, they resigned and organized the Volunteers of America (1896). While Ballington concentrated on the Volunteers of America, Maud organized the Volunteer Prison League to establish rehabilitation missions in prisons throughout the nation. In addition, she established welfare programs for prisoners' families, post-release employment counseling, and halfway houses, all supported by contributions from her lecture tours.[83]

Crittenton Services began when Charles Crittenton opened four missionary homes for "fallen women" in California. Kate Harwood Waller Barrett (1857–1925), who was educated in the Florence Nightingale Training School in nursing and attained her medical degree from the Women's Medical College of Georgia in 1892, contacted him because of her interest in the plight of prostitutes and unwed mothers. She opened Crittenton homes for unwed mothers, moving them in the direction of vocational training and skills for motherhood rather than moral proselytizing. In 1895 she established the National Florence Crittenton Mission, and as its vice president was in charge of more than fifty semiautonomous homes. Invited to the 1909 White House Conference for

Children, she later became a special representative of the Labor Department on a commission investigating moral grounds for the deportation of women aliens.[84]

Populism and the Settlement House Movement

Whereas COSs sought to differentiate between classes based on social Darwinism, settlement houses sought to reconcile class differences. The basic settlement house ideal was to have wealthy people move into areas where the poor and disadvantaged lived so that both groups could learn from each other. Canon Samuel Barnett, pastor of the poorest parish in London, established the first settlement house there in 1884. Toynbee Hall was based on the social gospel movement and attracted middle-class people to emulate Jesus by living among the poor. The first American settlement house was the Neighborhood Guild, established by Dr. Stanton Coit and Charles B. Stover on the lower east side of New York with the help of Dr. Jane E. Robers and Jean Fined. In 1889, Jane Addams founded Hull House in Chicago and Vida Scudder founded the College Settlement, a club for girls, in New York City. Soon Lillian Wald established the Henry Street Settlement, where she taught nursing to immigrant women. A great number of public health services arose from the Henry Street experience, including the Visiting Nurses Association in 1893. By 1910, there were more than four hundred settlement houses in the United States, mostly in Eastern and Midwestern cities.[85]

Settlement houses were run in part by client groups, and they emphasized social reform rather than relief or assistance. Three-fourths of settlement workers were women, and most were well-educated and dedicated to working on problems of urban poverty.[86] Early sources of funding were wealthy individuals or clubs such as the Junior League, and at first their founders tried to provide "culture" to members, such as art, music, and lectures. When they found a need, they added new features such as playgrounds, day care, kindergartens, baths, and classes in English literacy. Other services included art exhibits, lectures, and classes in homemaking, cooking, sewing, and shopping, especially for immigrant women who were not used to the facilities available in the United States such as grocery stores and the products they offered (fresh bread, milk, and canned goods). Settlement workers tried to improve housing conditions, organized protests, offered job training and labor searches, supported organized labor, worked against child labor, and fought against corrupt politicians. Over time settlement houses became centers of social reform, and clubs, societies, and political groups such as the Socialist party used them as bases of operation.

The most famous settlement house was Hull House in Chicago, established by Jane Addams and her friend Ellen Gates Starr in 1889 on the pattern of London's Toynbee Hall. It attracted many powerful women in its work. Among them, Jane Addams stands out. In her early years, after graduation from college, she was plagued by ill health. Unable to work, she traveled with Ellen Starr to England in 1887 and there became interested in Toynbee Hall. Returning to Chicago, she established Hull House and began her work in social reform. She became the most famous woman in America, a model of feminine virtue. She was

> a gifted scholar, a brilliant administrator, a shrewd tactician, and a marvel of a businesswoman, who handled an annual budget of several hundreds of thousands of dollars. But people kept insisting she was a saint.[87]

Addams influenced Theodore Roosevelt to mount a progressive reform platform in his presidential campaign in 1912, and became a leader in the Progressive party, although she considered resigning when it exhibited racist tendencies. With her founding of the International Society for World Peace, she became a "serious threat to national security."[88] Although she won the Nobel Peace Prize in 1931, when she died in 1935 she was considered by the FBI to be the most dangerous woman in America.

Addams was greatly influenced in her work by Florence Kelley (1859–1932), who changed her from a philanthropist to a reformer. Kelley, a Cornell graduate who became a socialist, was divorced in 1891 and moved to Hull House. There she worked for labor and political reform, particularly for children and immigrants. In 1892, reform Governor John Altgeld appointed her to the State Bureau of Labor Statistics, and she began to investigate factories and sweatshops in Chicago, involving Hull House women in her work. She became head of the National Consumers League and lobbied for fair labor practices, maximum and minimum work hours, and minimum wages for women.[89]

Mary O'Sullivan (1864–1943) also came to Hull House, where she interested Addams in the problems of working women. A labor leader and reformer, she organized the Chicago Women's Bindery Union in 1889. She and Addams organized a cooperative apartment house for working women, and women bindery workers held their union meetings at Hull House. O'Sullivan became one of Florence Kelley's twelve investigators into conditions in tenements and factory "sweatboxes" in 1892. In the same year, she became the American Federation of Labor's first woman organizer.[90]

Julia Lathrop (1858–1932) was appointed by Illinois Governor John Altgeld to the Illinois Board of Charities in 1893. During her tenure, she personally inspected all 102 county almshouses and farms in the state, along with all Cook County's charity institutions. A strong advocate of community care for mental patients, she became a charter member of Clifford W. Beer's National Committee for Mental Hygiene. Concerned with children, she helped Lucy Flower, Addams, and others in their fight for the first juvenile court system in the world, and Lathrop was the first woman to head a federal bureau: the Children's Bureau. There she instituted studies on child labor, mothers' pensions, out-of-wedlock births, juvenile delinquency, nutrition, and mental retardation.[91]

Lucy Flower (1837–1921), with Dr. Sarah Stevenson and others, helped found the Illinois Training School for Nurses in 1868. In 1886, she drafted legislation for a state industrial school for dependent boys, and although her bill was defeated, a private agency for that purpose was organized in 1889. She helped organize the Chicago Bureau of Charities, the Cook County Juvenile Court, the Protective Agency for Women and Children, and the Lake Geneva Fresh Air Association for poor urban children. Appointed to the Chicago Board of Education in 1891, she introduced kindergartens and manual and domestic training classes. She was the first woman to hold a statewide elective office in Illinois, as trustee to the University of Illinois.[92]

Grace Abbott came from work at Hull House to become director of the Immigrants' Protective League. With her sister, Edith Abbott, she joined the faculty of the Chicago School of Civics and Philanthropy, one of the first schools of social work in the nation.[93] Appointed to the staff of the federal Children's Bureau, she succeeded in having clauses prohibiting child labor written into all government war contracts during World War I. In 1921, she was named its head, succeeding its first director, Julia Lathrop.[94]

Dr. Alice Hamilton studied medicine at the University of Michigan, specializing in bacteriology and pathology. At Hull House she developed a well-baby clinic, and then went to the New England Hospital for Women and Children in Boston. There her interests in bacteriology led her to study medical problems of women in tenements and houses of prostitution. Later, she became a pioneer in industrial diseases.[95]

Hannah Greenbaum Solomon (1858–1942) became the first Jewish member of the Chicago Women's Club in 1877 and helped to establish the National Council of Jewish Women and the Illinois Federation of Women's Clubs (1896). In 1899, she was elected treasurer of the National Council of Women, and, with Susan B. Anthony and May Wright Sewall, represented it at the International Council of Women in Berlin in 1904. Working with Jane Addams and other social reformers on child welfare concerns, she helped to rehabilitate the Illinois Industrial School for Girls.[96]

Hull House and the many settlement houses throughout the nation provided forums and centers for women reformers. They led the way to community organization and group work practice within the profession of social work. Yet the settlement movement and the profession itself were primarily concerned with the white population. In fact, when Jane Addams tried to include African Americans in her work with settlement houses, she faced such opposition that a separate settlement house had to be opened for that group.

Child-Saving

Child-saving took impetus from the COS and settlement house movements. Whereas the settlement house movement worked diligently for child protective labor laws, COSs believed that poverty was inherited but that adult pauperism could be prevented by taking children out of bad environments. Before the 1870s, children were regarded as small adults, and childhood did not exist. From this perspective, their work was not exploitation but their duty to family, society, and God. As a result, children were required to work as soon as they were able, often in the mills by the age of three. They also were charged with adult crimes, tried as adults, and generally expected to maintain themselves. Even laws that required poor and dependent children to be taken from their parents and placed in foster homes or indentured were not for the benefit of the child's happiness—indeed, many would have probably preferred to remain with their families regardless of poverty—but to ensure good and moral work behavior throughout their lives.

... the first action to protect a child came when the Society for Prevention of Cruelty to Animals sued to have an abused child taken from her foster parents (Mary Ellen case, 1875).

Several trends changed this common perspective toward children. First, after industrialization child labor was not so necessary. Indeed, much of the concern of labor unions about child labor was not that the children were being exploited but that, hired in place of men, their wages held down those of adults. Second, with the decline in birthrate, children became more valued, especially among the upper classes, whose concern for their own children led to concern for all children. Also, this coincided with their growing interest in "saving" the lower classes. Third, the social reform movements of the 1800s began to redefine children as different from adults and protect them from abuse, neglect, and dependency. New knowledge available in psychology, sociology, and learning theories also contributed to a new perspective on the rights of children, and child welfare became a field in itself, as did juvenile justice.

Many would date the onset of the idea of *parens patriae* (the government taking the place of parents) from this time, but in fact the state had continuously intervened in child care, though usually to put children to work or keep them from becoming state dependents. Child protection became a new standard for social reformers, although the first action to protect a child came when the Society for Prevention of Cruelty to Animals sued to have an abused child taken from her foster parents (*Mary Ellen* case, 1875). Embarrassed that there was no such protection for children, both public and private agencies moved to organize. Adequate food, shelter, clothing, and medical care—part of the growing reform movements for all people—were more easily justified on altruistic grounds for children.

Benevolent societies formed to provide nurseries and day care for children of poor and working women, where before the only recourse for these women had been to put their children in orphanages. The earliest day care center in the United States opened in New York City in 1854, and enough more opened in the next three decades to found the National Federation of Day Nurseries in 1898. Private philanthropies also opened orphan asylums, such as the Benevolent Ladies Association Home, a facility for children whose mothers had died during birth or poor children whose mothers worked. Homeless mothers of good character could also be sheltered there. The idea was to isolate children from outsiders, including parents, to rehabilitate them through discipline and obedience to authority.

Children of African descent presented a special problem, for only a few people really cared about them. In Philadelphia in 1822, the Quakers founded an orphanage for the Care of Colored Children, followed by orphanages in 1835 in Providence and in 1836 in New York. White mobs burned Philadelphia's orphanage in 1838 and, during the Draft Riot of 1863, 500 white men burned the New York asylum. An orphanage in Albany indentured such children at the age of twelve. Here, a trust fund was established in payments of $100 per year by the indenturer, and given to the child at age twenty-one.[97]

"Contamination" by poverty was a major concern of both public and private child-savers. Therefore, taking children away from poor mothers was common practice, and outdoor relief and mothers' pensions were discouraged.

Reformers ... argued that it was better to break up a poor family than to risk accustoming children to life on the dole, which was so inherently demoralizing that it would transform them into lifelong paupers.[98]

Ironically, public agencies were more willing to give outdoor relief to mothers than were social workers, who argued that such aid should be given only if the mothers were closely supervised.

Until the 1870s, most children were placed in catch-all almshouses, their numbers doubling between 1856 and 1868. In 1875, the New York Board of Charities reported that 9 percent of all inmates were children (593) and nearly 300 over the age of two were "intelligent and in need of training." Following this report, New York passed a law prohibiting children's placement in poorhouses unless they "were defective, diseased, deformed, idiots, epileptics, or paralytics," that is, unfit for reform because they could never become self-supporting. In 1883, Pennsylvania passed a similar law.[99]

The orphanage movement was under way. Some states started statewide orphanage and placement systems; others required counties to provide them. The orphanages, however, were run on the almshouse model, with overseers earning their wages by saving on supplies. Mortality rates were about 20 percent.[100] Work morality was the major emphasis: rigid discipline, work schedules, and harsh punishments for rule infractions.

Perhaps the best known child-saver was Charles Loring Brace, who began the Children's Aid Society in 1853 (a national private agency that merged with Family Services in the 1960s). Brace believed that pauper families should be prevented from getting any kind of relief that would keep them together. His solution was to relocate children with families in the West, where they might learn the benefits of hard work in an untouched environment. For twenty years, haphazardly and without follow-up, often simply "taking" (kidnapping) children they felt were in need, agents loaded children on trains and shipped them to cities in the West, where they were "picked over" and chosen by families. Unfortunately, many families just wanted the extra help and badly mistreated the children. Many simply disappeared, either running away, getting lost, or dying. More than 50,000 children over a twenty-five-year period were shipped to the West, from 4,000 a year in the 1870s to about 500 in 1892.

The first Children's Aid Society was established in New York, with Boston in 1864 and most major cities following. Children's Aid Societies became adoption agencies with high standards for placement, requiring extensive knowledge of the child and his or her needs, a comprehensive study of available homes, and consistent supervision by the agency. Counseling and rehabilitation of parents were intended to keep families together, and this had priority over foster home placement. Adoption, which had been a simple agreement by the parties, began to require legal evidence of transfer of children similar to a registration of deeds. However, as early as 1851 Massachusetts required a judge to determine whether adoption was in the best interests of the child, along with consent of the natural parents.[101] By the late 1800s, orphanages, foster homes, and adoption were common.

Child-saving cut across all fields of reform, from public dependency to the establishment of juvenile justice systems. The first juvenile court law in the nation was drafted by the Illinois State Conference of Charities in 1899 and strongly influenced by such women as Jane Addams, Florence Kelley, and other Hull House workers. It was called "An Act to Regulate the Treatment and Control of Dependent, Neglected, and Delinquent Children" and dealt with children under age sixteen. The law provided a special juvenile courtroom and a separate record-keeping system and allowed for the appointment of juvenile probation officers. Within ten years, there were similar laws in twenty-two states, and by 1919 all states except Connecticut, Maine, and Wyoming had juvenile court laws.[102]

Undoubtedly much child-saving sprang from altruism, but other motives included the fear of pauperism, children's wages that lowered men's salaries, and the need to get children off the streets and out of criminal activity. For whatever reason, the public good required that children be "rescued," and as the movement progressed toward the twentieth century, there was a tacit acknowledgment, perhaps spurred by the new science of psychology, that children had special needs.

PUBLIC WELFARE EFFORTS

Although social welfare history usually stresses private philanthropy, in the late 1800s public welfare actually touched more people. Asylums, orphanages, workhouses, almshouses, and outdoor relief provided the necessities of life to the poverty-stricken. The Civil War brought greater centralization and more coordination to bear on the nation's massive needs, and in the 1880s governments slowly withdrew from subsidizing private organizations. They began to build their own service systems, especially in income maintenance, corrections, and institutional care for people with mental illness, retardation, or physical disabilities. Private charity interests continued with special groups of the deviant or distressed—unwed mothers, prisoners, immigrants, and children—but turned from income maintenance to professionalized casework. Gradually, their services were offered as additions to public services rather than in place of such services, and two systems of welfare developed.

Whereas private charities insisted that outdoor relief was more costly to society and more degrading to recipients, public welfare agencies, through their studies and statistics, noted that institutions cost society more in money, shattered families, longer-term care, and unhappiness. In addition, they were more difficult to supervise humanely. The public sector moved toward outdoor relief, although public monies continued to subsidize some private agencies, particularly those serving women and children. By the 1890s, few agencies except those serving the aged were subsidized. Instead, public monies were given to county boards of supervisors to provide outdoor relief. Cash grants ranged from $5 to $30 per month, but the more common kind of support was in food, clothing, or shelter.

During that period, poverty was severe even for those still employed. For example, in Lawrence, Massachusetts, the average salary was $500 a year in 1875, but a small family needed more than $600 simply to pay for essentials. Tenement rents in 1893, when wages dropped below $300, were often $200 a year. With depressions, or when people were injured or killed on the job, or when employers decided to lay off workers for any reason, disaster struck the common family. Added to this, massive immigration and the large "army" of tramps roaming the country necessitated a centralized and coordinated government system for adequate care of the poor, although "adequacy" was seldom achieved.

By the end of the century, the average wage in the United States was between $400 and $500 per year for a ten-hour day, six-day week, and poverty began at about $460 for a family of five. There were no employment benefits and unemployment was common. Women and children had to work, for men could not support their families alone. Almost 40 percent of the population lived in cities, and women made up 20 percent of the workforce.[103] Ten million people, or 12 percent of the total population, lived in poverty, and 4 million people received public assistance.[104] Almshouses in New York City gave outdoor relief to 209,092 people, compared with the 30,560 people aided in 1900 by private societies.[105]

Because the poor were so often ill, public health became an issue. The discovery of germs made public officials realize that some highly infectious diseases could be prevented through vaccination, aseptic treatment conditions, and better nutrition and sanitation among the poor. Although only a start was made in this era, the federal government moved toward national action. In 1878, foreign quarantine became the responsibility of the Marine Hospitals Service (forerunner of the Public Health Service). Emergency funds to prevent epidemics were appropriated in 1883 and a hygienic laboratory was added in 1887. The service took over foreign and interstate quarantine in 1893.

Public welfare monies were often used by politicians to buy votes. Immigrants used to the *padrone* system of their native countries were easily persuaded by money, food, and help in finding jobs. Officials gave special services to voters, but nonvoters such as women and children, regardless of need, went unaided. Friends and relatives of politicians were often financed from the public coffers, and politicians helped themselves; for example, in New York during the 1873–1878 depression, Boss Tweed stole $100 million from the New York City treasury. Serious irregularities in the Department of Public Charities and Corrections led to the complete suspension of outdoor relief from July 1874 to January 1875, and private agencies were flooded with desperate people seeking aid. Public relief was only partially resumed, primarily in distributing coal and giving aid to the blind. In 1876 and 1877, funds were allotted to be distributed through voluntary agencies.[106] In graft-infested Brooklyn, a municipal reform movement cut all outdoor relief in the winter of 1878, a period of depression and labor conflict, and desperate citizens rioted.[107]

The separation of private and public welfare continued as control moved from local overseers to state governments. Centralization brought the creation of state boards of charities and corrections, later to become state departments of public welfare. The first was in Massachusetts, in 1863, under the directorship of Dr. Samuel Gridley Howe (president for ten years), who emphasized the importance of keeping families together whenever possible and recommended humane treatment for those in institutions. The board's primary goal was to control and coordinate private and public agencies and to ensure legal standards of care.

Howe instituted a study in which board members inspected mental asylums, state hospitals, almshouses, industrial schools, and charitable institutions to which the state gave aid. From the survey, Howe developed a plan of inmate classification and regulations for administration. Because of concern for children, in 1869 a "state visiting agent" was appointed to attend the court trials of juvenile delinquents and to assume care for children not committed to reform schools—a forerunner of the juvenile probation officer.[108] In 1885, the state board of Massachusetts became the first to supervise charitable, medical, and penal institutions. Other states soon followed: Boards formed in Connecticut, New York, Wisconsin, Rhode Island, Pennsylvania, Michigan, Kansas, and Illinois. By 1897, sixteen states had state boards of charity.

The major results of such boards were better care and protection of dependent children because they were removed from poorhouses and placed in licensed children's asylums or foster care homes, more uniform and efficient administration of local public relief, a decrease in urban pauperism through the protection of immigrants, and improved care for the mentally ill. The state boards also gave a nationwide voice to social welfare by establishing the

American Social Science Association (1865), which later became the National Conference on Social Welfare.[109]

National organization was next, and Massachusetts, Connecticut, New York, and Wisconsin met in 1874 to form the Conference of Boards and Public Charities, a national network of private and public charities. In 1879, voluntary agencies were invited to participate in the conference's annual meetings. (The 1874 conference officially condemned outdoor relief in the middle of the 1873–1878 depression for demoralizing the workforce.) Within ten years, COSs dominated the conference, although it remained a forum for current thought and new policy. For example, in 1886 Frederick H. Wines questioned the pseudoscientific statistics that showed individuals to be the cause of poverty and crime, urging that the Conference look at the invention of labor-saving machinery, aggregation of capital in large and wealthy corporations, aggregation of population in urban centers, and the emancipation of women.[110]

At the seventeenth conference in 1890, Josephine Shaw Lowell argued that people should be given aid only "when starvation is imminent." Poverty or nonwork, in the majority's view, was a threat to a sound and moral economic system. She mentioned the obvious failure of public relief: the rising populations of poorhouses and mental hospitals and the growing number of unemployed vagrants. In rejoinder, Franklin B. Sanborn, secretary of the Massachusetts State Board, made a plea for outdoor relief or "family aid," saying that outdoor relief statistics often included medical care and burials and so were overstated. He concluded that except in hard times few able-bodied people were in poorhouses and that there would never be enough institutions for all the poor. He also deplored the idea that separating families was the best way to prevent dependency. As the century waned, private charities began to support government relief efforts. Many recommended mothers' pensions to keep families together, and most supported the move by the court system to create a juvenile justice system. By the end of the century, these trends had solidified. Public and private charities were clearly separated, and centralization of public welfare and outdoor relief had been accomplished.

PROFESSIONALIZATION OF SOCIAL WORK

Another post-Civil War trend was the professionalization of social work. In 1882, the newly formed Children's Aid Society of Pennsylvania began a training program, and in 1894 the New York Society conducted a course of twelve lectures on practical social problems. By the later 1890s, the Boston Associated Charities were paying workers to learn COS techniques and giving lectures on social and philanthropic topics. Mary E. Richmond (1861–1928) was instrumental in the professions development. In over forty years of practice, she defined casework and the importance of person-in-situation.

Richmond began her social work career as an assistant treasurer in the Baltimore Charity Organization Society and rose through the ranks to become its general secretary. She developed a consistent and coherent social work philosophy based on professional training and social research and maintained that both personal casework and social action were necessary to practice. In 1893, she began a series of educational conferences for friendly visitors, using social histories as case material; in 1897 she developed a plan and curriculum for a "school of philanthropic training." Both Edward T. Devine, executive secretary of the New York Charity Organization Society, and Robert de Forest, its president, supported her efforts, and in 1898 sponsored a course in applied philanthropy based on her ideas. This developed into the New York School of Philanthropy in 1901, offering a full academic year of classes for beginners in social services. The school, which depended on community agencies for field training, changed its name to the New York School of Social Work in 1919.

In 1899, Richmond published *Friendly Visiting Among the Poor* and, after numerous articles and lectures expounding her method, she published *Social Diagnosis* in 1917. The latter became the basic casework text for social work education. It taught the importance of social investigation before diagnosis and the need to base treatment on both insight and social action.[111] In 1909, Richmond was named director of the Charity Organization Department of the new Russell Sage Foundation in New York City, where she directed social research and developed further the methodology of social work. As the rift between tax-supported relief and private casework efforts developed, Richmond took the latter view, arguing that public outdoor relief, especially mothers' pensions, could not give the caring supervision that private social work practice provided. In addition, she noted the possibility of graft and unaccountability in public welfare and believed that private agencies would be more careful of how money was spent.[112]

In the same period, the Chicago School of Civics and Philanthropy was instituted under the direction of Hull House worker Julia Lathrop and Graham Taylor of the Chicago Commons Settlement. It became the Institute of Social Sciences in 1903–1904, under the Extension Division of the University of Chicago, and later the Graduate School of Social Service Administration, emphasizing research and social planning. Both it and the New York School were tied to city agencies for field placement instruction, a practice considered essential in the budding profession.

In the African-American sector after the Civil War, social welfare begun by free people of African descent a century before reached new heights in response to the atrocities being committed by whites. This is "race work," or "essentially community service coupled with the constant struggle for social justice and racial equality."[113] Martin and Martin say that black Americans

> built churches and schools in [unprecedented numbers and] made valiant attempts to bring into existing Black families the thousands of Black children ... left scattered and homeless by the war. White southerners ... were taking thousands of Black children under so-called apprenticeship laws [and using them] virtually as slaves.[114]

These movements were given impetus by the teachings of Alexander Crummell, an Episcopal minister who returned from his ministry in Liberia in 1873, and W.E.B. Du Bois, who considered Crummell his mentor and inspiration after they met in 1895. The two, in their many books and treatises, created a social work philosophy as crucial for African Americans as was Mary Richmond's *Social Diagnosis* for the early social work profession. Its main tenet was to instill "... in Black people the idea that race was a sacred entity worth fighting for...."[115] and it called for the "best tenth of the race to repay the sacrifices of their ancestors by dedicating their lives to the uplifting of Black people."[116] In answer to the call, African Americans took up the profession of social work as an extension to the race work in which they were already involved. The profession of social work continued on its two courses: that begun by the COS movement (which looked to individual casework to "cure" the distressed and deviant using the "medical model") and that following the settlement house movement (based on community action, group work, and social action and reform against structural problems of society, or the "structural model").

CONCLUSION: MOVING TOWARD REFORM

As society and social welfare entered the 1900s, the underlying motivations for aiding others—work ethic and Puritan morality—remained the same or became strengthened by new pseudoscientific reasoning. The Civil War's upheaval ensured federal supremacy over states' rights, but where it suited the purposes of the elite, states continued to act as they had, oppressing African Americans and exploiting child labor for the profits of the rich, for example. Social welfare had moved from the direction and influence of private philanthropists to centralization and bureaucratization, in both public and private sectors, and the two finally became separated. Yet the philosophies of blaming the victim, the morality of work, and the control of the poor by state, alone or under the direction of an economic elite, remained.

Social work moved from volunteer friendly visiting to a professional career, with goals, training, and an elaborate methodology of social diagnosis and social casework. It lost its elitist character as it split into two philosophies— the Charity Organization Society and the settlement house movements. Social reform movements still tried to control the poor and to teach Puritan and work ethic morality. Philanthropy, though it still existed, had distanced itself from social problems and was involved in "higher" issues such as the provision of public libraries, the endowment of colleges, and the funding of new social research.

The underlying issues of sexism, racism, and classism continued to direct the economic and political system of the nation. Social Darwinism, new scientific theories and information about diseases and medical practice, Freudian ideas about psychology, the new discipline of sociology, and the Cult of True Womanhood all gave legitimation to the exploitation of minority groups, including immigrants, women, and working people. Although labor unions were gaining power, they were also increasingly exploitative, especially of women and nonwhites. The Gilded Age, a period of immense accumulation of wealth for a very few, provides a showcase of exploitation. Although it freed some people so that they could begin social reform, that freedom—in suffrage, labor reform, social welfare, and political reform—came on the backs of others.

Social treatment progressed in new government and private agencies as the developing social work profession provided new methods and careful research on the causation and remedy for many social ills. Yet social control was an inextricable part of social welfare, advanced as much by the new technologies as was social treatment. It was visible and explicitly stated: in new regulations and procedures, the exploitation of workers, inattention to the needs of nonwhite people, and the repression, once more, of women. Prostitutes were blamed for sexually transmitted disease, woman workers were subject to low pay and terrible working conditions, married women were at the economic mercy of husband and society, widows were threatened with removal of their children, and professional women, under the guise of nurturing society, participated unknowingly in the control and exploitation of other women.

The following questions will test your knowledge and understanding of the content found within this chapter. For additional assessment, including licensing-exam type questions on applying chapter content to practice behaviors, visit **MySearchLab.**

1. The doctrine of nullification adopted by the South meant which of the following?

   a. They refused to follow laws with which they did not agree.

   b. They would not charge taxes they opposed.

   c. They refused to free slaves who were legally freed by state law.

   d. They threatened secession in order to protect slavery.

2. Which of the following was a practice of the American Federation of Labor (AFL)?

   a. It sought equal employment rights for women.

   b. It kept women out of the workforce through legislation.

   c. It helped women land better paying jobs.

   d. It prohibited admittance to women.

3. Black Codes mandated which of the following for African Americans?

   a. They could only own property in specific neighborhoods.

   b. They could only work as mechanics or artisans.

   c. They could be imprisoned for making too much money.

   d. Their children could be sold into slavery if they were unable to care for them.

4. Which of the following resulted in denied voting rights to many African Americans?

   a. The grandfather clause

   b. Jim Crow laws

   c. Black Codes

   d. Plessy *v.* Ferguson

5. What advice would you give an upper-class woman in the Civil War era?

   a. It is a mark of shame to work as a woman because only poor women work.

   b. It is her duty to be sexually passionate with her husband.

   c. Engaging in a social reform was deeply frowned upon since it required comingling with the poor.

   d. Charity work, teaching, and nursing were among acceptable careers.

6. You are working with a charity organization society and a family in need has come to you seeking assistance. How would you respond to their request for help?

   a. State that assistance would be offered if the breadwinner of the family died or had deserted them.

   b. Advise them to seek support from relatives, friends, churches, and employers.

   c. Deny them assistance unless they can prove each family member is able-bodied and worthy.

   d. Award assistance if the breadwinner of the family is a drunkard.

7. Discuss the changes implemented by the first state department of public welfare, launched by Dr. Samuel Gridley Howe.

Reinforce what you learned in this chapter by studying videos, cases, documents, and more available at **www.MySearchLab.com**.

Watch and Review

Watch these Videos

African-American Women and the Struggle for Civil Rights

Punching the Clock

Read and Review

Read these Cases/Documents

Jane Addams, "Ballots Necessary for Women" (1906)

Caroline Manning, "The Immigrant Woman and Her Job" (1930)

Abraham Lincoln, "The Emancipation Proclamation"

Secretary of Interior's Congressional Report on Indian Affairs (1887)

Jane Addams, "Twenty Years at Hull House" (1910)

Assess Your Knowledge

Go to **MySearchLab** to test your knowledge of key topics in this chapter with topic-specific quizzes. Conclude your assessment by completing the chapter exam.

8

The Progressive Era, War, and Recovery

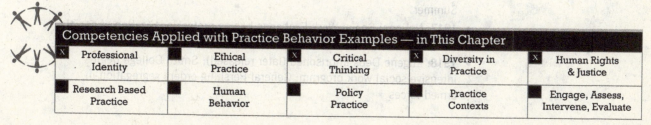

Competencies Applied with Practice Behavior Examples — in This Chapter				
X Professional Identity	Ethical Practice	X Critical Thinking	X Diversity in Practice	X Human Rights & Justice
Research Based Practice	Human Behavior	Policy Practice	Practice Contexts	Engage, Assess, Intervene, Evaluate

Times and Events

- **1900:** Booker T. Washington organizes National Negro Business League
- **1902:** New enforcement of Sherman Anti-Trust Law; National Reclamation Act passes to irrigate southwest deserts
- **1903:** National Women's Trade Union (NWTUL) forms
- **1905:** International Workers of the World (IWW, Wobblies) forms; New York begins treatment of mentally ill; first hospital social services department begins in Boston
- **1906:** San Francisco earthquake; Federal Employment Acts provides workers' insurances for federal employees
- **1907:** Gentlemen's Agreement limits Japanese Immigration; Lightner Witmer opens hospital for residential treatment of children with disabilities
- **1908:** Hannah Schoff organizes International Conference on Child Welfare in Washington
- **1909–1920:** States' Workers Compensation laws pass; states establish legislation for reporting sexually transmitted diseases
- **1909:** National Association for the Advancement of Colored People (NAACP) begins, led by W.E.B. DuBois; 700,000 acres of tribal land in Idaho and Montana opens to white settlement; First White House conference on Child Dependency
- **1910:** Immigrant Act Amendment excludes people likely to become burdens on society (poor, disabled, etc.); National Urban League forms; cure for syphilis found; Charlotte Gulich co-founds Camp Fire Girls
- **1911:** First statewide law on Mothers' Pensions passes in Illinois
- **1912:** Children's Bureau established under Department of Commerce and Labor; National Committee for Mental health (NCMH) begins (under Clifford Beers); Juliette Low founds Girl Scouts
- **1913:** Sixteenth Amendment (income tax) passes; Alien Land Law makes Japanese land ownership illegal; Alice Paul founds Congressional Union for Women's Suffrage (joins with Women's Party in 1917 to form National Women's Party)
- **1914:** Margaret Sanger found guilty of distributing contraceptive information; Seventeenth Amendment passes
- **1915:** Ku Klux Klan revives, first in Georgia, reaching 4 million members by 1925
- **1916:** Marcus Garvey begins Back to Africa Movement and United Negro Improvement Association (UNIA); Margaret Sanger organizes New York Birth Control League; NAACP marches on Washington to protest race violence
- **1916–1919:** uprising against African Americans takes place; 1919 Red Summer
- **1917:** National Social Work Exchange begins professionalization of social work
- **1918:** Eugene Debs imprisoned (later released); Smith College begins intensive social work program; General Pershing orders segregation in armed forces

- **1919:** Council of National Defense begins review of veterans benefits and psychiatric treatment; Veterans Bureau established (expanded in 1925 to include veterans' hospitals); Eighteenth Amendment (Prohibition) passes; Association of Professional Schools of Social Work becomes Council on Social Work Education (CSWE)
- **1920:** Vocational Rehabilitation is established in Department of Education; Jane Addams and Elizabeth Gurley Flynn, among others, become founding members of American Civil Liberties Union (ACLU)
- **1920:** League of Nations begins; Nineteenth amendment grants women's suffrage
- **1921:** Conference on Charities and Corrections becomes American Association of Social Workers
- **1921:** Johns Hopkins begins medical social worker training
- **1921, 1924:** Immigration Acts set up quotas based on national origin
- **1921:** Shepard–Towner Act established public health clinics
- **1924:** U.S. Immigration Acts restrict immigration by persons of African descent
- **1925:** Department of Justice introduces probation and parole services; Kentucky committee for Mothers and Babies formed, renamed Frontier Nursing Society in 1928; A. Philip Randolph organizes Brotherhood of Sleeping Car Porters
- **1926:** Senate passes law allowing unions to organize
- **1929:** Milford Conference proclaims casework the generic method of social work; New York Stock Market crashes, leading to Great Depression

THE PROGRESSIVE ERA

The Progressive Era—the period between 1900 and World War I—was a time of prosperity for the United States. For the general population, conditions of life improved as technologies changed the way of life: better roads and communication systems; electrification; better housing, water supply, and waste disposal systems; more amenities in terms of food, clothing, and other goods; and better hospitals and medical technology. The democratic thrust of the Progressive Era meant more citizen participation and an increase in government responsiveness and honesty, leading to secret ballots, direct primaries, and direct election of senators (the Seventeenth Amendment in 1914); civil service reform; regulation of campaign expenditures; accountability in government; the initiative, referendum, and recall; and local rule under city commission and city manager forms of government. New social legislation included antitrust laws, the Children's Bureau, child labor laws, and health and safety laws. The progressive income tax gave the federal government the means with which to govern on a national basis.

Questioning government policies and control of the economy by the elite became possible; for example, Louis Brandeis pointed out that low-paying industries and those who controlled them were subsidized by employees, families of employees, and society as a whole.[1] The radical voice of reform became strident as "muckraking" newspapers exposed big business, city bossism, graft, and corruption. Progressive reform was sought by a many-sided coalition of small businessmen, writers, settlement house workers, social workers, lawyers, clergy, farmers, labor reform movements, unions, women reformers and suffragists, middle-class clubwomen, men and women of African descent, and politicians. Many of the nation's intellectuals were members of this coalition: John Dewey, Paul Douglas, Jack London, Walter Lippmann,[2] and Charlotte Perkins Gilman. The growth of the Socialist party became one indicator: It had fewer than 5,000 members in 1900, but nearly 120,000 by 1912. Eugene V. Debs, its chair, ran for president in 1912, winning 6 percent of the popular vote—900,000 of 15 million votes cast—on a platform calling for government takeover and regulation of private industry.[3] In that election, more than 1,000 socialists were elected to public office.

The Progressive movement also was a reaction against big business and corporate profits. Under pressure, the government tried to intervene by enforcing the Sherman Anti-Trust Act in 1902, when the Supreme Court ruled against further incorporation of railroads by the Northern Securities Company. In 1906, the Interstate Commerce Commission (ICC) was given power to fix rates for railroad storage, refrigeration, and terminal facilities and for sleeping car, express, and pipeline companies. Telegraph and telephone companies were brought under ICC regulation in 1910.[4] In 1909, a 1 percent tax on corporate incomes over $5,000 was imposed; in 1913, the states ratified the Sixteenth Amendment, imposing progressive taxes on personal income.

Great trusts and monopolies formed or became stable, including Standard Oil, Consolidated Tobacco, and U.S. Steel. By 1914, supercorporations dominated coal, agrimachinery, sugar, telephone and telegraph, public utilities, iron and steel, railroads, oil, tobacco, and copper.[5] Between 1899 and 1929, total output of manufacturing increased by 273 percent,[6] and the gross national product had increased sixfold (see Figure 8.1). By 1910, 5 percent of the population owned nearly half the nation's property,[7] and in 1919 not quite 4 percent of all industrial organizations employed half the nation's workers and contributed more than two-thirds of the gross national product.

Poor laborers, whether men or women, were kept "in their places" by interlocking mechanisms of business, courts, social work, and government. "Protective legislation" based partly on social values that women were incapable of heavy work kept them in low-paying marginal jobs and gave employment

> **Poor laborers, whether men or women, were kept "in their places" by interlocking mechanisms of business, courts, social work, and government.**

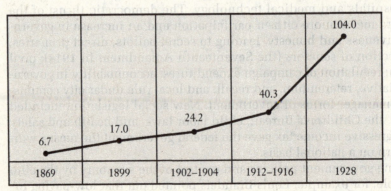

Figure 8.1

Gross National Product (billions of dollars)

to men who could work when and where women could not. Social Darwinism legitimated the eugenics movement, which advocated that all "inferior" people be sterilized so that their children would not "infect" society: immigrants not of Anglo-Saxon or Germanic stock, who were often English-illiterate; nonwhite people; criminals and prostitutes; the physically, mentally, or emotionally impaired, and often, public dependents and the poor. By 1915, twelve states had adopted sterilization laws based on the eugenics movement.[8] Dr. Harry Laughlin, a geneticist in the Eugenics Record Office, said in 1922:

> We in this country have been so imbued with the idea of democracy, or the equality of all men, that we have left out of consideration the matter of blood or natural inborn hereditary mental and moral differences. No man who breeds pedigreed plants and animals can afford to neglect this thing.[9]

In 1927, eight Supreme Court Justices, including Oliver Wendell Holmes, Louis Brandeis, and William Howard Taft, declared in *Buck v. Bell* that sterilization of the developmentally disabled, the insane, and the uncontrollably epileptic, among others, was constitutional. In his opinion, Justice Holmes stated that "... the principle that sustains compulsory vaccinations is broad enough to cover cutting of the Fallopian tubes," and that "three generations of imbeciles is enough."[10] By 1932, the Eugenics Society could boast that at least twenty-six states had compulsory sterilization laws and that thousands of "unfit" people had been prevented from reproducing.[11] In 1939, the Birth Control Federation planned a "Negro project" that, although not formally carried out, can still be observed in the "voluntary" sterilization of poor women—particularly African Americans and Hispanics—that occurred during the 1960s and 1970s. Involuntary sterilization was declared unconstitutional in 1939.

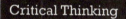

Critical Thinking

Practice Behavior Example: Use critical thinking augmented by creativity and curiosity.

Critical Thinking Question: What ideological values led some Progressives to take part in the Eugenics movement?

By the early 1900s, the United States had fulfilled its "manifest destiny" to control much of the continent. Now, in an era of worldwide imperialism, it began small imperialisms: Hawaii, Puerto Rico, Guam, and the Philippines were annexed in 1898, Cuba was made a protectorate in 1901, the Panama Canal Zone was in effect annexed by treaty in 1903, and the Virgin Islands were purchased from Denmark in 1917. Internally consolidated by railroads, the telegraph, and the telephone, northern European nations were engaged in wider imperialism: England and France peacefully divided up the African continent, and Russia, looking eastward, fought its losing battle with Japan. Landlocked Germany, surrounded by other nations eager to expand, began plans as early as 1903 to prevent the encirclement it feared from surrounding nations.

The new activities, new technologies, expansionism, and reforms that burgeoned after the Civil War burst into the twentieth century fueled by the Industrial Revolution. Speed became the new master of societies; gone were the leisurely agrarian settings that fostered extended families, time for local reforms, or even world diplomacy. Communication and transportation technologies made local emergencies national and even international; for example, the San Francisco earthquake in 1906 mobilized help from agencies all over the nation and brought scientists from Japan to help with the crisis. The quake and its fire destroyed nearly 30,000 buildings and ravaged the downtown area. About 200,000 people were left homeless and damage was estimated at $500 million, yet within a year, the city was back on its feet.

On June 28, 1914, Archduke Ferdinand, heir to the Austro-Hungarian throne, was assassinated. This brought a flurry of telegrams, telephone calls, threats, and pleas, and in the critical period between July 23 and August 4:

> there were five ultimatums with short time limits, all implying or explicitly threatening war.... In the final days the pressing requirements of mobilization time-tables frayed the last shreds of patience. And even before mobilizations were formally announced, armies prepared for war, making a shambles of the efforts of diplomats ... as time and the peace slipped away.[12]

Suddenly the world was at war, and neither time nor distance protected countries: Some people predicted that enemy air forces would bomb New York City. The country quickly adjusted to war conditions: Work in the munitions and supply business, in transportation, and in the production of steel led to such high profits that unemployment almost disappeared. African Americans from the South were recruited to work in northern factories, and the immigration of Mexicans was encouraged. More than 2 million African Americans came north, and more than 70,000 Mexicans entered the United States. In 1918, the same year that Czar Nicholas and his family were executed, Woodrow Wilson proposed the Fourteen Points on which the League of Nations was founded. For his work, he won the Nobel Peace Prize in 1919. However, in its new isolationism, the United States refused to join the League when it was formed in 1920.

After World War I, peace and prosperity returned for many. The average family could earn enough to live comfortably, particularly with credit now being offered for consumer purchases. Although the recession in 1921 brought widespread strikes, especially among dockworkers and steelworkers, standards of living continued to improve, and with higher profits and sales came high employment and a rise in real wages. A new belief in the "invisible hand" of the marketplace once more brought harsh reaction against public dependency.

Those who continued to help the poor or to work for social reform were considered un-American, and a "Red Scare" resulted from fear that the people's revolution in Russia might spread to the United States. It brought accusations of Bolshevism against socialists, suffragists, labor reformers, pacifists, settlement house workers, and social workers, and this encouraged many to get out of poor relief and into casework practice. Criminal syndicalism laws made it a felony to advocate violence for political change, and twenty-four states passed laws threatening jail for anyone displaying a red flag (350 people were jailed). Vigilantes attacked unionists and "reds," and loyalty oaths were instituted for teachers and other public employees. On one night in 1920, U.S. Attorney General Mitchell Palmer arrested 4,000 people in thirty-three states for being "radical aliens," and great numbers were deported.[13] People advocating political positions different from those in power were persecuted. For example, in 1918 Eugene Debs was sentenced to ten years (commuted in 1921) under the espionage and sedition laws, and Marcus Garvey, a Black Nationalist leader, was deported on trumped-up charges of mail fraud.

POPULATION MOVEMENTS AND IMMIGRATION

During the first two decades of the twentieth century, the U.S. population rose from 46.8 million to more than 100 million, with more than half living in the cities. Between 1920 and 1930, another 6 million moved from farms to cities.[14] Reasons for urbanization included immigration, a general migration to the cities, and an increase in migration of Mexicans and southern African Americans into unskilled nonfarm jobs. Urban industrial growth and incorporation made possible the undercutting of small businesses by large corporations, and in rural areas new agribusiness put tenant farmers and small owners off the land because they were unable to afford new high-production technology.

From 1900 until the Immigration Acts of 1921 and 1924, more than 19 million immigrants entered the United States,[15] of whom more than 75 percent came from Southern and Eastern Europe. By 1910, less than 20 percent of the population of New York City was native born.[16] Nearly two-thirds of the population was poor, and a third lived in desperate poverty. Women and children worked at lower wages than men, and men working full-time averaged between $400 and $500 per year, although it was estimated that the average family needed at least $600 to $800 to survive.[17] Wages were about 60 percent of basic subsistence.

Immigration Acts

Spurred both by the labor glut and social Darwinism, Congress passed the Immigration Act of 1907. Amended in 1910, it charged a head tax of $4.00 on each immigrant and listed those to be excluded: "idiots, imbeciles, the feeble-minded, insane, paupers, those likely to become paupers, people with contagious diseases, criminals, anarchists, children under sixteen unless accompanied by an adult, and laborers under short-term work contracts."[18] Quota restrictions passed in 1924 (in effect until 1965) were first based on national origin and the numbers of nationals in the United States according to the 1880 census, and then, in 1929, according to the 1920 census data. This effectively limited all Far Eastern immigration and greatly limited immigration from any Southern or Eastern European country.

Asian Exclusion

Although the Chinese Exclusion Act of 1880 was written primarily against the Chinese, it applied also to the Japanese, who came despite its restrictions and prospered. Their mutual benefit societies offered jobs to newcomers and education for children, and with their greater skills in horticulture they were able to compete with white farmers despite the high cost of the barren land they bought. To control this, Congress passed an alien land bill in 1913 forbidding Japanese aliens to own land. The Japanese circumvented it by incorporating with white partners or deeding it to their American-born children until 1920, when another amendment forbade this practice.

Japanese immigrants faced a rabidly racist American population. By 1905, newspapers, unions, the American Legion, and the California Farm Bureau were campaigning against the "Yellow Peril." Attacks on Japanese people and businesses became common: Even the Japanese scientists coming to help after the San Francisco earthquake were beaten. However, as a world power fresh from its victory over Russia, Japan could offer some protection to its nationals. Therefore, rather than banning Japanese immigration, President Theodore Roosevelt signed the infamous "Gentlemen's Agreement" with Japan in 1907, "voluntarily" limiting immigration to former resident aliens and their immediate families.

Because Japanese women could not immigrate unless they had relatives in the United States, Japanese men simply arranged marriages by proxy with women in Japan, but in the 1920 immigration amendment, Congress also forbade importation of "mail-order brides." By 1922, the Japanese had been declared "aliens ineligible for citizenship" (*Ozawa v. U.S.*, 1922), and the Chinese Exclusion Act of 1924 almost completely stopped their immigration until 1968. They remained a small group prospering in agriculture and service occupations: By 1919, they ran 47 percent of all hotels and 25 percent of all grocery stores in Seattle, for example.[19] By 1941, they raised 42 percent of California's truck-farm crops. However, at the onset of World War II, much of their wealth was seized and they were incarcerated in concentration camps.

Hispanic Immigration

Hispanic immigration, legal or illegal, has always been encouraged by U.S. business interests, despite the overt public outcry against it. In 1902, when the federal government passed the National Reclamation Act that watered the Southwestern deserts, white farmers could not meet the growing labor demands in truck and cotton farming, railroad construction, mining, and maintenance. They recruited Mexicans, who soon made up about two-thirds of the labor force. However, new agricultural technologies pushed them out and they moved up the California coast and into the Midwest as migrant workers. Another major recruitment era was World War I, and after the war agribusiness encouraged their immigration; in the 1920s, 500,000 workers and their families immigrated. Mexicans were specifically exempted from the Immigration Acts of 1921 and 1924.

With the onset of the Great Depression of 1929, Mexicans were no longer needed for farm work, and the Immigration and Naturalization Service (INS) created a border patrol to stop their illegal entry, making it a felony in 1929. Still, in the crop season, businessmen openly recruited them to the United States. After crops were in, neither their employers nor the law felt any obligation to return them to their homes. The company store system kept them in debt to their employers, and thousands were stranded without food, shelter, or clothing, and with no claim on schools, hospitals, or welfare. Their own mutual aid societies provided very limited help at times, and often the Mexican government itself appropriated funds to help its nationals stranded in the United States.

Between 1931 and 1940, only 22,000 Mexicans immigrated. Often they moved to cities, where they became strike-breakers in the great labor movements of the era and were subject to violence from other workers. Even those legally in the country had little protection from such attacks, and a movement to "repatriate" them began. Approximately half a million Hispanics unable to prove citizenship were deported, although the majority were in fact American citizens. Texas and California deported the largest numbers, but in Illinois and Indiana fully half of all Hispanics were "repatriated."

After World War II another Hispanic group, the Puerto Ricans, began to move slowly into the United States along the Eastern Seaboard. They, however, were American citizens, because Puerto Rico had been ceded to the United States at the end of the Spanish–American War and its people given citizenship in 1917 (Jones Act). As their island was slowly taken over by white landowners, they began to move to mainland cities. Although in 1899 they had owned 93 percent of their land, by 1930 absentee companies owned 60 percent.

Approximately half a million Hispanics unable to prove citizenship were deported, although the majority were in fact American citizens.

OPPRESSION OF AFRICAN AMERICANS AND NATIVE AMERICANS

Although social reformers took on nearly every other cause in the Progressive Era, the civil rights of African Americans were ignored. Over the history of the National Conference of Social Welfare, for example, only two programs were held on racial minorities.[20] Some settlement houses recognized their problems as they began to migrate to cities, but the few that actively tried to recruit African Americans found that their other clients refused to come. A few moderately successful settlement houses developed in large cities, but on the whole, African Americans were subject to rigid segregation or were blocked from even the meager social services that were provided other poor people. They were excluded from unions and from employment, although women found it easier to work, as domestics, than did men.

In 1900, nine-tenths of all African Americans lived in the rural South, but a new "enclosure movement" of their lands began after the Civil War, making them tenant farmers of their former owners or pushing them to Northern cities. Two million migrated: The largest number, 87,000, came to Washington, D.C., but Baltimore, New Orleans, Philadelphia, and New York each gained more than 60,000 African-American citizens.[21] In 1913, African Americans owned 550,000 homes, operated 937,000 farms, managed 40,000 businesses, and held $700 million in funds, even though more than 70 percent were literate. They had 40,000 churches, thirty-four colleges in the South, 35,000 teachers, and 1.7 million students in public schools,[22] although rigid segregation was still maintained in all facilities.

World War I brought thousands of African Americans to Northern factories. Thousands more entered the army—370,000 soldiers and 1,400 officers went into race-segregated units. More than half fought in France, often assigned to the French army. Among them, Henry Johnson and Needham Roberts were the first Americans cited for bravery, although African Americans were usually assigned menial chores. An official order from General Pershing in 1918 reinforced segregation: The prevention of contact between French and African-American officers was ordered so that white soldiers would not be offended, and contact between French women and African-American soldiers was forbidden. White officers could not eat, shake hands with, initiate conversations with, or commend African Americans.[23]

A great outpouring of hatred against African Americans took place during and after the War, related to the fear that they would take "white" jobs. In 1916, there were fifty-four lynchings, and despite a "silent march" of 20,000 protesters in Washington organized by the National Association for the Advancement of Colored People (NAACP), violence escalated. In East St. Louis on July 12, 1917, white workers drove nearly 6,000 African Americans from their homes and killed between 40 and 200. In 1918, there were sixty-four lynchings, and in 1919, with returning veterans seeking jobs, eighty-three African Americans were lynched and eleven burned alive. The Ku Klux Klan was revitalized: A rally at Kokomo, Indiana, drew 200,000 people. One of every eight white men belonged to the Klan at its height, and their terror was directed not only at African Americans, but also at Hispanics, Jews, and Catholics. Klan membership included senators, representatives, judges, sheriffs, and other government officials.

No African American could escape persecution, as the following account from 1918 demonstrates. Mary Turner, a pregnant woman, was hanged, doused with gasoline and motor oil, and burned.

> As she dangled from the rope, a man stepped forward with a pocket-knife and ripped open her abdomen in a crude caesarean operation. Out tumbled the prematurely born child.... Two feeble cries it gave—and received for answer the heel of a stalwart man, as life was ground out of its tiny form.[24]

The following summer, 1919, was called the Red Summer because of its violence. Over twenty-six riots broke out across the country: In Washington, Chicago, Omaha, and Knoxville, 170 African Americans were killed and 537 injured. They defended themselves and some whites died, as did whites who tried to help them. For example, in Omaha, a mob lynched and burned a man and hanged the mayor who tried to prevent his lynching.

African-American Leaders

Booker T. Washington was considered the "quintessential black" to white leaders: For example, Andrew Carnegie donated $600,000 in U.S. Steel bonds to Tuskegee with the stipulation that $150,000 be used to support Washington and his family so that he could continue his great work. He was invited to dine at the White House by Theodore Roosevelt, and some say that Roosevelt's defeat in 1912 had to do with his friendship with Washington, which alienated the South. Washington practically ruled "Black America" from 1895 to 1915,[25] sending annual messages to "his people" and having the final word on their political appointments. A strong advocate of vocational education, he urged them to seek economic rather than political advantage.

Among the more radical leaders was William Edward Burkhardt (W.E.B.) DuBois, a Harvard graduate whose mentor was Alexander Crummel. Martin and Martin[26] say that the early work of Crummel and DuBois

> gave early Black social workers ... a positive, forward-looking, spiritual outlook at a time of peonage, chain gangs, political disenfranchisement, de facto and de jure segregation, and lynching ... [and gave "race work"] a specialization in terms of its social problem focus ... in the purview of the budding profession called social work.[27]

After his return to America in 1894 from studies at the University of Berlin, DuBois became a professor of economics and history at Atlanta University, where he taught African Americans social reforms designed to promote social justice. However, he was appalled at the submissive attitudes of his African-American students. He and another Harvard graduate, William Monroe Trotter, organized a strategy-planning meeting in 1905 at Niagara Falls to demand civil, political, and social rights. This meeting, attended by Jane Addams, laid the groundwork for the NAACP, of which DuBois became the only African-American officer as director of research and publicity. In 1909, the First National Committee on the Negro met officially to form the NAACP; Florence Kelley and Lillian Wald were present. Trotter went on to form the more militant leftist National Equal Rights League. It consistently opposed segregation in such facilities as YMCAs and settlement houses and established the African-American press as a dominant force in the protest movement. The National Urban League, formed in 1910, had as its goals economic opportunity and civil equality through persuasion and conciliation. Its first executive officers were George Edmund Haynes, the first African American to receive a degree from the New York School of Social Work, and Eugene K. Jones. Also associated with the National Urban League were E. Franklin Frazier, Charles S. Johnson, and Forrester B. Washington—all leaders in social work. Frazier and Washington were, respectively, the second and third directors of the Atlanta School of Social Work, the first school to offer social work training to African Americans. The league's welfare component served as a channel for contributions from white benefactors to African Americans in need.

Many African-American men social workers in the early 1900s were ordained ministers influenced by the social gospel movement, social settlement movement, and the new science of sociology. Among them were George Edmund Haynes, Reverdy C. Ransom, Monroe N. Work, and Richard R. Wright, Jr. Haynes, Urban League co-founder and director, developed the first social work program at Fisk University and worked for interracial cooperation and understanding among Christians. Ransom, working in Chicago with, among others, Jane Addams, Clarence Darrow, Ida B. Wells Barnett, and Fannie Barrier Williams, influenced Illinois social welfare policies. He also developed church groups to help the poor and, with Jane Addams, the Institutional Church and Social Settlement, which helped newly arrived southern migrants. Work had special interests in health care and in his work at Tuskegee compiled records of every lynching in America to his time.[28] Wright became a community organizer for African-American unions in Philadelphia and developed a still useful definition of social justice: Service "... that gives all people the best opportunities to develop into the highest kind of personhood and to make the very best of their existence on earth."[29]

Marcus Moziah Garvey was the first radical nationalist of African descent in the twentieth century. His Negro Improvement Association advocated nationalism and a separate nation in Africa. The association's platform of racial separation, racial pride, and worldwide political liberation attracted millions of followers, mainly urban working-class African Americans. Garvey's goal was a united Africa under Africans, and in 1921 he declared himself provisional president of the new Republic of Africa. Raising more than $10 million, he organized cooperatives, factories, a commercial steamship venture, and a private army. In 1925, accused of mail fraud, he was deported to his native Jamaica, and died in London in 1940.[30] Amy Jacques Garvey, his second wife, played an active role as secretary, colleague, and leader in her own right in the organization.

African-American women were also leaders in the Progressive Era. Mary McLeod Bethune (1856–1913), the daughter of slaves, was perhaps the most influential woman of her time. Educated by missionaries, she started a girls' school in 1904 in Daytona Beach, Florida. Her class of five paid 50 cents each for tuition, and in two years she had 250 students. She paid her regular teachers $15 to $20 a week and relied heavily on volunteers. Later, she organized Bethune College, buying a former dumpsite for $250, and in 1922 amalgamated her girls' college with Cookman College, the first higher education institution for African-American men in Florida. Because its students were served unwillingly and inadequately in white hospitals,[31] Bethune–Cookman College had a fully equipped twenty-bed hospital on its campus.

Ida B. Wells Barnett (1862–1931), also a daughter of slaves, was a journalist and activist. Educated at Rust and Fisk Universities, she began her teaching career in 1884 at age fourteen. However, when she criticized the quality of education, she lost her job. Later, she bought an interest in the *Memphis Free Speech* newspaper and began an antilynching campaign. A protester against segregation, she sued the Chesapeake and Ohio Railroad for forcibly removing her from an all-white railroad car. Moving to Chicago, she organized local women in various causes and served as secretary of the National Afro-American Council. In 1910, she founded and became president of the Negro Fellowship League. From 1913 to 1916, she served as a probation officer in the Chicago municipal court. Although she took part in the 1909 meeting of the Niagara group, she refused to become involved in the NAACP because of its conservatism.[32]

Clubs such as those formed by Wells Barnett became the backbone of help for African-American women and families in the cities of the North. Darenkamp and colleagues say,

> ... the formation of black women's clubs represent a notable historical movement of this time. Along with fighting for equality for blacks and providing companionship, the black reform societies helped black women find employment, set up day nurseries and kindergartens, and established homes to protect young black women from sexual abuse. Like most middle-class white women of the era, black club women were middle class and educated but unlike many of their white counterparts the vast majority worked outside the home.[33]

African-American women's social work was a natural outgrowth of women's clubs and was based on African-American "fictive kinship ties." Martin and Martin define fictive kinship ties as

> care-giving and mutual-aid relationship among non-related Blacks that exists because of their common ancestry, history, and social plight.[34]

Prominent women social workers included S. Willie Layten, Eva Del Vakio Bowles, Maymie Leona Turpeau De Mena, and Thyra J. Edwards. Layten's goal was to integrate church work with social work, and in her position as first president of the Women's Convention of the National Black Baptist Convention she became active in every issue confronting African-American women. She encouraged women to train for social work, created settlement houses, and with social worker Florence Kelley created the National League for the Protection of Colored Women (NLPCW) to help Southern women migrants in New York City.[35]

Bowles worked extensively to integrate YWCAs, but, unhappy with her limited success, later opened African-American Ys. Given a federal grant, she established industrial and training centers for Southern women migrants and entertainment centers for World War I African-American soldiers.[36] De Mena joined Marcus Garvey's UNIA in 1925, first as assistant to Amy Jacques Garvey while her husband was incarcerated and then as a dynamic lecturer and recruiter for the organization.[37] Edwards organized the International Ladies' Garment Workers Union (ILGWU) in Chicago, and after the Depression became director of the Chicago Relief Association.[38] The Garvey Movement, Pan-Africanism, and radical Marxism were the inspirations for these women's social work, and they had to fight not only the racism of society and the budding social work profession but also the persistent patriarchal beliefs of African-American male social workers who had become accustomed to relegating women to "women's work," while professionalization belonged to men.

Native Americans

Native American activism, although repressed by the government and the Bureau of Indian Affairs, still existed in the Progressive Era. The Pan-Indian Society of American Indians was founded in the early 1900s to develop pride and a national leadership and to encourage educational and job opportunities; only a fourth of Native American children were being educated. A new religion also rose and was incorporated in 1919 as the Native American Church. Its sacramental use of peyote was thus protected from attacks by Christian missionaries.

Diversity in Practice

Practice Behavior Example: Recognize and communicate an understanding of the importance of difference in shaping life experiences.

Native Americans who fought in World War I were rewarded with citizenship, and in 1924 all became citizens, but they remained wards of the government. In 1928, appropriations for education were increased, and by the mid-1930s some boarding schools were replaced by day schools under the Johnson–O'Malley Act, which gave aid to states that provided public education to Native Americans.

Critical Thinking Question: Discuss the various acts of resistance to racism undertaken by Americans of color at the turn of the twentieth century.

LABOR AND THE UNIONS

The economy of the Progressive Era did not rise smoothly. There were depressions in 1907, 1910, 1919, and 1920 before the major crash in 1929. Each depression was accompanied by labor riots, strikes, and counteractions by police and courts. The depression of 1907–1908 paralyzed the country but led to the formation of such unions as the ILGWU. Major strikes, often led by women, broke out in 1909 when charities reported double the number of applicants in winter and quadruple the number in the spring.[39] In the depression of 1914–1915, a conservative estimate said 2 million people were jobless. In New York City, relief recipients increased by 23 percent in 1913 and 57 percent in 1914,[40] but charity expenditures increased only 14 and 17 percent, respectively. The New York Association for Improving the Condition of the Poor (AICP) paid men $2.00 a day for a maximum of three days for working for the city because the city could not afford to give them relief. In 1919, a vast wave of strikes broke out across the nation, and on Memorial Day in south Chicago police fired on a peaceful demonstration of workers, supporters, wives, and children, killing about thirty people, most of whom were shot in the back.[41]

Trade union membership declined throughout the early 1900s, from 3.2 percent in 1900 to a low of 1.5 percent in 1910. By 1920, it had surged upward to 6.6 percent.[42] Women were among the most active union organizers because the highly touted "protective legislation" proposed by unions and reformers benefited women far less than it did men. It stressed their inability to do hard labor or work long hours and cut back work hours, night work, heavy work, and overtime hours and reserved those jobs for men. If women won equal pay through their union activities, jobs went to men, who were preferred as workers for the same price. Protective legislation was first tested in 1908 in Oregon, where it set a national precedent for government intervention for women and children in the labor market. It also set a precedent for legal discrimination against women in terms of the jobs they could hold and the wages they would be paid, and contributed to channeling women into the rapidly expanding white-collar sector.[43]

In 1900 the average workweek for organized laborers was fifty-seven hours, whereas those in the building trades worked a forty-eight-hour week.[44] Unorganized laborers, such as steelworkers, worked a twelve-hour day and an eighty-four-hour workweek. Women and children often worked more than fifteen hours a day, at wages of about $1.50 for the day; for example, in 1905 a group of laundry workers in Illinois were hospitalized from exhaustion after working sixteen to twenty hours a day in the heat and dampness of steam-filled plants. Women were told that if they did not work on Sundays they need not come in at all.[45]

Women and Unions

Over 5 million women were employed in 1900, making up one-fifth of the nation's total workforce. By 1910, women comprised 25 percent of the labor force. A Women's Bureau survey during that period showed that 90 percent worked for economic reasons and that 25 percent were the principal wage earners of their households. By 1920, 25.6 percent of working women were in white-collar jobs, 23.8 percent in manufacturing, 8.2 percent in domestic service, and 12.9 percent in agriculture. A typical commercial laundry worker worked more than forty hours a week and took home less than $15.00 a month. In the same year, 75 percent of African-American women worked in agricultural labor, domestic service, and laundry work. In factories, they were paid less than were white women and up to a third less than men. The workforce was rigidly segregated, and amenities such as lunchrooms, cloakrooms, fresh drinking water, and clean toilets were provided only to white women.[46]

In the 1920s, fewer than 2 million of the 8 million wage-earning women were married, but by 1930 more than 3 million were married. Employers often refused to hire married women and often fired them when they married. Twenty-six states had laws prohibiting the hiring of married women.

Women were among the most active unionists because of the low pay and terrible conditions under which they worked. Industry-bred diseases were common, and women workers had a mortality rate more than double that of nonworking women and a third more than working men. In 1903, women founded the National Women's Trade Union League (NWTUL), which sought equal pay, an eight-hour workday, minimum wages, and full citizenship rights for women. The NWTUL was part of the American Federation of Labor (AFL), which tolerated but did not wholly support it, as AFL president Samuel Gompers vehemently fought both women's labor and "socialist movements."

Partly in response to AFL's refusal to help women and partly because of the socialist reforms taking place at the time, in 1905 radicals formed the Industrial Workers of the World (IWW), which advocated complete abolition of the wage system and the employing class. In the first five years of the century, it waged 13,964 strikes and 541 lockouts.[47] One such strike was against the mills in Lawrence, Massachusetts, where the governor sent 1,400 militiamen to back up police and state troopers. They were directed to "strike the women on the arms and breasts and the men on the head."[48] Strikers sent their starving children to strike supporters in other cities rather than end the strike, and the children aroused such sympathy that Lawrence mill owners refused to let any more leave:

> [T]roopers surrounded the railway station, clubbed the children and their mothers, and then arrested them. The mothers were charged with "neglect" and "improper guardianship."[49]

In 1909, when general strikes shook the nation, the NWTUL called a strike among garment workers against Leiserman and Company's Triangle Shirt Waist Factory. At the time, 80 percent of the garment workers were women, 70 percent were between the ages of sixteen and twenty-five, 65 percent were Jewish, and 26 percent Italian. Twenty thousand struck against the company. The police beat and clubbed them and threw them in jail. According to one judge who tried a young woman striker, "You're not striking against your employer … you're striking against God."[50] Yet every day up to fifteen hundred women joined the union. Middle-class women who had never before considered the plight of working women contributed money for bail and for relief.

This strike led to the founding of the ILGWU, which by 1914 was the third largest unit in the AFL. In 1913, the ILGWU signed the famous "protocol" contract, limiting work by gender. Only men could be hired as cutters and pressers, and the lowest-paid men had to earn more than the highest-paid woman, even for the same work. Cutters were paid $27.50 a week and finishers, examiners, and sample makers—jobs reserved for women—were paid $9.50, $11.50, and $13.00, respectively.[51] Modest gains of the strike included a fifty-two-hour workweek and limited overtime.

However, some of the most important demands for health and safety were ignored, and two years later the Triangle Shirt Waist factory caught fire. The factory, which had 500 workers, was on the top three floors of a ten-story building. Fire exits were kept locked to make sure employees did not steal from the company, and fire hoses were left unconnected. There was little chance for escape. Some women burned to death, others jumped from the windows, falling like "bundles of burning cloth" to their deaths. In all, 146 workers died. The judge fined the owners $75.00 for negligence.[52]

Among women important in the union movements were Bessie Abramovitz, Harriet Stanton Blatch (daughter of Elizabeth Cady Stanton), Elizabeth Gurley Flynn, Rose Schneiderman, Agnes Nestor of the glovemakers, Thyra J. Edwards of the LGWU, Mary Kenney O'Sullivan of the bookbinders, and Leonora O'Reilly. Abramovitz helped organize the Amalgamated Clothing Workers of America, one of the first unions to provide health care, housing, adult education, scholarships, and day care centers. Blatch organized the Equality League of Self-Supporting Women in factories, laundries, and garment shops. At its height it had 19,000 members. Flynn, a socialist, participated in twenty strikes and was arrested fifteen times between 1906 and 1926. Schneiderman organized for both the NWTUL and the ILGWU, becoming president of the latter. She also organized summer schools for working women, served as chairperson of the industrial section of the Women's Suffrage party, became secretary of the New York State Department of Labor, and was an unsuccessful candidate for the U.S. Senate. Franklin D. Roosevelt named her a member of the Labor Advisory Board in his administration.[53] Despite women's activities in the labor movement, they did not achieve top positions even in occupations they dominated numerically.

SOCIAL WELFARE IN THE PROGRESSIVE ERA

Several important changes took place in social welfare in the early 1900s. First, settlement house workers were ambivalent about joining the profession of social work and were progressively excluded from the profession of social work. Second, professionalization took the form of Mary Richmond's social diagnosis and casework method, which, although it considered the impact of environment on distress, remained oriented to personal rather than structural change. Third, bureaucratization and the use of scientific management techniques created new organizational structures and processes for accountability in the profession. Fourth, social workers, although they still protested that private charities could provide better psychic care to the distressed, formed new coalitions with public agencies that provided the funds for relief. For example, in 1914 they developed the Association of Public Welfare Officials in New York. Finally, although business interests were not altruistic, welfare became increasingly a business issue, and businesses encouraged welfare as a part of municipal reform to defuse political agitation and bypass political machines.[54]

In 1910, Kansas City organized the first Board of Public Welfare, followed in 1913 by Cook County in Chicago. In 1917, Illinois instituted a State Department of Public Welfare, and other states followed suit, with governors appointing heads of welfare. This innovation from traditional political appointments took public welfare out of politics except through the governor. Coll says,

> The reform spirit in which many social workers interpreted their role in the early twentieth century marked a departure from concern about pauperism to concern about poverty and a corresponding turnabout from the doctrine of personal fault to stress social and economic conditions as prime causes of hunger and squalor.[55]

After World War I, social reform was overwhelmed by a sense of prosperity and the belief that work would provide the final triumph over poverty. Spiraling prices and freely available credit increased profits and led the economy upward. The United States was the richest country in the world: By 1925, it was producing 55 percent of the world's iron, 66 percent of its steel, 62 percent of its petroleum, 52 percent of its lumber, 60 percent of its cotton, 80 percent of its sulfur, and 95 percent of its automobiles.[56] Demands for social insurance and public relief were considered a betrayal of the American way, and public dependents and social workers were seen as parasites or subversives. Settlement houses were believed to be hotbeds of radicalism, and gradually they became traditional social agencies, losing their autonomy as they took money from newly developing community chests. Professional casework, with its emphases on individual blame and middle-class morality, became the byline of the profession.

A new split in services for the needy emerged. The first cohort comprised professional social workers disassociating themselves from the "unworthy" poor through casework practice; the second was made up of public welfare bureaucrats, often political appointees without training. These latter were the "moral descendants" of overseers of the poor and were often chosen precisely for their antiwelfare stances. Poor relief remained extremely discretionary, based on personal values and beliefs relegitimated by the booming economy. Only the "morally deserving" were aided—often the aged, sometimes the handicapped, and white widows who could subject themselves to moral investigation. (Compare this trend with the split in services that created TANF in 1996.)

Religious, ethnic, and class differences continued to influence the provision of welfare. Protestant mission societies demanded church or Sunday school attendance as the price of assistance, and many new immigrants, particularly Catholics and Jews, avoided all church-related agencies, even nonevangelistic ones such as the YMCA. Language was also a barrier, and immigrants

After World War I, social reform was overwhelmed by a sense of prosperity and the belief that work would provide the final triumph over poverty.

were stereotyped as ignorant, slovenly, stubborn, and "inert" if they did not want, or could not afford, a middle-class lifestyle. Middle-class workers in both ethnic and mainstream agencies considered themselves better than those they helped, making them pay in the coin of humiliation for food, shelter, and clothing.

An enormous expansion of public education coincided with the great immigrations at the turn of the century. Kindergartens, vacation schools, extracurricular activities, and vocational education and counseling were offered by schools, and corporations, unions, churches, YMCAs, YWCAs, and settlement houses co-sponsored Americanization classes for immigrants.[57] Some states experimented with home teachers who took women to clinics, instructed them, and advised them on personal problems, housekeeping, and child care—the beginning of school social work. These *visiting teachers* paid little attention to girls, who were expected to stay home to help with housekeeping and younger children, but encouraged boys to stay in vocational education programs. Less money was spent for girls' education than for boys, and girls dropped out much more often.

Home economics classes were considered particularly important for immigrant women; however, few attended classes either because they had little time or because their husbands forbade it. For example, the immigrant population in Chicago in 1920 was over 300,000, but only 400 women attended "mothers' classes," and of these only 240 were regular students. Vocational education was highly supported for men. The Smith–Hughes Act of 1917 allotted 42 percent of its grants to schools of agriculture and 28 percent to trade or industrial schools. Seven percent went for general education and 23 percent for home economics courses for women. By 1920, most states had compulsory education to age fourteen, with a greatly lengthened school year. By 1923, there were sixty-eight land-grant colleges, twenty-four state universities, and seventeen colleges for African Americans.

Reforms for Children

At the turn of the century, one out of six children was gainfully employed—7 million children between the ages of ten and fifteen. No one knows how many under the age of ten worked, especially African-American children on southern farms, but 60 percent of farmworker children were employed by people other than their parents. Children worked in cotton, woolen, and silk mills, clothing and tobacco sweatshops, and coal mines and iron mills; up to 2.5 million worked in street trades.[58] Underage children working illegally were taught to hide when inspectors came. In 1900, Pennsylvania reported 120,000 children working in mines and mills, and New York reported some 92,000 employed who were under fifteen years old.[59] As textile mills moved south, employment of children increased until they made up 30 percent of all textile mill workers.[60] New labor laws and compulsory education began to make inroads on child labor: By 1910, only 2 million were working; by 1920, 1 million; and by 1930, about 667,000.

One of the most outspoken advocates against child labor was Irish immigrant Mary Harris Jones, known as Mother Jones (1830–1930). She fought for labor all her life, in the 1877 Pittsburgh railroad strike, the Haymarket riot of 1886, the Pennsylvania coal miners' strike in 1900, and the garment and streetcar workers' strikes in 1909. First an organizer for the Knights of Labor, she also organized for the United Mine Workers and the IWW. While supporting a textile mill strike in Pennsylvania in 1903, she found that 10,000 of the 75,000 mill workers were children, many of them maimed by machinery. She publicized their plight, speaking of

> Eddie Dunphy, a little fellow of twelve, whose job it was to sit all day . . . handing in the right thread to another worker.... Eleven hours a day . . . with dangerous machinery all about him . . . for three dollars a week. And . . . Gussie Ragnew, a little girl from whom all the childhood had gone. Her face was like an old woman's . . . little boys with their fingers off and hands crushed and maimed. . . . Philadelphia's mansions were built on the broken bones, the quivering hearts, and drooping heads of these children.[61]

Mother Jones marched her "children's army" to President Theodore Roosevelt's summer home, from Philadelphia to Long Island, feeding them with donations from people along the way. Although the president refused to see them, the nation became aware of the "crime of child labor," and shortly thereafter Pennsylvania passed a child labor law setting a minimum age of fourteen for child employment. Often beaten and jailed, Mother Jones continued until her death to "fight like hell" for children and the rights of labor.[62]

National intervention in child labor was prohibited by the Constitution, so reforms were fought out state by state. Although thirty-four states eventually passed child labor laws, they had so many loopholes that they were, for the most part, ineffective. The paradox is clear. Labor would benefit from the restriction of child labor, giving more jobs to men. However, labor standards for children would raise wages and reduce profits; therefore, although altruism won the day in law, loopholes and overlooked violations of the laws nullified the victory in favor of factory owners.

Child Labor and Social Reform

In 1902, Lillian Wald and Florence Kelley called a meeting of representatives of thirty-two settlement houses in New York City to discuss child labor, and in 1903 the group secured passage of a law regulating street trades. A national child labor committee was formed in 1904 as a clearinghouse against child labor, with such members as Edgar Gardner Murphy, Lillian Wald, Felix Adler (a crusader for housing reform), New York COS director Edward Devine, New York COS president Robert DeForest, and Jane Addams.[63] This committee influenced President Roosevelt to call the 1909 White House Conference on Child Dependency, which was attended by 200 prominent men and women. The conference went on record as favoring home care for children rather than institutionalization and recommended the creation of a public bureau to collect and disseminate information on children and child care.

In 1912, the Children's Bureau was established by William Howard Taft as a permanent part of the Department of Commerce and Labor. Its primary purpose was to protect children from early employment, dangerous occupations, and diseases. It advocated a minimum work age of fourteen in manufacturing and sixteen in mining, with documented proof of age, an eight-hour workday, and prohibition of night work. The first fifteen social workers ever employed by the federal government were hired to staff it, with Julia Lathrop as its director.[64] The bureau investigated and reported on all matters pertaining to child welfare and child life: infant mortality, birth rates, children's institutions, juvenile courts, desertion, dangerous occupations, accidents and diseases, child labor, and children's legislation. Its initial appropriation of about $25,000 was doubled, but was still far less than the money spent for animal research—$1.25 million.[65] The mortality rate for young animals at that time was lower than that of children.

All child labor reforms were called Bolshevik plots to "nationalize" children and families and were consistently declared unconstitutional. The Keating–Owens Bill to control child labor came to Congress in 1916 but failed to pass the courts; then an attempt to place a 10 percent tax on interstate commerce using child labor was outlawed. Finally, in 1924 a constitutional amendment was proposed, but was defeated by a lobby of manufacturers and Catholics, who called it a threat to family life. Nevertheless, by 1930, all states and Washington, D.C., had enacted child protection laws.

Mothers' Pensions

In the public arena, the most important social welfare reform of the Progressive Era was the granting of mothers' pensions—outdoor relief—to poverty-stricken widows. Social workers in private agencies consistently opposed this measure, claiming that outdoor relief would spread the contagion of pauperism to the next generation. They favored institutionalization: A study in New York found that COS workers had committed 2,716 children to orphanages solely because their mothers were poor, and almost another thousand whose mothers were ill.[66] However, this practice was increasingly questioned by settlement workers and judges in juvenile courts for, as Grace Abbott noted, mothers' child-caring contributions far exceeded their earning power in the marketplace.[67] Florence Kelley, speaking in favor of mothers' pensions, said,

> No money earned in the United States costs so dear, dollar for dollar, as the money earned by the mothers of young children.[68]

State after state chose to give mothers' pensions without consulting social workers in private agencies. The latter, faced with *faits accomplis*, demanded the right to investigate and administer the pensions using social casework to prevent recipients from "expecting relief as their right" and to "redeem" recipient families. They claimed that casework would ensure moral homes and proper upbringing for poor children. Convinced by their arguments as professionals and by the omnipresent public hatred of outdoor relief, states gave social workers the tasks they asked for. Their investigations were

> ... thorough if not humiliating. If accepted for aid—and the rejection rate was very high—the mother was assumed to be in need of "supervision." ... Why was a mother presumed to be competent to rear her children without caseworker supervision as long as the breadwinner was in the home but presumed to be incompetent when deprived of the breadwinner's support.... The growing profession of social work would doubtless have considered such a question impertinent.[69]

By 1911, twenty states provided mothers' pensions, and within ten years forty states allowed them. The first statewide law began in Illinois in 1911 as an addendum to the Juvenile Delinquency Code called the *Funds to Parents Act*. Wisconsin was next. The bills aimed at both providing for destitute children and establishing "moral" homes for children via a contract between the mother and the courts. If the agreement was violated by the mother, her children could be placed in foster homes or institutions. The programs were selective in the families they served, for there was still a strong reluctance to give outdoor relief. Recipients, therefore, were required to be of good moral character, widows, and white. Bell notes,

> Blacks were rarely admitted to this elite program for fatherless families, and as late as 1922 social workers reported that "low-type" families ... Mexicans, Italians, and Czechoslovakians were seldom helped. If they were, they usually received lower grants than "high-type" Anglo-Saxons.[70]

Most early laws confined aid to widows in the belief that assisting deserted mothers would encourage more desertion. By 1926, however, only five states still limited aid to widows. At local discretion, divorced mothers and those with husbands totally incapacitated, physically or mentally impaired, imprisoned, epileptic, or in an institution for the mentally ill were also included. Six states (Alabama, Georgia, Kentucky, Mississippi, New Mexico, and South Carolina) had no mothers' pensions. Coll says,

> In all states mothers' aid was not mandatory but at the option of county or municipality. So they were maintained only in a few towns. Ratios of children aided per 100,000 ... ranged from 1.4 to 331 in 1926. A few—Arkansas, Indiana, Texas, Tennessee, Virginia—aided less than 20 per 100,000.... By 1934, about half the aid to mothers ... [went] to cities of 50,000 or more.[71]

In 1926, maximum grants ranged from $70.00 a month in states such as California, Michigan, Indiana, and Ohio to $30.00 in Illinois, Iowa, Louisiana, Missouri, Montana, and Nebraska. In others, grants were made individually by administrative decision and according to need, although they could not exceed the cost of institutional care.[72] In California, women receiving mothers' pensions were called "gilt-edged widows," but in reality the payments were so low that welfare mothers still had to work, often as domestics or laundresses. In Chicago, where mothers' pensions began, Judge Pinckney's average award to mothers was $262 per year, and he was one of the most liberal judges.

Child and Maternal Health

The health of women and children was a primary concern of the Children's Bureau. Findings in 1909 indicated an unusually high infant and maternal mortality rate, higher for women than any cause except tuberculosis. The maternal death rate was 6.7 per 1,000 live births and more than 250,000 infants died before the age of one (10 percent). Poor clinical and obstetrical training were blamed, for at least half of all maternal deaths were considered preventable. Nearly 40 percent were caused by puerperal sepsis (bacterial infection caused by the delivering physician's dirty hands), toxemia, pelvic disproportion, and hemorrhage. As head of the Children's Bureau, in 1918 Julia Lathrop drew up a bill (later called the Sheppard–Towner Act) to establish public health clinics and hospitals. The bill was labeled a Bolshevik plot and an infringement on physicians' privileges, and opponents ridiculed its writer as an unmarried nonmother who presumed to instruct mothers on child care. Missouri Democrat James Reed went so far as to ask Julia Lathrop if she had ever been a mother to give her the right to talk about children. She replied, "No, sir, have you?"[73]

In 1921, after three years of lobbying, the Sheppard–Towner Act passed. Lathrop retired immediately before its passage, and Grace Abbott, newly appointed to direct the Children's Bureau, was given a five-year $1,252,000 grant to administer it. The program served nearly three thousand child and maternal health centers in forty-five states, and infant and maternal mortality dropped so significantly that the grant was extended for another two years. After the 1929 crash, a congressional committee ruled it too expensive, and although Congress dropped it, the program was reconstituted as part of the Social Security Acts of 1935.

One of the most important new health programs was the Kentucky Committee for Mothers and Babies (renamed the Frontier Nursing Society in 1928). Mary Breckinridge, a nurse, developed the program in 1925 to train nurse midwives in order to cut the alarming infant and maternal mortality rates in doctorless rural areas. Breckinridge hoped to gain federal Sheppard–Towner funds, but the director of Kentucky's Bureau of Maternal and Child Health Care stonewalled the federal grant application on the grounds that Kentucky's 2,500 practicing midwives, rather than outside nurses, should be trained. Breckinridge withdrew her federal proposal and raised money through women's committees to carry out her program.[74]

Medical and Psychiatric Social Work

As early as 1879 the National Conference on Charities and Corrections discussed mental illness and organized the National Association for the Protection of the Insane and the Prevention of Insanity. Its goals were research and education for better hospital policies and conditions, but it was opposed by hospital administrators and therefore failed after seven years. Psychiatric social work began on an organized basis in 1895, and New York State Hospital Services established its Pathological Institute in Albany in 1902 with a treatment program for the mentally ill. In 1905, Dr. Adolf Meyer was named chief of the New York State Hospital's Pathological Institute and moved it to Manhattan State Hospital. Meyer and his wife, a social worker, saw mental illness as maladjustment, and as Mrs. Meyer began to collect case histories, social workers became part of the mental health team. By 1906, the New York COS had established privately supported aftercare programs in each state hospital, and medical social work began to proliferate.

In 1905, the first social service department in a hospital was organized in Massachusetts General Hospital in Boston. Social workers went into the community to see patients in their homes and to investigate social conditions that had sent them to hospitals. Bellevue in New York City was established soon thereafter, and in 1907 Johns Hopkins established a social work outpatient section. In 1921, Johns Hopkins began a two-year program to train medical social workers. Between 1905 and 1917, more than a hundred hospitals in thirty-five cities hired hospital social workers, and in 1918 the American Association of Hospital Social Workers formed.

The mental hygiene movement began when a former mental patient, Clifford Beers, voiced his distress at his treatment over three years in mental hospitals (in his book *The Mind That Found Itself*). He founded the National Committee for Mental Hygiene (NCMH) and supported it himself, going deeply into debt, until in 1912 Henry Phipps donated $50,000 to the association. The Rockefeller Foundation and Russell Sage gave further support, and the NCMH began to look at broader concerns than mental hospital reform, over Beers's objections. The broadened mental hygiene movement focused on

- issues of the role of mental hygiene in education, criminology, and economic dependence;
- programs of "preventive" mental health and mental health treatment;
- research to define the "normal" personality (especially through improved child-rearing and education and the early detection and treatment of "abnormality"); and
- training a new generation of mental health professionals.[75]

Training mental health professionals referred especially to social workers, whose schools, professional associations, and journals were funded by the Russell Sage Foundation, the Commonwealth Fund, and the Laura Spelman Rockefeller Memorial Fund. Soon hospitals, private mental hospitals, and universities were establishing their own psychiatric care units. The mental hygiene movement led to the development of an alternative method to explain psychological problems, which had before been considered almost genetic in nature. This meant that mental disorder or deviance became a disease that could be prevented, detected, and treated. New diagnoses included the "maladjusted," the "psychopathic personality," and the "borderline patient." According to a text in use in the 1920s, people with personality disorders included paupers, prostitutes, misfits, criminals, drug users, bashful people, gypsies, old maids (by choice), unskilled laborers, dreamers and artists, deep thinkers, radicals and agitators, chronic grouches, peace-loving pacifists, and the over-studious.[76]

Veterans' services also had impact on the new mental hygiene movement. "Battle fatigue," a problem of soldiers returning from World War I, presented a different problem to the helping professions. No longer were the poor or deviant the only appropriate subjects for mental health care. The National Committee on Mental Hygiene and the Boston State Hospital collaborated to set up an intensive training program for social workers at Smith College in 1918. This program later became the Smith College School for Social Work, a model for psychiatric training for social work professionals.[77]

As early as 1896, Lightner Witmer developed the first psychological clinic in the United States (at the University of Pennsylvania) to introduce scientific knowledge about children and to train teachers, social workers, and psychiatrists. In 1907, he opened a hospital school for residential treatment of children with learning disabilities, and in 1909 Jane Addams and Julia Lathrop served on the advisory committee that established the Institute of Juvenile Research in Chicago. From these beginnings, Child Guidance Clinics began to open, funded in 1921 by the Commonwealth Fund for Prevention of Juvenile Delinquency. The Commonwealth Fund provided monies for many offshoots of the mental health movement: research on the causes and prevention of delinquency, establishment of an experimental system of school social workers, programs of direct public education, and the Child Guidance Clinics, which were actually demonstration projects.

The clinic personnel set up the first clinic in St. Louis and, when it became self-supporting, moved on to other cities throughout the nation. The clinics were oriented to providing "proper" child-rearing practices; that is, they stressed giving advice to parents and working with them, along with schools and courts, to prevent juvenile delinquency. Such clinics gave a tremendous impetus to the social work profession by stressing the need for trained caseworkers; they also set new standards for child care, based on new mental health knowledge and middle-class standards. A particular kind of conformity in child-rearing was intimated across class lines, and once again social welfare practices legitimated *parens patriae*, this time through mental health rather than poor relief.

Veterans' Welfare

Before the outbreak of war in 1914, veterans' pensions cost $174 million annually.[78] However, the war's terrible devastation made the nation eager to expand benefits for its survivors. In 1917, President Wilson appointed a Council of National Defense to review and recommend veterans' benefits, and a new benefit—the offer of readjustment and rehabilitation services for psychiatric problems such as shell shock—was added. Compulsory allotments were voted for families, at first paid by soldiers but later by the government. The War Risk Insurance Act was expanded to include voluntary insurance against death and total disability, medical and surgical hospital care, prostheses for those injured in service, and vocational rehabilitation.

By 1918, of the 4,744,000 in service, 116,000 had died and 204,000 were wounded, and by the mid-1920s, the Public Health Service had to increase its beds to 11,639 to accommodate veterans. Congress also authorized the use of beds in army and navy hospitals and in sixty national homes for disabled veterans. Because veterans' benefits were fragmented among the Bureau of War Risk Insurance, the Rehabilitative Division of the Federal Board for Vocational Rehabilitation, the Public Health Service, and the Armed Services, President Harding appointed a board (the Dawes Commission) in 1921 to establish the Veterans' Bureau. Benefits were further expanded in 1925, including the use of veterans' hospitals for veterans whose disabilities were not service-connected.[79]

During the war, the Red Cross provided canteens and clubs for servicemen, gave social services to men in military hospitals, and provided services to servicemen's families to help them cope with wartime separation. Although social work services had been previously provided for the nonpoor, they had been in assigned special categories, such as the mentally ill. The use of social work services for problems of "normal" (but stressed) people who were not poor gave a new impetus to the casework method in professional social work.

Aid to Blind People and Aid to People with Disabilities

Social workers objected to giving home relief to blind people because, they argued, flat grants did not take into account the degrees of need, discouraged industry, and made no provision for rehabilitation.[80] However, aid to blind people was approved by most people, and this was the first group to receive outdoor relief as a right, in Ohio in 1898. In 1915, Illinois required counties to grant $365 annually to blind people with incomes of less than $465 a year, and by 1925 twenty-seven states had aid to the blind programs.

Some states also aided programs for the disabled, such as the employment bureau opened by the New York COS to place the physically, mentally, and socially disabled in employment where their disabilities would not interfere with their work. After two years, the number of applicants averaged a hundred a month, and placements averaged eighty a month.[81] Vocational rehabilitation to help all categories of disabled people was established in 1920 in the Department of Education. The need continually outpaced the available federal funding, so not all in need were served.

Old Age Assistance

Pensions for the aged were one of the last reforms to be made, probably because society believed people should save for their old age or that relatives should support their aged parents. However, with new medical technologies and better nutrition people lived longer. Supporting them often went beyond the means of their children, and their small savings could not stretch through their longer old age. Many groups, including social workers, demanded that industry provide pensions, but they refused to do so voluntarily. Even if they had been willing, many aged people would have fallen outside their pension plans, such as women who had not worked, domestic workers, farmworkers, and day laborers.

By 1905, the Massachusetts Bureau of Statistics had noted the problems of the aged poor and recommended pensions as the only humane way of dealing with them (although Massachusetts decided against pensions in 1910). Both the National Conference on Charities and Corrections and the Progressive Party endorsed social insurance in 1912, including old age insurance. However, by 1914, only Arizona and Alaska had even limited plans, and fewer than 1 percent of workers were covered by private plans. After the war, pensions for the aged were tied to health insurance by such groups as the Consumers League, the Women's Trade Union League, and the American Association for Labor Legislation. This measure was fought by both employers and the American Medical Association, and old age pensions were lost in the battle.

As increasing numbers of the aged sank into poverty, dependence on public assistance grew, and by 1923 states were moving toward old age pensions. They helped "only persons of good character," however, and excluded people who deserted wives or husbands and those who had been tramps or beggars. Some states required fifteen years of residency and had limits on earned income and assets. Many also placed liens on recipients' property, to be claimed after death.[82] Montana, Nevada, and Pennsylvania passed limited voluntary bills in 1923, and the first mandatory bill was passed by California in 1929.[83] By 1929, eleven states had bills to provide pensions for the aged, and between 1929 and 1933 nineteen more enacted them.[84] Laws passed after 1929 were compulsory for the entire state. However,

> In 1929 only a little over 1,000 elderly persons received assistance, at a total cost of $222,000; by 1932 more than 100,000 persons were receiving OAA [old age assistance] at a total cost of $22 million a year.[85]

Most states set age eligibility for assistance at sixty-five, required that relatives support the aged if possible, set residency requirements, required recipients to be U.S. citizens, and ordered recipients to exhaust their savings before application.

Unemployment Insurance and Workers' Compensation

John R. Commons and John B. Adams of the University of Wisconsin led the fight for unemployment insurance, public employment offices, and regulation of industry. Although bills were introduced in a number of states, none passed until Wisconsin made unemployment insurance voluntary in January 1932 and compulsory in June of the same year. On the federal level, a bill was proposed to be administered by the Children's Bureau under a Federal Board of Unemployment Relief. It would have provided $125 million for the first six months, with another $250 million for the second. This bill also failed to pass, and not until the Social Security Act of 1935 was unemployment dealt with.

Workers' compensation, to help those injured on the job or the survivors of those killed at work, was first discussed at the American Sociological Association Conference in 1902 and again in 1905 and 1906. Despite the horrendous rate of industrial accidents at the time, Samuel Gompers and unions vehemently opposed workers' compensation, because they wanted welfare to be a union function and feared state intervention in union affairs.[86] However, the nation moved inevitably toward workers' compensation. Every year, half a million workers were injured in industrial accidents and 15,000 were killed. Employers blamed this on workers, saying that they knew the risks of the jobs when they took them. Courts generally supported this claim, although some states, including Massachusetts and Illinois, recommended industrial insurance to factory owners.

In 1906, under Theodore Roosevelt, the Federal Employment Act was passed, providing a minimum workers' compensation for federal employees, and in the same year the National Conference on Charities and Corrections appointed a committee on the issue. A National Conference on Workers Compensation was called in 1909, and shortly thereafter a major study was undertaken in Pittsburgh. This study, a comprehensive survey of all labor conditions in the entire city, was one of the most important social research efforts of the era. It was funded by the Russell Sage Foundation, and members of its committee included Paul Kellogg, a social worker; William H. Matthews, head of Pittsburgh Settlement House; Robert Woods, settlement house worker; Florence Kelley, director of the National Consumers' League; and John R. Commons, a well-known economist. The study looked at wages, hours, conditions of labor, housing, schooling, health, taxation, fire and police protection, recreation, and land values.

In 1910, Crystal Eastman published the final report of the study, "Work Accidents and the Law," arguing that the high rate of industrial accidents would continue as long as employers were not held responsible. After the Eastman report, thirty states investigated safety conditions in industry.[87] Ten states enacted workers' compensation laws in 1911, and by 1920 forty-two states had adopted her suggestions into law. Generally, they included compensation for workers and their survivors based on economic loss due to industrial accidents, employer responsibility for all accidents regardless of fault, and a voluntary insurance pool under public administration. Although many people were not covered and benefits were limited, it was a beginning.

Reformers tried to include health insurance in workers' compensation, but heavy opposition came from the medical profession, insurance companies, employers, Christian Socialists, superpatriots who saw all social insurance as "made in Germany," and, strangely enough, labor unions. Because of this, health coverage was dropped from consideration (except in some maternal and child health cases) until the major reforms of Medicare and Medicaid in the 1960s. Supporters of health insurance during the Progressive Era believed that illness was a more important cause of poverty than industrial accidents. They claimed it would not increase costs of medical care in the long run and that it would prevent poverty as it prevented illness. However, once more came the cry of Bolshevism and progress toward health insurance ceased. Katz says,

> In their struggle against social insurance measures opponents deployed the old American ideology of voluntarism, condemning the interference for the state, praising the efforts of private philanthropy, and stressing the importance of individual achievement. In place of voluntarism they held out the menace of social and racial degeneration, the destruction of the moral basis of American society, and the victory of other social systems, that is, socialism and Bolshevism.[88]

Juvenile and Criminal Justice

By the Progressive Era, the juvenile justice system had significantly changed the lives of poor children. *Parens patriae* influenced juvenile laws, new children's codes, the control of child labor, and mothers' pensions. Foster care, adoption, and protection for abused children were instituted by this time, as were separate facilities for delinquent children or probation under local courts for children committing federal crimes. The Federal Bureau of Prisons, organized in 1930, set up a national training school for boys, two detention centers, and federal prison camps.

For adults, the criminal justice system made much more use of probation, parole, and rehabilitation. In 1910, the New York COS led the way to a system of probation and fines for drunks so that they would not be incarcerated. For long-term offenders, commitment to a farm colony and hospitals for care and cure was recommended.[89] Federal prisons were established in 1890, and after riots in 1919 their conditions improved considerably. The Department of Justice introduced parole services and began probation investigations in 1925. In 1930, the Federal Bureau of Prisons expanded its services to include vocational training, recreation, and educational facilities, medical and dental care, and religious and cultural activities, and set up reformatories and correctional facilities for minor crimes and short-term sentences. A medical center was established for the physically and mentally ill.

Human Rights & Justice

Practice Behavior Example: Incorporate social justice practices in organizations, institutions, and society to ensure that these basic human rights are distributed equitably and without prejudice.

Critical Thinking Question: Identify social and economic justice practices in Progressive Era social work.

WOMEN'S MOVEMENTS AND PEACE PROTESTS

Women continued their reform movements in the Progressive Era, encompassing labor reform and children's welfare, the suffrage movement, the peace movement, and reforms related to sexuality. The areas of struggle, though often carried out by different groups, were related both by content and by interlocking memberships.

Suffrage

The suffrage groups that split after the Civil War coalesced in the 1900s into the National American Women's Suffrage Association (NAWSA). After a brief presidency by Carrie Chapman Catt (1849–1947), who succeeded Susan B. Anthony in 1900, Dr. Anna Howard Shaw (1847–1919), a Methodist minister and physician, became president. Although Shaw was an eloquent orator, she had almost no administrative skills and little tact. She consistently alienated men in power by attacking their politics, thus undermining their political support for women, and left NAWSA's administration in a shambles, with many of its staunchest supporters, such as Florence Kelley, resigning. Shaw resigned in favor of Jane Addams in 1911, and in 1915 the presidency was resumed by Carrie Chapman Catt.[90]

Catt, a tireless lobbyist, built NAWSA into a strong organization at both state and federal levels. She developed a "Winning Plan" of support and influence for legislative leaders in return for their favorable votes on women's issues, such as voting rights in party primaries and federal elections. During World War I, although Catt joined Jane Addams in forming the Woman's Peace Party, she supported Wilson's war policies. As reward, he threw his weight behind both suffrage and temperance movements. The prohibition amendment was passed in 1919, and suffrage was ratified in 1920. Its major goal attained, NAWSA became the League of Women Voters. In 1925, Catt founded the National Committee on the Cause and Cure of War and served as chair until 1932. She was also active in support of the League of Nations, for relief of Jewish refugees from Germany, and on behalf of the child labor amendment.

Politicians, unsure of the effect of the new women's vote, established the Women's Bureau in the Department of Labor in 1920 and passed the Sheppard–Towner Act for maternal and child health in 1921. Changes were also made in the civil service system, making it fairer to women, and in consumers' rights systems for pure food. However, women continued either not to vote or to vote with their husbands, and soon their effect on the national structure was discounted. After 1924, with the election of Warren G. Harding, the nation reverted to conservatism in terms of women's issues.

A more radical suffrage movement existed alongside NAWSA, merging into a peace movement that opposed Wilson's war policies. Among its leaders were Alice Paul, Lucy Burns, Rose Winslow, Crystal Eastman, and Mary Ritter Beard. Alice Paul (1885–1977), a devout Quaker, studied at the New York School of Social Work and lived at the New York College Settlement. She became disillusioned as a social worker and in 1906 went to England to work in settlements there. She joined the British suffrage movement led by Emmaline and Christabel Parkhurst, a radical group that practiced nonviolent resistance, including blocking roads and picketing homes and government buildings, and was jailed three times. Returning to the United States in 1910, she joined NAWSA but became impatient with its timid policies.

In 1913, Paul and her radical cohort formed the Congressional Union for Women's Suffrage.[91] It adopted a stance of active interference, including a spectacular suffrage parade in Washington, D.C., on the day of Wilson's inauguration in 1913. The parade became a riot, and troops were brought in to put down the crowd that was beating the women. The sympathy they aroused was short-lived, however, and in 1914 NAWSA withdrew its support of Paul. Although the suffragists never committed acts of violence, violence on a new scale was committed against them. Uniformed soldiers attacked women pickets blocking the White House, and by June 1917 they were being arrested. At first, the charges were dropped, but gradually the courts began to convict and jail them for up to six months. More than two hundred women from twenty-six states were arrested for blocking the streets, and ninety-seven were sent to the District of Columbia jail or the infamous Occoquan workhouse, where "the rats were so big dogs were afraid."[92] They were beaten at random, Alice Paul was tortured by being kept awake, and the authorities responded to hunger strikes by force-feeding the women by tube until their noses bled. Rose Winslow wrote,

> Yesterday was a bad day for me in feeding ... vomiting continually.... The tube has developed an irritation somewhere that is painful. Never was there a sentence like ours for such an offense as ours, even in England.... Don't let them tell you we take this well. Miss Paul vomits much. I do too, except when I'm not nervous ... we are making this hunger strike that women fighting for liberty may be considered political prisoners.... God knows we don't want other women ever to have to do this over again.[93]

The Congressional Union joined with the Woman's Party in 1917 to become the National Woman's Party, and Paul became its major spokesperson and organizer. After passage of the Suffrage Amendment in 1920, she drafted the first equal rights amendment in 1923. When it failed, she turned crusader for the League of Nations and founded and represented the World Women's Party at its meetings in Geneva. She continued as chair of the National Woman's Party from 1942 until her death in 1977, still seeking an equal rights amendment to end a societal sexism nearly untouched by the suffrage amendment of 1920.

Women and Health

The public health movement came at a time when women were still mostly excluded from regular medical practice. In 1920, for example, only 40 of 482 general hospitals accepted women as interns, and from 1925 to 1945 there was a 5 percent quota on women admitted to medical schools.[94] It was also a middle-class women's movement perceived as "cleaning society" as women cleaned their homes. Its financing was often justified with classist arguments about costs to the middle class of sickness among workers, absenteeism due to illness, and relief for orphans. Public health was closely related to the police; in fact, in earlier years it had been a police function, and public health workers continued to call on the police to enforce their mandates. Raids on tenements were commonplace, as police sought out disease carriers, including prostitutes, and such problems as typhoid were seen as visitations from God against sin.

Prostitution and Sexually Transmitted Disease

One major goal of the public health movement was to conquer sexually transmitted disease, and the method was to control prostitutes. Their health was not the issue, despite their high mortality rate after entering the field. The concern was to keep middle-class wives "clean" from infection by their husbands who used prostitutes. The men, however, were never blamed; the prostitutes were. Both men and women in the movement agreed on fighting prostitution, especially when "fallen sisters" obviously preferred prostitution to the back-breaking, low-paying jobs available to them.

A small minority of immigrant women prostitutes first caught the public eye, confirming social Darwinist, sexist, and nativist stereotypes. Women immigrants outnumbered men by the early 1900s, and many were young single women without family or friends, trying to survive in a new culture. The Immigration Bureau entered the battle to deport such "immoral" people as part of its sexually transmitted disease control program. Its commission found prostitution in virtually all ethnic communities but failed to note the power of poverty and the double standard in perpetuating it. Grace Abbott, then director of the Immigrants Protective League of Chicago, believed that poverty, loneliness, ignorance, and a desire for romance made immigrant women particularly vulnerable to sexual exploitation.[95] She condemned America's moral double standard and advocated that the Immigration Service pay less attention to keeping "immoral" women from immigrating and more to helping them to survive in America.[96]

Men transmitted such diseases across all class lines. In 1904, Prince Morrow, the chair of a committee investigating sexually transmitted disease, estimated that 60 percent of the adult male population would have either syphilis or gonorrhea within their lives (an estimated 450,000 new infections per year).[97] In 1910, a new estimate stated that 80 percent of urban males had sexually transmitted diseases and 60 to 75 percent of "marriageable" men had gonorrhea.[98] Syphilis caused sterility—for both men and their wives (as well as prostitutes)—and general paresis, a deterioration of the brain. Eight to 20 percent of insanity cases were linked to sexually transmitted diseases.

Children also suffered: In 1905, research showed that between 25 and 40 percent of all congenital blindness in infants was caused by gonorrhea from infected mothers,[99] and one of every four babies was blind. Wives were infected because doctors often colluded with husbands to keep sexually transmitted diseases secret even after they became detectable (for syphilis, with the Wasserman blood test in 1906) and curable (a 1910 arsenate compound destroyed the syphilis spirochete). Alexander Fleming's discovery of penicillin dropped the infection rate dramatically. Medical control was possible, but social ideologies prevented it. Many physicians would not discuss sexually transmitted disease, especially in public, for "by its nature it besmirched them." As early as 1903 the American Medical Association formed a standing committee on sexually transmitted disease, but because of its "dirty" nature, many hospitals would not admit sufferers as patients.

A study in 1914 estimated that between 28 and 100 percent of prostitutes had sexually transmitted diseases[100] and that infection of men was in most cases directly traceable to prostitutes. A later study by Dr. Howard Woolson, of the Bureau of Social Hygiene, estimated that there were at least 200,000 prostitutes in "a regular army of vice" and that 60 to 75 percent carried sexually transmitted diseases. An estimated 25 to 35 percent of the adult population was infected. He also noted that there was considerable shuffling back and forth between prostitution and low-paying jobs.

Legislatures took action to protect innocent wives: In Washington in 1909 and Wisconsin in 1913, laws required men to have physical exams before marriage, and by 1921 twenty states had similar laws. Sexually transmitted disease control was added to the U.S. Public Health Service in 1918, and by 1922 all forty-eight states had some kind of legislation requiring the reporting of sexually transmitted disease.[101] However, hiding the disease made the laws ineffective. Also, because wives were perceived as victims, they were not examined, so clandestine affairs or previous sexual liaisons continued to spread the disease. Finally, exams were not given carefully or the results examined because of doctors' belief in the morality of their clients, and therefore much disease simply escaped notice.

Police efforts severely reduced prostitution, and its regulation became a major issue. Because prostitution was considered "essential" for men, the men could not be regulated, but women could. One camp advocated moving all prostitutes to a particular red-light district under medical control. A wide variety of people opposed this, some feeling that medical regulation would give moral legitimation to the trade and others believing it was an infringement on the rights of freedom of women. Such eminent people as Theodore Roosevelt opposed the opening of a "tenderloin" district, calling for a war on commercialized vice rather than its regulation. Feminists and social workers such as Jane Addams and Maude E. Minier opposed such regulations because they controlled the lives of women but not the men who used them. Antiregulationists could also point to a study of European regulation by Abraham Flexner, who reported in 1914 that such containment and supervision was simply ineffective.[102]

In addition to wage-earning prostitution, there was a worldwide active "white slave trade"—women kidnapped and sold into prostitution. In 1873, Congress had passed an act aimed at breaking up this trade, and the Immigration Law of 1903 particularly excluded "prostitutes and persons who procure or attempt to bring in prostitutes or women for the purpose of prostitution." The law was strengthened in 1907 so that women immigrants who became prostitutes within three years could be deported. In 1904, a worldwide conference was held on white slavery, and in 1910, following its mandate, the United States made procurement of immigrant women for immoral purposes a felony. In addition, alien women living in a house of prostitution or employed in a place frequented by prostitutes could be deported.[103]

Abortion and Contraception

Abortion and contraception were also public health issues. Both were looked on as vice, and this closed the only avenues open to women who feared death in childbirth or the added burden of more and more children. Poor women still frequented abortionists, paying in pain and death, but middle-class women could arrange for "legal" abortions because of their "delicate conditions." In 1904, a symposium on abortion in Chicago, along with the Chicago Medical Society, came out against abortion. For a short time this influenced newspapers to drop their thinly disguised abortion ads and doctors to cut back on the number of abortions they performed. However, by 1908 the ads were back, producing an estimated $50,000 a year in revenue, and doctors resumed their profitable illegal practice on which city officials took protection payoffs.[104] It is estimated that after 1900 between 5,000 and 10,000 women died every year from botched abortions,[105] and by the mid-1930s, there was one abortion for every four pregnancies,[106] with about a million illegal abortions a year.

The fight for contraception was a fight against abortion, death in childbirth, and poverty. Pioneers included the socialist Emma Goldman (1869–1940), who as a midwife saw the desperate need for birth control and believed that women's control of their own reproduction was among their most important rights. Goldman gave the first public lecture on contraception, for which she was jailed. (Goldman also spent two years in jail for speaking out against the draft, and when the Red scare hit the nation after the war, she was among 248 leftists deported to Russia in 1919.)[107]

Another leader was Margaret Sanger (1883–1966), one of Goldman's students and founder of Planned Parenthood. A nurse among New York's immigrants, she saw her own mother die young from bearing too many children and like Goldman believed that women's emancipation began with control of their own bodies. She saw the terrible problems rising from lack of such control: too many children and the effects of illegal or homemade abortions. She wrote,

> I heard over and over again of their desperate efforts at bringing themselves "around"—drinking various herb teas, taking drops of turpentine on sugar, steaming over a chamber of boiling coffee or even turpentine water, rolling down stairs, and finally inserting slippery-elm sticks, or knitting needles, or shoe hooks, into the uterus.... Life for them had but one choice: either to abandon themselves to incessant child-bearing, or to terminate their pregnancies through abortions.[108]

Attending a woman who nearly died from an abortion and whom another pregnancy would kill, she heard her beg the doctor for contraceptive information. The doctor replied "Tell Jake to sleep on the roof." Three months later the woman was dead.

Sanger began her campaign for contraception by distributing handbills, some through the mail. She was arrested under the Comstock Act for sending out "obscene materials" and fled with her family to Europe. In Holland, she found that state-dispensed diaphragms had reduced maternal mortality by half. She returned to the United States in 1916 with more knowledge of contraception and opened the Brownsville Clinic in New York, conducting a house-to-house canvass to inform possible clients. Police closed her clinic and arrested Sanger and her sister, Ethel Byrne. Byrne was sentenced to thirty days in jail and began a hunger strike. After she went 103 hours without food, Commissioner of Corrections Lewis ordered her force-fed. Dangerously ill from the effects of the force-feeding, she was released on the promise she would not speak again of contraception.[109]

In Sanger's next clinic, which opened in 1917, physicians dispensed diaphragms smuggled in from Europe only to women whose medical history indicated that another pregnancy would be a health hazard. Other women were referred to sympathetic doctors.[110] Unable to get a license, Sanger turned over her Birth Control Research Bureau to physician Robert Layton Dixon, but he was also unsuccessful at obtaining a license. By 1927, Dr. Hannah Stone, the clinic's medical director, could demonstrate and prescribe diaphragms, but not until 1936 were doctors allowed to distribute contraceptives. The Depression, with its skyrocketing welfare costs, made contraception less socially offensive.[111] Although the American Medical Association in 1937 recognized that contraception was an important medical topic, it remained illegal until 1938, when a court ruling allowed physicians to import, mail, and prescribe devices. Even so, the under-the-counter racket in contraception remained a $250-million-a-year business because doctors were still unwilling to prescribe contraceptives.

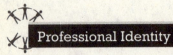

Professional Identity

Practice Behavior Example: Know the profession's history.

Critical Thinking Question: Compare and contrast the professional identity of social workers in the Progressive Era and today.

THE PROFESSIONALIZATION OF SOCIAL WORK

A professional association for social workers developed from community social work clubs affiliated with the Conference on Charities and Corrections, and the Intercollegiate Bureau of Occupations organized a separate social work bureau in 1913. In 1917, the National Social Work Exchange was organized; anyone who believed she or he was eligible was accepted as a member. By the end of World War I, there were seventeen schools of social work, and in 1919, under the leadership of Porter Lee, school representatives agreed on a standardized curriculum with casework as the major method. This group evolved first into the Association of Professional Schools of Social Work and then into the Council on Social Work Education. In 1921, the Conference on Charities and Corrections became the American Association of Social Workers—later the National Association of Social Workers—and members were required to have four years of experience or academic and professional training.

Professionalization also came through the fundraising community chests of charity organization societies. The first of these came in 1900, when the Cleveland Chamber of Commerce organized the Committee on Benevolent Institutions to accredit charities and evaluate methods for collecting and accounting for money. Altruism was only part of the goal, for the Hollis Amendment to the income tax law just before World War I provided tax loopholes for donors up to 15 percent of their income. In addition, those who supported community chests could decide which agencies would live and which would fail, and community chest boards, made up of locally prominent people, achieved great power over budgets and programs for member agencies.

Community chests became today's United Fund or United Way, whereas the service portion of charity organization societies evolved first into the American Association of Charities and then into the Family Welfare Association of America. In 1946, these organizations confederated into the Family Services Association of America. Settlement houses also became member agencies of United Way, losing their autonomy by accepting funds from community chests and losing their impetus for reform in the bureaucratization and professionalization of social work. During the same period, public welfare workers went from being overseers of the poor to county-level government bureaucrats in charge of investigating and doling out money to the "worthy poor." Thus the two historic themes of welfare—public and private charity—merged in the early decades of the century and parted in the 1930s to become public welfare and family casework services. Social reform movements that stressed that poverty was caused by economic and social issues solidified into the settlement house movement; this movement lost its voice for reform in the newly prosperous nation.

By 1929, there were 4,600 social workers belonging to forty-three chapters of the American Association of Social Workers (founded in 1921). Almost as many belonged to the American Association of Hospital Social Workers and the American Association of Psychiatric Social Workers. Twenty-five programs led to master's degrees in social work (MSW) and a new professionalism that would legitimate social work and gain support from state legislatures, foundations, and philanthropists. Psychoanalytic casework was the method of choice, and social workers could now come to the profession equipped with learnable skills as well as goodwill. New human behavioral theories became the knowledge base of the profession, which subsequently moved away from its historic mission of care for the poor. Veterans' services, the mental health movement, Child Guidance Clinics, the growth of an organized theory of social development, the growing interest in psychology, and Freudian psychoanalysis became the threads that bound the profession together. At the Milford Conference of 1929, social casework was proclaimed the generic method of social work in both purpose and methodology regardless of practice setting.

CONCLUSION: NEW FREEDOMS AND OLD CONSTRAINTS

From the Progressive Era and World War I to the stagnation and Depression of the 1920s, social reform and social work took separate paths. Social reform had virtually ended by 1920, and social work had become a middle-class profession. The government's reform legislation had bureaucratized county and state departments of public welfare, with more regularized funding and more accountability. The move away from institutionalization of the poor was almost complete and pensions, though far from adequate, were the trend of the future.

Although we often think of this era as one of increasing equality, in reality America had lost little of its classism, racism, or sexism. The gains made by labor unions were primarily for men, and women's secondary status in the job market was confirmed in most states by law. The polarization of classes had increased, and the great wealth of the few insulated and isolated them from the problems of the poor. By 1929, 5 percent of the population owned half the nation's wealth, and 42 percent of all families earned less than the $1,500 required for minimum health and decency for a family of five.[112] Racism based on economic problems and exacerbated by attitudes of social Darwinism existed as though the Civil War and Emancipation had never happened.

In this era, each social movement contributed to the new definitions of deprivation, dependency, and public and private social welfare responsibilities. Social reform also set forth *ideals* of equality for workers, people of color, and women and laid the bases for future civil rights action. Finally, the era clearly crystallized the scope and method of professional social work and set it apart from social reform. Concern with poverty, whether for the benefit of the needy or to maintain a low-wage workforce for business, became the domain of government bureaucrats. The new domain of social work became casework—mental health, psychiatric casework, school social work, medical social work, and so on—for people who could afford such services or were entitled to them as members of society.

As the government under Herbert Hoover continued to support big business as a right, unemployment began to push the economy into its downward spiral toward the stock market crash of 1929. Despite the many warning signals, the nation continued to operate as if economic realities did not exist: The "invisible hand" of the marketplace would set everything right, and the new profession of social work would, through casework, set to rights the growing number of the unemployed and poor. Suddenly, however, the bubble burst, and the United States faced a crisis that could destroy it.

> **The new domain of social work became casework—mental health, psychiatric casework, school social work, medical social work, and so on—for people who could afford such services or were entitled to them as members of society.**

The following questions will test your knowledge and understanding of the content found within this chapter. For additional assessment, including licensing-exam type questions on applying chapter content to practice behaviors, visit **MySearchLab.**

1. *Buck v. Bell* legalized which action?
   a. Preventing women from being hired for jobs that required heavy work.
   b. Barring nonwhites from purchasing property.
   c. Jailing anyone advocating violence for political change.
   d. Sterilizing the developmentally disabled and people deemed insane.

2. Which of the following contributed to the "Red Scare"?
   a. Refusal to help the poor or contribute to social reform.
   b. Native Americans leading violent revolts to reclaim land rights.
   c. Working in public relief and supporting social reform.
   d. An epidemic disease that caused disfigurement and insanity.

3. Which statement best describes immigration laws or practices in the early 1900s?
   a. All immigrants were eligible to receive public aid assistance.
   b. Hispanic immigration was encouraged by U.S. businesses.
   c. Japanese immigration was encouraged due to their advances in agriculture.
   d. The "Gentlemen's Agreement" signed by Roosevelt allowed immigrants to come to the U.S. as long as they already had a job offer.

4. The Triangle Shirt Waist Factory brought attention to what labor issue?
   a. Employees being forced to work without lunch breaks or rest periods.
   b. Workers not being paid for hours they worked.
   c. Harassment and abuse in the workplace.
   d. Health and safety practices.

5. What insight would you offer a middle-class woman in the early 1900s who was seeking an abortion?
   a. Since she is a middle-class woman, she could arrange for a legal abortion.
   b. A middle-class woman who had an abortion would be publicly shamed as a murderess because she could financially afford to care for the baby.
   c. She would have to get her husband's permission in order to get an abortion.
   d. It would be extremely difficult to find a doctor who would perform an abortion illegally.

6. What warning would you give someone in the early 1900s about sexually transmitted diseases?
   a. The majority of insanity cases were linked to sexually transmitted diseases.
   b. Doctors frequently colluded with patients to keep STDs secret from their spouses.
   c. Men and women could be tested for STDs at any time and were jailed if detected.
   d. Most doctors refused to treat STDs because it was considered "dirty work."

7. Discuss the focus of The National Committee of Mental Hygiene launched in 1912 under Clifford Beers.

MYSEARCHLAB CONNECTIONS

Reinforce what you learned in this chapter by studying videos, cases, documents, and more available at www.**MySearchLab**.com.

Watch and Review

Watch these Videos

Trials of Racial Identity in Nineteenth-Century America

The Lives of Southern Women

The Women's Rights Movement in Nineteenth-Century America

Read and Review

Read these Cases/Documents

Keating-Owen Child Labor Act of 1916

Upton Sinclair, from The Jungle (1905)

Herbert Croly, from Progressive Democracy (1914)

Assess Your Knowledge

Go to **MySearchLab** to test your knowledge of key topics in this chapter with topic-specific quizzes. Conclude your assessment by completing the chapter exam.

9

The Great Depression and Social Security for Americans

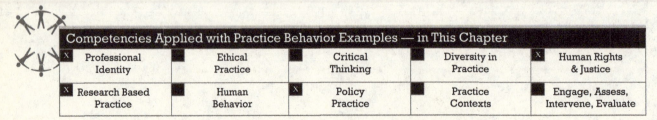

	Competencies Applied with Practice Behavior Examples — in This Chapter				
X Professional Identity	■ Ethical Practice	■ Critical Thinking	■ Diversity in Practice	X Human Rights & Justice
X Research Based Practice	■ Human Behavior	X Policy Practice	■ Practice Contexts	■ Engage, Assess, Intervene, Evaluate

Times and Events

- **1930:** Depression deepens; Wallace D. Fard founds Nation of Islam
- **1931:** Jane Addams shares Nobel Peace Prize; New York Association of Federated Workers organizes and social workers begin to unionize
- **1932–1972:** USPH syphilis study recruits African American men, leaves them untreated
- **1932:** "Bonus Army" marches on Washington for promised benefits, (Hooverville); Roosevelt elected President
- **1933:** Roosevelt's "Grand Design" begins: Federal Emergency Relief Act (FERA), National Industrial Recovery Act (NIRA), Public Works Administration (PWA) and Civil Works Administration (CWA) put into operation under Harry Hopkins; Frances Perkins appointed Secretary of Labor; Roosevelt appoints "Black Cabinet," including, among others, Mary McLeod Bethune, A. Philip Randolph, and Robert C. Weaver
- **1934:** Indian Reorganization Act partially repeals Dawes Act and restores tribal rights; Elijah Mohammad succeeds Fard as leader of Nation of Islam
- **1935:** Social Security Acts of 1935 (SSA) establish social insurance programs
- **1935:** (Old Age Insurance [OAI]), Workers' Compensation, Unemployment Compensation), public health programs (maternal and child health services, vocational rehabilitation, public health clinics) and public assistance (Old Age Assistance [OAA]), Aid to the Blind [AB], and Aid to Dependent Children [ADC], Mary McLeod Bethune founds National Council of Negro Women; National Labor Relations Act supports unions' rights to organize
- **1936:** Bethune appointed director of Division of Negro Affairs of National Youth Administration; Walsh-Healy Act abolishes child labor; NAACP Counsel Charles Houston wins right for African Americans to enter University of Maryland Law School
- **1937:** Congress of Industrial Organizations (CIO) forms; Federal Housing Administration (FHA) established
- **1938:** National Labor Relations Act (Wagner Act) legitimates unions
- **1939:** SSA adds Survivors' Insurance to OAI (OASI); World War II in Europe begins; leading activists such as A. Philip Randolph, Ralph Bunche, and John Davis question NAACP's strategies, move to National Negro Congress
- **1941:** United States joins World War II; Great Depression ends; Roosevelt bans discrimination in defense factories, establishes Fair Employment Practices Committee (FEPC); Lanham Act provides welfare services for communities affected by war
- **1942:** Congress of Racial Equality (CORE) forms under James Farmer; Japanese Americans, German Americans, and Italian Americans interned; Servicemen's Dependent Allowance Act provides family allotments; women enter branches of Armed Forces, including Army Nurses, Women's Auxiliary Corps (WAC), Women's Voluntary Emergency Services (WAVES), Women's Air Force Service Pilots (WASPS), Marine Corps Enlisted Reserve, and Coast Guard; segregated African American and Native American units go to war
- **1943:** CORE challenges segregation with sit-ins; A. P. Randolph assumes CORE coleadership

- **1944:** G.I. Bill passes with benefits in education, housing, and employment for returning veterans
- **1945:** World War II ends: Hiroshima and Nagasaki bombing kills more than 200,000; United Nations established
- **1946:** National Mental Health Act passes to care for needs of veterans, later for general populace; Truman establishes President's Committee on Civil Rights
- **1947:** House Un-American Activities Committee (HUAC) established, Communist labeling includes social workers
- **1948:** Truman desegregates Armed Forces; Eleanor Roosevelt authors Universal Declaration of Human Rights; Dixiecrats form States Rights Democratic Party
- **1950:** Ralph Bunche wins Nobel Peace Prize; Office of Civilian Defense integrates servicemen's health, welfare, and recreation services

The years between the complacency of the 1920s and the social revolt of the 1960s taught us many lessons. Although society clung to work ethic traditions, the Great Depression of the 1930s demonstrated that social and economic forces rather than individual fault created poverty, hitting both the wealthy and poor laboring classes. The Social Security Acts of 1935 were the most important social legislation in American history, though retaining ideals and traces of legislation predating the Elizabethan Poor Laws of 1601. Among these were definitions of worthy and unworthy poor, a low-wage workforce kept in line by social programs, the influence of the elite in the programs to prepare future workers, and the dedication to work as morality.

As the federal government assumed care of the poor, the social welfare system effectively split into two sections: the private sector, staffed by professionals inspired by psychoanalytic and social development theories, who treated middle-class clients with emotional problems; and the public sector, which provided income assistance to the poor. The public sector was further split: local public relief offices, staffed by people hired by political appointees, and the state and federal bureaucracies, staffed with more highly educated civil servants and often administered by professional social workers.

The Social Security Acts provided a safety net for many, but some still fell through.

The Social Security Acts provided a safety net for many, but some still fell through. Racist attitudes among welfare workers discouraged minorities from public assistance programs for which they might qualify. People in intact families unable to support their families through work did not qualify for Social Security's Old Age and Survivors Insurance program, unemployment insurance, or public assistance. County poor relief and general assistance programs were usually their only recourse. Mothers with dependent children, already suspect because they were disattached from a male breadwinner, were increasingly devalued when they sought public assistance. Although war efforts and unionization could lift most white male laborers from poverty, these other groups remained stigmatized and needy.

World War II changed the economic system of the United States from consumer to military production as demands for war matériel brought more prosperity. It was immensely profitable because it was ultimately consumable—as fast as weapons were produced they became outdated, and if used were destroyed. Moreover, war production was capital-intensive, rather than labor-intensive, so as more sophisticated automation developed, workers and their demands became less important in profit making. Hard-won unionization became increasingly oriented to management's needs once basic rights were secured. During the war, women and people of minority groups went into the labor force and, for the first time, made good wages. They created a new middle class and taught their children to reach for equality. When the war ended, women displaced by returning veterans went back to childbearing with a vengeance, producing the generation of children known as the baby boomers. Many minority people kept their jobs because of unions and because, remembering the lessons of World War I, the nation kept many veterans out of the labor market by financing their educations. This newly created middle class changed the demographic face of America as they took higher-level jobs, moved to the suburbs, and left the inner cities to the poor.

THE GREAT DEPRESSION

The Great Depression did not crash full-blown on the economy in 1929. There were many warnings: high unemployment, lack of consumer buying, loss of homes and farms as mortgages failed, and strikes and riots when workers could no longer earn a family wage. However, the business boom in the early 1920s led to faith that the economy would right itself. In fact, President Herbert Hoover urged companies to high production and high prices with a "supply-side" economics: Provide the goods people want, they will buy, and once more the economy will rise. This essentially conservative wait-and-see philosophy could not deal with the deepening depression. Different from former depressions, it was based on "paper money": stocks and bonds for the rich and easy credit for the poor. Workers—the vast underpinnings of any economy—had scant real money to purchase goods. A 1929 study by the Brookings Institution showed that although $2,000 per year was needed for basic necessities, almost 12 million families, or nearly 40 percent of the population, had annual incomes of less than $1,500, and another 30 percent made less than $3,100 per year.[1] Credit lent a false sense of security because payments could be delayed "until things got better," but as consumers lost their jobs, creditors foreclosed.

The whole economic structure collapsed in October 1929. A spiral of falling sales, rising unemployment, declining income, further production cuts, and more unemployment began. In some cities, unemployment reached 40 percent and in some counties, 90 percent. The gross national product, at an all-time high of $103 billion in 1929, fell to $55.6 billion in 1933, and did not reach pre-Depression levels until 1941.[2] By 1933, manufacturing was 20 percent below its 1929 level. Average weekly wages were down 35 percent and aggregate corporate profits, which had hit a record $8.7 billion in 1929, dropped to minus $2.7 billion in 1933.[3] Unemployment increased in nine months from nearly 3 million to over 4 million; three months later, in May 1930, it was at 4.6 million, and by September 1930, over 5 million were unemployed. By the spring of 1931, over 8 million were jobless, and by 1932, one of every four people formerly in the labor force was unemployed and one of every five was on welfare.[4]

The first people laid off were Hispanic and African-American men. By 1932, 56 percent of all African Americans were unemployed, and by 1933 nearly 18 percent of African-American family heads were certified for relief.[5] Next to go were African-American women, as white women displaced them in domestic labor. White blue-collar men lost their jobs next, and finally white women working in food and garment industries. White-collar workers and people in sales managed to hold on into the 1930s.[6]

By 1935, 30 percent of African Americans were on relief rolls,[7] twice the relief rate for whites. It was worse in the South: In Atlanta, 65 percent were on relief and in Norfolk, Virginia, 81 percent were. In some areas, a de facto slavery returned; in others, communists began to organize African Americans into cells by offering to help them deal with white employers, renters, and welfare agencies. Lynchings nearly doubled in the South as white unemployment worsened, and African Americans in the North lived in absolute squalor. Men rarely found work, and women worked at any jobs they could find. Domestics made an average $6.17 per week and did white families' weekly washes for 50 cents each.[8]

Wage-earning women in 1930 numbered more than 10 million. Because of the protective legislation of the Progressive Era, they worked primarily at "women's jobs" rather than in heavy industry. As husbands lost jobs, wives went to work in the expanding clerical and human services sector—jobs men refused to take because of low pay.[9] Minimum wage levels for women rose dramatically; in New York in 1934, for example, they climbed 16.6 percent in eighteen months while men's rose only 3.4 percent. However, their wages were still so low that employers preferred to hire women over men.[10] Ninety percent of women who worked did so for economic reasons and 25 percent were the family's principal wage-earners. In 1920, only 23 percent of married women worked, but the numbers increased to 28.9 percent by 1930 and 36.7 percent by 1940.[11] Fewer than a third of all employed women were married.[12] The Depression destabilized the family: The marriage rate per 1,000 unmarried women declined from 92 in 1920 to 68 in 1930, and the birthrate went from 27.7 per 1,000 in 1920 to 21.3 in 1930 and 18.4 in 1933.[13] Although divorce rates showed no appreciable change, suicides and desertions increased.

Problems were compounded by a massive drought all the way from Virginia to Arkansas. Moreover, new farm technologies threw tens of thousands of workers off farms, forcing them to cities and adding to unemployment and dependency there. Because the Depression was worldwide, the market for farm exports dropped to $2.5 billion in 1932, less than half that of 1919. Individual farm incomes dropped from $945 annually in 1929 to $379 per farm in 1933, although farm production fell less than 5 percent.[14]

Not until 1931 did Congress enact the Wagner–Rainey Bill over Hoover's veto. It authorized the Reconstruction Finance Corporation to make loans to tide companies over this "self-limiting" crisis. Believing in the power of private sector charities, Hoover instituted a national voluntary fund-raising drive through the Emergency Committee on Employment to ensure cooperation among private and public charities so that no one would be cold or hungry. However, the committee became merely a clearinghouse for correspondence, advice, and encouragement and gave little real aid.[15] Public relief expenditures skyrocketed to $54 million by 1931. Seventy-four percent of relief expenditures ($31 million) came from public funds during 1929 while in 1930 all relief expenditures doubled, with 75 percent ($51 million) coming from public funds. States tried to meet the demand: In 1931, New York, under the governorship of Franklin D. Roosevelt, disbursed funds to cities and counties for outdoor relief and work projects, and seven more states followed suit before 1932.[16]

Charities struggled valiantly to turn the tide of poverty and to prove the value of private casework methods to counsel people out of poverty. However, by 1931 they had given up and placed responsibility for relief on the federal government. Family welfare associations (formerly Charity Organization Society, COSs) and the National Federation of Settlements argued that poverty was societal rather than personal failure, and for all practical purposes the social work profession gave over income maintenance to public welfare. Between 1929 and 1932, public relief expanded eightfold but still provided less than an average of $30 per recipient a year.[17]

Social Revolt and Temporary Relief

Demonstrations, strikes, and riots occurred nationwide as the Depression worsened. In March 1930, more than a million people demonstrated in dozens of cities, demanding relief. Some forty workers were killed in strike-related incidents, and between 1933 and 1934 troops were called out in sixteen states.[18] Petition drives, at least three with more than a million signatures each, demanded government action. Unemployment councils fought against evictions, protested cutbacks in what little welfare there was, and demanded a massive program of relief. The New York Unemployment Council, for example, claimed to have prevented 77,000 evictions between 1930 and 1934. Across the nation, 2 million people were involved in unemployment movement actions, with thousands jailed or hurt and fourteen killed.[19]

In 1932, between fifteen and twenty thousand World War I veterans marched on Washington, demanding early receipt of the bonuses they had been promised by 1945. They and their families erected shacks across from the White House, but after a month Hoover dispatched soldiers to burn "Hooverville." Hoover vetoed the early bonus bill but Congress overrode the veto, granting half the "adjustment compensation certificates" to be paid to veterans in 1937. When the Federal Economy Act cut veterans' pensions and benefits, veterans marched again in 1933 and 1934, and the protest became so severe that in 1934 Congress rescinded the act. More than 10,000 veterans stranded in Washington were assigned to work camps in the Civilian Conservation Corps, and another 7,000 were sent either to special work camps if they were disabled or to the Works Progress Administration. The bonus payment, made in 1937, put nearly $3.5 billion into the hands of veterans.[20]

Workers turned to the left: Communists played a major role in San Francisco's longshoremen's strike, in Toledo independent radical socialists demonstrated, and in Minneapolis the Trotskyite Social Workers party led a general strike.[21] Six million workers organized in three years. Other citizens took political action. A retired California physician named Townsend started a movement to give federal pensions to every worker over age sixty-five—$200 per month, returnable to the government if unspent and financed by a sales tax. By 1935, he had 25 million signatures and 3 million people in Townsend clubs across the nation.[22] In 1935, Huey Long, the reform governor of Louisiana, set up the Share the Wealth party, with 27,000 clubs around the nation and a mailing list of 7 million names. Long unsuccessfully challenged Roosevelt's presidential candidacy and was assassinated in 1935.[23]

As governor of New York, Roosevelt, with social worker Harry Hopkins, had provided benefits and work projects for the unemployed. As president, understanding that only emergency measures would quell the growing social unrest, he sent Labor Secretary Frances Perkins to Europe to study social programs

that had staved off revolt there. The 1934 landslide victory of Democrats in Congress mandated a restructuring of the economy, and Roosevelt's subsequent actions strengthened the executive branch of the government enormously in the area of economic security. He expanded the cabinet and doubled the number of civilian government employees during the Depression years.[24]

Roosevelt's Emergency Measures

Roosevelt's wealth predated the Civil War, and he did not have social Darwinistic "training." He believed in social justice and felt that the government was obligated to help the distressed.[25] His Federal Emergency Relief Act (FERA), administered by Harry Hopkins, was based on the belief that relief from unemployment was a right, and that any work, even digging holes and refilling them, was preferable to direct relief.[26] The Roosevelt administration determined to give the estimated 70 percent of those without work jobs until they could be reabsorbed into private employment.[27]

Roosevelt believed that Keynesian economics—demand-side consumerism—was the key to economic health. This meant, briefly, that putting money in the hands of consumers would increase buying and begin the upward spiral of the economy. Roosevelt intended to do this by saving farms and homes, reducing farm production, hiring out the unemployed in public works, and supporting manufacturers so that they could hire the unemployed. His temporary measures, the Federal Emergency Relief Act (FERA) and the National Industrial Redevelopment Act (NIRA), were passed in 1933. Both were declared unconstitutional and were replaced, respectively,

Professional Identity

Practice Behavior Example: Know the profession's history.

Critical Thinking Question: How do fluctuations in the economy during the twentieth and twenty-first centuries effect social work as a profession?

with the Social Security Acts of 1935 and the Works Progress Administration. However, during the time they were in operation, they reduced unemployment; controlled savings, investment, and consumption; and developed mechanisms to keep people out of the labor market.[28]

Federal Emergency Relief Act (FERA)

Roosevelt gave Harry Hopkins almost unlimited authority as director of FERA, with $500 million in grants to disburse for direct relief. Hopkins took office in May 1933, and by the end of the next month had paid out $51 million to forty-five states, Washington D.C., and Hawaii, putting about 20 million people on the relief rolls. By the end of the year, $324.5 million had been distributed. Half ($250 million) went to states on a matching basis—one federal dollar for every three state dollars—and another $250 million was distributed on need alone. No more than 15 percent of the total could go to any one state, and although states had to bear part of the cost, there was no formal plan for determining "shares." States that raised the most got the most.

To qualify for FERA funds, each state had to establish an emergency relief authority to receive and disburse federal monies on estimates of need, using means testing.[29] Rents and medical care expenses were paid directly to landlords and health providers. FERA provided direct relief to both individuals and families, but work relief was encouraged. Discrimination against people of color was "to be avoided" but was not forbidden: A disproportionate amount of FERA money went to rural areas in the South. One of FERA's most far-reaching effects was to legally end the distribution of federal funds through voluntary or private agencies, adding impetus to the profession's move away from poverty work. Aubrey Williams, a social worker and deputy administrator of the Works Progress Administration, said,

> the sooner social work as a profession can turn its back on direct relief as
> a valid form of social treatment, the better off will be the nation and the
> higher the standing of social work.[30]

No set guidelines for relief giving existed except for means testing, so FERA workers' discretion determined eligibility, grant amount, and work relief. They checked real property and bank accounts; conducted interviews with recent employers; canvassed families, relatives, friends, and churches for other support; and visited recipient families once a month. Work relief was supposed to be paid in cash but was often in-kind.[31] In the three years of its existence, FERA spent over $3 billion.

National Industrial Recovery Act (NIRA)

NIRA instituted federal control of production, prices, and the rights of workers in industry. Its codes were intended to end cutthroat competition, raise prices, limit output, and provide for reasonable wages. It also reaffirmed the 1932 Norris–LaGuardia Act restricting federal courts from issuing injunctions against unions engaged in peaceful strikes, thereby legitimating unions and collective bargaining. For the first time, courts supported workers rather than employers. Unionization, which had been in a decline since 1920, began to pick up, and by 1935 unions had 3.7 million members.

Within half a year the ten largest industries in the nation agreed to come under NIRA.[32] Although it was declared unconstitutional in 1935, in its two years of existence it set standards for 2.5 million employers and 16 million workers. In that time, employment rose by 2 million, production rose from

62 percent to 79 percent of 1929 levels, and the gross national product increased from $55.6 billion to $72.2 billion.[33] Yet in 1935, 20 percent of the labor force was still unemployed.

Title II of NIRA created the Public Works Administration (PWA) with $3.3 billion given to industry for public improvement of the societal infrastructure, such as bridges, schools, parks, and roads. The Civil Works Administration (CWA) was folded into PWA and given a $400 million budget. However, neither PWA nor CWA used the money to increase employment. When NIRA was declared unconstitutional in 1935, it was replaced by two major programs: the *National Labor Relations Act* (1938), also called the Wagner Act, which aimed at controlling labor and management practices; and the Works Progress Administration (WPA)[34], which encapsulated the social programs of NIRA (PWA and CWA) (note: the Public Works Administration (PWA) was declared unconstitutional and mutated into the Works Progress Administrations (WPA)). Passage of the Wagner Act was aided by the excesses of industries vis à vis workers: more than $9 million spent between 1933 and 1936 on strikebreakers, labor spies, and munitions; a General Motors executive proposal offering a general force of 500,000 men to overthrow the government;[35] and Republic Steel's arsenal of 352 pistols, 64 rifles, 245 shotguns, 143 gas guns, and 2,707 gas grenades to be used against strikers. The Wagner Act outlawed company-dominated unions, heard unfair labor practices, and gave the Labor Relations Board power to determine bargaining units and petition courts to enforce its decisions.[36] It set a minimum wage (25 cents an hour, increased to 40 cents by 1945), a forty-four-hour workweek (forty hours in three years), and a minimum age of sixteen for child labor in industries of interstate commerce.[37]

Massive unionization of unskilled workers followed, joining together in 1937 to become the Congress of Industrial Organizations (CIO). By 1939, there were 10.6 million members in organized labor: 5 million in the CIO and 4.6 million in the AFL. African-American workers were welcomed into the CIO, but the Wagner Act allowed discrimination against women. Although NIRA administrator Hugh Johnson, Secretary of Labor Frances Perkins, and Eleanor Roosevelt opposed differential wages for men and women, about a quarter of the codes, covering nearly 17 percent of all workers, allowed lower wages for women.[38] The Walsh–Healy Act of 1936 abolished child labor and set standards for workers in industries with sizable federal contracts. In 1939, twenty-one states still had no minimum wage laws for women, and thirty states still lacked eight-hour workday laws.

The Works Progress Administration (WPA)

Roosevelt's first job program was the Civil Works Administration, established in 1933 under the direction of Harry Hopkins. Workers were paid at regular rates for civil works already in progress, but the program lost money, and along with PWA, the CWA became the Emergency Work Relief Program under FERA. Roosevelt's Grand Design, however, envisioned a better program, one that paid money directly to the employee, and on this basis he instituted the Works Progress Administration in 1935 to hire workers until the economy revived or until the Social Security Act became operative. WPA was funded at $4.9 billion, but in its short lifetime spent $10 billion. WPA paid less than did regular employment, but wages were higher than poor relief, and by 1936 WPA employed one-third of all unemployed Americans at minimum security wages in nearly 8 million jobs. From 1935 to 1941, more than 2 million men per month were on WPA payrolls, with a peak of 3.25 million in November 1938. WPA financed more than 250,000 projects and spent $11 billion in the construction of roads, bridges, libraries; painting of murals; cultural projects for unemployed artists, actors, writers, and musicians; and myriad other works.[39] Macarov notes,

> work relief during the depression was more expensive than direct relief would have been ... whether the work accomplished was worth the extra cost is debatable, but that it would have been cheaper to give out checks is hardly questionable.[40]

Other New Deal Programs

Between 1930 and 1934, more than 4,000 banks failed because unemployed home and farm mortgage holders defaulted. Although banks foreclosed, they could not recoup their losses because they could not resell the homes. "Runs" on banks by depositors trying to get back their savings occurred, and Roosevelt declared "bank holidays," forbade gold payments and exports, and established penalties against banks that hoarded gold. His emergency banking bill led to the Federal Reserve Bank system, enabling the Treasury Department to regulate the banking industry.[41] The Federal Deposit Insurance Corporation (FDIC) was instituted to provide federal insurance against loss of depositors' savings.

More than 250,000 families lost their homes in 1932, and in every month in 1933 a thousand more lost theirs. To combat this, Roosevelt set up the Home Owners Loan Corporation, through a Federal Housing Authority, to give insured loans for home repair, to refinance mortgages in danger of failing, and to grant new mortgages for prospective home purchasers.[42] A later bill, the 1937 Housing Act, provided for federally subsidized housing.[43]

As farm income fell, farmers threatened a nationwide strike. In response, Roosevelt authorized the Agricultural Adjustment Act (AAA, 1933) to provide money for the purchase of new farm technology and limit farm production by paying farmers to slaughter their animals and leave their fields empty. However, only large farmers could afford the new technology, and marginal and tenant farmers, particularly African Americans, lost their land. The number of tenant farmers decreased by 303,000, with African Americans constituting 56 percent of the decrease. Not until 1935 were farmers receiving federal help required to keep the same number of tenants, and by then the move to the cities was nearly complete. The AAA also bought surplus food under the Federal Surplus Commodities Corporation, which it then distributed to the poor.

By 1935, Roosevelt had instituted the Farm Credit Administration (FCA) to administer all federal agricultural agencies, including the AAA. Farm income rose from $2.5 billion in 1932 to more than $5.9 billion in 1935. Although in 1940 there were about 6 million farms, this was a loss of nearly 200,000, almost entirely in farms of African Americans.[44]

Youth Programs

Roosevelt established programs with the dual purposes of removing young people from the job market and giving them work training. The National Youth Authority (NYA) kept young people in high schools or colleges by giving them jobs to support them during their education. The Civilian Conservation Corps (CCC) employed young people to work in the preservation of natural resources in conservation camps. Young men between the ages of eighteen and twenty-five from relief families worked on reforestation, soil conservation, and flood control. They were given board and room and $30 a month, of which $25 was sent to their families. More than 2.75 million participated during the life of CCC, which was terminated in 1942.

Eleanor Roosevelt and Women in the New Deal

Eleanor Roosevelt (1884–1962) worked in settlement houses in the early 1900s and at age eighteen joined the National Consumers' League to work in the labor movement. She married her cousin Franklin in 1905 and provided constant support to him in his political career, particularly after his crippling attack of polio in 1921. While rearing six children, she continued her interest and activities in social causes and public affairs. She worked at Red Cross canteens for soldiers during World War I, encouraged the appointment of Frances Perkins first as New York's state industrial commissioner and then as U.S. Secretary of Labor, and was instrumental in such forward-looking social legislation as the National Youth Authority. She also worked to improve conditions for the mentally ill, coordinated the League of Women Voters' legislative plans, and was an active member of the Women's Trade Union League and the Democratic Party. She also developed (with Franklin) the National Polio Center at Warm Springs, Georgia, and taught sociology, economics, and government at the Todhunter School in New York City, of which she was part owner.

Eleanor brought an unprecedented number of women into Roosevelt's administration: Ellen Woodward, Hilda Worthington Smith, and Florence Kerr, all of whom held WPA appointments, and Lorena Hickok, a social worker who researched the impact of the New Deal programs. Eleanor also encouraged the rejuvenation of the women's division of the Democratic Party under the leadership of Molly Dawson.[45] Because of the president's disability, Eleanor did much of the ceremonial and public relations work of the presidency, including the inspection of government works projects. She actively supported civil rights legislation and helped to financially support the NAACP. She publicly resigned from the Daughters of the American Revolution after it denied African American operatic soprano Marion Anderson permission to sing at Constitution Hall, arranging a concert at the Lincoln Memorial that was attended by 75,000 people. She argued for ending discrimination in the armed services and defense employment, supported student socialist groups, provided a forum for women's causes, defended social welfare programs, and served as advocate for Jewish refugees, especially when the president refused admission of Jewish children to the United States during Hitler's pogroms. She brought poor Southern textile workers, Northern garment workers, African-American civil rights workers, and student activists to dinner at the White House so her husband could hear them, although he seldom acted on their issues.

After her husband's death, Eleanor continued to be the most effective woman in American politics. She encouraged Truman to push forward with civil rights and to maintain the temporary Fair Employment Practices Commission. As American delegate to the United Nations in 1945, she was the fundamental author of the Universal Declaration of Human Rights passed by the General Assembly in December 1948. A commissioner of the U.S. Commission on Human Rights in 1953, she spoke out against the McCarthy communist hunts. Retiring in 1953, after Dwight D. Eisenhower became president, she continued to work in the American Association for the United Nations. Her last official position was a chair of President Kennedy's Commission on the Status of Women, to which she was appointed in December 1961 and held until her death in 1962.[46]

Human Rights & Justice

Practice Behavior Example: Incorporate social justice practices in organizations, institutions, and society to ensure that these basic human rights are distributed equitably and without prejudice.

Critical Thinking Question: Did FDR's New Deal programs promote lasting social and economic justice outcomes?

SOCIAL INSURANCE IN THE UNITED STATES

European social insurance programs began with Germany's Chancellor Otto von Bismarck's plan (1879) to subvert growing socialist influences. It provided workers in mines and factories insurance against illness, job accidents, and old age and disability. By 1889, the program required contributions from workers, employers, and the government. By the 1900s, all European countries had some form of social insurance based on commitment to full employment. Bell says,

> As European nations adopted comprehensive social welfare programs, they also made a commitment to maintain full employment ... [reflecting] a conviction that everyone should have the right and opportunity to work.... Nowhere is the difference in values between other industrialized nations and the U.S. more striking than around the issue of full employment.[47]

The American social insurance movement began in 1906, when the American Association for Labor Legislation (economists and political scientists) began to investigate labor conditions. Its main tenet, based on evidence indicating poverty as structural rather than personal, was that

> social insurance was not charity but a basic human right, and that problems arising from poverty, age, sickness and accident ought to be guaranteed by the state rather than relying on either private charity or the benevolence of employers.[48]

In 1912, delegates to the National Conference on Social Welfare endorsed social insurance, and it became a part of Theodore Roosevelt's 1912 presidential platform. A 1913 study by Isaac M. Rubinow showed that between 80 and 90 percent of all wage-earners earned less than they needed to support families. The first state social insurance law was passed in Arizona in 1915, but was declared unconstitutional. Massachusetts passed the first state worker's compensation law in 1916, but the first unemployment insurance law was not passed until 1932.

By 1935, thirty states already had their own Old Age Assistance (OAA) programs, twenty-seven had Aid to the Blind (AB) programs, and a few had Aid to the Disabled (AD). The federal Vocational Rehabilitation program was set into the Department of Education in 1920. In the private sector, corporations began to expand social insurance as a good investment because it kept people on the job and loyal, decreased their tendency to strike, and led to more satisfactory job performance. Pension plans also made possible the retiring of elderly workers and the hiring of younger, quicker, and cheaper workers.[49]

However, during the Depression, massive nationwide needs could not be met by any local organization, public or private. National action was required. Rather than a reactive program, however, Roosevelt envisioned a proactive Grand Design for national income support, with social insurance for the *worthy* poor (related to work participation) and public assistance for nonworking yet dependent people (the aged, dependent children), categories still considered *unworthy* poor. The Grand Design intended that no citizen should be deprived of the basic necessities of life, yet it was not completely altruistic. Its social control elements included "raising children up properly," maintaining a low-wage work force, and controlling the rebellious needy. Nevertheless, it was a major ideological step toward social morality and government responsibility.

... during the Depression, massive nationwide needs could not be met by any local organization, public or private. National action was required.

In June 1934, Roosevelt instituted the Committee on Economic Security. Its members included the secretaries of labor, the treasury, and agriculture; the attorney general; and Harry Hopkins, administrator of FERA, with Frances Perkins, Secretary of Labor, as chair. The committee's charge was to build a "Grand Design" so that no citizen would go "ill-housed, ill-clothed, or ill-fed." In defense of his proposal, Roosevelt addressed Congress to this effect in 1934:

> People want decent homes to live in; they want to locate them where they can engage in productive work; and they want some safeguard against misfortunes which cannot be wholly eliminated in this man-made world of ours.... The complexities of great communities and of organized industry ... [compel us] to employ the active interest of the nation as a whole through government in order to encourage a greater security for each individual who composes it.[50]

To avoid the charge that the "Design" was unconstitutional, Perkins suggested that the Social Security Acts be financed through the taxing powers of the federal government, a ploy upheld in court despite arguments against it.[51]

Although inclusion of a health insurance plan was considered, the American Medical Association opposed it so strongly it was dropped, so it would not threaten the entire program. Aid to Dependent Children, originally intended to be placed under the Children's Bureau to give aid to all poor children, including those in intact families, was given at the last minute to the Department of Labor. Unfortunately, this removed the focus from children, placing it instead on mothers' morality and work ethic considerations.

Submitted in 1935, the Social Security Acts were amended and became law in August 1936. They set a precedent for final federal responsibility for citizen well-being not seriously questioned until the 1990s. A revolutionary act in itself, SSA borrowed heavily from the past, expecting many of the Depression needs to "wither away" as the "invisible hand" of the market revived, and it continued to categorize the poor as worthy (those who had been connected with the labor market) and unworthy (those peripheral to it):

> Frances Perkins ... and Edwin Witte ... who guided the 1935 law through ... believed that open-ended government handouts to citizens must be avoided. In their view temporary "relief" payments to unemployed people, and minimal "public assistance" programs for dependent children and old people, had to be kept separate from "social insurance" programs that workers would earn as a matter of right through regular tax contributions from themselves or their employers.[52]

The SSA left many gaps: no provision for unemployed able-bodied workers, time-limited unemployment benefits, no health insurance, neglected disabilities, coverage of only certain kinds of employment (thus excluding millions), and extremely low benefits.[53] Galper says it was an extension of state activity into the social welfare arena to meet corporate needs, used to socialize the costs of production to government rather than elite. Such costs included

- preparing (through job training) and maintaining the labor force;
- subsidizing low or irregular wages; and
- stimulating consumer purchasing power by an influx of cash benefits during periods of high unemployment or recession.[54]

However, SSA filled the immediate needs of those needing help, both poor and rich, and set into law national provisions for citizens in need.

The Social Security Acts set up two systems: federal social insurance for people connected in some way with the labor force, and federal/state categorical public assistance. The former provided direct payments from the federal government to retirees and their survivors or dependents; and the latter gave grants partly financed by the federal government but administered on state and local levels. Each state submitted a proposal to qualify for SSA funds, which had to include merit hiring, sound administrative procedures, fair hearings, and adequate records on which to compile annual reports. Categories eligible for aid were the aged (over sixty-five), blind, surviving children, and dependent children. Under separate titles, the Social Security Acts provided for crippled children and their vocational education, maternal and child welfare, and the administration of the unemployment compensation laws.

The Acts were actually two separate pieces of legislation: a payroll tax and a pension plan. Harry Hopkins, its first director, said,

> I have never liked poverty. I have never believed that with our capitalistic system people have to be poor. I think it is an outrage that we should permit hundreds and hundreds of thousands of people to be ill clad, to live in miserable homes, not to have enough to eat; not to be able to send their children to school for the only reason that they are poor.[55]

Now he had the power to do something about it.

PROGRAMS OF SOCIAL INSURANCE BASED ON SOCIAL SECURITY ACTS

Although the politics of the era changed part of the shape and intent of SSA, it passed as the basis for federal services for the "general welfare." Thus, its impact went beyond income transfer:

- It legitimated both state and federal income redistribution.
- It established local federal Social Security offices for administration of redistribution to the worthy poor.
- It established federally mandated state Bureaus of Social Aid for administration of categorical assistance to the "unworthy poor." These later combined with county offices for public welfare to provide all public assistance services.
- It ended most federally funded income redistribution by private agencies.
- It mandated the establishment of state offices for employment services and workers' compensation.
- It provided public health services for the poor and established guidelines for state-administered county health departments.

SSA established two insurance programs for the deserving poor (those who had worked or were working): Old Age and Survivors Insurance (OASI) (Title II) and Unemployment Compensation (Title III). Workers' compensation, provided to workers injured on the job or their survivors, developed state by state rather than being part of the national act. However, it is another program of social insurance.

Old Age and Survivors Insurance (OASI)

Originally this title provided only for retirement pensions for people over sixty-five, along with their spouses, and was designated Old Age Insurance (OAI). Because it was not means-tested, social work services were not required, so it was outside the purview of the social work profession. Monies collected from both employer and employee were paid into a reserve fund, with amounts originally based on actuarial tables developed by the secretary of the treasury. In 1937, employers and employees paid 1 percent of the first $3,000 earned, with no benefits over $85. A death benefit was also established. Most workers became eligible by working forty quarters (three-month periods), but farm and domestic workers, casual day laborers, and officers or crew of sailing vessels, federal or state employees, and charity employees were not eligible at all.[56]

Survivors' insurance (OASI) was added in 1939, providing pensions for widows and children of deceased workers. Disability coverage was not added until the 1950s (OASDI), and health insurance (Medicare) was added in 1965 (OASDHI). Most worker categories, including the self-employed, were added in the 1950s, and now coverage is nearly universal. Although at first workers could not earn income and still collect their pensions, this was relaxed, allowing earnings of OASDI retirees to be factored in for income tax determinations.

To gain support for its passage, OASI was presented as an insurance program, with participants viewed as investors contributing to the fund on actuarial models. However, rather than insurance, OASI is a regressive tax, with only a tenuous relationship between contributions and benefits. The program was placed in the newly created Social Security Administration, and the Treasury Department was designated to collect taxes paid by workers and employers [Federal Insurance Contributions Act (FICA) and Self-Employment Contributions Act (SECA)]; to prepare and disburse payments; and to maintain the trust fund (actually, three separate trust funds).

> **To gain support for its passage, OASI was presented as an insurance program ... However, rather than insurance, OASI is a regressive tax ...**

Unemployment Compensation: Title III

The Social Security Acts of 1935 mandated that states and employers provide insurance for workers unemployed through no fault of their own. Based in the Employment Security Administration of the U.S. Department of Labor, taxes for the Unemployment Compensation (UI) program are collected by the U.S. Department of the Treasury. Federal funding for *administrative* program costs began with $4 million in 1936, increasing over the years by each state's labor force estimates. States pay out *grants* through taxing employers, who may offset taxes up to 90 percent of estimates by paying into the state unemployment fund. Every state administers its own unemployment compensation program, and these vary state to state. Unemployment insurance provides regular cash benefits for a limited time to people who have worked a base period and then been let go from regular employment. At first the base period for coverage was forty quarters, or the equivalent of ten years. Unemployed workers must file for benefits and must be willing, able, and available for work, but benefits cannot be denied for refusal to accept work where conditions are below those prevailing in the community or if the job does not meet the applicant's qualifications.

Amounts of grants have some relationship to the amount formerly earned by the employee but also take into account number of people in the family. In any case, the grant is always much less than former wages.

Within a short period after passage of the Social Security Acts, all states established such funds, along with agencies to administer the state programs and provide employment services (now called state Employment Security Commissions). One purpose was to prevent layoffs, so employers with stable employment records pay reduced taxes: Employers hiring eight or more people for twenty months or more pay a 3 percent tax on their payrolls. Excluded from this tax originally were farm and domestic employers, the government, railroads, and nonprofit organizations, although most are now included. Railroad employees were covered in 1938 by a special railroad retirement plan, and federal government employees were brought into the program in 1954. In 1956, the program was amended to cover four, rather than eight or more, employees.

Workers' Compensation: State Social Insurance

Workers' compensation came state by state rather than through national legislation. Most states set up their programs under state Departments of Labor or independent workers' compensation boards through private insurance agencies. Employers almost always fund such programs, although some states contribute funds and some employees might contribute to medical care. States can impose a penalty against employers that do not have insurance. Premiums are based on company size and nature of risk. Many states still exclude agricultural workers, domestic workers, and workers in casual employment.

Workers' compensation provides benefits to victims of work-related accidents and illnesses regardless of fault, although workers must prove that their injuries were not from gross negligence, willful misconduct, or intoxication. Benefits for disabled workers or the survivors of dead workers reflect the worker's wages at the time of injury or onset of illness. They are given in cash and without means testing to spouses until they remarry and to children until they reach a state-set age. Benefits can be limited by time, amount, or extent of disability (temporary or permanent). Many states pay for the total length of the disability, including life, and some pay medical benefits. Some have a maximum number of weeks for temporary disability. Medical services, rehabilitation, and job training may be provided, although some states limit this liability.

In 1970, the National Occupational Safety and Health Act (OSHA) began to set standards for safe and healthy work conditions and authorized the National Commission on Workers' Compensation Laws to evaluate situations. The commission recommended compulsory coverage, no exemptions for small firms and government employees, coverage for all types of workers, coverage of all work-related diseases, and weekly cash payments at two-thirds of the gross wage up to a weekly benefit equal to 100 percent of the average weekly wage in the state. Also, it recommended no limits for permanent total disability benefits or for medical services and physical rehabilitation.[57] The interest of the federal government in occupational safety demonstrated that more federal intervention might be forthcoming. However, both the Reagan and Bush administrations and Republican-led Congress of the early 1990s limited the financing, standards, and scope of OSHA.

PUBLIC ASSISTANCE PROGRAMS
OF THE SOCIAL SECURITY ACTS

Although social insurance is considered an entitlement, public assistance is not. It is for those considered undeserving because they have not made the most of opportunities to work or save. The public assistance provisions of the Social Security Acts set up categories of the unworthy poor, much as in the Elizabethan Poor Laws of 1601. The categories were Old Age Assistance (OAA, Title I), Aid to the Blind (AB, Title C), and Aid to Dependent Children (ADC, Title IV), which in 1950 added the caretaking parent to the grant (Aid to Families with Dependent Children, or AFDC). The categories were instituted as temporary measures that would "wither away" as the market provided jobs and income or as social insurance benefits took over. Recipient grants were based on federal–state sharing, and states determined both needs and the grant levels on which the federal share was based.

Eligibility, based on means testing and home investigations, was at the discretion of workers, which meant that they could make value judgments as to who deserved help. Blaming the poor for their poverty was still a keynote of assistance, even among the most forward-looking reformers. Harry Hopkins said,

> The means test is our one way of keeping panhandlers off the rolls. It calls for the most detailed prying into the lives and habits of every applicant for relief.[58]

Needs and grants for aged, blind, and disabled people were set low and those for children were set even lower. Public assistance categories were first placed under the Social Security Administration until Truman put them into the Department of Health, Education, and Welfare (DHEW). During the Reagan administration, the Department of Education was made a separate office and DHEW became the Department of Health and Human Services (HHS).

Old Age Assistance (OAA)

Old Age Assistance (OAA) was set up to provide an income for people over age sixty-five who did not have enough savings for retirement or had never worked. Until health and nutrition lengthened our lives, these people had not been much of a problem. They either died or their children took care of them. However, children with families of their own could no longer support their aging parents, and the poorhouse seemed costly and inhumane. Therefore, OAA was established as a form of outdoor relief for the elderly.

Under the original act, the federal government paid half the grant amount in any quarter up to $30 per month, along with 2.5 percent of the costs of administration. Eligible people were all those over sixty-five who fell below state grant levels and were ineligible for OASI. Federal age eligibility was sixty-five, but until 1940 states could set it as high as age seventy. No citizens could be excluded, and states could not demand that people reside in the state for more than five of the preceding nine years. OAA was a partial answer to the Townsend Movement, but was not as ubiquitous or generous.

Aid to the Blind (AB) and Aid to the Disabled (AD)

Aid to the Blind (AB) was for people judged legally blind by medical authorities. Again, the federal government paid for half the grant up to $30 per month and for 5 percent of administrative costs. Aid to the Disabled (AD) was added to the Social Security Acts in 1956. Later it was called Aid to the Permanently and Totally Disabled (APTD), with state-appointed doctors deciding eligibility. At first disability meant only physical disability, but the definition was later amended to include mental and emotional disability.

AB, APTD, and OAA were moved to Social Security in 1971, redefining these groups as "worthy poor, and adding "D" for Disabled (OASDI)." Because OASDI paid less than had some states, given their standards of need, those states moved to reduce their benefits to OASDI levels. However, the government required them to supplement the federal grant up to their former standards of need so that recipients would not lose income because of the move. With the establishment of Supplemental Security Income (SSI) in 1972, a federal floor was set for aged, blind, and disabled people, providing a basic guaranteed annual income (GAI) not necessarily connected with work history for all people in this group. Although SSI remained a public assistance program (means-tested), as were the preceding categories, the Social Security Office administered distribution of benefits.

Aid to Dependent Children (ADC)

Aid to Dependent Children (ADC) was the most controversial categorical program of the Social Security Acts. Originally, the Children's Bureau was expected to administer it, and provision was to be made for all needy children, including those in intact families. However, for political reasons it was taken from the Children's Bureau and restricted to

> children under age sixteen who were deprived of parental support or care by reason of the death, continued absence from the home, or physical or mental incapacity of a parent, and who were living with father, mother, grandfather, grandmother, brother, sister, stepfather, stepmother, stepbrother, stepsister, uncle or aunt, in a place of residence maintained by one or more of such relatives as their own home. (Title IV, 55A 1935)

Mothers were not included in the grants until 1950, when the program became AFDC and in 1962 it was moved to the Department of Health, Education, and Welfare when it was established.

The wording of the bill designates dependent children as those deprived of "parental support" rather than those in need. This allowed for worker discretion in deciding the definition of *support*, and in some states it came to mean the presence of a father figure available for "emotional support," rather than financial need. Thus, if welfare workers suspected that a woman was involved with a man, whether or not he contributed financial aid, the family could be put off the program. This gave rise to "suitable home" and "substitute parent" policies in which welfare workers could take away grants if they considered the home "immoral." Moreover, because "unsuitability" was often equated with neglect, it gave workers power to remove children from mothers they considered unworthy. Eligibility determinations often excluded out-of-wedlock children, those from divorced parents (because the mothers were considered sexually immoral), and African-American children, because of the racism of workers who believed African Americans "always manage to get along."

Appropriations for 1936 were $24,750,000 and as much as needed thereafter, with the federal government paying up to one-third of the first $18 for the first child and up to one-third of $12 for each succeeding child per month. (Contrast this with the federal input of half of $30 for aged and blind adults.) ADC had to be given across each state at the same grant level, and a one-year residence requirement was allowed (later struck out as unconstitutional). Although ADC allowed mothers to care for their children at home, only those judged "fit and proper" by investigators were allowed to do so. The rest had to find jobs or alternative means of support, voluntarily give up their children, or have them taken away under neglect statutes. Local administrators could require eligible mothers to work as a condition for the grant.

Federal financing for ADC was probably enacted only because it was tied to other, more popular bills. Although some believe that disinterest led to ADC's meager provisions, intentional neglect because of institutional sexism and racism was the more likely cause. By November 1936, while forty-two states were receiving money for Old Age Assistance, only twenty-six were receiving ADC monies, although it had been legislated in all but three states (Alabama, Georgia, and South Carolina) by the end of 1935.[59] In 1936, 162,000 families received $49.7 million in benefits, or about $307 per family for the year.[60] The basic eligibility requirement for ADC was need, set by state standards and determined by needs testing. Although now fewer children were placed in orphanages, and to that extent ADC was a positive step, grants were always low and the threat of removal of children always present.

AFDC became a federal–state program, with the federal government contribution based on a formula depending on state-set levels of need. The program was severely cut back under the Reagan administration but continued until 1996, when it was replaced by the Temporary Assistance to Needy Families (TANF) program under the 104th Congress's Personal Responsibility and Work Opportunity Reconciliation Act.

MATERNAL AND CHILD WELFARE ACT: TITLE V

Title V under the Social Security Acts set up preventive and remedial health care for children, providing

- child welfare services for the care of homeless, dependent, and neglected children, and those in danger of becoming delinquent. Money would be given to states on plans developed jointly by state departments of public welfare and the Children's Bureau;
- vocational training and rehabilitation for crippled and physically handicapped children; and
- programs for maternal and child health, including prenatal and birthing care for mothers, and eventually some contraception, school nurses, public health programs, and the Women's, Infant's, and Children's food program (WIC).

This title was placed in the Children's Bureau. In 1936, $3,800,000 was approved, with grants to be given under the authority of the chief of the Children's Bureau, the secretary of labor. Each state was allotted $20,000 plus part of $1,800,000, depending on the proportion of state-to-national live birthrate. Another $980,000 was available for grants according to financial need of the states. State health agencies were required to administer these programs, with states contributing funds on a matching basis.

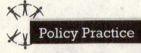

Policy Practice

Practice Behavior Example: Know the history and current structures of social policies and services; the role of policy in service delivery; and the role of practice in policy development.

Critical Thinking Question: In what way is the Social Security Act a continuation of or departure from the Elizabethan Poor Laws?

THE PROFESSIONALIZATION OF SOCIAL WORK

Because the Social Security Acts moved federal funding from private to public agencies and most professional social workers were with private agencies, it fostered the split between professional social workers and public welfare. Public assistance was delegated to two parallel agencies: county welfare offices, which distributed general assistance, poor relief, and various residual programs of medical and burial assistance; and state Bureaus of Social Aid. Workers in the first were hired by local directors, who often were political appointees. Bureaus of Social Aid were established at the county level under a central state administration to administer Old Age Assistance, Aid to the Blind, Aid to Dependent Children, and later, Aid to the Permanently and Totally Disabled.

In effect, then, the United States had three parallel programs of income redistribution: OASI (under the Social Security Administration) and two public assistance programs (Bureaus of Social Aid and county welfare offices). Neither the Social Security Administration nor county welfare offices required professional social workers, though for different reasons: OASI was an entitlement program, needing no personal investigation or surveillance, and county welfare offices required only a high school diploma or two years of public work for its workers. (See Table 9.1 for a summary of programs.)

A new breed of activist arose to champion the cause of the poor: the workers in Bureaus of Social Aid. Typically, young college graduates staffed the new federal offices: teachers, salesmen, and engineers unsocialized to "professionalism" and deeply critical of it as a defense of status and a tool of oppression. They became the rank and file of new social services unions, which gained 15,000 workers in the 1930s.

Table 9.1 **Parallel Income Maintenance Programs: Social Insurance and Public Assistance**

Social Insurance Federally Mandated Social Security	Public Assistance	
	Federal/State Funds Categorical Programs	State/County Funds Poor Relief, General Assistance
OAI: Old Age Insurance 1935	ADC: 1935	
OASI: Add Survivors 1950	AFDC: Add Parents 1950	Medical Assistance
AD: Add Disabled 1956	*AB: Aid to Blind 1935	Burial Assistance
Medicare (HI): 1965	*OAA: Old Age 1935	Medicaid: 1961
Workers Compensation: 1935	*AD: Disabled 1951	
Unemployment Compensation	SSI: Supplemental Security Income 1971 TANF: 1996	

*Moved to Social Security (OASDI) in 1971.

As early as 1931 workers of the Jewish Federation in New York City organized the New York Association of Federation Workers, and a little later the first strike in social work history occurred. This laid the groundwork for social work trade unions in the public sector, the first of which was the Home Relief Employees Association (December 1933). By 1938, 14,500 people belonged to social work locals, and the American Association of Social Workers included an estimated 10,560 of the 60,000 social workers in the nation. Eighty-three percent of those unionized were in public agencies.[61] Though concerned with their own job issues, they were also aware of the needs of their clients. Within a year, their successes had encouraged new unions in Chicago, Cincinnati, Cleveland, Detroit, Minneapolis, Newark, Philadelphia, and Pittsburgh.[62]

However, Red-baiting campaigns in the late 1930s and the McCarthy witch hunts after World War II brought the downfall of social work unions and activists. Many social workers were in fact communists or socialists, including Mary Van Kleeck, who attacked the New Deal because of its commitment to the needs of the elite rather than the needs of the poor at the May 1934 meeting of the National Conference of Social Workers. Bertha Capen Reynolds, a graduate of Smith, identified with both communism and the rank-and-file movement, saying that "caseworkers were employed to see that society was not troubled by [the economically unsuccessful]."[63] Although she was deeply respected in the profession, she never worked again as a social worker after the McCarthy Red scare. The Bertha Capen Reynolds Society was established in her honor in 1985. It is now called the Social Welfare Action Alliance (SWAA).

"Professional" social workers turned to social casework, usually based on psychoanalytic models or new developments in family–child relationships. By 1937, child services and family agencies were merging because of the similarity of their practice base and middle-class clientele. Freudian psychosexual development theories and an emphasis on "inner self" created a ripe field for casework practitioners and gave "scientific" support to personal blame theories. These "prescribed" psychoanalytic treatment as "cures," lending more credence to the medical model of social work than the social/structural model. Ehrenreich says,

> social workers more and more became psychotherapists ... concerned with the life cycle problems of the middle class, their theoretical base widened ... behavior modification and learning theory, existentialism and humanist therapy, transactional analysis and gestalt therapy, systems theory and "social ecology" and a dozen varieties of family therapy and group work joined.... Freudian psychodynamic theories as part of many social workers' armamentarium of approaches and techniques. What was "social" about these techniques few ever asked.[64]

From the psychodynamic perspective, the *presenting* problem was not the *real* problem. Requests for help, such as paying bills or dealing with authorities, were believed either to mask emotional problems or be indicative of psychological inability to cope with such problems. Disposing of the immediate problem, such as heat turnoff or need for food, was seen as

> unprofessional, potentially destructive, and [creative of] even further dependency. All casework services have to be ... "constructive" parts of a "plan." ... [T]he coercive aspects of the casework relationship ... stemmed from the structural position of the agencies which gave them enormous power over clients.... They were extensions of other authoritative agencies—the police, the schools, the health agencies—or the key to desperately needed benefits.[65]

Freud's dictum "happiness is to love and to work" reinforced work as therapy for troubled souls. Moreover, Freud's differential psychosexual development theories for men and women reinforced women's secondary status in work and in the home. It also gave society scapegoats for the perceived growth of juvenile delinquency—mothers who put their own needs over those of their children by remaining in the labor market.

Research-Based Practice

Practice Behavior Example: Use research evidence to inform practice.

Critical Thinking Question: Discuss the continued effect of psychological research on social work practice.

WORLD WAR II

Although the Social Security Acts alleviated some basic subsistence problems, war was the real reason for the end of the Depression. War came to Europe when Germany invaded Poland in 1939, but its gestation was much earlier. Germany was brought to its knees by World War I, and the "democratic" government of the Weimar Republic, imposed by its victors, collapsed in 1927. As the worldwide depression intensified, the German economic situation worsened, precipitating Hitler's rise to power. Although a 1923 coup d'état failed, by 1930 his Nazi party had gained 107 seats in parliament, and by 1931 the Nazi party had 800,000 members. In the next election, Hitler won 11 million votes against Hindenburg's 18 million, and in 1933, with 96 percent of the vote, became Chancellor with dictatorial powers. In 1935, he formed a Rome–Berlin Axis with Mussolini's fascist regime, and in 1936 Germany and Japan, under Emperor Hirohito, signed the Anti-Comintern Pact, and Japan declared war against China.

The United States was an ally of Britain and Poland but had signed a Neutrality Act in 1937. Furthermore, it was involved in its SSA program development, a new recession, and strikes by half a million workers. However, by 1939 Roosevelt had to acknowledge America's European alliance as Germany invaded Poland. Still, not until Japan attacked Pearl Harbor on December 7, 1941, did the United States finally enter the war in an uneasy alliance with China and communist Russia.

Internment of Japanese Americans

As the United States went to war, its selective racism showed on many fronts. One of the most crucial was the internment of Japanese Americans. The first action against the Japanese took place on state and local levels: The legislature of California passed a bill denying elections of Japanese Americans to state government, state and federal police raids intensified, and more than 2,000 people of Japanese descent were arrested.[66] Most such cases were thrown out for lack of evidence, but this, according to California Attorney Earl Warren, merely "reflected the cunning of the Japanese." Japanese businesses were forced to close and citizens illegally detained, evicted, and fired. At least three dozen violent attacks were documented.

In 1942, Roosevelt proclaimed western California, Oregon, Washington, and southern Arizona as areas where no Japanese, German, or Italian aliens could reside. A War Relocation Board moved a small number of Japanese, German, and Italian aliens from "sensitive" military areas and restricted their movements.

Because Italy's fascist government had joined Nazi Germany in the "Axis alliance," about 10,000 Italians the FBI suspected of being "fifth-columnists" were stripped of their constitutional rights; hundreds were arrested, forced to carry special identification cards, observe curfews, or face internment. Among those targeted were Joe Dimaggio's father and Ezio Pinza, the opera singer.[67] However, only Japanese Americans as a group were pressured to resettle. The Federal Reserve Bank was ordered to protect their property, but most sold it at low prices, and businesses and farms went at losses.

Japanese Americans were detained and then transported, without any semblance of trial or due process, to barbed-wire concentration camps. By fall 1942, more than 112,000 people, two-thirds of them citizens, were interned in ten camps under military guard. Allowed few personal possessions, they were housed in partitioned-off barracks with inadequate supplies. Small monthly wages were paid to those who would work. Local camp governments were established under the direction of the War Relocation Authority, with a council selected from the prisoners. The internees underwent constant political screening to ferret out disloyalties, and their demonstrations and riots were generally fruitless. A few thousand students and workers in special agricultural assignments were released, and many joined the army, in which their segregated unit was the most decorated in World War II. Some 6,000 renounced their U.S. citizenship. In 1943, more than 10,000 relocated to the east coast.

In 1944, one-third of the prisoners were allowed to leave the concentration camps, and in late 1944 the order to hold them was rescinded. Most returned to the West coast and over the next two years 800 returned to Japan.[68] The cost to the United States for the evacuation was about $250 million, and Japanese American losses have been estimated at $400 million or more. The internees formed the Japanese American Citizens' League to formally protest the evacuation and its losses to them, and by 1946 it was pressing for compensation. By 1950, nearly 24,000 were filed, totaling $132 million, but the government paid only $38 million, less than 10 percent of the estimated losses. In 1980, the Commission on Wartime Relocation and Internment of Civilians recommended that 60,000 survivors should receive $1 to $2 million,[69] but this was still minimal in the face of Japanese American losses from the internment.

The War Years

The federal government had refused since 1932 to hire married women whose husbands were already employed (Federal Economy Act, married person's clause) and fired 1,600 of those whose husbands held federal jobs. At the same time, 77 percent of the nation's school systems refused to hire married women as teachers, and half dismissed those who married. In Texas, women who worked in railroad companies were fired if their husbands earned over $50 per month. As late as 1939, legislatures in twenty-six states were considering bills to bar married women from all employment. A live-in domestic in New York earned $34 per month, and the Women's Bureau thought $6 per week was an adequate salary for a seventy-two-hour workweek.[70] Because of the recession, both government and private employers began to fire women. Norman Cousins, echoing the public sentiment of the day, said in 1939,

> There are approximately 10 million people out of work in the United States today.... There are also 10 million or more women, married or single, who are jobholders. Simply fire the women, who shouldn't be working anyway, and hire the men. Presto. No unemployment. No relief rolls. No depression.[71]

When the Japanese attacked Pearl Harbor, the United States had already been gearing up for war for two years. More and more people were being recruited to factory work: African-American men from the South, Puerto Ricans, Mexicans and Mexican Americans, women, and even young people. Factory recruiters paid high school principals to send them students, and the minimum age for employment was reduced from eighteen to sixteen. Military and civilian demand pushed the economy upward. In 1940, the gross national product was $99.7 billion, and in a total population of 132.1 million, the number of workers in the labor force was 55.6 million, with 540,000 people in the armed services and civilian employment at 47.5 million. The unemployment rate was 14.6 percent, or 8 million workers. Sixty-four percent of the working population made annual wages of under $2,000 and 84 percent made under $3,000.

With the Selective Service Act of 1942, factories were left inadequately staffed to produce sufficient amounts of goods and war matériel . More than 16 million men were transported for military reasons; women, wives, and family followed them. Another 16 million moved for job reasons.[72] When war employment soaked up the residue of unemployed men, employers turned to women. They were recruited not only into the "women's" labor market, but also into war production plants. The War Manpower Commission estimated that only 29 percent of America's 52 million adult women had jobs and told them they were shirking their patriotic duties if they did not work. During the first two years of war, twenty states and Washington, D.C. enacted emergency laws to extend maximum daily or weekly working hours for women. Laws against night work were modified in eight states, and in four states various occupations previously covered by protective legislation were exempted. By February 1943, *Fortune* magazine suggested drafting women if they did not come forward to work.[73]

Nearly 11 million women had jobs before 1940, and 3 million were looking for work.[74] By 1940, nearly 16 million women of a total female population of 50.1 million were working full-time despite discrimination, lower pay, and segregated job classifications. Of the female workforce before the war, 48.4 percent were single, 36.4 percent were married, and widows and divorcees made up 15.1 percent. Labor force participation of women over age fourteen increased from 25 to 36 percent.[75] During the war, the percentage of single women workers decreased to 40.9 percent, while those married rose to 45.7 percent. Two million women went to work in offices, half in the federal government. By 1945, the wartime peak, 19.5 million women were employed, excluding those in the Red Cross and military service. By 1950, women were 32 percent of the labor force.[76] Three-fourths of new women workers were over thirty-five, 60 percent were married, and the majority had children of school or preschool age.[77]

Before the war, 40 percent of African-American women—1.5 million—worked (compared with 25 percent of white women). More than half were in service occupations such as domestic employees (72 percent) and 20 percent were farm workers. By war's end in 1945, 2 million African-American women were working, with 18 percent in factories and the greatest increase in manufacture of metals, chemicals, and rubber. Their numbers as factory workers quadrupled, and there was a noticeable and permanent decrease in their employment as domestic workers.

Pay for women changed with war employment as the federal government endorsed equal pay for equal work in government and war-connected jobs, and unions fought for equal pay so that men's pay would not be reduced. Union membership for women, which had been 500,000 in 1937, reached 3,500,000 by 1940. By 1944, women constituted 22 percent of trade union member-ship.[78] Still, in many jobs women received lower pay even when equal pay clauses were written into labor contracts. The National War Labor Board de-fended employers against women on the grounds that they would leave the labor force with the end of the war. Although some 700,000 workers received industrial training in the last half of 1941, only 1 percent of these were women. By 1943, unemployment had virtually ended, with a rate of 1.2 percent—about 1 million unemployed. Twenty-four percent of all women of working age were in the labor force. By 1945, with a population of 105.5 million, the gross na-tional product was $211.9 billion, and civilian employment rose 11.1 percent, reaching 52.8 million.[79] Total employment in 1946 was 56.7 million, of whom 15.8 million were women.

The presence of women in factories led to improved working conditions in many ways, including company cafeterias, a few day care centers, transporta-tion facilities, rest breaks, and some shopping and banking facilities on plant sites. In 1942, the federal government allotted $400,000 to assist local com-munities in funding child care, and the 1943 Lanham Act authorized money for day care centers in 1943, but few communities came up with matching funds to build them. Day care centers were expensive (up to $6 per child) and inconveniently located, and their hours open did not consider the travel needs of working women. Thus, they operated at only a quarter of capacity and were too cost-ineffective to continue. With the end of the war, the issue of day care centers as needed facilities faded away, replaced by the feeling that, at best, day care centers made it easy for mothers to be neglectful and, at worst, they were part of a leftist plot to destroy the American family. A 1945 bill asking for $30 million to continue day care centers failed, with some congressmen arguing that "women should be driven back to their homes." Although a bill for $20 million to continue centers through 1946 did succeed, it included no money for expansion and soon all federal support for day care ended.[80]

The War and People of Minorities

Although many nonwhite people shared in the benefits of the Roosevelt years, the country still maintained a racist bias. For example, the Civilian Conservation Corps had a racial quota that limited participation; Federal Emergency Relief, National Industrial Recovery, and Agricultural Adjustment Act monies were given discretionarily according to race; the National Labor Administration had codes with discriminatory pay rates; and government employment was discriminatory and offices were segregated. Roosevelt, in political debt to the Southern aristocracy, refused to support antilynching laws and would not endorse a broad civil rights program.[81] Although he appointed more than one hundred African Americans to federal positions between 1933 and 1940, it was always at lower levels: William Hastie was appointed to the third U.S. Circuit Court, the highest African-American judicial appointment up to that time; Robert C. Weaver was given a post in the Department of the Interior; and E. K. Jones took a post in the Commerce Department, Laurence Oxley in the Labor Department, Ira D. Reed in the Social Security Administration, and Mary Bethune in the National Youth Authority.[82]

The 1928 Merriam Survey gave impetus to major changes in Native American affairs under Commissioner Charles J. Rhoads. In 1933, Roosevelt appointed John Collier as commissioner (a post he held until 1946). Collier, who had been active in supporting Native Americans since the 1920s, instituted major changes under the Indian Reorganization Act of 1934 (the Wheeler–Howard Act), and most Native Americans had the right to decide whether they would participate in the changes. The act stopped allotment of Native American lands to white people and ended the forced assimilation of their cultures, allowed Native Americans to develop their own constitutions and elect tribal councils, created a fund to provide credit for agriculture and industrial projects so that Native Americans could develop tribal business corporations, and gave them over a million acres of new land. Health and school services were improved. The act also allowed for preferential hiring in the Bureau of Indian Affairs to Native Americans. The Secretary of the Interior, however, could still veto constitutions and make rules for tribal elections, and he also continued to supervise expenditures and regulate land management. Almost 25,000 Native Americans entered the armed services, most as draftees, and almost twice as many left reservations to work in war industries.[83] They came back as veterans entitled to such services as rehabilitation, education, housing, and jobs, and became the fathers of the generation that rebelled in the 1960s.

Before the war, partly in response to Roosevelt's New Deal, African Americans began to become Democrats. (He received about one-fourth of their vote in 1932, but in 1940 received 53 percent.) In 1944, the Supreme Court ruled that they could not be barred from primaries in Southern states, and by the late 1940s an estimated 600,000 African-American voters were registered. By the time of World War II, they had become more vocal in their demands for equality. They had migrated to urban areas, become educated, and participated in the Works Progress Administration, the National Youth Administration, and vocational training. Their victories were few but steady: By 1940, 73 percent of African-American men in the labor force had blue-collar jobs, despite tremendous resistance to their employment, and despite resistance to their induction, more than a million men and women of African descent served in the armed forces, though in segregated units. For the first time, they could enter combat units rather than be assigned to menial chores, and they could now enter the Army Air Corps and the Marines. Although African-American officers were commissioned and sent to integrated officers' training schools, segregation continued for the regular soldier in living quarters and in training and recreation.

On the home front, their activism continued. In 1940, the Urban League had a membership of 26,000 in 46 branches, and the NAACP had 481 branch offices and 85,000 members nationwide. The latter's attention focused on the South, pushing for antilynching laws and laws to end quasi-peonage and debt slavery, for educational and employment opportunities, for equitable treatment in courts, for equal pay for work equal to that done by white workers and access to labor unions, and for the fair distribution of public education funds and the end of segregated facilities.

In 1943, the Congress of Racial Equality (CORE) began to challenge segregation in restaurants, swimming pools, and municipal facilities in Northern and border states and staged its first sit-in at a restaurant in the Chicago Loop. CORE was inspired by the Gandhian tactics of nonviolence and by the militancy of a new leader, A. Philip Randolph. Randolph, son of an African Methodist minister, had won recognition for the Brotherhood of Pullman Car Porters after twelve years as a labor organizer. Protesting unfair labor practices, he threatened Roosevelt with a march on Washington by 50,000–100,000 black workers. In efforts to dissuade him, Roosevelt asked him, Walter White of the NAACP, and T. Arnold Hill, acting executive of the Urban League, to end plans for the march, but Randolph was adamant. In response to the threat, Roosevelt wrote an executive order barring discrimination in war industries and the armed services on June 25, 1941, and Randolph called off the march.[84]

This first Fair Employment Practices Committee met widespread defiance and was ineffective because it lacked power to punish offenders. Its institution touched off, in 1943, the worst series of riots by white workers since 1919. In a Mobile, Alabama, shipyard, African-American workers were promoted and white workers rioted until troops were called in to quiet them. There were riots in Harlem, and in Detroit thirty-four people died in job riots. Because African-American labor was necessary to the war effort, both the National Defense Advisory Committee and President Roosevelt spoke out against discrimination. This, along with the growing protest movements, fostered a second Fair Employment Practices Commission (FEPC) in 1943. Soon, African-American workers held 1 million factory jobs, union membership increased to 500,000, and their number in government increased from 50,000 in 1939 to 200,000 in 1944. The proportion of African Americans in war-related industries increased from 3 to 8 percent during war years, but layoffs at the end hit them much harder than whites. Since then, their unemployment has remained consistently double that of whites.

Not until the war ended did President Truman abolish segregation in army units and end discrimination in firms doing business with the federal government. As the war ended, however, racism once more took its toll. White people mobbed and attacked neighborhoods where African Americans lived and lynched returning veterans. Truman refused to recant his civil rights stand, however, and set forth a civil rights platform for the 1948 presidential election. Although he won the election on the African-American city vote, it cost him the Southern vote and his proposed civil rights bill failed in Congress, which continued to refuse legislation to protect voting rights. Not until 1951 was lynching finally made a federal offense. However, racially motivated lynchings continued throughout the twentieth century.

Social Welfare Services: The War and After

During the war, Roosevelt turned to problems of dislocation and distress related to the war itself. In November 1940, he named the administrator of the Federal Security Agency as coordinator of the Office of Health, Welfare, and Related Defense activities. This office provided services for training camps and their civilian communities. In 1941, he placed the Office of Civilian Defense in the Office of War Management to integrate servicemen's health, welfare, and recreation services with defense activities. By 1943, these had been integrated into the Office of Community War Services under the Federal Security Agency, serving both armed forces and the civilian population.

The Community Facilities Act of 1941 (Lanham Act) provided federal funds for construction of houses, schools, day care centers, hospitals, water and sanitation plants, and recreational facilities. Routine physical health care was encouraged: During the war years, the Emergency Maternal and Infant Care program (1943) served more than 1.2 million military wives with 230,000 infants. Inoculation programs for all children were undertaken through public health services.

Education became a major service goal when Army examinations showed an illiteracy rate of one in five among inductees. The U.S. Office of Education was expanded to make federal aid available for elementary and secondary education and for agricultural extension services in rural areas. In addition, it awarded enormous government contracts for research in engineering, science, and civil aeronautics; education in defense industries; management; and the Reserve Officers Training Corps (ROTC).[85]

More than 16,535,000 servicemen went to war. The death toll for Americans was 292,000 in action and 114,000 from other causes. Nearly 700,000 were wounded. While the servicemen were gone, some never to return, the government concerned itself with helping the families who had given up fathers, sons, and husbands to the national need. The Servicemen's Dependent Allowance Act of 1942, under the War Department, provided family allotments. At first paid half-and-half by the serviceman and the government—by 1943, $797 million— by 1945, allotments totaled $3 billion, with the government paying $2 billion.[86]

After the war, major social legislation centered on veterans, both because the nation believed they deserved reward for services to their country and in order to avert a major economic catastrophe. We had learned from World War I: The release of millions of soldiers into the job market when millions were laid off as the war economy declined would have produced a massive depression. Although the Selective Training and Service Act of 1940 provided that inductees be reemployed at the end of service in positions of like seniority, status, and pay, the government took steps to keep veterans out of the labor market. The first was the 52–20 Plan, which provided veterans $20 each week for a year, whether or not they were disabled or involved in battle.

The second was the Servicemen's Readjustment Act of 1944, called the G.I. Bill of Rights. Its only eligibility requirement was that the veteran had served during a specific time. It provided stipends to support veterans and their families while the veterans went to school for vocational education or higher education, paid for tuition, and subsidized home loans, business and farm loans, unemployment insurance payments, and veterans' employment services. G.I. Bill expenditures were $3.4 billion in 1946 and $9.3 billion in 1950—23 percent of that year's federal expenditures.[87] In addition to averting a depression, the G.I. Bill upgraded the quality and earning power of the American workforce for a generation. The National Mental Health Act of 1946, in response to the mental health needs of veterans, began to fund research and training in mental health and to establish community mental health services. This led to even more programs and agencies for social work professionals.

Women After the War

The nation made a radical turnabout regarding women's work at the end of the war. Within two years, 14 million veterans returned to civilian work, and the number of women working as operatives and craftspeople dropped by over a million. Where they had been recruited and had won many gains for all workers because of the labor shortage, now it became their patriotic duty to leave the factory and return to marriage and family roles in the home. The Selective Service Act of 1942 contained a tacit assumption, because it guaranteed veterans the jobs they had held before the war, that women would want to go home. Frances Perkins, secretary of labor, insisted that their war effort was only temporary and they would return to the home when men came back. However, this did not acknowledge that many women had to work and that, for the first time, they had been paid reasonable wages. Many did not want to give this up. In a UAW poll asking if women would work after the war if jobs were available, 98.5 percent of single women, 100 percent of widows, and 68.7 of married women said yes.[88]

Unions helped little in retention of women's jobs after the war: In Detroit, for example, the AFL–CIO had between 300,000 and 350,000 women members by war's end. Yet when layoffs occurred, 41 percent of men laid off were offered new jobs at 8.5 cents lower per hour (the average wage of Willow Run workers was $1.23 an hour), but less than 3 percent of women were offered other jobs, and those who were lost more than 48 cents per hour. Layoffs for women were always higher than for men, with the old excuses of "heavy work," late hours, and women needed at home. A clause in a contract between United Steel and Wire and Local 704 said,

> When a man is the youngest employee in a classification involved in a reduction of force … he shall be permitted to bump any woman filling a job designated as a man's job … in case of plant-wide layoffs, women employees holding duly designated men's jobs will be laid off before any man employee.… A woman employee is not permitted to bump a man employee off a man's job.[89]

Women protested and picketed, but in general to no avail. In the two months following VJ Day (Victory over Japan), women were laid off at rates of 75 per 1,000, twice that of men. By the end of 1946, 2 million women had been fired from heavy industry, and some companies reinstated old policies of not hiring women.[90]

In 1946, the Women's Bureau held a conference on union contract provisions affecting women. The majority of the recommendations were for equal treatment rather than protection of women because of their "frailty." The bureau held that pregnancy should not be grounds for dismissal and that women returning after maternity leave be given their former jobs at current salary. Job classification and wage rates should be set by job, not by sex, and no new employees should be hired if women were available for upgrading.[91] A 1947 bureau report showed that 1 million fewer women were employed, and that although half were actively seeking work, there was an obvious shift to unemployment insurance and later to the welfare rolls. By 1953, 1 million women were seeking jobs, of whom African Americans made up the largest percentage.[92]

Women as workers faced increasing hostility after the war, fired by the growth of the social sciences and the social work profession's casework emphasis. The new information on child development, the Freudian interpretation of the roles of women and psychosexual development, and an intense concentration on the problem of juvenile delinquency blamed absent mothers for all kinds of problems. "Latchkey children"—given keys to get into their homes while their mothers were at work—were investigated by welfare departments, juvenile justice systems, and the growing number of family and children's agencies. The family and children's agencies, though unlikely to serve poor children whose mothers had to work, researched the problems of juvenile delinquents in terms of parent–child relationships and the "mental illness" of women who worked (that is, took on male roles). Their conclusions were very useful to a government trying to reduce the labor force and to men returning from war to their previous roles, indicating that the working mother was an affront to the rights of children for "good parenting" and the American way of life.

Although it is likely that the concentration on juvenile delinquency came from new reporting, new casework theories, and the fact that young people could not get jobs because veterans were returning to employment in a time of economic downswing, the whole issue was used to influence women to return home and participate in the baby boom. Women who entered male fields after the war—law, mathematics, physics, business, industry, technology—were discriminated against[93] because the "psychic maladjustment" that made them want to leave home made them poor business risks. Fewer than half of both men and women believed that women should have equal chance at jobs, even if they were sole breadwinners.[94] It was said that

> feminism represented a neurotic reaction to male dominance and a deep illness which encouraged women to reject their natural sex-based instincts.[95]

This made the case against women in the workforce on moral, political, economic, and "scientific" grounds.

Three million fewer women were employed in 1946 than at wartime peak, and between 1945 and 1947, 2.7 million women were removed from industrial employment.[96] However, by 1950 female employment neared its top wartime level. Need for money was still the main reason women worked: In 1947, 31 percent of all families still had incomes below $2,000 and 50 percent earned less than $3,000.

THE RESURGENCE OF SOCIAL WORK

Shortly after the war, the economy began to pick up because of the massive backlog of demands for consumer goods. The return of veterans; the almost forcibly reduction in the female labor force; and the ideology that women ought to be in the home, with babies and supported by husbands, led to an increase in marriages and a baby boom that meant a new market. Soon after the war ended, the birthrate reached a high of 26.6 births per 1,000.[97] As people could afford to move into the suburbs because of G.I. Bill home loans, the isolation of women from one another began, contributing to their loneliness and depression. Moreover, as they moved far from their mothers, the normal channels for learning about homemaking and child care were closed off. Once more, social professionals took over, and all "failures"—misbehaving or unhappy children—were the mothers' fault.

Treatment continued to be skewed by the idea of woman as dependent, nonassertive, and emotionally immature. Women who wanted to work were judged mentally ill, or worse, to be destroying their families and children. Although social workers believed deviance arose from the environment, the environment in question was not social and economic conditions, but home, early training, and how children dealt with authority, especially around the learning of toilet training and eating. These produced different disorders that could be "cured" by social work treatment.

The fear of juvenile delinquency began to alter the national consciousness as well as that of the profession. Between 1940 and 1960, the number of cases rose from 200,000 to 813,000, and Cloward and Ohlin's idea of a "deviant subculture," in which children learned criminal behavior from their peers, began to obfuscate the structural and economic reasons for delinquency. The profession of social work expanded and grew on this new emphasis of mental illness—called an epidemic—and by 1955 some 558,000 people resided in psychiatric hospitals, with about 200,000 new admissions a year.[98] Mental health clinics had 300,000 more clients, and the community mental health program began.

Women who wanted to work were judged mentally ill, or worse, to be destroying their families and children.

In addition to juvenile delinquency, social work's interest turned to drug abuse. During the first two decades of the century, alcohol consumption had been the "morality issue" of social welfare. This ended with Prohibition, but Prohibition itself created two massive organizations devoted to crime management: organized crime, which provided alcohol to those who wanted it, and enforcers of the Prohibition amendment, the bulk of whom were in the Treasury Department as "revenuers." When Prohibition was rescinded in 1933, both organizations turned to the business of newly illegal drugs (marijuana, cocaine, and heroin). Where previously drug abuse had been a medical problem, with relatively low costs for society, now it was a legal problem and a mental health problem, and the costs skyrocketed.

The number of social workers expanded in the 1930s from 31,000 to 70,000. The number of professional organizations also expanded: By 1930 they included the American Association of Medical Social Workers, the National Association of School Social Workers, the American Association of Psychiatric Social Workers, and the American Association of Social Workers. Members of these organizations made up less than 25 percent of social workers; the remainder were not affiliated or were in public assistance jobs and organizations.[99] By 1939, the American Association of Schools of Social Work required two-year Master of Social Work programs. In 1946, the National Council on Social Work Education was formed, and in 1952 it became the accrediting body for American and Canadian schools of social work until 1970, when Canada set up its own council.

Fees for service and private practice began: In 1943, Jewish Family Services in New York began to charge fees, and other family agencies followed suit with sliding fee scales. Now community centers and organizations for young people such as the Girl Scouts and YWCAs set up paid "memberships" for participation. The profession moved away from service and into support by middle-and upper-class clientele. Though parents could learn about child development and the skills of parenting from experts, lower-class clientele were not welcome, because they were not "treatable." By 1960, 9 percent of social work clients were in the upper socioeconomic class and 48 percent were in the middle class.

Group work practice was professionally recognized in the 1930s. Early settlement work led the way to its development, but group work developed primarily from the work of Mary Follett (1868–1933). Follett, a theorist in the field of organization and bureaucracy, adapted Frederick Taylor's scientific management to humanistic management. From 1908 to 1920, she developed community centers within neighborhood schools and worked for minimum wage legislation. Her 1924 book *Creative Experience* detailed her theory of *humanistic management* and posited a new form of democracy based on spontaneous organization, or grassroots development through the creative interaction of people and groups. Group work was legitimated with the Association of Group Workers and the Social Work Research Association (1949). Near the same time, the Association for the Study of Community Organization was also formed, based on Follett's theories and settlement house experiences.[100]

While social work continued on its course, a split arose. On one side were the proponents of psychosocial casework, defended by such eminent social workers as Gordon Hamilton and Florence Hollis. On the other were "functionalists," who believed that although psychosocial investigation might be interesting, social work practice belonged in the here and now, and psychosocial practice's demand for long-term relationships, differential diagnoses, and setting of long- and short-term goals controlled rather than served clients. Among functionalists, Jessie Taft argued for a process model of helping, and Ruth Smalley argued against client control. Virginia Robinson's presentation,

"A Changing Psychology in Social Work," written in 1930, was heavily influenced by Otto Rank and challenged Freud's paternalistic models. Robinson said that casework should focus on the relationship between client and environment, the client should be central, and the worker–client relationship was to strengthen rather than control clients. John Ehrenreich says,

> The functional school sustained a serious and coherent effort at dealing with the welfare state and its implications for social work theory, practice, and professional status.... It sought to rethink radically the relationship between the social environment and the individual. But it never convinced more than a minority.[101]

The debate between the functional school and psychosocial casework grew bitter and threatened to end all the professional gains made. Although the debate has never really ended, Helen Perlman's eclectic problem-solving model, which focused on systems and could incorporate either type of casework, helped to bridge the gap and reunited, however uneasily, the casework profession.

Reorganizing Federal Social Welfare Efforts

After the war, President Truman asked former President Hoover to head a commission to study the federal bureaucracy and make recommendations. From this study, the Federal Security Agency and several other domestic agencies were formed into a single cabinet-level department, the Department of Health, Education, and Welfare (DHEW),[102] which then housed the Social Security Administration. Some new legislation was passed: the national school lunch program of 1946, the Housing Act of 1949, a special milk program for poor children in 1954. The Housing Act authorized 135,000 public housing units per year, but only 25,000 to 40,000 per year were built in the following decade. The houses built under this act and the G.I. Bill promoted the movement of middle-class whites to the suburbs, while people of color and poor people moved into the central cities. Most social legislation other than for veterans took the form of incrementing existent programs after the war, including new provisions added to laws, expanded eligibility, and increased payments in both public assistance and social insurance.

THE AMERICAN DREAM

After World War II, flush with the victory of democracy over fascism, veterans returned to a G.I. Bill of Rights that promised them their former jobs, higher education, and new homes—under the Veteran's Administration (VA). They stepped back into good jobs newly enhanced by unionism or could realize their dreams of education and profession. Even groups formerly discriminated against benefited: They had their taste of good wages supported by unions and could develop more stable home lives based on their better incomes. The middle class expanded, and it seemed that the American Dream was coming true.

The boom in consumerism produced by new higher wages and the move to the suburbs was joined by the "war business." "Corporate statesmen"—leaders of national corporations appointed to public offices during the War—grew in influence as the economy swung upward. What was good for business was assumed good for the nation, and war was extremely profitable—war matériel either became obsolete or was blown up. These business leaders, along with government officials and war advisors, came to be known as the "military–industrial complex." Support of war in other countries, in the guise of "saving the world from communism," became a goal of our corporate-influenced government, and wars backed by the United States exploded—in emerging countries in the Near East, South and Central America, and the Far East. A "shadow government" began to dictate foreign policy for the United States.

CONCLUSION: MOVING TOWARD THE FUTURE

As the nation moved into the 1950s, a new configuration to life and to social welfare began. The social legislation of the 1930s and the nation's adaptation to the war had created a welfare state, however minimal its provisions, for most of the needy groups in society. Poverty was changing: Now the workforce had some power to demand living wages, but groups without the capability for unionization were little better off than before. People of color, inspired by their earning power during the war and the advances they had achieved with little if any help from social institutions, were also demanding rights.

However, backlash soon emerged in race riots, the communist hunting of the McCarthy era, and the recalcitrance of both county relief and the Bureaus of Social Aid to extend benefits to those who were eligible but who were not "morally correct." During the next decade, the profession of social work would have little to do with issues of reform but would continue to firm up its psychological intervention techniques. Although researchers were well aware of the problems of people oppressed because of poverty, race, and sex, their work had little impact on society's orientation to the poor—still blamed for their poverty—or the distressed, now mentally ill rather than disadvantaged.

The children who reached adulthood during the 1950s have been called the Silent Generation, yet this might be only in comparison to the eruption of mass social movements in the 1940s. Surely the problems were there, and recognized, throughout the 1940s and 1950s: the unrest of people of color, the baby boom, the white flight to the suburbs, and growing urban unrest. Perhaps this generation taught its children that life did not have to be unfair. People of color and women for the first time had been treated equally, and they learned despite the postwar attempts to suppress them. They had money and could earn more, protected by fair employment laws. They became educated and vocal, and taught their children that their oppression was not only immoral but illegal. Automobiles gave them physical mobility, and television widened their perceptions to the world rather than the neighborhood. The emphasis on education helped them to question not only local political situations, but those of the world.

The causes of gender and civil rights were nurtured during World War II, and many of the changes in social welfare sprang from changes during the war and its aftermath. The G.I. Bill made money available to a great number of people and created a new middle class. In addition, new technologies made the world smaller in both physical and mental senses, adding to the immediacy of new social welfare programs. The profession of social work had altered nearly completely from the provision of income maintenance for the poor to an accent on mental health for the middle class, and social workers had become professionals rather than reform voices crying in the wilderness. New services to children, veterans, and the middle class; new research into developmental theories and the knowledge bases of sociology, education, psychology; and an elaboration of skills and techniques via social casework and group work legitimated the profession as a part of American society.

The following questions will test your knowledge and understanding of the content found within this chapter. For additional assessment, including licensing-exam type questions on applying chapter content to practice behaviors, visit **MySearchLab.**

1. Roosevelt believed that the key to economic health was Keynesian economics, which was defined as:
   a. demand-side consumerism.
   b. supply-side consumerism.
   c. putting money into the hands of big business so they could generate more jobs.
   d. creating tax breaks and funding assistance programs.

2. Which statement about workers' compensation is true?
   a. The state is responsible for funding 100% of the cost of the program.
   b. It provides benefits to victims of work-related injuries regardless of fault as long as the incident was not due to gross negligence or misconduct.
   c. Workers' compensation is not required by the state.
   d. All workers, regardless of industry, are automatically granted workers' compensation benefits.

3. During the Great Depression, who would qualify for Old Age Assistance?
   a. Anyone over age 60.
   b. Anyone who had never worked and didn't have enough savings for retirement.
   c. Anyone who had been widowed after age 65 by the breadwinner of the family.
   d. Anyone who suffered a disability or ongoing health problems that would prevent them from working until retirement.

4. Which statement regarding Unemployment Insurance (UI) is true?
   a. It is granted to workers who have been fired for misconduct from a job.
   b. Workers will receive UI as long as they are willing and able to work after having been laid off.
   c. Workers can be denied UI for refusing a job that does not meet their qualifications.
   d. UI is automatically granted to workers who have been terminated involuntarily from a job.

5. You are working for a public assistance program under the Society Security Acts. A client comes to you asking for assistance. Your determination of whether the client receives help is based upon:
   a. Your own personal value judgement.
   b. A strict set of criteria required by state law.
   c. Standardized investigations administered by a neutral third party.
   d. Availability of funds and resources.

6. A single mother who is seeking assistance from Aid to Dependent Children asks you for your advice on how to qualify for the program. What factor would negatively influence her eligibility?
   a. Having Native American children; they would qualify under a different grant program and thus would be rejected.
   b. Being involved with a man who could potentially provide for her and the children.
   c. Being widowed or abandoned by her husband.
   d. Being married to a man who was a drunkard or a criminal.

7. Describe how the workforce changed for women after the war ended.

Reinforce what you learned in this chapter by studying videos, cases, documents, and more available at **www.MySearchLab.com**.

Watch and Review

Watch these Videos

Responding to the Great Depression: Whose New Deal?

Read and Review

Read these Cases/Documents

Negro Workers and Recovery (1934)

Flint Sit-Down Strike (1936)

Assess Your Knowledge

Go to **MySearchLab** to test your knowledge of key topics in this chapter with topic-specific quizzes. Conclude your assessment by completing the chapter exam.

10

Civil and Welfare Rights in the New Reform Era

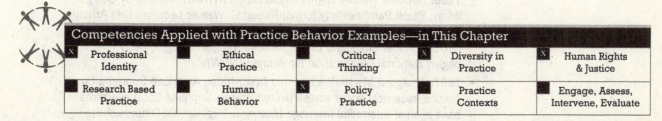

Competencies Applied with Practice Behavior Examples—in This Chapter				
X Professional Identity	Ethical Practice	Critical Thinking	X Diversity in Practice	X Human Rights & Justice
Research Based Practice	Human Behavior	X Policy Practice	Practice Contexts	Engage, Assess, Intervene, Evaluate

Times and Events

- **1950:** Incapacitated fathers category added to AFDC (AFDC-I)
- **1952:** Eisenhower becomes President; Immigration and Naturalization Act removes racial barriers to immigration
- **1953:** "Termination" frees Native American societies from federal wardship; Eisenhower approves removing gays from federal employment
- **1954:** *Brown v. Topeka Board of Education* ruling by Supreme Court bars racial segregation in public schools, overturning *Plessy v. Ferguson*
- **1955:** Rosa Parks refuses to give up bus seat, sparks Montgomery bus boycott; Roy Wilkins heads NAACP; AFL and CIO merge; Oveta Culp Hobby becomes first U.S. Secretary of the Department of Health, Education and Welfare (HEW); Emmett Till lynched in Mississippi
- **1956:** OASI program adds disability (OASDI) and classifies mentally ill as disabled
- **1957:** Federal troops enforce school integration in Little Rock; Civil Rights Act of 1957 protects African American suffrage; Southern Christian Leadership Conference (SCLC) founded by Dr. Martin Luther King, Jr. and Ralph Abernathy; Eisenhower reactivates food stamp/surplus program
- **1960:** John F. Kennedy elected President; college students found Student Non-Violent Coordinating Committee (SNCC), begin Freedom Rides to South
- **1961:** AFDC adds unemployed parent category (AFDC-UP); African American Robert C. Weaver appointed head of Housing and Home Finance Agency
- **1962:** Kennedy's Manpower Development and Training Act (MDTA) begins; Title XX of SSA provides states with money for programs for the disadvantaged, stimulating "purchase of service" grants to private agencies; Student Democratic Society (SDS) founded
- **1963:** President Kennedy assassinated, Lyndon B. Johnson becomes President; peace marchers attacked by Birmingham (AL) police; Medgar Evers murdered in Mississippi; Martin Luther King, Jr. leads march on Washington; Betty Friedan reactivates U.S. feminist movement with *Feminine Mystique*
- **1964:** Civil Rights Act passed; Economic Opportunity Act (EOA) establishes Equal Employment Opportunity Act (EEOC) and Equal Opportunity Office (OEO); King receives Nobel Peace Prize; Twenty-fourth Amendment outlaws poll taxes
- **1965:** Medicare and Medicaid operationalized; Voting Rights Act of 1965 passes; Older Americans Act instituted; Congress passes Elementary and Secondary Act (ESEA)
- **1966:** National Welfare Rights Organization (NWRO) founded by George Wiley; Black Panther Party forms; Robert C. Weaver becomes first African American cabinet member (Secretary of Housing and Urban Development [HUD]), Model Cities and Urban Renewal programs begin; Betty Friedan begins National Organization for Women (NOW)
- **1967:** Thurgood Marshall appointed first African American Supreme Court Justice; race riots occur across United States; Supreme Court overturns bans against interracial marriage (*Loving v. Virginia*); OEO funds shifted from grass roots organizations to local politicians

- **1968:** Martin Luther King, Jr. and Robert Kennedy assassinated; Civil Rights Act of 1968 outlaws discrimination in housing; Law Enforcement Act (LEAA) passes; Shirley Chisholm becomes first African American woman elected to Congress
- **1969:** American Indian Movement (AIM) occupies Alcatraz

After the upheavals of the 1930s and 1940s, the nation entered the next decade almost with a sigh of relief. War hero Dwight D. Eisenhower was elected president in 1952, and on the surface, prosperity reigned. However, there were troublesome undercurrents. First there was the fear that the Soviets would obtain the atomic bomb and threaten the peace of the world. Next came a backlash against the Social Security Acts as a "communist plot," and a new Red Scare exacerbated by the Korean conflict. Finally, there was an increasing ideological frustration that the promises of equality of the 1930s and 1940s were still unfulfilled in the fifties.

On Truman's order, the atomic bomb eliminated Hiroshima and Nagasaki even though surrender talks were in progress. The Chinese communists under Mao Tse-Tung flexed their muscles in Korea and defeated U.S. forces at the 38th parallel. Renewed fear of communism led to the establishment of the Federal Employee Act and the House Un-American Activities Committee (1947), under leadership of Senator Joseph McCarthy, who charged the Roosevelt and Truman administrations with "twenty years of treason" because of their social programs. The committee launched a hunt for communists, and the Internal Security Act (McCarran Act) passed Congress, establishing six concentration camps to house political prisoners and allowing imprisonment without trial for those suspected of treason.

By 1953, a great number of dissidents were in jail or in hiding, for everyone was suspect. Thousands of teachers, social workers, journalists, screenwriters, government workers—guilty of usually nothing more than organizing unions, belonging to the Communist Party during the wartime alliance of the United States and Russia, attending a radical meeting, or supporting liberal causes—lost their jobs for refusal to cooperate with investigatory committees. Under pressure of investigation, the labor movement pulled back from radical action, liberals renounced their social programs, libraries removed controversial books, and books teaching communism or socialism were banned. Ethel and Julius Rosenberg were executed for giving the secret of the atomic bomb to Russia. Schools, universities, and many public organizations required loyalty oaths as criteria for employment. As welfare workers resisted the label of "soft" or "pink," eligibility regulations tightened and benefits were withdrawn from recipients.[1]

By 1954, McCarthy's accusations became so outrageous that he was censured by the Senate and removed from the committee. However, by then Federal Bureau of Investigation procedures were firmly in place. Anyone voicing differing opinions might be investigated. Great numbers of dossiers went into FBI files, including those of civil rights activists such as Dr. Martin Luther King, Jr.

Roosevelt's emergency relief measures during the Depression, new educational opportunities, unionization, and veterans' benefits opened up new resources to nonwhite minorities. During the war, they earned wages competitive with white people to support their families. Now they were unwilling to give up those gains. New political channels opened to them through voting, their presence in unions, and legislation and court cases that supported their citizenship. However, their frustration and that of the poor was invisible, for it did not affect the lives of the upwardly mobile middle class. Tension grew as those who had shared, however briefly, in economic equality in unions, labor, and the war effort taught their children to expect equality. The struggle became ideological as well as economic.

Unionization and veterans' benefits had empowered white laborers in the 1930s; now those winnowed out of success—women, the aging, and people of color—began to fight. Television added a new dimension: "Around the world" became next door as Americans watched famines, wars, riots, oppression, and death over evening meals. We saw people dying in Korea, the justice system manhandling peaceful demonstrators, and poverty in a society of affluence. We saw war becoming the basis for economic prosperity: From 1945 to 1970, the federal government spent 69 percent of its total budget on defense ($1 trillion). In the Kennedy–Johnson era, the defense budget increased dramatically, and by the end of the 1960s, 10 percent of all jobs were tied to the defense budget.[2] We saw young people's lives traded for monetary profit and foreign countries invaded in the name of economic prosperity. And we began to ask why.

As we found answers, social revolution erupted. Students rioted and people of minority groups staged demonstrations demanding equality. Women, joining civil rights groups, saw class and race hatred compounded for them by sexism. Welfare and economic rights became intimately related with civil rights in the new ideological struggle. Idealists and pragmatic politicians developed new social programs and expanded civil rights: Presidents John F. Kennedy and Lyndon B. Johnson joined the battle, claiming that the United States, having the power to create a great society, should do so. But the bubble of idealism lasted less than a decade. The internal political stresses of the War on Poverty and the disastrous and expensive Vietnam War led to a conservative backlash that undermined the 1960s-inspired movements, and all too soon welfare cutbacks and civil repression returned.

THE STATE OF THE NATION UNDER EISENHOWER

Dwight D. Eisenhower became president in 1952, a respected war hero in a time of reasonable prosperity for middle and upper classes. The gross national product rose from $100 billion in 1940 to $286.5 billion by 1950, and by 1960 it was $400 billion.[3] Unemployment reached only 4.5 percent in the early 1950s, and although it rose to nearly 7 percent in 1958, it returned to 5.7 percent in the next decade.[4] A series of mild recessions occurred between 1961 and 1963, and nearly 2 million people were added to the unemployment rolls. By 1960, almost 40 million people, or 22.4 percent of the population, lived below the poverty line of $3,022 for a family of four.[5] Urban unemployment was exacerbated as a displaced farm population moved to the cities. Between 1940 and 1969, the number of farms owned and operated by African Americans decreased by 87 percent, from 680,000 to 90,000.[6] Within three decades, 16 million white people and 4 million African Americans moved to the cities, and by 1950, 64 percent of the U.S. population was urban.[7]

With the population changes, patterns of family life altered as drastically as during the Industrial Revolution. New middle-class families moved to the suburbs, leaving inner cities with a poor and increasingly African-American population. Consumerism boomed as more people could afford a "home in the country," and the baby boom meant even more buying. By 1960, the U.S. birthrate nearly equaled that of India. The age of marriage lowered: 14 million women were engaged by the time they were seventeen (1960), and the average age at marriage for women was below twenty. Sixty percent of all college women dropped out to marry before they earned their degrees.[8]

Although consumerism and mobility increased material goods, "personal good" suffered. The community bonds of family and friends ruptured, and the separation of poor from wealthy, white from nonwhite, grew. Young white mothers, in the suburbs far from their older women relatives, became isolated and depressed. Mental health and parenting programs overtly aimed at helping women find happiness as wives and mothers. Poor women were increasingly defined as mentally ill or deviant on two counts: poverty and "unwomanliness" because they worked. "Pockets of mental illness" were found in low-income areas, especially after the Joint Commission on Mental Illness and Health reported in 1960 that stress-creating situations such as poor health, poor housing, unemployment, and poverty should be considered in planning for mental health.

After World War II, emotional problems took on new meaning. Whereas *mental illness* had been stigmatized and hidden, now *mental health* became the right of every American. The social work profession argued that all social problems could be solved with casework treatment and psychoanalytic techniques, and the power of the profession increased synergistically with new mental health funding. Two innovations moved the focus of treatment from mental hospitals to the community: The use of tranquilizers became widespread after 1954, and the federal government declared mental illness a disability, making patients eligible for up to half their community care under OASDI. A study by Alfred Stanton and Morris Schwartz (1954) demonstrated that the mental hospital itself made people sicker, and the exodus to community care began. Despite more people being admitted to mental hospitals, the mental hospital population showed a definite decrease by 1957.[9]

Tranquilizer use was particularly problematic for women. Any doctor could prescribe them for any reason, and women were increasingly vulnerable as they became more isolated and depressed. Sex roles predicted they would be happy with their suburban homes and families, and those who were not were often labeled mentally ill and in need of medication. Tranquilizers became a panacea for unhappiness, and their misuse often resulted in emotional dependency, addiction, or ongoing and irreversible physical or emotional damage. The mental health movement and the excessive use of tranquilizers also put a great number of people under surveillance and paved the way for a more subtle behavioral control.

SOCIAL PROGRAMS IN THE 1950s

Few new social programs were instituted under Eisenhower, but eligibility and benefit levels of public assistance were expanded. Theorists and researchers concluded that, except for some "pockets of poverty" and personal "case poverty," America's poverty problem was solved. Concern for the aged provided a constant pressure, and conferences on aging in 1950 and 1951 kept the nation aware of their need for services. Private benefit plans expanded under pressure from unions: By 1962, their expenditures were more than 11 percent of the total expended for workers' pensions and health care ($9.8 billion).

Social Insurance

Increasing numbers of people became covered under social insurance until, by 1961, 90 percent of the potential population was covered.[10] By 1950, wives or divorced mothers with entitled children—to age eighteen, or twenty-one if still in school—were included in survivors' grants. In 1956 disability insurance was added to OASI (now OASDI), and mentally ill people were classified as disabled. In 1957, people disabled before the age of eighteen became entitled to their own, rather than survivor's, benefits.[11] The age of eligibility was reduced to sixty-two for retiring and sixty for dependent spouses (age fifty if disabled). Dependent spouse survivors' benefits were increased to 82.5 percent of the deceased worker's entitlement at age sixty-two, or for young spouses caring for children, to 75 percent of the entitlement plus an equal amount for the children.[12] The income subject to social insurance taxes reached $3,600 in 1951 and was $7,800 by 1967, with a tax increase from 2 percent to 6.65 percent.[13]

Public Assistance

During this same period, while costs for social insurance increased from $47.0 billion in 1950 to $123.9 billion in 1960,[14] public assistance expenditures increased from $2.3 billion in 1950 to $3.3 billion ten years later. Although the number of aged recipients (OAA) decreased from 2.8 million in 1950 to 2.2 million in 1965,[15] numbers of recipients on the whole increased by 13 percent. The AFDC population boomed along with the baby boom. By 1960, AFDC rolls had increased to more than 3 million people, and expenditures by 92 percent to more than $1 billion. During 1961, the first year under Kennedy, the number of AFDC recipients rose another half million, and expenditures rose another $2 million.[16] However, structural rather than personal reasons caused the increase:

- Simple population growth, especially with the baby boom, accounted for many of the new cases. Between 1940 and 1970 the nation's population increased over 50 percent and the number of children under age fourteen increased by 80 percent.
- The number of divorces doubled between 1935 and 1970. Whereas in the 1940s 60 to 70 percent of families were eligible because of death or incapacitation of the father, by 1971 nearly three-fourths of all applicants were separated, divorced, or unmarried, and 5 percent of fathers had deserted.[17]
- The out-of-wedlock birthrate tripled between the beginning of World War II and 1968, from one in twenty-five births to one in ten. Of the fathers absent from home, 28 percent were not married to mothers of children being served.
- Legislation and court decisions extended coverage to needy children without regard to the marital status of their parents. In 1950, in addition to adult caretakers of dependent children, states could also choose to include incapacitated breadwinners in grants (AFDC-I). In 1961,

states could choose to add unemployed parents to the rolls (AFDC-UP), although only half did so (the family was dropped when the breadwinner worked more than 100 hours per month).[18] Thus, parents and nonworking adults became part of the AFDC population. To society, this meant that women were "rewarded" for not having a husband's support and men were "rewarded" for not having jobs. Two of the strongest values in society were violated.

- Ideas about employability changed. One reason for the Social Security Acts' ADC program was to remove women from labor force competition with men. Another was the rationale that a mother could care for her children more cheaply and more competently than could day care or institutionalization. But wives and mothers worked during and after the war, so AFDC became increasingly difficult to justify on those grounds.[19]
- The great displacement of agricultural workers to the cities added thousands of women, many of them African American, to AFDC rolls, and racist hostility toward the program increased.

To "contain" AFDC, states restricted eligibility, reduced need levels, restricted residency requirements, and tried to embarrass recipients and new applicants by publishing their names or closing entire caseloads, forcing the needy to reapply.

To "contain" AFDC, states restricted eligibility, reduced need levels, restricted residency requirements, and tried to embarrass recipients and new applicants by publishing their names or closing entire caseloads, forcing the needy to reapply. Fewer applications were accepted: In 1948, 66 percent were accepted, compared to only 54 percent in 1958.[20] Especially in the South, families might be put off public assistance when it was assumed they could find work in the fields. Mandell says,

> The welfare system has been used as an instrument of economic exploitation by communities and states that needed cheap labor. This has been especially true in the southern states. For example, the farm policy adopted by Arkansas in 1953 required able-bodied mothers and older children to accept employment whenever it was available. This policy was responsible for 38.6 to 58.6 percent of all closings between [19]53 and [19]60.[21]

A classic example occurred in 1961 when the city manager of Newburgh, New York, closed all cases and allowed them to reopen only under grossly stigmatizing conditions: Applicants had to prove they had applied for city jobs and had not left other jobs voluntarily, and they had to reapply at police offices. All new cases had to be reviewed by the city manager and active ones by the city attorney. All able-bodied men had to work and vouchers rather than cash were given. Upon appeal, the state welfare board would not allow the new regulations, but the months they were in effect were painful for many.[22]

The greatest hostility was directed against women because of their "sexual immorality," the "great numbers" of out-of-wedlock children, and, again, the implication of mothers in causing juvenile delinquency. Part was a racist attack against the burgeoning nonwhite welfare population (in 1948, 31 percent of the recipients were nonwhite, and by 1974, 48 percent were nonwhite).[23] States gave their workers wide discretion in defining the "suitability" of the home, and the higher the rolls, the more stringent the requirements became. "Suitable homes" meant homes where no out-of-wedlock children lived and women had no men friends—no "men in the house." In further refinement of dependency, "need" became lacking a "father substitute" rather than needing money. Thus, children of women with men friends were not considered needy even if the friends contributed nothing economically. Violation of either suitable home or substitute parent policies, or even the accusation of such violation, could mean loss of grants.

In 1960, twenty-three states had "suitable home" rules, and such policies allowed Louisiana, in 1960, to remove 22,000 out-of-wedlock children from the rolls, 95 percent of them African American.[24] However, Arthur E. Fleming, Secretary of the Department of Health, Education, and Welfare (DHEW) under Eisenhower, charged that this action violated the intent of the Social Security Acts of 1935. Upon his threat to withdraw all federal welfare funds if the recipients were not reinstated, Louisiana's Governor Davis capitulated. In Arkansas, Governor Faubus proudly asserted that "8,000 illegitimate children were taken off the welfare roles during my term of office." In Florida, AFDC applicants with "unsuitable homes" were told to place their children in foster care or institutions or face court action to have them taken away. Only 186 of 2,908 families complied; the rest withdrew their welfare applications,[25] which is what the department really wanted anyway. Handler says,

> Sexual promiscuity, men in the house, divorce, remarriage, and so forth ... patterns of sexual behavior outside of conventional moral standards are tolerated by the public as long as the public is not called upon to support those who engage in such activities. The poor must stay married or become celibate.... As the price of survival, the poor are required to engage in certain behavior not required of the rest of society or to forego amenities and pleasures enjoyed by others.[26]

AFDC workers were investigators" whose purpose was to find ways to reduce rolls. They investigated employers, banks, credit agencies, and often neighbors; such a practice

> assumes dishonesty ... and applicants ... [must prove their] statements. The punitive administration of intake is, ostensibly, to protect the public by excluding applicants who do not qualify. It also protects the welfare rolls by using stigma as a rationing device.[27]

Investigations could take place at any time of the day or night, often with the cooperation of police. Workers "raided" women's homes looking for evidence such as men's shoes under the bed or clothes in the closet and assets that would not be purchasable on AFDC grants. These "midnight raids" continued even after the Supreme Court declared them unconstitutional in 1967. Investigators also kept information from recipients: amounts of grants, rights to fair hearings, and other programs. Clients asking for their rights were perceived as "challenging" and might lose their grants or their children—risks they could not afford. Although every kind of documentation was needed to qualify for AFDC, disqualification required very little, perhaps only an anonymous report from a neighbor.

Suitable home rules, farm work provisions, and residency requirements were disproportionately applied to African-American families moving north.[28] The removal of grants from the homes of out-of-wedlock children halted in 1961 when Arthur Fleming, secretary of the Department of Health, Education, and Welfare under Kennedy, ruled that support could not be removed unless the welfare department found new "suitable homes" for the children.

Diversity in Practice

Practice Behavior Example: Gain sufficient self-awareness to eliminate the influence of personal biases and values in working with diverse groups.

Critical Thinking Question: How do personal biases, shaped by social identities like class, race and gender, inform notions of "suitable" and "unsuitable" homes?

"Substitute father" or "man in the house" requirements were eliminated in 1968, under the *King v. King* decision, and residence requirements ended in 1969 with the *Shapiro v. Thompson* decision.

CIVIL RIGHTS BEFORE KENNEDY

In 1948, the Dixiecrats in Congress—Southern Democrats led by Strom Thurmond—successfully challenged the Democratic party's support of civil rights when it defeated Truman's bill to reestablish the Fair Employment Practices Commission, eliminate segregation in public transportation, and outlaw poll taxes. Hostility to civil rights continued throughout Eisenhower's administration (although a federal antilynching law was passed in 1951). Segregation was deeply ingrained in both North and South: seventeen states and Washington, D.C. required it, and four states—Arizona, Kansas, New Mexico, and Wyoming—authorized it at local option.

Economic and political oppression meant that the nonwhite median income was 51 percent that of white families in 1947 and 56 percent in 1962. In 1952, 5.4 percent of African Americans were unemployed, compared to 3.1 percent of white workers, and in 1970 African-American workers had 7.2 percent unemployment versus 4.5 percent white unemployment.[29] Generally, African-American unemployment remained double that of white unemployment in spite of the poverty programs of the late 1960s.

African Americans

The NAACP's policy of taking grievances to court increased the legal rights of people of minorities. Thurgood Marshall, Walter White, and William Hastie led the battles against segregation, along with Charles Hamilton Houston, Vice Dean of Howard University Law School.[30] In three court cases in 1950, the Court struck down segregation in schools and dining cars, saying that unequal rights were more than physical facilities, and in 1954 it ruled in *Brown v. Topeka Board of Education* that separate educational facilities were inherently unequal. This overturned the separate-but-equal doctrine of *Plessy v. Ferguson* and became the turning point in the civil rights movement. However, it also revitalized the white backlash by the Ku Klux Klan, White Citizen's Councils, and vigilante groups.[31]

Elected police and justice officials refused to enforce the federal rulings, and African Americans realized that legal victories were not enough. In Little Rock, young people tried to enter Central High School, and as white adults attacked them, Governor Orval Faubus proclaimed that they would never enter white schools. His resistance finally provoked President Eisenhower to send federal troops to enforce the ruling. Still, ten years after the *Brown* decision, only about 2 percent of segregated schools had been integrated, and fifteen years later almost 80 percent of African-American youth were still in segregated facilities.[32] Dye and Zeigler say,

> the *Brown* decision meant nothing to the overwhelming majority of Negroes, whose frustrations were intensified by the discrepancy between the declarations of the Supreme Court and the behavior of the local officials. Legally they were victorious, but politically they were impotent, since the South stubbornly refused to abide by the decisions of the Court.[33]

Segregationists renewed social Darwinist arguments against school integration with new "scientific" proof from researchers Arthur Jensen and Richard Hernstein, among others. They argued that inherited intelligence differences among racial groups required different educational techniques and that the national IQ would be lowered by higher African-American birthrates. However, the tests they used showed a white cultural bias. New tests indicated that better economic and learning environments improve test scores; for example, African-American children in the North often had higher scores than white children in the South.

Militancy increased with the evidence of the ineffectiveness of court action. The Congress of Racial Equality (CORE), founded in 1942, began a series of sit-ins in the North in 1955. The Nation of Islam, a religious group advocating separatism, became more vocal under the charismatic Malcolm X, who led African Americans to reexamine their oppression by whites and be proud of their African heritage. However, the key to mass civil rights activity came in December 1955 in Montgomery, Alabama, when Rosa Parks, a woman who had been a political activist for many years, refused to give up her bus seat to a white man and was jailed. This triggered a decade of protests and demonstrations, beginning with a year-long municipal bus boycott led by the young minister Martin Luther King, Jr. Although King and his coworkers were subjected to threats, violence, false arrest, and imprisonment, they persevered, and after thirteen months the buses were desegregated.

King was a student of the nonviolent tactics of Indian leader Mahatma Gandhi. Educated at Morehouse College, Howard University, and Boston University, he preached a new social gospel. Adding religion to resistance, he gave spiritual and civil leadership to people of color and the white liberals who fought alongside them. After the Montgomery boycott, he helped to organize the Southern Christian Leadership Conference (SCLC) in Atlanta, which became the central organizing body for passive resistance. During one of his imprisonments, King won the Nobel Peace Prize, accepting it in the name of all those working for equality.

Young people in the South became increasingly active in demonstrations and sit-ins, but there was little organization among these student groups until 1957, when Ella Baker, a graduate of Shaw University and long-time civil rights activist, organized an SCLC youth conference attended by about two hundred delegates from Southern communities in twelve states. The group subsequently met monthly to coordinate student demonstrations across the South. In 1960, it became the Student Non-Violent Coordinating Committee (SNCC) and organized demonstrations across all color, age, and income lines, with the ideals of nonviolence and passive resistance.

SNCC then organized "freedom rides"—busloads of activists going to Southern communities to register voters and support civil rights activities. In 1961, at Anniston, Alabama, the first freedom bus was burned. Later, riders in Birmingham were attacked by white mobs. According to FBI files, the FBI itself helped to precipitate the mobbing of two busloads of freedom riders by providing the Birmingham Police Department with a detailed itinerary. Police, under Commissioner "Bull" Connor, passed this to the Ku Klux Klan and agreed to come to the bus terminal 15 or 20 minutes after the expected arrival, giving the Klan time to attack the demonstrators with pipes, chains, and baseball bats.[34] By September of that year, freedom riders had worked in more than a hundred cities in twenty states. At least 70,000 students of all ethnicities participated, with 3,600 students arrested and 141 students and 58 faculty members expelled from their universities for political action.

Television brought an immediacy to civil rights because, for the first time, people far removed from such problems viewed firsthand the paradox of freedom denied in a free country, police brutalizing the innocent, and the efforts of elected officials and the police in defense of, often the cause of, violence. Through television, citizens observed the gentleness and firm resolve of Martin Luther King, Jr. and the pacifism of young people as they were beaten, set upon by police dogs, and even murdered without official response. The image of the police became for many Eugene "Bull" Connor directing firehoses and police dogs against children, women, and old men. For some, this was the end of innocence and belief in the American system. The civil rights struggle was no longer "somewhere and someone else": It was a national disgrace.

Other protests began among Native Americans, Hispanics, the young, welfare activists, and women. Most protests were modeled at first on King's nonviolent example. Social workers were far from the forefront in this movement; generally, they argued caution rather than activism.

> **Social workers were far from the forefront in this movement; generally, they argued caution rather than activism.**

Native Americans

In 1949, Congress began to turn Native American programs over to state governments to rid itself of the "Indian problem." In 1953, it began the process of "termination," ending federal supervision of the tribes and freeing Native Americans from government wardship. Termination gave certain states the right to overturn or replace laws of the 1934 Reorganization Act. Supporters of termination included land-hungry whites and members of Congress seeking to cut costs, along with some tribal members. Between 1954 and 1960, several dozen tribes were terminated from federal guardianship.[35]

Ostensibly, termination gave Native Americans the same privileges and responsibilities as other citizens. In fact, many necessary support programs were abandoned through termination. The problems Native Americans had are exemplified in the case of Wisconsin's Menominee tribe: The state created a county from the former reservation and immediately billed Native Americans for property taxes. They were unable to pay, and lost sanitation services, police and fire protection, and highway maintenance. Their tax base was too small to support adequate schools and health services, and their sawmill and forest holdings were endangered. Many lost their homes and life savings.

Some tribes, such as the Klamath in Oregon, were not treated so harshly—they were given interim financing, transportation and moving costs, and help with jobs and housing. However, from the Native American perspective, termination was another kind of oppression. Native American groups such as the National Congress of American Indians (founded in 1944) worked vigorously against it. Nevertheless, between 1954 and 1960 several dozen groups were terminated. Although President Kennedy ended termination, it had become a rallying point for activism. In 1961, the National Indian Youth Council was created, with a Red Power ideology, and in the next decade 194 instances of protest or civil disobedience occurred. Of these, 141 were legal suits and formal complaints, and the rest were protests such as delaying dam construction, occupying government facilities, picketing, and sit-ins.[36] The economic status of Native Americans grew increasingly worse. By 1960, unemployment had risen to 38 percent, compared to 5 percent for all males.[37]

Hispanic Americans

Traditionally, Hispanics in the United States have been agricultural workers. In the general social unrest after World War II, when the average annual income of Hispanic Americans was $2,600 (1956), Mexican Americans (Chicanos) began to organize for political action. During the next decade, when Hispanic income had increased about a third—still less than half that of white people[38]— more organizations were formed: the Mexican American Political Association, the Association of Mexican American Educators, the Mexican American Legal Defense and Educational Fund, and the Political Association of Spanish Speaking Organizations, a coordination council. However, they were all relatively ineffective.

Excluded from labor unions, Hispanic agricultural workers were continually denied economic advancement until Cesar Chavez organized the National Farm Workers Association. Some small strikes brought victories, but in 1965 police began harassment and brutality in California, while the hated Texas Rangers were brought in to enforce the growers' demands in Texas. Strikers and their leaders were imprisoned. Despite Anglo violence, Chavez kept the movement nonviolent and joined in 1966 with the Agricultural Workers Organizing Committee to form the United Farm Workers Organizing Committee.

More militant groups formed in the civil rights years: the paramilitary Brown Berets and the Chicano Moratorium Committee, La Raza Unida (California, South Texas, Colorado, California), the United Mexican American Students, and finally, a more violent group, the Chicano Liberation Front in Los Angeles, which claimed credit for a number of bombings of Anglo institutions. Under La Raza Unida in Denver, Corky Gonzales organized school strikes and action against police brutality. La Raza ran as a third party, undercutting Democratic strength in the area, and although it was unsuccessful in the elections, it helped Hispanics to become recognized as a united political force.[39]

The most militant of the Chicano groups was the Alianza Federal de Mercedes, formed in 1963 by Reies Tijerina, who in 1966 took his grievances to the New Mexico government at Santa Fe. At the same time, another group of Chicanos made citizens' arrests of forest rangers for violating old land boundaries, but Tijerina's group was arrested and tried for civil disobedience. In 1967, Tijerina was arrested at an Alianza meeting and taken to the courthouse at Tierra Amarilla, where later a group of armed Chicanos tried to arrest the district attorney. Some officials were wounded and in retaliation a number of Hispanics camping at a nearby picnic ground were detained without adequate shelter or water by armed police and hundreds of national guards, who claimed that Tijerina planned to take over northern New Mexico. Tijerina was charged with insurrection but acquitted for lack of evidence. However, he was jailed in 1969 because his wife had burned two national forest signs (government property).[40]

Until the 1930s, Puerto Rico was an agricultural colony based on sugar production, with the amount of land natives could own determined by the U.S. government. Massive strikes against U.S.-dominated business led to the Independence Party, under the leadership of Harvard-educated Pedro Albizu Campos. In March 1937, government officials massacred marchers in Ponce, and police raids led to armed revolt in five cities, with hundreds killed and 2,000 arrested for advocating independence. In 1948, Puerto Rico was given permission to elect its own government, and it became a commonwealth in 1952. Soon after, Operation Bootstrap began to industrialize the island and help it pull itself out of the poverty U.S. ownership had created. Possible investors were promised cheap labor and no taxes, and soon U.S. agribusiness had taken over so much land that Puerto Rico had to import food. By 1970, 80 percent of all industry in Puerto Rico was owned by U.S. corporations.[41]

Increasingly, Puerto Ricans were moving to the mainland, especially along the East Coast. By 1940, there were 70,000 Puerto Ricans in the continental United States, and from 1946 to 1955, 406,000 entered. In the next decade, immigration dropped drastically, but in 1966 alone 121,000 Puerto Ricans came to the Midwest and West.[42] During the 1950s, one-fifth of the Puerto Rican population left the island, encouraged by the government to migrate both to relieve unemployment on the island and to work on the mainland as cheap labor. In the United States, when they could find work, they became concentrated in blue-collar jobs, with women in sales and clerical jobs.[43] During the civil rights years, the Puerto Rican average income decreased from 71 percent to 59 percent of the national average.

Although the civil rights demonstrations of Puerto Rican Hispanics were less noted than were others, they did occur, particularly under the leftist-leaning Young Lords in Chicago. During the Johnson years, such groups were active in organizing programs for school breakfasts and lunches and providing protection against police brutality and advocacy assistance against social welfare agencies.

Chinese Americans

During World War II, China became an ally of the United States, and in 1943 Congress repealed the Chinese Exclusion Act. After the war, Chinese war brides were taken out of the regular immigration quota, and Chinese began to immigrate, about 90 percent of them women. Thirteen thousand Chinese Americans had served in the armed forces, 17 percent of the Chinese American population. On their return as veterans, they took advantage of such benefits as the G.I. Bill. Barred from laboring jobs by the anti-Chinese attitudes of unions, they became educators, researchers, doctors, lawyers, accountants, nurses, ministers, white-collar workers, and social workers. By 1970, 24 percent of all Chinese American men had college degrees, double the U.S. average and higher than any other ethnic group.

However, the McCarthy Red Scare soon lit the fires of anti-Chinese racism again, especially after the Chinese Revolution that made China a communist state in 1949. The political situation of Chinese Americans worsened during the Korean conflict (1950–1953), when China supported the North Koreans against U.S. forces. McCarthy and people with his perspective urged that Chinese Americans be incarcerated, as had been the Japanese, because they were a danger to the U.S. war effort. Although this did not occur, Chinese in the United States were once more suspect.

Many, especially the elderly, lived in poverty. Because of Chinese traditions of family and benevolent associations, only about 25 percent of those eligible for public assistance actually received it; whenever possible, the Chinese took care of their own. As the nation entered the War on Poverty, some civil rights agitation did occur, especially in the great Chinatowns of California and New York. Mostly this centered on housing needs, because 60 percent of Chinese American dwellings were substandard. In the past, the Chinese Consolidated Benevolent Associations (CCBA) had served as the Chinese voice for civil rights and welfare, but now they were joined by more activist groups: the Chinatown Park and Recreation Committee, Chinatown Coalition for Better Housing, and the Chinatown Neighborhood Improvement Resource Center, a coalition of several activist groups.[44]

CIVIL RIGHTS IN THE KENNEDY–JOHNSON YEARS

When John F. Kennedy won the presidency in 1960, people took his victory as a sign of a new era of liberalism. His Democratic party had lost power in the South, where white Dixiecrats opposed social programs that would benefit people of color, and among white urban workers, who had traditionally been Democrats because of Roosevelt's social insurance programs. Now African American urban Democrats were competing for jobs with white erstwhile Democrats, and the balance of power was shifting. If the Democrats helped the African-American urban poor, they would alienate both the white urban workers and the Southern aristocracy.[45]

Because Kennedy needed Southern support, his response to the needs of African Americans was politically difficult. For two years he temporized, but by the summer of 1963 he could not ignore the facts his own investigators brought him: Poverty was widespread in America, and nonwhites were systematically discriminated against in all facets of American life. Although he urged people to ask what they could do for their country rather than what the country could do for them, he began to understand the responsibilities a country had to its people, particularly a country that had the power to end poverty and discrimination.

In 1963, prolonged demonstrations and riots broke out throughout the South. In Mississippi, Air Force veteran James H. Meredith tried to enroll at the University of Mississippi but was stopped by Governor Ross R. Barnett himself. Twelve thousand federal troops, marshals, and national guardsmen were rushed to campus to put down the riots.[46] However, the key demonstrations were in Birmingham, Alabama, where in a massive voter campaign African Americans marched to the registrar's office to demand registration. An escalation of white violence brought Martin Luther King, Jr. to lead the demonstration, and he was arrested and jailed by "Bull" Connor. Eight white church leaders of all faiths—Catholic, Jewish, and Protestants—denounced King and chided the African-American community for following him. President Kennedy alerted Attorney General Robert Kennedy that intervention might be needed, and upon King's release April 20, violence began again.

By May 1, nearly a thousand people had been imprisoned. King called on African-American children to march on May 2, and although Bull Connor held off for a day, he finally attacked them, some no more than six years old, with firehoses, clubs, and dogs.[47] More than 2,000 people participated in subsequent demonstrations. Kennedy sent a mediator to intervene, and after six days of rioting, on May 10 Birmingham agreed to desegregate lunch counters, restrooms, fitting rooms, and drinking fountains. The city officials acted in good faith over the next three months, setting up a biracial committee, desegregating public facilities, and releasing 2,400 demonstrators from jail. However, on May 11—the day after the agreement—the Ku Klux Klan retaliated, bombing King's brother's home and the motel housing King's temporary headquarters, and a counter-riot ensued.

More riots broke out in Virginia, Maryland, and Georgia. Cambridge, Maryland, was under limited martial law for more than a year. In Mississippi, Medgar Evers, a World War II veteran, led a demonstration of 700 people. He was assassinated on June 12.[48] Until then, Kennedy had pursued a "sophisticated tokenism," but on the eve of Evers's death he began to compile a civil rights bill that guaranteed equal accommodations and gave the attorney general power to file suits to enforce the Fourteenth and Fifteenth Amendments. It remained bottled in Congress, and unrest grew worse: An estimated 1,412 demonstrations took place in the summer of 1963.

On August 28, King led a march of 250,000 people, including 60,000 whites, on Washington; standing before the Lincoln Memorial, he spoke of his dream of peace and civil rights. Eighteen days after the march, a church was bombed in Birmingham and four children were killed and twenty-one injured. This was the twenty-first bombing of establishments or homes of African Americans, and the twenty-first time the bombers were not apprehended. Over the year, there were more than 10,000 racial demonstrations, and more than 5,000 African Americans were arrested for political activities.[49]

Kennedy was assassinated on November 22, 1963, and although they mourned, African Americans continued their demonstrations, including a school boycott in Chicago involving 220,000 children. White resistance escalated, and demonstrators were arrested and confined for "insurrection" under Truman's McCarran Act. However, Kennedy's death gave the nation and Congress the moral thrust to attend to his civil rights bill that, along with the War on Poverty, became the legacy of democratic action in the 1960s.

JOHNSON AND THE GREAT SOCIETY

Lyndon B. Johnson assumed the presidency with a belief that the people had mandated a new day, one in which social welfare and civil rights were intimately connected. He called for a War on Poverty, and with his advisors—a liberal intellectual elite—drew up a coordinated attack on the many fronts of discrimination. Johnson's philosophy was "not a hand out but a hand up" and linked personal change with social reform. Although the poor were still considered "unmotivated," new theories pointed out the structural reasons for their lack of employment, and both personal rehabilitation and change in opportunity structures became the cornerstones of the War on Poverty. The job-related poverty programs focused on men; the poverty strategy for women was to secure their right to welfare, not to get them into the labor force.[50] The many-pronged attack on poverty began with the passage of the Civil Rights Act in July 1964. In November Johnson was reelected by a landslide, and Congress passed his Economic Opportunity Act the same year and the Voting Rights Act in 1965.

The Civil Rights Act and Continued Protest

Black Protest

The Civil Rights Act of 1964 was the first significant entry by Congress into the civil rights field since the Civil War. The bill was still opposed by the Dixiecrats, and as a joke or as a last-ditch effort to defeat it, Howard V. Smith, a Virginian congressman, attached an amendment to the bill outlawing sex discrimination. In the ensuing discussion, Representative Martha Griffiths and Senator Margaret Chase Smith fought to have it retained.[51] The bill passed both houses by more than a two-thirds vote with the amendment intact. By its provisions:

- It became unlawful to apply unequal standards in voter registration or to deny registration for irrelevant errors or omissions on records or applications.

- Discrimination and segregation became illegal in places of public accommodation and in all establishments whose operation affected interstate commerce or whose discriminatory practices were supported by the state.
- The attorney general was authorized to undertake civil action on behalf of people so denied. Those who refused to abide by the law were considered in contempt of court and subject to fines or confinement without trial by jury, thus circumventing local politics.
- The orderly desegregation of schools was called for.
- A congressional committee was to study deprivation of the right to vote and to inform the president and Congress of its actions.
- All federal agencies and departments were required to end discrimination in order to receive federal funds. The withdrawal of federal grant money was an innovation in enforcement.
- Discrimination in employment or labor unions with twenty-five or more people was forbidden.[52]

The Civil Rights Act made all discrimination illegal on a federal, and therefore nationwide, basis. It forbade discriminatory employment practices based on race, color, religion, sex, or national origin and created the Equal Employment Opportunity Commission (EEOC) to enforce civil rights.

Racial demonstrations became, if anything, more violent after the act passed in July, perhaps because

> masses do not revolt until they perceive the possibility of actually bettering their lot in life, while at the same time perceiving that their attempts to do so are being thwarted.[53]

White resistance was overwhelming. The summer of 1964, when the bill was passed, was a Red Summer equal to that of 1919, and the summer of 1965 was known as the "long hot summer," with riots in Watts (in Los Angeles), in Newark, New Jersey, and in Detroit. As late as 1970–1971, there were 250 race riots of various sizes in the nation.[54] The murder of white civil rights workers such as Viola Liuzzo, Michael Schwerner, Andrew Goodman, and James Chaney shocked the nation. Although an FBI agent witnessed Liuzzo's murder, the Southern jury refused to convict the murderer, who was finally convicted in federal court of depriving her of civil rights. He was imprisoned but released after ten years.

Because African Americans could not participate in the Democratic party's delegate selection in Mississippi, the Student Non-Violent Coordinating Committee sponsored its own election of delegates to the National Democratic Party Convention in 1964, under the name of the Mississippi Freedom Democratic party. Their delegates were denied seats and SNCC lost faith in the whole process of peaceful demonstration. It removed white people from its leadership in 1965 and from its membership in 1966. Stokely Carmichael became its chairman, and "Black Power" became the password. Its leaders—including Carmichael, H. Rap Brown, and John Lewis—defined Black Power as

> political and economic power and cultural independence of black people to determine their destiny individually and collectively, in and out of their own communities.[55]

Much of the theoretical underpinning of Black Power came from Malcolm X, of the Nation of Islam. After having visited Muslim countries in Africa, he determined that liberation required political organization and involvement. Early in 1965, he founded the Organization of Afro-American Unity (OAAU) in Harlem, a united-front organization to encompass all liberation groups and organizations (but no white groups). Malcolm X was assassinated in February 1965, but his teachings were passed on to other separatist/nationalist organizations. We must note that the "Nation of Islam" was a religio-political organization, a splinter group that did not encompass American Islam as a whole.

James Farmer charted the new direction for the Congress of Racial Equality on Malcolm X's insights. His major target was African-American economics, and he urged the development of cooperatives in the South and community programs for self-help in Northern ghettos. Farmer could not support Black Power within CORE and so stepped down, leaving the directorship to Floyd B. McKissick, a graduate of Morehouse College in Atlanta and the Law School of the University of North Carolina. In 1968, Roy Innis succeeded McKissick, with policies of self-help, government aid to African-American capitalists, and private business involvement.

Huey Newton and Bobby Seale organized the Black Panthers in Oakland, California in 1966, rallying around Malcolm X's statement that self-defense and freedom by any means were the ways to equality:

> We should be peaceful, law-abiding, but the time has come to fight back
> in self-defense whenever and wherever the black man is being unjustly
> and unlawfully attacked. If the government thinks I am wrong for saying
> this, then let the government do its job.[56]

Armed Black Panthers monitored police who used unnecessary force, protested rent evictions, informed welfare recipients of their legal rights, taught classes in African-American history, and demanded school traffic lights in a street where several African-American children had been killed while crossing.

Eldridge Cleaver, author of *Soul on Ice*, became their minister of information, and the Black Power movement took another turn. Cleaver believed that destruction of capitalist imperialism was necessary to gain power for people of color. Under his leadership, Marxist–Leninism became the new ideology, and Black Panthers formed alliances with communists, the Student Democratic Society (SDS), and the Young Lords—a Chicago-based Puerto Rican militant group—and shifted its emphasis to internationalism.

Women's Protest

By 1960, 40 percent of all American women were working in full- or part-time jobs and made up about a third of the labor force. Sixty-eight percent were in blue-collar or traditional female professions. Nearly half were mothers of school-age children, and many were middle class. Their individual freedom was still secondary to the needs of their husbands, however. In 1962, a Connecticut court ruled (*Rucci v. Rucci*) that

> a wife must both be a solicitous helpmeet and perform her household
> and domestic duties ... without compensation.... A husband is entitled
> to the benefit of his wife's industry and economy.[57]

Kennedy appointed the first Presidential Commission on the Status of Women in 1961, chaired by Eleanor Roosevelt. The commission deplored the trend to blame women for juvenile delinquency and confirmed in 1966 that the EEOC should take action against sex discrimination.[58]

Women had worked actively for civil rights and against the war in Vietnam. In those battles they learned the rhetoric of equality and methods of political action, and also that men did not consider them equal partners even in those activities. In both the SDS and SNCC, for example, they were rarely allowed to speak and continued to perform "women's work"—making coffee, taking notes, and doing secretarial labor. A famous quote from Stokely Carmichael was that "the only position women had in the movement was prone." Realizing that their issues were a part of the larger struggle, women argued that patriarchy was the oldest and most basic form of oppression. When their voices went unheard, many split off from men-dominated groups to form protest movements of their own.[59]

Betty Friedan's systematic look at women's oppression added support to women's struggle. She talked of the romanticization of domesticity, the infantilization of women, and the transformation of the suburban home into a comfortable concentration camp. In 1966, 300 women and men organized the National Organization for Women (NOW), and Friedan was named its president. Its goal was to bring women into full participation as equals in American society. In 1967, NOW adopted a Bill of Rights urging the Equal Rights Amendment, joined the Women's Commission in calling on the EEOC to enforce antidiscrimination legislation, and worked for equal and unsegregated education, maternity leaves that preserved job security and seniority, tax deductions for child care, inexpensive day care centers, reform of the welfare system, and equality of benefits.[60]

Discussion of abortion as a woman's right began in the early 1960s, and NOW picked up the issue, advocating the right to contraceptive information and devices and safe legal abortions. Health care organizations also advocated legalized abortion as a medical issue, and laws were passed to permit it in certain instances. The War on Poverty established family planning programs and clinics, and Medicaid began to pay for abortions for poor women.

Youth Protest

The youth movement was one of disenchantment from the "establishment"— groups and institutions that made the rules and laws many young people considered immoral. Young people demonstrated against colleges and universities, the Vietnam War, and the draft. Their protests were often brutally repressed by police, and university authorities denied the right of students to speak out. Demonstrations against the invasion of Cambodia in May 1970 and the killing of student protestors at Kent State (Ohio) and Jackson State (Mississippi) Universities virtually closed down the country's college and university system.[61] Youth became heavily involved in Senator Eugene McCarthy's bid for the Democratic presidential nomination in 1968. He made the war in Vietnam and the youth movement his causes and hundreds rallied to him. During the Chicago nomination convention in August 1968, confrontations between the police and the thousands of young people there became violent. Many were arrested and jailed, and for some imprisonment, in both prisons and mental hospitals, continued for years.

The youth movement was, in essence, a protest by middle-class young people against the materialism of their elders. Its concerns were the nation's continued injustices against the poor and people of color and the government's involvement in the internal affairs of other nations for profit. Young people turned from materialism and sought new ways of life offering freedom and creativity in such forms as communal living and, later, involvement in drugs as a way to heightened awareness. By 1973, the youth movement had crumbled. No longer looking outward to change the world, young people turned increasingly inward. Their search for new awareness and freedom was far from selfish in the beginning. That what they sought could not be found in an unresponsive government is, perhaps, one of the shames of our society. Other than some success in their protests against the war in Vietnam and the lowering of the voting age, few real benefits emerged from their struggle. However, Nixon's administration did end the Selective Service Act (draft) in response to their protests.

The Gay Liberation Movement

Human social evolution has produced many sexual styles, socially acceptable or not, according to societies and times. Until after the Civil War, the few state regulations that applied to homosexuality were generally based on religious or moral grounds and referred to sodomy, prostitution, indecent exposure, and so on. According to William Eskridge, this social construction of sex and gender categories reflected a reification of the roles of men and women returning to "normalcy" after the Civil War. He says this

> ... arose out of increased social and economic opportunities for women, which fueled not only a robust feminist movement, but also a reaction that emphasized rigid gender lines and roles. Faced with the newly independent woman, middle-class men grew obsessed with cultural reinforcements for manliness.[62]

Homosexuality, along with other sexual alternatives, became identified as "sexual perversion" during the Victorian era—the time of the "pure" wife on the pedestal versus the prostitute; "Women's Sphere" in social work, education, and nursing; the Comstock Law outlawing the mailing of birth control information as pornography; "red lighting" city districts to control prostitution; and so on. By the turn of the twentieth century, there were major subcultures of homosexuals in most big cities, along with new definitions for those "deviating" from male or female roles: sexual degenerates and psychopaths. Homosexual activity was generally labeled sodomy, indecent exposure, or "a crime against nature," and police action and enforcement targeted at homosexuals stimulated the creation of new laws to regulate same-sex intimacy.[63]

In the 1930s, child molestation became a national hysteria, and legal control of sexuality shifted from female corruption, such as prostitution or birth control, to male sexual aggression. Policing became increasingly aggressive, and penalties for homosexual activity included prison sentences and/or castration, called "asexualization." As medicine and psychiatry bloomed, it became fashionable to view alternate sexuality as mental illness, and offenders sent to mental hospitals received medical solutions: prefrontal lobotomies, massive injections of male hormones, electroshock, and other aversion therapies.[64] By the 1940s, antigay laws were used to arrest homosexuals, censor homoerotic publications, close down meeting places such as gay bars, and exclude gays from the Armed Services. National security was the rallying cry, claiming that homosexuals could be blackmailed for information. Under-Secretary of State Sumner Welles, despite his friendship with Franklin D. Roosevelt, was removed from his post because of his homosexuality, and accusations of homosexuality, true or otherwise, became key tools in prosecuting America's antiespionage campaign.

From 1947 on, the FBI under Director J. Edgar Hoover triggered unprecedented homophobia under the "national security" banner. Between 1946 and

1961, as many as a million lesbians and gay men were redefined as sexual psychopaths and given criminal punishments.[65] In 1953, President Eisenhower, in an executive order, added the homosexual category as grounds for investigation and dismissal from federal employment, and within two years more than 800 federal employees resigned or were terminated. Because the government shared its military and police records with companies contracted by the Defense Department, by the 1960s over 2 million private sector employees were blacklisted.[66] In addition, gay people with jobs requiring a license were denied their licenses and their livelihoods—doctors, teachers, pharmacists, and so on. Interestingly, the American Civil Liberties Union (ACLU) upheld such actions on the basis of the perceived security risk.

Gay Liberation had its tentative beginnings in the late 1940s and early 1950s with the founding of the Mattachine Society in Los Angeles and the Daughters of Bilitis in New York and San Francisco. Generally, these organizations remained hidden because of the illegality of homosexuality in many areas and the threat of persecution. Mostly social groups, they devoted themselves to research and education rather than the active repeal of antigay laws. However, in 1961 Franklin Kameny, reduced to poverty because of license laws, organized the Mattachine of Washington Society to promote political activism. In 1964, when the Civil Rights Acts were being passed, he said:

> I do not see the NAACP and CORE worrying about which chromosome and gene produced black skin or about the possibility of bleaching the Negro. I do not see any great interest on the part of B'nai B'rith Anti-Defamation League in the possibility of solving the problems of anti-Semitism by converting Jews to Christians. In all of these minority groups, we are interested in obtaining rights for our respective minorities as Negroes, as Jews, and as homosexuals. Why we are Negroes, Jews, and homosexuals is totally irrelevant, and whether we can be changed to white Christians or heterosexuals is equally irrelevant.[67]

Active resistance began when, on June 27, 1969, New York City police raided the Stonewall Inn, a gay bar, and patrons fought back. The "Stonewall Riot" incident is widely accepted as the beginning of Gay Liberation, of which the major group is the Gay Activist Alliance. The alliance used a nonviolent but militant strategy to persuade homosexuals to perceive themselves as an oppressed minority. The two major legal bases for the struggle of gays to reclaim their civil rights are the Constitution's First Amendment Freedom of Speech clause and Title VII of the Civil Rights Act of 1964. Three struggles overlap: to protect private gay spaces (homes, cars) against prying and intrusion by the police; to assert control over the institutions of gay subculture (gay bars, restaurants); and for equal gay citizenship— "public equality and equal treatment on their merits as employees, soldiers, immigrants, and parents."[68]

The Voting Rights Act and New Legal Rights

The Voting Rights Act of 1965, along with Johnson's Affirmative Action Order in 1968, effectively ended legalized segregation. Almost a million southern African Americans registered to vote within three years, and by 1970 nearly 70 percent of eligible voters were registered.[69] Local sheriffs and judges who had been instrumental in denying civil rights to African Americans became vulnerable to the new voting blocs. In 1964, there were only about 100 elected officials in the nation who were of African descent, but in 1965 approximately 70 more were elected and by 1968 there were 248. By 1980, there were more than 4,900 elected African-American officials in offices ranging from county clerks to mayors and judges. The first to serve in a presidential cabinet was Robert Weaver, in 1967, named the secretary of Housing and Urban Development (HUD), and Andrew Brimner became the first to serve on the Federal Reserve Board. Thurgood Marshall was appointed to the Supreme Court, and Patricia Harris became the first ambassador of African-American descent.[70]

One of the most important legal decisions during the Kennedy administration was the *Gault* decision. Before then, because of the tradition of *parens patriae* in juvenile justice, children had no real legal rights. Even minor offenses such as shoplifting or status offenses could mean years of detention in children's institutions, often to age of majority. The *Gault* decision secured due process for juveniles and gave young people the same rights as adults in the justice system, including adequate notice of charges and rights to counsel, to confront accusers, to avoid self-incrimination under the Fifth Amendment, and to cross-examination.

Under Johnson, new legal rights included the assignment of counsel to those unable to afford attorneys and, in 1966, the *Miranda* decision, which mandated clarifying a suspect's rights before his or her arrest. The *Miranda* decision began to be circumvented immediately with the 1972 decision denying the right to counsel in police lineups. Judicial and administrative decisions also strengthened the rights of the aged, mentally ill and developmentally disabled people, prisoners, and juveniles.

SOCIAL PROGRAMS IN THE KENNEDY–JOHNSON YEARS

Poverty was easier to deal with than civil rights. The Social Security Administration's reports on poverty from 1959 census data, Attorney General Robert Kennedy's firsthand reports, and books such as Michael Harrington's *The Other America* (1962) and Dwight MacDonald's *Our Invisible Poor* (1963) pointed out the hidden pockets of poverty in the cities, among the aged or disadvantaged, or in rural areas such as Appalachia that existed even in this time of affluence.

President Kennedy's 1962 plans were modest: some advances in public assistance, the extension of unemployment insurance and liberalized OASI benefits, an increased minimum wage and an increase in AFDC benefits, a new housing act to create more jobs in construction, some training bills, and financial and technical aid for depressed regions. To stimulate consumer buying and corporate investment, he also cut personal and corporate income taxes.[71] He sought prevention rather than cure when possible: In 1963 alone, the Department of Health, Education, and Welfare (DHEW) spent $130 million for basic and support services, personnel training, research, construction of residential facilities, income maintenance, and maternity and infant care programs, including health screening programs, especially in high-risk populations.

Kennedy's Social Security Amendments

The most important changes for social welfare by far were those of the Social Security Amendments of 1962, called the Service Amendments. In 1961, Kennedy appointed a twenty-five-member Ad Hoc Committee on Public Welfare with members from both public welfare and private social work. They were charged to recommend methods leading to adequate financial assistance, efficient administration and organization of public assistance offices, research into the causes of dependency and family breakdown, and provision of rehabilitation services by trained personnel. The guiding ideals were still that

- people would not work if they could get welfare and
- rehabilitative services by social workers could return recipients to the workforce.

The committee gave full support to social work's claim that casework and psychoanalytic intervention could "cure" the problem of motivation and strengthen the family, and that this would cause a drop in welfare rolls. Its major recommendation was that schools of social work receive enough funding to train new workers to "rehabilitate" AFDC families. Other recommendations included

- support for unemployed and incapacitated parents;
- research and demonstration projects on out-of-wedlock births, dependency, and family breakdown;
- the removal of residence requirements for public assistance;
- new funding for day care;
- vouchers rather than cash for recipients who could not manage money; and
- money earned by children to be exempted when figuring family eligibility or grant levels.

Kennedy's message to Congress in 1962 dealt solely with public dependency, reiterating the "blame the victim" and work ethic stances of most public assistance rhetoric. He called for a "new" approach to dependency:

> a return to seeking causes within the individual, buttressed by job training and employment services for the dependent and those who might become dependent.[72]

To carry out this new approach, the Social and Rehabilitative Service (SRS) was established in the Department of Health, Education, and Welfare.

Massive funding was provided to schools of social work and new standards were set to ensure that workers could provide adequate services: caseloads of no more than sixty (patently impossible as rolls continued to rise), one supervisor for every five caseworkers, home visits to improve family functioning, homemaker services, a "service plan" for every child, and guardians when adult clients misused AFDC funds. Group homes grew rapidly in this period, and many children were removed to such homes or to foster care. Institutionalization was also an option: There were approximately 306,000 children in institutions at the time. Of these, 23 percent were labeled neglected and dependent, a third were adjudged juvenile delinquents, and a little over a third were in homes and schools for children with mental and physical disabilities.[73]

Employment was the most important goal, and AFDC recipients who refused training without good cause were removed from the grant (although their children remained recipients). Success of the amendments was measured in terms of the new financial independence of former recipients, but unfortunately the rolls continued to expand, now faster than unemployment rates, and "services" became increasingly suspect. Whereas in 1955, 3 percent of all children were receiving AFDC, in 1970, 8.5 percent were on the rolls.[74] Although the numbers of people in poverty dropped by nearly half from 1960 to 1969, AFDC rolls more than doubled, from 2.9 million to 7.3 million. Expenditures tripled in the same period, from $1 billion to $3 billion, and by 1972 had increased tenfold, to $10.3 billion.[75] In 1961, in real dollars the average monthly AFDC payment was $117 per family. A decade later, it was $183, or about $49 per person (compared with per capita income of $307 in the general population).[76] Levitan, Rein, and Marwick say,

> There is no evidence that the provision of social services for welfare recipients has induced labor force participation.... The failure of social services to "rehabilitate" welfare recipients led to a new emphasis on concrete programs related to employability. The emphasis shifted to day care, family planning, manpower training, and compensatory education.[77]

Under Johnson, the Social Security Acts were further amended, first with the massive health programs of Medicare and Medicaid in 1964 (operationalized in 1965), and then with further AFDC amendments in 1967.

The Economic Opportunity Act of 1964

The Economic Opportunity Act of 1964 (EOA) was overtly aimed at calming riots and providing job training and employment for the poor and people of color—those most likely to rebel. Several programs led the way to or enhanced the programs of the War on Poverty. One was Kennedy's Manpower Development Training Act (MDTA) in 1962, designed to deal with institutional causes

The Economic Opportunity Act of 1964 (EOA) was overtly aimed at calming riots and providing job training and employment for the poor and people of color—those most likely to rebel.

of unemployment by training people for better jobs. Johnson incorporated both the funding and the ideals of MDTA into the Title I and IV programs of the Economic Opportunity Act. Another Kennedy program, the Area Redevelopment Act of 1961, gave financial and technical aid to depressed regions by luring new industries to areas of regional unemployment and expanding industries already there. Johnson built on this program with Titles III and V of the Economic Opportunity Act of 1964 and the Economic Development Act of 1965, funding industries in depressed areas in Appalachia, New England, the Coastal Plains, the Ozarks, the Upper Great Lakes region, and a poverty-stricken sector in the Southwest.[78]

Title I included Job Corps training centers for out-of-school and unemployed youths, work training programs to help young people stay in school, and work study programs to enable them to go to college. Unfortunately, job training programs were often run by white middle-class people who believed that lack of motivation, rather than unavailability of jobs, caused unemployment. Participants came because they were paid for their attendance, but many perceived the programs as childish and inauthentic, teaching people to use alarm clocks and public transportation, for example, or filling out job applications when there were no real jobs available.

Unlike Roosevelt with his Works Progress Administration, Johnson did not attempt to create new jobs. According to Ehrenreich, this would have implied

> a direct government role in corporate investment decisions, a step that Johnson-era America was not ready to take and that the poor never gained enough power to demand.[79]

Although jobs became increasingly available at the same time as the training programs,

> it was the war in Vietnam, not the war on poverty ... that both stimulated the economy and provided "jobs" (although often fatal ones) for many of the poor.[80]

Title III provided grants and loans to buy or improve real estate, reduce debts, construct buildings, operate family farms, and participate in cooperative associations, particularly in rural areas. Title IV targeted especially African-American-owned businesses and investment opportunities by providing small business loans for African-American entrepreneurs, although others could qualify.

Title V, Work Experience Programs (WEP), permitted businesspeople to use funds from the MDTA (1962) and Vocational Education Act (1963) to hire low-income and minority people, including AFDC recipients; money was channeled to the workers through the businesses. WEP also established Volunteers in Service to America (VISTA) to work in programs for Native Americans, migrant workers, or people in need in Washington, D.C., Puerto Rico, Guam, American Samoa, the Virgin Islands, and the Trust Territory of the Pacific Islands. VISTA volunteers also worked in agencies for the care and rehabilitation of mentally ill and developmentally disabled people.

Title II, Community Action Agencies, was the most controversial. It gave money directly to grassroots public or nonprofit agencies established by the poor, bypassing the traditional channels of state and local governments, United Ways and social agencies, and political parties, although many traditional agencies also shared in the funding. A key term was *maximum feasible participation* of the poor. There were very different interpretations of how much "maximum participation" was feasible. To liberals and the poor, it meant that they had to be represented in developing goals and policies and in maintaining the programs receiving federal funds by administering and working in them. To mayors, governors, and traditional social agencies, it meant that people whom they had previously controlled now had massive funds and needed neither advice nor control. The Office of Economic Opportunity (OEO), which administered the programs, was under attack from the first by mayors and political machines, and legal suits were filed against its programs.

Community Action Programs (CAPs) were the local arms of the OEO. Their services included advocacy against public and federally funded private agencies that discriminated or withheld services; job training and employment services; Head Start, a nursery school for deprived children; Upward Bound, teaching remedial educational skills so that young people might enter college; day care centers for employed parents; neighborhood recreation centers to enhance the lives of children in poverty; and neighborhood health and family planning centers. The New Careers Program trained tens of thousands of indigenous paraprofessionals to work in social agencies, increasing the numbers of social workers but threatening the profession's argument that only highly trained social workers could give services. It provided career ladders, increased on-the-job experience, and gave in-service training and release time for college. Legal Services Organizations (LSOs) provided class actions against established agencies: By 1968, there were approximately 250 LSOs, with 1,800 lawyers initiating more than 25,000 cases per year against schools, welfare departments, mental hospitals, police, city administrations, and courts. Other programs included mental health family-centered care, adult basic education, information and referral centers, police relations programs, and volunteer programs.

Although a manifest purpose of the EOA was to enable social agencies that qualified for OEO funds to be innovative and responsive to the needs of their clients, this rarely happened. Rather, agencies took the federal money and used it to expand their clientele in poverty areas while they maintained the same attitudes and intervention modalities: belief in personal fault and the efficacy of casework. For example, community mental health centers expected to pioneer new services remained attached to their entirely conventional outpatient services, although they now offered them in poor communities.[81] Funds intended to create neighborhood health centers were captured by hospitals for institutional expansion. School systems took the funds but did not use them to innovate. Ehrenreich says,

> in the end, despite the successful reorganization of many agency
> practices and attitudes, the poverty program failed to reform the service
> delivery system, much less to eliminate poverty.[82]

The fight against OEO was effective. In late 1966, Congress cut back and restricted the scope of the CAPs, and legislation in 1967 required OEO funds to be channeled through the offices of mayors. The fight went out of the OEO movement. Many mayors already had political control, or the agencies were so innocuous as to not matter anyway.[83] President Johnson, sensing the failure of the War on Poverty and concerned about his loss of support, abandoned the OEO to throw the nation's resources behind the war in Vietnam. The most important immediate reason for the failure of the OEO was the false assumption that "no one had a vested interest in maintaining poverty"[84] when in fact many people found it profitable. Moreover, indigenous leaders of the civil and welfare rights battles were co-opted by the good government pay, and this loss of leaders devastated both movements. Furthermore, a major tenet of the OEO was to train the disadvantaged to take jobs in society. As with other such programs, this "work ethic" basis was inauthentic, for the jobs simply did not materialize no matter how effective the training. Finally, the OEO did fulfill its latent purposes and so was no longer needed: It quelled the rebellious by giving them some benefits, co-opted the leaders, and put control back in the hands of those who needed a cooperative low-wage workforce.

Programs Amended Under Johnson

Medicare

Medicare was added to social insurance (OADSI), making it Old Age, Survivors, Disability, and Health Insurance (OASDHI). Medicare was an insurance-like system with two programs (Part A and Part B) to provide health care for people over age sixty-five and people with disabilities on Social Security. Part A was compulsory, and a "premium" was automatically deducted from monthly OASDHI checks, and Part B was optional, with an added premium for expanded services. General revenues, rather than the premiums, paid most of the cost. The program was operated through private mediaries such as Blue Cross/Blue Shield, to which the government paid a 2 percent administrative fee.

Part A paid for part of the costs of hospitalization, with deductibles paid by patients according to length of stay: skilled nursing home care for up to 100 days, 80 percent of outpatient diagnostic tests, and up to 100 home nursing visits per year following hospitalization. Part B had a higher yearly deductible plus monthly premiums and paid 80 percent of "reasonable" expenses for physicians' and surgeons' services, more home nursing visits, mental health care, and a number of medical appliances and diagnostic tests. For hospital stays of more than ninety days, a patient could draw on a sixty-day lifetime reserve, and hospice care for the terminally ill was provided.

Medicare did not pay for such needs as eyeglasses, dentures, hearing aids and batteries, prescription drugs not given by health professionals, and home care for fragile, nonambulatory, or senile people when other adults in the family worked. Recipients got no money: Vouchers went directly to the health services. Because Medicare paid only "reasonable" costs, patients had to pay all "unreasonable" or overcosts. When Medicare was exhausted, recipients paid their own way, relying on private insurance plans, or, having sold their assets, turning to public assistance (Medicaid).

Medicaid

Medicaid's forerunner was the Kerr–Mills Bill of 1958. A means-tested public assistance program rather than social insurance, it was administered through state departments of public welfare or public health. Like Medicare, Medicaid was a voucher program, with payment going directly to health care providers. Funded through general revenues, it was given on an open-ended basis to the participating states depending on per capita income, with grants-in-aid of 50–83 percent of Medicaid costs. The Health Care Financing Administration (HCFA) administered Medicaid under the Department of Health and Human Services (formerly Department of Health, Education, and Welfare).

Medicaid's primary target was people on public assistance, although others below the poverty line might be covered if states so chose. States also had to give Medicaid for people in other selected categories, such as children under twenty-one in foster homes or institutions for whom public agencies provide some financial support. In general, Medicaid paid for all costs of hospitalization, doctor's services and calls, prescriptions, diagnostic testing, emergency services, doctor's visits, and extended nursing home care for the aged or those with long-term disabilities who had exhausted other payment alternatives (including Medicare). Also, depending on different state guidelines, Medicaid might pay for eyeglasses, hearing aids, dental care, false teeth, prostheses, appliances, and other equipment. Medicaid funds were also paid to train professional medical personnel and facility inspectors, and for administrative needs such as information systems. By the end of 1964, thirty-nine states had Medicaid programs, five were establishing them, and six had decided not to. In 1982, thirty-four states chose to provide for the medically needy (in addition to public assistance recipients), but still only about three-fifths of poor households were covered.

Because health care providers understood that Medicaid was guaranteed by the government, highly inflated medical costs, not only for Medicaid recipients but also for the general public, occurred. Ironically, many health care services and physicians would not take Medicaid clients, leaving them to rely on a limited number of physicians and hospital emergency rooms rather than the preventive health care envisioned by those who developed the Medicaid program.

Social Security Amendments of 1967

During 1967, the Department of Health, Education, and Welfare underwent reorganization. One of the most interesting changes was the creation of the Assistance Payments Administration in AFDC. This divorced income maintenance functions from social services functions and split public welfare departments into two sections: social services, whose workers provide counseling services and services to neglected, abused, or dependent children and older people; and assistance payments, whose workers determine eligibility and set amounts of grants based on state levels of need, number in family, and their own discretion. Purchase of services from the private sector, for such treatment as mental health care, drug abuse, or family services, was also authorized.

The social work community had been for some time arguing that services to the poor should not be connected with whether or not they received financial aid. The National Association of Social Workers (NASW) supported the split in services as clients' right to self-determination, acknowledging that need did not necessarily call for services.[85] However, the split in services caused some unfortunate consequences. Services personnel were required to have bachelor's degrees (in any field), but assistance payments (AP) workers needed no more, generally, than a high-school education. Therefore, less-educated workers, often with harsh values regarding work and sexual morality, were AFDC's gatekeepers and had real power over subsistence issues. Services workers could only suggest to AP workers that clients' financial needs (beyond grants) be filled—more food, for example, or the purchase of a refrigerator or bedding.

In effect, the split in services made the more-educated workers powerless except in an advisory capacity and caused dissension within departments of public welfare.

Social services for children included protective services for the abused and neglected; licensing of foster homes, day care centers, and institutions; and placement services (foster care, institutionalization, or adoption) for children who could not remain with their biological parents. Workers were required to maintain contact with both biological and foster parents for the duration of need, and they could also request permanent termination of parental rights. In 1968, state and local departments provided services for 656,000 children, or 80 of every 10,000, and private agencies served another 219,000 children. In fiscal year 1968, child care cost $499.7 million, a 13 percent increase over 1967. Of that, only 9 percent was federal money, with over half coming from the state and the rest from the local level. Day care took the most—more than 60 percent.[86]

The sexual morality of single mothers remained an intense issue among AFDC policymakers. One result was a freeze on the number of out-of-wedlock or deserted children who could receive aid; however, this was overturned in 1969 because it punished needy children.[87] In 1970, 5.6 million children were on AFDC, an increase of 900,000 from 1969, and family planning program services under Medicaid began to be offered to AFDC clients. Some, especially African-American men, perceived this as race genocide, but in general women hailed it. Workers, whether services or AP, continued to believe society's sex and race stereotypes of their clients: that "most welfare mothers are promiscuous" and that "black women are worse (in sexual immorality) than are white women."[88]

Some states also chose to provide protective services to dependent aged or disabled adults, for many were subject to "granny beating" or mistreatment from those with whom they resided. Also, service workers in some states licensed nursing homes for elderly or disabled people and day care or group homes for developmentally disabled adults. Guardians were assigned as needed for either child or adult dependents.

The 1967 amendments made employment and training top priorities. The major AFDC work program was the Work Incentive Program, first called WIP, an appropriate name soon changed to WIN. It required AFDC parents with no children under the age of six to register for work training and job placement. Any adult who refused to enroll, unless incapacitated or needed at home, was disqualified for benefits (although the children still received their portion of the grant). Children out of school and over age sixteen also had to register or be disqualified. WIN was a joint Public Welfare and Labor Department program that in the long run cost more, with fewer long-term benefits, than would have simple grants. New work incentives developed and day care monies became reasonably generous. Work expenses, such as payment for uniforms and transportation, were paid by the departments of public welfare. Very importantly, the "$30.00 and a third" disregard was instituted: that is, working parents could keep the first $30.00 they earned, along with a third of the remainder of their income, without a deduction in AFDC benefits.

Other Kennedy–Johnson Social Programs

Food Programs

On his first day in office, Kennedy doubled the Surplus Commodity Program (reactivated by Eisenhower in 1957) by which the Department of Agriculture bought surplus food from farmers and distributed it to the poor. Concerned that this was a "white" diet—white flour, white rice, white lard—without nutrition, he instituted in selected counties a Food Stamp Program through the Department of Agriculture (aimed also at supporting farm prices). Under the Food Stamp Program, people purchased "vouchers" including a "bonus" amount determined on family size and assets beyond the dollar value of the stamps. Stamps were redeemable for any U.S.-grown foodstuffs, but no alcohol, tobacco products, or cleaning or paper products were allowed. Because the whole amount had to be purchased at one time (later twice a month), poor families often could not afford to buy them from their meager AFDC or general assistance allowances.

Johnson formalized the Food Stamp Program, extending it to all states that wanted it (although at first only twenty-two elected to have it). Over the next two decades, the benefit levels rose and coverage was increased from only those on public assistance to those qualifying as needy under state guidelines. In addition, food stamps became free rather than having to be purchased, increasing their use among eligible people. He also revamped the National School Lunch Program and the Special Milk Program and made money available for school breakfasts and lunches to Community Action Agencies, schools, and groups such as the Young Lords or CORE.

Mental Health and Developmental Disability

Concerned very personally with the lack of services for his sister, who was developmentally disabled, in 1962 Kennedy appointed a mental health panel that presented the Mental Health Act to Congress in 1963. Though not passed until after Kennedy's death because of resistance from the American Medical Association, the act provided for construction of mental retardation facilities and community mental health centers, comprehensive services, and education and consultation to upgrade the nation's services. It also provided funding for the training of more social workers. Although Johnson's administration aimed at more practical aid, such as job training and housing, he did agree on the training of new social workers and continued their educational funding under the Social Security Amendments of 1967.

Housing

In the 1940s and 1950s, federal grants for housing averaged $2 billion a year, increasing in the 1960s to $7 billion. In 1961, Kennedy proposed to desegregate all federally funded housing, and in 1962 the government spent $820 million for housing for the poor (although it allowed $2.9 billion in subsidies for middle- and upper-income levels). An array of agencies administered the programs directed primarily at middle- and upper-income families on the assumption that the poor would take over housing vacated by them. In 1966, the many agencies dealing with housing were consolidated into a superagency, Housing and Urban Development (HUD), and expenditures reached $16 billion for construction guarantees and another $12 billion for mortgage guarantees. HUD administered

- Urban Renewal, to construct middle-class housing and tear down slums;
- mortgage guarantees for all income classes;
- public housing; and
- housing for special groups, such as the aged and disabled.

HUD also brought housing programs up to date. The 1949 Federal Housing Administration was modified to help lower-income families, and new public housing and housing for special groups was constructed. Urban Renewal was a mixed blessing, giving money to rid cities of slums but displacing many of the poor those slums had sheltered. So many African Americans were left homeless that Urban Renewal was often called "Negro Removal." In the period between 1949 and 1964, an estimated 177,000 family dwelling units and 66,000 individual family units were razed by Urban Renewal, which replaced only 68,000, of which only 20,000 were for low-income people.

In 1966, the Model Cities Program began under HUD, its goal to provide assistance to cities to coordinate their welfare activities in "a massive and comprehensive effort to rebuild or restore entire sections and neighborhoods of slum and blighted areas."[89] In 1968, HUD was authorized to provide 6 million new dwellings for low- and moderate-income groups, with a budget of $2.6 billion, of which $412 million was earmarked for Urban Renewal. By 1971, it approached $10 billion, excluding loan insurance and guarantees, whereas Model Cities was budgeted at about $390 million a year.[90]

Specialized Programs

The Older Americans Act of 1965 developed from the National Conference on Aging (1950), the Committee on Geriatrics (1951–1956), and the 1961 White House Conference on Aging. These conferences created the Administration on Aging to fund community planning services and training, establish state agencies on aging, support research and demonstration projects to study the status of the elderly, and provide grants for community service programs. Amendments in 1967 extended the provisions and increased funding for community planning and innovative demonstration projects. It gave State Aging Offices the responsibility for statewide coordination and planning. Under Nixon in 1973, the Older Americans Comprehensive Amendments established the National Clearinghouse on Aging, increased grants for State and Area Agencies on Aging, gave training and research money for multidisciplinary centers of gerontology, and established multipurpose senior centers. It also provided for community service employment for the elderly, administered by the Department of Labor. The Retired Senior Citizens' Program and Foster Grandparents program were created, and nutrition programs were authorized in senior citizens' centers.[91]

The Elementary and Secondary Education Act (ESEA) of 1965 offered grants and services to schools serving low-income areas including inner cities, bilingual communities, and Native American schools. Before the act, such schools had low property tax bases and therefore lacked new and high-quality educational materials and facilities. They were very often staffed by teachers fresh out of college (because older, more experienced teachers often had the right to fill vacancies in newer suburban schools), who were unable to provide new and innovative teaching materials or could not cope with the needs of these children. ESEA money helped to provide better buildings, better teaching materials, and more experienced teachers attracted by the chance of creating innovative educational experiences. For Spanish-speaking children, ESEA provided bilingual classes.

Another Kennedy program, the Juvenile Delinquency and Youth Offenses Control Act, was funded at $10 million a year for three years. It researched the social causes of delinquency and developed innovative empowerment programs such as Mobilization for Youth (MFY), on the Lower East Side of New York City. MFY offered comprehensive services to youth gangs to break the cycle of delinquency and crime and organized the groups themselves to search out and provide services to young people. Under Johnson's Economic Opportunity Act, such innovative programs continued. One of the best known was Haryou—Harlem Youth Opportunity program—which offered supportive services and self-help and training classes for the youth of Harlem.

WELFARE, CIVIL RIGHTS, AND THE SOCIAL WORK PROFESSION

Only after 1964 did social work interest turn to social action and civil rights, especially in schools of social work. With an influx of activist students, often supported by government grants, schools became more flexible and varied, offering tracks in community organization, administration, and policy. Courses on ethnic minorities were established and enrollments of people of minority groups soared. By the early 1970s, almost 25 percent were nonwhite students, and many civil activists had joined the schools as students.[92] This new generation worked to empower rather than change their clients. At the same time, in Community Action Programs, paraprofessionals who served clients with great skill and care overturned the professional social work belief that only highly trained social workers could deliver human services.

In 1967, a new challenge confronted traditional service orientation. Under the leadership of Dr. George Wiley, a chemist turned advocate, welfare workers, welfare recipients, civil rights workers, members of the Student Democratic Society, poverty program workers, and a large number of VISTA volunteers met to establish a National Coordinating Committee of Welfare Rights Groups to plan welfare demonstrations. In the summer of 1967, they formed the National Welfare Rights Organization (NWRO). By 1969, NWRO had more than 22,000 dues-paying members in 523 local groups, the most members it ever had, which was around 2 percent of adult recipients of public assistance.[93]

NRWO's members militantly demanded publicity about welfare rights and benefits, information heretofore kept classified, and after extended struggles prepared and distributed handbooks on client rights to welfare mothers. They continued to demonstrate: In Philadelphia, when the welfare department refused requests for school shoes for their children, welfare mothers went en masse to a blood bank to sell their blood and purchase shoes. Of the twenty-seven who came, twenty-five were rejected because of anemia resulting from poor nutrition.[94] In 1969, NWRO, the Association of Black Social Workers, the radical student-based Social Welfare Workers Movement, and a newly formed women's organization, Women of the American Revolution, took over the National Conference on Social Welfare. Doors were barred and they demanded that the conference donate $35,000 to NWRO and the conference attendees another $25,000. Those demands went unmet, but negotiators agreed to seek an increase in minority membership and to focus the following annual conference on poverty and racism. At the 1970 National Conference on Social Welfare, Johnnie Tillmon, an AFDC mother from Watts and 1970 NWRO chair, told the assembled social workers

> If it hadn't been for you people who administer social services, we would
> have no organization. We organized because we were tired of being beat
> around by social workers.[95]

NWRO lobbied for a minimum guaranteed income of $6,500 for a family of four, the poverty level at the time, but was generally ignored. The idea of single mothers supporting families on welfare was an important challenge to key values of marriage and the work ethic, but NWRO argued that

> work in the home is a valuable aspect of the nation's productive efforts and that women have a right to be paid wages for caring for children in their homes.[96]

In the long run, NWRO was unsuccessful in lobbying for increased benefits or increased coverage. Although the idea of a guaranteed annual wage was seriously considered by President Nixon, Congress refused the Family Assistance Plan that would have instituted it.

Although some welfare workers organized in support of welfare clients and the new young activists took their part, mainline social workers remained conservative and casework-oriented in their approach. They cautioned the National Welfare Rights Organization, felt threatened by proposals to use paraprofessionals in their agencies and to train bachelor's level people in social work, and feared the new people they now had to deal with—Hispanic and African Americans, welfare department staffs, community action agency personnel, and poverty agencies.

CONCLUSION: LOOKING BACK ON THE 1960s

Near the end of his second term, Johnson, worn down by the demands of the War on Poverty and the failure of the war in Vietnam, decided not to seek reelection. White backlash, protests by people of color, and failure in Vietnam meant his defeat on both international and domestic fronts. However, his dedication to the Vietnam War (1969–1975) was much higher than to the War on Poverty: Vietnam cost the federal government $120 billion, whereas the Economic Opportunity Act of 1964 spent only $15.5 billion from 1965 to 1973, less than a tenth of the amount spent on the war.

The civil rights movement splintered: Militancy and Black Power movements, along with Red Power movements among Native Americans and Brown Power movements among Hispanics, ruled the day. In 1966, there were riots in forty-four cities, and in the 1966 elections Republicans gained forty-seven seats in the House of Representatives. Reagan became governor of California.[97] According to Dye and Zeigler,

> The angry mood of the public was also reflected in Congress, where President Johnson's proposal of a federal open housing law was killed by a Senate filibuster. In the same session, limits were imposed upon the authority of DHEW to divert funds from schools failing to desegregate ... a trend toward repressive legislation directed against those who were responsible [for] ... urban violence.[98]

Although the Open Housing Law passed in 1968, it was probably in response to the slaying of Martin Luther King, Jr. rather than a liberal action.[99] The backlash against civil rights and welfare rights continued throughout the election year of 1968. Both Democrat Hubert Humphrey and Republican Richard Nixon moved their rhetoric closer to the conservative side. Status quo and law and order were the keynotes of this election year.

Neither the Social Service Amendments of 1962 nor the Economic Opportunity Act of 1964 reduced welfare rolls, nor did they quell civil unrest. However, social justice prevailed more during the 1960s than since the 1930s, and perhaps since before the 1300s. The idea of service as a right, even though translated through the work ethic ideology, brought more people into programs and helped more than ever before. Relief programs came under federal standards that shared their costs even though "need levels" were determined by the states. In addition, thousands of new social workers were trained and thousands of paraprofessionals were given jobs in the social service system.

Looking back, we found benefits in the increased level of social insurance through OASDI and Medicare. Coverage was extended to over 90 percent of the population, but it still excluded federal government employees, railroad employees, irregularly employed farm and domestic workers who did not have minimum income for coverage, and self-employed people earning less than $400 annually. Benefit levels came under indexing; that is, they rose with the cost of living. Medicaid underlaid social health insurance for the nation. Civil rights legislation became a permanent part of the polity. Perhaps the greatest benefit of this was the emphasis on education and the movement of minority group persons, however slowly, into better and higher-status jobs.

Gains from the War on Poverty were few. Although community action agencies still exist, their major efforts are tied very securely into local governments. Head Start and Upward Bound programs continue, but at lower funding levels and with far less autonomy and innovation. Maximum feasible participation became a thing of the past, many programs were severely cut, and public assistance programs remained stigmatized. Poor people remained in the secondary labor market and in the secondary welfare system—marginal jobs and inadequate public assistance.

We learned many things from the 1950s and 1960s. Perhaps the most enduring lesson is that the threat of rebellion engenders accommodation, but when its force is dissipated, renewed denial of services occurs. Moving into the Nixon years, control of the poor and other minorities tightened. Even during the Carter administration gains for social justice were few and, during the Reagan years, repression again became society's goal, fulfilled in the Clinton administration. However, the Decade of the Dream—of freedom and social justice—did happen. The shame is that, unless repression becomes severe enough to cause rebellion, it may not happen again.

We learned many things from the 1950s and 1960s. Perhaps the most enduring lesson is that the threat of rebellion engenders accommodation, but when its force is dissipated, renewed denial of services occurs.

The following questions will test your knowledge and understanding of the content found within this chapter. For additional assessment, including licensing-exam type questions on applying chapter content to practice behaviors, visit **MySearchLab**.

1. *Brown v. Board of Education of Topeka* made which ruling?

   a. It prohibited nonwhite teachers from teaching in public schools.

   b. It concluded that segregation in private schools is legally protected.

   c. It argued that separate education facilities were inherently unequal.

   d. It denied students outside of the district from being bussed in to attend "better schools."

2. Which statement best describes "freedom rides"?

   a. Busloads of activists going to Southern communities to register voters and support civil rights activities.

   b. Free transportation offered to citizens in poor communities to assist them in getting public assistance services and resources.

   c. Nationwide journeys taken by activists fighting for segregation.

   d. Bus tours of pacifists who promoted freedom from fighting.

3. In 1949, the government began the process of termination for Native Americans, which meant Native Americans:

   a. were no longer considered American citizens.

   b. no longer owned the land they lived on.

   c. would be wholly governed by U.S. laws with no exceptions.

   d. would be freed from U.S. government control.

4. Which provision was included in the Civil Rights Act of 1964?

   a. Discrimination in employment with 10 or more people was forbidden.

   b. Desegregation would take place in Northern counties only.

   c. All federal agencies were required to end discrimination in order to receive federal funds.

   d. Segregation in public schools would be effective immediately, but private schools would be exempt.

5. What advice would you give someone under the Work Incentive Program?

   a. If the person has children under age 18, he or she must register for work training and job placement.

   b. Any adult who refuses to enroll is disqualified for benefits (unless he or she is disabled or needed at home).

   c. Children over age 18 have to register or be disqualified.

   d. Adults can be fined for failure to register.

6. What advice would you give someone seeking a program for medical assistance?

   a. Medicare is granted only to those who are over 65 and are on disability with Social Security.

   b. If Medicare is exhausted, he or she can appeal for additional funding assistance.

   c. Both Medicare and Medicaid recipients can receive a cash grant that will allow them to pay for medical expenses as they are incurred.

   d. Since Medicaid is guaranteed by the government, virtually all hospitals and physicians are required to take Medicaid clients.

7. Discuss the major changes implemented by the Housing and Urban Development agency in 1966.

MYSEARCHLAB CONNECTIONS

Reinforce what you learned in this chapter by studying videos, cases, documents, and more available at www.MySearchLab.com.

Watch and Review

Watch these Videos

Rosie The Riveter

Rev. Dr. Martin Luther King

Creating Apartheid in South Africa

Read and Review

Read these Cases/Documents

John Lewis, Address at the March on Washington (1963)

Fannie Lou Hammer, Voting Rights in Mississippi (1962–1964)

Stokely Carmichael and "Black Power" (1966)

Student Nonviolent Coordinating Committee, Statement of Purpose (1960)

Southern Manifesto on Integration (1956)

Assess Your Knowledge

Go to **MySearchLab** to test your knowledge of key topics in this chapter with topic-specific quizzes. Conclude your assessment by completing the chapter exam.

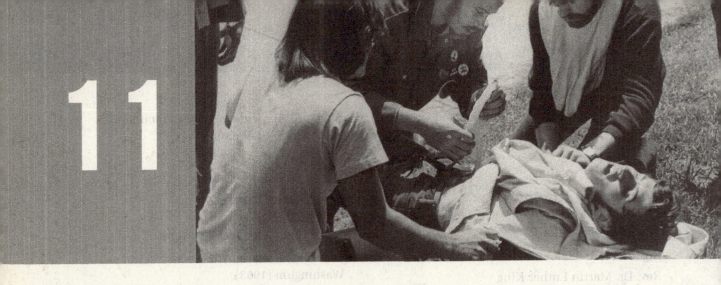

11

The Return to the Past

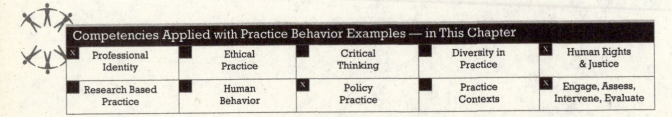

Competencies Applied with Practice Behavior Examples — in This Chapter				
x Professional Identity	▪ Ethical Practice	▪ Critical Thinking	▪ Diversity in Practice	x Human Rights & Justice
▪ Research Based Practice	▪ Human Behavior	x Policy Practice	▪ Practice Contexts	x Engage, Assess, Intervene, Evaluate

Times and Events

- **1968:** Lyndon Baines Johnson elected president; new social work associations include National Association of Black Social Workers, Association of Puerto Rican Social Services Workers, Asian American Social Workers

- **1970:** Kent State and Jackson University antiwar protesters killed; NASW adds Educational Legislative Action Network (ELAN); Nixon authorizes COINTELPRO

- **1971:** Adult public assistance categories transferred to social insurance, Talmadge Amendments to AFDC program, WIN participation mandated; *Swann v. Charlotte Mecklenburg Board of Education* upholds busing to end segregation; American Indian Social Workers Association forms; Alaskan Native Americans lose land titles; AIM members removed from Alcatraz, occupy Wounded Knee; CSWE accredits baccalaureate social work programs

- **1972:** Cost of Living Adjustments (COLAs) added to OASDHI and food stamp program; Title IVD of Social Security Amendments creates Notice to Law Enforcement Officials (NOLEO), requires AFDC mothers to sue "absent pappies" for child support; Title XX capped by Revenue Sharing Act

- **1973:** Comprehensive Education and Training Act (CETA) established; *Roe v. Wade* legalizes abortions; ERA stalls in Congress; National Gay and Lesbian Task Force begins; Civil Service Commission denies right of federal government to exclude gays from employment

- **1974:** Supplemental Security Income (SSI) begins; Block Grants take the place of open-ended Title XX; Housing Act shifts federal resources to states' revenue-sharing plans; Child Abuse and Treatment Act established; Mohawks occupy Adirondack forest preserve; Nixon resigns presidency

- **1975:** Developmentally Disabled Bill of Rights Act passes; Vietnam war ends

- **1976:** Jimmy Carter elected president; Mexican immigration capped at 20,000 persons, 120,000 for Southern Hemisphere

- **1977:** United Racist Front forms from Nazi Party of America, National States' Rights Party, and Federated Knights of the Ku Klux Klan

- **1980:** Ronald Reagan elected president; Child Welfare Act changes foster care; Carter signs $27 million Native American land trust fund; new EEOC guidelines ban sexual harassment; states may refuse Medicaid payments for abortion

A RETREAT FROM THE WELFARE STATE

The 1960s were a time of flower children, psychedelics, free love, and rock and roll, when everything was touched with beauty, and love was the key word; when dreams grew into possibilities and possibilities could come true. We did not know how precious this time was until we lost it, but we knew with finality it was over when our children, demonstrating against U.S. involvement in Cambodia in 1970, were shot at Kent State University. That the killings were accidental is unimportant. The government was there with its show of force in the National Guard, and the guns were there to back up their power. Death by our own hands was the result. Others had died in the 1960s, but they died for the dream. With Kent State, the dream died.

As Johnson withdrew from his failures at home and abroad, the backlash that plagued him in his second term of office accelerated. The election of President Richard M. Nixon began the retreat into conservatism. Increasingly severe recessions racked the economy during the 1970s, with that of 1975 equal to the Great Depression, leading to an even greater economic crisis from 1981 to 1982. By 1970, manufacturing had declined to 25 percent of all employment, 17 percent of employment was in service occupations, and the government employed 18 percent of all workers.[1] The gross national product grew during the 1970s from $982 billion to $2,369 billion, but because of inflation, real median family income grew only 5 percent. In May 1980, the overall unemployment rate stood at 7.8 percent, with the rate for African Americans twice and the rate for teenagers three times the overall rate.

Despite its failure to end poverty, the Kennedy–Johnson legislation had a significant effect in reducing it. Although the Office of Economic Opportunity received less than $6 billion in all—not even 1 percent of the federal budget—from 1965 to 1968, 20 million people rose above poverty levels by 1969. Yet as OEO programs ended, poverty began to climb and by 1982 had jumped to 15 percent of the population. One notable exception was among the aged: Social Security increases (OASDI) were tied to cost-of-living adjustments (COLAs) in the 1970s, and poverty among the elderly fell by about one third, from 35.2 percent to 24.5 percent. It then decreased by another third, leaving only about 12 percent of the aged in poverty by the 1980s.[2]

Nixon's tenure, supported by a conservative backlash, moved the nation away from citizen and individual rights and toward the monolithic power of the transnational economy. On the domestic side, he dismantled most Great Society programs and gave their control over to states. This, soon to be called the New Federalism by Ronald Reagan, continued with revenue-sharing programs in which money formerly used for national social programs was given directly to states in block grants. To combat civil dissidence and growing social unrest, Nixon poured funds into law enforcement (Law Enforcement Assistance Administration, LEAA) and, suspicious of radical dissidents, authorized the COINTELPRO (counter intelligence program). Using the Federal Bureau of Investigation, his administration investigated and infiltrated dissident groups,[3] and by his reelection in 1972 most civil and human rights movements had ended (although the women's movement remained strong). Moreover, believing his executive powers placed him above the law, he used illegal activities to root out the intentions of his political enemies. This led to his forced resignation and the trial and imprisonment of his top aides, although he was pardoned when President Gerald Ford took office.

On the international level, Nixon used the Central Intelligence Agency (CIA) to keep the United States embroiled in the internal affairs of other nations. Although U.S. participation in the Vietnam War ended in 1973, pressures from the military–industrial complex—corporations with interlocking memberships in the government and military—involved the United States almost immediately in Cambodia. U.S. foreign policies supported covert activities and overt weapons sales in nations ripe for revolt, such as Chile and Brazil, providing a profitable market for U.S. war matériel. In addition, his administration added to the power of transnational corporations through investments and tax breaks that depleted the general revenue and increased the flow of jobs to foreign countries. These transnational corporations owed allegiance to no country or government. During the 1950s, massive industrial conglomerations began, and between 1965 and 1974, just under 13,000 companies merged. In 1973, transnationals invested more than $165 billion in foreign companies, and the share of taxes they paid to the United States declined from 30 percent of federal revenues in the 1950s to 16 percent by 1978.

Nixon's New Federalism revenue sharing cut up general revenues and distributed them directly to the states. This actually channeled more money to cities than had the Johnson programs, but it made social agencies compete with each other and with other urban programs for a share of the federal pie. Most programs suffered cutbacks, although Nixon expanded the Food Stamp Program and provided funds for child nutrition and rent subsidy programs. Food stamp expenditures rose from $550 million in 1970 to $4.4 billion in 1975—a sevenfold increase—and more than doubled again by 1981, to $10 billion. Public assistance became increasingly restrictive about work and training even though jobs grew scarcer. As the middle class became more vulnerable to runaway inflation and as jobs closed down, the outcry against the poor led to taxpayers' revolts, most notably Proposition 13 in California, which set an upper limit on the amount that could be used for social spending (including even police and fire departments).

Nixon continued to support civil rights, but not with Johnson's fervor. Three important changes were enacted: The Equal Employment Opportunity Commission (EEOC) was given power to sue firms that discriminated, the Office of Federal Contract Compliance Programs (OFCCP) could impose sanctions against federal contractors for not hiring people of color, and the Fair Housing Act was amended to prohibit sex discrimination. The EEOC, OFCCP, and the Justice Department increased their activities against institutional discrimination.

After Nixon's resignation and Ford's uneventful term, Democrat Jimmy Carter was elected in 1976. Both Ford and Carter maintained holding patterns, although Carter tried to move the nation toward social progress with a new welfare reform bill aimed at a guaranteed annual income (GAI), inflation reduction, and more jobs. Carter's federal appointments reflected his civil rights stance: Of the 298 federal judges he appointed, 23 percent were minorities, 15 percent were women, and many had records of sympathy toward civil rights and equal opportunity.

After the 1960s, the social work profession began its own retreat to conservatism, with social action declining and staid professionals thoroughly ensconced in the mental health movement. The defeat of the War on Poverty brought a mood of indifference, passivity, and resignation, leading to fewer enrollments in action programs in schools of social work.[4] However, the National Association of Social Workers (NASW) tried to encourage professional action by adding two lobby arms: in 1970 the Educational Legislative Action Network (ELAN) and in 1976 the Political Action for Candidate Selection (PACE) lobby.

The Council of Social Work Education (CSWE) began to accredit baccalaureate programs in 1971, and the NASW began to admit their graduates to membership. By 1976, NASW membership was 70,046, or 17,000 more than in 1970, and in 1975 schools of social work granted more than 43,000 MSW degrees. Between 1970 and 1976, social work jobs increased by 79,000. Caucuses also formed to represent minority interests. In 1968, new associations included the National

Policy Practice

Practice Behavior Example: Understand that policy affects service delivery and actively engage in policy practice.

Critical Thinking Question: Do changes in presidential administrations affect the day-to-day practice of social workers?

Association of Black Social Workers, the Association of Puerto Rican Social Service Workers, the Asian American Social Workers (in California); in 1971 the Association of American Indian Social Workers formed.[5] By 1982, there were 384,000 social work jobs, with 88,000 in professional associations. Two-thirds of these were held by women and 19 percent were held by nonwhites.[6]

SOCIAL PROGRAMS IN THE 1970s

Although President Ford did not tackle welfare reform, Presidents Nixon and Carter expanded social insurance incrementally. In addition, each proposed basic guaranteed annual income (GAI) plans to provide a national minimum income through benefits and tax credits. Nixon's Family Assistance Plan (FAP) would have replaced Aid to Families with Dependent Children (AFDC) and unemployment insurance for every family with at least one child. Incentives would have been paid to encourage parents to enter the workforce, with job training programs and day care facilities greatly expanded.[7] FAP failed in the Senate on its first submission (1969), but seemed likely to pass when reintroduced in 1971, despite its GAI aspects. However, Nixon's Watergate problems left it to die in Congress.

President Carter's Better Jobs and Income Proposal was a negative income tax plan for all poor people regardless of family status. To be administered by the Internal Revenue Service, it would have consolidated AFDC, Supplemental Security Income (SSI), and Food Stamps under one cash benefit plan. Carter's plan was similar to FAP in provision for a federal minimum income guarantee, benefits with work incentives, job training, and child care. Under the program, those "expected to work" would have received at least $2,300 per year, with increasing benefits for family size and a possible basic yearly income of $6,100 before any disregards. The "not expected to work"—the aged, blind people, people with disabilities, and parents with children under age seven—would have received a minimum of $4,200 for a family of four. Federal monies disbursed to state and local governments would have created 1.4 million public service jobs and training slots for training useful in the private sector.[8] The proposal failed in Congress.

Human Rights and Justice

Practice Behavior Example: Advocate for human rights and social and economic justice.

Critical Thinking Question: Would passage of a negative income tax advance social and economic justice?

Social Insurance

Old Age, Survivors, Disability, and Health Insurance (OASDHI)

There were two major policy changes in social insurance in the 1970s. The first was legislation in 1972 that granted cost-of-living adjustments based on the Consumer Price Index, which rose 27 percent from 1970 to 1974 and another 15 percent by 1976. Thus, with every increase in cost of living, additional benefits were paid to recipients. The second was the transfer of all adult public assistance categories from public assistance to social insurance in 1971. This meant that recipients of Old Age Assistance, Aid to the Blind, and Aid to the Permanently and Totally Disabled were placed under the OASDI programs, with the effect of drastically increasing the number of entitled people without regard to work history. This led to the creation of Supplemental Security Income (SSI), a public assistance program in the Department of Health and Human Services (DHHS).

The Social Security Amendments of 1978 changed the method by which coverage was determined so that, rather than counting quarters of the year for coverage, workers were credited with a quarter year of employment for each $250 of earned income. Fully covered workers could now retire at age sixty-two, though with reduced benefits. Surviving spouses could collect benefits at age sixty-two or, if disabled, at age fifty. Surviving unmarried children would collect benefits until age eighteen (or nineteen if still in school), and children born out of wedlock qualified as survivor dependents. Children with continuous disabilities would qualify to age twenty-two, when their own OASDI benefits would begin. For disability coverage, people had to be permanently unable to work and not yet sixty-five years old, and to have worked for a certain period before disablement.

Social welfare expenses boomed during the 1970s because of new entitlements and inflation. In 1970, expenditures reached nearly $146 billion, about 17 percent of the gross national product, and then almost doubled, to $290 billion, in 1975. With private expenditures included, 28 percent of the GNP went to social welfare in 1970. By 1976, social insurance accounted for 44 percent of welfare expenditures, increasing to 52 percent by 1983.[9] More than $55 billion a year went for retirement, with another $28 billion in benefits to disabled workers, dependents, and survivors.[10]

The federal share of expenditures for social programs increased (as opposed to state monies): By 1970, it was somewhat more than 50 percent, but by 1978 it was 61 percent.[11] By 1983, total expenditures hovered at about 19 percent of the GNP. Wildavsky suggests that inflation caused between 35 and 45 percent of the increase between 1965 and 1975.[12] Food stamp benefits were also tied to the Consumer Price Index, and therefore increased proportionately with inflation.[13]

Income maintenance varied widely by geographic area and type of program. (In 1979 in Mississippi, for example, a family of four on AFDC received $101 monthly whereas an OASDI family received $580.) Social Security for a retired couple paid $431 a month, and SSI paid between $189 and $284. Unemployment benefits averaged about $350 monthly, including dependent allowances in the few states that paid them, and in a number of states, maximum benefits payable to survivors or workers killed on the job were lower than those for temporary disabilities.[14] As of 1980, no family could receive more than 150 to 180 percent of the former worker's benefit, so the greater the number of children, the less per capita was received.

One reason for the generosity of Congress in OASDI payments was that, early in the 1970s, the program had surpluses not since matched. In 1970, OASDI collected $35 billion in taxes and paid out $32 billion. However, the worsening economy changed the surplus situation by 1975, and in 1979 benefits of $104.3 billion exceeded contributions of $103 billion. The deficit increased in the early 1980s, and prices increased faster than wages. Because they were COLA-indexed, OASDI benefits rose faster on average than workers' take-home pay—19 percent faster by 1980. In 1981 OASDI paid out $145 billion while collecting only $140 billion.[15]

Most people receive much more than they put into the Social Security system, and pensions depend on current legislation rather than on legislation at the time the person becomes eligible. Benefits are paid from current funds rather than the so-called trust or reserve fund, and funds collected from people now being paid are being contributed by workers today. According to Handel,

The Social Security system in America made its first payment on January 31, 1940, to a retired unmarried woman who died thirty-five years later at the age of one hundred ... for a total tax contribution of about $22.00 she received more than $20,000 over the thirty-five-year period. Her payment in 1940 was $22.54, and in 1974 was $109.20.[16]

Unemployment Insurance

The recessions of 1969–1971 and 1974–1975 were moderated by the expansion of unemployment benefits. The period of eligibility was extended and offices were kept open nights and weekends. People were eligible for unemployment insurance if they had worked for a base period, which varied by state. Most states restricted benefits for students, pregnant women, and people unemployed because of marital or family obligations. Also, people fired from jobs for misconduct or refusing suitable work were treated differently, the waiting period for unemployment insurance delayed. Most states figured benefits on base pay, with minimum and maximum levels, and a few states added extra for dependent children.

Approximately 20 percent of the population is not covered by unemployment insurance, although more than 90 percent of jobs are covered. Employers with fewer than four employees are not covered, and people looking for first jobs or having only brief employment do not qualify. Moreover, many employers do not hire full-time or let employees go before the base period is covered so they need not pay unemployment insurance taxes. This secondary labor market, providing neither social insurance nor company fringe benefits, is a prime employer of young people, women, and people of color.

Public Assistance Programs

Public assistance after the Johnson years had several themes: the promiscuity of welfare mothers; the laziness of recipients; and fraud, including secret jobs; use of money to support communes; lying; and cheating. Heffernan says,

> The personal fault theme was supplemented by a belief that current welfare programs ... encouraged withdrawal from the labor force, family splitting, and migration ... for the purpose of receiving aid.[17]

Social Darwinism was still active. For example, in 1974 William Shockley, a Nobel Laureate in physics, advocated paying the "unfit poor"—those who did not pay income taxes—for eugenic sterilization at the rate of $1,000 for each point they fell below IQ 100. The bonuses, placed in a trust fund, would be doled out over the individual's life span. He noted that

> $30,000 put in a trust for a 70 IQ moron potentially capable of producing twenty children might return $250,000 to taxpayers in reduced costs of mental retardation care.[18]

Obviously, his greatest interest was in control of women, because men can father many more children than twenty. He also established a sperm bank for contributions from men of "genetic superiority."[19]

Supplemental Security Income (SSI)

The move of adult categories—blind, aged, and disabled adults—out of public assistance and into social insurance meant that these groups were finally recognized as "deserving poor." The change had two major results. On one hand, it channeled even more hostility toward "undeserving" AFDC recipients. On

The move of adult categories—blind, aged, and disabled adults—out of public assistance and into social insurance meant that these groups were finally recognized as "deserving poor."

the other, the new SSI program gave the nation a guaranteed annual minimum income except for AFDC recipients. The move meant that grants were less in some states than people received under the categorical programs (AB, AD, and OAA). This was particularly true for disabled people because of stricter federal medical certification for disability. To remedy this, SSI, a federal public assistance program funded through general revenue and tied to COLAs, was legislated in 1972 and put into effect in 1974. Means testing and social services were provided through local departments of public welfare.

With SSI, people falling below states' standards of need received an additional cash grant beyond OASDI grants. For eligibility and grant determinations, recipients were allowed no more than $1,500 in liquid assets ($2,250 for a couple), homes had to be worth less than $25,000, and cars worth less than $1,200. Referral to vocational rehabilitation was required for blind and disabled people under age sixty-five. Spousal or child income was counted as resources, but the first $65 earned and $20 per month of income were disregarded. States had to provide supplements up to state levels of need until SSI payments exceeded the total spent on former OAA, AD, and AB, when the federal government picked up the extra costs.

Aid to Families with Dependent Children

Despite the social protest movements of the 1960s, gains for AFDC families were soon lost. The National Welfare Rights Organization had made two proposals that were given serious consideration by the legislature. The first, cost-of-living increases, succeeded as a joint legislative–welfare reform effort in 1967. However, states would not give up their rights to set standards of need and the Supreme Court upheld their position.[20] The second proposal, eligibility by declaration (1969), allowed welfare departments to rely solely on applicants' statements without in-depth verifications. New York City used it with apparent success for some time, but in general it was so modified at the local level that it was ineffective.[21]

In the 1970s, hostility increased toward AFDC recipients. Slippage of civil rights—the rights to privacy, equal protection under the law, and due process—continued apace. Searches for "men in the house" and midnight raids continued in spite of Supreme Court decisions,[22] and other regulations were ignored or finessed. For example, residence requirements, though unconstitutional, were used under the guise of "inappropriate housing" and decided at the discretion of welfare workers. Welfare workers again had free discretion to remove those not meeting their standards from AFDC rolls. AFDC grants continued to be minimal: In constant dollars, between 1970 and 1981, average benefits declined by almost 20 percent, and even with food stamps benefits dropped by 9 percent.[23]

The Talmadge amendments of 1971 made participation in the Work Incentive Program (WIN) mandatory for all adult recipients with children age six or over. Because there were not sufficient spaces in the WIN training programs, "creaming" took place because administrators wanted good success records. In 1971, more than half of those in WIN programs were white, and 40 percent were men.[24] That WIN did not work seemed beside the point: It was required not for its effectiveness, but because of the desire to punish those who did not work. Senator Russell Long said,

Of 250,000 welfare referrals found appropriate and referred to the Work Incentive Program during its first twenty-one months, less than

60 percent were enrolled in the program ... and out of the 145,000 who were enrolled, one-third subsequently dropped out. Only 13,000 welfare cases have been closed following participation in the ... program.[25]

Because the WIN appropriation was $500 million, the closing of a welfare case cost approximately $35,500, or enough to support each family at welfare rates for about nine years.

Child Support and Dependency Programs

In 1972, Title IV.D. of the Social Security Acts was enacted for child support enforcement. Officially called Notice to Law Enforcement Officials (NOLEO), it was more often called the "absent pappy" law. It required AFDC mothers to file suit against their children's fathers to collect back support. As early as 1960, Kaplan concluded that

> absent fathers of needy children, like their families, tend to be poor, and even the most vigorous law enforcement does not create income. Collections from fathers are grossly inadequate to meet their families' needs. The unemployment and underemployment of men, particularly ... [African-American men], appear to be the most pressing problem.[26]

Mothers, often against their will, became instruments of the law in compelling support from fathers, under threat of the loss of their AFDC benefits. Some had to sign warrants or complaints with the district attorney, others had to swear out paternity suits, and some had to submit to lie detector tests.[27] The law also opened Social Security and income tax records to help the new Offices of Child Support locate absent parents and permitted garnishment of federal wages and stipends to pay delinquent support orders.

In 1978, there were five times more mothers above the poverty level than below who were not receiving court-ordered payments, and of men ordered to support, two-fifths rarely paid anything and one-tenth paid only sporadically. In 1979, 34.6 percent (2.5 million) of 7.1 million children under twenty-one received child support payments. Over one-third of all fathers were not required to pay anything because of limited earning ability, and the amounts ordered bore little relationship to the man's income. After a year or two, in most cases, noncompliance was the rule rather than the exception. On average, African-American fathers are more conscientious about child support payments, and the poor are at least as conscientious as are middle- or upper-class fathers.[28]

Social Services (Title XX, 1962)

This open-ended act provided federal reimbursement to states up to 75 percent of costs for new programs for the disadvantaged. Ninety percent of social services money had to be spent for people on public assistance, with the remaining amount to be used for child care and family planning services, and for services to people with developmental disabilities; drug addicts, alcoholics, and children in foster care. State welfare departments saw it as a way to gain more federal dollars. Instead of developing new services, states began to charge the government for services they had traditionally provided. "Purchase of services" grants to private agencies were unusually generous, stimulating the growth of the "personal social service" industry—casework treatment—and encouraging social workers to enter private practice or organize private consultant firms.[29] States were reimbursed 50 percent of the cost in 1956, 75 percent in 1962, and up to 90 percent in 1975.

In 1972, to control flyaway costs, Congress capped the program at $2.2 billion through the Revenue Sharing Act. The "open invitation" policy ended. With federal money limited, newly developed services deteriorated and purchase of services from private agencies—for mental health counseling, drug abuse, child care—dropped abruptly. Therefore, in 1974 legislators created Social Security Act "block grants" for which agencies competed, with costs capped at a "permanent" ceiling of $2.5 billion (raised to $3 billion for 1982). Now *only 50 percent was required to be spent on services for the poor*. Block grants were allocated to states on the basis of population, with state matching required, usually at 75:25 ratio. Some services qualified for a 90:10 ratio, especially administrative and staff development and social work education.

In the new block grant system, states had to plan comprehensively to develop social services. Each service had to have at least one of the following goals:

- Reduce the dependency of clients.
- Help them gain economic independence (get off the welfare rolls).
- Prevent or remedy the neglect, abuse, or exploitation of children and adults unable to protect their own interests, including the preservation, reuniting, or rehabilitation of the family system (leading to family preservation programs).
- Provide for the least intrusive care, usually community-based or home care rather than institutional care.
- Secure institutional care when other kinds are inappropriate and provide services to those so placed.

About 10.6 million people received social services in 1978, of whom about 30 percent were AFDC clients, 37 percent other people in poverty, and 13 percent people receiving services not related to income level. Child day care was the most costly item, totaling $732.3 million, and $324.8 million went for homemaker services, although only 11 percent of homemaker services went to AFDC families.

Because of the caps, mental health agencies withdrew many mental health services, cutting some of the most frequently provided: counseling, day care, child protective services, health-related services, homemaker services, transportation, and family planning. In addition, community mental health services neglected the great numbers of mentally ill being released from hospitals. The result was a national shame: homeless men and women wandering the streets of large cities without food, clothing, or shelter, living and often dying with nobody to care.

Concern for children, especially those born out of wedlock, came to the fore again in the 1970s. Programs to combat child abuse and neglect continued to receive increased funding, and in 1971 Congress passed the Comprehensive Child Development Act to provide funds for comprehensive high-quality day care. However, President Nixon vetoed it on the grounds that it would destroy the family, duplicate already existing services, and establish communal child-rearing against American values.

One unanticipated consequence of block grants was the move toward taking children from parents not considered "adequate." New institutions, foster care, and group home situations proliferated, with higher funding than for in-home preventive services. During this period, about 700,000 children were placed away from their parents, about 400,000 in various types of foster care and another 300,000 in institutions. One-third of the latter were placed in corrections facilities.[30] Thus, rather than giving support to intact but unstable

During this period, about 700,000 children were placed away from their parents, about 400,000 in various types of foster care and another 300,000 in institutions.

families, millions were spent for child placement after families had disintegrated or deteriorated. Looking at yearly costs per child by type of care, homemaker services, family day care, and day care centers cost between $2,000 and $3,000 per child. For remedial care, $5,200 per child was spent yearly for foster home care, $15,400 per child for group home care, $18,600 for each child in group residences, $34,000 per child in general institutions, and $42,100 for each child placed in secure detention facilities.[31]

Institutional classism, sexism, and racism are all evident in such placements: More poor children and children of color are placed in institutions, and boys and girls are placed differentially, girls more often for status offenses and boys for offenses that would be criminal if committed by an adult.[32] (Nearly half were locked up because of running away from home, being truant, or not being wanted at home.)

Professional Identity

Practice Behavior Example: Know the profession's history.

Critical Thinking Question: Discuss how the rise in conservatism affected social welfare programs and social workers.

OTHER SOCIAL WELFARE PROGRAMS

Food Stamps

Food stamp expenditures were $35 million in 1965, $550 million in 1970, more than $4.4 billion by 1975, and $10 billion in 1981.[33] In 1977, recipients were no longer required to buy food stamps, and "bonuses" figured on income level and number in household were simply given to eligible recipients. Still, many eligible people did not receive food stamps because, among other problems, they were not informed about the program or their eligibility, certification requirements were too difficult, offices were inaccessible, and using stamps was embarrassing to proud people. During the late 1970s, eligibility levels were changed several times, resulting in a 2.5 million drop in users between 1976 and 1978. Worsening economic conditions still pushed the number of food stamp users to new heights before the 1980s began.[34]

Comprehensive Education and Training Act (CETA)

CETA arose from the Manpower Development and Training Act of 1962, the Economic Opportunity Act of 1964, and the Emergency Employment Act of 1970. Nixon's administration established the program in 1973 to provide entry-level jobs in the private sector for young urban minority people and the chronically unemployed. In 1977, for example, five-sixths of CETA employees were school dropouts averaging below sixth-grade reading ability. One-half were from single-parent families, their family sizes were nearly twice the national average, and their family's per capita income was less than one-third of the total population's average. Eighty percent had previous arrests and 75 percent prior convictions. More than one-third had never held a twenty-hour-a-week job for longer than one month.[35]

State and local governments determined the extent of the program by how much they spent in matching funds. In 1974, however, a severe recession added millions to the unemployment rolls in the private sector and eliminated the competition for jobs there. In response, CETA became an employment agency for temporary public service jobs, in government and social agencies, that were to be picked up with local funding when CETA subsidies ended.

However, almost two-thirds of the 6 million CETA jobs, which cost the federal government nearly $24 billion, ended when federal subsidies terminated. From 1974 to 1979, CETA was one of the largest government agencies, and spent $55 billion during the eight years of its operation.[36]

Education and Youth Programs

The remnants of the OEO, including Head Start, Upward Bound, Talent Search, and Job Corps, were moved to other agencies and continued with varying success. Substantial evidence indicates that Head Start had a positive effect on nearly every aspect of early childhood development, including the inhibition of serious educational and behavioral problems.[37] Disadvantaged children were less likely to be in special education classes, more likely to be in their regular grade at school, and more likely to graduate from high school, enroll in college, and obtain a self-supporting job. They were also less likely to be arrested or on welfare when adults. In 1983, Head Start served 400,000 children at a cost of $907 million and reached about 20 percent of four- and five-year-olds from disadvantaged homes.[38]

Upward Bound and Talent Search programs encouraged young people to continue their education. Nearly 60 percent of Upward Bound students entered college and remained at least two years, and in 1976 Talent Search placed between 75 and 90 percent of its students in postsecondary institutions. Job Corps was not so successful, with only 30 percent completing vocational training from the corps. Nevertheless, in 1977 those who did earned $1,250 more annually ($1,500 for women) than young people in the same life situations who were not in Job Corps, and they generally obtained jobs with higher status and better working conditions. Trainees were also more likely to attend college and were 35 percent less likely to engage in criminal activities.[39]

In 1965, the Education for All Handicapped Children Act was added to the Elementary and Secondary Education Act (ESEA). It mandated that school districts provide appropriate educational opportunities for educationally impaired children. The act aimed for basic skills improvement, consumer education, bilingual education, and the acquisition of instructional materials and equipment. It was revised and extended in 1975 (Developmentally Disabled Bill of Rights Act), before which students with physical or mental handicaps could be taught in classrooms separated from the conventional classroom. With the revision, every child was required to have an individualized program in the least restricted feasible environment—the regular classroom where possible—with teachers specifically trained in special education. The federal government paid a substantial portion of the added costs to school districts. Because the federal government has no direct legal authority over public schools, the law was passed to protect the constitutional rights of disabled students.

Five-sixths of all ESEA funds were designated for educationally deprived and disadvantaged children, and grants were allotted according to the number of children from low-income families in the school district. Special grants were also given for migrant, neglected, and delinquent children. ESEA was credited with eliminating over 40 percent of the difference in reading achievement between nine-year-old white and African-American children after 1965. In 1982, 10 percent of monies for bilingual programs were cut from ESEA by the Reagan administration, with another 50 percent to follow in 1983. For remedial instruction and related services, however, $3.5 billion was provided in 1984.[40]

Housing

Nixon, Ford, and Carter did little in the area of housing. The Model Cities Program, along with public housing and Urban Renewal, was deemphasized by the Nixon administration in 1973 and effectively terminated by the Housing Act of 1974, which shifted federal resources to revenue-sharing strategies. Low-rent public housing, home loans for low-income families, and rent supplement programs were made available to the poor, along with special Department of Housing and Urban Development programs for the aged (HUD Title 8). The U.S. Department of Agriculture also gave home loans to farmers, and HUD administered the Office of Indian Housing. Most such programs were means-tested, with the exceptions of Veteran's Housing Assistance and guaranteed mortgage loans from the Federal Housing Administration and HUD.[41]

Juvenile Protection and Adult Corrections

In 1974, Congress amended the Juvenile Justice and Delinquency Prevention Act. Secure institutions and jails were overused and became "schools of crime" for children institutionalized for noncriminal and minor delinquencies. There were almost no rehabilitative programs, and children in such institutions were often subject to physical abuse.[42] Another reason for the legislation was increasing estimates of child abuse in the home—between 60,000 and 2 million cases per year. Estimates indicated that half of the approximately 2 million children who ran away from home annually were physically and sexually abused by relatives and other adults and that at least six children were beaten to death by adults on an average day.[43]

The Child Abuse and Treatment Act (1974) accelerated the development of state programs to aid the mistreated child, established the National Center for Prevention and Treatment of Child Abuse and Neglect at the University of Colorado Medical Center, authorized runaway shelters and hotlines, and promoted research and professional training in the areas of child abuse and protection, although funds were not allocated until Carter's administration. The Child Welfare Act of 1980 provided funds and federal regulations to alter the pattern by which children were removed to foster care, of whom there were 500,000 in 1980.

Attention to violent crimes during the Nixon years led to the Law Enforcement Assistance Administration (LEAA) in the Department of Justice in 1968. It conducted and funded research, promoted efforts to improve personnel in the field of corrections, and encouraged demonstration projects. Between 1969 and 1972, its budget rose from $60 million to $700 million,[44] providing impetus to the training of people to work in criminal justice.

Society has great faith in the justice system, but the fact is that it perpetuates institutional racism and classism. A study of the legal and social characteristics of 2,419 consecutive felony probation cases found that those most likely to be labeled as felons were defendants who were older, nonwhite, and poorly educated, had prior records, and were defended by court-appointed attorneys. These groups are also more likely to receive severe punishments, such as imprisonment or death for rape and murder. Former Attorney General Ramsey Clark says,

Racial discrimination is manifest from the bare statistics of capital punishment. Since we began keeping records in 1930, there have been 2,066

Negroes and only 1,751 white persons put to death. Hundreds of thousands of rapes have occurred in America since 1930, yet only 455 men have been executed for rape—and 405 of them were Negroes. There can be no rationalization or justification of such clear discrimination. It is outrageous public murder, illuminating our darkest racism.[45]

Lesser punishments also show bias: Parole often depends on the value judgments of parole board members, corrections officers, and others in power. The safest risk, according to their biases, are middle-class white educated men, with white-collar rather than skilled or unskilled job training. African Americans had about one-half the chance of early release of whites at the same educational level.[46] The growing numbers in prison seem to validate our beliefs in the growing crime rate, but it is the reporting of crimes that is increasing. Because of racist and classist bias, there is a winnowing out of white, middle-class, white-collar men, and those left are generally people of color, especially African-American men, and the poor.

During the 1980s, there were about 5,000 city and county jails, 400 state and federal prisons, and a variety of other detention centers. In some states, the cost of imprisonment for one inmate was above $20,000 per year, not including the cost of his or her family's support if he or she went on AFDC. On an average day, about 1.3 million people were confined. Spending for prisons and jails rose 50.9 percent during the first half of the 1980s, and in 1983, $10.4 billion was spent on corrections, up from $6.9 billion in 1980. Spending for police, courts, and prisons came to $39.7 billion in 1983.[47] The number of correctional officers more than doubled, to nearly 100,000.[48]

Human Rights and Justice

Practice Behavior Example: Understand the forms and mechanisms of oppression and discrimination.

Critical Thinking Question: Why does the institutional discrimination of oppressed groups persist despite legal protections?

CIVIL RIGHTS IN THE 1970s

Although the 1964 Civil Rights Act brought some lasting benefits to people of color and to women, the Equal Employment Opportunity Commission was unable to keep up with complaints in the 1970s. In 1974, nearly 57,000 people filed complaints that took more than two-and-a-half years to resolve, leaving a backlog of 100,000 cases by 1980. By 1982, the backlog was 5,000 to 10,000 cases.[49]

Native Americans

Native American protests became more radical after the Civil Rights Act of 1964, for although the War on Poverty brought some benefits in temporary jobs and training, systematic discrimination continued. Literacy tests and the gerrymandering of district lines, especially in Western states, were rampant, although more Native Americans began to serve in government office. (From 1900, only two dozen had served in state legislatures and only a handful in the U.S. Congress, although Charles Curtis, born in 1869 on the Kaw reservation, served as representative for fourteen years, senator for twenty, and vice president under Hoover.)

During the 1960s and 1970s, tens of thousands of Native Americans were encouraged to leave reservations for the cities. One-half to three-fourths of

Native American protests became more radical after the Civil Rights Act of 1964, for although the War on Poverty brought some benefits in temporary jobs and training, systematic discrimination continued.

urban relocatees returned to reservations after a few years because of continued poverty and discrimination in jobs and housing. Still, by 1980, half of all Native Americans lived in metropolitan areas. In 1968, the government acted to attract industry to some reservations, and by 1972 there were 200 factories there, though only half the jobs went to Native Americans. By the late 1960s, the gross income from agriculture on reservations was $300 million, of which Native Americans received only about $100 million.[50]

With the beginning of the Indian Health Service in 1955, the health of Native Americans improved markedly. Mortality rates declined and life expectancy increased: Between 1955 and 1971, the infant death rate decreased by 56 percent and the maternal death rate by 54 percent, and deaths from tuberculosis, gastritis, and influenza pneumonia declined by 86, 88, and 57 percent, respectively. Still, Native Americans die younger than any other group, and infant mortality on some reservations is comparable to that of undeveloped countries.[51] In 1970, two-thirds of all the U.S. population sixteen- to twenty-four years old had finished high school, compared to 50 percent of Native Americans in urban areas and 25 percent in rural areas.

The American land-grab of Native American lands continued: Until Native Americans abandon use and occupancy of land they have aboriginal title to it, and as recently as 1971 Alaskan Natives held aboriginal title to nine-tenths of Alaska. Therefore, in 1970 a judge held that an oil pipeline could not be laid across the Yukon until permission was obtained. However, "on December 14, 1971, Congress took note of the Alaskan Natives' aboriginal title and extinguished it."[52] In return, Congress gave the Native Americans a business corporation for each of their 220 villages to manage the land they would be allowed to take back from selected areas. It also agreed to pay them something less than a billion dollars from North Slope Oil revenues, but there is no deadline for payment. Eighty thousand Native Americans were affected by the act, so each would have 1/80,000 of a share in the corporation; however, their shares could not be sold until 1991, so they realized very little from the agreement. The only tangible benefit was a cash dividend, which in 1974 amounted to about $181 each.[53]

In 1973, the American Indian Policy Review Commission, the first top-level investigative commission in Indian affairs since the Merriam Report in 1928, was formed. Its members were five Native Americans and seven senators and congressmen, the majority from states with large Native American populations. In 1975, they ruled that tribes are sovereign political bodies with power to enact and enforce their own laws, and that a special trust relationship still exists between them and the U.S. government.[54] In 1977 their full report was issued:

> From the standpoint of personal well-being, the Indian of America ranks at the bottom of virtually every social statistical indicator ... the highest infant mortality rate, the lowest longevity rate, the lowest level of educational attainment, the lowest per capita income, and the poorest housing and transportation in the land.[55]

Of all men in the United States in 1977, 74 percent were employed, but only 56 percent of Native American men worked. Native American women averaged less than $400 a year for their employment. Rural residents lived in greater poverty than did those in cities. Thirty-four percent of Native Americans had an annual income of $4,000 or less, as compared with 15 percent of the total population; only 22 percent earned $10,000 or more, compared with 47 percent of the general population.[56]

Forced assimilation of Native Americans still existed. A prime example was the taking of Native American children from their families as part of the general discretionary trend of welfare and mental health workers,

> ... placing these children in white foster homes or institutions. In some areas 25 to 40 percent of all children are taken from their homes. Social workers argue the homes of poor Native Americans are not "fit" places for children.... [T]he poverty and "dirt" in the lives of Native Americans are fundamentally the result of the destruction of Native American resources ... over hundreds of years of colonial oppression.[57]

Among Native American protest groups, the most radical was the American Indian Movement (AIM). In 1969, after student protesters occupied the no-longer-used prison island of Alcatraz, a hundred AIM members replaced them, arguing that their treaty rights guaranteed them unused federal lands. They were forcibly removed in 1971. In 1973, AIM led an armed occupation at Wounded Knee on Pine Ridge Reservation, arguing that the tribal government was dominated by whites. Federal agents and disguised army units occupied the reservation with an armed struggle that lasted seventy-one days, with two Native Americans killed and two federal officials wounded. Up to 300 Native Americans were involved. Illegal wiretapping and paid witnesses led to the defeat of the suit against AIM, but a dozen suspicious murders and accidents later happened to AIM members, with few arrests or convictions for the crimes. The Eighth Circuit Court of Appeals reversed a lower court's dismissal of complaints that their constitutional rights had been violated when the military intervened in a domestic problem with Air Force planes for surveillance and high-ranking military officers on hand, under the direction of Alexander Haig, vice chief of staff under Nixon. The court decided that

> ... the use of military forces to seize civilians can expose civilian government to the threat of military rule and the suspension of constitutional liberties.[58]

In 1974, a group of Mohawks occupied a forest preserve in New York's Adirondack State Park, claiming its 600 acres, along with 9 million additional acres in New York and Vermont. In September, the state went to federal court seeking to evict the Mohawks, and they countered with a suit charging that the land had been usurped by fraud. On appeal, they were granted rights to considerable land in the state. Furthermore, in 1975 armed Menominees occupied the Alexian Brothers' novitiate building, and as a consequence, a committee was formed to supervise contacts between Native Americans and police, which was successful in improving police behavior. In 1979, the Supreme Court upheld a 1974 decision that treaties reserved fishing rights for Native Americans differently than for whites and recognized tribal rights to fishing resources. However, this led to a significant backlash of congressional bills aimed at breaking treaties, overturning court decisions, and exterminating land claims.[59]

In the 1970s, three dozen tribes created the Council of Energy Resources (CERT) to protect their interests. They hired a former Iranian oil minister to help them with contracts because they rarely received the correct royalties in dealing with white Americans for the development of coal, oil, and other resources. CERT obtained several million dollars of grants for technical assistance and reservation industrialization. Throughout this time, however, the government tried to co-opt CERT because Native American lands included one-third of the strip coal mining resources of the West and half the uranium outside public lands.[60]

Feagin says,

> Native American lands have been taken for dams, reservoir projects, national parks, and right of ways for roads. The sale of lands to private lumbering and mineral interests—200,000 acres in 1970—continues....
> Large proportions of the usable land in reservations have been leased to whites.[61]

By 1973, some 300 land claims had been heard and over $300 million awarded to Native American societies. However, this represents less than 4 percent of the amount claimed. In New York and Maine, the Oneida society's claims against the government have returned some illegally taken land. An agreement providing for the acquisition of 300,000 acres to be held in trust for Native Americans was developed, and a $27 million trust fund was signed by Jimmy Carter in 1980.[62] In 1984, appropriations included $254 million to the Bureau of Indian Affairs for the operation of Indian-controlled boarding and day schools, and an additional $69 million went to the Department of Education to support the education of Native American children in public schools.[63]

Reaganomics hit Native Americans hard. After 1980 average unemployment on reservations jumped from 40 percent to a devastating 80 percent, and in some societies average income fell to $900 per year for a family of four. Because Native Americans receive no state or local aid, they had to rely on the federal government for help, yet programs that benefited them, such as CETA, the Economic Development Administration, Housing and Urban Development, and Health and Human Services, were cut drastically.

Japanese Americans

Although Japanese Americans suffered personally and economically from their internment during World War II, they soon began to recoup their losses. In 1950, Japanese American activities in Hawaii led to statehood, and Daniel Inouye, a war hero, became the first Japanese American in the House of Representatives. Spark Matsunaga was second in 1962, and Inouye then became the first Japanese American senator in 1964. Patsy Takemoto Mink became the first Japanese woman in Congress. Whereas these congresspersons came from Hawaii, in 1976 Samuel Hayakawa was the first Japanese American senator from the mainland, reelected in 1982.[64]

In 1970, there were 591,000 Japanese Americans in the United States, with the heaviest concentrations in Hawaii (217,307) and California (213,280). Their median family income was $12,500 (all incomes median $9,600), although Japanese American women earned much less than men, at $5,880 (compared to $5,122 for white women). Only 7.5 percent lived below the poverty level. By this time their education level was higher than any other population group: Nearly all had finished high school and over half the men and one-third of the women were college graduates. By 1980, Japanese American median family income was $22,025.[65]

Japanese Americans continued to protest their illegal internment during World War II. In January 1983, Gordon Hirabayashi, who was jailed in 1943 for arguing against internment, sought to have his conviction set aside (along with that of Fred Koromatsu) on grounds that government lawyers had concealed important evidence at his trial: a naval intelligence report contradicting the army's claim that widespread disloyalty among Japanese Americans required their evacuation and internment. The "proof" that convicted them was a decoded intelligence statement suggesting that Japanese Americans working in aircraft plants had cabled production figures to Tokyo—figures printed ten days before in the *Los Angeles Times*. A star witness could not connect those cables to a single American citizen of Japanese ancestry. The U.S. Court of Appeals for the District of Columbia heard a $12 billion damage suit brought on behalf of all surviving internees. A federal district court judge dismissed the suit on statute of limitations grounds, but the Circuit Court finally reversed the dismissal and granted compensation to plaintiffs.

A resurgence of racism against Asians across the country was evident in the 1980s recessions. Peter Irons says,

> From California to Boston, violence against Asians has spread, as the "Rambo syndrome" and "Japan-bashing" have become respectable. The murder of Vincent Chin in Detroit and the wave of attacks on Vietnamese and other Indochinese refugees testify to the ugly strain of racism the Reagan Administration has done little to counter.[66]

Other Asian Americans

In 1970, there were 435,000 Chinese and 343,000 Filipinos in the United States. During 1973, immigration brought in approximately 21,700 Chinese, 30,000 Filipinos, and 5,500 Japanese. There were 1.5 to 3.5 million Asian immigrants from 1970 to 1980, and by 1980 Chinese had surpassed Japanese as the nation's largest Asian group. One-half million Indochinese immigrated to the United States in 1970, of whom two-thirds were from Vietnam. This last group was particularly threatened when they settled around the Gulf of Mexico, with incidences of burning in effigy and harassment of fishermen by the Ku Klux Klan.[67]

Mexican Americans

In 1970, Mexican Americans numbered more than 4.5 million, with almost 80 percent living in Arizona, California, Colorado, New Mexico, and Texas. Their median family income was $6,972 (though substantially lower in Texas), whereas that of all families was $9,600.[68] One-quarter of the Mexican American population lived below the poverty level. Approximately 17 percent of all children in the Southwest were Mexican Americans, but only 4 percent of the 325,000 teachers in the Southwest were Mexican Americans. Significant provisions were made for bilingual education under ESEA (1968), and in 1974 the *Law v. Nichols* decision determined that schools could not ignore the language problems of non-English speakers, yet we continued to weaken bilingual programs. In 1979, more than 50 percent of Mexican American children did not finish high school, and one-quarter had less than an elementary school education. In 1982, the Supreme Court ruled that all children, including illegal aliens, had to be provided schooling without tuition in U.S. schools.[69]

Little real progress was made to ensure equality for Mexican Americans, partly because of lack of differentiation between Mexican American citizens and illegal immigrant Mexicans. Officially, legal immigration was limited: There were new restrictions in 1960, and in 1965 the Immigration Act limited immigration from the Western Hemisphere to 120,000. In 1976, an immigration cap of 20,000 was placed on Mexico. However, whenever more labor is needed, growers support illegal immigration. Four to seven million undocumented Mexican laborers—*braceros*—entered the United States between 1920 and 1980. Whole families came to the United States, where they had no legal protection. Despite abuses, even death (for example, a truckload of Mexican laborers were left in a locked truck to die in the desert early in the 1980s), they are afraid to go to authorities for help. Because workers picking crops are often paid by the basket, their children work in the fields, too, without adequate shelter, food, or health care. Although hiring of American children is prohibited by law, Hispanic children—whether illegal immigrants, legal immigrants, or Hispanic Americans—rarely have such protection. Major canneries and food producers do not bother to ask who has picked the baskets of food turned in for pay.[70]

In the mid-1970s, nearly all employers of Hispanics refused government help in finding American workers to replace Mexican workers who had been caught. There were no legal penalties against employers who knowingly hired undocumented workers, and although a 1982 Senate bill would have imposed fines as high as $10,000 and jail, it failed in the House. It was widely condemned by supporters of agribusiness based on Hispanic labor: A Heritage Foundation report said that imposing sanctions on employers who hire illegal aliens would cause significant economic disruption and that immigrants, both legal and illegal, have been "net contributors to the nation's economy." It recommended increased enforcement efforts by the U.S. Border Patrol, an increased quota for immigrants, and the establishment of a legal guest program rather than fines for growers. The Reagan administration passed an immigration bill in 1987 that allowed 350,000 "guest workers" into the United States at any one time and granted amnesty to those who entered the country before January 1, 1980.

Hispanics were always targets of hate groups such as the Ku Klux Klan and the Aryan Nation, especially in towns bordering Mexico. Overt action, however, always becomes more common as unemployment worsens. Most Americans would not work at such hard labor and low pay as do Hispanic farm workers, yet this is only a rallying cry to stir up hatred and action against those who are "different."

Puerto Ricans and Cubans

The 1974–1975 recession that brought cutbacks in the petrochemical industry left the island of Puerto Rico, a commonwealth of the United States, in permanent recession. *Puertoriquenos*, pushed out by the recession and encouraged to migrate to the mainland, came in great numbers. However, life was little better for them: In 1976 over 16 percent of Puerto Rican men and 22 percent of Puerto Rican women were unemployed. Except for Native Americans, Puerto Ricans are the poorest of all citizens in the United States. In 1980, when there were 2 million *Puertoriquenos* on the mainland, their median income was $9,900, one-half the national average.[71]

Puerto Ricans faced discrimination in more than employment and housing. For example, a federally funded survey by the Hispanic Health Council found that of 153 Puerto Rican women in Hartford, Connecticut (1980), fully half had been sterilized. Women told interviewers they had signed consent forms without understanding them. The rate of sterilization in Puerto Rico has been between 30 and 35 percent for many years, encouraged by the government as a means of controlling population and welfare costs.[72] Sterilization for poor women of all ethnicities is a pervasive, though usually undocumented, reality of welfare life. Puerto Rican activist groups include Aspira, which tries to provide educational opportunities for young people, the Puerto Rican Legal Project, the Puerto Rican Defense Fund, the League of Puerto Rican Women, the Puerto Rican Teachers Association, the Puerto Rican Forum, and the Puerto Rican Family Institute.

A more recent group of Hispanic people came to the United States from Cuba after Castro's revolution. The first wave were professional and monied classes fleeing from nationalization of their wealth, so they were extremely conservative. In 1980, a new influx began of people poorer and less educated.[73] Unable to find work, they swelled the welfare rolls and competed with Miami's African-American low-wage workers. Tensions between the two groups were severe, sometimes resulting in riots: In 1980, a major riot broke out in Miami, with three days of extensive burning and looting. It left sixteen dead and 400 injured, and caused $100 million in property damage.[74] In Miami alone, by 1982 Cubans constituted 39 percent of the population, as compared to 44 percent white and 17 percent African American.

African Americans

Although significant gains were won for people of color in the 1960s, enforcement of civil rights remained problematic. A major issue during the 1970s was school busing to enforce desegregated education. In 1971, in the *Swann v. Charlotte-Mecklenburg Board of Education* decision, the Supreme Court upheld busing. However, whites opposed it as being against the "neighborhood school"—a thin veil for racism, because at least 44 percent of all children, regardless of color, ride buses to school, and fewer than 4 percent are bused for the purposes of desegregation.[75] Some school districts quietly and effectively integrated their schools, but many continued the battle into the 1980s, where it disappeared not because schools were integrated, but because of little enforcement under the Reagan administration.

The same lack of civil rights enforcement was evident in employment. African Americans, despite educational gains, remained unemployed and underemployed at far greater rates than white people; their unemployment rates are consistently double those of whites. In 1970, 56 percent of young African Americans twenty-five to twenty-nine years of age were high school graduates, and 10 percent had college degrees. In 1979, 75 percent had high school diplomas and 21 percent had at least some college. By 1980, the African/Caucasian differential in years of school had effectively ended. However, this did not significantly increase their chances of employment.[76] In recessions, they lose jobs at twice the rate of white workers—last hired, first fired. Official estimates of unemployment seriously underestimate real joblessness, subemployment, and underemployment. Those not counted, according to a nationwide study in 1980, were discouraged workers taken off the official unemployment rolls because they stopped trying (3.5 percent), part-time workers (5.4 percent), and full-time workers at poverty wages (9.5 percent). This brought the real unemployment rate significantly above official levels. In the 1981–1983 recession, African-American unemployment generally went above 20 percent and, in some areas, for young men between ages seventeen and twenty-five, it soared to over 50 percent.[77]

Although few African Americans reached political eminence, a few became leaders, including Barbara Jordan, congressperson from Texas; Shirley Chisholm, who in 1972 declared her candidacy for presidency; Andrew Young, formerly an aide to Martin Luther King, Jr., the U.S. representative to the United Nations, and then mayor of Atlanta; and Reverend Jesse Jackson, who launched an unsuccessful bid for the presidency in 1984 under the banner of the Rainbow Coalition. African-American mayors have included Marion Barry of Washington, D.C., Tom Bradley of Los Angeles, and Richard Hatcher of Gary, Indiana.

Violence against minority groups continued partly because of a resurgence of the Ku Klux Klan. Although by 1970 Klan membership dropped to an estimated 2,000, by spring of 1976, it was reinvigorated, growing, and engaged in activities

> such as protesting busing in Boston and Louisville, joining the textbook fight in Charlestown, West Virginia, creating a scandal in the New York state prison system, burning crosses from California to Maryland, going to court to sue and be sued, and appearing on national talk shows.[78]

Estimates of Klan membership in the late 1970s ranged from 2,000 to 10,000 members, with 30,000 to 100,000 sympathizers. The Klan's racial hatred is based on belief in white supremacy, fear of loss of jobs to people they believe to be inherently inferior, belief in "pollution" of the national "gene pool," and hatred of African Americans and Jews as matters of religious and economic ideologies. Their most potent belief is a fundamentalist Christianity, although they espouse no particular denomination. They do espouse traditional values for women, the importance of home and family life, and male supremacy, but they began to admit women (and Catholics) to their membership in the 1970s.[79]

White supremacy groups include the Klan, the Aryan Nation, and neo-Nazis. Although some authorities believe they are essentially harmless, others feel that violence by the Far Right is a real danger in the United States. One group of the Aryan Nation—the Order, the Sword, and the Arm of the Lord—has robbed banks and killed. The dirty work of the Aryan Nation is often done by young "skinheads" preparing for race war. Paramilitary camps span the country and include significant numbers of neo-Nazis as participants or trainers. Some have "security forces," run national book services, distribute paramilitary training manuals, and publish books on making bombs, explosives, and other weapons. The United Racist Front, formed in 1979, is a coalition of the National Socialist (Nazi) Party of America, the National States' Rights Party, and the Federated Knights of the Ku Klux Klan. It was implicated in a 1979 Greensboro, North Carolina, incident at which American Communist party members and union officials were slain at an anti-Klan rally.[80] Raphael Ezekial, a professor of psychology, says that hate groups

> have very dangerous things to tell us: ... that racism has deep roots, that terror is widespread in this country, and that more people than we like to think can be moved by unsophisticated ideas.[81]

Women

The women's movement during the 1970s became more politically aware if more fragmented, its values based on a deep-seated conviction that personal problems of women, such as poverty and low-wage work, spring from political causes. The National Organization for Women remained the strongest group. By the late 1970s, membership was nearly a quarter of a million. NOW worked for two major goals: passage of the Equal Rights Amendment (ERA) and the rights of women to control their reproduction through birth control and abortion. ERA was the overt issue, and although there has been much controversy over it, the amendment stated simply that

> Equality of rights under the law shall not be denied or abridged by the United States or by any State on account of sex.

In the 1960s, ERA was endorsed by Presidents Johnson and Nixon. In 1972, the Senate joined the House in approving ERA, and sent it to the states for ratification. Twenty-one ratified it quickly, but by the spring of 1973, a significant counterattack had begun, stalling it three short of the needed three-fourths approval. In response to the backlash, some states even began rescission processes. For all practical purposes, ERA is now a dead issue for the United States, though many states have their own ERAs.

Foes of ERA insisted that it would have brought a military draft for women, unisex toilets, and enforced Lesbianism, and that it would have forced women dependent on men into the labor market. To counteract women's liberation movements, antifeminist organizations began. For example, Happiness for Women (HOW), created in 1971, boasted 10,000 members within a year and 15,000 by 1981. It was "dedicated to the preservation of the family, preservation of the masculine role as provider, and preservation of the feminine role as wife, mother, and homemaker." Members supported

> God's divine plan, the family structure, removal of Communist and Socialist teachings from the schools, removal of radical elements of Women's Liberation Movement teachings from the schools, teaching the joys of womanhood to young girls, preservation of femininity, restoration of morality, elimination of drug abuse, return to patriotism, and the election to government of men and women dedicated to God, Family, and the Country.[82]

It was one of the organizations leading to the Moral Majority, which claimed that feminism was the primary cause of breakdown in family and marriage patterns because it takes away women's "right" to stay in the home. Moreover, it claimed feminism to be anti-God because it rejects male supremacy and so must be eliminated to restore traditional values. Abortion was a major issue because it concerned the sacredness of life. Ironically, many in the Moral Majority supported both the death penalty and massive arms buildups and opposed public assistance, on the basis that the latter encouraged out-of-wedlock births and interfered in the rights of the church to care for its own. The Moral Majority was the forerunner of the Christian Coalition.

Teenage pregnancies were also an important issue to women in this period. Between 1963 and 1978, premaritally conceived births increased 25 percent for white teenagers and 50 percent for African-American teenagers. Out-of-wedlock births represented nearly 11 percent of all live births in 1970 and 15.5 percent in 1978. Although rates for African Americans declined, they remained about six times those for whites. During the 1960s, white unwed teenagers began to keep their babies rather than giving them up for adoption, as many as 76 percent in 1976, increasing to 93 percent by 1978, creating a real shortage for white adoptive parents.[83]

Despite the religious backlash against birth control programs, many were funded: The Bureau of Indian Affairs made family planning available in 1965, the Children's Bureau began to support family planning through state health departments in 1966, the 1967 OEO amendments included family planning funds for the parents' division of Head Start, and in 1975 the Office of Child Development initiated research and demonstration projects. Under Medicaid and through family planning clinics such as Planned Parenthood, funds came from Title XX or Title X of the Public Health Act. Sixty-three new fertility-related laws were passed in 1981, the largest number since 1973.[84] In 1983, influenced by pressures from far-right groups, the Department of Health and Human Services proposed that family planning clinics receiving Title X funds should be required to notify parents before prescribing contraceptives for teenagers. This "squeal rule" triggered some 65,000 protests, four to one against the regulation, but it was passed and implemented in many states.

The abortion issue struck at the heart of the reactionary religio-political system of the United States, then as now. Although abortion is less dangerous than carrying a fetus to term, especially for teenagers, legal abortions became increasingly restricted. In the 1950s and 1960s, many states had reformed abortion laws to permit it in certain instances, particularly in the first trimester. Still, laws restricted abortion until the *Roe v. Wade* decision in 1973 upheld women's rights to decision in the first two trimesters of pregnancy, declaring that the interest of the woman was paramount in the first three months. The court explicitly rejected the idea that life begins at conception and that the fetus is a person protected by the Fourteenth Amendment.

After *Roe v. Wade*, legal abortions approached one-third of all pregnancies. New programs developed to help women with their abortion decisions, the most useful of which was probably that Medicaid would pay for abortions for poor women. However, the conservative backlash increased, and in 1976 a constitutional amendment banning abortion was proposed: the Hyde, or Human Life, Amendment. Although it was defeated, Congress imposed increasingly strict limits on the use of federal funds for abortions. In the 1980 *Harris v. McRae* decision, the Supreme Court ruled that states were no longer required to use Medicaid funds for abortions for otherwise eligible women except in cases of rape or cases where the pregnancy endangered the woman's life. However, government standards for what constitutes proof of rape are so narrow as to render this exception almost useless. The number of Medicaid-funded abortions dropped from 300,000 in 1977 to 17,983 in 1981.[85] Since the Reagan administration, there has been increasing political momentum to overthrow *Roe v. Wade* and make all abortions illegal, even for pregnancies that result from rape or incest.

Gay Liberation

The gay liberation movement took on greater national significance with the formation first of the Lambda Defense and Educational Fund in 1972 and the National Gay Task Force in 1973 (now the National Gay and Lesbian Task Force). The Lambda Fund defended civil rights of homosexuals in employment, housing, education, child custody, and the administration of justice, working solely through the court systems. It paid for legal representation on behalf of homosexual clients and maintained a national network of attorneys willing to take cases pertaining to homosexual rights. In 1986, Lambda counted over 7,000 people as regular contributors. The National Gay and Lesbian Task Force, a clearinghouse for federal legislation affecting homosexuals, coordinated the activities of local homosexual groups, worked with the media to facilitate a more accurate portrayal of homosexuality, and assisted foundations and associations working with the homosexual community. It was the prime organizer of the October 1979 March on Washington for Lesbian and Gay Rights, attended by just under a quarter of a million people.[86] Although few gains were made for homosexuals, since 1983 most of the larger U.S. cities have enacted gay rights laws and more than half the states have repealed sodomy statutes.[87]

In New York City in 1970, the police raided a gay bar (the Snake Pit) and arrested 167 patrons. One was killed in the melee. Enraged by the raid's brutality, even mainstream politicians, including Congressman Ed Koch, argued for change. Gay groups gained access to police chiefs, mayors, and human rights offices. When Koch became mayor in 1978, one of his first acts was to prohibit discrimination based on sexual orientation in all municipal agencies, including the police department. Similar access and results were gained in Washington, D.C., and Los Angeles.[88] In San Francisco, gay political power increased with the election of Harvey Milk as supervisor and George Moscone as mayor in 1978. Both were assassinated, but by 1981 San Francisco had integrated openly gay police officers into their troops and gay-bashers were being prosecuted.

Gays pursued equality in the courts based on First Amendment rights and the Civil Rights Act of 1964 (Section VII). In 1972, the Supreme Court decided that the First Amendment allowed students to form Student Democratic Societies, and based on that precedent in 1974 the University of New Hampshire was required to recognize a gay student group. In 1973, the Civil Service Commission notified federal agencies they could no longer deny jobs to homosexuals (*Scott v. Macy*, 1965). Whereas the Ninth Court of Appeals ruled that an openly effeminate man, a gay man, and a Lesbian couple had no sex discrimination in employment claims under Title VII because they were harassed for sexual orientation rather than sex (*De Santis v. Pacific Telephone & Telegraph*, 1979), later Title VII decisions applied by the Equal Employment Opportunity Commission (EEOC) makes gender stereotypes irrelevant to job decisions and protects workers against gay bashing in places of employment.[89]

As the Religious Right grew in strength, so did heterosexism and hostility. The epidemic of acquired immune deficiency syndrome (AIDS) is a case in point. Despite the fact that its consequences were always fatal, not until it began to infect heterosexuals did the national government begin to fund research adequately. In fact, AIDS among homosexuals was labeled as God's curse

> ... AIDS among homosexuals was labeled as God's curse against their sins and trivialized with jokes reaching as high as the presidential level.

against their sins and trivialized with jokes reaching as high as the presidential level.[90] A quote from Senator Jesse Helms exemplifies this:

> The government should think twice about spending much money fighting a disease brought on by deliberate, disgusting, revolting conduct.[91]

This is despite the fact that, more and more, AIDS became a heterosexual disease. By 1995, it was the number-one cause of deaths for all Americans age twenty-five to forty-four.[92] No discussion of bigotry and AIDS is complete without mention of the Reagan administration's role in suppressing information about the disease. Surgeon General C. Everett Koop was pressured to downplay the existence and spread of AIDS as well as the role of condoms in prevention; pressure on Koop mysteriously eased up after Reagan was reelected. Attempts in the mid-1990s to eliminate the office of Surgeon General altogether reflected the Far Right's desire to place public health decisions in the hands of politicians who lack even a basic understanding of epidemiology.

CONCLUSION: TIGHTENING THE REINS

Throughout the 1970s, conservatism increased. Where legislation could not be denied, as in the case of civil rights, it was supported. However, in dealing with women, children, people of color, and the poor, programs became increasingly more restrictive and even hostile. The hostility was augmented with the upsurge of groups devoted to male supremacy and their own brands of morality, ranging from such physically violent groups as the Ku Klux Klan and neo-Nazis to ideologically violent groups such as the Religious Right.

The election of Ronald Reagan in 1980, and his reelection in 1984, should have been no surprise to those watching the reactionary trends so evident in politics. With the overt backing of the Far Right and the Moral Majority, he saw his election as a mandate to enforce certain ideological beliefs, among them the Christianization of American politics, the return to patriarchal marriage and family norms, the breakup of social programs that supported people outside marriage and outside the work ethic, and the retreat from civil rights. In addition, his adherence to a war ethic—a "refusal to blink"—is "reasonable" given the reactionary trends of the 1970s. To intervene in sovereign nations for the sake of the economy or to end the world in defense of a principle is not beyond the pale of such beliefs.

The following questions will test your knowledge and understanding of the content found within this chapter. For additional assessment, including licensing-exam type questions on applying chapter content to practice behaviors, visit **MySearchLab.**

1. Which statement regarding the Social Security system is true?
   a. Most people receive much less than they put into the Social Security system.
   b. Most people receive much more than they put into the Social Security system.
   c. Pensions depend on the legislation at the time the person becomes eligible.
   d. Benefits are paid from a reserve fund or a trust fund.

2. Under which condition would a worker likely be denied Unemployment Insurance?
   a. Being laid off due to a restructuring.
   b. Being laid off from a small company with only 10 employees.
   c. Having met the state's base period requirements.
   d. Having been fired for misconduct.

3. In the 1970s, the struggles with the AFDC program included which kinds of problems?
   a. Applicants were being denied after false accusations of undisclosed income.
   b. Lack of state funding meant the program would close down altogether.
   c. Welfare workers began striking in protest of unreasonable work conditions.
   d. Regulations were being ignored or applied as desired by the welfare workers.

4. Which was an example of a criterion required for states to meet the "block grant" system?
   a. Providing ongoing housing, food, and clothing to help justify the program.
   b. Offering institutional care as a first step.
   c. Providing job retraining to increase their marketability in the job market.
   d. Proving that all able-bodied family members, including children over 14, were employed.

5. How would a block grant welfare worker in the 1970s handle a situation in which the parents were deemed unfit to care for their child?
   a. The welfare worker would come into the home to provide training and in-home assistance to bring the home environment up to suitable standards.
   b. The child would be placed in a foster home or institution.
   c. The parents would be given 30 days to improve the home environment or would face jail time or fines.
   d. In order to keep the family intact, the entire family would be moved into an institution to be cared for.

6. You are a welfare worker advising a disadvantaged family who has a child who will be starting school this year. What might you tell them about the Head Start program?
   a. The Head Start program has proven to be effective in helping students perform well in school.
   b. The Head Start program is geared only toward helping special needs students.
   c. Children who complete the Head Start program have the same dropout rates as those who do not go through the program.
   d. The focus of the Head Start program is to prevent substance abuse and generate drug awareness for school-age children.

7. Discuss the benefits in education and conflicts in employment that Mexican immigrants faced in the 1970s.

Reinforce what you learned in this chapter by studying videos, cases, documents, and more available at **www.MySearchLab.com**.

Watch and Review

Watch these Videos

English—Who Needs It

Abortion Wars

*Understanding Forms of Oppression and Discrimination

Read and Review

Read these Cases/Documents

Cesar Chavez, from "He Showed Us the Way" (April 1978)

The Gay Liberation Front, Come Out (1970)

Lyndon B. Johnson, The War on Poverty, (1964)

Tori Derricotte, Black in a White Neighborhood (1977–1978)

Assess Your Knowledge

Go to **MySearchLab** to test your knowledge of key topics in this chapter with topic-specific quizzes. Conclude your assessment by completing the chapter exam.

_____
* = CSWE Core Competency Asset

12

The Reactionary Vision

Competencies Applied with Practice Behavior Examples — in This Chapter				
■ Professional Identity	X Ethical Practice	X Critical Thinking	■ Diversity in Practice	■ Human Rights & Justice
■ Research Based Practice	■ Human Behavior	X Policy Practice	■ Practice Contexts	■ Engage, Assess, Intervene, Evaluate

Times and Events

- **1981, 1982:** Omnibus Reconciliation Acts (OBRAs) pass to balance federal budgets on the backs of the poor, change OASDI and AFDC requirements and benefits; Supreme Court upholds parent notification before abortion; Sandra Day O'Connor first woman Supreme Court Justice
- **1982:** Tax Equity and Fiscal Responsibility Act passes; Agriculture and Food Act restricts food stamps; OBRA consolidates programs into Block Grants, caps title XX; eliminates federal–state matching requirements; maternal and child health care provisions severely cut; schooling for illegal alien children required
- **1983:** CETA ends, Job Partnership Training Act (JPTA) begins; Harold Washington becomes first African American mayor in Chicago; Martin Luther King day proclaimed national holiday; Japanese Americans compensated for WWII internment
- **1984:** Medicare deductions increased; homeless set up tents across from White House
- **1986:** Gramm–Rudman–Hollings Act (GRH) massively cuts federal social programs; diagnostic related categories (DRGs) established for Medicare
- **1987:** Urgent Relief for Homeless Act passes; Farmers' Home Administration slashes financing for rural housing; Immigration bill allows Mexican "guest workers," grants amnesty to illegal immigrants
- **1988:** Family Support Act undermines public assistance and social insurance; Commission on Interstate Child Support enacted; Free trade agreement between United States and Canada begins; Congress passes Civil Rights Restoration Acts over Reagan's veto; George H. W. Bush elected President
- **1989:** African American Douglas Wilder becomes Governor of Virginia; David Dinkins becomes first African American Mayor of New York; Colin Powell becomes Chair of Joint Chiefs of Staff
- **1991:** Home Ownership and Opportunity for People Everywhere (HOPE) initiative established for homeless people; Clarence Thomas confirmed as Supreme Court Justice; Bush signs Civil Rights act of 1991 to strengthen earlier law
- **1992:** Bill Clinton elected President

BITING THE CONSERVATIVE BULLET

The elections of Ronald Reagan and George H. W. Bush were the emerging tip of a reactionary iceberg. Faced with a downward-spiraling economy, Reagan promised to eliminate the proliferation of government regulations that "strangled private enterprise" and to balance the budget regardless of who had to "bite the bullet." Bush followed his lead. The ideas were not new: Nixon had begun to limit social spending and institute fiscal change, along with privatization and federalized block grants. Nevertheless, until the Reagan administration, although questions about the process of social responsibility to the poor were raised, most politicians did not advocate its end. However, powered by belief in supply-side economics and unduly influenced by corporate America and a monied and media-wise Religious Right, Reagan began the dismantling of the fallback subsistence programs of the Social Security Acts of 1935. His legitimation was simple: He believed that America was ordained by God to carry out traditional morality and work values no matter the cost. As a spokesperson of the Moral Majority, the Reverend Jerry Falwell stated the aim simply:

> America's commitment to individualist values, hard work, and the acquisition of property and wealth is divinely inspired.[1]

A clearer statement demonstrating the synergy of religion, economics, and politics would be difficult to find.

Reagan's *domestic* social policies constituted a return to pre-Civil War ideology, as in the Pierce veto of Dix's Ten-Million-Acre Bill. His *tax* policies led us back to pre-1932 supply-side economics, or government support to the wealthy that would "trickle down" to the poor. His *international* policies included a rabid fear of the Soviet threat. Moynihan says,

> the United States government was ... in the throes of a consummate obsession with an expansion of communism—*which was not happening* ... all this in the cause of fighting a cold war that was over![2]

Given these policies, Reagan's goals were to balance the budget without cutting military preparedness and to eliminate social programs except for a safety net for the "truly needy." His safety net program was two-tiered: Those covered by social insurance—workers—would keep most benefits, and the nonworking poor would see programs substantially cut to encourage their return to the workforce or workfare.

Winifred Bell says that Reagan's election heralded a return to

> old-fashioned virtues of economic individualism, unfettered private enterprise, and a very limited role for government.... [Social programs were] vigorously attacked for their overwhelming cost, depressing effect on savings and private investments, and as ill-conceived liberal efforts.[3]

Reagan had far-reaching support among conservatives, the elite, and fundamentalist religious groups. The political Far Right supported less federal government, free enterprise, and traditional sex roles: men supporting their families and women homemaking and rearing children. The Religious Right, a conglomeration of fundamentalist and evangelical groups, supported political action to enforce morality and assumed the role of watchdog of public morality. According to Midgley, its vision

> extols traditional values, the virtue of the family and local community, statutory sanction over moral behavior, capitalist economic ideals, and a rigorous antiwelfarism rooted in a traditional antagonism to state intervention in social affairs.[4]

Patriarchal values dominated its perspective on women and the Protestant work ethic provided an intense focus on men as family wage earners.

Three morality-based issues permeated Reagan's policies. First was the sanctity of the nuclear family and the maintenance of its traditional male/female roles and statuses. This ideology ignored the fact that two adults working full-time at minimum wages remained in poverty, or that the number of female-headed families was growing exponentially. The second was the morality of income-producing labor at any wage, and its converse, nonwork, as immorality. The third was less precise: superpatriotism and religious belief in the God-ordained future of America. Protection of the "American way of life," and "making the world safe for democracy" rationalized hostility toward other nations, increased war production, and fostered a "dare you to cross this line" attitude.

REAGANOMICS: THE CONSERVATIVE POLITICAL ECONOMY

Reaganomics was, basically, a belief in supply-side economics: High production would keep a large supply of goods on the market, people would continue to buy, and buying more would produce more jobs, producing more money to buy more goods. An upward-spiraling economy would, through taxes on the greater volume of sales and increased income, move revenue upward to the government, and government investments in corporations via business tax breaks, subsidies, and contracts would add more productivity, leading again to higher employment and more consumerism.

Aside from the human problems of losses of jobs and income, Reaganomics had several fatal errors. First, in a recessionary economy with reduced employment causing limited income, fewer people could buy the increased goods, and those with money did not need more basic production items. Second, the 1981–1983 recession was not a "natural economic cycle" (therefore self-limiting), but a deliberate Reagan decision to trade unemployment for lower inflation rates. (Economists say that an unemployment increase of at least a million for two years will reduce inflation by a single percentage point.) According to Levitan and Johnson this

> precipitated a deep recession which brought the highest jobless rates since the 1930s and transformed the marginal income losses of rising prices into the total income losses of forced idleness. His sweeping tax and spending reductions further skewed income distribution in favor of the wealthy, slashing federal benefits for low-income Americans while significantly reducing the tax liability of the rich.[5]

It was estimated that from 1980 to 1984 there was a net transfer of income of $25 billion to the richest fifth of the population.[6]

Third, high production induces buying if prices are lowered through competition. However, the Reagan agenda maintained high prices to garner more taxes from higher income. Fourth, government corporate investments led to increases in production technology that eliminated jobs and moved jobs to foreign countries. Finally, government spending increased while revenue was cut by tax breaks for the wealthy and for corporations. Moynihan says,

> President Reagan ... never understood the onset of fiscal instability. His first budget director David A. Stockman ... did in time see what he/they had done. He pleaded for new revenues. Was greeted with amiable incomprehension. He would write of this as "a willful act of ignorance and grotesque irresponsibility."[7]

Reaganomics bore great similarity to pre-1929 economics. The saving grace for the 1980s was safety net programs going back to Roosevelt, such as bank insurance, federally supported mortgages, and social programs. These Reagan duly set about to destroy, leaving a decimated economy.

Polarization of incomes grew with each year of the Reagan and Bush administrations as the rich grew richer, the poor grew poorer, and the middle class shrank. Those at the top remained there: The richest 2 percent controlled

- 30 percent of all financial assets
- 50 percent of all stocks in private hands
- 71 percent of all tax-free bonds
- 20 percent of all real estate
- 39 percent of taxable bonds.

The wealthiest 6 percent of families owned 57 percent of all the nation's wealth and the top 16 percent owned 75 percent.[8]

The Reagan and Bush administrations virtually abolished corporate income taxes and drastically reduced personal income taxes for the rich. During his first year in office, Reagan slashed business taxes by an estimated $169 billion and, in the next six years, reduced individual taxes by $500 billion.[9] By 1984, families earning over $100,000 had net gains exceeding $20,000, while from 1980 to 1984 taxes of the poorest one-fifth of Americans rose by 22.7 percent—a net loss of $240.[10] From 1977 to 1988, the bottom 80 percent of families in the United States lost income while the top 5 percent gained 49.8 percent.[11] The poor paid higher net federal income taxes in 1990 than in 1980. According to Piven and Cloward, the reorganized federal tax structure

> promote[d] a massive upward redistribution of income. New investment and depreciation write-offs favor[ed] large corporations over small businesses; 80 percent of the benefits [went] to the 1,700 largest corporations (which have generated only 4 percent of all new employment over the past twenty years) ... [with losses] estimated [at] $750 billion in federal revenue.[12]

The federal debt increased four and a half times over the Reagan administration,[13] and when Reagan left office the deficit was $1 trillion.[14]

Between 1978 and 1984, poverty rose by 41 percent for white families and 25 percent for African Americans.[15] By 1982, more than 9 million more families had fallen below the official poverty line ($7,450 in 1980), with a 5.5 million increase just from 1980,[16] and in 1983, 35.5 million people (7.3 million families) were in poverty, an increase of 38 percent from 1978.[17] Between 1968 and 1984, African-American income rose from 73.2 percent of white income to 84.8 percent, but by 1982 it had returned to 55.3 percent of white income, virtually the same as in 1960.[18]

Capital gains taxes were cut from 33 to 28 percent to benefit the wealthy during the Bush administration.[19] Although Bush had promised "Read my lips: No new taxes," Reagan-established structures led to unprecedented budget deficits. Karger says,

> Throughout the late 1980s, Congress and the Reagan, then Bush administrations, postponed the day when the budget would have to be reconciled with the Gramm Rudman Hollings Deficit Reduction Act.... [F]acing a huge revenue shortfall in 1990, the Congress and the President [Bush] ... created ... a deficit reduction bill.[20]

The Gramm–Rudman–Hollings (GRH) Act bill included reductions in entitlement programs and defense spending, increases in user fees for government services, tax increases (especially "sin" taxes on alcohol, liquor, and luxury

From 1977 to 1988, the bottom 80 percent of families in the United States lost income while the top 5 percent gained 49.8 percent.

items such as boats), and reduced interest payments on the national debt.[21] The deficit at the end of George H. W. Bush's administration was $4.6 trillion,[22] rising a billion dollars a day.

THE NEW FEDERALISM

Reagan's New Federalism was Nixon's block grant program warmed over. It represented a reversal from societal responsibility to societal disregard for the poor and became the guideline not only for the Reagan/Bush era but for the Republican-dominated Congress of 1994, with its excessively punitive "Contract with America." Reagan's New Federalism had two facets: (1) reprivatization of services for the poor by private charities and churches and (2) the assumption by state governments of Aid to Families of Dependent Children (AFDC), Supplemental Security Income (SSI), and food stamps, while the federal government took full responsibility for Medicaid. The former paralleled pre-1935 aid to the poor and the latter substituted local/state standards for federal standards.

Privatization

Privatization—federal funding of services to private for-profit agencies such as hospitals, nursing homes, day care centers, drug rehabilitation centers, and even prisons—was intended to save money through competition. In fact, competition often eliminated services to the poor because financially secure agencies could lobby for and receive higher funding. Agencies with low- or no-fee bases could not afford lobbyists or could not compete. The result was poorer services for the poor and higher client rates for public agencies. Palmer and Sawhill say,

> The dismantling of the public sector social service delivery system [was] defended as a way to obtain cheaper, more effective, more flexible and efficient, and more innovative services [through contracting out].... [F] ew of these benefits have been realized.... Contracted out services were no cheaper than those performed by the public service agency ... and were more difficult ... to monitor.[23]

The concept of privatization is not new to social welfare, because social work began in service to the poor through private agencies. However, making profit from the poor dates much earlier: to asylums, poorhouses, institutions, and orphanages. Profit-making agencies can set their own client profiles, whereas public agencies serving the poor have fewer dollars to serve an ever-increasing poverty population. Privatization is instrumental in the polarization of social services. Hospitals are an example: Those that have privatized can select low-need, low-risk consumers, whereas public hospitals must fill the gaps in health care among the poor, whose problems are often more costly and extreme.

Privatization is, in fact, a step backward from public and social responsibility because when there is no access to care, a socially moral government has an obligation to provide. Finally, privatization abrogates the application of broad-based standards and regulations that prevent discrimination or abuse. Given that abuse and discrimination have occurred throughout our past when government standards were not enforced, we should not have allowed that to happen again.

George H. W. Bush followed the conservative move to privatization of social services and expanded services for corporations and the wealthy. His "kinder, gentler nation" did not address the growing numbers of the poor, increasing homelessness, higher school dropout rates, and decreased employment, particularly among minority groups. His attention focused much more intently on international rather than domestic efforts, and the deterioration began with Reagan expanded.

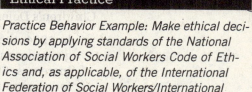

Ethical Practice

Practice Behavior Example: Make ethical decisions by applying standards of the National Association of Social Workers Code of Ethics and, as applicable, of the International Federation of Social Workers/International Association of Schools of Social Work Ethics in Social Work, Statement of Principles.

Critical Thinking Question: What ethical dilemmas accompany the privatization of social welfare services?

New Federalism: Returning Programs to States

Reagan's proposed tradeoff—federal payment for Medicaid while states assumed responsibility for AFDC, SSI, and food stamps—was turned down by Congress, though Congress severely cut funding for those programs. Legislation that led to cuts included the Omnibus Budget Reconciliation Act (OBRA) of 1981, the Tax Equity and Fiscal Responsibility Act of 1982, the Agriculture and Food Act of 1982 (which provided new eligibility restrictions and spending cuts for food stamps), the Deficit Reduction Act of 1984, the Gramm–Rudman–Hollings Act (GRH) of 1986, and the Family Support Act (FSA) of 1988. Program cuts and losses of revenue were compounded with each new bill under the pretense that money was being retargeted to the needier:

> In fact ... in no entitlement programs were real (inflation-adjusted) benefits increased ... when eligibility levels were reduced ... benefits declined nearly a fifth, from 88 percent of the official poverty threshold in 1970 to 71 percent in 1981.[24]

Under the New Federalism, all social welfare programs lost an average of 7 percent during Reagan's first three years, but

> cutbacks totaled 29 percent in child nutrition; 13 percent in welfare and food stamps; 17 percent in compensatory education; and 60 percent in employment and training programs. Spending for means-tested programs dropped from 13.3 percent of total federal expenses in 1980 to 11.1 percent in 1983, though universal programs [social insurance] rose from 40.8 to 42.9 percent.[25]

Approximately 400,000 to 500,000 families whose adult members worked were put off AFDC, losing extra benefits such as food stamps and Medicaid in the process, and another 300,000 families suffered severe cuts in benefits. States were no longer required to give cost-of-living increases for SSI. Almost half of all people with disabilities lost Old Age, Survivors, and Disability Insurance (OASDI) because of presumed "malingering." Other programs important to the poor were cut: Among them, Legal Services lost most of its funding, planned construction of public housing and veterans' hospitals was reduced, Vietnam veteran counseling centers were eliminated, and the Comprehensive Education and Training Act (CETA) program was abolished.

Of all programs devastated by Reaganomics, children's programs were hit hardest. The average number of children on AFDC per 100 children in poverty dropped dramatically from 71.8 percent in 1979 to only 52.5 percent in 1982, despite the increase of about 1 million children in poverty.[26] Low birth weight, prenatal death, and prematurity increased, especially among children of color, ranking the United States eleventh in infant mortality. According to the Children's Defense Fund,

> In 1984, the Reagan cuts imposed on poor children [saved] the federal government a million dollars an hour . . . [to] offset new Reagan increases: $9 million an hour on defense, $1 million more on tax breaks for corporations; $10 million more an hour on tax breaks for the wealthy; $2 million more an hour on interest on the national debt, to which we add $23 million an hour.[27]

All told, domestic spending for human resources was cut by $101.1 billion, of which $65.4 billion came from programs that provided benefits to poor families.[28]

Omnibus Budget Reconciliation Acts (OBRAs), now an accepted part of our fiscal culture, are intended to balance the national budget by equal funding cuts across all programs. However, certain programs are "more equal" than others; that is, some programs such as defense were given funding breaks and exemptions from the first OBRA (1981), so later cuts were not as drastic. On the other hand, because the deficits abetted by such exemptions had to be made up, other programs—usually social programs—were cut enormously at the beginning, and, even though protected and/or exempted from further OBRA cuts, were crippled.

The Omnibus Budget Reconciliation Acts of 1981 and 1982 reduced federal matching costs for Medicaid, set new eligibility and income limits on many social programs, and gave Reagan about half the cuts he proposed in income maintenance programs of SSI, food stamps, and AFDC. OBRA consolidated more than ninety categorical programs into four blocks, with a 20 to 25 percent reduction in federal funding for each. Block grants fostered competition among agencies for scarcer resources, a strategy that left them fighting for existence rather than serving their clients. Moreover, because private enterprise could compete for the grants, the for-profit service industry burgeoned, particularly in child care, nursing homes, and for-profit hospitals.

OBRA also capped Title XX, the Social Services Amendment, at $2.7 billion, replacing it with the Social Services Block Grant and eliminating federal regulations and state matching requirements earmarked for the poor. Because states no longer had to match funds, many reduced programs by up to 50 percent of previous funding. A study in 1982 showed that only about a fourth of federal cuts were replaced in employment, job training, compensatory education, health, and social services programs. In fact, some states reaped savings on the cutbacks because they no longer had to pay the 25 percent matching costs.[29] States reported significant increases in mental health problems as programs were reduced at the same time unemployment increased: More than thirty-eight states detailed increases in severe child abuse and molestation, suicides, and broken marriages. In 1983, thirty-two states reported less child care than in 1981, with the total expenses for such programs dropping by 14 percent.[30]

The Gramm–Rudman–Hollings Act (GRH) of 1986 was intended to make "fair" across-the-board cuts to end the federal deficit by 1991. It exempted some key health and income maintenance programs and made modified cuts in others, but these programs had already been cut massively by earlier Reagan bills.

Protected programs—that is, those given modified cuts—included OASDI, AFDC, Child Nutrition, food stamps, Medicaid, SSI, Veterans' Compensation and Veterans' Pensions, the Women, Infants, and Children Nutrition program, Medicare, federal input into state unemployment benefits, the Social Services Block Grant, and health programs for migrants, veterans, Native Americans, and communities.

Unprotected programs cut across the board by GRH included Head Start; general revenue sharing; rural development; ESEA grants; training, employment, and rehabilitation services; low-income energy assistance; special services to elderly and other groups; health research; housing assistance; and consumer/occupational health and safety programs. Most administrative costs (in Medicare, for example) were not exempt, so that even if benefits remained intact, administrative cuts ensured delays or cutbacks in worker-intensive services. In 1987, federal spending for education, employment and training, and social services was reduced by $827 million, Medicare administration by $74 million, low-income energy assistance by $81 million (29 percent), and $104 million was taken from nonexempt programs such as child support enforcement. New units of housing were reduced by 2,500–4,000 from the 97,000 authorized in 1986, and Legal Services, already drastically cut, lost another $13 million.[31]

Defense did not suffer, although supposedly it bore half of the GRH cuts. Because it had more funds to begin with, the remainder was still extremely high. Also, President Reagan had wide discretion on defense and exempted virtually all military personnel accounts and the entire Strategic Defense Initiative ("Star Wars"). Finally, in a clever sleight of hand, half the savings from cost-of-living adjustments and pensions were credited to defense on the basis that many of those affected were government employees, such as retired military and civilian defense department personnel and civil service retirees. However, most of the pensions cut were governmental only by a stretch of the imagination: longshoremen's and harborworkers' compensation benefits or black lung disability benefits, for example.[32] In all, in 1986 the defense budget was still roughly double 1980 levels (an estimated $268 billion).

Though intended to end the deficit, GRH failed because 60 percent of the deficit ($131 billion out of $217 billion) stemmed from tax policies that granted more tax breaks than the budget could afford. GRH neither broadened the tax base nor brought in more revenues. Supporting a triple-failsafe defense system, with enormous cost overrides and without increased taxes, was another unrecoverable waste. Finally, the enormous tax breaks given to the rich and allowed to multinational corporations, with little if any reinvestment in the government, continued to drain revenue from the nation.

PRUNING THE PROGRAMS

Although statistics, demonstration projects, and successful social programs proved beneficial both to recipients and to society, the nation entered a cutting frenzy under Reagan, focused on programs traditionally serving disadvantaged groups: people of minorities, the aged, women, and blue-collar workers.

Old Age, Survivors, Disability, and Health Insurance

Changes to OASDI began in 1981 and continued throughout the Reagan/Bush era: postponement of cost-of-living adjustments (COLAs) for six months, increased deductions and optional premiums for Medicare A and B, taxes on one-half of all Social Security benefits for people whose incomes exceeded $34,000, raises in amounts subject to taxes, and decreases in future benefit levels to 70 percent for retirement before age 67.[33] Resident aliens became subject to the same withholding taxes as U.S. citizens, and nonresidents paid a 30 percent tax on half of all earnings.[34] By the George H. W. Bush administration, the amount of payroll taxes charged to both employers and employees was 7.65 percent each (the self-employed paid 15.3 percent for FICA). Of each of these dollars 73 cents went to OASI, 8 cents to the Disability Insurance (DI) program, and 19 cents to the Health Insurance (HI or Medicare) program.[35]

Whereas the taxable wage base for OASI in 1990 was $51,300, it increased yearly (to $61,200 by 1995). All wages up to $125,000 could be taxed for Medicare, and by 1994 HI tax was applied to all earnings. By 1994, retired people age sixty-two to sixty-five could earn $8,040 and those age sixty-five to sixty-nine could earn up to $11,060 without penalty (one dollar of every two earned, no limit after age seventy).[36] Older people not on OASDI could buy into Medicare's Part A by paying premiums, in 1994, $245 a month, and into optional Part B (Supplemental Medical Insurance or SMI) for $46.10 per month (1995). In an attempt to limit Medicare costs, the Reagan administration developed diagnostic related group (DRGs) categories. Under DRGs, health care providers were paid a set amount for all patients admitted with certain categories of ailment. Additional ailments at the time of admission were not paid for, and when the "reasonable costs" for the category had been paid, the patient had to be released. Often, seriously ill patients were sent home to care for themselves or to nursing homes not set up to provide intensive medical care.

By 1992, 132 million workers, along with their employers, paid Social Security taxes, and 42.6 million beneficiaries received $24.5 billion per month.[37] Of these, 37.2 million received OASI benefits and 5.5 million were on disability allotments. About 30.2 million (70.8 percent) received benefits based on work records, and 12.4 million (29.2 percent) got spousal or dependent supplements. Of this latter group, 5.5 million were widowed and surviving parents, 3.3 million were spouses, and 3.6 million were children under the age of nineteen.[38] By 1995, the monthly benefit for a single retired worker was $98, and for worker and spouse it was $170.[39] In 1992, the average *private* pension was $599 per month, versus $1,205 for federal military retirees and $1,423 for federal civilian retirees; roughly three-fourths of federal retirees also qualify for Social Security. The average age of military retirement is forty-two for enlistees and forty-six for officers, meaning that "a typical military pensioner spends more years collecting benefits (thirty-five) than earning them (twenty-two)."[40]

During the Reagan administration, people with disabilities suffered disproportionately under presumptions that they did not have true disabilities. Disability reviews, beginning in 1980, increased termination from the programs fourfold. Sixty percent of those cut off won reinstatement, and although the government saved 10 percent while they were in appeal, costs for reinstatement were between $27 million and $69 million. Claimants were required to use federally appointed doctors who, it was discovered, overbilled and marked up lab fees by 300–400 percent. Of the thousands of doctors hired, 108 actually did 22 percent of all the exams and earned an average of $348,672. Six doctors earned more than $1 million each, and one received $3 million in one year.[41] Congress later enacted legislation more cautious in disqualifying beneficiaries with disabilities.

Unemployment Insurance and the New Poor

Beginning in 1979, the unemployment rate began to climb, and by May 1980 national unemployment was 7.8 percent. White unemployment was 5.8 percent, African-American unemployment 11.8 percent, and Hispanic unemployment 8.9 percent. Unemployment for all teenagers was 19.2 percent, but for minority youth it was nearly 60 percent. A total of 12 million people lost their jobs, but according to Ehrenreich the actual number of unemployed reached more than 35 million, or 23.9 percent of the working population.[42] Six and a half million workers could find only part-time employment and 1.8 million were "discouraged workers," people no longer on the official unemployment rolls.[43]

In a time of increasing unemployment, the unemployment insurance program itself came under attack. Whereas in 1975 over 75 percent of all unemployed workers were covered, by 1980 that number had dropped to 50 percent, and by 1988 to a record low of 31.5 percent.[44] In 1978, with 7.6 million people unemployed, unemployment insurance benefits were $31 billion. However, in 1982, with 10 million unemployed, less than $24 billion was paid out,[45] although payments rose to $30 billion in 1983 as unemployment increased.[46] Because the Reagan administration reduced the number of weeks of unemployment insurance available, unemployed people were more quickly forced into marginal jobs or onto public assistance. Of the officially unemployed— those registered with unemployment insurance offices—nearly 60 percent received no unemployment benefits, and payments averaged only 46 percent of before-tax earnings.[47] However, much like OASDI, unemployment insurance is a good investment and does not contribute to the federal deficit, generally taking in more than is paid out.[48]

The primary labor force employs people permanently, at reasonable wages and with fringe benefits, and entitles them to Social Security programs. The secondary labor force includes people working at marginal jobs or in part-time or low-paying jobs. Businesses employing people from the secondary labor force are usually small and highly competitive (such as fast-food chains) and hire for less than full time at low wages, firing their employees before they qualify for fringe benefits or for OASDHI. Over one-third of all jobs were in the secondary sector in the 1980s, and they were predominantly held by women, young people, and people of color.[49]

Reform legislation in the Reagan administration, in addition to forcing many regular workers into the secondary labor market, threw thousands more into it through cuts in AFDC, SSI, and OASDI and by ending the Comprehensive Education and Training Act (CETA) in 1983. CETA had employed 400,000 poverty-level workers through public and private nonprofit agencies, but Reagan replaced it with the Job Training Partnership Act (JTPA), subsidizing the private sector to retrain the adult unemployed and to train disadvantaged youth to have marketable skills. JTPA was another "trickle down" program, but it served fewer people than CETA and people less disadvantaged, "creaming" its JTPA workers to ensure program success.

Even in full-time covered work, workers' control over their employment continued to wane rapidly. Many in the forty-to-sixty age group found themselves unemployed after years on the job, at a time when their earnings should have been highest and would have led to future higher Social Security benefits (impoverishing their families in the present and reducing their retirement security). Companies used government tax breaks and investments to "retool" and roboticize factories and jobs disappeared. "Job skidding" occurred, in which the newly unemployed found jobs, but at salaries significantly lower than former earnings; for example, an electronics job typically paid 61 percent of a factory job. Between 1979 and 1984, an estimated 11.5 million people lost their jobs through plant closings, job relocations, and technical innovations.[50]

Unemployment implied a moral judgment against workers because they could not fulfill the major societal role of family support. This took an emotional toll, keeping them quiet about job changes and cutbacks. It also helped to destroy unions and their fight for workers. Abramovitz says,

> Reagan signaled the end of the post-war labor/management pact in 1981 when he fired over 11,000 striking air traffic controllers ... combined with antilabor appointments to the national Labor Relations Board, implicitly granted employers permission to revive long-shunned antiunion practices: decertifying unions, outsourcing production, and hiring permanent replacements for striking workers.[51]

Farmers constituted another group of the new poor. According to Devine and Wright,

> The rate of farm poverty dropped dramatically from more than 50% in 1959 to about 11% in 1990.... This ... does not reflect a major turnaround in the economics of the family farm so much as a continuous replacement of small-scale, economically marginal family farming operations by large-scale agribusiness enterprises. In fact the size of the farm population shrank from more than 15 million in 1959 to less than 5 million in 1990.[52]

While small farms died, the government supported large agribusiness by refusing to put a $500,000 lid per farmer on government subsidies. Some large farmers collected as much as $20 million in government support in 1986.[53] As in the past, the support of agribusiness and new technology forced small farmers off their farms, out of ownership positions, and into whatever labor they could find.

Public Assistance Programs

Supplemental Security Income

Beginning in 1974, this program by 1993 served over 4.5 million people. Of these, more than 60 percent were considered disabled, 33 percent were aged, and the remaining were blind. To become eligible, people could have assets of no more than $2,000 ($3,000 for couples). To encourage work, $65 and half of all additional earnings per month were disregarded. Average monthly grants in 1993 were $221 for the aged, $351 for blind people, and $361 for those with disabilities. Women, who comprised 58 percent of all

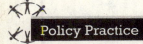

Policy Practice

Practice Behavior Example: Analyze, formulate, and advocate for policies that advance social well-being.

Critical Thinking Question: Was AFDC intended to be a poverty alleviation program? What elements of the program facilitated economic mobility?

SSI recipients, made up 74 percent of aged recipients, 57 percent of the blind, and 55 percent disabled. From the time SSI began in 1974 until 1993, the number of recipients increased from 3,216,000 to 5,984,000.[54] Reagan/Bush procedures for SSI were identical to AFDC (discussed next), including retroactive and windfall payments, workfare, and loss of casual or inconsequential earnings, such as from blood donations.

Aid to Families of Dependent Children (AFDC)

AFDC, always the most stigmatized program, received Reagan's harshest cuts. Antiwelfarism took on an even stronger "moralistic" stance against women (and their "fatherless" children). Before Reagan, AFDC served approximately 3.7 million families (about 11 million people), with grants totaling about $14 billion. Of these families, 88 percent were headed by women. AFDC supported 51.7 percent of poor white families and 43.9 percent of poor African-American families. Seven million children, of whom 3 million were under age six, received AFDC grants.[55] During the Reagan administration, the average grant was $1,264.40 per child per year (compared with foster care at $3,753.69 per child per year and $16,712.55 per year for institutionalization).[56] The number of families on AFDC fell by over 300,000 from 1981 to 1982, even though those years constituted the most severe recession since 1929. By 1983, the poverty rate had increased to 15.3 percent, up from 11.7 percent in 1979.[57]

Through OBRA and GRH cuts, cash benefits to over 10.3 million people were cut by 15 percent,[58] based on new assumptions about income:

1. *Assumed income* meant that eligibility workers could assume income, received or not, from stepfathers, court-ordered support from absent parents, Earned Income Tax Credits (EITC) (prorated and deducted from grants each month), and "windfalls"—gifts, insurance benefits, small inheritances (also prorated and deducted).

2. *Allowable assets* were reduced to $1,000 except for a home and a reasonably priced car, one burial plot, one funeral agreement, and marketable real estate (exempt for six months, when repayment from proceeds was expected).

3. Persons above *eligibility caps* were ineligible: in 1981, caps were set at 150 percent of state need levels and increased in 1984 to 185 percent of state need levels.

4. *Age limits for children*, lowered to age sixteen under Reagan, were restored by George H. W. Bush to age eighteen.

5. Eligibility and benefits were determined on *retrospective budgeting* of the previous month's income, prorated at AFDC levels and expected to last as long as AFDC grants even if the client had no money.

6. *New work provisions* eliminated the $30 and a third disregard on earnings, placing an effective 100 percent tax on wages. Previously, people on public assistance could keep the first $30 and another 30 percent of what they earned each month by working. Now there was no benefit incentive to work. Those who lost jobs could not reapply for a year, and work costs were standardized regardless of real costs of transportation, tax deductions, meals, union dues, and so on: $75 for full-time and $50 for part-time work, $160 a month for each child's care.

7. *Other regulations* included reporting of casual income, such as tips or blood donations; immigrants' sponsors income counted as applicant's income for three years; deduction of some vendor payments such as food stamps; pregnancy care moved from first to third trimester; pregnant women were expected to work until the sixth month; state option for emergency AFDC could be provided while applications were being processed.

8. AFDC for the Unemployed Parent (AFDC-UP) was allowed at state option.

The results of the $30-and-a-third disregard reduction immediately eliminated many working women from AFDC with less than a month's notice. Also, depending on state regulations, they lost Medicaid and food stamp benefits.

Forty percent of all AFDC recipients who left the program had incomes below poverty levels for at least the following year, according to a study by Zinn and Sarri. A quarter of their respondents said they had run out of food at least seven times in the year after having lost benefits, and half at least once. A major problem was the loss of Medicaid: Poor people are not healthy people, and in this sample, typical of the poor, one in seven had serious chronic illnesses such as cancer, diabetes, epilepsy, hypertension, sickle cell anemia, and arthritis/rheumatism.[59]

The Family Support Act (FSA) of 1988

Although these laws changed the *processes* of AFDC, Reagan's 1988 legislation changed its *structure*. No longer a program aimed at supporting children and women's roles in the home (however punitive the regulations), AFDC now became a work ethic program in which women and men were required to "pay back" their welfare grants by working or participating in activities oriented to future work (education and training). This most significant change removed from poor women—at least those on public assistance—all assumed roles as mothers, replacing them with worker roles formerly applied only to men.

FSA 1988 embodied the sexual morality and work ethic values of the Religious Right. It aimed first to decrease AFDC rolls by changing recipient behaviors and second to intensify pressure on clients, their families, and state/local agencies to get off the welfare rolls and into work. The law included provisions for education, training, and employment, including subsidies for expenses, child care provisions, and transitional support as families moved from welfare to work and child support enforcement provisions. It required states to implement AFDC for Unemployed Parents (AFDC-UP) by October 1990, and every single parent (with children over age three or one, at state discretion) or at least one parent in intact families had to participate in work or training programs. There were exemptions: those caring for children under age three or without good day care; the ill, incapacitated, or elderly or those caring for such; people working, attending school, or in the second or third trimester of pregnancy; and those for whom states could not provide Job Opportunity and Basic Skills (JOBS) programs, the Community Work Experience Program (CWEP), or on-the-job training (OJT).

The new idea of "case management" developed under FSA 1988 as welfare workers developed contracts with recipients for their future careers. Those who refused contracts or work programs could lose AFDC eligibility. Recipients who volunteered for JOBS, which replaced WIN, got first chance at the program. JOBS was capped at $600 million in 1989, based on states' previous WIN costs and Medicaid federal matching rates. Child care costs were outside the cap, reimbursed at federal Medicaid matching rates, and states were required to provide day care for every AFDC recipient in the JOBS program. JOBS included basic and remedial education, job skills training, job readiness programs, job search, and job development and placement services, or, at state discretion, school, vocational, technical training, or JTPA programs.

CWEP was the fallback program, requiring recipients to work off their grants. CWEP-eligible people who worked received the same grants as exempt people or those for whom no work was available; in other words, they worked for nothing. "Workfare," sometimes called "slavefare," was justified on grounds such as the need to learn a skill, get off welfare, and get into employment, as well as the notion that no one should get "something for nothing."

Child Support Enforcement Provisions revised the Child Support Enforcement Amendment of 1984, tightening up Title IV.D. (Notice to Law Enforcement Officials, or NOLEO). FSA 1988 instituted the Commission on Interstate Child Support to revise the Uniform Reciprocal Enforcement of Support Act, which traced and returned nonpaying parents across state lines and allowed immediate wage withholding of delinquent support. This instituted processes for collection of support from absent parents through written warnings, reports to credit agencies, garnishment of wages, civil and criminal charges, seizure of federal and state income tax refunds, property liens, seizure and sale of property, and bond-posting by the absent parent. FSA produced a particularly important change: It required judges and other officials to establish statewide standards for amounts and collection of child support. Former discretionary awards were no longer legal. Periodic review and adjustment of child support grants were required every three years in AFDC cases. FSA required states to set up 50 percent paternity establishment quotas, to increase by 3 percent every year after 1991, the federal government to pay up to 90 percent of the lab costs. "Paternity establishment quotas" meant that the welfare departments had to establish a certain number of named fathers for each child per year. Fifty dollars of any recovered support was disregarded for grant levels and Medicaid continued for four months for children losing AFDC because of increased child support payments. Despite the intent of FSA, support collection remained low.

Other provisions of FSA 1988 stipulated that minor children who were pregnant or mothers had to live with a state-appointed adult, such as a parent, legal guardian, foster parent, or other adult relative. An important provision, used extensively by the first President Bush, was the waiver of AFDC regulations to establish demonstration programs. Some states cut benefits if a child did not attend school, froze benefits if the client had another child while on welfare, restricted access to general assistance, paid to have the contraceptive Norplant embedded, encouraged marriage by paying higher benefits to married couples, paid recipients to move to higher-benefit states, or required school attendance or even marriage for unwed mothers on AFDC.

FSA 1988, despite its punitive intentions and results, explicitly acknowledged that states could no longer overlook child care needs. It also beefed up child support mechanisms, required statewide standards for child support, and established AFDC-UP for intact families. In retrospect, although none of these positives worked well, primarily because of lack of state resources, they constituted substantive changes in AFDC legislation. Unfortunately, the moral issues they involved became more important than the substance, and morality became the guideline for what was to follow.

BASIC NEEDS PROGRAMS

Reaganomics and Nutrition

The AFDC program provided more food on a regular basis than most poor people would otherwise have had, and the cuts it underwent threw millions into hunger. Beyond that, a major target of Reaganomics cuts was nutrition programs: food stamps, school meals, and nutrition for women and children.

Food Stamps

By 1982, *almost 8 million people* of the 22 million receiving food stamps lost their eligibility under the Reagan cutbacks. Fifty-four percent were children under age eighteen, and 78 percent were unable to work because of age, disability, or dependent care. New eligibility regulations totally excluded strikers and temporarily unemployed workers and eliminated more than 200,000 students, leaving an estimated 50,000 students still eligible. These cuts "saved" the government an estimated $7 billion but took their toll in human well-being, because with food stamps households bought 50 percent more food than they would otherwise.

Almost 70 percent of food stamp families were headed by women. In 1980, the average monthly food stamp allowance per person was $34.34, or about 44 cents a meal. Even if this amount—an average of $1,638—were added to a family's annual income, it would still fall about $960 below the poverty threshold.[60] In 1988, after much damage had already been done, Congress passed the Hunger Prevention Act, which increased food stamp allotments, increased access to food stamps for the homeless (who had been denied because they did not have addresses), and allotted federal funds for outreach to the hungry. Food stamps were also made available, at state discretion, at banks or post offices or through the mail.[61]

School Lunch Program

The government's largest child nutrition effort, the school lunch program, suffered Reagan *cuts of 30 percent*, dropping 3 million children. In 1982, despite the cuts, it still served 23.6 million children at a cost of $2.9 billion. However, prices were raised, thereby eliminating many children marginally able to buy lunches, and the quantity and quality of the lunches was lowered dramatically. Lekachman says,

> In the new order, pickle relish and catsup count as vegetables, jam masquerades as a serving of fruit, cookies and cakes define themselves as bread, and the egg in the cake substitutes for meat. A hearty lunch for an adolescent might be two slices of cheese, one-fourth of a cup of grape juice, one cupcake, a cup of whole milk (four, not eight ounces), and a quarter cup of canned peaches.[62]

Until 1981 the goal of this program was to provide one-third of a child's daily nutritional needs, and the Department of Agriculture concluded that poor children got one-third to one-half of their daily nutrition from school lunches.

In response to public outrage, the administration withdrew the changes in school lunch standards, but they crept back as school lunch sizes decreased and costs increased. The school breakfast program, a supplemental program usually carried out by community groups or agencies with surplus commodities, some federal funding, and private donations, now reached only about one-third of eligible children, while the summer lunch program reached only 16 percent.

The Women, Infants, and Children Nutrition Program (WIC)

WIC also suffered *a 30 percent reduction.* It had been available, at the option of state departments of public welfare and local charitable agencies, to provide supplementary food grants for women during pregnancy and children to age four. All monies except for administration costs came from the federal government, and the only regulation, aside from means-tested eligibility, was that a local agency administer the program. Numerous counties throughout the nation refused to include WIC programs in their social offerings, thereby limiting the use of WIC in any case. Nationally, only 2.4 million—fewer than half of those eligible—received WIC food (valued at an average of $378 per year) in 1983.

Yet even that small amount markedly reduced the incidence of low birth weight, with results in savings for long-term care estimated at three dollars for every dollar spent. The cost of WIC was about a dollar a day per recipient. The Center for Disease Control found that WIC reduced anemia in infants and helped to prevent retarded physical growth, susceptibility to contagious diseases, and mental retardation. The nutrition WIC provided was estimated to save $20,000 to $40,000 each in remedial care for low-birth-weight infants, $1,400 a week for hospitalization for undernourished children, and between $0.5 million and $1 million over a lifetime for children requiring institutional care for retardation.[63]

Hunger is an ever-present problem for millions in the United States today. It is not only a statistic: it is real and painful. In a recent book, a woman confides,

> I keep praying I can have the will to save some of my food so I can divide it up and make it last.... On Friday, I held over two peas from the lunch. I ate one pea on Saturday morning. Then I got into bed with the taste of food in my mouth and I waited as long as I could. Later on in the day I ate the other pea.
>
> When there are bones I keep them... I am almost ashamed to tell you, but these days I boil the bones till they're soft and then I eat them. Today there were no bones.[64]

Reaganomics and Health Care

Public health care programs included Medicare, Medicaid, temporary disability insurance, worker's compensation, general hospital and medical care, armed forces and dependents care, school health, other public health activities, veterans' hospital and medical care, medical vocational rehabilitation, and OEO health and medical care. In addition, many private agencies provided health care: nursing homes, the Visiting Nurses Association, extended care homes, and so on. Public funds paid $144,204,000 for health care in 1983, with another $202,921,000[65] in private care. Federal costs of health care in 1991 were $204.1 billion, while state and local care was $79.1 billion.[66]

Under OBRA, Medicare and Medicaid underwent significant changes, and four block grants replaced a variety of programs. Block grants included Alcohol, Drug Abuse, and Community Mental Health; Preventive Health Services; Community Mental Health Centers; and Maternal and Child Health Services.

Medicare

In 1984, at the same time Social Security cost-of-living increases were cut, the Medicare deductible rose to $400 from $356, and recipients had to pay everything over $100 (up from $89) per day from the 61st to 90th day and everything above $200 a day, up from $178, for lifetime reserve days. The basic premium rose from $14.60 to $17.90 per month (an increase of 15.5 percent) as of January 1, 1987. Medicare payments to hospitals were frozen for all of 1986, and physicians' payments were frozen through March 1986. As a result, the elderly got less care or had to pay more from their own income for medical services.[67] Medicare provided services for 30.5 million people during the Reagan years, with costs of $63.1 billion that rose another $10 billion the next year, the first year of the George H. W. Bush administration, 1989.

Medicaid

Along with the raising of Medicaid eligibility limits, cutting many poor people off Medicaid, the program itself underwent structural changes and funding cuts. After Reagan took office, all states cut back on matching funds, in turn allowing massive federal cutbacks. As eligibility for AFDC and SSI was cut, so was eligibility for Medicaid, and 700,000 children were thrown off. State options were reduced: Children in poor non-AFDC families who had been covered until age eighteen (twenty-one if still in school) were only covered to age five. A report from the Congressional Budget Office in 1983 estimated costs for Medicaid for three years at $520 million—about half the estimate of Defense Department annual waste from inefficient spare parts procurement.[68] In addition, OBRA made changes in Medicaid that enhanced states' abilities to limit benefits and deregulated prices for many services.[69]

Maternal and Child Health Program

The Maternal and Child Health Program, Title V of the Social Security Act, suffered a 47 percent cutback when it was placed into an OBRA block grant even though there was an 84 percent increase in demand related to high unemployment. The grant collapsed seven programs into one: Basic Maternity and Infant and Child Health Care, Crippled Children's Services, services for children with disabilities on SSI, lead-poisoning prevention, sudden infant death syndrome, genetic screening and hemophilia treatment services, and adolescent pregnancy programs.

The funding cuts were particularly devastating for pregnant women. Maternal and Child Health Services block grant programs served 17 million children and pregnant women in 1981. After OBRA, there was a severe reduction in prenatal care and an increase of death rates for all infants between 1981 and 1982. The death rate of infants in Washington, D.C., for example, exceeded that in Cuba and Jamaica.[70] In Florida alone, only 38 percent of 65,000 pregnant low-income women got comprehensive prenatal care, and in Michigan 10,000 of 140,000 delivering mothers had fewer than five of twelve recommended prenatal visits after OBRA.[71]

Babies whose mothers receive no prenatal care are three times more likely to suffer low birth weight and greater risks of birth defects and death. According to Raymond Wheeler,

> We can document decreases in illness, in infant and maternal deaths, in premature births, and in the incidence of iron deficiency anemia and retarded growth among children of the poor ... these reductions in illness

and death have accrued most significantly by women, blacks, and American Indians, and in the ten states with the highest incidence of poverty and malnutrition.[72]

The U.S. infant mortality rank fell from sixth place to a tie for last place among the twenty industrialized nations as nearly 40,000 of the 3.6 million babies born in 1984 died before their first birthday. African-American babies suffered twice the toll of white babies.[73]

Such cuts make no ethical or even financial sense, because the cost of care for low-birth-weight or damaged babies is astronomical. States have studied the cost–benefit ratio of health maintenance programs and have generally found that, in the long run, they save money. A Texas study found, for example, that the state saved eight dollars in avoided medical costs for every dollar spent on preventive services, and a North Dakota analysis demonstrated a drop of one-third in Medicaid costs for children who received preventive health care.[74] A $10 cost to immunize against all childhood diseases can save $500,000 to $1 million dollars for children with mental retardation caused by measles. The Center for Disease Control showed that $180 million for measles vaccination saved $1.3 billion in medical care and long-term services for deafness, blindness, and mental retardation.[75] All children up to one year, along with poor pregnant women, could have been covered for about $120 million—roughly the cost of 100 MX missiles and a third of what the federal government spent in 1982 for inspection of animal care facilities to ensure humane treatment.[76]

Alcohol and Drug Abuse Block Grant

In October 1986, Reagan launched a massive new war on drugs, after having taken away 46 percent of drug funding via block grants. His program was to distribute $100 million to state-run alcohol and drug abuse treatment centers, but this did not recoup losses from cuts already made, such as the 25 percent cut in state treatment programs in 1982, through OBRA. The block grant consolidated many programs dealing with drug abuse, alcoholism, rehabilitation, and mental health concerns surrounding substance abuse. The resulting system, the Alcohol, Drug Abuse, Mental Health Administration (ADAMHA), became a program in progress, however, constantly changing and consolidating more programs into its block grant.

A most controversial part of the Reagan war on drugs was the establishment of urine testing for drug detection for federal employees as part of job eligibility. The General Accounting Office (GAO) noted that such testing (for federal employees) was vague, ineffective, and potentially unconstitutional (Fourth Amendment protection against unreasonable search and seizure), with unmeasurable benefits and high costs, yet it has entered society, and nationwide drug testing is not uncommon. A black market in clean urine samples developed to evade drug use detection, and, to overcome this, many businesses required a witness to watch the urine sample being taken.

Housing in the 1980s

According to Rubin and colleagues, in 1970

> there were two low-income housing units ... for each low-income renter household (income below $5000). By 1983, that situation was reversed ... two low-income renter households for each low-income unit ... [and] of the 2 million renters with incomes less than $3000 per year, 86 percent paid more than 60 percent of their incomes for rent.[77]

By 1985, there were 4 million fewer housing units available than renter households needing them.[78] From 1983 to 1987, the number of poor households increased by 300,000 to 7.5 million, yet, even taking inflation into account, the number of units that rented for less than $300 declined by nearly 1 million, in great part lost to disrepair and abandonment. After 1981, the number of new federally assisted housing units being constructed dropped from more than 200,000 to approximately 25,000.[79]

Housing policy under Reagan had two foci. For upper-income groups, tax policies underwrote housing costs through income tax deductions of property taxes and mortgage interest. In fact, these deductions cost the Treasury more in two years, during the Reagan administration, than did the total outlay for subsidized housing over the last half-century.[80] On the other hand, there was an "open market" policy for the poor—in other words, they took their chances on finding housing they could afford. Although Reagan officially endorsed housing allowances, federal subsidy programs for rent were reduced and funds for the maintenance of public housing were cut. During the Reagan years, the budget of the Department of Housing and Urban Development was slashed by 76 percent.[81] Under Gramm–Rudman–Hollings, the Farmers' Home Administration reduced direct loans for rural housing in 1987 to $2 billion, or $91 million less than in 1986 and $1.2 billion (37 percent) less than in 1985.[82]

Cutbacks in housing meant, of course, more homelessness. By 1987, the Department of Health and Human Services estimated that 3 million people were homeless,[83] of whom children were the fastest-growing group.[84] Many of the homeless were former mental patients with little awareness of their rights, although a great number also were those pushed out of work, off the farms, and into the cities by unemployment and consequent loss of their homes. To bring attention to their plight, in 1984 advocacy groups erected tent cities to shelter the homeless (reminiscent of Hooverville) across from Reagan's White House. An estimated 5,000 to 10,000 homeless people in Washington, D.C. fasted until President Reagan agreed to renovate a deserted government building into a model home for the homeless.

Reagan later reneged because the cost estimate was $5 to $10 million. The GAO then developed a lower-cost shelter—four huge barrack-like rooms—grossly unlike the model shelter promised. When homeless advocacy groups protested, the government ordered the homeless once more into the streets.[85] Although shelter was later provided, this demonstrated clearly—in ways that statistics hidden in charts and books could not—the reluctance of the government to provide for those obviously unable to provide for themselves.

The answer to homelessness is to provide homes that people with low incomes can afford. However, the nation seems uninterested in increasing the number of low-cost housing units; rather, short-term shelter has been the response to need. In 1986, $80 million was appropriated for transitional housing, and in 1987 Congress passed an emergency homeless bill—the Urgent Relief for the Homeless Act—of $500 million providing for sleeping rooms and shelters.[86] In 1988, $100 million was authorized, but Congress appropriated only $65 billion, of which $20 million was for transitional housing.[87]

George H. W. Bush took limited leadership in the housing dilemma. Expenditures for HUD in 1990 were $22.8 billion, although only $1.6 billion was targeted for low-income housing programs.[88] He pursued home ownership (Cranston–Gonzalez National Affordable Housing Act) rather than shelter housing, and in 1991 Jack Kemp, Secretary of HUD, developed the Home Ownership and Opportunity for People Everywhere (HOPE) initiative, committing $3.1 billion over two years for the purpose of selling public housing units to tenant management groups.[89] This was as much political as altruistic: One intention was surely to divest the government of ownership, maintenance costs, and overall responsibility for public housing.[90] Despite the growing need, the number of families assisted by HUD, 3.1 million in 1980, grew to only 4.4 million by 1991.[91]

Education and Training

One of Reagan's first acts of office in 1981 was to rescind $440 million in funding for Title I of the Elementary and Secondary Education Act (ESEA). This program, developed especially to serve disadvantaged and handicapped children, had provided compensatory education to minorities and the poor, funding for bilingual education for Hispanic children, and extra services for Native American and African-American children. More than half the children ESEA served before 1981 were children from minority groups: 29 percent African American, 21 percent Hispanic, and 4 percent other groups. New policies subsumed the Emergency School Assistance Act, intended to help schools desegregate, into the new block grant system, which was then cut by 35.3 percent (about $269 million), and desegregation funds were virtually eliminated. Although Head Start continued, the number of children it reached was drastically reduced.

In higher education, Basic Education Opportunity Grants (BEOGs), legislated in 1972, had been a major source of financing for disadvantaged youth bound for college. Among those it served, 70 percent were from low-income households (below $12,000 annual income) and 57 percent were minority students. OBRA severely cut BEOGs (renamed Pell grants), and all college grants, loans, and work–study support became more difficult to get and more costly as loan interest rates rose sharply. Financial aid offices were required to assume that parents would contribute $750 toward students' costs whether or not that money was actually available. Despite the cuts, Pell grants in 1983 provided $2.8 billion to needy students, and for 1984, $4 billion was appropriated for all student aid programs.[92]

Federally guaranteed loans and work–study employment reached 9 million students in 1983, attesting to the level of need even with reductions in funding. However, a great many young people were shunted away from higher education. Bell says that keeping certain people—the poor and minorities—out of school will create an educationally segregated elite and make more people available for the labor market. She adds,

> This is a good illustration of how selective programs can be manipulated to keep poor people poor and to nip aspirations in the bud.[93]

Many young people formerly supported by grants and loans dropped out of school to help their families. Enrollment of African-American students dropped rapidly: In 1980, about 11 percent of college graduates were African Americans, but in the 1984–1985 school year the number declined to 8.8 percent. Although a few top-ranked African-American colleges graduated record numbers, dropout rates at predominantly white schools were abysmal. In graduate and professional schools, African-American enrollment declined by 11.9 percent between 1980 and 1984, and the percentage of African-American faculty and administration, never very large, decreased by 4.3 percent.[94] According to a study by the College Board, federal aid to postsecondary students dropped from $22.2 billion to $20.7 billion in constant dollars after 1980, with the 1988 budget calling for another $2 billion in cuts.[95]

Critical Thinking

Practice Behavior Example: Use critical thinking augmented by creativity and curiosity.

Critical Thinking Question: In the United States, why is there no consensus on the role that government should play in the provision of social services?

CIVIL RIGHTS UNDER REAGAN AND BUSH

The attack on social programs from 1980 forward was paired with an attack on civil rights. Administration policies clearly demonstrated that programs for empowerment or human rights were to be underfunded or withdrawn. Reagan, and later Bush, called for an end to quotas, even though they had never been part of the affirmative action program, and began to talk about the "angry white male" as undergoing "reverse discrimination." Budgets for civil rights enforcement agencies were slashed and civil rights opponents were appointed to the Civil Rights Commission and the Supreme Court. In 1990, the first President Bush vetoed civil rights legislation that might have mitigated such actions and in 1991 appointed conservative Clarence Thomas, an outspoken critic of affirmative action, even though he benefited from it, as Supreme Court Justice.

To recapitulate, the civil rights gained in the two decades preceding the Reagan years included

- The Civil Rights Act of 1957, which established the Justice Department's Civil Rights Division to sue for voting rights
- The Civil Rights Act of 1964, which barred discrimination in public schools, facilities, employment, and federally financed activities
- The Voting Rights Act of 1965, which broadened guarantees of the right to vote
- The Civil Rights Act of 1968, which forbade housing discrimination
- The Educational Amendment of 1972, which made it illegal to discriminate on the basis of sex in schools receiving federal support
- The Rehabilitation Act of 1973, which barred discrimination against people with disabilities
- The Civil Rights for Institutionalized Persons Act of 1980, which gave civil rights protection to prisoners, the mentally ill, and other institutionalized people.[96]

Attacks on civil rights through the courts opened the way to charges of "reverse discrimination" and quota-setting. Although the intent of affirmative action was to redress centuries of institutional inequities, majority people thrust away the historical focus and centered on immediate present effects of affirmative action for individuals. For example, in *Bakke v. Regents of the University of California* in 1978, Bakke charged reverse discrimination and quota-setting because he was denied admission even though his grades were higher than those of people admitted to slots reserved for minority people. The Supreme Court ruled in favor of Bakke, but upheld the university's right to reserve slots for minority students. This decision opened the way for other such court battles and accelerated the trend away from social equity for nonmajority people.

Reagan's personal support for institutional discrimination was clear: He filed a "friend of the Court" brief against a 1983 Supreme Court decision that upheld a Boston decision to fire 700 white workers rather than more recently hired minority workers. The basis for the Court's decision was past discrimination in hiring. The Supreme Court rejected, by close margins, Reagan's argument to limit affirmative action claims to actual victims of past bias. For example, when the Cleveland fire department claimed promotions should not follow racial lines, the Court voted that half of promotions be reserved for qualified minority candidates; in sheetworkers' unions in New York and New Jersey, it provided that nonwhite membership had to be doubled to 29.3 percent by August 1987. Although Reagan encouraged voluntary compliance with fair employment and antidiscriminatory rules, he continued to argue against federal or court intervention in businesses to ensure remedial action. His position rejected class action suits, quotas, numerical affirmative action goals or timetables, and compensation for past discrimination.

Civil rights battles for gays began in earnest in the 1980s and made slow progress, based on First Amendment freedom of speech rights and Civil Rights Act Title VII, which federally prohibits sex discrimination in the workplace. The Reagan administration, enforced by the Moral Majority, validated a moralistic approach to homosexuality even at Supreme Court levels, where antigay Chief Justice Warren Burger held sway. According to Eskridge,

> By treating sex as dirty conduct rather than expression and "homosexuals" as presumptive sodomites rather than citizens, the Burger Court did what it could to preserve the remnants of the 'closet.' "Don't ask, don't tell" sums up the Burger Court philosophy.... While the Court did not require antigay policies, it permitted states to choose such options.[97]

At first, courts circumvented the First Amendment, ruling that homosexuality is conduct—often criminal conduct—rather than speech. On this basis, suppression of gay "subculture"—bars, social gatherings, literature, mailings, and so forth—could not be termed "speech." Gay-bashing, although an assault crime, was not deemed a hate crime. Civil Rights Title VII was for a time bypassed by determining that the rights of "deviants" *should* be controlled. In 1979, the Ninth Court of Appeals ruled (*De Santis v. Pacific Telephone and Telegraph*) against sexual harassment claims (brought by an openly effeminate man, a gay man, and a Lesbian couple) because—splitting numerous hairs to make the case—they were discriminated against not for their *sex*, as prohibited by Title VII, but by their *sexual orientation*.[98]

Since that time, however, courts and the Equal Employment Opportunity Commission (EEOC) have reinterpreted Title VII to make gender *stereotypes* irrelevant to job decisions and to protect workers against sexualized harassment and treatment, though as of 1995, gay and bisexual men still earned 11 to 27 percent less than straight men.[99] About a third of all states have adopted Equal Rights Amendments, and gays have fought and won inclusion in most, and since 1981 an increasing number of states and cities have adopted laws affirmatively protecting gay people against private discrimination and violence.

Funding for civil rights action declined 9 percent from 1981 to 1983, and the budgets for the EEOC and the Office of Federal Contract Compliance Programs (OFCCP) were reduced 10 and 24 percent, respectively. EEOC staff was cut by 12 percent, and OFCCP staff dropped by 34 percent.[100] As a result, the number of employment discrimination cases brought by the EEOC and the Justice Department declined by half during Reagan's tenure, although the number of complaints increased by nearly 50 percent. Cases with "no cause" findings (not guilty of discrimination) increased by a third. OFCCP complaints against government contractors for discrimination in hiring dropped from fifty-three in 1980 to eighteen in 1983, with only five in 1982.[101]

In the Department of Health and Human Services, thirty violations by recipients of federal funds were put on hold rather than pursued.[102] Between 1980 and 1983, there was a 25 percent drop in support for enforcement activities such as class action suits against employers and government contractors.[103] There was little action against civil rights violations in prisons and mental hospitals. In housing, only six fair-housing suits were filed during Reagan's first thirty months in office, compared to forty-six for Carter in the same time period.

In education, Reagan even argued against the long-fought battle for busing to end school desegregation, although the Supreme Court upheld busing in October 1986. In Washington state, when citizens filed a referendum against busing, the Justice Department held that the referendum was racially motivated and therefore unconstitutional, but when Reagan took office this stance was reversed.[104] Moreover, under his tenure, the Justice Department filed only one school desegregation case and delayed release of findings in eighty-six investigations. The number of such investigations by the Department of Education dropped from 10.4 percent in February 1981 to 4.4 percent in January 1982.

In addition to stonewalling efforts *for* civil rights, Reagan supported actions *against* such rights. For example, his administration exempted 300 small colleges from laws barring sex and race discrimination and tried to grant tax exemptions to larger schools practicing discrimination. In one such instance, the Justice Department tried to withdraw a suit from the Supreme Court that would have denied tax-exempt status to the Goldsboro Christian Schools for racial discrimination, and Bob Jones University, which forbade interracial dating and housing. The Supreme Court ruled against the Justice Department in these instances.

The Civil Rights Commission, investigating Reagan's own record of employment, claimed it evidenced sexism and racism:

> [T]hrough the first two years of the Reagan administration, appointments were 8 percent female and 8 percent minority (4 percent black); Carter's appointments were 12 percent female and 17 percent minority (12 percent black).[105]

Rather than respond to the commission's charges, Reagan fired three of its six members and tried to fire two others. He then created a new eight-member commission with members whose civil rights views matched his own.[106]

> **In addition to stonewalling efforts for civil rights, Reagan supported actions against such rights.**

Some gains were made despite the administration's tacit approval of institutional racism, primarily because of the increased education and political action of people of color in earlier decades. The number of elected officials of African descent at all levels of government rose from 1,472 in 1970 to 5,606 in 1983, and numbers of African-American and Hispanic mayors increased, to 248 and 47, respectively.[107] Nevertheless, the move toward civil rights slowed considerably with increasing conservatism in the nation and Reagan's personal involvement in discrimination.

Under the George H. W. Bush administration, a new kind of civil rights became available: The Americans with Disabilities Act (ADA) protects the rights of people with physical, emotional, or mental impairments that limit "one or more major life activities." It

- requires employers to reasonably accommodate qualified applicants or employees with disabilities (unless there is a hardship);
- prohibits state and local governments from discriminating in any program, benefit, policy, or activity;
- requires government agencies with fifty or more employees to identify and change physical and programmatic barriers;
- requires that physical barriers in public facilities be removed, or alternative methods provided;
- prohibits discrimination in public accommodations, although private clubs and religious organizations are exempt;
- requires new transit systems to be accessible and older ones to have one car per train accessible;
- requires special transportation for people with disabilities who cannot use public transportation;
- requires the provision of speech, vision, or hearing equipment to allow equal participation in accommodations or services; and
- requires telephone companies to offer telephone relay services to people with disabilities, although they must buy their own equipment.

Importantly, ADA allowed people with AIDS-related disabilities to claim disability, making them eligible for the many programs heretofore denied them.

THE COSTS OF SOCIAL WELFARE

Estimating Poverty

Some people believe that vendor payments—food stamps, housing subsidies, and Medicaid—should be counted when estimating the poverty rate. However, such calculations are an illusion: Payments actually go to the service provider, not the poor.

> Thus, at market value, an AFDC mother with two children ... "received" an additional $1287 in 1979 because she was covered by Medicaid ... of course she did not receive a dime.... Poor people receive medical services, not income; the latter goes to providers.[108]

In 1982, then, the poverty rate was "reduced" from 11 percent to 9.4 percent because a family of four receiving Medicaid coverage had $547 "released" (or available) to spend on goods other than medical care—an extra $45.58 per month.

However, without the vendor payments the person would either not get the services or take the money needed to pay for them out of food money. It is not really "received" money. Besides, as Ehrenreich says,

> [T]he question of whether 20 million or 34 million or 50 million Americans are "poor" is surely an indecent one; the lowest of these figures is a national scandal.... No matter how poverty is measured, the decline in poverty that began in the sixties slowed and then stopped in the seventies; since 1978, the numbers below the poverty level have steadily risen.[109]

How Much Did Welfare Cost in the Reagan Era?

In 1980, all social programs constituted only 18.7 percent of the gross national product (GNP). All means-tested cash transfers came to $30.1 billion, increasing to $39.9 billion in October 1985, and OASDI payments were $252.7 billion in 1980 and $388.6 billion in 1985. Health and medical care cost $3.9 billion, veterans' benefits $2.6 billion, and education $141.2 billion.[110] Although public assistance (AFDC and SSI) made up only 2.7 percent of the total GNP in 1980, it actually decreased in 1983.[111] By 1984, OASDI and Medicare constituted 35 percent of all social welfare expenditures, at about $220 billion, whereas all costs of public assistance totaled $80 billion.[112]

Individual taxpayers are misled into thinking social welfare programs, particularly public assistance, take the biggest bite from our tax dollars, but in fact the per capita tax cost we each paid for public assistance was about $30.16 per month during the Reagan years. This was more than in earlier years: In 1960, per capita cost was about $1.87 per month, in 1970 about $6.60, and in 1980 $26.01.[113]

Under George H. W. Bush, although expenditures for social programs seemed to expand, the Reagan cuts had slashed many programs beyond repair. What was left was almost the bare minimum, subject to inflation and future cuts even in entitlement programs. Table 12.1 shows social program costs in the middle of the Bush administration.[114]

Table 12.1   Social Welfare Expenditures Under Public Programs, 1991 (billions, current dollars)

	Total ($)	Federal ($)	State/Local ($)	Percentage of Federal (%)	Per Capita
OASI	564	454	111	67	2,196
Public assistance	180	113	67	80	705
Health	69	30	40	63	271
Veterans	33	32	1	43	126
Education	277	19	258	98	1,083
Housing	22	19	3	7	84
Other	20	10	10	87	77
All health and medical	315	213	103	50	1,234
Total	1,165	677	490	58	4,542

Source: U.S. Bureau of the Census, Statistical Abstracts of the United States: 1994 (114th Ed.), Table 572, p. 370.

THE INTERNATIONAL ELEMENT

By the end of his tenure, Reagan had moved away from his warlike stance toward the Soviet Union and overt interference in the internal affairs of nations such as the Dominican Republic. George H. W. Bush moved even further. Anticipating world economic leadership for the United States, he proposed a "New World Order" in which stability depended not on a balance of war power but on cooperation and the "beneficent intervention" of the United States.[115] He envisioned a *Pax Americana*, with the United States setting standards for economic cooperation and becoming the watchdog of world peace. His view of America as the world's peacekeeper became evident in the Gulf War against Saddam Hussein, the Grenada invasion to "save" American students allegedly held there against their will, and in drug wars in Panama. His support of rich Kuwaitis and their oil was economic rather than altruistic, although publicity focused on Saddam Hussein as a worldwide threat. The assault on Grenada seemed to have little meaning except for muscle-flexing, however, and the invasion of Panama appeared to be an interference in the domestic affairs of another nation, although justified as politically necessary. The arrest and trial of General Manuel Noriega, erstwhile President of Panama, on drug import charges, was a strange step, calling into question both the right to interfere in other nations and, because there was some evidence Noriega was employed by the CIA, the whole issue of covert activity.

Nevertheless, by the time the first President Bush left office, America's isolationist perspective had disappeared on the federal level, although it was still present in the minds of workers displaced in the job market by foreign labor. The nation was well under way in becoming wedded to transnational corporate control of the global economy.

CONCLUSION: PAST IDEOLOGY IN A POSTINDUSTRIAL WORLD

There is no doubt that the Reagan and George H. W. Bush administrations made deep inroads on social welfare in the United States. Reagan, with a few strokes of his pen, set back human and civil rights for decades, or perhaps four centuries, depending on one's perspective:

> The president clearly did seek to turn back the social policy clock.... Given his way, the president would have eradicated most of the hallmarks of the Great Society and would have shrunk the social insurance programs to a scope more nearly approximating their New Deal origins. On the civil rights front the president would have scrapped the federal government's role as a "commanding general" in the war for equal opportunity ... broad goals, quotas, and timetables would have been replaced by individual disciplinary action according to rather narrowly interpreted rules.[116]

These reactionary administrations redefined those who disagree with traditionalism as malcontents, deviants, and the un-American. Levitan and Johnson say,

> The inequities and hardships imposed by the Reagan administration's economic and social policies cannot be construed as merely a response

This set the stage for a society whose politicians believe cutbacks in social programs and laissez-faire civil rights are the appropriate way of conducting a county.

to the demands of an angry public. Reagan social welfare policies, founded on right-wing ideology, have never been ratified by the voting public, and they deviate sharply from the American commitment to opportunity and compassion.[117]

Reagan's ostensible attack on big government, Ehrenreich argues, was an attack on the idea that government can or should protect people against the power of corporations, landlords, and merchants. The attack on "entitlement" programs is an assault on the idea that economic well-being is a political right. The attack on the ... legal services program, on affirmative action programs, on laws regulating corporate behavior is an attack on the laws and institutions that enable people to express their rights.[118]

That Reagan only led this attack, and that millions of Americans followed in this battle against justice, is an even more terrifying statement about the state of our society. The George H. W. Bush years solidified what Reagan began simply by not dealing adequately with domestic issues. This set the stage for a society whose politicians believe cutbacks in social programs and laissez-faire civil rights are the appropriate way of conducting a county. Even Democratic President Clinton did not search for a way out of the morass. Rather, despite his rhetoric, he took his cues from the legacy of the Reagan/Bush years: workfare, time-limited public assistance, and personal responsibility for failure (although he seemed to understand the institutional causes and repercussions of this approach). The moral degradation of society appeared likely to continue well into the next century.

The following questions will test your knowledge and understanding of the content found within this chapter. For additional assessment, including licensing-exam type questions on applying chapter content to practice behaviors, visit **MySearchLab.**

1. An example of the morality-based issues in Reaganomics included which of the following?

   a. Stay-at-home mothers who maintained the traditional male/female family roles.

   b. Working mothers who "did it all" and could do so independently of a husband.

   c. Protesting and striking until fair wages were provided to workers.

   d. Embracing the "melting pot" of America which included a variety of cultures and religious beliefs.

2. Reaganomics was primarily defined as:

   a. A demand-side economy where consumer demand controlled the economy.

   b. The belief that keeping a large supply of goods on the market would prompt buying and thus more jobs to support the increased sales activity.

   c. An economic system where taxes generated funds for welfare services, financial support, and resources.

   d. An economic strategy to financially support small businesses and the creation of new businesses which would generate new jobs.

3. Federal funding of services to for-profit agencies such as hospitals and day care centers was part of which system?

   a. Reaganomics

   b. Privatization

   c. CETA

   d. Medicare

4. Quotas led to accusations from "angry white males" claiming what violation?

   a. Reverse Discrimination

   b. Breach of the Civil Rights Act of 1964

   c. Affirmation Action

   d. Privatization

5. A friend with severe hearing loss tells you that he has trouble participating in staff meetings at work because he isn't able to understand most of what is said. What advice would you give him?

   a. He is only protected under the ADA if his disability will not create an unreasonable hardship on his employer.

   b. Hearing loss does not qualify him under the ADA so his employer is not obligated to provide any accommodation for his hearing disability.

   c. He qualifies under the ADA and his employer is obligated to provide a reasonable accomodation so he can participate in staff meetings.

   d. His employer is obligated to provide an accommodation for any ADA-qualified employee regardless of the expense of the accommodation.

6. You are working with a family who is seeking assistance under the Family Support Act of 1988. What is a feature of the program that you need to mention to the family?

   a. Recipients are eligible for only six months of assistance.

   b. Recipients must qualify under specific provisions that include having children under age 3 or being severely ill, elderly, or disabled.

   c. Recipients must pay back 50% of the welfare grant awarded to them within five years.

   d. Recipients of the program are required to "pay back" their welfare grants by working or participating in education or training programs.

7. Analyze how the civil rights laws impacted employment for whites and minority citizens in the United States.

Reinforce what you learned in this chapter by studying videos, cases, documents, and more available at **www.MySearchLab.com**.

Watch and Review

Watch these Videos

* Engaging the Client to Share Their Experiences

Read and Review

Read these Cases/Documents

Jesse Jackson, Common Ground (1988)

Assess Your Knowledge

Go to **MySearchLab** to test your knowledge of key topics in this chapter with topic-specific quizzes. Conclude your assessment by completing the chapter exam.

---

* = CSWE Core Competency Asset

13

The Decline of Social Responsibility

Competencies Applied with Practice Behavior Examples — in This Chapter				
■ Professional Identity	X Ethical Practice	■ Critical Thinking	■ Diversity In Practice	X Human Rights & Justice
■ Research-Based Practice	■ Human Behavior	■ Policy Practice	X Practice Contexts	■ Engage, Assess, Intervene, Evaluate

Times and Events

- **1992:** Bill Clinton elected President; gross federal debt $4.2 trillion; Stewart B. McKinney Assistance Act for the Homeless reauthorized; Carole Moseley-Braun first African American woman elected to U.S. Senate
- **1993:** Clinton stimulus package begins Empowerment/Enterprise Zones; Americorps, College Tax Credits inaugurated; Rodham Clinton Health Security Act fails in Congress; Free Vaccines for Children program (VFC) begins; Jocelyn Elders appointed Surgeon General
- **1994:** "Contract with America" formulated; Clinton Omnibus Crime Bill begins; Head Start reauthorized; School to Work Opportunities Act funded; U.S. Steelworkers of America, UAW, and International Association of Machinists merge
- **1995:** National Home Ownership policy sets up partnerships between HUD and private banking systems; Congress alters tax structure to aid wealthy families; Supreme Court rules that preferential treatment based on race is almost always unconstitutional; Million Man March on Washington D.C. organized by Louis Farrakhan, Nation of Islam leader
- **1996:** PWRORA passes Congress, TANF replaces AFDC and subsumes other assistance programs; Administration for Children and Families (ACF) Department instituted; Children's Block Grant consolidates children's services; Telecommunications Act provides Internet hookups for schools; Defense of Marriage Act (DOMA) passes; Supreme Court rules in *Bush v. Vera* and *Shaw v. Hunt* that using race as a factor in creation of congressional districts is unconstitutional
- **1997:** Balanced Budget Act (BBA) passes, creates surplus; State Children's Health Insurance Program (SCHIP) established; Education IRAs created; Congress prohibits public housing from lowering tenant rents because of TANF loss of income; Clinton formally apologizes for Tuskegee syphilis experiments, forms President's Commission on Race Relations
- **1998:** Supreme Court decision *Oncale v. Sundowner* allows claims for same-sex harassment
- **1999:** Section 8 housing vouchers increased by 103,000
- **2000:** Senior Citizens' Freedom to Work Act passes

CLINTON AND THE REPUBLICAN CONGRESS

The election of President Bill Clinton in 1992 seemed a mandate for reform of the Reagan/Bush legacy of enormous deficit and corporate power; increasing unemployment, crime, and poverty; and the growing polarization of rich and poor. He came to office with three major promises: a crime bill, health care reform, and welfare reform. New anticrime legislation was easy because a bipartisan Congress was already calling for reform, but the National Health Insurance bill failed because of opposition from the increasingly powerful health insurance lobby (and backlash against Hillary Rodham Clinton, who led its development).

Faced with a recalcitrant Congress answerable both to a politically powerful Religious Right and economically forceful transnational corporations, Clinton chose politics over principles and backed away from other promises.

First to go was his promise to end discrimination against gays in the military, although as Commander in Chief of the Armed Forces he could have ordered it. However, his major retreat was in welfare reform. Despite his protestations of care for children, this politically driven president, concerned with upcoming elections, after two vetoes signed the Personal Responsibility and Work Opportunity Reconciliation Acts (PRWORA, 1996) with its pernicious welfare reform bill titled Temporary Assistance to Needy Families (TANF). To the dismay of those who trusted him, he fulfilled his promise to "end welfare as we know it" by ending sixty years of the citizen entitlements established in the Social Security Acts of 1935.

The Reagan tax structure that sent the country spiraling into deficits could not be reversed because Omnibus Budget Reconciliation Acts (OBRAs) and deficit-reduction bills had become part of the legislative structure. Clinton was able to curtail their effects to some extent: When he entered office in 1992, the gross federal debt—the sum of debt held by the public and debt the government owes itself—was $4.2 trillion, mounting at a rate of $1 billion a day. In 1993, Clinton and the Congress enacted a five-year deficit reduction package of spending cuts and higher revenues. By 1995, the rate of growth had slowed to about $800 million a day ($9,600 per second),[1] and by 1998, under the historic 1997 Balanced Budget Act (BBA), the federal budget had a surplus of $69 billion and the federal debt was reduced by over $50 billion.[2] As Clinton set about repairing the budget, he cut thousands from the government workforce, changed the military procurement system to avoid purchase of overpriced goods, and reduced excessive budgets in federal bureaus.[3] He also raised the tax rate for corporations over $10 million by 1 percent (to 35 percent)[4] and closed more than seventy military bases.

The Clinton presidency ended with a reduced national debt and an economic surplus. George W. Bush, elected president under a cloud of questions about the election's validity, continued policies that disenfranchised the poor and benefited the rich, and within months the surplus disappeared into a new recession.

Practice Contexts

Practice Behavior Example: Keep informed, resourceful, and proactive in responding to evolving organizational, community, and societal contexts at all levels of practice.

Critical Thinking Question: Discuss why Clinton did not promote a more generous social welfare agenda.

WELFARE AS WE KNEW IT

The "Contract with America"

Before the 104th Congress, the political pendulum swung to the Far Right, which, in concert with the increasingly powerful Religious Right, created a "Contract with America." The ten-item document was signed by 237 Republican candidates and dedicated to a new moral America (with a balanced budget). In the context of the "Contract," blame for the national deficit was laid not to faulty tax structure or unwise fiscal planning. Rather, it was defined as lack of "personal responsibility" of public dependents, primarily women. With the disintegration of the Soviet Union, our Cold War enemy had disappeared, so we chose a new one for a Colder War: women disattached from men and "choosing" to increase an unneeded surplus labor force by having more children.

The 104th Congress, sworn in midway into the Clinton term (January 1995), was the first Republican-controlled Congress in forty years. Its "Contract with

America," ranging from a balanced budget to the reestablishment of Reagan's "Star Wars" initiative, overtly promised to end social programs and give tax breaks to the wealthy—in other words, to take welfare from the poor and give it to the rich. The "Contract" led the way to the most overtly anti-woman, anti-poor legislation ever passed in the United States.

Whereas previously our sexist, racist, and classist values were mostly unwritten, legislation based on the "Contract" placed them squarely within the legislative structure of American polity. It undermined most programs of the Social Security Acts of 1935, which for sixty years had provided a safety net against catastrophe. "Welfare reform" became "recipient reform" as Congress capped spending, set up even harsher work requirements, and block-granted programs to defederalize them. The savings, supporters claimed, would be applied to the federal deficit. The direction was clear: Take away welfare as we *knew* it and substitute welfare as we had only *guessed* it—support for the wealthy through tax breaks and investments in corporate structures.

The budget-balancing cuts, seven times those of Reagan's first Congress, were far from even-handed. Although means-tested programs were only 25 percent of entitlements, they faced 45 to 62 percent of the cuts. All other programs lost about 1 percent of their funds, but low-income programs lost 13 percent.[5] Cuts or cutbacks included elimination of the summer jobs program, which served about 600,000 poor youth between ages fourteen and nineteen; five Housing and Urban Development (HUD) programs, which provided temporary shelter and social services for some 600,000 homeless people (slashed by 40 percent); the federal education program for disadvantaged elementary school students, reduced by one-sixth (more than $1 billion); and Legal Services, cut by almost one-third and proposed for elimination.[6]

The attack on the poor began in the first hundred days of the 104th Congress. With new political power, it reiterated the elements of the Nixon/Reagan/Bush proposals:

- Privatization: opening public programs to private competition
- Defederalization: moving power from federal to state governments
- Welfare for the wealthy and corporate entities.

In many cases, Congress instituted cuts by denying allocations before legislation was even considered. Casualties of this maneuver included the Environmental Protection Agency, National Labor Relations Board, Occupational Safety and Health Administration, Department of Commerce, Arts and Humanities Endowments, Federal Election Commission, Legal Services Corporation, and Economic Development Agency.[7]

Restructuring Public Assistance: Losing the Safety Net

In the 1990s, there were, on average, fewer than 5 million AFDC households,[8] of which children comprised about 67 percent. Of these children, 60 percent were less than six years old and 13 percent were above the age of eleven, indicating that most AFDC mothers stayed on welfare only while their children were very young. Although a persistent racist myth claimed that most AFDC recipients were African American, only about one-third actually were. In fact, their numbers on AFDC declined during the 1990s, from about 45 percent to about 37 percent. In the mid-1990s about 40 percent of AFDC recipients were white, Hispanics made up 18 percent, and Native Americans made up 1 percent.[9]

AFDC grants were about 38 percent of the poverty line, and the maximum grant in 1995 was $388 per month.[10] The AFDC program cost about 1 percent of the federal budget and about 2 percent of state budgets.[11] There were fewer than three people (2.9)[12] in the average AFDC household, indicating a lower fertility rate than in non-AFDC households. Only about 1 percent were under age eighteen, belying the myth of the excess of teenage single mothers on welfare. On average, mothers had four years of work experience, and only 26 percent relied solely on AFDC for support,[13] receiving some combination of family help, employment, and AFDC. In general, 9 percent received public housing subsidies, 14 percent rent subsidies, and 87 percent food stamps in addition to AFDC. About 50 percent left AFDC within two years, while 85 percent were off the rolls after eight years.[14]

In 1996, President Clinton and the 104th Congress passed the Personal Responsibility and Work Opportunity Reconciliation Act (PRWORA) and its welfare reform bill, TANF. To carry out new welfare laws, Congress established the Administration for Children and Families (ACF) in the Department of Health and Human Services (DHHS). Congress then eliminated AFDC and parts of SSI and the Food Stamp program at the national level, merging them into public assistance block grants and capping the federal share at reduced funding. Capped programs also included housing (HUD and Section 8, public housing, Native American housing, rural loans, rental, repair, farm labor housing) and work programs and training programs under the Family Support Act's JOBS program. The combination of caps and block grants meant an overall reduction in state and federal funding, an elimination of categories of service, and a removal of federal obligations and standards. Because states could use block grants as they chose, some programs were dropped entirely and the money spent at state discretion.

Block-granted food programs received about $59 billion less over four years, replacing the Food Stamp Act (1977), Child Nutrition Act (1966), National School Lunch Act, Emergency Food Assistance Act (1983), Hunger Prevention Act (1988), Commodity Distribution Act of 1987 (although commodities might still be distributed), and the WIC program (one of the truly successful nutrition programs of our time).[15] The Child Protection Block Grant, set to replace foster care, adoption programs, and family preservation and support systems, was vetoed by President Clinton in February 1996. However, the nation's governors met and passed a resolution allowing states to opt for a capped entitlement grant for foster care, adoption, and independent living funds that could then be transferred to other activities, as each state chose.[16]

The new Child Care Block Grant consolidated six programs for public assistance: the Child Care and Development Block Grant (CCDBG), AFDC Child Care services, Transitional Child Care services, the At-Risk Child Care program, the Dependent Care Block Grant, and the Child Development Association Scholarship program. Funding for this block grant was cut by more than $350 million the first year and $2.5 billion over the next five years. An estimated 370,000 children would lose child care assistance by the year 2000 and states could divert up to 20 percent ($400 million) of the grant to other services or eliminate them altogether, because matching requirements were ended.[17]

More established block grants underwent massive cuts, including Community Services grants, Title XX Social Services, Preventive Health programs, and Educational Block Grants. Education was hard hit: Clinton's new Goals 2000 remained unfunded, ESEA was slashed by more than a billion dollars, and poor young people were priced out of college loan programs.

In addition, Head Start, School Improvement Programs, the Safe and Drug Free Schools program, and Summer Youth Employment were cut by millions. Low Income Energy Assistance lost a billion dollars.[18]

HUD lost $6.4 billion, almost a fourth of its budget, meaning that tenants would pay an average of $83 a month more for subsidized housing even though public assistance was cut by $800 million. Family planning clinics lost $193 million in the face of a drive against out-of-wedlock parenthood.[19] All programs for aliens, except refugees and those over age seventy-five, were cut except for medical emergencies (though later some were restored). All told, domestic spending for human resources was cut by $101.1 billion, of which $65.4 billion came from programs that provided cash or in-kind benefits to families.[20]

The Structure of TANF

TANF was a comprehensive (and bipartisan) plan to rid the United States of responsibility for the poor...

TANF was a comprehensive (and bipartisan) plan to rid the United States of responsibility for the poor by demanding work for a time-limited period: two years for any one stay on assistance, with a five-year lifetime maximum. TANF replaced AFDC programs and the Job Opportunity and Basic Skills (JOBS) program of Reagan's Family Support Act (1988) and ended all entitlements to public assistance. Monies equivalent to each state's fiscal year (FY) 1994 allotment for these programs, along with monies gleaned from other program cutbacks, were given to states as block grants. For economically troubled states, TANF had a $2 billion federal matching contingency fund; and its Rainy Day Loan Fund had $1.7 billion to loan to states on a revolving basis. It also had a "performance" bonus of $1 billion over five years which gave states more money if they cut more recipients per year than their quota, and an "illegitimacy reduction" bonus fund of $20 million a year from 1999 to 2002 to be divided each year among the five states with the greatest success in reducing out-of-wedlock births without increasing abortions.

Along with the conservatism that swept PRWORA through Congress was the strong belief—common in the late 1880s and part of our public assistance heritage—that local administration served to better control the poor. "Devolution" was, therefore, a prominent aspect of TANF: Administration first devolved to states, territories, and tribes; then to counties, and at times even to cities, communities, or organizations. Each state, territory, or tribe determined its own eligibility and benefit levels, and each had to spend 80 percent of their FY 1994 budget (called "maintenance of effort," or MOE) or be penalized dollar for dollar. MOEs were reduced to 75 percent if states met work quotas: 25 percent of caseloads either working or off the rolls by FY 1997, 50 percent by 2002. Program administration could cost no more than 15 percent of the block grant, and, at state discretion, up to 30 percent of the block might be transferred to the CCDBG, with 10 percent available to the Social Services Block Grant, which provides services to children and families with income up to 200 percent of poverty.

Block grant monies were used for any plan that furthered TANF purposes, allowing local entities such as counties or community entities to administer new or old programs. With devolution, counties (or other entities) submitted their plans to "partner" with the state, setting goals for developing job placements, job training programs, and educational arrangements. States could accumulate unspent TANF funds, and both 1997 and 1998 showed low levels of expenditures, probably due to uncertainty about allowed flexibility. Final regulations were released in 1999, after which most states spent more, investing in a wide range of services such as transportation, child care, job training, substance abuse treatment, and so on.

With the advent of TANF, state public assistance rolls diminished drastically. By 1999, 2.4 million families received cash assistance, a 52 percent reduction from the early 1994 level of 5 million. Federal and state expenditures for cash assistance benefits in FY 1999 totaled $12.4 billion, or $10.6 billion less than in FY 1994. Since PRWORA specified that funding remain at 1994 funding levels, available federal funding remained stable. The annual TANF allocation was $16,500 million, and supplemental grants in 1999 totaled another $161 million.[21]

Basically, TANF required that, within a twenty-four-month period of cash aid, adult recipients engage in either work preparation, work training, or education (with some restrictions) or in employment to take them off public assistance rolls. Any assistance required parents to work or be in a work-related activity. If not, benefits to them and their children could be eliminated at state discretion. Whether or not they found work, after twenty-four months their TANF grants ended for them and their children. States could readmit clients after a time they (the states) set, but recipients could only receive grants for a maximum of sixty months (lifetime limit). In addition, states had the option to give noncash aid or vendor payments after TANF grants ended and might exempt up to 20 percent of their caseload from the twenty-four-month rule.

At the federal level, TANF had various rules and exemptions: employment and training might or might not be TANF subsidized; job search and job skills training counted for only up to six weeks before the twenty-fourth month limit set in; vocational training put off the time count for only twelve months. Allowable work activities included subsidized or nonsubsidized work in the public or private sector, community work experience, on-the-job training, satisfactory attendance at secondary school, and provision of child care services to other TANF recipients. Teenage mothers had to live with parents or responsible adults and be engaged in high school or GED education to receive aid; convicted felons and known drug abusers might be denied cash aid, though their children received grants. States had to provide child care if they demanded work, and they could not penalize mothers for nonwork if child care was unavailable.

Single parents were required to be in work-related activity for twenty hours each week the first year and for thirty hours per week by 2002. Two-parent families worked thirty-five hours per week. Each TANF client had an Individual Responsibility Plan (IRP) agreeing to send children to school; immunize them; cooperate with child support enforcement in determining paternity; give to TANF any support payments they received (up to their TANF grant level); and engage in education, training, and job placement services as required by the state. TANF cut Medicaid, SSI, and food stamps for illegal and legal aliens. However, the Balanced Budget Act (BBA) of 1997 restored aid to legal aliens, though at lower rates.

States had great latitude in designing their welfare-to-work programs. For example, some states penalized parents if children were absent from school, some required teenage mothers to marry the fathers of their children, some waived time limits or residency requirements in cases of family violence, and so on. Some allowed two-year postsecondary education to count as training. Some states imposed family caps, refusing to increase grants for children born while mothers were recipients. (Studies of the family cap in New Jersey indicated little connection between fewer children and the cap, probably in part because the increase was so low [about $67].) However, the number of abortions rose.

Privatization of welfare functions was also part of state plans. As an example, Florida contracted with Lockheed-Martin IMS to provide all welfare functions, from eligibility determination to job training and placement, in three Florida counties. Lockheed had already won contracts to provide limited services to TANF clients in twenty-one Florida counties.[22]

Support from Absent Parents

Support from absent parents remained an ongoing issue. In 1990, children received only $14 billion of the $48 billion owed, and despite the Child Support Recovery Act of 1992, which made it a federal crime to fail to pay child support across state lines, only $15 billion of absent parents' $50 billion obligation was collected. In 1992, the average yearly amount collected for AFDC families by support agencies (Title IV-D) was $2,695 for AFDC families and $3,258 for non-AFDC families.[23]

The Clinton administration made support collection a priority. Clinton, using his executive authority, directed the Treasury Department to offset child support debts against most federal payments, such as income tax returns. He ordered federal agencies to deny parents who were in arrears loans, loan guarantees, and loan insurance. Clinton also implemented the Federal Case Registry and National Directory of New Hires to track nonpayers across state lines (3.5 million delinquent parents found by 1999) and implemented paternity-establishment regulations denying public assistance to women who would not name the fathers of their children. He also required all federal job hires to comply with child support enforcement. His Deadbeat Parents Punishment Act (1998) set up multi-agency task forces to track nonpayers who crossed state lines to avoid child support, making such activity a felony.[24] Clinton's efforts doubled absent parents' collections from 1992 to 2000. Still, about 29.2 percent of those who received child support remained in poverty, and about 10 percent of welfare families—those perched between eligibility for TANF and the poverty level—became ineligible for even TANF's meager benefits.[25] By 1998, resources for child support enforcement were increased by 53 percent, and in 1999 Clinton's budget allocated $3.2 billion to support enforcement programs.[26]

Jail sentences remained the most popular penalties for nonsupport at state levels. Other penalties at both state and federal levels included garnishment of wages, seizing of income tax refunds and property, and revoking of drivers', professional, and trade licenses. DNA and blood testing was used to determine paternity, and a Parent Locator System based on social security numbers was established, along with a more stringent Interstate Enforcement Agreement.

Ethical Practice

Practice Behavior Example: Apply strategies of ethical reasoning to arrive at principled decisions.

Critical Thinking Question: Discuss the conflicts between the provisions in TANF and social work values.

Child Care

Given the welfare-to-work imperative, funding adequate child care was a major problem in carrying out TANF's work requirements. Thirteen million children, including 6 million infants and toddlers,[27] were already in child care before TANF. Work requirements meant that the children of the estimated 3 million TANF recipients soon to enter the labor force would need child care. However, good child care was scarce: Responsible parents would not want their children in most. In 1995, six of every seven centers gave mediocre to poor care and one in eight jeopardized children's safety and development. Eighty percent of states required no credentials or training for child care staff, and in 1997 only 6 percent of child care centers were accredited by the National Association for the Education of Young Children. Home care was little better: In 1994, one in three homes providing care could have conceivably hindered children's development. Forty percent of placements for infants and children under age three had care poor enough to endanger their health, safety, and development.[28]

Child care is, of course, extremely expensive. Families earning less than $14,400 spend 25 percent of their income for child care, with annual costs of $4,000 to $12,000 for preschoolers and infants.[29] Still, some help was available. Congress promised to maintain its appropriations of $2.3 billion for the already established Social Services Block Grant, although it cut each year's appropriation for the next three years and provided only $1.7 billion each for 2000, 2001, and 2002. Under PRWORA, Congress expanded the Act for Better Child Care, passed in the late 1980s, to become the Child Care and Development Block Grant (CCDBG), with about $2.3 billion a year funding. CCDBG authorized $20 billion to the states from 1997 to 2002 and added discretionary monies from the Child Care and Development Fund (CCDF), totaling $4.6 billion for each year.[30] Other resources included free Head Start programs, which enrolled 800,000 children in 1997. States could supply additional funds, including up to 30 percent of their TANF grants, and TANF would match states' individual day care funds up to $600 million. In addition, the Child and Dependent Care Credit (CDCC) of $2.8 billion a year, along with Earned Income Tax Credit (EITC), was available to working families who made enough money to have tax liabilities, and about half of all states offered state tax credits.

Still, although child care resources benefited an average of 1.8 million children each month, another 15 million were waiting for adequate child care. Only 12 percent of eligible children received federally funded child care in 1999. In FY 2002, twenty-eight states still had waiting lists or had frozen applications.[31] Rationing was normal: Full-time rather than part-time care was supported and TANF "leavers" were guaranteed preference, with others placed on waiting lists until there was enough money to cover them.[32] TANF required mothers to work; it also required states to provide child care. However, half the states did not, so to that extent TANF has failed both the grand plan and TANF recipients. When child care could be provided, parents generally received certificates or vouchers from their states' CCDBG to pay child care providers in care centers or family day care, or caregivers in the family's home. Some states reimbursed providers directly through contracts, in addition to offering certificates to families. In 1997, states spent almost $98 million on improving the quality of child care services—teacher training programs, health and safety improvements—about the required 4 percent of their block grants.[33]

Another question, of course, concerns society's right to deprive children of parental love and support. Without a qualm, TANF sends to work the only parent in one-parent families and tries to place children in inadequate, often dangerous child care situations. Thayer says,

> This ... approach [destroys] the tradition that full-time parenting, by rich or poor, is socially useful. Welfare reform obviously seeks to separate poor single mothers from children, either during the work day or forever. The costs of child care will probably justify shoving welfare children into assembly-line and profit-making orphanages ... [or] foster homes....[34]

What was our real goal in this effort?

Certainly TANF saved money for the government and for taxpayers. But consider that public assistance cost only about 1 percent of the federal budget anyway. A change in federal priorities, say at the corporation level, could easily make up for 1 percent. Of course, money was not really the issue, nor was it the reason for TANF. Those can only be found in our societal values.

The Place of Values in TANF

Throughout history, a surplus worker population threatening traditional patriarchal beliefs has led to concerted attacks on women, their sexuality, and their production of children.

Throughout history, a surplus worker population threatening traditional patriarchal beliefs has led to concerted attacks on women, their sexuality, and their production of children. This appeared in early conquest and colonization from 6000 B.C.E. forward, the "witch" burnings of the fourteenth century, America's colonization, and the rape and murder of women in tribal wars of the 1990s in Serbia and Bosnia, for example, and the Hutus and Tutsis in Africa. In America it took the guise of a "Contract," taking food from children to punish their mothers for sexuality—the bearing of children either out of wedlock or as public dependents. Note the misogynistic wording of the Personal Responsibility Act's mission statement (H.R. 4). The intent of Congress is

> To restore the American family, reduce illegitimacy, control welfare spending, and reduce welfare dependence.[35]

"Restoring the family" means a forced return to monogamous marriage for women, "reducing illegitimacy" places the responsibility for the conception of children solely on women, "control welfare spending" threatens the withholding of subsistence to women and children, and "reducing welfare dependency," gives stringent but inauthentic work requirements (because no jobs are available) and indicates that it does not matter whether women cannot find means of support: After two years of public assistance, they and their children will be "thrown away."

The Religious Right helped to define the act, demonstrating its intimate connection with the political economy of oppression. The act's two major thrusts were Puritan (sexual) morality for women and the work ethic for adult recipients, most of whom are women. As Ehrenreich says,

> [T]he welfare mother makes an ideal scapegoat for the imagined sins of womankind in general. She's officially manless, in defiance of the patriarchal norm.[36]

The first thrust of TANF was that women on public assistance (particularly unwed teen mothers) did not take "personal responsibility" for having children. They then became public dependents, and, by extension, created and maintained the massive federal deficit. This hyperbole was used to promote the ideas of both the government's decreasing social responsibility to the poor and its increased financing of welfare for the wealthy. Furthermore, the loss of public support for children was also their mothers' fault: Because they did not take "personal responsibility" for their sexual activities in producing children, they became "personally responsible" when their children went cold and hungry. Moreover, their lack of "responsibility" saddled the "moral" (working, married) public with a monstrous budget deficit, so that the public pays for their "sins."

There are strange conceptual gaps here, one of the first being that the cost of AFDC, at about 1.5 percent of the federal budget ($22.3 billion of $1.5 trillion) is hardly enough to send the government into bankruptcy. However, an even stranger gap in the mission is that there is little mention of the "personal responsibility" of men in impregnating women, becoming fathers, and supporting their families (except that paternity must be proved before women can receive public assistance). Conception is not parthenogenic: Men share the responsibility by half.

Another hiatus in thinking is to deny the complicity of adult men in teenage pregnancy. In fact, the fathers of most children born to teenage mothers—at least 51 percent—are generally over the age of twenty-one. Moreover, many such pregnancies are not chosen by teenagers: Girls under the age of eighteen are the victims of about half of the nation's rapes each year, and as many as 65 percent were victims of sexual abuse in their childhoods. Teenagers who have out-of-wedlock pregnancies, on the average, were less than ten years old at the time of the first abuse, and the offending male was twenty-seven.[37]

The solutions Congress offered were, not strangely, patriarchal in nature and oriented to control by men, relatives, or other authorities. First, unwed teenagers—even rape victims, in some states—were refused grants unless they married (either the fathers or men who would adopt—it appeared that any man would do). Next, they were required to live with parents or other adults, ignoring the fact that about 65 percent of unwed teens do remain with adults. Ancillary services for housing were denied. New monies were provided for "special homes" where unwed pregnant teens would receive "close supervision" to keep them moral, and for adoptions, foster care, and orphanages to take their children from them to placements more conducive to raising children with good middle-class values.

TANF is clearly punitive, for fear of losing their children has been a control mechanism for women public dependents for centuries. Its bases are punishment of women and control of the upbringing of children to be "moral" adults. Congress's "solutions" actually could be traced back centuries: girls being "married off," relatives taking responsibility for "wayward" girls, institutions for the "sexually immoral" who became pregnant (penitentiaries or almshouses), orphanages or fostering-out of children to teach them to live like "moral" people, and, of course, denial of subsistence to women with dependent children. Intentions are clear: Women need to be controlled from their first onset of sexuality and the penalty for being "uncontrolled" might be starvation and homelessness. Although we do not say "death," as with women the colonial fathers drove into the forest to die, we "out of sight, out of mind" such women—what happens to them is their "personal responsibility," not ours.

Women do not have babies to access the minuscule amount they could receive from public assistance. Therefore, to believe that ending public assistance will end out-of-wedlock pregnancy—especially because most unwed mothers do not receive public assistance—is extremely naïve. Or, perhaps, it is not naïve at all to incite the public in order to hide what is really happening. At best, denying assistance to poor families will send them into less legal channels to support their children or, before that happens, it will increase abortions. At worst, it will starve children, send them into the streets to die or be killed, or increase their alienation and hostility to the affluent society that has denied them the rights of citizenship. More than that, it will demonstrate to us all that social morality no longer has a place in the United States.

The second thrust of TANF was the issue of work. According to TANF, it "is the intent of Congress to help, cajole, lure, or force adults off welfare and into paid employment": in other words, to *require* them to accept jobs or lose their eligibility for assistance. To accomplish this, Congress placed a two-year one-time and five-year lifetime limit on receiving assistance, cut job subsidies and job training after two years, and required job participation and day care placement for children over age one. Given the reduction of jobs and wages in our economy, expecting women to support themselves totally after two years was simply another sleight of hand to ease the public conscience. Obviously, work, work training, and workfare are meant to punish, reform, and control rather than to provide legitimate routes off the welfare rolls. Moreover, as in other such programs, those most likely to find jobs anyway are "creamed," leaving a hard core of people with few skills and no support—social Darwinism at its best.

We know from past experiences—from the 1960s forward—that job training programs are ineffective and enormously expensive. An example from Texas: In 1994 $1.6 billion was spent on workforce training, half of which was paid for by the state. However, in a program where a thousand employees helped recipients in jobs and job training, only thirty-one recipients actually got training, a ratio of more than thirty workers for each recipient trained. The General Accounting Office reported that the federal government spent more than $25 billion per year on 154 work assistance or development programs administered by fourteen agencies—an average of $156 million for each agency.[38]

It is unrealistic to believe that two years of job training could address the problems of poverty in the United States. Training and retraining, particularly when funds for those tasks are cut to the bone, will not replace jobs destroyed because of new technologies or those moved to other countries. The fact is that we have a surplus worker population that, in general, will be limited to much lower income than what they earned over the past fifty years. Nor could we rely on the growing number of service jobs, because they do not produce enough income to take people from poverty. We must look at work in a different light—*productivity beyond income*—because no matter how heavily we flagellate those who cannot find work, they cannot find what does not exist.

Our society needs new definitions for work. The idea of income-producing labor as a moral stance grew from the needs of a ruling elite from about the fourteenth century. This has both blocked our perception on the importance of other productivity, such as raising children, and served to maintain a compliant workforce to further benefit that elite. As William Raspberry says,

> It is no longer necessary for everybody to work to produce the things we need, [nor] to look at open-ended economic growth as the main solution to our social ills ... [nor] to think of full employment as an achievable (or even desirable) goal.... [According to Jeremy Rifkin, we need] a full-fledged debate on how to have productivity gains so that everybody is better off ... [a new] social good.[39]

Our expectation of income-producing work for every person is anachronistic and serves to punish people, demoralizing them into alienation and apathy until they believe in and act on their "sins." However, we continue to demand workfare for the poor even though their work is unneeded and unavailable.

According to a study by the Center for Study of Policy Attitudes, Americans in general still believe it is the responsibility of the government to care for the poor. Eighty-four percent said that society has a moral obligation to help the poor and 85 percent said the government should create jobs for those who want to work. Ninety-two percent felt that a reduction in poverty would be a good investment and 73 percent said it would reduce racial tension and crime. In addition, 58 percent said the wealthy should pay more to finance care for the poor.[40]

Other polls conducted in the late 1990s demonstrated the extent to which society blames public assistance recipients in ways that are inherently sexist, racist, and classist. In one poll, 65 percent of respondents believed that public assistance encouraged poor lifestyles (i.e., immoral, lazy, etc.), discouraged work behavior (80 percent), encouraged women to have more children (57 percent), and kept them in poverty (51 percent). However, 90 percent of public assistance recipients were women, mothers raising children alone. Only 7 percent of recipients were two-parent households, and even fewer were headed by fathers. The public's aversion to public assistance also has a racist flavor: Because a greater percentage of African and Hispanic Americans are poor than are whites, they are more likely to receive public assistance. Of those receiving public assistance, 38 percent were African American and nearly 25 percent were Hispanic.[41]

Society shows little recognition of the special needs of the desperately poor that prevent regular employment, such as health and nutrition problems, disabilities of all sorts, lack of education, unavailability of secure child care, and so on. The most distressing aspect of our reluctance to provide adequate assistance is lack of recognition that many of these programs, such as AFDC, food stamps, and general assistance, were originated to benefit children. Although public assistance programs needed massive changes to correct their inadequacies (particularly in terms of value stances), their focus remained on children. However, TANF has almost removed children from consideration with its emphasis on work and women's sexual morality. TANF's time limits and penalties neglect the reality that punishing parents means denying children access to adequate food, clothing, shelter, health care, and education. By dwelling on the presumed faults of the parents, TANF, legislators, perpetrators, and society in general visit the "presumed" sins of the parents upon their children.

Did TANF Work?

From the standpoint of numbers off public assistance rolls, TANF was a success. The recipient caseload declined by 53 percent from August 1996 to June 2000,[42] when it constituted only 2.1 percent of the U.S. population, down from 5.5 percent in 1993.[43] Steadily decreasing during the first year of the millennium, the number on public assistance rolls in June 2000 was 5,780,543 individuals, down to 5,382,063 in June 2001.[44] However, social responsibility demands more: that former recipients' (leavers') incomes be high enough to lift their families from poverty.

There is no doubt that, on the wings of a burgeoning economy at the end of the century, overall poverty declined, including the poverty of AFDC or TANF families. Both inflation and unemployment were low in 1999, at 2.2 percent and 4.4 percent, respectively, and the country had attained a budget surplus of about 2 percent of GDP. According to Sheldon Danziger,

> The favorable economic conditions led to increased employer demand for workers and welfare reform mandated increased labor supply from single mothers. As a result, the labor force participation rate of single mothers increased and welfare case loads decreased substantially in a period of only a few years.[45]

However, an important caveat in the welfare-to-work debate is the equating of single working women with TANF clients, while they actually are very different. In fact, the income of the very poor—generally 20 percent of female-headed families with children—actually fell during the early years of welfare reform. Although their earnings and overall incomes rose between 1993 and 1995, from 1995 to 1997 they began to decline. Two million families, or 6 million people, lost an average of $580, even with food stamps, housing subsidies, the EITC, and earned income. Among the poorest 10 percent, incomes fell about $810, or by one seventh.[46]

Some loss was due to an apparent lack of knowledge by the poor about eligibility for food stamps, emergency cash, or Medicaid—services of which caseworkers should have kept clients informed. While between 1995 and 1997 the number of people living in poverty fell 3 percent, the number receiving food stamps dropped 17 percent; in 1995 food stamps aided 88 percent of poor children, but by 1998 only 70 percent received them. In 1995, 57 percent of poor children received cash assistance, but by 1998 that was down to about 40 percent. In constant 1999 dollars, median welfare benefits decreased considerably from 1972, when their value was $11,400. In 1979 median benefits were $7,690, in 1989 $6,030, and by 1999 only $4,289.[47] Fewer than one-third of those who left TANF (leavers) received food stamps—about 30 percent—and only about a third of former recipient adults reported having Medicaid coverage.[48]

Census Bureau data and those from studies conducted on post-TANF families differ in interpretation. By 2000, for the seventh year in a row, poverty was down, the poverty rate for African-American and Hispanic households was the lowest ever, and the overall child poverty rate was lower than since 1976, at 16.2 percent,[49] still very high among industrialized nations, and not including EITC, food stamps, and other noncash benefits. An index including the latter benefits placed child poverty at around 10 percent.[50] While some conclude that this data indicates the success of welfare-to-work plans, state-specific studies and one national study found that many welfare leavers remained poverty-stricken because of low-wage jobs. In the national study, 29 percent of a representative sample of leavers who worked in 1997 earned hourly wages below $5.75, less than $1.00 per hour above the federal minimum of $4.75, and state-specific studies found that many received much less than this.[51] Leavers who had been off welfare for some time earned no more than recent leavers, suggesting wages remain static over time.[52]

An August 2001 study by the Center on Budget and Policy Priorities belied the common assumption that as families moved from welfare to work increased earnings automatically translated into reduced poverty. Families headed by working single mothers in the late 1990s earned more money because of the strong economy, EITC benefits, child care, and TANF supplements, but their increased earnings were fully offset by the decline in government safety net programs. Although some families benefited, many were pushed far deeper into poverty. The poverty rate for families headed by single working mothers stagnated between 1995 and 1999 at 19.4 percent, after government benefits and taxes were taken into account. In 1995, this group, including many TANF leavers, fell a total of $5 billion below the poverty line after government benefits, and by 1999 their rate fell $6.3 billion below poverty, about $1,505 for each person.[53]

By 2001, hourly wages (in 1999 dollars) among leavers averaged $7.15, representing annual earnings of $16,320 if people could work at least thirty-five hours per week. However, only 68 percent of former recipients worked a full workweek; about one-quarter worked at night or on irregular schedules, making child care arrangements more difficult; and health and other personal difficulties precluded many from regular work. Danziger says that,

> ... despite the large caseload reduction, the national poverty rate has fallen rather little. Many who have left welfare for work remain poor.... [E]conomic hardship remains high, because, given their human capital and personal characteristics, many former, as well as current, welfare recipients have limited earnings prospects in a labor market that increasingly demands higher skills.[54]
>
> ... About one-third of ... leavers say ... they did not have enough to eat in the past year [and] [m]ore than half ... worried that their food would run out before they got money to buy more.... About half ... report that food did not last or they did not have money for food at some time in the past year, either often or sometimes.[55]

Institutional racism remained a factor: three of five TANF families were members of minority races or ethnic groups. African-American families comprised 37 percent and Hispanic families made up 23 percent.[56] In addition, 75 percent of the people on TANF were children.

Class action suits challenged TANF. The most questionable rules were time limits and the rights of legal aliens. Many challengeable issues were based on federal and state statutes such as Title VI of the Civil Rights Act, the Americans with Disabilities Act, and laws affecting workers, such as minimum and prevailing wage laws and laws protecting workers' health and safety. In a study of 100 cases, 77 percent were won: Grounds for litigation included civil liberties questions of denial of assistance for drug-related felonies, the two- and five-year time limits on eligibility, and the exclusion of legal aliens from aid.

At the state level, violations included forcing high school students to leave school for workfare; paid and unpaid work assignments that did not protect health and safety; treating TANF recipients differently from other workers or dependent populations; family cap provisions; and reduced benefits for recipients moving from other states. Required community work is forced volunteerism, especially when such work involves religious organizations, and teenage residency requirements also are in question.[57]

Human Rights & Justice

Practice Behavior Example: Engage in practices that advance social and economic justice.

Critical Thinking Question: How can social workers premote social and economic justice durring periods of restrictive social welfare programs?

OTHER SAFETY NET PROGRAMS IN THE CLINTON ERA

Supplemental Security Income (SSI)

Since the 1970s, SSI provided supplemental income to people who were aged and disabled. The program continued to grow during both George H. W. Bush and Clinton terms, with people with disabilities the largest number of recipients. By 1994, there was a backlog of 700,000 eligibility applications for people with disabilities; although those with more obvious disabilities, such as

AIDS, were accepted before formal decisions. Of those on SSI in 1993, about 86,000 were blind, 1.5 million were aged, and 4.5 million had disabilities. Children were the fastest-growing group, of whom the largest segment were those with developmental disabilities (44 percent).[58]

Unfortunately, new legislation fell most severely on children with disabilities. PRWORA tightened SSI eligibility by eliminating functional disabilities, so that only the more restrictive medical diagnoses could be used. Those most likely to lose benefits were children with multiple impairments, where none is severe enough to meet medical disability requirements but in combination create disablement. Approximately 38 percent of children with mood disorders, pulmonary tuberculosis, mental retardation, burns, intracranial injuries, schizophrenia, and arthritis lost benefits. People unhappy with the cuts demanded another review, but even so the number of children receiving SSI dropped by more than 100,000 from a peak of 955,174.[59] SSI was also denied to illegal aliens and legal aliens, until they became citizens or had worked in the United States for at least ten years. The 1997 Balanced Budget Reconciliation Act, however, restored benefits to noncitizens who were receiving assistance as of August 22, 1996.

In 1999, 6.5 million individuals received SSI payments. Of these, 1.3 million were over age sixty-five, 79,291 were blind, and 5.2 million were disabled, with 847,063 children under age eighteen. Average monthly payments were $368, with about $289 a month for older persons ($642 for a couple); $402 for blind people; and $388 for those with disabilities. The average grant for children was $450.[60] In 2000, 6.3 million people received federal SSI payments, with average monthly benefits ranging from $254 for people over age sixty-five to $445 for blind and disabled children. In 2002, 6.4 million were estimated to be eligible.[61]

For those receiving SSI but considered employable after medical recovery, SSI had a continuation of payments provision to allow recipients to complete a vocational rehabilitation plan that was underway. Provisions also covered necessary work expenses for the blind (BWE), for the impaired (IWE), for children completing school (until age 23), and for those working toward self-support (PASS). At least partially as a result of such provisions, by December 2000 about 6.7 percent of the total disabled caseload was working.[62]

Earned Income Tax Credits (EITCs) and Child and Dependent Care Credits (CDCCs)

In 1975, President Ford signed EITCs into law, creating a refundable income tax credit for low-income workers. President George H. W. Bush added new credits for health care and for parents with newborn children, and Clinton expanded the program substantially in 1993, giving a tax cut to 15 million workers and including poor workers without children, making work the only prerequisite for reverse income tax grants. By 1995, about 20 million low-wage workers received tax credits of $500 per child. In that same year, however, the House Ways and Means Committee's Republican majority moved to save $23 billion over seven years by reducing or eliminating EITC benefits for two-thirds of the working poor, including all childless workers. This excluded more than 4 million people with incomes of $350 to $450 a month, increased the tax burden on more than 14 million low- and middle-income taxpayers (those with two or more children lost an average of $305 per year) and expanded eligibility to families with incomes up to $100,000. EITC cost about $28 billion in 1995, and all but $1.5 billion went to families making less than $2,500 a month.[63]

By 1997, Clinton secured a $500 per child tax credit for 27 million families, including 13 million children from families with incomes below $30,000.[64] Credits ranged from 7 cents to 40 cents per dollar earned, phasing out when earnings reached $500–$600 a week. In 1997, federal spending for EITC was about $27 billion, $10 billion more than federal cash welfare payments.[65] A significant marriage penalty applied to EITC when two-parent income overshot eligibility levels; although two single-parent families could access EITC, an intact family with the same number of children could not. Since its beginning in 1975, the number of taxpayers claiming EITC has increased from approximately 6.2 million to 19.4 million.[66]

The Child and Dependent Care Credit (CDCC), managed by the Treasury Department, was another tax benefit for workers with children or adult dependents. If families did not earn enough to pay taxes, however, they could not claim CDCCs. To qualify for full benefits, family income had to exceed $30,000. As of 2000, the credit was expanded to those making up to $59,000, at a cost of $5 billion over five years. Under certain circumstances, both CDCC and EITC credits could be available to families.[67]

Social Insurance

Old Age, Survivors, and Disability Insurance (OASDI)

Before Clinton entered office, incremental changes within OASDI had placed limits and some cutbacks on retirement, disability, and health care aspects of OASDI. Outlays for the program under Clinton were $66 billion (nearly four times the annual cost of AFDC), expected to grow another $17 billion before the year 2000.[68] To justify its attack on the program, Congress accelerated its charges that Social Security—especially Medicare—would bankrupt the nation. In fact, OASDI (without Medicare) continued to run a surplus: Since 1937, $4.3 trillion has been paid into OASDI and $3.9 trillion paid out in benefits. Less than 1 percent has been spent on administrative costs, making it the least expensive and most productive income transfer program in the United States. In 1995, its surplus was $60 billion, expected to rise to $100 billion by 1999.[69]

We need to understand the myth that OASDI will bankrupt the government. As FICA funds come into the trust fund, surplus revenues must be placed in special-issue government securities, which can be borrowed by the government to use as it needs and pay back with interest. OASDI is *not* part of the national operating budget (although Medicare [HI] is), but is like a bank, which the borrowers (government) can bankrupt through profligate spending and a refusal to pay back. The problem, then, is that the government wants to renege, causing the trust fund to bankrupt, not the other way around. As Moynihan says,

> Clearly, Social Security is not causing the budget deficit. In fact, surplus Social Security revenues are invested ... and in this way actually help [repay] the deficit.[70]

Under George H. W. Bush in 1990, Congress removed OASDI from the Gramm–Rudman–Hollings federal deficit calculations, but in practice it is

> To justify its attack on the program, Congress accelerated its charges that Social Security—especially Medicare—would bankrupt the nation.

still included in the "unified budget." This enables part of the deficit (the government debt to the trust fund) to be hidden and part to be blamed on OASDI recipients.

Thus, Social Security itself came under attack by Congress after 1994. While the program itself had strong support among the "over-age-fifty" lobby, particularly represented by the American Association of Retired Persons (AARP), increments through Cost-of-Living Adjustments (COLAs) continued to be cut. Though COLAs are intended to keep pace with cost of living expenses, in 1999 the COLA was only 1.3 percent, equal to the first COLA in 1975. The highest pension most retirees could earn without losing benefits was $15,500.[71]

In April 2000, the Senior Citizen's Freedom to Work Act was enacted, eliminating the earnings test for people over age sixty-five. It "set" earnings limits for persons through age sixty-nine at $17,000 in 2000, $25,000 in 2001, and $30,000 in 2002. Benefits were withheld at the rate of $1 for every $3 of earnings above these exempt amounts.[72] In December 2000, nearly 39 million people (excluding those on disability) received OASI payments, at an average monthly benefit of $787.80. Men's average benefit was $951.50, whereas women's was $729.80. Benefits for white workers averaged $807.60, whereas those for African Americans was $652.70.[73] In the same month, nearly 7 million disabled persons received OASDI supplements. Benefits for white persons averaged $677 and those for African-American persons averaged $588. Men's average benefit was $883, whereas women's was $661.[74]

Eligibility for Disability Insurance (DI) is based on an SSA-appointed doctor's assessment of client capability to work and whether that person is engaged in significant gainful employment. Since 1999, a person is considered gainfully employed by earning $700 a month. Earnings below $300 automatically qualify the recipient, and between $300 and $700 require that, before eligibility is granted, work-related circumstances and client capability to perform the work must be considered. Increases in significant gainful earnings are pegged to increases in the national average wage index and were not affected by the 1999 change.[75]

Since the Reagan years there has been debate on raising the retirement age for Social Security benefits. Smith says,

> There is no mistaking an increase in the retirement age for anything other than a benefit cut ... [it] means reduced lifetime benefits for all beneficiaries and lower monthly amounts for those who begin to receive benefits before attaining the new, higher retirement age.[76]

In 1999, 36 percent of retired workers and spouses received half their income from Social Security, and 35 percent relied on it for 50 to 89 percent of their support. The remainder—29 percent—depended on Social Security for nearly all their income—90 to 100 percent.[77]

The question of partially privatizing Social Security arose in the conservative 1990s. Partial privatization meant that people would put part of their FICA taxes into individual retirement accounts of their own choice. Because benefits from private accounts are related to contribution size and return on investment, lower-earning workers have less to invest or put at risk, according to Marcia Greenberger, co-president of the National Women's Law Center.[78] This would be a harmful situation for older women, because any change taking away retirement-income guarantees leaves them at risk. As it stands, Social Security

... offers lifetime guaranteed benefits, higher returns for low-earning workers, cost-of-living adjustments and spousal benefits for widows and divorced women ... [and] is just too risky ... because, on average, women earn less money and live longer than men.[79]

Social Security is not gender-neutral, although it was intended to be, and has already built-in inequities such as a reduction in spousal benefits when widowed, retirement income geared to spouse's benefits, and so on. Because hiring practices and wage decisions are patriarchal in nature, women generally draw smaller retirement benefits than do men. They work for fewer years because of child-rearing responsibilities and at lower wages because high-paying jobs are generally denied them (78 cents to men's dollar). Women also outlive men, so they live on smaller benefits for a longer period of time. In 1999, Social Security was the only source of income for 2.5 million women—26 percent of all older women who are single—automatically consigning them to live below the poverty level,[80] whatever that might be at the time.

Nutrition Programs: Food Stamps, WIC, and Child Nutrition

Food and nutrition programs remained remarkably stable over the decade leading into the new millennium. The Food Stamp Program, extended in 1990 with the Mickey Leland Memorial Domestic Hunger Relief Act, was reauthorized through 1995. By 1992, participation was at 27 million, more than 10 percent of the U.S. population. More people became eligible by instituting disregards of child support, educational aid, income earned by school children, excess shelter costs (above state AFDC level), income tax refunds, a $131 income disregard (in most states), and disregards for all but $135 of recipient-paid medical expenses.[81] PRWORA 1996 had a significant effect in reducing participation: In 1995, there were 26.6 million participants, but by 2000, 17.2 million.[82] Benefits averaged $73.25 per month.[83]

By 2001, many states had completed the transfer from actual paper stamps to electronic debit cards, and some—Indiana, for example—included cash assistance. The cards look and function much like those used for automatic teller machines and are updated monthly electronically, so that recipients do not have to come in to get stamps or wait for checks in the mail. The cards save money in printing, shipping, and administrative costs, and, more important, relieve clients of problems of accessing their benefits and loss of self-esteem at groceries and other vendors.

In 1994, the WIC program served 5.4 million participants at a federal cost of $2.6 billion, reaching 60 percent of those eligible. Reauthorized in 1995, it was allotted nearly $3.5 billion, an increase of $260 million, but received no incremental funding through 1998. The Clinton administration supported modest increases: In 1999, 2000, and 2001, the number of participants remained at about 7.2 million, at a cost of about $3.8 to 4.1 million.[84]

PRWORA 1996 ended expansion of school breakfast programs and the Summer Food Service Program, but their use remained stable. From 1999 through 2001, on an average day, the breakfast program served 5.7 million children, with 83.3 percent of all breakfasts served free, at a federal cost in 2001 of $1,443.9 million. The School Lunch Program, which received no significant cuts, increased by 5 percent from 1994 to 1997,[85] but in 1999, 2000, and 2001 continued to serve about 1.3 million children.[86] About 57 percent of those lunches were free, and children paid a varying rate for the rest. Commodities distribution suffered a cutback with the 1988 Omnibus reforms, from $1,075 million in 1988 to $730.5 million in 1989 and a low of $406.7 in 1996, but has grown incrementally since then, with an expenditure in 2001 of $703.6.[87]

Malnutrition presents significant problems in growing children, among them adverse learning effects, iron deficiency anemia, stunted growth, and nagging hunger that endangers full participation in our society. In addition, poor nutrition among pregnant women often results in low birth weight, high infant mortality (7.6 deaths per 1,000 live births overall, 15.1 among African-American children),[88] and children unable to fulfill their physical and mental potentials. Perhaps this is yet another evidence of the "starvation principle" of social Darwinism—if we don't need them, don't feed them.

Homelessness and Housing

In 2001, an Urban Institute study reported that 75 percent of homeless people were men, 85 percent of whom were single. The homeless population was 40 percent white, 40 percent African American, 10 percent Hispanic, and 8 percent Native American. Four-fifths were 25 to 54 years of age; 86 percent reported health problems; and 55 percent had no medical insurance. Two-fifths were parents of minor children, and 15 percent had at least one child homeless with them.[89] In 1997, families with children represented 36 percent of those in homeless shelters. According to the Children's Defense Fund,

> Children who are homeless or constantly moving from one dilapidated place to another suffer numerous serious and long-lasting consequences: poor health, missed school, and emotional damage.[90]

Almost all the homeless reported incomes below 50 percent of the poverty level, and 40 percent of all homeless people said they had gone without food for at least one day in the previous month.[91] Veterans constituted 23 percent of homeless people.[92] Another study estimated that 700,000 people a night, or 2 million a year, were homeless, with shelters often filled to capacity and 26 percent of shelter need was unmet.[93]

In the 1990s, nonprofit agencies operated 85 percent of the approximately 40,000 homelessness assistance programs. They included about 9,000 food pantries, 5,700 emergency shelters, 4,400 transitional housing programs, 3,500 soup kitchens, 3,300 outreach programs, and 3,100 voucher distribution programs. Food pantries served more than a million people a day, and soup kitchens provided meals for 522,000 a day. Emergency shelters housed about 250,000 people.[94] Government programs extending aid to the homeless included the Stewart B. McKinney Assistance Act for the Homeless, reauthorized in 1992, the Emergency Food and Shelter Program, and, to provide permanent housing, the Homeless Assistance Grants and the Housing Certificate Fund. None were sufficient to the need. Although both Presidents George H. W. Bush and Clinton made home ownership the key to their housing policies, the supply of low-rent housing decreased (by 900,000 units from 1993 to 1995), while need increased by 24 percent.[95]

In 1996, about 1 million HUD-assisted families received some income from AFDC/TANF: 260,000 in public housing, 80,000 with Section 8 housing vouchers and certificates, and 250,000 in project, based Section 8 housing. One quarter of all TANF families lived in assisted housing, paying about 30 percent of their incomes in rent, and more than 5.3 million households had "worst case housing needs"—lived in substandard housing or paid over

50 percent of their income in rent.[96] Yet Congress (from 1995 on) required that public housing authorities delay reissuance of the approximately 1.4 million HUD Section 8 vouchers and certificates, reducing the annual supply by about 40,000. HUD also has Community Development Block Grants, Rural Housing and Economic Development, Elderly Housing (Section 202), and Disabled Housing (Section 811).[97]

In 1997, Congress *prohibited* public housing authorities from lowering tenant rents in response to loss of income from TANF (to protect housing authorities from loss of revenue), meaning that people with reduced grants from TANF and those put off TANF, with problems of low-wage and irregular employment, probably were unable to pay their rents and were evicted. Many landlords refused to rent to TANF recipients. The nonpoor continued to benefit from mortgage interest tax deductions, which are the primary mechanism to promote home ownership—in 1995, rebates amounted to $83.3 billion.[98]

Finally, racism increased in the housing market. The Association of Community Organizations for Reform Now (ACORN) reported that, based on data filed with HUD by lenders in thirty-five cities, 33 percent of African Americans were refused mortgages in 1997, up from 25 percent in 1955, while rejections for Hispanics rose from 22 to 28 percent in the same period. Minorities received a lower share of conventional mortgages and a higher percentage of government mortgages.[99] ACORN itself has since been discredited, but the study's accuracy remains intact.

HEALTH CARE IN AMERICA

Health Insurance

President Clinton entered office with clear mandate to design a national health insurance program. He delegated its development to Hillary Rodham Clinton, who led a bipartisan committee representing both public and private interests. The most radical opposition came from health insurers: Their power had grown in the Reagan/Bush era through privatization of managed care. Privatized managed care with government sponsorship actually began when diagnostic-related groups (DRGs) were created by private insurers involved in Medicare and Medicaid programs (purchase of services at state option). To save money, DRGs defined the hospital stays of patients under their programs, substituting fiscal for medical decision making.

By the time the Rodham Clinton Health Security Act came to Congress in September 1993, private insurers were already providing for one quarter of all Medicaid recipients and more than half of all AFDC recipients. By June 1994, all but eight states had Medicaid managed care programs in at least some communities. Rodham Clinton's proposal was in fact managed care, but it was defeated as privatized managed care became the course of health care in the United States.

Managed care is based on contracts between health insurance companies and health providers to coordinate medical services and cut costs, often through Health Maintenance Organizations (HMOs) and Preferred Provider Options (PPOs). It became part of the government health care process under Reagan's privatization plans, with contracts for Medicare and Medicaid. DRGs were designed to contain costs. Medicare utilizes managed care DRGs for its

patients and offers a variety of Medicare Plus plans. Medicaid recipients are in most cases required to seek medical care at designated HMOs.

Though some believe managed care coordinates services and cuts costs, resulting in better utilization of health care, others believe it is a threat to quality care and " ... a bureaucratic system that ... forces doctors to place saving money before saving lives....[100] In fact, a study among physicians found that 57 percent of respondents felt "pressured to limit referrals," and that this often compromised patient care.[101] The vocabulary of managed care includes "trade secrets," which impose gag orders on physicians about contracts; bonuses, offered for limiting care and referrals to specialists; "medical necessity," a catch phrase allowing insurers rather than physicians to determine medical care; "capitation rates," a limit to the number of patients seen; and of course "case management," in which insurers rather than medical personnel decide the care needed. With all this, health services in the United States have become oriented to profits for the insurers (and for some physicians) at the cost of good medical care.

Case management arrived in the social work vocabulary at about the same time, probably in response to severe program cutbacks. It overlapped managed care in mental health delivery systems, which often required health insurance contracts, but spread throughout public and private agencies. Generally, "case managers," a new category of worker, coordinated services for all client needs, viewing them as "whole persons" rather than cases. However, case management is still a cost-containment mechanism: Often case managers have little or no social work training and, as the "first line" clients meet, are often gatekeepers for their own agencies and for referrals to other agencies.

National Health Insurance died quickly after its defeat during the Clinton administration. Although health measures depending on privatized care were later passed, none had the scope of a national insurance. As early as 1993, the Vaccines for Children (VFC) program provided free vaccines to doctors and other established agencies to immunize uninsured children and those covered by Medicaid. States used their own funds to extend the program so that more children could be vaccinated. The program extended immunization clinic hours and created registries to identify children who were not completely immunized. By 1996, 78 percent of all children were fully immunized, up from 55 percent in 1992, and vaccine-preventable disease declined to all-time lows at less than one-seventh their levels in the mid-1980s.[102]

In addition, Clinton's administration was successful in creating the State Children's Health Insurance Program (SCHIP) under the Health Care Financing Administration (HCFA) Title XXI as part of the Balanced Budget Act (BBA) of 1997. SCHIP provided $48 billion over ten years to cover other medical services for noninsured, non-Medicaid children in families with income less than 200 percent of the poverty line. Each state had great flexibility in developing its own plan: extending Medicaid or producing new plans financed by matching Medicaid rates; requiring cost-sharing by parents; block grants; covering children for twelve months after family income increases or eligibility is lost for other reasons; and so on. "Presumptive eligibility" provided coverage to new applicants for SCHIP,[103] and by the end of the Clinton administration more than 3.3 million children were enrolled in SCHIP at a federal cost of $4.3 billion. Yet in the late 1990s, 14 percent of American's children still had no public or private health insurance.[104] In 2000, the federal cost share of Medicare was $213 billion; Medicaid, $107 billion; Veterans' programs, $18 billion; Native American Health Care, $2.8 billion; $1.3 billion to build community health centers; and $900 million for maternal and child health clinics. Still, 36 million non-elderly Americans remained without medical insurance, including 29 percent of whites, 33 percent of African Americans, and 54 percent of Hispanics.[105]

Medicare

Whereas the privatization of health care was already well under way in Medicaid and nursing home care, Medicare had been considered untouchable. Nevertheless, it proved irresistible and Congress attacked it. Cuts were tied to increased premiums for the 37 million beneficiaries; new medical Individual Retirement Accounts (IRAs) ($3,000 out-of-pocket spending required); and an end to federal caps on health provider fees. In addition, annual government-sponsored "health fairs" were required so that private health care insurers could market their own "Medicare Plus" programs. This meant that private health care programs would receive Medicare funding and would also have federal support to market private "Medigap" programs.

The rationale for cutting Medicare was that the nation should not burden its children with future taxes. However, tax breaks for the wealthy of about $245 billion were also proposed—repeal of the corporate alternative minimum tax ($22.5 billion over seven years), increased write-offs and deductions ($47.8 billion), and capital gains tax breaks indexed to inflation ($78.6 billion). That provided the wealthy up to $290 billion, at a loss of about $629 billion to the poor. If we add in Medicaid cuts ($192 billion) to the $270 billion taken from Medicare, about half the roughly $1 trillion in reduced spending Congress wanted—$452 billion—came from these medical programs. As House Minority Leader Richard Gephardt said, "It doesn't take Einstein to figure it out, just drop the tax cuts and we don't need to cut Medicare."[106]

The powerful AARP fought against the destruction of Medicare, but retaliation from Congress was swift. It launched an investigation of AARP (which represents 33 million members) and charged it with using monies inappropriately or illegally. In addition, it attacked social agencies that came to the defense of the poor in support of Medicare with the Istook amendment to the appropriations bill funding the Departments of Labor, Health and Human Services, and Education. The amendment prohibited "individuals and nonprofits from receiving federal grants if more than 5 percent of their [own] private and non-federal funds are used for advocacy." This effectively muzzled many nonprofit groups and charities. However, no such restrictions were placed on other groups receiving federal funding; for example, Lockheed and Intel together received more than $54 million from the federal government in 1994 but could use any nonfederal funds to lobby without restriction.[107]

In 1970 there were 20.5 million Medicare recipients, but by 1994 that number had increased to 36.9 million. The value of the trust fund in 1970 was $32 billion and in 1994 $132.8 billion.[108] At the same time, Medicare covered only 53 percent of the average senior's annual medical expenses. Preventive care services remained insufficient to help seniors remain healthy. Routine annual physicals, vision tests, and hearing aids were not covered, and the program continued its fee-for-service cost-sharing structure, often leaving clients with high costs. Medicare spending represented 17.6 percent of every dollar spent on health care in 1999.[109]

Medicaid

In 1994, Medicaid provided care for more than 35 million people. Nearly two-thirds of Medicaid patients were people with low incomes, mostly receiving public assistance. The program paid for one-third of all births in the United States, more than a quarter of all emergency room visits, and 37 to 50 percent of long-term care of the approximately 1.5 million people in nursing homes—the elderly and young with disabilities, including people with AIDS—at an annual average cost of $38,000 each. Fifty percent of Medicaid clients were children, but they took only 18.5 percent of its costs. Aged Medicaid clients (11.5 percent) took 28.4 percent of costs and those with disabilities nearly 39 percent. Each elderly patient cost $9,862 on average, whereas Medicaid paid $9,226 for each client with disabilities and $1,360 for each child.[110] Medicaid was merged into block grants without matching state fund requirements, which portended not only a loss of federal funds but a 30 percent loss in state funds.[111] Eligibility rules became more stringent, so that of 22 million children covered by Medicaid, about 4.4 million would be dropped, with no provision for new health coverage.[112]

Privatization of care for Medicaid-covered children came even before the 104th Congress demonstrated a lack of concern about mandated programs, and it increased with loss of federal standards. For example, although children were entitled to Early and Periodic Screening, Diagnosis, and Treatment (EPSDT), privately managed contracts did not guarantee it. In a study examining thirty-three contracts (in twenty-three states and Washington, D.C.), 82 percent did not require it. Although 59 percent of the contracts required *plans* for EPSDT, only twelve contracts specified that immunizations were required, eight gave providers the option of giving immunizations, and three referred children to public health departments.[113]

Besides children, the elderly and disabled clients of Medicaid also were at risk. In 1995, Medicaid paid about 70 percent of the costs of nursing home care for 1.5 million residents. The Medicaid cut of at least $192 million meant that with reduced federal and state funding, 350,000 nursing home residents lost coverage, along with 1.4 million people with disabilities.

The Balanced Budget Act of 1997 allowed states to force most Medicaid patients to enroll in managed care entities: Managed care organizations (MCOs) and primary care case managers (PCCMs)—physicians, group practices, physician assistants, or nurse practitioners—would serve them. States must give clients a choice of at least two, and providers are required to give patients information on rights and responsibilities, covered services, benefits available out-side the managed care entity, and so on. There are also grievance and appeal procedures. In 2000, the federal share of Medicaid was $107.5 billion.[114]

SOCIAL ISSUES

The Clinton Stimulus Package (1993) provided nearly $6.5 billion in tax incentives, particularly an investment tax credit for small businesses through Empowerment/Enterprise Zones, put 100,000 new officers on the streets through the Omnibus Crime Bill, increased spending on transportation, accelerated the Home Investment Partnerships program (similar to HOPE, the George H. W. Bush bill), and provided funds for environmental cleanups. In addition, it increased the time limit for unemployment compensation and provided $4 billion for extended unemployment compensation.[115]

Empowerment Enterprise Zones

The purpose of the Empowerment Enterprise Zone Bill was to put money into blighted or disadvantaged areas. In 1993, it set up nine empowerment zones (six urban, three rural) and ninety-five enterprise zones. Each urban empowerment zone received a $100 million block grant for social services such as child development and drug treatment, and each rural zone got $40 million. Enterprise zones received up to $3 million for social services. Business owners received tax deductions for each zone-area resident employed, up to $3,000 (20 percent of the first $15,000 of employees' salaries or wages), and some training expenses.

There is no doubt that areas and people benefited from the program, through better schools, more social services, and more small businesses, but perhaps direct investment into families rather than another layer of infrastructure would have produced more lasting effects. Latent functions, aside from the political, included

- provision of tax havens to make more money for the already moneyed;
- pacification of those who are overtly served,[116] encouraging conformity;
- creation of jobs for social workers;
- conflict issues of poverty—classism, racism, and sexism—converted to "social problems" that imply solutions; and
- crediting the powerful for their concern for the nonpowerful.[117]

Crime Control

The Clinton Omnibus Crime Control Act of 1994, approved quickly by Congress, allowed for $30 billion to be spent over six years, with $5.4 billion for prevention programs, $7.9 billion for new prison construction, and $8.8 billion for increased police forces. It also instituted the "three strikes and you're out" plan for habitual criminals: life imprisonment after three convictions. The bill applied the death penalty to over fifty new crimes, although it specified that jurors were not required to impose the death penalty and that it could not be imposed on the incompetent, people with mental retardation, or children under age nineteen. Adding to the Brady Gun Control bill, the act also banned at least 150 brands of semiautomatic weapons.

Unfortunately, the latent functions of this "lock-'em-up" program intensified action against people who were poor or from minority groups. The bill grew out of not only fear of increased crime, but also from the Reagan war on drugs, which ghettoized neighborhoods in poverty, closing them off for further crime and police action. Disproportionate reporting and apprehension of suspects, along with more convictions and more severe punishment for crimes committed by African Americans and other minorities, are a given in the United States. Heightened efforts to stop the drug business by making more arrests and giving longer sentences made this bill another weapon not only against crime but also against the urban poor.

In the seven years between 1991 and 1998, violent crime dropped by 25 percent, yet prisons and jails held 1,860,520 inmates, or one in every 147 adult Americans (Russia's prisons held one in 146 citizens).[118] The growth of the prison population was responsible for only about 25 percent of the drop in the crime rate. The rest came from changes in the crack cocaine markets, greater efforts by police to get guns off the streets, and the strength of the economy. In turn, the growth of the prison population came from longer sentences for violent and drug-related crimes, more mandatory minimum sentences, and more difficulty in obtaining parole.[119] Almost one in three African-American men in their twenties was under some form of criminal supervision on any given day in 1995, and by 1999, 46 percent of all inmates serving a year or more were African Americans. Hispanics constituted 18 percent of the prison population and whites 33 percent.[120]

In the Clinton decade, most illicit drug users were white—an estimated 9.9 million, or 72 percent of all users, whereas 2 million were African American (15 percent) and 1.4 million were Hispanic (10 percent). Yet African Americans constituted 36.8 percent of those arrested for drug violations, over 42 percent of those in federal prisons, and 58 percent of those in state prisons.[121] Among persons convicted of drug felonies, 32 percent of white defendants received prison sentences, whereas the rate for African Americans was 46 percent. The rate of imprisonment for African-American women (for all offenses) was more than eight times that for white women, and Hispanic women's rate of imprisonment is nearly four times that of white women.[122]

Social costs of pursuing a hard line on criminal justice are inestimable, especially given the racist nature of prosecution. People convicted of felonies lose their right to vote, and so can no longer participate in governance. Harsh guidelines such as "three strikes, you're out" means that a disproportionate number of young African-American and Hispanic men are likely to be imprisoned for life for drug-related offenses, virtually warehousing them into old age.[123] Aside from the cost of maintaining enough prison space for these men, their imprisonment means an end to any kind of family or fatherhood, poorer lives for their spouses and children, and higher social costs for the ensuing poverty of their families.

Education

In 1994, Clinton reauthorized Head Start and proposed his Goals 2000: Educate America Act, but it remained unfunded. His School to Work Opportunities program established job training programs, apprenticeships, and vocational education systems for young people not going to college, with a $125 million appropriation for 1995.[124]

To aid the college-bound, he designed the National Community and Service Trust Act—Americorps (1993)—which enabled prospective students to volunteer two years of community service in exchange for tuition or student loans and a living allowance. The program also provided health and child care benefits. Volunteers could serve in educational, public health and safety, environmental, or social welfare positions before, during, or after college. A direct federal student loan demonstration program was also enacted, but as a compromise with banks it was phased in to provide 60 percent of all new loans by the 1998–1999 academic year.[125]

Clinton also created College Tax Credits, the largest single investment in higher education since the 1940s. Called the Hope Scholarship, it provided a $1,500 tax credit for the first two years of college. Also, the $1,000 Lifetime Learning Tax Credit reimbursed families for 20 percent of their tuition and fees (up to $5,000 per family) for college, graduate study, or job training. Student financial aid doubled during the Clinton administration: Over 3.8 million students received Pell Grants in 2001. The 1997 Balanced Budget Act also created Education IRAs: For each child under age eighteen, families could invest $500 a year tax-free if used for college expenses.[126] In addition, the expanded 21st Century Community Learning Centers program provided after-school centers. In fall 1999, 30,000 new teachers were hired under Clinton's seven-year plan to hire 100,000 teachers to reduce class size. Further, the 1996 Telecommunications Act provided Internet service to almost 47,000 schools and libraries by E-Rate (education rate).[127]

Employment and Jobs

From the 1950s to the 1990s, the country lost about half its manufacturing jobs as automation and robotization replaced human work. This major loss of good-paying jobs was exacerbated by the loss of 1 million more manufacturing jobs between 1990 and 1995. An additional 6 million workers went to part-time employment. In 1994, despite 3 million new jobs created, poverty rose from 11 percent to 15 percent and real wages fell by 2.3 percent. About three-quarters of the 2.8 million "long-tenured" workers who lost full-time jobs in 1991 and 1992 had found new employment by 1994, but fewer than a third were employed in full-time jobs that paid equal or higher wages.[128]

In 1994, the minimum wage approached a forty-year low in constant dollars, with nearly 20 percent of full-time workers earning less than the poverty level. Moreover, they lost benefits: Those with employer-paid pension funds declined by 25 percent, and an estimated 43.4 million lost health insurance (up 1 million since 1993). Meanwhile, corporate profits were at a forty-five year high, and chief executives, who in 1972 made forty times the average pay of workers, made 140 times as much in the 1990s. Only about 11 percent of the labor force was unionized, although, hoping to gain clout with size, the three largest industrial unions—United Auto Workers, United Steelworkers of America, and International Association of Machinists—decided to merge.

This created a 2-million member union second in size only to the National Education Association.[129] The minimum wage was raised in 1997 to $5.15 per hour, yet on that wage a family of three was still below the poverty line.

Economic growth under Clinton created more than 22.5 million jobs, of which 92 percent were in the private sector. In 1995, unemployment was at 7 percent, but by 2000 it was 4.0 percent, with unemployment for African Americans falling from 14.2 percent in 1992 to 7.3 percent in October 2000, and unemployment for Hispanics from 11.8 percent in 1992 to 5 percent in October 2000.[130] Coincidentally with the election of President George W. Bush, the boom that pushed us into the new millennium suddenly died. By March 2001, unemployment had begun to rise: Between November 2000 and November 2001, the number of unemployed workers rose by 2.5 million— from 5.7 million to 8.2 million.[131] Factory employment fell in 2001, bringing the total number of manufacturing jobs lost since July 2000 to 1.2 million. The services industry, where most Americans work, lost 221,000 jobs between November 2000 and November 2001. The 330,000 payroll jobs lost in November 2001 came on the heels of a loss of 468,000 jobs in October, the biggest one month loss in twenty-one years.[132]

From January through August 2001, there were 1.2 million layoffs, exceeding the year-end total for 2000 by 83 percent. Since August 2000, the jobless rate for workers age forty-five and older jumped 23.5 percent, while that for workers age twenty-five to forty-five rose 20.7 percent.[133] In November 2001, 2.4 million workers had been unemployed fifteen weeks or longer, an increase of 16 percent from October, and 1.2 million workers were out of work for twenty-seven weeks or longer, an increase of 32 percent from October, the largest one month increase since these data began in 1948. Unemployment benefits expire after twenty-six weeks, and the number of workers without benefits was, in November 2001, at the highest level in ten years.[134]

AFFIRMATIVE ACTION AND CIVIL RIGHTS

The Reagan civil rights and affirmative action reversals were based on the idea that protecting the civil rights of some defined groups could entail a kind of discrimination against other groups and was thus forbidden by the equal protection clause (Fourteenth Amendment) of the Constitution. This theme permeated the senior Bush's presidency. In 1989, the Supreme Court (in *City of Richmond v. J.A. Croson Co.*) ruled that states could not give preference to minority-owned firms in awarding contracts (although federal set-aside programs were exempt). In another case (*Wards Cove Packing v. Antonio*), people claiming discrimination had to produce proof that an employer intended to discriminate against employees. Congress, aware of the political uproar of such reversals brought, brought new legislation for restoration of civil rights, but Bush vetoed the first bill (1990) and rejected a 1991 compromise. However, legislation was finally developed to reverse some such decisions (including the *Wards Packing Company* case). (The bill also allowed punitive and compensatory damages for sexual discrimination cases and "cases of discrimination against people with disabilities and members of religious groups,"[135] the latter leading to the Americans with Disabilities Act.)

During the 1990s, the Supreme Court continued the path set for it in the Reagan/Bush years, reinterpreting laws concerning affirmative action and civil rights in an increasingly restrictive manner. With the appointment of Clarence

Thomas by President Bush, the Court's work became driven by a core of conservatives chosen from Reagan onward: Chief Justice William Rehnquist, Justices Antonin Scalia and Clarence Thomas, and frequent allies Anthony Kennedy and Sandra Day O'Connor. A number of affirmative action cases came before this court. In a five-to-four vote, it stopped short of striking down a program to help minority-owned businesses win federal construction projects. The ADA-RAND Corporation lost on a bid for federal road construction to higher-bidding Mountain Gravel, a minority-owed business. The Supreme Court sent the case back to the Appeals Court for closer study, but warned that "racial classifications must serve a compelling government interest and must be narrowly tailored to further that interest."[136] This narrowing of definition meant more restriction in awards, jeopardizing programs under which federal agencies award more than $10 billion a year in contracts to minority-owned firms. In fact, the interpretation led the Pentagon to end most awards to minority contractors.

Another important case dealt with the redrawing of voting districts to include minority representation. The Voting Rights Act of 1965 had outlawed gerrymandering that denied voting rights to people of minority groups, and amendments in 1982 went a step further, allowing redistricting to ensure African-American representation. Separate charges were brought by Louisiana and Georgia that the creation of African-American majority districts violated the rights of white voters to a color-blind society.[137] The Court, voting in July 1995 with a five-to-four majority, said that when race is the predominant factor in a districting plan, aggrieved white voters could file suit and force the lines to be withdrawn.

During the Clinton administration, funding and staffing for six major civil rights agencies dropped 10 percent, according to the U.S. Commission on Civil Rights, despite a doubling of complaints and cases at some agencies. Most showed marked declines both in number of investigations and number of complaints closed since 1994. The Department of Education Office of Civil Rights, for example, closed 282 fewer cases in 1999 than in 1994, although the number of complaints received over the period rose by 1,326. At this agency, 144 reviews were initiated in 1994 as opposed to 76 in 1999. Also, from 1994 to 2000, staffing fell from 821 to 707. In 1998, the Clinton administration sought a substantial increase in funding, but funding grew only moderately for two agencies and declined for the other four, probably due to Clinton's lack of attention to them because of scandal and impeachment problems.[138]

President Clinton's stand on civil rights for gays was demonstrated when, under pressure from the Pentagon and Religious Right conservatives, he reneged on his promise to change the "don't ask, don't tell" policy on gays in military services. Military discharges of gays rose in 2000 by 17 percent to the highest total in recent years. In all, 1,212 members of the Armed Services were discharged during FY 2000, compared with 1,034 the year before and 1,145 in 1998. Of the total, 106 were cases in which military members stated their homosexuality. The others were discharged for homosexual acts.[139]

Although many states and cities passed Equal Rights laws that included gays in their protection, the conservative 104th Congress, encouraged by the Religious Right, passed the Defense of Marriage Act (DOMA, 1996) to deny federal recognition of same-sex marriages recognized by states. This effectively denied same-sex couples such basic considerations as

… bereavement or sick leave to take care of a partner or partner's child; pension or Social Security continuation when a partner dies; the ability to keep a jointly owned home if a partner goes on Medicaid, dies, or becomes sick; joint tax returns and exemptions for primary relationships on estate taxes; veteran's discounts on medical care, education, and home loans; immigration and residency for partners from other countries.[140]

DOMA also violates the Full Faith and Credit Clause of Article IV of the Constitution, which provides that the court judgments of one state shall be recognized as valid in other states.[141]

Many states and cities now have laws protecting gays from discrimination and defining gay-bashing as a hate crime. Yet in 2000, all states except Hawaii and Vermont refused marriage licenses to gays, nineteen states still criminalized sodomy, and six states criminalized same-sex sodomy, leaving doors open for prosecution. For lesbian or gay parents, child custody was almost always denied when former spouses objected, and three states officially prohibited gays from adopting children, although the prohibition was de facto in most others. Informally, many states and communities refused employment to gays applying for civil positions, such as those in teaching or police work. However, the Supreme Court decision in *Oncale v. Sundowner Offshore Services* (1998) allowed claims for harassment by someone of the same sex, and this could reopen the issue for lower federal courts. Moreover, the Department of Education and the Seventh Circuit Court of Appeals decided that an educational institution's failure to provide relief to gay students harassed by homophobic classmates is sex discrimination.[142]

PRIVATE CHARITY

In the 1990s, President George H. W. Bush validated Reagan's efforts to decrease federal social programs by calling on private individuals and agencies to become "a thousand points of light" to help their neighbors at the local level in times of hardship. Begging the question as to how many points of light can lift the darkness of poverty and despair, this rationalization for lack of social responsibility continued into the new millennium. Although we Americans believe we are charitable—and we may be, to people we know—we rarely generalize altruism across barriers of economic class and race. In part this is because of social values such as the work ethic and social Darwinism; another part is that we think we pay enough in taxes and charitable contributions so that, if people are poor, it is their own fault.

Whereas the government's retreat from social responsibility is patent, is it true of private charities? Many charitable organizations are highly funded by the government; for example, the government provides 96 percent of funding for Volunteers of America, 80 percent for United Cerebral Palsy, 78 percent for CARE, 65 percent for Catholic Charities, and 51 percent for settlement housing and neighborhood centers.[143] Moreover, most of what we call nonprofits have little to do with aiding those in need. They are thousands of educational, health care, arts and cultural, religious, research, civic, and membership organizations. They own a trillion dollars in assets and account for 10 percent of America's gross domestic profits.[144] In 2000, a total of $203.5 billion was donated to charities and other nonprofits.[145] However, little of that was earmarked for the poor or our neighbors fallen on hard times.

Expecting that church-affiliated agencies would help their local poor, PRWORA 1996 included the "charitable choice" option, meant to allow programs otherwise disqualified as religious-oriented to access TANF funds.

Later, Congress extended that concept to federal drug treatment and community development programs. Yet almost two-thirds of states report no requests for such funding. Whereas thirty-one states and Washington, D.C., awarded no government welfare contracts to religious groups, fourteen states reported sporadic use of the program, and five states—Arkansas, Indiana, Missouri, Ohio, and Texas—embraced it, spending hundreds of thousands or even millions of dollars.[146]

The idea of corporate charity—that corporations are obligated to advance the welfare of the nation—arose in the 1970s. However, the main thrust of corporate charity is "cause-related marketing," in which corporations can expand their markets by supporting worthy aims.[147] By supporting orchestras, symphonies, and museums, they reach upscale consumers without the high cost of advertising broadly. Wagner says

> For example, SCM Company, which sponsors museum exhibitions, admits that it would cost $51 million per year on advertising for five years to reach the customers it now does on $200,000 a year.[148]

American corporate giving was $11.02 billion in 1999, about 1.3 percent of pretax income and a jump of 14.2 percent over the previous year. Business owners have learned that "good corporate citizenship polishes a good name."[149]

According to Wagner, charity is rarely concerned with the social change of structures that impact our most vulnerable citizens. For example, the concern with homelessness in the late 1970s was not oriented to the need for good jobs, the housing crisis, or the need to improve and restore social benefits. Rather, defined as an issue of sympathy by social service, mental health, and church leaders, it created a whole new industry: shelters and soup kitchens, mental health and substance abuse counseling aimed specifically at street people, "Hands Across America" rallies, and Second Harvest food collections.[150]

As of 2000, charities had a great deal of money. The ten largest U.S. charities, ranked by total income, were: Lutheran Charities, $3.7 billion; National Council of YMCAs, $3.6 billion; Salvation Army, $2.7 billion; United Jewish Community, $2.4 billion; American Red Cross, $2.4 billion; Catholic Charities, $2.33 billion; Good Will Industries, $1.65 billion; Boys and Girls Clubs, $800 million; American Cancer Society, $666.9 million; and Planned Parenthood, $660 million. Executive officers were extremely well paid in salary and benefits: The highest paid CEO worked for the Girl Scouts of America at $648,790; the lowest paid worked for Lutheran Services at $91,467.[151] A redistribution of some of the wealth owned by charities to our most vulnerable citizens would probably provide enough points of light to end poverty in America.

WELFARE FOR THE WEALTHY AND CORPORATE WELFARE

Capital Assets and Tax Cuts

To carry out their plan to expand benefits to the wealthy, Congress in 1995 again altered the tax structure for families with capital assets. Among the benefits was a new 50 percent exclusion from taxation for the sale of real estate, securities, and other assets, effectively lowering capital gains tax rates from a range of 15 to 28 percent to 7.5 to 19.8 percent. In addition, capital gains were indexed to inflation, and so the corporate rate on capital gains dropped from

35 to 28 percent. Earnings from retirement accounts were no longer taxed, and exemptions on estate taxes would increase over six years to $750,000.

As social welfarists, we watched many Clinton efforts with approval, such as educational tax credits and the increase in EITC, which extended tax credits to 6 million additional low-income citizens.[152] However, the Balanced Budget Act of 1997 primarily benefited the wealthy. While the middle 20 percent of families got a tax break of $153 a year, the bottom 40 percent actually got nothing. Only 2.4 percent of children in the poorest one-fifth bracket qualified for EITC, and, although the education tax credit gives tax reductions to those with incomes up to $100,000, low-income children are not as likely to attend college, so nearly one-half of education credits go to the wealthy.[153]

In the 1990s, the Republican budget plus tax cuts redistributed wealth from the poor to the richest 1 percent of American families giving each, on the average, about $19,000 per year in tax breaks. More than half of all tax relief went to families earning more than $100,000 per year, and for the top 1 percent totaled more than all tax breaks for all families with incomes less than $50,000. In fact, people who earned under $10,000 a year paid nearly 10 percent more in taxes than they had before the so-called tax breaks.[154]

Cuts in corporate, capital gains, and estate taxes provided about one-half of total tax relief nearly exclusively to the super-rich. In 1998, the top tax bracket for capital gains—sale of stocks, bonds, and similar assets—was 20 percent, down from 28 percent; the minimum corporate tax was eliminated; and the estate tax exemption was raised from $600,000 to $1 million. These breaks gave the richest 5 percent of families 83 percent of the benefits from the three cuts.[155] There was also a major increase in the tax deductibility of contributions to Individual Retirement Accounts. The average after-tax income of the richest 1 percent of Americans grew by 157 percent between 1979 and 1997, while after-tax income for the poorest fell. The top 1 percent, in other words, had as much after-tax income as nearly 100 million Americans with the lowest incomes.[156] In the 1999 tax bill, 59 percent of the benefits went to the wealthiest 10 percent of households and the fully one-third of all capital gains tax breaks went to taxpayers whose annual capital gains income exceeded $1 million.[157]

In June 2001, President G. W. Bush and the Congress passed a new tax bill benefiting the wealthy. Among the benefits were an expansion of education IRAs that raised the $500 per year limit to $2,000 for those with incomes up to $220,000 and an increase in allowable contributions of IRAs: $3,000 a year in 2002 and $5,000 in 2008. Though his administration also used some of the fast disappearing surplus to give many Americans a $300 to $600 instant tax rebate, about 35 million of the poorest—those without income or who earn too little to pay income tax—received nothing, and the rebates were taxable for the 2001 tax year.[158] It was likely that the $1.35 trillion tax cut passed in the spring of 2001 was the major reason for the vanishing surplus left by the Clinton administration, in addition to the September 11 attack and subsequent war.[159]

Corporate Welfare

According to a *Time* magazine study,

> During one of the most robust economic periods in our nation's history [beginning in 1997], the Federal Government has shelled out $125 billion in corporate welfare, equivalent to all the income tax paid by 60 million individuals and families.[160]

The government supports the corporate system in myriad ways:

- Direct legislation
- Tax breaks and subsidies
- Interest write-offs for corporate debt
- Provision of infrastructure demanded by corporations
- The maintenance of a public assistance system
- Direct purchases of goods and services

Direct legislation benefiting corporations was demonstrated by the preservation of the $110 million Market Protection Program, which protects such corporations as McDonald's, Pillsbury, and Ernest & Julio Gallo from competition.[161] Congress even allows corporations to define its laws: For example, the Environmental Protection Agency's Clean Water Act was revised to ease anti-pollution requirements and allow more incursion into such natural resources as forests and wetlands. Ivins said,

> lobbyists for the Chemical Manufacturers Association and International Paper ... [literally rewrote] the Clean Water Act.... Under the Republican revision, 70 percent of the marshlands now protected will once more be open to exploitation.[162]

The 104th Congress's emphasis on laissez-faire corporate behavior was another aspect: By reducing funding to the Occupational Safety and Health Administration OSHA), it enabled corporations to ignore costly health and safety requirements. In addition, despite antitrust and antimonopoly laws, Congress ignored massive corporate mergers.

In 1994, the Office of Management and Budget found $51 billion in direct subsidies to industries and $53 billion in corporate tax breaks. A 1995 report showed that corporate subsidies to 129 private industries totaled $87 billion, ranging from export promotional funds for giant food companies to transportation and interest-rate subsidies for manufacturing and utilities and the underwriting of defense industry worker recreation programs.[163] Although Congress cut billions in social programs in 1995, it reduced corporate tax breaks only by about $1.5 billion.[164]

Interest write-offs for corporate debt, the preservation of infrastructure to meet corporate demands, and the maintenance of public assistance for corporate benefit are perhaps not quite so obvious. Because of quick corporate mergers and capital turnaround, corporations borrow high-interest corporate loans, on which much interest is lost, costing the government millions in revenue. Increased corporate debt necessitates immediately increased profits, so corporations rid themselves of the least profitable elements—workers—or go to part-time no-fringe-benefit workers. Loss of wages and benefits leads to greater use of public assistance programs, so the government actually subsidizes the downsizing of corporations. Karger says,

> the government tacitly assumes the social costs of corporate competition in the new global economy.... [B]y allowing corporations to create a floating labor force, the government agrees to mortgage its future ... [because] an unstable labor market means fewer tax revenues.[165]

At the same time, under threat of loss of corporations, local, state, and federal governments invested in new roads, advanced communications systems, and public facilities. This further plunged them into deficit spending and the reduction of social programs.[166]

Corporate lobbying is not the only way to gain support from Congress. Financial support paid to election funds, while its influence is denied by the recipients, is worthy of note. For example, the American financial industry contributed to the reelection of almost every member of the House and Senate Banking committees—the fifty-one members of the House Banking Committee received at least $4.6 million in 1991–1993, with even more contributions in 1995. At one fund-raiser in 1995, the Republican party received $11 million from wealthy individuals and corporations. Is it coincidental that the 104th Congress under Republican leadership gave huge tax breaks to many of America's largest corporations?[167]

Between 1991 and 2001, forty-one companies contributed a total of $150 million to federal candidates and parties through cash contributions to political action committees (PACs), individual contributions from executives and their families, and unlimited "soft money" contributions—perks, favors, and gifts.[168] Primary targets are members of the House Ways and Means and Senate Finance Committees, who, since 1991, have collected $9.7 million from top tax-avoiding companies.[169] From 1989 through June 2001, energy industries contributed $209 million to political campaigns, though they already paid the lowest corporate tax rate in America (5.7 percent in 1998). Five accounting firms whose job is to find corporate tax loopholes contributed $29 million, and industries benefiting from special research and experimentation (R&E) credits—primarily pharmaceutical and computer industries—donated $148 million.[170] In the 2000 election cycle, corporate donations[171] included:

Corporation	Amount (millions)
AT&T	$4.3
Microsoft	$3.4
Citigroup Inc.	$3.1
Verizon	$2.7
Goldman Sachs Group	$2.6
UPS	$2.5

Tax loopholes and corporate-pricing schemes also contributed to corporate welfare. In 1998, using legal tax dodges around the 1986 tax law, twenty-four large companies received income tax refunds. Write-offs for stock options, depreciation, and other tax breaks gave refunds of $186.8 million to Chevron, whose 1998 profit was $708 million; MCI Worldcom, with profits of $2,742.2 million, received $112.6 million; Pepsico, with $1,583 million in profits, was refunded $302 million; and Pfizer, with profits of $1,197.6 million, got back $197.2 million.[172] Multinationals also avoided $45 billion in taxes in 2000 by artificially fixing prices in overseas trade, overpricing goods sold in the United States, and underpricing goods purchased. Examples of overpricing goods coming into the country include $5,655 for a toothbrush or $5,000 for a flashlight; and examples of underpricing include $1.58 for a ton of soybeans, $528 for a bulldozer, and 82 cents for a prefabricated metal building.[173]

One of the biggest beneficiaries of corporate welfare is the war industry, through the military–industrial complex—interlocking memberships in corporate boards, the military, and politicians. Congress began to reconstruct Reagan's antimissile defense system ("Star Wars") against attack from "rogue" governments such as Iraq and Korea or "accidental actions" by Russia and China.[174] To accomplish this, the House Appropriations Committee, which had stripped social programs of more than $10 billion for FY 1996, found an extra $7 billion beyond the $258 billion requested by the president for the Defense Department. It targeted the money for projects neither requested nor planned by the Pentagon. Of the $7 billion, more than $4.1 billion (81 percent) was intended for arms contractors in states represented by senators and representatives sitting on either Armed Services or Defense Appropriations Committees.[175]

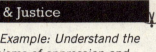

Human Rights & Justice

Practice Behavior Example: Understand the forms and mechanisms of oppression and discrimination.

Critical Thinking Question: Why is there more political support for corporate welfare programs than social welfare programs?

For "Star Wars," where $70.7 billion was spent under Reagan (more than double the $32.6 billion the government claimed was spent), Congress added another $625 million to the $3 billion President Clinton requested for 1996.[176] The Cold War was over, the plan would violate arms agreements from 1973 to the latest START accords, and nuclear arms production had ended in 1992, yet Congress persisted in its costly and scientifically improbable "Star Wars" plan. Corporations lobbied heavily for the new funds and succeeded: For example, Northrup Grumman Corporation received $493 million to keep factories open for the sole production of the B-2 (Stealth) bomber ($2 billion each), even though it is similar to other military aircraft.[177] Four Aegis cruisers—two more than requested by the Navy—were commissioned for the home states of William S. Cohn of Maine, Republican chairman of the Armed Services Seapower Subcommittee, and the GOP majority whip, Trent Lott, of Mississippi.[178] To the military construction budget ($106 billion), Congress added $346 billion for forty-four unsolicited projects.[179]

Although initially wary of the Strategic Defense Initiative (Star Wars), Clinton bowed to pressure from the Pentagon and a coalition of "true believers" and arms manufacturers—companies such as Lockheed Martin, Raytheon, Boeing, and TRW, who had spent more than $35 million on lobbying and $6.9 million in campaign contributions since 1997.[180] The "Contract with America" of the 104th Congress called for a national missile defense system, and its proponents gained enough support to develop a modified plan, the National Missile Defense (NMD). Scaled back from Reagan's Star Wars because of the end of the Cold War, NMD aimed to defend the United States from accidental missile launches from Russia or China, or from attack by "rogue states" such as Iraq or North Korea.[181]

NMD research and development was funded at $3 to $5 billion per year until summer 1998, when a congressional panel chaired by Donald Rumsfeld asserted that the risk of attack by a rogue state was much higher than previously predicted. His report, along with missile tests by Iran and North Korea, led Clinton in January 1999 to more than double NMD funding to $10.5 billion over the next six years. A bill declaring it government policy to deploy the system as soon as possible was passed in June 1999. In his final year in office, President Clinton added an additional $2.2 billion to NMD funding, bringing the total over the next five years to $12.7 billion. On coming into office, G. W. Bush promoted NMD even more vigorously, calling for an overhaul of U.S. defense strategy, with the defense screen at its core. Strangely, in a grim vision of the future, during the Clinton administration, Robert Walpole, a national intelligence officer for strategic and nuclear programs, stated that

... in the coming years, U.S. territory is probably more likely to be attacked with weapons of mass destruction from nonmissile delivery means (most likely from nonstate entities) than by missiles.[182]

Nonmissile delivery is anything from a suitcase to a truck bomb or other low-tech "delivery vehicle"—methods least effectively deterred by the NMD system.[183] On September 11, 2001, when terrorists struck America, NMD became peripheral to defense.

In 1998, national defense cost $268 billion and in 1999 $274 billion. By 2000, expenditures had grown to $294 billion, with estimated expenses in 2001 of $299.1 billion.[184] In 1998, national defense cost $268 billion, while TANF outlays were approximately $13 billion. By 2000, expenditures for national defense had grown to $294 billion, while TANF cost the government about $15.5 billion.[185]

Globalization, the International Economy, and American Social Welfare

On September 11, 2001, the people of the United States experienced globalization as we had never expected. The tragic attacks on the World Trade Center and the Pentagon—symbols of our economic and military power—shocked us to awareness that the technologies of international trade brought with them the dangers of nations without barriers, a world without walls. Who would have guessed that our full-blown awareness of the "New World Order" would come not through our prowess in transnational profit making, but through the anguish of terrorist attacks?

Globalization—the interlocking of all systems of ecology and human society throughout the world—is the natural outcome of free market capitalist expansion. International economic pacts on trade and financing dictate every nation's economic policies, including those of social welfare. Although America's economic and political leaders have global economic interests, they remain isolationist with regard to the by-products of their profit making: environmental pollution, poverty, health crises, crime, and war. With the end of the Cold War in the Reagan era, what corporate leaders saw as a *fait accomplis* since World War II—the "New World Order"—became a fact of international policy.

Because any nation's social programs depend on government spending, and because our nation's economic well-being is powered by transnational corporations, we need to understand that corporations determine the thrust of social welfare. Corporations are legal entities without concern for the common good except as it affects their goal, and notwithstanding the good and decent people who staff them, profit is that goal. Workers are the costliest parts of production, and it makes sense that cheaper labor means more profit.

From that perspective, we can more easily understand the withdrawal of help for workers and for the secondary labor force comprised most often of women and minorities. They are just not needed and will not be as long as technology and low wages in developing countries keep production high. Requiring work or earned income for programs such as TANF is an unrealistic demand: good-paying jobs are not available. Low-paying service jobs leave workers even deeper in poverty and despair. At the end, they and their children—the potential next generation of workers—can simply disappear.

However, corporations do feed the government. In 1994, the top 500 U.S. corporations produced 63 percent of the gross national product. For that, the government pays corporate welfare handsomely: depending on who tallies the statistics, from $85 billion to $125 billion annually in government subsidies. However, we unknowingly pay a much higher cost. Transnational corporations have stepped outside the national scope to form their own trade agreements, and although nations may sign the treaties, they are written by transnational corporations. The North American Free Trade Agreement (NAFTA), for example, took an estimated 395,000 jobs from the United States to Mexico, where workers earn about $5.00 a day as compared to the U.S. minimum wage of $5.15 per hour, or compared more strikingly with the production worker wage of $17.70 per hour.[186]

Money is not the primary cost, however. The loss of our social morality, the loss of people productive in ways other than income, the loss of the environment to the wastemaking of the corporations—these cannot be recouped. The American poor, women, people of color, and other "unwanted" groups represent a conceptual microcosm of what is happening in the rest of the world. Ignoring the needs of individual nations or the purpose of the United Nations as a global overseer, transnational corporations have formed their own worldwide trade organizations to foster profits, and they are recolonizing the peoples of the world to their own purposes.

The Organization for Economic Cooperation and Development (OECD) is composed of nations in the Northern Hemisphere. Ninety percent of all transnationals are based in the Northern Hemisphere, more than half from five nations: France, Germany, the Netherlands, Japan, and the United States. Their organizations include the World Trade Organization, the World Bank, and the International Monetary Fund (IMF), which carry out and support trade agreements such as the General Agreement on Tariffs and Trade (GATT), which has been called a corporate "bill of rights." The European Economic Community (EEC), thought at first to be a union of nations, protects European trade, whereas NAFTA protects North American trade. They are not in competition: They protect their corporations from government infringement on profit. General Motors and Ford exceed the combined gross domestic product of all sub-Saharan Africa, and fifty-one of the largest 100 world economies are corporations. Transnationals hold 90 percent of all technology and product patents in the world, and handle 70 percent of all trade.[187]

The World Bank and the IMF were intended to aid the Southern nations in economic development. However, when such nations do not meet service payments on those loans, the financial institutions step in to tell them what social programs they must abolish and what and how much they must produce for export. Formerly self-supporting nations, now in debt, must import food and other necessities. Their social programs, including education, health, employment benefits, and public assistance, have been slashed. In 1992, the interest paid on those debts exceeded $160 million—more than two and a half times the size of all foreign aid.[188]

In 2000, the World Bank and the IMF forgave some $34 billion in loans to their twenty-two poorest nation debtors, ostensibly to help them develop programs to help their poor. Just the service on their probably unpayable debts cripple many such developing nations. For example, Zambia owes the World Bank and the IMF nearly twice its annual gross national product—$5.5 billion—and pays $168 million a year on debt service. Therefore, the country supports education at only $70 million and health at $76 million. Somewhat less than half of these nations' debts were forgiven, and that depended on conditions that they continue economic, social, and governance reforms.[189]

Transnationals, either directly or indirectly through such mechanisms as the World Bank and IMF, command 80 percent of all land cultivated for export crops.[190] Although fostering an expanding international trade system, more than half the earth's population—over 3.5 billion people—are too poor to buy those goods. A fifth of the population of the Southern Hemisphere goes hungry every night, a quarter lacks access to even a basic necessity like safe drinking water, and a third—more than 1 billion people, 70 percent of them women—live in a state of abject poverty.[191]

The seeming all-encompassing power of the transnational corporations include the Multilateral Agreement on Investments (MAI), which gave them a kind of "citizen power" within nations to:

1. open all sectors of a nation's economy to foreign companies;
2. require states and localities to treat foreign companies the same as local companies;
3. make it unnecessary to hire locally or pay local wages; and
4. allow investors to directly challenge laws and seek monetary damages in international courts.[192]

The MAI

> would accelerate economic globalization by severely restricting the ability of national and local governments to regulate corporate investment, including social, economic, and environmental goals. It would give investors and corporations unprecedented legal standing to directly sue governments in international courts for breaking the agreements' rules.[193]

The world is rife with new or proposed economic agreements. The European OECD put into effect its euro currency system on January 1, 2002. Mexico, El Salvador, Guatemala, and Honduras signed an economic accord in June 2001 to promote tourism, trade, education, and antidisaster planning and to improve road, rail, air, and sea links. Mexico also has free trade agreements with Costa Rica and Nicaragua and is negotiating with Panama and Belize,[194] in addition to its NAFTA agreement. The thirty-four Western Hemisphere nations, excluding Cuba, plan to create the world's largest free-trade zone (Free Trade Area of the Americas, FTAA), to stretch from the Arctic to the tip of South America.[195] In Africa, thirty-five countries ratified a pact for an Organization of African Unity (OAU), which intends to set up an African Central Bank, a court of justice, a single currency, and a parliament.[196]

These agreements represent *economic* rather than national or global interests or concerns. Representatives of the G-8 nations—the United States, Japan, Germany, France, Britain, Italy, Canada, and Russia—meet regularly to plan for economic corporate growth. Social issues are usually given short shrift, although in 2001 they did create a health fund of $1.88 billion to help poor nations fight AIDS.[197] Usually, though, when global issues conflict with profit, nations and world organizations tend to be less charitable. For example, the 1997 Kyoto Protocol, intended to reduce greenhouse gas emissions to the 1990 level, was rejected by G. W. Bush despite its acceptance by 178 other nations and despite power plant emissions in the United States exceeding those of 146 other nations combined.[198] His reason: Energy production would be harmed. Other U.S. actions against ecological problems include cutting aid for global warming to Third World countries revocation of EPA reductions on arsenic in drinking water from 50 to 10 parts per million (lumber and mining industries lobby); and plans to allow mining and oil drilling in the Alaskan Arctic

National Wildlife Refuge. Corporations have their own reasons for denying help with social issues. Becker notes that

> Profit-oriented companies will not invest the half-billion dollars and more required to research and develop effective drugs for major diseases if they cannot price them sufficiently high to recoup their investments.[199]

Although present-day agreements on antiterrorism have visibly united the world, economic treaties previous to September 11 already had united the political economy of the world through transnational corporations. The terrorist attacks on America were a logical aftermath of terrorist attacks elsewhere that gained little international attention or retaliation: America has become the *symbol* of transnational corporate power over the nations of the world and of homogenization, forced and otherwise, of people and of cultures.

CONCLUSION

The 104th Congress and Presidents G. H. W. Bush and Clinton legitimized control by the wealthy in the legislative, judicial, and administrative branches of government, undercutting the promises of the nation for equal opportunity and equal treatment under the law. In addition, they reinvested patriarchy—control of women, children, and workers—with a new "morality" that defies humankind's vision of social morality.

We know how to end poverty. Guaranteed annual incomes such as SSI and EITC, even if only a toe in the door, would move people beyond scratching for existence in America. The mechanisms are there, through Social Security and the Internal Revenue Service. What we lack is the moral foresight to accomplish it. We have taken another road, forcing the burdens of harsh values on the already overburdened poor while we pay homage to the rich. Our social aim today is not to end poverty but to make profits, and the targets of society's largesse are not the poor but the rich.

This has set new patterns into society, patterns that divide us and set us against one another. They include rivalries among the poor and near-poor, growing dissension between white and nonwhite people, the polarization of income, and a tacit approval of violence on both private and political levels. This new "tribalism" is often based on race and demonstrates itself in local militia groups, the rise of hate groups such as the Aryan nation, the bombing in Oklahoma City, and increasingly violent federal retaliation against dissidents such as the Branch Davidians at Waco or the siege at Ruby Ridge. Gil says,

> History reveals that societal violence ... can be traced to the use of coercive measures concerning the organization of work and the exchange and distribution of products of work.... Coercive measures became institutionalized ... [which justify] established, inegalitarian conditions of life and work.[200]

We have created a "Third-World citizenry" within the United States, a neocolonization of our disadvantaged.[201] With wage labor controlled, a segment of our population walled off in urban ghettos killing one another and being killed in "drug wars," and social programs limited, proscribed, and deteriorated, a small group of moneyed elite nevertheless continues to increase profits and reap rewards in the destruction of lives.

> **We know how to end poverty. Guaranteed annual incomes such as SSI and EITC, even if only a toe in the door, would move people beyond scratching for existence in America.**

Like those citizens in the United States whose lives are Third World in nature, we have neglected to understand the impact of corporate power and arrogance on the Third World nations themselves. In retrospect, we should not have been so surprised at the heartbreaking 9/11 attack on America, since America is the symbol, warranted or not, of inequality among people and their lives and work across the world. Nor can we predict the impact of the war against international terrorism on social welfare within the United States, except that it will be costly. This is not a war about nations or governments; rather, though we may refuse to recognize it, this war is about world economics, the decline of national cultures, and the ease of use of technologies to destroy instead of construct—factors that, in fact, war has always been about.

The following questions will test your knowledge and understanding of the content found within this chapter. For additional assessment, including licensing-exam type questions on applying chapter content to practice behaviors, visit **MySearchLab**.

1. The Contract with America, created by Congress and the Religious Right, stated that the national deficit was a result of which of the following?

   a. A faulty tax structure.

   b. "Personal responsibility" of public dependents.

   c. Unwise fiscal planning.

   d. Lack of true patriotism and devotion to the church.

2. How is corporate welfare defined?

   a. Corporations privately funding public assistance programs.

   b. Banks using a portion of the interest payments from corporate loans to fund welfare programs.

   c. Company employees volunteering their time at public assistance agencies.

   d. Government's bestowal of money grants and or tax breaks for corporations.

3. Managed care is based on contracts between which two groups?

   a. State government and health providers.

   b. Federal government and health insurance companies.

   c. Health providers and health insurance companies.

   d. Federal government and health providers.

4. Which of the following was an impact of the 1993 Empowerment Enterprise Zones?

   a. Tax breaks for the lower class.

   b. Tax havens to make more money for the wealthy.

   c. Religious control over public assistance programs.

   d. Fewer social worker jobs in favor of funding educational and training programs.

5. You are on a jury for a court case of a defendant who has just received his third conviction for a crime punishable with the death penalty. Which of the following is a potential outcome for the defendant based on the "three strikes and you're out" plan?

   a. If he is over 18, he will likely face the death penalty.

   b. He can face the death penalty even if he has impaired cognitive functioning.

   c. The jury is forced to impose the death penalty if he is found guilty.

   d. The jury cannot be forced to impose the death penalty, so the jury decides his fate.

6. A female coworker has complained that a woman in her office has made repeated romantic advances toward her that make her feel extremely uncomfortable. Does she have a case for sexual harassment in the eyes of the law?

   a. Yes, the Supreme Court has ruled that claims for same-sex harassment are valid.

   b. Only if she lives in California or Texas since these are the only two states that recognize same-sex harassment.

   c. No, the law recognizes sexual harassment only as a violation between males and females.

   d. The courts have not ruled on same-sex harassment cases and therefore, do not have a position on this issue.

7. Discuss the fundamental problems with the TANF program in the 1990s.

Reinforce what you learned in this chapter by studying videos, cases, documents, and more available at **www.MySearchLab.com**.

Watch and Review

Watch these Videos

* Learning from the Client to Co-create an Action Plan
* Developing an Action Plan

The Great Contradictions of the Twentieth Century

The Historical Significance of the 2008 Presidential Election

Read and Review

Read these Cases/Documents

Δ Ethical Dilemmas

Δ Substance Abuse: Frank

Assess Your Knowledge

Go to **MySearchLab** to test your knowledge of key topics in this chapter with topic-specific quizzes. Conclude your assessment by completing the chapter exam.

---

* = CSWE Core Competency Asset
Δ = Case Study

14

Spiraling Down to Welfare Past

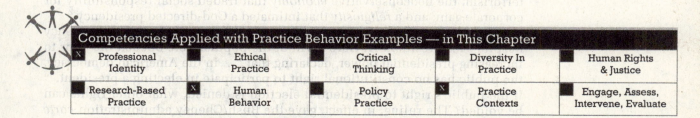

Competencies Applied with Practice Behavior Examples — in This Chapter				
X Professional Identity	■ Ethical Practice	■ Critical Thinking	■ Diversity In Practice	■ Human Rights & Justice
■ Research-Based Practice	X Human Behavior	■ Policy Practice	X Practice Contexts	■ Engage, Assess, Intervene, Evaluate

Times and Events

- **2000:** Pax Americana planning for Iraqi War; Supreme Court gives Bush presidency
- **2001:** President Bush and Vice President Cheney sworn into office; "New Freedom Initiative" added to ADA; terrorist attack on World Trade Center and Pentagon; war declared on terrorism, preemptive strike on Iraq; ESEA reauthorized, No Child Left Behind program begins; creation of Faith-Based and Community Initiatives in Office of the President; "Jobs and Growth Plan" initiated by Bush
- **2002:** Compassionate Capital Fund established in DHHS, ACF
- **2003:** Invasion of Iraq; Supreme Court rules racial diversity in schools legitimate (*Gratz v. Bollinger*); Medicare Modernization Act promotes Medicare Advantage; Partial-Birth Abortion Ban legislated
- **2004:** WIC reauthorized
- **2005:** Supreme Court prohibits death penalty for those age 18 and under (*Roper v. Simmons*); TANF reauthorized under DRA
- **2006:** Tax Relief Healthcare Act; Medicare D Prescription Plan begins; Supreme Court upholds partial-birth abortion legislation (*Gonzales v. Carhart* and *Gonzales v. Planned Parenthood*)
- **2007:** Higher minimum wage legislated; Supreme Court ruled Partial-Birth Abortion Act does not place "undue burden" on pregnant women; expansion of Head Start under the School Readiness Act; No Child Left Behind Act reauthorized; Bush vetoes SCHIP expansion twice; SCHIP reauthorized; Tea Party begins; Barack Obama and Hillary Rodham Clinton vie for Democratic presidential nomination against John McCain and Sarah Palin
- **2008:** Barack Obama elected president

THE BUSH/CHENEY PRESIDENCY

The new millennium began with the elections of President George W. Bush and Vice President Dick Cheney, a conservative Supreme Court and Republican Congress, a national surplus of $230 billion, and a booming economy. Yet, within a few years, the economy faltered, the surplus had become an immense deficit—estimated at $9 trillion in 2007[1]—and the Bush/Cheney administration had begun a course of neocolonialism, secrecy, and military–industrial power that degraded America's global reputation and depleted American social welfare, trading social responsibility for corporate gain. A spiraling synergism of polity, economy, and religion marked the Bush/Cheney presidency: the *politics* of war for oil resources and purported national security against terrorism; the neoconservative *economy* that traded social responsibility for corporate gain; and a *religiosity* that intimated a God-directed presidency.[2]

The Supreme Court decision that awarded George W. Bush the presidency despite Vice President Al Gore's win of the popular vote opened the door to increasing presidential power, declaring that "… in the American democracy, the public has no constitutional right to participate in electing a president."[3] If the public's right to presidential election is denied, what other rights can be voided? The ruling, in effect, gave the Bush/Cheney administration *carte blanche* to ignore constitutional guarantees of citizen rights, especially after the September 11, 2001, attack on the World Trade Center and the Pentagon. Under the umbrella of national security against the "war on terrorism," Bush and Cheney structured a "Homeland Security" agency with unknown powers under the "state secrets privilege" doctrine; challenged Congress and the judicial system by delaying requests and demands for information; secreted or destroyed tapes and documents deemed accusatory; and promoted the profit interests of cronies and corporations.[4]

Oil and War

On the international level, the Bush/Cheney administration ignored the United Nations and the Geneva Convention as it launched pell-mell into a preemptive strike against terrorism. Through misinformation, patriotism, fear of weapons of mass destruction (WMDs), and outright lies, the administration manipulated American patriotism and outrage and conveniently located terrorism in Iraq. There, President Saddam Hussein had been dealing with Russia and China to open an eastern pipeline that could destroy Western control of Iraq's oil resources. Control of oil resources as a national goal of the United States emerged in the 1940s, orchestrated by the military–industrial complex— politicians, corporate leaders, and the military—and required a strong presidency. The political construction of such a presidency, over a period of more than thirty years, culminated in the Bush/Cheney election. Within the context of his own created war on terrorism, Bush became Commander-in-Chief.

The plan for attacking Iraq was completed in September 2000, before the Bush/Cheney election, by a conservative "think tank" developing a *"Pax Americana* Blueprint,"[5] needing only a reasonable incident to be activated. The 9/11 attack became that incident. By conflating terrorism with Saddam Hussein's eastern pipeline plan, as resource theorist Michael Klare says,

> ... oil was no longer a commodity but had become a national security matter under the purview of the Department of Defense and warranting protection at any costs, including the use of military force.[6]

This became clearer in hindsight, when in 2007 President Bush developed documents giving "preferential access" to Iraq's oil reserves to ExxonMobil, Chevron, BP, and Shell.[7]

By 2004, America's war costs were $400 billion, twice that of all NATO nations combined,[8] and in 2008 the wars in Iraq and Afghanistan were estimated as costing about $195 billion.[9] The Iraqi war alone cost about a million dollars a day. Inestimable were the costs in human life: by 2008, 4,000 American servicemen and women, about the same number of nonservice support persons, and untold numbers of Iraqi persons and families were killed. In addition, nearly 24,000 Americans were wounded in combat, and from March 2003 to the end of 2007 more than 30,000 noncombatant injuries occurred.[10]

Religion and the Presidency

The Religious Right's fundamentalist beliefs in the 1990s, having already influenced national policy-making, were furthered as Bush, their co-religionist, took office. As a "God-directed" president, he represented both political leader and religious crusader with a double mission: to instill morality into American laws and to spread Christianity throughout the world, especially among its Islamic peoples.[11] With the ideal of "Charitable Choice," Bush and his conservative

Congress overruled the constitutional premise of separation of church and state and instituted new "faith-based" programs. A Supreme Court ruling (*Hein v. Freedom from Religion Foundation*) forestalled protests by forbidding taxpayers to challenge alleged violations of separation of church and state.

Despite the moral overtones of administration and Congress, scandals rode the presidency. Most were covered up or ignored until they reached the public eye, when underlings took the blame, resigning, being grudgingly let go, or facing charges themselves rather than allowing them to reach the Oval Office. Some did reach the courts: among the most egregious was the political firing of eight U.S. attorneys by Attorney General Alberto Gonzales for political purposes and the coverup of the actions of Karl Rove, who might have encouraged the firings. Among the most important changes in the court system during the Bush/Cheney tenure was the Supreme Court's swing to the right. The Bush/Cheney presidency succeeded in changing the conservative margin on the Court by replacing Sandra Day O'Connor with conservative Justice Samuel Alito and appointing Chief Justice John Roberts. This court heralded in a doctrine of judicial restraint in at least six cases in 2007, clearly evidencing conservative support of the Bush administration.

The Conservative Economy and Poverty

Bush's faith-based initiatives crossed the boundaries between church and state.

Bush's faith-based initiatives crossed the boundaries between church and state. The senior Bush's rhetoric of a "thousand points of light" morphed into George W. Bush's "compassionate conservatism." Social programs seemed to receive the brunt of conservatism; compassion was reserved for the nation's moneyed elite. Despite presidential protests that tax cuts would invigorate the economy by providing more jobs and increasing consumer confidence, a clear relationship emerged among tax cuts, rising unemployment, and a looming recession.

The Bush administration gave tax cuts to corporations and the wealthy that reduced capital gains tax rates, lowered corporate interest rates and allowed high debt levels; and promoted federal budget deficits as an alternative to raising taxes. Under estate tax laws of 1999, 6.6 percent of wealthy estates (those over $5.25 million) brought in federal revenues of $20 million. Under the George W. Bush administration, estate taxes were to be phased out by 2010. Therefore, the top one percent of the wealthiest Americans who would otherwise pay estate taxes, in effect, received a 36 percent tax reduction, enabling an even more top-heavy wealth-based American aristocracy.[12] By 2004, more than $2 trillion in tax cuts were aimed primarily at the top 2 percent of earners, and budget deficits were projected to reach $5 trillion by 2010.[13] Meanwhile, by August 2006 wages had fallen by more than 2 percent from 2003.[14] Unemployment was 5 percent by the end of 2007, and from January 2001 to November 2007 inflation had risen by 26.4 percent, predicting an inevitable recession in 2008.[15]

Government favors for personal friends and corporate interests (crony capitalism) also provided benefits, such as nonbid contracts in Iraq and for hurricane disaster relief; secrecy for friends in personal, political, or financial scandals; and publicly financed rescues for private financial interests.[16] The spiraling deficit was not considered a problem, but rather viewed in terms of the desire of foreign nations, who held $2 trillion of the deficit,[17] to invest in the United States.[18] By 2006, the federal deficit was nearly $9.1 trillion and growing.[19] Interest alone was nearly $430 billion a year.[20] Fueled by loss of construction jobs and the falling housing market, income polarization increased: whereas the top 40 percent of the population earned 73.3 percent of all income, the lowest 40 percent earned 12 percent by 2006.[21] Institutional discrimination manifested itself clearly in wages, by sex, marital status, age, and ethnicity (see Table 14.1).

Poverty guidelines in 2007 began at $10,120 for one person, rising to $20,650 for a family of four, and advancing incrementally by about $3,500 for each person thereafter. More than 37 million Americans lived at or below that

Table 14.1 Householders' Median Income, 2006

Group	Median Income ($)
U.S. population	48,201
Married couple households	69,716
Women-headed households	31,818
Men working full time	42,261
Women working full time	32,515
Under age 65	54,726
Age 65 and older	27,798
White households	52,243
African-American households	31,969
Hispanic households	37,781
Asian households	64,238

Source: U.S. Census Bureau, Current Population Reports: Consumer Income, "Income, Poverty, and Health Insurance Coverage in the United States: 2006." Table 1. "Income and Earnings Summary Measures by Selected Characteristics: 2005 and 2006." (Washington, D.C.: U.S. Department of Commerce, Economics and Statistics Administration, 2007), pp. 5–6.

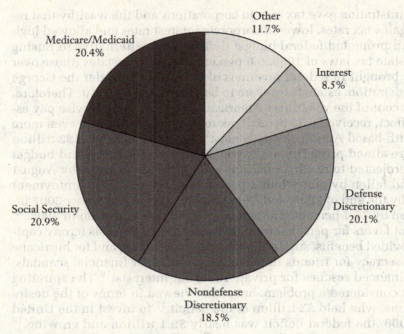

Figure 14.1
Federal Outlays in 2007

line,[22] although about 56 percent of poverty-level-or-below households had at least one member who had worked in the previous year, 20 percent of these full time (2003).[23] By contrast, the average income for CEOs was $10.8 million a year,[24] about 369 times the average worker's salary. The highest paid company chief earned $469 million in 2006, or $150,000 per hour.[25] Barbara Ehrenreich makes the point that

> By eliminating other people's jobs, top management can raise its own income. In the last few years, outsourcing has reaped the greatest rewards for CEOs: compared to other firms, compensation has increased five times faster at the 50 U.S. firms that do the most outsourcing.[26]

As the costs of the wars in Iraq and Afghanistan cut ever more deeply into the national budget, stable and reasonably waged employment became scarcer. The focus on foreign wars distracted us from domestic social welfare issues. Social welfare programs, with few exceptions, suffered actual budget cuts or held at pre-2001 levels that, given inflation, further curtailed their funding (see Figure 14.1).

SOCIAL WELFARE IN THE BUSH/CHENEY ADMINISTRATION

Faith-Based Initiatives

Among Bush's first acts as president was to create the Office of Faith-based and Community Initiatives (OFBCI) and to establish agency centers in the Departments of Justice, Housing and Urban Development, Labor, Education, and Health and Human Services (DHHS). Soon after, centers also were created in the Departments of Agriculture, Homeland Security, and Commerce.[27] In DHHS, under the auspices of the Agency for Children and Families (ACF), the Center for Faith-Based and Community Initiatives (CRBCI) created the "Compassion Capital Fund" (CCF) with initial funding of $141 million to support grassroots organizations, including religious organizations, in expanding their social service programs. Since its inception in 2002, more than $148 million has been awarded to more than 3,000 organizations that provide, among other services, day care, gang-prevention programs (Helping America's Youth), mentor programs for children of prisoners, and controlled-substance abstinence education.[28] Church-based community programs became eligible for federal funding for programs that addressed issues such as illegitimacy, marriage, and personal responsibility for moral choices in life.[29] In 2007, 50 percent of all faith-based service agencies received federal funding and nearly one-third received more than half of their operating budget from federal funds.[30] Since 2003, twenty-seven states have enacted legislation to increase the delivery of social services by faith-based agencies,[31] and in 2007 DHHS gave awards totaling $57,840,781 to 387 faith-based and community social service agencies.[32]

Levels of Income Security

The line from basic well-being to abject poverty measures income security, the need for social welfare programs, and the extent to which society responds to those in need. From the colonial period to the present, in America the first level of income security is employment, especially for men, with preferred support within marriage for women and their children (inherited wealth and fame might also be included). The second level is Social Insurance Programs (Social Security, OASI, SDI), Unemployment Insurance (UI), and Workers' Compensation. Public assistance (general assistance, SSI, and TANF) is the third level. There is a fourth level, survival by any means, but that takes us into areas of homelessness, desperation, and criminal activities where, as a society, we prefer to place blame rather than take responsibility.

The First Level: Employment

Employment in America

The U.S. employment-scape changed dramatically during the Bush administration. More than 140 million persons were employed in 2005, but nearly another 8 million were available for work but unemployed, 5 million of these because of "plant closings or moves, slack work, or the abolishment of their positions."[33] Manufacturing lost 3.1 million jobs between January 2007 and September 2007, despite Bush's new "Jobs and Growth Plan," which was supposed to add 5.5 million new jobs between June 2003 and the end of 2004 alone. (Each job created by the plan since 2001 cost $871,000.)[34] Unemployment and underemployment for discouraged or part-time workers meant that about 4.7 million persons were looking for work, and the Bureau of Labor Statistics (BLS) estimated that if the number of underemployed people were included, the unemployment rate in 2007 would have been 8.4 percent. In addition, the number of people without jobs for more than 26 weeks (after their Unemployment Insurance had run out) was 89 percent higher in 2007 than when Bush took office.[35]

New information systems, computers, and robotics, among other innovations, made much physical work nearly obsolete, and outsourcing jobs to countries with cheaper labor further limited reasonably waged working-class jobs in the United States. The AFL-CIO estimated that between 2000 and 2007 more than 525,000 white collar, software manufacturing, and customer service jobs, along with 3 million U.S. manufacturing jobs, were eliminated,[36] and health care and retirement benefits were lost with the jobs. The AFL-CIO membership declined from 20.1 million in 1983 to 14.4 million in 2005, also reported that government statistics lied about high domestic growth (GDP) in the Bush administration. Half of all U.S. growth reported in this "phantom GDP" actually took place in foreign subsidiaries of American corporations, which did not provide employment, wage, health, or retirement benefits in the United States.[37]

African Americans and Hispanic Americans were most likely to be fired as corporations cut employment. Although African Americans comprised 12.4 percent of the U.S. population, they were only 10.8 percent of the workforce. Hispanic Americans, who comprised 14.8 percent of the U.S. population, were only 13.1 percent of the employed.[38] Median income for white Americans increased from $50,262 in 1974 to $60,000 in 2004 (adjusted for the 19 percent inflation rate), while African-American median income increased from $31,833 to $35,010.

The influx of women into low-wage employment was another change. By 2005, nearly half of all workers were women. This was due, in part, because with inflation a family with one worker at minimum wage could no longer support a family, and in part because TANF required recipients to work after two years on assistance. However, from 1974 to 2004, the median income for white women in their thirties increased more than fivefold, from $4,021 to $22,030, while that of white men dropped slightly, from $41,885 to $49,081. Median incomes for black men dropped from $29,095 to $25,600, and median incomes for black women nearly doubled, from $12,063 to $21,000.[39]

The Earned Income Tax Credit (EITC)

The EITC, although not an antipoverty program, is probably America's best program for reducing poverty. By 2003, it had lifted 4.4 million people from poverty, including more than 2.4 million children,[40] with 22.1 million households receiving $39.2 billion in EITCs.[41] Up to 86 percent of eligible workers apply for it,[42] and states have followed the federal government's lead in developing their own EITC programs. By 2007, eighteen states and the District of Columbia had adopted or substantially increased EITCs.

Available only to workers who file income taxes, EITC directly reduces tax liability rather than giving tax exemptions or deductions. Low-wage earners whose tax credit exceeds their liability (below $11,340) receive tax refunds plus an additional payment that varies based on the number of children.[43] In tax year 2006, a single mother with two children could claim a tax credit of 40 percent for every dollar earned up to $11,340. Families earning between $11,340 and $14,810 received a maximum credit of $4,536, and beyond $14,810 the credit was lowered by about 21 cents on the earned dollar, ending for earners above $36,348.[44] Earners without children received a maximum of $412 in addition to their income tax refund.[45]

Veterans Benefits

Veterans benefits are linked to family income and have inflation-based cost-of-living increases. In 2000, the maximum allowable benefit, after income was deducted, was $9,304 for single veterans and $12,186 for veterans with

dependents. Only veterans with Congressional Medals of
Honor are guaranteed pensions regardless of income, at $600
a month. Survivors of veterans killed during military service
might be eligible for pensions based on income and ability
to work, and surviving spouses receive about two-thirds of
the deceased spouses' pensions, about $6,026 if they have
no other earnings.[46]

Americans with Disabilities Act

In 2001, President Bush added the "New Freedom
Initiative" (NFI) to the Americans with Disabilities Act
(ADA), with funding to train for new technology, open
new educational and employment opportunities, and promote increased
access to community life by allowing those considered "homebound" to
occasionally leave their homes without losing Medicare coverage. His request
included monies for additional transportation services to increase access to
employment and for travel services demonstration plans.[47] DHHS's Office
on Disability, through Medicare and Medicaid, also offers a wide variety of
research and development for the NFI.

The Second Level: Social Insurance

Old Age, Survivors, and Disability Insurance

OASDI served 48.5 million people in 2005 at a cost of $520.8 billion.[48] Com-
monly called Social Security (OASI), the program for elders, their spouses, and
their dependents provided benefits in 2005 to about 30 million clients at a
monthly average of $1,002 for single persons, $1,660 for married couples, and
$938 for the estimated 3.5 million survivors.[49] The Bush administration tried
to cut back or privatize Social Security pensions, but was unsuccessful. Even
so, because of inflation and deductions for the Medicare Prescription Drug
(Medicare D, see later), people lost real income during Bush's tenure.

Pensions for disabled persons (SDI, of OASDI), workers' compensation,
Supplemental Security Income (SSI), and veterans benefits provided for about
7.3 million disabled children and adults, averaging $967 per month in 2005.
Disabled persons included 1.8 million adults with visual impairments,
3.6 million with hearing or speech difficulties, and 14.3 million with cognitive, mental, or emotional difficulties.[50] Even though officially disabled, at
least 57 percent were employed full time, with a median earning of $22,000
for those with nonsevere disabilities and $12,800 for those with severe disabil-
ities.[51] Poverty and race intersected with disability: In 2006, disability rates
for African Americans, Native Americans, and Alaskan Natives were highest,
at 24.3 percent, with a 20.9 percent rate for Hispanics, and although the poverty rate for people without disabilities was 10.6 percent, 17.6 percent of those
with disabilities were poor.[52]

Applications for SDI in 2007 faced a record backlog of 750,000 people, who
waited an average of 520 days for hearings. Reasons for the backlog included
Congressional budget cutting in the Social Security Administration (SSA) ($1
billion since 1998), nonreplacement of staffing (staffing was at its lowest in
34 years), and new SSA responsibilities, such as eligibility determinations for
Medicare D (6.7 million since 2005), immigrant-related employment determinations, and enforcement of Homeland Security regulations.[53]

Practice Contexts

*Practice Behavior Example: Recognize that
the context of practice is dynamic, and use
knowledge and skill to respond proactively.*

Critical Thinking Question: What social
welfare needs are an outgrowth of the
wars in Afghanistan and Iraq?

Unemployment Insurance (UI) and Workers' Compensation

UI remained virtually unchanged in the Bush/Cheney presidency. The first fallback for the laid off, it provides about 60 percent of former earnings for 26 weeks after job loss. In 2004, 3.6 million unemployed people used all their UI benefits before finding another job,[54] and the average benefit period was 15.3 weeks. Total benefits paid were $31.2 billion, at an average of 35.5 percent of normal working wage.[55] In most states, TANF recipients are not eligible for UI.

Workers' Compensation faced new challenges under Bush. A Department of Labor program, it continued to provide partial wage replacement, medical treatment, and vocational rehabilitation to workers and their dependents. However, traditional safety goals of Workers' Compensation were undermined by Bush through changes in the Occupational Safety and Healthy Administration (OSHA), the office that sets safety standards and regulates worker conditions. The president, favoring private industries, set new OSHA regulations and reduced OSHA's funding, staffing, and investigatory resources. "Voluntary compliance standards" took the place of government regulation. In addition, Bush appointed leaders of corporations, many of whom were his friends or cronies, to regulate their own standards, thus maximizing business profits at the cost of worker safety. This resulted in looser safety regulations such as truckers' driving hours, logging in forests, and corporate mergers, but increased corporate profits.

Before these changes, job-related deaths and injuries had steadily declined, but by 2005 more than 6,800 workplace-related deaths and 4.2 million injuries and illnesses occurred. Looking at the Bush administration's statistics, fatalities and injuries seemed to have declined, but health experts said that recategorization of recognized injuries by the Bush administration were the reason for these apparent declines. Moreover, they advised that undocumented workers, who refused to report potential or actual accidents for fear of deportation, now performed many of the most dangerous jobs. Moreover, OSHA officials said that the apparent increase in Bush funding (2006) represented a $6.7 million cut in real-dollar terms because of inflation and was insufficient to maintain OSHA's programs.[56]

The Third Level: Public Assistance Programs

General Assistance, Poor Relief, Transitional Assistance

Forty states offer general assistance, sometimes called "poor relief," to people ineligible for any other cash assistance. Ten have residency requirements, and twenty require drug and alcohol testing and treatment, if warranted. Only two states pay more than 55 percent of the poverty threshold, and one pays only 12 percent.[57] Transitional assistance is available to families leaving TANF, providing at least six months of Medicaid when recipients leave welfare for work.

Supplemental Security Income (SSI)

SSI provides support beyond public assistance in cash grants and Medicaid disability eligibility when basic needs for income are not met by any other program. In the Bush presidency, nearly a million more people qualified for SSI, increasing the program's rolls from 6.6 million to 7.3 million,[58] indicating both an increase in poverty and the failure of TANF "welfare-to-work" programs. Average monthly benefits in 2004 were $351 for aged persons, $463 for blind persons, and $444 for those who were otherwise disabled.[59]

Temporary Assistance to Needy Families (TANF)

Whereas AFDC was an individual grant program, serving 80 percent of all eligible families, TANF became a state block grant by which states established welfare-to-work programs, reducing the number of eligible families to 48 percent.[60] Over the next ten years, caseloads declined by nearly 60 percent, from more than four million recipients to fewer than two million.[61] However, the reason for the decline was not recipient's success in finding jobs. Rather, the rising economy probably accounted for a 40 percent decrease and greater use of EITC was responsible for another 30 percent decrease. By 2005, 1,980,000 families (4,491,000 recipients) were on TANF rolls.[62] Reauthorized until 2010 under the Deficit Reduction Act (DRA) of 2005 (Bush's OBRA), TANF's funding remained capped at the 1996 level of $16 billion, with a basic grant of $13.7 billion for cash assistance, $2 billion for emergency aid, and $319 million for supplemental grants.[63] Medicaid provided states with optional Transitional Medical Assistance (TNA) to persons leaving TANF for up to a year depending on earned income (in thirty-seven states a parent working full-time for $7 an hour earns too much to qualify for Medicaid).[64]

By 2002, 47.2 percent of TANF clients were looking for work, and 27.5 percent had given up looking.[65] Few held jobs consistently for a year, both because jobs were not available and because many clients were relatively unemployable because of poor job and educational skills; mental, physical, and emotional problems; and situational problems, such as domestic violence, substance abuse, or unstable housing.[66] Institutional discrimination took its toll, both in caseload numbers and employment success: After TANF's onset, African Americans comprised 39 percent of TANF recipients; whites, 30 percent; and, Hispanic Americans, 26 percent. (Asian Americans were 2.1 percent and Native Americans were 1.3 percent of the caseload.) Fewer than one-third of African-American TANF recipients found jobs, compared to over half of whites.[67] In 2003, the number of "no-work, no-welfare" woman-headed families in poverty was 400,000. By 2006, the number had increased to roughly a million women and two million children.[68]

The DRA reauthorization brought stringent changes to TANF. Required caseload reduction, or maintenance of effort (MOE), was reset to base year FY 2005, meaning that at least 50 percent of one-parent families and 90 percent of two-parent families had to be engaged in work activities or states would lose proportional funding. Also, work participation was increased, beginning at that 50 percent base and increasing by 5 percent each year.[69] Program activities also changed, including an end to individual job plans, which became "readiness for work" assessments; drug testing for applicants and recipients; and cuts in what could be included as job time. For example, educational homework (unless under formal supervision), arranging for child care, or finding shelter in domestic violence situations could no longer count toward job time. Remedial reading, writing, and math programs could no longer be counted for basic core activities; vocational education was limited to twelve months over a recipient's lifetime; and any training taking more than two years to complete, including those that might result in bachelor degrees, were excluded.

Substantive changes included marriage promotion, such as premarital and marriage education; marriage mentoring and enhancement programs; divorce reduction education; and advertising campaigns on the value of marriage. Two of the changes actually might have been positive: Child support money could now be channeled to families rather than being retained for state and federal expenses, and the Out-of-Wedlock Birth Bonus to states with lowered illegitimacy rates on their TANF rolls was eliminated. In addition, states could exempt 20 percent of their caseloads from federal time limits, using accumulated MOE funds to provide a variety of other state benefits.

Child day care for TANF parents, which was required by law, continued to fall short in numbers of providers and in their regulations. Approximately 13 million infants, toddlers, and preschoolers per day—three of every five—are cared for by someone other than parents.[70] The only growth in the number of day care facilities was in faith-based ministries at least partly funded by ACF, with few regulations or oversight because they were trusted to be "safe." Nevertheless, charges of neglect and abuse have been filed against them in at least the same proportion filed against non-faith-based agencies. For example, in Indiana faith-based day care ministries have only four regulations, with three or four inspections a year, whereas licensed centers have sixty pages of regulations and may be inspected often. In the first five months of 2006, sixty ministries were charged with abuse or neglect, whereas only eighty-five non-faith-based centers were so charged, even though there are many more of them.[71] The Social Services Block Grant (SSBG), TANF funds, MOE funds, and the Child Care and Development Fund (CCDF) help support day care for TANF families.

In 2006, CCDF received $1.9 billion and the SSBG received $975 million specifically for child care.[72] The Bush administration funded CCDF at more than $2 billion,[73] child abuse programs at $95 million, child support and enforcement programs at $4.5 billion, and foster care and adoption services at $6 billion.[74] The Adoption and Safe Families Act (ASFA) was created to find new permanent homes for children removed from their homes for abuse or neglect, a change from the family reunification ideals of the past.[75] Child Protective Services reported that neglect was the most common form of maltreatment reported, and reunification with parents the most common outcome after exiting foster care. The number of children adopted from foster homes increased 40 percent from 1998 to 2003, with most children being adopted by their foster parents.[76]

Objectification of clients is a major fault in public assistance.

Although these efforts seem to indicate concern, they are remedial and do not meet poor children's basic subsistence needs. In 2004, America ranked fortieth in infant mortality, below Cuba, Taiwan, and most of Europe, with a neonatal death rate of 6.8 deaths for every 10,000 births. For African-American babies, the rate was the same as Saudi Arabia's, at 13.7 for every 10,000 births.[77] Childhood poverty can result in elevated rates of heart disease, diabetes, hypertension, cancer, infant mortality, organic brain damage, and so on.[78] The death rate for people born into poverty is, in later life (between the ages of 25 and 64), about "… three times higher than for the affluent, [with] a life expectancy that is considerably shorter (approximately 9 years)."[79] Yet, in TANF, we trade what may be children's lives for the right to enforce work upon their parents, especially their mothers.

Objectification of clients is a major fault in public assistance. We do not see recipients as mothers and fathers caring for children, homeless and hopeless men living in cardboard boxes on the street, children going hungry and cold or sick and dying. They are not brothers or sisters, veterans, the unemployed, the desperate. They are faceless shadows we pass on the street, "cases" or "welfare caseload," and they become mere statistics, pawns in political battles of those who represent others. The Bush administration's success in privatizing TANF offices, which "sells" public assistance to corporations such as Lockheed or IBM, has turned people into numbers and quotas, "boxes" on production lines keyed to net profit. Their personhood and their privacy are ignored through agency intrusion into marriage or the "capping" of grants when children are born to families receiving TANF. Even their homes are not safe from TANF intrusion. Although "midnight raids" were declared unconstitutional in the 1960s and 1970s, the Supreme Court let stand a California law requiring home searches without a warrant, because, according to the judges, "they are not seeking evidence of crime but are intended to determine whether welfare recipients qualify for benefits."[80]

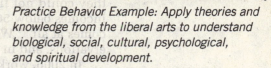

Human Behavior

Practice Behavior Example: Apply theories and knowledge from the liberal arts to understand biological, social, cultural, psychological, and spiritual development.

Critical Thinking Question: How does rhetoric—like "income insecurity" or "food insecurity"—effect public understanding of social inequalities?

In the same way poverty became "income insecurity," hunger has turned into the less ominous "food insecurity" under the Bush/Cheney administration, which defines it as lack of access to enough food for healthy living. U.S. Department of Agriculture (USDA) figures in 2003 reported that 36.3 million Americans were "food insecure," up from 31 million in 1999. Of those, more than 13 million were children, and 31.7 percent of families with children reported at least one member going hungry at times.[81] Children suffering from food insecurity are undernourished and hungry, generally in poor health, and susceptible to infections, sore throats, and stomachaches. More than one million children are anemic, which can negatively influence cognitive development and academic achievement and may lead to behavior problems later in life. "Food insecure" teenagers have higher levels of anxiety and irritability, aggressive and oppositional behaviors, and, among 15- and 16-year-olds, more depressive and suicidal behaviors.[82]

Food and Nutrition Programs

Food programs feed one of every six Americans daily.[83] Most programs are funded through the USDA and include commodity programs, food stamps, school programs, and Women, Infants, and Children (WIC) Nutrition Program. In addition, local communities provide food at food banks, emergency shelters, and soup kitchens, which, although originally stopgap in nature, are now an ongoing part of family life. In 2003, 3.5 million families had to use a food pantry at least once during the year, and nearly half of these families also received food stamps.[84]

The Commodities Food Program (CSFP) provides surplus food, including canned tuna fish, peanut butter, cheese, cereal, and canned fruits and vegetables, to hungry people. In an average month in 2006, CSFP provided food to 423,000 people over age 60 and to 40,000 women, infants, and children through the WIC program at a cost of about $107 million.[85] In 2007, President Bush proposed to eliminate the program because this population could also receive food stamps. However, CSFP clients receive food stamps in addition to CSFP, and its elimination would have significantly cut the diets of an estimated 440,000 seniors and more than 30,000 WIC recipients.[86]

The Food Stamps Program (FSP), which is usually distributed via electronic debit cards, as is TANF, served about 26.7 million people, including more than 13 million children (half of all recipients) in 2006, with an average monthly household benefit of $214.28, or, for the 26,672,000 individual recipients (an average of $3.14 a day, about one dollar per meal).[87] Eligibility is based either on public assistance participation (TANF, SSI, poor relief) or on an annual income less than $20,650 (monthly, $1,667) or $155 a month for a single person). Some expenses, such as dependent care, shelter costs, child support, and out-of-pocket medical expenses are deducted for eligibility purposes. At least twenty hours of work availability is required, and nonworking adults are denied food stamps except for three months out of each three years. In 2000, about 400,000 applicants were denied because, even though willing to work, they could not find jobs. Of these, 40 percent were women, 82 percent had incomes below 50 percent of the poverty threshold, and 57 percent had no incomes at all.[88] Work requirements were waived in 39 states, many Indian reservations, and in locations where unemployment was higher than 10 percent.

In 2006, working-age women made up 28 percent of food stamp recipients, and nearly half of all recipients were children. Nine percent were over age 60. Almost half lived in households where at least one person worked, and fewer than 13 percent had incomes above the poverty line. Thirty-nine percent had incomes at or below half the poverty line, over two-thirds had no countable resources, and the remainder averaged about $4,137 in annual income. In 1990, 42 percent of food stamp households received public assistance and 30 percent had some income, but by 2006 only 13 percent received public assistance and only 19 percent had earnings.[89] The percentage of food stamp households with no cash income of any kind doubled to 14 percent from 1990 to 2006.[90]

In 2006, the USDA's School Lunch Program provided lunches for more than 30 million children from low-income families at a cost of about $8.2 billion.[91] The USDA's School Breakfast and Special Milk programs provided free or reduced-price breakfasts to poor children (others paid full price) for almost 9 million children in 2004.[92] The milk program decreased significantly after TANF, but lunch and breakfast programs grew steadily from 5.27 million free lunches and nearly a half million reduced-price breakfasts in 1996 to 6.99 million free and almost a million reduced-price breakfasts in 2006.[93] In addition, the Child and Adult Care Food Program (CACFP) provided meals and snacks in summer camps, day care centers (children and adults), and local health clinics. Children in homeless shelters could receive three meals a day.[94] CACFP served 2.3 million participants in 1996, and ten years later served 3.1 million.[95]

The Women, Infants, and Children Program (WIC) aided more than 860,000 people as of April 2004, half of them children and 25.7 percent infants. Hispanics were the largest group of participants (39.2 percent), of whom about 46,000 were migrant farm-worker families[96]; with whites next at 34.6 percent; African Americans at 20 percent; Asian and Pacific Islanders at 3.5 percent; and Native Americans at 1.6 percent.[97] Over 60 percent of WIC enrollees had incomes at or below the poverty line. WIC's reauthorization in 2004 added more foods, more nutritious foods, and new health, education, and nutrition programs to the program, including a 24-hour helpline for nutrition problems of children.[98]

Local donations supply most food pantries, and the federal government supplements them through The Emergency Food Assistance Program (TEFAP) and faith-based Charitable Choice funding. Over 4 million low-income families use food pantries (food distribution) or soup kitchens (meals prepared and served at sites) in any given year. Working parents with children make up nearly half of their recipients, and, of these, 46 percent also receive food stamps. Local charities and national organizations such as Second Harvest are the brokers between food companies and local pantries.[99]

People without Homes

In 2003, the number of unhoused people was about 3.5 million, of whom 1.35 million (39 percent) were children under age 18 (nearly half under age 5).[100] On any given night, 750,000 people were without homes: 43 percent were single men, 17 percent were single women, and 40 percent were members of homeless families.[101] According to the National Coalition for the Homeless, 35 percent of those without homes are Caucasians, 49 percent are African Americans, 13 percent are Hispanics, 2 percent are Native Americans, and 1 percent are Asian Americans. Given that only about 12 percent of our American population is African American, the continuing racism underlying our nation's polity and economy is clearly evident.[102] Approximately 22 percent of single adults have severe and persistent mental illness, 65 percent have addictive disorders,[103] and chronic physical, social, and emotional problems are common. Shelters were usually filled to capacity: In twenty-four cities studied in 2005, 32 percent of families requesting emergency shelter were turned away.[104]

Rural areas have even fewer shelters, so many without homes lived temporarily with others or moved from place to place. Among children and youth, 35 percent stayed in shelters, 34 percent were with family or friends, and 23 percent lived in motels or "elsewhere," including vehicles (59.2 percent) and makeshift housing such as tents, boxes, caves, or boxcars (24.6 percent).[105] Between 2003 and 2006, the number of homeless public school students increased 50 percent.[106]

With the Bush/Cheney wars, the number of homeless veterans increased, estimated in November 2007 to be one-fourth of all homeless.[107] Homeless women veterans face unique problems: Of their 260 programs, the National Coalition for Homeless Veterans had only eight programs to address women's needs. Only a few shelters had special buildings or floors for women, even though separate facilities were crucial for their recovery, especially considering fear of sexual abuse.[108]

As the Bush recession increased, the housing crisis worsened. Rent and utility costs rose by 8.5 percent as early as 2002, and incomes among the already poor fell by 1.6 percent.[109] For some 8.5 million low-income people needing housing, only about 6.7 million affordable rentals were available, resulting in a shortage of 1.8 million units.[110] The Bush/Cheney administration apparently had disengaged itself from providing low-income housing assistance to the poor.

HEALTH CARE UNDER THE BUSH/CHENEY PRESIDENCY

Medicare

Traditional Medicare changed little in the Bush administration, although Medicare Advantage (Medicare C) was promoted as a substitute, Medicare B premiums were converted to an income tax base, and the new Medicare D, for prescription drugs, was instituted. The Medicare B premium conversion meant that people with incomes less than $80,000 now paid $93.50 a month for coverage and those with incomes above $200,000 ($400,000 for joint returns) paid $161.40 a month.[111] Big changes happened, however, in Medicare Advantage and Medicare D, and the true advantages were not for consumers, but for private health insurers and pharmaceutical companies.

Medicare Advantage actually began in 1997 as Medicare+Choice, a privatized fee-for-service plan expanded by the Bush administration first in 2003 under the Medicare Modernization Act (2003) and again in 2006 with Bush's Tax Relief Healthcare Act. Touted as a better insurance program than traditional Medicare, Medicare Advantage actually had many disbenefits, such as little or no choice in health service providers; corporation-dictated service caps; limited services, such as no away-from-home emergency care; and copayments, such as for lab fees. Life-saving treatments such as chemotherapy were much more expensive, if covered at all.[112] Benefits accrued to private insurance corporations, increasing their subsidies while removing many restrictions. The cost to consumers was about 19 percent more than traditional Medicare,[113] or $65 billion a year.[114]

The Medicare D Prescription Drug Plan was another privatization scheme. Begun in 2006, with an option that allowed deductions from monthly Social Security benefits, consumers could choose among insurance companies approved by SSA. The insurance and pharmaceutical corporations set nonnegotiable drug prices in three expense tiers and could change both drugs offered and prices annually. After prescription costs reached $2,400, consumers had to pay all costs up to $3,850, when "catastrophic coverage" began (the donut hole). Seniors could change insurance companies each November, but the various plans were so numerous and so complicated that such decisions were extremely difficult. Seniors could only enroll when first eligible; otherwise they paid a continuing late-enrollment penalty. State options to help the poor with Medicare D included Medicaid, Medical Assistance programs, and the free "Extra Help" Medicare prescription drug benefit. In the "Extra Help" plan, eligibility was means-tested and was generally limited to $4,000 for an individual and $6,000 for a married couple.[115] Some states chose instead to provide their seniors the PACE program (Programs of All-inclusive Care for the Elderly), a joint Medicare and Medicaid program.[116]

Pharmaceutical companies lobbied hard for Medicare D, spending more than $155 million to members of Congress and over $800 million on political campaigns in 2005 and 2006.[117] Because of Medicare D's privatization, prices for common brand name drugs increased 6.2 percent in 2006, employee health insurance costs by 2008 nearly matched corporate profit in the average *Fortune* 500 corporation,[118] and the five largest pharmaceutical firms in the United States enjoyed a 45 percent increase in profits in 2006. Realistic estimates put the cost of Medicare D at more than $1 trillion, although the government's estimate was $400 billion.[119]

Medicaid

Medicaid changed little during the Bush/Cheney administration, although spending declined in 2006, probably because of the shift of drug expenses to Medicare D; more aggressive investigation of fraud; changes in treatment of high-cost patients, such as those with AIDS or hemophilia; and moving the elderly from nursing homes to home health care.[120] About 7.4 percent of Americans aged 75 and older lived in nursing homes in 2006, compared with 8.1 percent in 2000 and 10.2 percent in 1990,[121] and by 2006 the percentage of those 85 and older decreased to less than 16 percent in nursing home care.[122] Another reason for the decline was the 2.3 percent increase in funding for the Older Americans Act (OAA) in 2007 ($31.4 million).[123] OAA has consistently aided elders with nutrition programs and other health services, keeping them from being forced into nursing homes prematurely, promoting good nutrition, and preventing those with chronic health conditions from getting sicker. Still, in 2007 Medicaid experienced a 10.7 percent cost hike and was expected to spend a record $330 billion in 2007.[124]

State Children's Health Insurance Program (SCHIP)

Forty-seven million Americans were without health insurance in 2006,[125] and the cost of health care was more than $6,000 per person and rising. SCHIP was created in 1997 to give health care to children in families too poor to afford health insurance but with incomes too high to qualify for Medicaid. In 2005, more than 6 million children were enrolled in SCHIP, with another 9 million eligible,[126] at federal expenditures of $5 billion.[127] In 2007, Congress twice proposed legislation to increase SCHIP funding to $35 billion over five years, but President Bush vetoed both bills, claiming the program was for children only, that it would cover 5.8 million adults (pregnant women and young adults to age 25), and that it would extend insurance into middle-income groups. In addition, he said that private insurance firms would be harmed because families would drop them to enroll in SCHIP. Although 28 percent of children newly enrolling in SCHIP had private insurance previously, half had lost it because of parental job loss or because the premiums were too high. Only 2 percent had canceled private insurance to join SCHIP, and they had to wait a year without insurance to do so.[128]

Bush countered with a bill funded at $4.77 billion, ending coverage for 840,000 children and some pregnant women. He vetoed both Congressional bills, and after the second veto Congress sent him the bill he wanted, extending coverage into 2008 at current levels and waiting for a change in administration that would allow further funding.[129]

Other Health Programs and Issues

Veterans Care

Before 2000, the number of veterans with service-connected disabilities had declined substantially, but the Bush/Cheney wars brought a massive influx of veterans who required more extensive health care than the Veterans Administration (VA) could provide. No medical or administrative staff was added to the VA despite its increased work load because of the Iraq and Afghanistan wars. Of the approximate 1.5 million troops sent to Iraq, there were at least 30,327 combat wounds and an estimated 30,000 noncombat injuries. In addition, at least 20,000 U.S. troops not classified as wounded have signs of brain injuries, and more than 150,000 might have suffered head injuries.[130]

To the military's shame, those suffering posttraumatic stress disorder (PTSD) often were discharged for "bad behavior," denying them veterans' health care benefits.[131] Shoddy conditions at veterans' hospitals and recovery units were only symptoms: delayed treatments, overdue benefits, and inattention to both physical and mental health needs were apparent. Approval for disability benefits fell by two-thirds from 2001 to 2005 despite the increase in need, and applications for those benefits have a backlog of at least 400,000. Suicide among both active-duty personnel and veterans is twice that of other Americans.[132] Between 1995 and 2007, there were almost 2,200 suicides among active duty soldiers, and among veterans at least 6,256 suicides in 2005 alone

> To the military's shame, those suffering posttraumatic stress disorder (PTSD) often were discharged for "bad behavior," denying them veterans' health care benefits.

(120 per week average). For veterans aged 20 through 24, the rate was estimated at between two and four times higher than civilians the same age. The number approved for disability payments fell by two-thirds from 2001 to 2005.[133]

Faced with a seemingly indifferent government, difficult duty tours that stretch for fifteen months, and lingering stress disorders, one solution is suicide, another is desertion. At the highest rate since 1980, there has been an 80 percent increase in desertions since 2003 and another 42 percent since 2006. About 9 in every 1,000 soldiers deserted in 2007—about 5,000—compared to about 7 per 1,000 in 2006, or 3,301.[134]

Indian Health Service (IHS)

Of the 1.9 million Native Americans, one-third live on isolated reservations, tribal lands, or other established Indian areas, and most Alaskan natives reside in villages. These poorest groups in the nation receive extremely limited health care. The Indian Health Service (IHS) and tribal groups together operate 48 hospitals, 272 health centers, 40 school health clinics, and 154 smaller health stations and satellite clinics, along with 34 urban programs.[135] Federal appropriations for 2007 were $3.2 billion to serve 1.9 million Native Americans and Alaska Natives on reservations and 600,000 in urban clinics. Still, the average cost for mainstream health insurance plans is 40 percent greater than IHS funding. In 2000, IHS annual appropriations stood at $28 billion,[136] while President Bush's budget request for 2008 totaled $4.1 billion.[137] IHS achieved some success in bettering health in 2006; however, tuberculosis, streptococcal infections, nutritional and dental deficiency, diabetes, and poor mental health are much higher among Native Americans than for other Americans,[138] as are mortality rates for alcoholism, cervical cancer, car crashes, homicide, and suicide.[139]

The Hill–Burton Act

Under the Hill–Burton Act of 1946, about 300 health care facilities are obligated to provide free or reduced-cost care to the poor in exchange for hospital construction funds granted from 1946. Because of the move from public to private hospitals, this is primarily restricted to emergency patients, who can then be released without further treatment after specific dollar amounts of care have been provided.[140]

Substance Abuse and Mental Health Services Administration (SAMHSA)

Generally speaking, services for mental health care are scattered across DHHS, and SAMHSA concentrates on mental illness and drug abuse. Approximately 54 million Americans have mental illnesses, and about 23 million struggle with substance abuse. In 2007, the Bush/Cheney administration, following its avowed pattern of reduced social responsibility, cut SAMHSA funding by $36 million. Another source of funding is Medicaid, which pays for between 50 and 60 percent of public mental health services for its eligible clients, providing for inpatient, outpatient, and physician services (it may impose time limits for treatment of substance abuse). States also have options for rehabilitation and case management under Medicaid, and prescription drugs are the fastest-growing area of Medicaid spending.[141]

Criminalization and incarceration of the mentally ill is a growing and ominous trend. More than 16 percent of those in prisons or jails are severely mentally ill but receive neither proper medication nor psychiatric support. In addition, the mentally ill serve longer sentences, and their recidivism rates are significantly higher than those of other prisoners.[142] The Law Enforcement and Mental Health Project was added to SAMHSA in 2000 with the goal of diverting the mentally ill to treatment programs. Among those program goals were continuing supervision and periodic review for nonviolent offenders; centralized case management; coordinated social services; training for enforcement and judicial personnel to identify needs of the mentally ill; and provision of outpatient or inpatient treatment in order to dismiss charges or reduce sentencing. In addition, it funds programs for life-skills training, job placement, vocational training, education, health care, and continuing treatment and psychiatric care.[143]

EDUCATION

Head Start was expanded in 2007 through the School Readiness Act, which stressed competition among providers, coordination of children's programs, and an "investment perspective" to ensure fiscal responsibility. The Act provided more children access to Head Start and provided teacher training.[144] In 2005, 907,000 children, were enrolled in Head Start with a federal appropriation of almost $7 billion.[145] Ten percent of its children were under 3 years old, 34 percent 3 years old, and 56 percent 4 years old. Head Start's importance in preparing children for school, rather than just providing day care, cannot be underestimated, because it teaches poor children skills they often do not learn at home. For example, Handler and Hasenfeld note that poorer students are more likely to lack verbal skills, and that

> ... one- and two-year-old children from professional families are exposed to approximately 150,000 more words *per week* than children with families on welfare, and the inequalities for learning and development persist when these children enter school.[146]

The reauthorization of the Elementary and Secondary Education Act (ESEA, 2001) brought the No Child Left Behind (NCLB) program, based on accountability for educational results, parental school choice, greater local control and flexibility, and an emphasis on research-based education. Tests for adequate yearly progress in math and reading are given in grades three through eight to ensure basic proficiency, with assessments broken out by poverty, race, ethnicity, disability, and limited English proficiency. A problem arose in the disability area, because the American Disabilities Act (ADA) required mainstreaming of disabled children, which lowered some schools test scores. As a consequence, those schools needing the most help might have lowered funding. School districts failing to make progress, as reflected in standardized test scores, could be restructured, while those that met or exceeded objectives were eligible for State Academic Achievement Awards. Children learned to take tests very well, but, because teachers were encouraged to teach to the test to attain higher scores, education on required topics suffered. Those children from lower social/economic levels had less language proficiency, lowering test scores again.

NCLB was reauthorized in 2007, but education as a whole suffered drastic budget cuts. The Department of Education's budget dropped from $55.92 billion in 2007 to $54.92 billion in 2008. Of 141 programs proposed for elimination, 42 were in the Education Department. Among them were programs for disadvantaged students applying for college and vocational education programs, totaling nearly $1 billion in cuts. The Department's biggest budget item,

Title I grants to high-poverty schools, was increased by $200 million, but the increase was reserved exclusively for NCLB, and 29 states saw their Title I allotments decline.[147]

In K-12 public schools, diversity and desegregation again became an issue because of recent decisions by Bush's conservative-packed Supreme Court. Although in 2003 the Supreme Court ruled that promoting racial diversity in education settings was a legitimate criterion (*Gratz v. Bollinger*),[148] it struck down race-based enrollment in *Parents v. Seattle School District* and *Meredith v. Jefferson County Board of Education*. Plans for voluntary integration in Seattle and Louisville were also declared unconstitutional, with the Court stating that any solution to segregation that considers race is highly suspect. With this ruling, Chief Justice John Roberts and his conservative cohort undermined the landmark *Brown v. Board of Education* ruling of 1954, demonstrating contempt both for legal precedent and the authority of local communities.[149]

Today, problems in schools threaten not only students' education, but also their safety. Substance abuse remains a growing problem. In a 2003 survey, half of high school seniors had used illicit drugs and more than three-quarters of seniors had tried alcohol. Bullying, in person or by computer, has reached a danger point. Schools are no longer safe havens: 6 percent of high school students said they had recently carried a weapon—gun, knife or club—to schools to protect themselves. Even more frightening, disaffected youth, often depressed, bullied loners,[150] have perpetrated mass killings of students and teachers. From 1992 to the Columbine shooting in April 1999, 18 students and teachers had been killed in school massacres. By 2008, 56 people have been killed.[151] Parents and children are rightfully afraid, and school lockdowns and guards in the halls are increasingly common.

At college levels, low- and middle-income students, women, and minority students are increasingly squeezed out of higher education as programs and funding are slashed, remedial courses eliminated, and other programs remain underfunded at 2006 levels.[152] Congress has tried to remedy the cuts by increasing Pell grant maximums for needy students, cutting interest rates on subsidized student loans, capping monthly payments for low-income borrowers, and creating a debt-forgiveness program for graduates who take public service employment. Still, rising tuition and college housing costs, which make college more problematic for women and minority students in any case, have resulted in an increasingly white, male, and wealthy student body.

JUVENILE AND CRIMINAL JUSTICE SYSTEMS

Juvenile Justice

The number of children in the juvenile justice system continued to increase: More than 2 million juveniles were arrested in 2005, nearly 100,000 for violent crimes and over 40,000 for property crimes. In 2005, the Supreme Court prohibited the death penalty for those age 18 and under (*Roper v. Simmons*). Boys committed about 70 percent of all offenses, and youth under age 15 accounted for about a third of all offenses. Of this younger group, 29 percent were girls.[153] Although African-American youth comprised only 17 percent of all juveniles in 2004, they accounted for 46 percent of arrests for violent crimes, compared to 52 percent for white youths.[154] Institutional discrimination through the police and the courts accounts for much of this difference.

One of every four violent crime victims was a juvenile, and most juvenile victims were girls. Most juvenile rape victims were ages 14 or 15, and most rapists were at least seven years older. In 2005, 109,000 runaways were arrested, of whom 58 percent were girls and 35 percent were under age 15. Runaways accounted for nearly half of all missing children, and 80 percent of the remaining were abducted, usually by family members.[155] Grants totaling almost $88 million were allocated in 2007 to fund group homes, juvenile detention centers, and transitional living programs (including maternity group homes). Another $15 million was provided for abstinence education, particularly for children, including runaways, homeless, and street youth.[156]

Increasingly, juveniles are being tried as adults and face harsh adult punishments even though, generally, their offenses are not serious. Approximately 200,000 youths every year are tried as adults. Since 1990, the incarceration rate for juveniles increased by 208 percent. Often placed with adult offenders, they are at grave risk of assault, suicide, and death. Discrimination also affects how juveniles are charged and incarcerated. A study in California, for example, found that about 70 percent of jailed juveniles were African American or Hispanic.[157]

Criminal Justice System

The stricter approach to crime in the 1990s resulted in harsher drug laws, the "three strikes" legislation, and a boom in jail and prison construction. According to Mark Robert Rank, in 1999

> ... the United states spent $147 billion on justice expenditures, including police, courts, corrections, [and] legal activities, ... an increase of more than 300 percent since 1982.[158]

By 2002, the United States had the highest incarceration rate in the world, with more than two million people in state, federal, and local prisons. From 2000 to 2005, the number of probationers rose from 1.1 million to 4.2 million, and those on parole from about 220,000 to nearly 800,000, meaning that nearly 1 percent of the American population was under the control of the criminal justice system.[159] Women made up about 23 percent of the nation's probationers and 12 percent of parolees. Approximately 55 percent of adults on probation were white; 30 percent African American, and 18 percent Hispanic.[160] The Sex Offender Registration and Notification Act (Adam Walsh Act) was legislated in 2006 to surveil released sex offenders, raising constitutional questions as to privacy and punishment for crimes.

The 1990s three strikes law increased the number of inmates ages 55 and older, many of whom will die in prison. Their number rose 33 percent from 2000 to 2005, far above the 9 percent increase in the general prison population. In the South, which has the harshest sentencing laws, the rate rose an average of 147 percent (from 1997 to 2007). Prisoners are not eligible for Medicare or Medicaid, but they have constitutional rights to health care, thus states must fund their care and medications. Many inmates are frail, sick, or debilitated and suffer from chronic conditions such as arthritis, high blood pressure, bad backs, age-related dementia, and Alzheimer's. States often neglect inmates' care due to lack of funding. For example, in 2006 California found an average of one inmate a week dying of neglect or malpractice, and a federal receiver was appointed to oversee the prison system.[161] The cost of imprisonment per person is estimated at $18,000 to $31,000 a year,[162] and these people are there for life.

OUR "ISM-RIDDEN" SOCIETY

Throughout these chapters, institutional discrimination has appeared in almost every program mentioned, even at the highest levels of legislation, administration, and the judicial system. Despite the obvious achievements of a few, such as the successes of both an African American, Barack Obama, and a woman, Hillary Clinton, in the Democratic primary of 2008, "isms" continue to symbolize our ways of hating those who are not "us." Today isms intersect in our quiet neighborhoods, our cities, states, and rural areas, and in our minds and hearts.

In the past decade, we have reworked some of our oldest "isms" (racism, sexism, and discrimination against the poor, classism) and found some that were hidden. The immigration dispute exemplifies xenophobia or ethnocentrism, long a part of American culture, and the war against terrorism has brought forth our rarely spoken Christian-centrism in Islamophobia (an irrational fear or condemnation of all Muslims or Islam)[163] against Islamic people, both in America and around the world.

Racism

African Americans

Racism appears in all aspects of social welfare and even in Supreme Court decisions on school integration. Economically, as of 2007 the gap in median income between African Americans and white Americans was 61 percent, the same as in 1997.[164] Politically, violence and neglect are demonstrated by such incidents as the Jena Six, where white teens brought back the spectre of lynching and were "admonished" while African-American teens who confronted them were charged with assault and one with attempted murder. Multiple protests freed the boy accused of murder from unfair criminal charges, but noose incidents have since appeared across the country. President Bush's response to hurricanes Katrina and Rita evidenced deep-grained discrimination: His emergency programs failed for the majority of victims, who were poor and African American. The Federal Emergency Management Agency (FEMA) provided a grossly inadequate number of temporary toxin-embedded travel trailers, in a "trailer park gulag"[165] where families still wait for promised housing. Bush's plans more than succeeded, however, as white and/or wealthy victims received the earliest attention in rebuilding homes and casinos and white contractors received no-bid FEMA and unsupervised repair contracts. Another example (among many) of institutional racism is reminiscent of last century's syphilis studies on African Americans: a clinical trial in twenty cities with high minority populations subjected hundreds of people, unconscious because of gunshot wounds and car crashes, to an experimental blood substitute rather than traditional treatment with blood and saline solution. Of the 349 receiving the blood substitute, 46 died, while of the 363 given traditional treatment, 30 died.[166]

Hispanics and Immigration

Hispanic American citizens are a significant portion of the low-wage working population, along with illegals who come to the United States for employment, and their wages are lower than most working the same jobs. Legal or otherwise, they often were advised to avoid programs such as TANF, Medicaid, and food stamps, and their fears of deportation or denial of citizenship led to participation rates significantly below those of the general population. Nearly one-quarter of all children in poverty have an immigrant parent.[167]

Hispanics lag behind in educational achievements and access to higher education, further limiting their employment and financial success. We hide our prejudices behind the immigration debate, where real efforts at immigration reform are fiercely opposed by conservatives. Their answer was to secure the Mexican border with 700 miles of new fencing. The Secure Fence Act, authorized by President Bush at $1.2 billion in funding, included cameras, underground sensors, light towers, and radar for about 300 miles,[168] but this was unlikely to end the influx of people seeking a better life. It is merely symbolic of our prejudice against "outsiders" and is epitomized in a statement by Representative Steve King (R. Iowa), who wants to electrify the wall with

> … the kind of current that would not kill somebody, but it would simply be a discouragement for them to be fooling around with it. We do that with livestock all the time.[169]

Native Americans

Another set of "others," Native Americans are discriminated against not so much by action, but by neglect. Belonging to sovereign societies within the United States, their lives are determined in great part by the Bureau of Indian Affairs (BIA), which is chronically underfunded. For example, large BIA budget cuts not only affect the educational quality of Native American children, but leave them in physical danger, in schools with inadequate ventilation, plumbing, and fire-escape routes. Although the BIA is required to finance tribal schools at a per student average for their state, the rules have been ignored because of insufficient funding.[170] In 2003, of these poorest Americans, 23 percent lived below poverty levels and 40 percent were unemployed.[171] Some are poorer than others: the Blackfeet society, for example, had a 34 percent poverty rate and 70 percent were unemployed.

Over the centuries, the BIA has leased Native American lands to oil, timber, and agricultural corporations and other commercial entities. Revenues are paid to Native Americans through the Individual Indian Trust, but payments have been erratic and much less than is truly owed, due as much to purposeful intent as to bureaucratic error. A recent lawsuit (*Cobell v. Norton*), filed on behalf of a half-million Native Americans, sought redress for unpaid revenues. It demanded payment of all unpaid revenues for the past century, $176 billion, to individual landowners ($352,000 per plaintiff). Gale Norton, Secretary of the Interior, was held in contempt for willful delays, destruction of records, and denying notice of the suit to the Native Americans involved.[172] In 2011, the lawsuit was settled in favor of Native Americans.

Sexism in the United States

Women

From our discussions concerning TANF, children in poverty, employment, and so on, it is clear that sexist discrimination still exists in our society. The controversial issue of abortion vividly reveals persistent attempts by a patriarchal society to control women. Since the passage of *Roe v. Wade*, state legislatures have tried to end or regulate abortion. In 1989, the Supreme Court allowed parent notification, waiting periods, and provider regulations;

in 1992 it allowed state regulation if "undue burdens" were not placed on women (*Planned Parenthood v. Casey*); and in 2000 it held unconstitutional a Nebraska law banning late-term abortions (*Stenberg v. Carhart*). Bush and Congress passed the Partial-Birth Abortion Ban in 2003. It did not provide "health exceptions" for pregnant women with medical emergencies, and the law was challenged, but upheld, in 2006 (*Gonzales v. Carhart* and *Gonzales v. Planned Parenthood*). The federal ban and the Nebraska case were alike: The difference in outcome was due to the composition of the Court, as Bush appointed conservatives Samuel Alito and John Roberts.[173] In 2007, the Court ruled 5–4 that the banning of late-term abortions did not place undue burdens on women.[174]

Another Supreme Court decision affecting women (and potentially all workers) was the wage discrimination case brought by Ledbetter (supported by the government's own antidiscrimination agency) against Goodyear Tire (1998) (*Ledbetter v. Goodyear Tire*). Having worked at Goodyear for twenty years, she found that her salary was 40 percent lower than that of men doing the same job. The corporate-biased court ruled 5–4 that this discrimination, while existing, was irrelevant, because the complaint was not filed within 180 days of when it first occurred. That decision was later overturned.[175]

Heterosexism

Few changes have occurred in discrimination against gay, lesbian, and transgendered people, although there is apparently less tolerance for heterosexist bias in the public media. In the military, the "don't ask, don't tell" protocol continued to exist until changed during the Obama administration. One positive change occurred in 2003, when the Supreme Court struck down a Texas law that criminalized sodomy on the grounds that states could not interfere in private sexual practices (*Lawrence v. Texas*). In addition, nine states, many major corporations, and more than seventy colleges and universities have banned discrimination based on gender identity.[176] In 2004, Massachusetts found that its constitution provided for same-sex marriage, challenging Congress's 1990 legislation of the Defense Of Marriage Act (DOMA), and although many states still ban same-sex marriage, they recognize same-sex civil unions on equal-protection grounds.[177] A major failure was the deletion of the Matthew Shepard Amendment from the Defense Department's authorization bill, which would have allowed FBI enforcement for hate crimes against gay and transgendered people (2007).

CONCLUSION: WHERE ARE THE SOCIAL WORKERS?

Since its beginnings, social work's mission has been to aid the helpless and poverty-stricken among us and to take action against social structures that perpetuate social and economic injustice. That content is required today in every CSWE-accredited social work program, and social work research examines in depth the consequences of and solutions to poverty and discrimination. Every mission statement, in social work programs or agencies, endorses our mission to ensure justice for those with whom we work. However, there seems to be a disconnect from mission to practice: We rarely practice in areas directly connected with clients in poverty or victims of direct or institutional discrimination. Rather, we practice in "tidier" areas, perhaps more personally rewarding ones, such as ensuring mental health for people who find themselves at odds with their lives. We ignore the intersections of "isms," such as racism, sexism, and classism, without realizing the broader consequences of our neglect.

We have edged or been edged out of these most elemental levels for many reasons, including society's need to maintain its racist, sexist, and classist status quo. For example, public assistance is confined to a small percentage of our population, takes only a small piece of governmental budgets, and is, by nature, a public responsibility; inadequate housing has no effects on educational attainment or employment; TANF requirements that mothers work have no consequences for the emotional well-being of their children. Whenever we have been involved in social action and have realized successes (the Social Security Acts of 1935, the 1950s' amalgamation of state and federal welfare into AFDC, the gains of clients' rights in the 1960s), we have then abandoned the field, leaving it to nonprofessional workers, political appointees, and civil servants.

Our desertion of mission leads us to "accommodate" injustices rather than to use our many resources to end them. The National Association of Social Workers (NASW) reports that it has nearly 150,000 members, and a Census Bureau Survey says there are over half a million professional social workers in the nation. Ten thousand social work educators teach in more than 200 programs, with more than 3,000 individual members of Council on Social Work Education (CSWE) and over 400 members of Baccalaureate Program Directors (BPD).[178] As social responsibility spirals downward under the Bush/Cheney imperial presidency, where created foreign wars have distracted the nation from attention to the needs of our most vulnerable, we should be at the forefront of social change.

Why are we not?

> **We have edged or been edged out of these most elemental levels for many reasons, including society's need to maintain its racist, sexist, and classist status quo.**

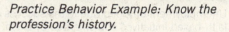

Professional Identity

Practice Behavior Example: Know the profession's history.

Critical Thinking Question: How has the focus and context of social work practice changed over the last hunderd-plus years?

The following questions will test your knowledge and understanding of the content found within this chapter. For additional assessment, including licensing-exam type questions on applying chapter content to practice behaviors, visit **MySearchLab**.

1. Providing government favors for personal friends and corporate interests is referred to as which of the following?

    a. Crony capitalism

    b. Carte blanche

    c. Compassionate conservatism

    d. State secret privileges

2. Which of the following affected employment during the Bush/Cheney administration?

    a. Companies minimized outsourcing jobs in favor of hiring American workers.

    b. Manufacturing jobs skyrocketed due to increased consumerism.

    c. New technology made many physical labor jobs obsolete.

    d. Unemployment dropped due to the success of the faith-based initiatives implemented by Bush.

3. Which statement about the Earned Income Tax Credit program is true?

    a. While it was a popular program because it awarded tax refunds, it was unsuccessful in moving people out of welfare.

    b. It was considered the most effective program for reducing poverty in America.

    c. It was a benefit available to anyone who earned income in the previous year.

    d. Federal grants from this program were automatically awarded to anyone below the poverty line.

4. Which Supreme Court case ruling in 2005 prohibited the death penalty for those 18 and under?

    a. *Roper v. Simmons*

    b. *Stenberg v. Carhart*

    c. *Lawrence v. Texas*

    d. *Cobell v. Norton*

5. You are working with a client with diabetes who is incarcerated. What should your client expect in regard to health and medical care coverage while in jail?

    a. Prisoners are eligible for Medicare.

    b. Prisoners are eligible for Medicaid.

    c. Prisoners rely on state funding for their medical care and medications.

    d. Federal grants specifically for prisoner health care will provide any health care needed.

6. When working with Hispanic Americans and immigrants, what factor should you keep in mind when discussing their options for public assistance?

    a. The fear of deportation or denial of citizenship makes them less likely to participate in any kind of public assistance program.

    b. The religious beliefs of most Hispanic Americans argue that relying on public assistance is immoral.

    c. They tend to rely on public assistance programs more than any other group.

    d. They tend not to trust the ethics of social workers of public assistance programs.

7. Discuss the significant changes in the employment market in the United States during the Bush/Cheney administration.

Reinforce what you learned in this chapter by studying videos, cases, documents, and more available at **www.MySearchLab.com**.

Watch and Review

Watch these Videos

Marrying Kind

* Keeping up with Shifting Contexts

* Attending to Changes and Relevant Services

* Providing Leadership to Promote Change

Read and Review

Read these Cases/Documents

Δ A Narrative in New Masculinity

Δ Community to Community: A Unique Response to Long-Term Disaster Relief

Δ Volunteer Experiences with the Neighbors Helping Neighbors Program

Δ Medical Social Work: Annie

Assess Your Knowledge

Go to **MySearchLab** to test your knowledge of key topics in this chapter with topic-specific quizzes. Conclude your assessment by completing the chapter exam.

---

* = CSWE Core Competency Asset
Δ = Case Study

15

Political Stonewalls

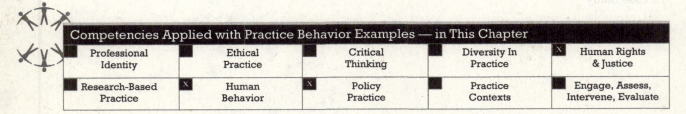

Competencies Applied with Practice Behavior Examples — in This Chapter				
☐ Professional Identity	☐ Ethical Practice	☐ Critical Thinking	☐ Diversity In Practice	☒ Human Rights & Justice
☐ Research-Based Practice	☒ Human Behavior	☒ Policy Practice	☐ Practice Contexts	☐ Engage, Assess, Intervene, Evaluate

THE BITTER REMNANTS OF THE BUSH ADMINISTRATION

As Obama campaigned for the presidency on a vision of hope, the nation slid into what would become known as the *great recession*. Analysts and commentators have used this concept to describe the economic recession the country and much of the world started to experience in late 2007. Although this is not the first time *great* has been used to describe a recession,[1] the current recession is great in that recent data reveal that it is the worst economic downturn since the great depression of the 1930s.[2,3] In this recession, the national debt was about $400 billion, overall unemployment in the double digits and for minority workers between 25 and 30 percent, manufacturing and construction down, banks and companies in debt to the government or bankrupt, homes at a rate of foreclosure not seen since the 1930s, wars in both Iraq and Afghanistan, and citizen despair at the chaotic state of the Union. Civil anguish led to two kinds of backlash: first, the creation of a new Far Right conservatism, with a goal of shrinking government power (from which came the Tea Party); second, to what extent the government could attempt to solve the nation's problems and create hope for the future.

These diametrically opposed stances threw the political economy into chaos even before the 2008 election, the theme being to "throw the rascals out." Radical conservatives and libertarians, such as Alaskan Governor Sarah Palin (or politicians newly radicalized for the sake of elections, such as John McCain) clamored for the status quo in terms of spending and taxes. Just as vocal and angry about the state of the nation were those seeking positive changes for the general welfare, including social programs such as health care, a rising economy, and greater employment as they rallied around the motto of "Yes we can." Primary elections were fought hard and noisily, with potential candidates on the Democratic side funneling down finally to Barack Obama, with Hillary Rodham Clinton a close runner-up and Joe Biden the vice-presidential nominee. Republicans finally chose John McCain and Sarah Palin as running mates. These candidates presented a phenomenon in itself, because neither a person of African descent nor a woman had ever entered the race for president, though Geraldine Ferraro had earlier been a vice-presidential candidate.

THE HISTORICAL SIGNIFICANCE OF THE 2008 ELECTION

For the first time in American history, a president of African-American heritage—Barack Obama—was elected, bringing the reality of equality under law finally into existence. On the national level we began to look again at what equality meant, and on the global level the election reaffirmed the proof of American democracy. While the election did not end racism in America, we now had a powerful impetus to free future generations of that form of immorality.

In much the same way, the status of women in America received needed attention. Not only did Hillary Rodham Clinton run for president, in itself a coup, but she was appointed Secretary of State in a time of global turmoil, like former Secretary Madeleine Albright, in a position equal to men dealing with nations that traditionally treated women as less than human. In addition, we note that Alaskan Governor Sarah Palin ran for Republican vice president with John McCain. Geraldine Ferraro had tried for this office (as a Democratic candidate) in the 1994. However, Palin made her mark as an outspoken and respected spokesperson for the Far Right, claiming her status as a "maverick," a new role model for many American women.

The Obama election also brought a Democratic majority into the House of Representatives. However, this was a short-lived victory. Although Obama and the Democratic Congress worked for bipartisan agreements, Republicans, along with a few conservative Democrats, began block voting and turned down social proposals and attempts to bring in more revenue by taxing the wealthy and corporations. As a result, the nation had a "do-nothing" Congress, and in the mid-term election (2010) a disgruntled electorate threw the rascals out again, returning a Republican majority to the House. Thus the political economy became mired, concretized as the Republican "party of No" refused to compromise or support Obama's proposals for health care—a major social welfare plan—or stimulus package to ward off the recession (to be discussed later).

Policy Practice

Practice Behavior Example: Understand that policy affects service delivery and actively engage in policy practice.

Critical Thinking Question: How does the political composition of the executive, legislative and judicial branches affect the outcome of social welfare policies?

THE ECONOMIC MORASS

With Republicans pointing the finger at Obama for not solving the economic crisis, the public joined them in blaming him for being unable to turn around the burgeoning recession. However, according to Ettlinger and Linden,[4] the single most important factor in the massive deficit's cause was . . .

the legacy of President George W. Bush's legislative agenda. . . . Changes in federal law during the Bush administration are responsible for 40 percent of the short-term fiscal problem. [We] estimate that the tax cuts passed during the Bush presidency [reduced] government revenue collections by $231 billion in 2009 . . . [and his administration policies increased . . . federal debt interest payments by] $218 billion . . . in 2009.

Had President Bush not cut taxes while simultaneously pursuing two foreign wars and adopting other programs without paying for them, the current deficit would be only 4.7 percent of gross domestic product this year [2009], instead of the eye-catching 11.2 percent . . . fiscal irresponsibility, regulatory indifference, fueling of an asset and credit bubble, a failure to focus on jobs and incomes, and inaction as the economy started slipping. . . .

Obama entered the presidency while politics was concretized around two ideals—ideals that were sincere but gave no room for compromise on the massive problems confronting the nation. Republican politicians, harking back to the Reagan "trickle-down theory," took the stance that promoting social ideals, including paying for Social Security and Medicare, would cost too much. Raising new revenue by taxing the rich and corporations would hurt the capitalist economy. Tea Party radicals joined them in calling for less government interference in state and private lives, along with the demand to end the national deficit and pay off the national debt. On the other hand, liberals, mostly Democratic politicians, were willing to compromise on some issues but were appalled that conservatives would not "provide for the general welfare" as the constitution provided. Clearly, it appeared that conservative politicians were once again trying to balance the budget on the backs of the needy and/or helpless.

SOCIAL WELFARE IN THE OBAMA ADMINISTRATION

Obama's Signature Acts: Health Care and Stimulus Acts

Obama's presidential campaign and his first three years as president focused on several key issues, especially the economy and health care. A month after he took office (February 17, 2009), Congress passed his first major bill, the American Recovery and Reinvestment Act of 2009, also known as the Stimulus Act. Its purpose was to "stimulate" the economy, in deep recession since 2007, and it allocated $787 billion to "jump start" the economy and salvage between 900,000 and 2.3 million jobs.[5] When the depth of the recession climaxed in late 2008, major investment firms and commercial banks, such as Lehman Brothers and Bear Stearns, filed for bankruptcy. The Stimulus Act bailed them out with $700 billion, and in addition allocated $288 billion in tax cuts; $224 billion to extend unemployment benefits, education, and health care; and $275 billion for job creation. These latter amounts were to be allocated over ten years, but the bulk of the money was spent in the first three years.

The Patient Protection and Affordable Care Act (Health Care Law, also known as Obamacare) was Obama's second signature legislation, signed into law on March 23, 2010. The law allocated $900 billion in new funding to lower health care costs, expand health care coverage to more people, and eliminate barriers to quality health care. The nine titles of the bill were to:

1. change the current system by eliminating refusal for pre-existing conditions, creating an American Health Benefit Exchange so that individuals and small employers might access health coverage by refunding tax credits for those whose incomes were between 100 and 400 percent of the federal poverty threshold, and instituting a plan requiring people to buy health coverage or pay a penalty;

2. expand Medicaid coverage to lower-income individuals, enhance federal support for the Children's Health Insurance Program (CHIP), make enrollment procedures less difficult for Medicaid and CHIP, improve Medicaid services, and provide greater flexibility for long-term services and supports;

3. improve quality and efficiency of health care to all persons, especially Medicare and Medicaid, by linking payments of services to quality of outcomes, supporting research to better educate consumers concerning divergent medical interventions, reducing the Medicare Part D prescription coverage gap (donut hole), and establishing an Independent Medicare Advisory Board to ensure the program's sustainability;

4. prevent chronic illnesses and improve the overall public health of the nation by establishing an interagency prevention council, identifying barriers to preventive health care services, and offering federal grants for pilot programs to demonstrate better health and best prevention practices;

5. improve training, recruitment, and retention of health care workers so as to increase and diversify the health care workforce, and to establish a workforce commission to evaluate health care needs and strategies to meet the needs;

6. establish new requirements for health industry transparency by providing public information and seeking to prevent fraud and abuse in health care programs;

7. promote access to medical innovations by establishing a process to allow the FDA to license new treatments bio-similar or interchangeable with previous licensed product or therapies, and make more affordable medicines for children and underserved areas;

8. establish a voluntary self-funded long-term care insurance program called the Community Living Assistance Services and Supports (CLASS) program to purchase community living assistance services for persons with functional limitations; and

9. impose a new excise tax of 40 percent on insurance companies with any health care plan with an annual premium that exceeds the threshold of $8,500 for individual coverage and $23,000 for family coverage.

These signature policy initiatives are extremely important to understand and analyze social welfare policy trends since Obama took office in January 2009. We now examine specific social welfare policy trends during the Obama administration, especially but not exclusively through his economic stimulus package and health care law.

Policy Practice

Practice Behavior Example: Analyze, formulate, and advocate for policies that advance social well-being.

Critical Thinking Question: What impact does the Health Care Reform Law have on lower-, middle-, and upper-class Americans?

Unemployment, Homelessness, and Housing

Major objectives of the American Recovery and Reinvestment Act (Stimulus Act) were to reduce unemployment and to save almost a million American jobs. The Obama administration contended that a minimum of 900,000 jobs would be saved by October 30, 2010, though in actuality only 640,329 jobs were saved. Indeed, the unemployment rate increased significantly after the Stimulus Act passed. The unemployment rate was 7.8 percent when Obama took office in January 2009. Table 15.1 shows that the national unemployment rate increased in eight consecutive months, peaking at 10.1 percent in October 2009 and remained high at 9.2 percent as of June 2011.

Table 15.1   U.S. Unemployment Rates, 2007–2011

Year	Jan	Feb	Mar	Apr	May	Jun	Jul	Aug	Sep	Oct	Nov	Dec
2007	4.6	4.5	4.4	4.5	4.4	4.6	4.7	4.6	4.7	4.7	4.7	5.0
2008	5.0	4.8	5.1	4.9	5.4	5.6	5.8	6.1	6.2	6.6	6.8	7.3
2009	7.8	8.2	8.6	8.9	9.4	9.5	9.5	9.7	9.8	10.1	9.9	9.9
2010	9.7	9.7	9.7	9.8	9.6	9.5	9.5	9.6	9.6	9.7	9.8	9.4
2011	9.0	8.9	8.8	9.0	9.1	9.2						

Source: Bureau of Labor Statistics, 2011.

Table 15.2 **Housing Vacancy Rates by Units, 2007–2010**

Year	1 Unit	2 or more units	5 or more units
2007	2.4	8.3	8.5
2008	2.5	8.8	8.8
2008/r*	2.5	9.0	8.7
2009	2.3	8.7	8.7
2010	2.2	9.2	9.5

*/r: Revised, see quarterly or annual report for explanation.

Source: Current Population Survey/Housing Vacancies and Homeownership, Series H-111, Bureau of the Census, Washington, D.C. 20233, 2011.

Though the Stimulus Act was intended to reduce unemployment and therefore preclude the likelihood of more homelessness, between 2008 and 2009, the number of homeless persons in families increased by 3.6 percent and the number of sheltered households (those who used emergency shelters or transitional housing programs) with children increased by 6.9 percent.[6]

Another way to examine how the great recession affected the living patterns of persons and families is to review data on housing vacancy rates. According to the U.S. Census Bureau, "a housing unit is vacant if no one is living in it at the time of the interview, unless its occupants are only temporarily absent." Table 15.2 shows that during the year when the recession officially started, the housing vacancy rate for two or more and five or more units was 8.3 and 8.5, respectively. However, by 2010, those rates had increased to 9.2 and 9.5, respectively. Multiple housing units are usually apartment dwellings, and they serve as a major source of shelter for the working class and both working and non-working poor persons. Thus, the increase in multiple housing vacancy rates from 2007 to 2010 (with some fluctuation in 2008 and 2009) could suggest that economically vulnerable persons were either driven into homelessness or frequently displaced from one apartment unit to the other. The frequent housing displacement of individuals and families could be attributed to evictions or the need to move to a unit that is less expensive.

Human Rights & Justice

Practice Behavior Example: Understand the forms and mechanisms of oppression and discrimination.

Critical Thinking Question: Is the Stimulus Act an example of corporate welfare or social welfare policy?

Human Rights and Justice

Poverty and TANF

Obama spoke very little about poverty and public welfare issues in his campaign, and he offered few explicit ideas about these issues as president. He often has used the slogan "a rising tide raises all boats," intimating that there is no need to specifically target the poor or those with significant social and economic challenges, apparently assuming that the Stimulus Act could improve the lives of us all. Obama's lack of poverty-specific policies seems to suggest that there is no need to specifically target the poor who have fewer skills and significantly more social and economic challenges. By the end of 2009, the Stimulus Act had not demonstrated improvement among the poor: in fact, the number of people and families in poverty increased between 2007 and 2009.

Table 15.3   Number and Percent of Persons Below Poverty Level by Race, 2007–2009

Year	All Races		Not Hispanic White		Not Hispanic Black		Asians		Hispanic	
	n	%	*n*	%	*n*	%	*n*	%	*n*	%
2007	37,276	12.5	16,032	8.2	9,237	24.5	1,349	10.2	9,890	21.5
2008	39,829	13.2	17,024	8.6	9,379	24.7	1,576	11.8	10,987	23.2
2009	43,569	14.3	18,530	9.4	9,944	25.8	1,746	12.5	12,350	25.3

Note: Numbers in Thousands.

Source: U.S. Bureau of the Census, Current Population Survey, Annual Social and Economic Supplements, 2011.

As shown in Table 15.3, the number of all people living in poverty increased from 12.5 percent in 2007 to 14.3 percent in 2009. For those living below the poverty line, the increase was from 10.8 percent in 2007 to 12.5 percent in 2009. Finally, the situation for families headed by a female householder also worsened in that their poverty status rose from 30.7 percent in 2007 to 32.5 percent in 2009. Interestingly, for African-American families headed by a female householder, the percentage of families in poverty was the same for 2007 and 2009, at 39.7 percent.

The data on the average number of recipients of the Temporary Assistance for Needy Families (TANF) program also suggest the lack of effectiveness of Obama's Stimulus Act. Table 15.4 presents TANF recipient data from 2007 to 2010. In 2008, when Obama won the presidential election, an average monthly number of 3,795,007 persons received TANF. By 2010, when Obama was in office for two years, the average monthly number of total TANF recipients had increased to 4,376,347. To help people on TANF, Obama created a $5 billion TANF emergency fund that states could use for basic assistance, short-term non-recurrent benefits, or subsidized employment. States had to demonstrate an increase in caseloads to receive the emergency funds. However, Congress failed to extend the TANF emergency fund in the fall of 2010. Instead, in

Table 15.4   Number of TANF Recipients, 2007–2010

Year	Total Recipients
2007	3,896,081*
2008	3,795,007*
2009	4,154,769*
2010	4,376,347**

*Calendar Year (January–December); Including adults and children

**Calendar year average is based on data for nine months.

Note: Numbers in Thousands

Source: Temporary Assistance for Needy Families, U.S. Department of Health and Human Services, Administration for Children and Families, 2009–2011.

November of 2010, it passed the Claims Resolution Act, which extended the TANF block grant program of $16.5 billion through September 30, 2011. One problem with the Claims Resolution Act is that it reduced funding for TANF supplemental grants to 17 relatively poor or rapidly growing states. Each year since TANF was established, these grants have helped these states to supplement the regular block grant funding to meet the needs of their recipients. The Claims Resolution Act reduced these grants to 66 percent of their original funding through June 30, 2011. This reduction had diminished these states' ability to provide needed welfare services.

Although the TANF Emergency Fund and the Contingency Resolution Act helped to cushion the effects of the recession somewhat, economically vulnerable persons still suffered. Mothers on TANF still had difficulties finding employment, especially African-American and Hispanic mothers. When they could locate employment, it was in very low wage jobs that provided little to no health care or other benefits. These mothers also are more likely to be the first to be laid off in touch economic times, which means that they are likely to return as TANF recipients. Additionally, about 25 percent of newly unemployed persons who leave TANF apply for unemployment insurance, and about half of this number receives the benefit.[7] The problem, however, is that because of higher rates of job instability and employer layoffs, TANF leavers who receive unemployment insurance get less money.[8]

One of the most recent controversial changes to welfare policy as it pertained to TANF was Florida's law that required all recipients of their TANF program to be tested for illicit drugs.[9] Signed into law by Florida Governor Rick Scott in May 2011, the law required recipients to pay for their drug tests, and those who tested positive could be denied benefits for a year. If recipients fail a second time, they will be denied benefits for three years. Those who failed the test can designate a third party to receive the benefits on their children's behalf. Most states do not require such comprehensive and obtrusive drug testing, but Florida's law might serve as a precedent if it holds up under appeal. Consistent with the historic justifications, Governor Scott said that the new law reinforces personal responsibility and prevents Florida's taxpayers from supporting the drug addictions of the poor.[10] This justification relies heavily on prominent notions and stereotypes of the poor as social deviants who need to be regulated and castigated. The law went into effect on July 1, 2011.

The deleterious impact of the recession on TANF mothers also have grave consequences for their children. Child poverty data show that children experience poverty more than all other persons. For example, in 2009, the first year of the Obama administration, child poverty was over 6 percent higher than the poverty rate for all persons.[11] Although roughly 63 percent of U.S. children attain adulthood without ever experiencing poverty, about 10 percent of children experience conditions of persistent poverty.[12] Relative to white children, African-American children are 2.5 times more likely to live in poverty and seven times more likely to be persistently poor.[13] Furthermore, children who live in TANF-recipient households are at a very high risk of experiencing persistent poverty throughout their childhood.

The great recession also lead to an increase in the number of persons receiving food stamps (now called SNAP).[14] According to the U.S. Department of Agriculture,[15] over 12 million more persons received food stamps in fiscal year 2010 compared to fiscal year 2008. Likewise, almost 6 million more households received food stamps in fiscal year 2010 as compared to fiscal year 2008. The data

According to the U.S. Department of Agriculture, over 12 million more persons received food stamps in fiscal year 2008 compared to fiscal year 2010.

on the increase in the number of food stamps recipients reinforce the 2009 U.S. Department of Agriculture report on food security. The report found that there were more food insecure households in 2009 compared to 2008 and that 50.2 million people live in such households, 17.2 million being children.[16] Food insecure households are those in which one or more persons in the household were hungry over the course of a year due to the inability to afford sufficient food.[17] Like most data of this kind, black and Hispanic households experienced greater food insecurity rates than did other households. A final indicator of the injurious effects of the great recession related to poverty is numbers associated with the WIC (Women, Infants, and Children) program. In 2008, the year Obama was elected, there were 8.705 million WIC participants. In 2010, the number had increase to 9.175 million participants.[18]

During the first few years of the Obama administration, a few changes took place under the SNAP program. On June 17, 2009, the old paper coupon system was completely replaced by the Electronic Benefits Transfer (EBT) system as the nationwide way to distribute benefits to SNAP recipients.[19] Some states, however, had phased in the EBT before 2009. In addition, provisions of the Farm Security and Rural Investment Act of 2002 were implemented. This Act created new eligibility and certification standards for recipients of food stamps, and the provisions gave states greater flexibility in their food stamp eligibility practices.[20] For example, states now have the flexibility to exclude some forms of income of applicants or recipients who are not considered under the state's TANF and Medicaid programs.

Education and Crime

A consistent finding in social science research is the relationship between social class and violent crime. Persons who have lower socioeconomic status, which includes lower educational levels, tend to be at more risk of committing violent and street-related crimes.[21] Thus, it can be argued that two characteristics of vulnerability in America are low educational level and risk of committing violent crimes. Several commentators have written about the low high school graduation rates and the poor state of public school education and funding in America. Data from the Children's Defense Fund's 2010 report, *State of America's Children*, reveal the following:

- "The U.S. spends almost three times as much per prisoner as per public school pupil.
- Black students are more than three times as likely as White or Asian/Pacific Islander and twice as likely as Hispanic students to be suspended from school.
- Forty-six percent of Black high school students, 39 percent of Hispanic, and 11 percent of White students attend the 2,000 'dropout factories' across our country, where less than 60 percent of the freshman class will graduate in four years with a regular diploma.
- Teachers in high poverty schools are more likely to have less experience, less training and fewer advanced degrees than teachers in low poverty schools." (p. G-1)

Those who live in lower-income communities are especially victimized by poorly funded and low-performing schools, and their high school completion rates are lower than average.

Those who live in lower-income communities are especially victimized by poorly funded and low-performing schools, and their high school completion rates are lower than average. Whereas nationally, about 72 percent of public school students graduate on time, the rates are significantly lower for students who live in lower-income communities and who are disproportionately black and brown.[22] Obama's effort at addressing the education problem was to include money in the Recovery and Reinvestment Act of 2009. In the Act, Obama included $5 billion to improve early learning programs, included Head Start, Early Head Start, child care, and programs for special needs children. The Act also included $77 billon for reforms to improve elementary and secondary school education, providing $48.6 billion to help states stabilize their education budgets and to help states to accomplish the following:

- "make improvements in teacher effectiveness and ensure that all schools have highly qualified teachers;
- make progress toward college and career-ready standards and rigorous assessments that will improve both teaching and learning;
- improve achievement in low-performing schools, through intensive support and effective interventions; and
- gather information to improve student learning, teacher performance, and college and career readiness through enhanced data systems."[23]

Because of the abysmal data on public school education and graduate rates, much of the school reform debate focuses on the use of educational vouchers. Educational vouchers are tuition certificates that parents can use to pay for their children to attend both public and private schools.[24] These vouchers can be paid by government or private funds. The use of public vouchers, sponsored by taxpayer money, to pay for private school education has generated considerable controversy. Those on the political Right favor vouchers because they say they provide parents in low-income areas the choice to remove their children from persistently failing schools. They also contend that vouchers would infuse the element of competition into primary and secondary school education and would help eliminate *poorly* performing public schools.[25] Moderates like President Obama tend to oppose the voucher idea and support the continuation of public school education. They also tend to focus on the dynamics of the school milieu that they view as impediments to successful student learning, such as the need for greater teacher and principal accountability, higher teacher salaries, and more resources to improve failing schools. Some, like former Washington, D.C. school chancellor Michelle Rhee support the elimination of the tenure system, which provides lifetime employment for teachers, merit pay for teachers, and the removal of educators and principals who consistently produce poor results.[26,27] Those on the Far Left focus on correcting the inequities in the funding structure of public education. They advocate for the elimination of property taxes as the major funding source of public education and significant increases in state and federal funding for public education.[28,29] These advocates maintain that the exclusive reliance on local property taxes creates wide disparities in educational funding between higher-income and lower-income communities.[30,31]

The educational disaster in many of the nation's low-income communities and its link to persistent poverty perhaps reveal itself best through the prevalence of crime and mass incarceration. Data from the FBI show that violent crime has gone down in recent years in the United States in both small and

Human Behavior

Practice Behavior Example: Know about human behavior across the life course; the range of social systems in which people live; and the ways social systems promote or deter people in maintaining or achieving health and well-being.

Critical Thinking Question: What are some of the short- and long-term consequences of unequally funding public schools?

large cities and metropolitan areas.[32] The data also reveal that drug-related arrests, especially in many of the urban centers in America, have increased.[33] Most of the offenses are nonviolent crimes of possession and distribution and many of those arrested are young males in low-income communities.[34] Drug-related arrests often take on a racial feature in that those arrested are most likely to be young African-American and Hispanic males.[35] Michelle Alexander[36] contends that the racial feature of drug-related and other nonviolent arrests constitutes a new era of "Jim Crow" in that it has led to the mass incarceration and disenfranchisement of mostly young, African-American males. This new form of Jim Crow, she suggests, serves a social control function by locking up young men who are deemed deviants and threats to community stability. She also argues that this mass incarceration justifies the marginalization of these men and the denial of essential resources to combat the roots of the problem, which are poverty and racism.

Much of the mass incarceration that Alexander speaks about has been facilitated by the federal "three strikes and you're out" law passed in the 1990s under the Clinton administration. This law established many new federal capital crimes, authorized life sentences for some three-time offenders, and allocated over $16 billion for the expansion of state prisons and local law enforcement agencies.[37] In 2009, 2,284,900 persons were incarcerated.[38] High incarceration levels have placed a tremendous strain on state budgets and have led to jail overcrowding. In California, prison overcrowding led inmates to file lawsuits claiming that the state did not provide adequate medical and mental health services in the prison system. Inadequate health services had caused many inmates to die unnecessarily or to prolong their illnesses. In 2011, the cases reached the U.S. Supreme Court, and, in a 5 to 4 ruling, the Court ruled that California had to sharply reduce its inmate population of 145,000 to prevent unnecessary death and suffering due to prison overcrowding.[39]

Another strategy that has been used to prevent prison overcrowding is the drug court system. A significant number of arrests and incarcerations are for nonviolent drug-related offenses.[40] Increasingly, states and local jurisdictions are using drug courts as a way to adjudicate these offenders. Drug courts are for drug-addicted persons who can receive treatment while under the supervision of the criminal justice system.[41] Usually for a term of a year, these courts require participants to: (1) enter intensive drug treatment; (2) be held accountable by the drug court judge for meeting their obligations to the court and the broader society; (3) be regularly and randomly tested for substance use; (4) appear in court often so that their progress can be reviewed by the judge; and (5) be rewarded for making progress and sanctioned when they do not meet their obligations.[42] These courts have shown much success but critics say that the strategy is too soft on drug-related crimes.

The Obama administration has not spent much time on drug-related issues, but Obama's National Drug Control Strategy was released in May of 2010. It attempts to achieve a balance among prevention, treatment, enforcement, and international cooperation.[43] However, consistent with many of his other social policy initiatives, Obama's policy does not address head on the problem of poverty and its intersection with racial inequality. To be fair, Obama's Justice Department has attempted to eliminate the differential sentencing between powder and crack cocaine arrests, but the Obama administration still appears to downplay the important role economic and racial inequality plays in arrests and conviction rates.

SOCIAL ISSUES AND VULNERABLE POPULATIONS

The 2007 recession targeted economic issues and had devastating effects on the economically vulnerable. However, social vulnerabilities—sexism, racism, heterosexism, ageism, and ableism—often intersect with economic realities. A review of some social indicators helps us understand the degree of vulnerability among women; people of color; lesbian, gay, bisexual, and transgender (LGBT) persons; the elderly; and persons with special needs. Although focusing many efforts on the economy and health care, the Obama administration has taken important steps to assuage social vulnerabilities among some of these groups.

Women

Since the 2007 recession, the gender picture has been complex. During the early years of the recession, men experienced unemployment more than twice as much as did women, which accounted for about 71 percent of the jobs lost from December 2007 to June 2009.[44] However, from June 2009 to May 2011, men's unemployment rates, regardless of race, decreased as women's increased.[45] In addition, men have made gains more than women in almost all of the major sectors of the economy.[46] In 2009, women continued to lag behind men at 80 percent of their median weekly earnings.[47] Although this represents an improvement from the late 1970s when women's earnings were at 62 percent of men's, wage discrimination continues.

According to the U.S. Equal Employment Opportunity Commission (EEOC), women experience three types of workplace discrimination: caregiver discrimination, wage discrimination, and harassment based on sex.[48] Typical examples of current caregiver discrimination include supervisors' reduction of workloads and denying promotions for mothers, because of the belief that these women are less committed to their careers and have less time for work assignments and responsibilities.[49] These forms of discrimination continue to reduce women's opportunity to advance their careers by reinforcing attitudes and stereotypes that support patriarchy and the notion that women's work should be confined to the private sphere.

To address wage discrimination among women (and other individuals), President Obama signed the Lilly Ledbetter Fair Pay Act in January 2009, which was his first bill signed as president.[50] This law overruled a 2007 5 to 4 U.S. Supreme Court ruling[51] (*Ledbetter v. Goodyear Tire & Rubber Co.*) that restricted the time that persons could file wage discrimination law suits with the Equal Employment Opportunity Commission (EEOC) to 180 days after an employer first issued a discriminatory paycheck.[52] Ms. Lilly Ledbetter, plaintiff, claimed years of discrimination by the Goodyear Tire Company in Gadsden, Alabama, which resulted in lower pay increases over time. She alleged that although her initial compensation was similar to her male counterparts', over time numerous discriminatory performance evaluations from her supervisor lowered her present salary. Filing suit in 1998, in the U.S. District Court of Northern Alabama, the court ruled that her claim was unsubstantiated and that she should have filed separate discrimination charges within 180 days for each time she received an unequal pay check. In short, the ruling meant that plaintiffs could not claim that current acts of wage discrimination were based on cumulative past acts of discrimination.[53] On appeal, the Ledbetter Act relaxed the conditions under which plaintiffs could file for and receive compensation for wage discrimination so that they did not have to swiftly perceive that they had endured discrimination and promptly report it. It gives women and others who may experience wage discrimination more protection under Title VII of the 1964 Civil Rights Act.

People of Color

The 2007 recession has had devastating but differential effects on people of color. Unemployment rates during the recession have been consistently higher for African and Hispanic Americans compared to white or European Americans.[54] For example, in 2009, the annual unemployment rate for white Americans was 8.5 percent, 14.8 percent for African Americans, and 12.1 percent for Hispanic Americans[55] (though the unemployment rate for Asian Americans was 7.3 percent). By June of 2011, the disparity between white and black unemployment had doubled: the white unemployment rate was 8.2 percent while the black unemployment rate was 16.5 percent.[56]

Throughout America's history, including Obama's tenure, people of color have had less household and per capita income than non-Hispanic whites. For example, in 2009, non-Hispanic white median household income was $54,461, for African Americans it was $32,584, and for Hispanics it was $38,039. Only Asian-American household median income exceeded that of non-Hispanic whites.[57] Per capita income patterns were similar: in 2009, non-Hispanic whites, $30,941; African Americans, $18,135; and Hispanics, $15,063. Asian Americans had the highest per capita median income of the groups of color ($30,653), which was slightly lower than that of non-Hispanic whites.[58] Additionally, people of color were most likely to suffer poverty more than non-Hispanic whites, with a quarter of African and Hispanic Americans falling below the poverty level in 2009, compared to 9 percent of non-Hispanic whites (see Table 15.3).

People of color also tended to have less health insurance and more home foreclosures than did non-Hispanic white persons. In 2009, 21 percent of African Americans and almost a third (32.4 percent) of Hispanic Americans lacked health insurance, compared to 12 percent of non-Hispanic whites.[59] From these numbers, it would appear that Obama's health care plan, which attempts to expand Medicaid coverage to a larger number of Americans, may help address some of the health challenges people of color disproportionately confront.

Finally, the home mortgage catastrophe disproportionately afflicted people of color. Between January 2007 and the end of 2009, foreclosure rates per 10,000 loans were estimated at 790 for African-Americans, 769 for Hispanics, and 452 for non-Hispanics.[60] Among recent borrowers during the same period, an estimated 8 percent of African and Hispanic Americans lost their homes compared to 4.5 percent of non-Hispanic whites.[61] Furthermore, the racial disparity in home foreclosure rates persisted even across income lines: higher-income people of color foreclosed at a higher rate than similarly incomed non-Hispanic whites.[62] These foreclosure numbers suggest that people of color were less likely to have the financial cushion to withstand economic downturns than non-Hispanic whites, and that they were targeted more often by greedy mortgage lenders aggressively marketing to families of color, ostensibly to circumvent charges of racial discrimination.[63] Known as "reverse redlining," mortgage lenders intentionally marketed subprime, no-down payment, and interest-only loans to families of color whom they knew were at risk of defaulting.[64] However, these same lenders, in league with Wall Street bankers, would benefit from these defaults by selling these loans for a profit.[65]

Many people of color, especially African Americans, believed that President Obama's election would improve their lives and that a black president and former community organizer in poor communities would be sensitive to their plight. However, President Obama has not advocated or brought about any race-specific social policies to improve the conditions of communities of color. Instead, the Obama administration appeared to choose the "racial neutral" path of governing and social policy development, which maintains that race-specific policies generate cross-racial antagonism that might be perceived as reverse racism.[66] Race-specific policies also would render Obama vulnerable to criticisms of racial favoritism, which would be inconsistent with the "one America" motto that characterized his campaign. Although Obama never ran as a race-specific candidate, many people of color still hoped that he might end some of racism's contemporary manifestations.

LGBT Persons

Since the Defense of Marriage Act (DOMA) of 1996, marriage rights have become a major civil rights issue affecting LGBT persons because the DOMA mandated marriage be defined as a legal union between one man and one woman.[67] Several states have included this issue as a referendum and, by June 2011, six states had made it legal for LGBT persons to marry. Advocates of marriage equality for LGBT persons contend that denying these rights to LGBT persons violates the fourteenth amendment of the U.S. constitution.[68] They argue that marriage is an individual right that should transcend all group classifications, so the government has no right to express moral disapproval of groups of people.[69] Supporters of gay marriage also say that promoting marriage is a good thing for gay and lesbian persons and for the broader society[70,71] because married people tend to be healthier, happy, and live longer, and are more connected to their communities.[72,73] Marriage equality supporters also say that allowing LGBT persons the opportunity to marry reinforces the value of monogamy.

Opponents of LGBT marriage contend that one of the standards to determine whether a right should receive equal protection under the fourteenth amendment is whether it is deemed a component of the nation's history and tradition.[74] They argue that since gay and lesbian marriage does not represent the nation's history and tradition, only marriage between one man and one woman should receive constitutional protection. Also, opponents say LGBT marriage violates biblical doctrine and pollutes and confuses children about the definition of normal and healthy sexual relations, presenting data showing that children from same-sex parents are harmed socially and psychologically. Finally, LGBT marriage opponents maintain that allowing same-sex marriage would open the floodgate to legitimize other undesirable marriage possibilities such as polygamous, incestuous, and adult–child relationships.

During the Obama administration, the marriage equality debate continued, along with other LGBT rights issues. In 2010, President Obama ordered the state department to no longer constitutionally defend the DOMA, because he believed that sections of the law might be unconstitutional.[75] In both 2009 and 2010, President Obama expanded benefits for same-sex partners of federal employees,[76] including family assistance services, hardship transfers, re-location funds, healthcare, sick leave, and medical evacuation services.[77] Although these benefits helped sex-partners achieve some degree of equality, he stated that existing federal law precluded him from allowing same-sex federal partners from having the same benefits as did heterosexual married couples.[78]

Perhaps Obama's most significant gesture toward LGBT equality was his signing, in 2010, of the repeal of Clinton's 1994 military policy of "Don't ask, don't tell" (DADT). The DADT policy prohibited the military from discriminating against or harassing LGBT personnel who do not disclose their sexual orientation/preference and excluded openly LGBT persons from military service.[79] Though some saw DADT as a movement toward LGBT equality, others interpreted it as dehumanizing for LGBT military persons because they still had to keep their sexual orientation a secret. President Obama echoed the latter sentiment while signing the repeal by stating: "No longer will tens of thousands of Americans in uniform be asked to live a lie, or look over their shoulder in order to serve the country that they love."

Although he was applauded for repealing DADT and expanding benefits to same-sex federal employees, Obama was still criticized for not supporting same-sex marriages.[80] However, in May, 2012, Obama declared his acceptance and of support of gay marriage as public opinion on marriage equality moved toward greater acceptance. A Gallup poll released in May 2011 reported that for the first time since it has been collecting data on the subject, a majority of Americans (53 percent) say that same-sex marriage should be legal.[81] For now, the matter still remains unresolved, as both proponents and opponents of LGBT marriage equality appear to be entrenched.

The Elderly and Disabled

Considerable attention in the Obama administration has been given to the solvency of Social Security and Medicare, largely due to political debates about the federal government's debt and deficit levels, which accelerated after the Republicans took control over the House of Representatives in 2010. Before that takeover, Obama's Social Security reforms, which focused on taxing those with incomes above $250,000, received resistance from both Congressional Democrats and Republicans.[82] Democrats said his focus should be on the economy rather than Social Security, while Republicans claimed taxing the rich to assuage Social Security spending was wrong. The Republicans House take-over pushed Obama, along with Congressional Democrats, to address debt and deficit issues more prominently. New House GOP Budget chairman Paul Ryan introduced in his budget plan the recommendation to establish private health care plan options as a way to reform Medicare.[83] During this period, Republicans increased their recommendations to cut Social Security benefits, at least for future recipients.

Discussions over cutting and privatizing Social Security and Medicare have scared many elderly persons, especially those in poverty who depend heavily on the two programs for survival. In 2009, 8.9 percent or 3.4 million of persons 65 and older were living below the poverty line,[84] but one analysis revealed that nearly 14 million more elderly Americans 65 and over would experience poverty had it not been for Social Security benefits.[85] For the elderly, the recession has caused many to pay more for housing, health care, transportation, and food, and their fixed income status means no new income can be generated. Elderly poverty is exacerbated by race and gender, with people of color and women experiencing significantly more poverty than whites and men.[86] The 2010–2011 debate over reducing Social Security and Medicare benefits or privatizing these programs focused mainly on reducing the country's debt and deficit, giving much less attention to the likely consequences of increasing elderly poverty. Will more attention in the Social Security debate be given to elderly poverty, or will increasing poverty among this group be a conceded as a necessary liability of reducing the nation's debt and deficit?

For the indigent disabled, Supplemental Security Income (SSI) has been a major source of relief since the early 1970s. During the 2007 recession, the Obama administration included a one-time economic recovery payment of $250 to certain recipient groups, one of those being SSI recipients.[87] In 2010 there were 7.5 million recipients of the SSI program with average monthly payments of $476, representing a slight increase from 2009 when there were 7.2 million recipients with average monthly payments of $474.[88] Federal expenditures for SSI cash payments increased from $42 billion in 2008 to $45.9 billion in 2009[89] though such increases do not suggest automatic future growth. Under pressure from the Republicans, President Obama seemed willing to institute across-the-board social spending cuts including SSI.

Although the SSI program received little attention during the Obama-Republican ongoing debate, it is part of the overall social safety net for vulnerable groups like the indigent disabled. Because of this, on June 30, 2011, over 60 professional and advocacy organizations, including the National Association of Social Workers, signed a letter to President Obama requesting that he preserve and not reduce funding for the SSI program for children with mental disabilities.[90] The letter delineates the struggles of low-income families with mentally disabled children and counters critics who say the program for these children is too costly and allows for fraud and abuse. The proliferation of children diagnosed with attention deficit disorder, autism, and other mental conditions is taxing for all families, but especially low-income families who lack the resources to adequately grapple with their children's condition. Spending reductions in the SSI program for this population would mean increasingly more children being underserved and neglected, and not having the opportunity to achieve their positive potential.

PORTENDING THE FUTURE

Thus far, this chapter has discussed the Obama administration's social welfare policies, how the poor and vulnerable have fared under his term, and other social welfare trends in the period. Obama's signature legislations—the Economic Stimulus and Health Care Laws—represent substantive government spending and a quasi return to fundamental principles and practices of liberalism. The question of the constitutionality of portions of Obama's Health Care Law must be decided by the Supreme Court. Time will tell if the American electorate will endorse these principles and practices in the 2012 presidential election.

Tea Party Movement

Several events emerging during the Obama administration may have major political implications for the future. The first is the emergence of the Tea Party Movement. The Tea Party arose almost immediately after Obama was elected to challenge the massive governmental spending embedded in Obama's economic stimulus package but especially during the 2009 health care bill debate. The official principles that guide the Tea Party are fiscal responsibility, limited government, and the affirmation of the free market.[91] Members of the Tea Party Movement embrace more conservative beliefs on a variety of issues than do Republicans generally. They are more likely to define themselves as "very conservative" and President Obama as "very liberal." Although most Republicans state they are "dissatisfied" with Washington politics, Tea Party followers are more likely to describe themselves as "angry." Additionally, Tea Party supporters believe that excessive governmental spending and social welfare programs are a violation of the U.S. constitution.[92] In the 2010 congressional mid-term elections, a significant number of Tea Party-backed candidates won elections and helped the Republicans gain control of the U.S. House of Representatives that they lost in the 2006 mid-term elections.

The long-term consequence of the Tea Party has yet to be revealed but a few observations deserve attention. First, its impact on the American political landscape generally and the Republican Party specifically has been poignant and dramatic. The Tea Party is largely credited for not only helping the Republicans re-gain the House of Representatives in 2010 but also for preventing the Obama administration and congressional Democrats from including and being able to pass a government option in the Health Care Law. They also have gained the support of many prominent Republican elected officials, some of whom openly identify themselves Tea Party candidates. What remains to be seen is whether additional Republican candidates for office openly and officially seek the support of the Tea Party and whether the Tea Party Movement has sufficient momentum and power to challenge the hegemony of the Republican Party over conservative politics.

Mid-Term Elections

The 2010 mid-term elections was a second event with potentially significant political consequences for Obama and the political agenda of Democrats. The 2006 congressional and 2008 presidential elections signaled for some a major shift in the political mood of the nation. Obama's message of hope and change galvanized the political Left as they saw an opportunity to overturn the national grip of the Republicans over the political landscape for the previous eight years. Furthermore, Obama's message, charisma, and seemingly tempered political views attracted many moderates and those generally characterized as swing or independent voters. Obama's election helped to secure a congress completely controlled by Democrats, and for the first time since the start of the Clinton administration, Democrats controlled the legislative and executive branches of government.

All of that changed in November 2010 when the Republicans won over 60 seats to regain control of the House of Representatives and narrowed the majority of Democrats in the Senate. Obama already had problems unifying his party on key issues and was unable to get bipartisan support in the House on many key legislative proposals, including his signature policies. An indication of this political gridlock was the debate over the federal budget and deficit. When they gained control, House Republicans vowed not to approve a federal budget without substantive spending cuts and approved a $61 billion budget reduction. Congressional Democrats cast Republicans as mean spirited,

lacking compassion for the poor and middle-class Americans. These debates culminated in April 2011 and almost forced a shutdown of the federal government until Republican and Democratic leaders reached an eleventh-hour compromise.[93]

The debate over federal government spending demonstrates how Republicans flexed their political strength, and this led some to contend that the Republicans, not the Democrats, are showing leadership in fiscal affairs. These commentators suggest that Obama and the Democrats are reactionaries and that Obama began to seriously consider spending cuts only after the Republicans regained the House. Indeed, the April 2011 release of the Republicans' budget by House GOP Budget Committee Chairman Paul Ryan steered up considerable controversy and forced Democrats and Republicans to react to it. The budget's title is "The Path to Prosperity" and it recommended, among other things, to repeal President Obama's Health Care Act, to establish private health care plan options as a way to reform Medicare, and to block grant Medicaid.[94] Obama and other Democrats say the Ryan budget is draconian and radical, and that it dismantles the federal safety net for the poor and the elderly. However, with the 2011 federal deficit at $1.267 trillion and the federal debt over $14 trillion, the Republicans will continue to place federal spending at the center of U.S. political debates, forcing Obama to consider reductions that may alienate his party base. Coupled with a continued high unemployment rate and other indicators of a slow economy, Obama is vulnerable on the domestic policy front. The 2010 mid-term elections that catapulted the Republicans back into power appear to be Obama's Achilles' heel. Obama's hope might be that the Republicans' radical spending cut proposals could turn off many moderate and independent voters who desire a balance between needed governmental spending and free market solutions.

The Arab Spring

A final event with major potential implications was the winter and spring 2011 uprisings (called "Arab Spring") in several Middle Eastern and African countries, prominent among them being Egypt, Tunisia, Syria, and Libya. These Arab nations are predominantly Muslim, and each uprising was spawned by discontent over long-term dictatorships and prolonged economic turmoil. In March 2011, Obama along with NATO forces launched an air attack on Libyan President Moammar Gaddafi's military. Obama's rationale was based on humanitarian concerns, suggesting that Gaddafi's brutal military reprisals of rebel forces in the country constituted major atrocities that could not be overlooked.[95] Nonetheless, Obama later decided against a land invasion in Libya.[96]

The Arab uprisings could have major political implications for the Obama administration and for Obama's ability to fund his domestic social welfare agenda. Many people have applauded the uprisings as a sign of hope that Western style democracies could emerge in these countries and that the United States could generate more allies in the fight against terrorism. However, these countries have diverse political leanings and some fear that more extreme forms of government based on Islamic fundamentalism could take hold.[97] They suggest that if this occurs, more money and military resources would have to be spent protecting Israel and the United States against potential terror attacks.[98] The Obama administration is already mired in two wars, and though Obama has considerably reduced the U.S. military presence in Iraq and has set a deadline for military withdrawal in Afghanistan, some on the political Left fear that these wars will continue.

The continuation of these wars, especially the one in Afghanistan, and the potential for the Arab nation uprisings to produce radical Islamic leaders might compel the Obama administration to spend more revenue on military campaigns. Although the spring 2010 killing of Al-Qaida leader, Osama Bin Laden, was viewed as a major victory in the war against terror and helped to boost Obama's approval ratings, some suggest that the killing might motivate and mobilize more terrorist activities worldwide. If this is so, Obama may become preoccupied with international terrorism and attenuated in his ability to gain support for domestic social welfare spending. Indeed, the intensification of these international events may make Obama a primary target for the same criticism he and others on the political Left levied against George W. Bush in the 2008 presidential campaign. Just as Bush then was cast as an unregulated imperialist, Obama may come under a similar attack from those within the Democratic Party, especially those on the far or progressive Left. These attacks may foster further divisions within the Democratic Party and may undermine the fragile political coalition that was able to pass Obama's social welfare legislation.

Social Work and the Obama Administration

During the Obama administration, major social work organizations like the National Association of Social Workers and the Council on Social Work Education have officially supported Obama's domestic policy agenda. Although much of the public social work dialogue has focused on the impact of the recession on cuts in social services, almost equal attention also appears to be given to how clinicians can avoid harsh consequences of the recession on their private practice. This dialogue demonstrates the continued split in social work along the micro/macro dimensions of practice. To be sure, most social workers probably remain aware and knowledgeable about Obama's domestic policy agenda, if only superficially. However, because macro practitioners are more concerned with the broader political and economic implications of social welfare policy development, their attention to Obama's social policy agenda may be more pronounced and persistent.

It is still too early to comprehensively assess the social work profession's response to both Obama's foreign and domestic policies, but a brief perusal of social work's premiere journal, *Social Work*, revealed that for 2009 through half of 2011, only one article appeared that specifically focused on the Obama administration and its policy agenda.[99] Since the Reagan revolution of the 1980s, much, if not most, of social work's practice thrust has moved increasingly toward clinical and private practice. This trend is reflected in surveys that show social work students' overwhelming desire to pursue a career in private and some sort of clinical practice.[100] Although interventions at the micro level of human function and behavior are critical, there is a tendency to depoliticize the individual and de-emphasize the effects of macro social patterns on individual choices and behavior. Indeed, Obama's economic stimulus and health care laws may have fostered this trend even more in that both policies include substantive money for the expansion of mental health services. If social work continues to trend more toward the "person" component of the "person-in-situation/environment paradigm," it may miss an opportunity to capitalize on its traditions of social activism and policy practice and employ them as vehicles to address the rising social problems associated with the current great recession.

> **If social work continues to trend more toward the "person" component of the "person-in-situation/environment paradigm," it may miss an opportunity to capitalize on its traditions of social activism and policy practice.**

THE WORLD IN TURMOIL

In the months of winter 2010 and throughout 2011, nature, as if in sympathy with human disasters, killed tens of thousands as earth erupted in tsunamis, spewing volcanoes, floods, droughts, wildfires, tornados, severe heat, and killing cold in usually temperate areas. Added to the starvation, displacement, and deaths brought about by natural disasters were those made by humankind: internecine warfare such as that in Somalia, the Arab Spring, or between Israel and Palestine, and the global economy's seemingly inevitable collapse as nation by nation faced reneging on their international debts and fell into the black hole of recession. Without bailouts of faltering countries by Germany, England, France, and the International Monetary Fund (IMF), the euro, which held together the European Economic Community, seemed destined to fail. Poverty, unemployment, and an overall agitation led to demonstrations and riots across Western Europe. Only Asian countries, particularly China, seemed immune. We cannot underestimate the importance of suddenly worldwide availability of electronic media, particularly cell phones, which immediately united and called to action like-minded people across nations and cultures.

In the United States, citizen unrest increased as the economic recession remained static despite predictions of growth. A quarter of America's children lived in poverty by the end of 2011, and the official poverty rate remained at about 9 percent but did not include those who were underemployed or had given up hope of jobs. In addition, the unemployment rate of most people of color was at least double that of the general public, adding to the misery of the already disadvantaged.

"Flash groups," brought together via the Internet, for (usually) benign purposes, morphed into protest movements, the first being "Occupy Wall Street" in New York City. The Occupy Movement spread throughout the nation quickly, and into at least 120 universities. While there seemed to be no consistent policy demands, anger toward America's 1 percent who hold most of its wealth, banking institutions holding fortunes while continuing home foreclosures, along with other anti-consumer activities, and the cry for jobs clearly indicated their overriding malaise. They rallied for the "99 percent" of Americans who had little money and no power in America. Within a few months, cities and universities attempted to rid their parks and areas from occupiers, citing unsanitary conditions and rising crime as rationales and as a hedge against the accusations of constitutional rights to free speech and peaceful congregations. As the Occupy Movement persisted, more police action began, and in November of 2011 in Davis, California, the spraying of tear gas directly into the faces of peaceful demonstrators evoked Kent State University's use of force against our children (and by our children).

Meanwhile, in the nation's capitol, the argument over deficit reduction continued as if nothing was happening among the nation's citizens. The overt problem was clear: how the nation could reduce its deficit—what it owed versus the revenue it could produce. The recognized but more covert issue: The 2012 election, when Republicans hope to throw out President Obama, his programs, and Democrats across America. The stalemate's lines were clearly drawn: Conservatives, primarily Republicans answering to the Tea Party and the Far Right, refused to eliminate tax breaks for the wealthy or to impose new taxes, seeking revenue from cutting social programs; Democrats, including President Obama, supporting a mix of spending cuts and tax increases on the wealthy and unwilling to cut social programs. When no compromise was reached in Congress, the dilemma was turned over to a "Super-Committee" comprised of six Republicans and six Democrats, who admitted their own failure after a few weeks. Thereafter, a 10 percent cut in all programs, including the Pentagon but entitlements such as Social Security and Medicare, was scheduled to take effect in 2013.

As Nero fiddled while Rome burned, so Washington politicians fiddled—unaware or unconcerned—while America smoldered.

CONCLUSION: AFTERWORD

Cycles of Power

More than twenty-five years ago, A New History of Social Welfare was conceptualized on the premise that a dynamic synergy of politics, economics, and religion determines social welfare policies and practices in a society. We noted that the institution of social welfare fluctuates to fill in gaps left by those institutions. From colonial times, our nation moved slowly toward social morality in provision for the disadvantaged, but in the last forty years national welfare efforts have spiraled steadily downward as conservative politics became more intensely integrated with an increasingly religious fundamentalism and an economy based on control of oil resources. Visible across the administration of at least nine presidencies, beginning with Nixon, the trend includes increased privatization of programs; decreased federal attention to poverty, civil rights, and income equity; and burgeoning support of the wealthy and of corporations. Today, the boundaries of social welfare are drawn ever more tightly as the other institutions expand. To most appearances, the social work mission—aid to the disadvantaged—has disappeared from most traditional practice.

The election of conservative and oil-rich George W. Bush as president put presidential power behind the push of those moving toward corporate and elitist control of the nation. Set on creating a powerful presidency, Bush seized on the 9/11 attacks as a serendipitous excuse to strike at Iraq, take the post of Commander in Chief, and undermine a host of constitutionally guaranteed rights. With the nation focused on the contrived war, concern with domestic issues, including social welfare, waned. A strong neo-conservative coalition oriented toward work ethic morality began to dismantle social programs and intensify penalties for those deemed unworthy. Neo-colonialism aimed at Middle East oil resources enriched the elite, while the nation began to fall into deep recession that neither President Obama nor the "do-nothing" Congress could or would repair.

The consequent internationalization of the American economy resulted in dismantling both the labor force and social programs. Privatization and defederalization of social programs ensured control by vested interests at state levels, where it is easier than at federal levels. Karger says,

> economic strength translates into political power . . . corporations can blackmail local and state governments by threatening plant closures, relocating operations offshore, and laying off large numbers of workers.[101]

Moreover, state control meant reductions in federal standards, requirements, and safeguards, resulting in loss of long-time citizen protections.

Another trend is more frightening: legislative actions and concepts portending a slow genocide for "socially indigestible" people such as women and their dependent children, the aged, people with disabilities, and people belonging to minority groups. There were already increases in poor health, poor nutrition, disease, homelessness, and crime that, if continued, would automatically reduce our "unwanteds," along with their "problems" and costs to society. Devine and Wright note,

> In the highly segmented and technically sophisticated labor market . . . the unskilled cease to function as an industrial reserve army. Instead, they [become] a dependent surplus population [with] . . . ever-increasing expenditures necessary to contain [it].[102]

"Containing" the poor is expensive, but redefining them as "deviants" or "underclass" absolves society of guilt. Macarov says,

> the manner in which poverty is viewed as deviance, and refusal to work is considered the cause, dates back to the Puritan's dictum that those who will not work should not be permitted to eat . . . an attitude not conspicuously absent from the public mind today.[103]

Cycles of History

Looking at history, these same patterns emerge on ever-widening levels. As groups gain power, they desire more power; they seek wealth because wealth buys power and luxuries, and somehow religions fall into place to give them moral legitimation. Such legitimation produces social values, some of which are ancient and some which emerge with each new cycle of conquest. The values "stick" in our societies as truths to which we owe allegiance. The most ancient is probably patriarchy, which gives rise to the oppression of women; legitimizes the private ownership of land; and gives an elite the use of women, children, slaves, workers, and outsiders as tools to work. Moreover, patriarchy could be considered the "father" of such more recent values as White Privilege, capitalism, social Darwinism, and other modern-day values. White Privilege and patriarchy (in all its forms, not just as oppression against women) are now so pervasive that they are nearly invisible in Eurocentric societies. In particular, White Privilege's racism has been a major pillar of America's economy since colonial times.

The Work Ethic is another value in full flower today. It validated the New World's conquest, the rape of native cultures, and slavery as a means to wealth and power and today justifies our society's "meanness" in terms of social programs: the harsh TANF regulations, reductions of social programs, refusal to deal with health and nutrition needs, unemployment, movement of jobs to others countries, and so on. Abetted by social Darwinism and the ethic of individual responsibility, it labels, discards, and denies social and economic justice to a growing number of persons disadvantaged by the present-day political economy. Although benevolent values such as democracy, egalitarianism, and charity remain part of the American social ethos, they are very often whispers on the wind, blown away by the primacy of these other values or twisted in support of our meanest personal or national goals.

The "Why" of Values Analysis

Throughout our *New History*, we identified and analyzed how American social values affect and perpetuate social welfare and social justice policies, procedures, and programs. In doing so, we also identified the sources of our own values and discovered how former historical perspectives are by nature Eurocentric, androcentric, and elitist. By examining social treatment and social control in terms of underlying values, we gained new insights into the persistence of social institutions that harm the most vulnerable while claiming to have their best interests at heart. If social work is to truly meet the needs of the disadvantaged, we need to understand that values, while powerful, are not necessarily truths, and that to accept them at face value limits our participation in the primary mission of social work. Using a values analysis, we can look at the underlying policies and, perhaps, mediate those that are harmful.

Toward the Future

Social welfare does not exist in a vacuum but is a product of the "moral state," influenced by and dependent on the political economy of the nation. Therefore, its policies are fundamentally political and responsive to the requirements of the few who hold economic power. In this sense, "welfare" has nothing to do with the common good. It is a tactic, a strategy, playing on the needs of certain groups, promising them aid in return for their conformity to oppressive systems. Its purpose is to reify systems of power and maintain control for the betterment or profit of those in power. Only the arena is different: from small tribal societies in 6000 B.C.E. to the world economic political system today.

The winners are the same: those who redefine all kinds of morality to fit their own world views. The losers are the same: those who, for whatever reasons, are shunted from power. And the spoils remain the same: increasing accumulations of wealth and power beyond all reasonable world reality.

We began this journey through the history of social welfare by talking about love. Yet, our topics have seemed far from the idea of love and very much about social control of our society's vulnerable groups. For women, it has meant giving only enough to eke out their lives if they are dependent on public resources. For the poor, welfare has meant providing benefits to quell their revolt against inequities. For people who are "different," whether in appearance, religion, or other characteristics, it has meant depriving them of equality in human rights so that they can be exploited. Racism in America has complicated and augmented exploitation of each of our oppressed groups.

Some of us see social evolution as linear, progressing from past to future, and we often picture our historical cycles as a wheel rolling ever onward. However, looking at social welfare from the perspective of the synergy of politics, economics, and religion, we might better perceive a wheel spinning on its axis rather than its rim. It does not go forward; it remains ever in motion but grinds our lives ever finer. And while it grinds out our social evolution, our moral evolution stays at the hub of the wheel, unchanged and unchanging in past and perhaps future millennia.

From the time humankind began, four species characteristics have existed: curiosity, the use of tools (including use of people as tools), greed, and altruism. The first three have led us into a new global society, very often at the cost of the fourth. But we do not have to continue on that path: We can choose love instead. It is unconditional love for humanity in all its colors, forms, and features that inspires the best part of social welfare, and we must not become blind to that vision. Love is not enough to change the world, but it is surely the best place to begin. And there is still time.

The following questions will test your knowledge and understanding of the content found within this chapter. For additional assessment, including licensing-exam type questions on applying chapter content to practice behaviors, visit **MySearchLab**.

1. How did the "party of No" contribute to social welfare reform?
   a. It championed for "no more cuts" to health care programs.
   b. It fought for a stimulus package to ward off the recession.
   c. It supported Obama's plans that no one would be left behind.
   d. It didn't support social reform; instead it fought against any reform proposals.

2. What is unique about the Florida welfare laws as they relate to TANF eligibility?
   a. There are no time limits on public assistance.
   b. Recipients are not required to work after two years of assistance.
   c. All recipients are drug-tested and those who test positive are denied assistance.
   d. The program is funded entirely through private contributions.

3. The term used to describe households in which one or more persons were hungry over the course of a year due to the inability to afford sufficient food is:
   a. food insecure
   b. food deficient
   c. food poor
   d. food limited

4. Which statement about education vouchers is true?
   a. Parents can use them only to pay for their children to attend private school.
   b. The vouchers are donations from private contributors.
   c. They are ineffective because students must attend school in their district.
   d. They can be used for private or public school education.

5. What actions would a member of the Tea Party most likely take in regard to welfare programs?
   a. Increase taxes in order to expand social welfare programs.
   b. Minimize cash assistance and increase job training and education efforts.
   c. Cut welfare programs as much as possible since they are unconstitutional.
   d. Completely revamp welfare programs so they are managed entirely by religious organizations.

6. It is 2008 and you, a person on a minority race, are considering buying your first home. What should you know as you begin talking to mortgage companies about a loan?
   a. You are eligible for a "reverse redlining" tax break.
   b. Mortgage companies receive tax credits for loaning to minorities.
   c. Mortage companies target minorities because they knew they are most at risk for defaulting on their loans.
   d. Racial discrimination practices will likely prevent you from getting approved.

7. Discuss the relationship between education and crime and describe how Obama's Recovery and Reinvestment Act of 2009 would positively affect both.

Reinforce what you learned in this chapter by studying videos, cases, documents, and more available at **www.MySearchLab.com**.

Watch and Review

Watch these Videos

Δ MS-13 Gang Life

Δ Intersex

Δ Questioning Islamic Traditions

Δ The In-Crowd and Social Cruelty

Read and Review

Read these Cases/Documents

Δ Social Workers Involved in Political Action

Δ Dylan James

Δ Chelsea Green Space and the Power Plant

Assess Your Knowledge

Go to **MySearchLab** to test your knowledge of key topics in this chapter with topic-specific quizzes. Conclude your assessment by completing the chapter exam.

Δ = Case Study

Notes

Chapter 1

1. Naomi Brill, *Teamwork: Working Together in the Human Services* (New York: J. B. Lippincott, 1976), pp. 12–15.
2. Phyllis J. Day, "Social Welfare: Context for Social Control," *Journal of Sociology and Social Welfare*, Vol. VII (March 1981), p. 42.
3. *Webster's* New Collegiate Dictionary, 1980, p. 406.
4. Ibid., p. 1282.
5. Beulah Compton, *Introduction to Social Welfare and Social Work: Structure, Function, and Process* (Homewood, IL: The Dorsey Press, 1980), p. 78.
6. Mary Ski Hunter and Dennis Saleeby, "Spirit and Substance: Beginnings in the Education of Radical Social Workers," *Journal of Education for Social Work*, Vol. 13, no. 2 (Spring 1977), pp. 60–67.
7. Marc L. Miringoff and Sandra Opdycke, *American Social Welfare: Reassessment and Reform* (Englewood Cliffs, NJ: Prentice Hall, 1986), p. 2.
8. *Webster's* New Collegiate Dictionary, 1980, p. 1094.
9. Cheikh A. Diop, *The Cultural Unity of Black Africa: The Domains of Matriarchy and of Patriarchy in Classical Antiquity* (London: Karnak House, 1989).
10. Edna Bonacich, "Racism in Advanced Capitalist Society: Comments on William J. Wilson's *The Truly Disadvantaged*," *Journal of Sociology and Social Welfare*, Vol. XVI, no. 4 (Dec. 1989), p. 43.
11. David Wagner, *The New Temperance: The American Obsession with Sin and Vice* (Boulder, CO: Westview Press, 1997), pp. 4–5.
12. Ibid., p. 8.
13. My thanks to Professor Jerome Schiele for pointing out my omission of this extremely important American social value and to Professor Schiele and Professor Joe R. Feagin for helping me to define it.
14. Jerome H. Schiele, "Mutations of Eurocentric Domination and Their Implications for African American Resistance," *Journal of Black Studies*, Vol. 32, no. 4 (March 2002), pp. 439–463.
15. Ibid., p. 441.
16. Joe R. Feagin, *Racist America: Roots, Current Realities, and Future Reparations* (New York: Routledge Press, 2000), p. 29.
17. Ibid., p. 175.
18. Ibid., p. 128.
19. Patricia Hill Collins, *Black Feminist Thought*, 2nd ed. (New York: Routledge Press, 2000), pp. 70–72.
20. Kingsley Davis and Wilbert E. Moore, "Some Principles of Stratification," *American Sociological Review*, Vol. 10 (1945), p. 246. Quoted in Miringoff and Opdycke, *American Social Welfare*, p. 8.
21. Miringoff and Opdycke, *American Social Welfare*, pp. 9–11.
22. Ibid.
23. Melvin Tumin, "Some Principles of Stratification: A Critical Analysis," *American Sociological Review*, Vol. 10 (1953), p. 380. Quoted in Miringoff and Opdycke, *American Social Welfare*, p. 11.
24. U.S. Census Bureau, "*Measures of Household Income Inequality*," Washington, D.C., 2001. Available online at www.census.gov/hhes/www/img/incpov00/fig.12.
25. U.S. Census Bureau, "*Income, Poverty, and Health Insurance Coverage in the United States: 2009*." Washington, D.C., 2010: U.S. Government Printing Office.
26. U.S. Census Bureau, "Current Population Survey Annual Social and Economic Supplement," Washington, D.C., 2010, Table HINC-05. Available online at http://www.census.gov/hhes/www/cpstables/032010/hhinc/new05_000.htm. Accessed February 13, 2011.
27. U.S. Census Bureau, "*Net Worth and Asset Ownership of Households: 1998 and 2000*," Washington, D.C., 2003. Available online at www.census.gov/prod/2003pubs/p70-88.pdf. Accessed February 13, 2011.
28. Linda Levine, "The Distribution of Household Wealth," Penny Press, November 18, 2010, http://economic-legislation.blogspot.com/2010/11/distribution-if-household-wealth.html. Accessed March 9, 2012.
29. William J. Wilson, *The Truly Disadvantaged* (Chicago: University of Chicago Press, 1987). Wilson's thesis was, in brief, that as African Americans became middle class they left the urban ghettos, leaving those who remained as a "culture" based on class rather than race. Lack of motivation, not discrimination, was the barrier to success. Although this was not Wilson's intent, his description of underclass is now taken to describe poor urban African Americans as deviant. This has created a new social Darwinism. In the most common rendition, *underclass* refers to chronic, concentrated, inner-city minority impoverishment accompanied by extreme social isolation and exceptionally high rates of social pathology of all sorts, according to Devine and Wright in *The Greatest of Evils*.
30. U.S. Department of Health and Human Services, "The 2011 HHS Poverty Guidelines," *Federal Register*, Vol. 76, no. 13 (January 20, 2011), pp. 3637-3638. Available online at http://aspe.hhs.gov/poverty/11poverty.shtml. Accessed February 13, 2011.
31. U.S. Census Bureau, "Poverty Thresholds for 2010," Washington, D.C., 2010. Available online at www.census.gov/hhes/www/poverty/data/threshld/index.html. Accessed February 13, 2011.
32. U.S. Census Bureau, "*Income, Poverty, and Health Insurance Coverage in the United States: 2009*." Washington, D.C., 2010: U.S. Government Printing Office.

33. U.S. Census Bureau, "Current Population Survey: 2009." Annual Social and Economic Supplement. Available online at www.census.gov/hhes/www.cpstables/032009/hhinc/toc.htm.

34. LaDonna Pavetti. "Safety Net's Response to the Recession," presented before the House Subcommittee on Income Security and Family Support (October 8, 2009). Center on Budget and Policy Priorities. P.2. Available online at www.cbpp.org/cms/index.cfm:fa&view&id=2945. Accessed July 30, 2010.

35. Pavetti, "Safety Net's Response," p. 4.

36. U.S. Census Bureau, Current Population Survey: 2007 and 2008. Annual Social and Economic Supplements, Table 4. "People and Families in Poverty by Selected Characteristics: 2007 and 2008." Available online at www.census.gov/hhes/poverty/data/threshold08.html. Accessed July, 22, 2010.

37. U.S. Census Bureau, "Current Populations Reports," P. 60-235, (published August 2008), Table 697. Persons Below Poverty Level by Selected Characteristics: 2007. Available online at www.census.gov/hhes/www/income/histinc/ho1AR.html. Accessed July 22, 2010.

38. U.S. Census Bureau. "Current Population Survey: 2007 and 2008." Annual Social and Economic Supplements. Table 4. People and Families in Poverty by Selected Characteristics, 2007 and 2008. Available online at www.census.gov/hhes/www.poverty/data/threshold08.html. Accessed July 22, 2010.

39. Children's Defense Fund, "Every Child Deserves a Fair Start", Washington, D.C., Children's Defense Fund, November 2001. Available online at www.childrensdefense.org/fairstart-faqs.hy.

40. Children's Defense Fund, "Welfare Reform Fund Briefing Book." Washington, D.C., Children's Defense Fund, 1995, p. 34.

41. Feagin, *Racist America*, p. 138.

42. Ibid.

43. Joe R. Feagin, Racial and Ethnic Relations, 2nd ed. (Englewood Cliffs, N.J.: Prentice Hall, 1984), p. 177.

44. U.S. Census Bureau. "American Indians by the Numbers," http://www.infoplease.com/spot/aihmcensus.html. Accessed March 5, 2012.

45. Ibid.

46. Stephen Ohlemacher, "Race Disparities Continue, Report Says," *Journal and Courier* (Lafayette, IN, November 14, 2006, p. A3).

47. Ibid.

48. Rosemary Sarri, Elisabeth Cramer, and Virginia du Rivage, *Highlights: Socio-Economic Status of Women in Michigan and the United States* (Ann Arbor: The University of Michigan Institute for Social Research and the School of Social Work, 1983), p. 6.

49. James H. Rubin, "Study: Race Still Factor in Mortgage Denials," *Courier-Post* (New Jersey), July 19, 1995, p. 12D.

50. Children's Defense Fund, *State of American's Children Yearbook 2005* (Washington, D.C.: CDF, 2005) p. 94.

51. Children's Defense Fund, *State of America's Children Yearbook 1995* (Washington, D.C.: CDF, 1995), p. 117.

52. Molly Selvin, *Journal and Courier* (Lafayette, IN), April 23, 2007, p. A1. (Reporting in *Los Angeles Times* via AP.)

53. Calculated from U.S. Census Bureau, "Current Population Survey 2007 and 2008," Annual Social and Economic Supplements. Table 4, ibid.

54. ChildStats.gov. "America's Children: Key National Indicators of Well-Being, 2011." Source: U.S. Census Bureau Current Population Statistics, School Enrollment Supplement. Federal Interagency Forum on Child and Family Statistics. http://www.childstats.gov/americas-children/edu4.asp. Accessed March 9, 2012.

55. "Women's Earning as a Percentage of Men's, 1951–2010." http://www.infoplease.com/ipa/A0193820.html. Accessed March 12, 2012.

56. U.S. Census Bureau, "Poverty in the United States: 2005," (Washington, D.C.: U.S. Government Printing Office, 2006). Taken from Annual Social and Economic Supplement Table 3: "Poverty Status of People by Age, Race, and Hispanic Origin, 1995–2005." Available online at www.census.gov/hhes/www.poverty/poverty05/pov05hi/html.

57. Charles Zastrow, *Introduction to Social Welfare Institutions: Social Problems, Services, and Current Issues* (Homewood, IL: The Dorsey Press, 1982), p. 465.

58. Gregory Benford "A Scientist's Notebook: Sex, Gender, and Fantasy," *Fantasy and Science Fiction* (September 1995), pp. 117–118.

59. U.S. Census Bureau, *American Fact Finder* (Washington D.C.: U.S. Government Printing Office, August 2, 2005), p. 1. Available online at http://factfinder.census.gov/jsp/saff/SAFFInfo.jsp?_pageId=tp4_disability.html. Accessed July 5, 2007.

60. U.S. Census Bureau, *Statistical Abstract of the United States: 2007* (Washington, D.C.: Government Printing Office). Table 549 Supplemental Security Income: Recipients and Payments: 1990–2004, p. 359.

61. Norman Goroff, "Humanism and Social Work: Paradoxes, Problems, and Promises" (mimeograph) (West Hartford, CT: University of Connecticut School of Social Work, 1977).

Chapter 2

1. Compton quotes W. G. Sumner on the definition of an institution: "An institution consists of a concept (idea, notion, doctrine, interest) and a structure.... The structure is a framework or apparatus, or perhaps only a number of functionaries, ... [that] holds the concept and furnishes instrumentalities for bringing it into the world of facts and action," in *Introduction to Social Welfare and Social Work: Structure, Function, and Process* (Homewood, IL: The Dorsey Press, 1980), p. 31. Neil Gilbert and Harry Specht say that an institution is a network "of relationships that are generally accepted as the way of carrying out these essential social functions ... human activities such as child-rearing and the production, consumption, and distribution of goods ... raising and training the young," in *Dimensions of Social Welfare Policy* (Englewood Cliffs, NJ: Prentice Hall, 1974), p. 4.

2. Neil Gilbert and Harry Specht, *Dimensions of Social Welfare Policy* (Englewood Cliffs, NJ: Prentice Hall, 1974), p. 3.

3. As with the Ku Klux Klan or in situations of conquest over other polities. For example, the Ku Klux Klan influences and/or is part of the polity because it coerces behavior in American society. In war, a society coerces another society, taking power over it.

4. Gilbert and Specht, *Dimensions of Social Welfare Policy*, p. 3.

5. David Macarov, *The Design of Social Welfare* (New York: Holt, Rinehart & Winston, 1978), p. 23. 6. Walter A. Friedlander, *Introduction to Social Welfare*, 5th ed. (Englewood Cliffs, NJ: Prentice Hall, 1961), p. 4.

6. National Association of Social Workers, *Encyclopedia of Social Work* (New York: NASW, 1977), Vol. II, p. 1503.

7. Klein (1968), Romansky (1971), and Martin Wolins (1976), discussed in Compton, *Introduction to Social Welfare and Social Work*, pp. 28–29.

8. Ralph Dolgoff and Donald Feldstein, *Understanding Social Welfare*, 2nd ed. (New York: Longman Press, 1984), p. 95.

9. Peter R. Day, *Social Work and Social Control* (London: Tavistock Publications, 1981), p. 12.

10. The concepts of residual and institutional social welfare are taken from Harold L. Wilensky and C. N. Lebeaux, *Industrial Society and Social Welfare* (New York: Free Press, 1965).

11. The phrase is taken from William O. Ryan, *Blaming the Victim* (New York: Pantheon Books, 1971).

12. The idea of minimal subsistence level for public assistance is based on the concept of poverty level developed by Mollie Orshansky in the 1960s.

13. June Axinn and Herman Levin, *Social Welfare: A History of the American Response to Need*, 4th ed. (New York: Longman, 1996).

14. Frances Fox Piven and Richard Cloward, *Regulating the Poor* (New York: Random House, 1971).

15. James B. Rule, *Insight and Social Betterment: Applied Social Science* (New York: Oxford University Press, 1978).

16. Jerome H. Schiele, *Human Services and the Afrocentric Paradigm* (New York: Haworth Press, 2000).

17. Patricia Hill Collins, *Black Feminist Thought: Knowledge, Consciousness, and the Politics of Empowerment*, 2nd ed. (New York: Routledge, 2000).

18. Diana Pearce, "Farewell to Alms: Women and Welfare Policy in the Eighties." Paper presented at the American Sociological Association Annual Meeting, San Francisco, Sept. 1982.

19. Personal correspondence with Jerome H. Schiele, April 14, 2004.

20. Ibid.

21. Collins, Black Feminist Thought, p. 18.

22. Ibid., p. 273.

23. Ibid., p. 18.

24. Ibid., pp. 69–70.

25. Referring to Hazel Carby, *Reconstructing Womanhood: The Emergence of the Afro-American Woman Novelist* (New York: Oxford University Press, 1987), p. 22.

26. Although education and health services are part of the institution of social welfare, each has developed its own professional mandates and functions. For this reason, they will be discussed only in terms of the social services each provides rather than with their primary focuses of education and health care.

27. National Alliance to End Homelessness, TANF Emergency Contingency Fund, (Washington, D.C.: National Alliance to End Homelessness, March 9, 2009). Available online at www.endhomelessness.org/content/article/detail/2200

28. Charles Zastrow, *The Practice of Social Work* (Homewood, IL: The Dorsey Press, 1985), p. 375.

29. Alfred J. Kahn, *Social Policy and Social Services* (New York: Random House, 1973), p. 29.

30. Dolgoff and Feldstein, *Understanding Social Welfare*, p. 285

31. Ibid.

32. Ernest Greenwood, "Attributes of a Profession," in Neil Gilbert and Harry Specht (eds.), *The Emergence of Social Welfare and Social Work*, 2nd ed. (Itasca, IL: F. E. Peacock Publishers, 1981), pp. 231–240.

33. National Association of Social Work Code of Ethics. Taken from the NASW Code of Ethics as presented in Zastrow, *Practice of Social Work*, pp. 516–517.

34. Peter Day, "Social Work and Social Control," from discussion paper #3 (British Association of Social Workers, 1973), p. 3.

35. Council on Social Work Education, "Educational Policy and Accreditation Standards," (Alexandria, VA: Council on Social Work Education, 2010), p. 8.

36. Peter Day, *Social Work and Social Control*, p. 4.

37. Ibid., p. 16.

38. Hannah Arendt, *On Revolution* (New York: Viking, 1963), pp. 74–75. Quoted in David Wagner, *What's Love Got to Do With It?* (New York: New Press, 2000) p. 1.

Chapter 3

1. Williams, Chancellor, *The Destruction of Black Civilization* (Chicago: Third World Press, 1987), p. 100.

2. Asante, Molefi, *The History of Africa: The Quest for Eternal Harmony* (New York: Routledge, 2007).

3. Quoting Lady Flora Louisa Lugard, *Tropical Dependency* (London, 1911), in Bennett, *Before the Mayflower*, p. 5.

4. W. Flinders Petrie, *Social Life in Ancient Egypt* (London: Constable and Co., 1923), p. 110.

5. Max Weber, *Ancient Judaism* (New York: Free Press, 1952), p. 252; and Noel Timms, *Social Work* (London: Routledge & Kegan Paul, 1973), pp. 17–18.

6. Karenga, Maulana, *MAAT: The Moral Ideal in Ancient Egypt.* (New York: Routledge, 2004).

7. H. W. F. Saggs, *Everyday Life in Babylonia and Assyria*, 2nd ed. (New York: G. P. Putnam's Sons, 1967), p. 29.

8. Taken from Samuel N. Kramer. Quoted in Dolgoff and Feldstein, *Understanding Social Welfare*, p. 30.

9. Saggs, *Everyday Life*, pp. 66–68.

10. Ibid., p. 138.

11. Ibid.

12. Dolgoff and Feldstein, *Understanding Social Welfare*, p. 30.

13. Sarah B. Pomeroy, *Goddesses, Whores, Wives, and Slaves: Women in Classical Antiquity* (New York: Schlocken Books, 1975), pp. 12–13.

14. Amaury De Riencourt, *Sex and Power in History* (New York: Dell Publishing, 1974), p. 76.

15. Weber, *Ancient Judaism*, pp. 32–33.

16. De Riencourt, *Sex and Power*, p. 87.

17. Merlin Stone, *When God Was a Woman* (New York: Harcourt Brace Jovanovich, 1976).

18. Deuteronomy 22:23–25; Leviticus 21:19.

19. Deuteronomy 22:23–25.

20. Deuteronomy 24.

21. De Riencourt, *Sex and Power*, p. 79.

22. Bennett, *Before the Mayflower*, pp. 10–11.

23. Weber, *Ancient Judaism*, p. 258.

24. Isaiah 58:5–7.

25. Walter Trattner, "The Background," in Neil Gilbert and Harry Specht (eds.), *The Emergence of Social Welfare and Social Work*, 2nd ed. (Itasca, IL: F. E. Peacock Publishers, 1981), p. 22.

26. Pirke Avit 3:8 and 1:2. In Dolgoff and Feldstein, *Understanding Social Welfare*, p. 32.

27. Deuteronomy 15:8.

28. Leviticus 19:9; Deuteronomy 24:19–22.

29. Deuteronomy 23:24–25.

30. Dolgoff and Feldstein, *Understanding Social Welfare*, p. 32.

31. Marc L. Miringoff and Sandra Opdycke, *American Social Welfare: Reassessment and Reform* (Englewood Cliffs, NJ: Prentice Hall, 1986).

32. De Riencourt, *Sex and Power*, pp. 170–174.

33. Dolgoff and Feldstein, *Understanding Social Welfare*, pp. 28–29.

34. De Riencourt, *Sex and Power*, p. 182.

35. Michael Loewe, *Everyday Life in Early Imperial China* (New York: Harper & Row, 1968), p. 30.

36. Ibid., p. 31.

37. Ibid., pp. 70–75.

38. Dolgoff and Feldstein, *Understanding Social Welfare*, p. 29.

39. Loewe, *Early Imperial China*, pp. 61, 68.

40. De Riencourt, *Sex and Power*, pp. 161–177.

41. Mary Daly, *Gyn/Ecology: The MetaEthics of Feminism* (Boston: Beacon Press, 1978), pp. 145–146.

42. De Riencourt, *Sex and Power*, pp. 77–78.

43. Ibid., p. 132.

44. Ibid., p. 156.

45. Pomeroy, *Goddesses*, p. 202.

46. Dolgoff and Feldstein, *Understanding Social Welfare*, p. 36.

47. Pomeroy, *Goddesses*, p. 228.

48. David Macarov, *The Design of Social Welfare* (New York: Holt, Rinehart & Winston, 1978), p. 76.

49. Pomeroy, *Goddesses*, p. 202.

50. Gerald Handel, *Social Welfare in Western Society* (New York: Random House, 1982), p. 225.

51. Pomeroy, *Goddesses*, p. 228.

52. Ibid., p. 198.

53. Marc Bloch, *Feudal Society: The Growth of Ties of Independence*, Vol. 1, translated by L. A. Maryont (Chicago: University of Chicago Press, 1964), p. 61. Quoted in Handel, *Western Society*, p. 31.

54. Matthew 7:30 and 9:24.

55. This is discussed in the Gnostic Gospels; De Riencourt, *Sex and Power*; and Michael Baigent, Richard Leigh, and Henry Lincoln, *Holy Blood, Holy Grail* (New York: Dell Publishing, 1982).

56. John 8:3–11.

57. Matthew 19:8–9.

58. Luke 8:2–54; Acts 9:17.

59. Galatians 3:28.

60. Timothy 2:9–15; Ephesians 5:22–24.

61. De Riencourt, *Sex and Power*, p. 154.

62. D. Constantalelos, *Byzantine Philanthropy and Social Welfare* (New Brunswick, NJ: Rutgers University Press, 1968), p. 11; and Macarov, *Design of Social Welfare*, p. 76.

63. Mark 10:25; Luke 6:20.

64. Dolgoff and Feldstein, *Understanding Social Welfare*, p. 36.

65. Handel, *Western Society*, p. 49.

66. Handel, *Western Society*, p. 48.

67. Ibid., p. 34.

68. Ibid., p. 35.

69. De Riencourt, *Sex and Power*, p. 41.

70. Ibid., p. 154.

71. Ibid.

Chapter 4

1. Ralph Dolgoff and Donald Feldstein, *Understanding Social Welfare*, 2nd ed. (New York: Longman Press, 1984), p. 39.

2. Amaury De Riencourt, *Sex and Power in History* (New York: Dell Publishing, 1974), p. 156.

3. David Macarov, *The Design of Social Welfare* (New York: Holt, Rinehart & Winston, 1978), p. 97.

4. De Riencourt, *Sex and Power*, p. 194.

5. Thomas Thompson, "Concepts and Practices of Charity in Early Islam," (mimeograph and personal correspondence), n.d., p. 1.

6. Maulana Muhammad Ali, *A Manual of Hadith* (Lahore: Ahmadiyyih Anjman Isha'et Islam, n.d, but c. 1955–1960).

7. Thompson, "Concepts and Practices," p. 15.

8. Ibid., p. 18.

9. Lerone Bennett, Jr., *Before the Mayflower: A History of the Negro in America, 1619–1964* (Chicago: Johnson Publishing Company, 1966), p. 18, quoting Alexander Chamberlain.

10. Justine Glass, *Witchcraft: The Sixth Sense* (North Hollywood: Wilshire Book Co., 1973), p. 108.

11. Frances Gies and Joseph Gies, *Women in the Middle Ages* (New York: Barnes and Noble, 1978), pp. 27–31.

12. Frances Gies and Joseph Gies, *Cathedral, Forge and Waterwheel: Technology and Invention in the Middle Ages* (New York: HarperCollins, 1994), p. 109.

13. Joseph R. Strayer and Dana C. Munro, *The Middle Ages 395–1500* (New York: Appleton-Century Crofts, 1970), p. 130. Quoted in Dolgoff and Feldstein, *Understanding Social Welfare*, p. 41.

14. Richard W. Southern, *The Making of the Middle Ages* (New York: Dell Publishing, 1982), p. 50. Quoted in Dolgoff and Feldstein, *Understanding Social Welfare*, p. 42.

15. Herbert J. Muller, *Freedom in the Western World: From the Dark Ages to the Rise of Democracy* (New York: Harper & Row, 1963), p. 67. Quoted in Gerald Handel, *Social Welfare in Western Society* (New York: Random House, 1982), p. 32.

16. Gies and Gies, *Women in the Middle Ages*, pp. 1–16.

17. Gies and Gies, *Cathedral, Forge and Waterwheel*, p. 50.

18. Ibid., p. 51.

19. Carolyn Merchant, *The Death of Nature: Women, Ecology, and the Scientific Revolution* (San Francisco: Harper & Row, 1980), pp. 1–3.

20. Ibid., pp. 46–47.

21. *The Hutchinson Family Encyclopedia*, http://195.152 .156.15/encyclopedia/88/MOOO3688.ht, Helocon Publishing, 2000.

22. Gies and Gies, *Cathedral, Forge, and Water Wheel*, p. 269.

23. Ibid.

24. "Capital and Labour—Population: The Growth of the Proletariat," www.history.rochester.edu/steam/ lord/3-1.1.

25. Michael Baigent, Richard Leigh, and Henry Lincoln, *Holy Blood, Holy Grail* (New York: Dell Publishing, 1982), p. 49.

26. G. G. Coulton, *The Medieval Scene* (Cambridge: Cambridge University Press, 1930), p. 1. Quoted in Handel, *Social Welfare*, p. 32.

27. Walter Trattner, "The Background," in Neil Gilbert and Harry Specht (eds.), *Emergence of Social Welfare and Social Work*, 2nd ed. (Itasca, IL: F. E. Peacock Publishers, 1981), p. 25.

28. Walter A. Friedlander and Robert Z. Apte, *Introduction to Social Welfare*, 4th ed. (Englewood Cliffs, NJ: Prentice Hall, 1955), pp. 9–10.

29. Gies and Gies, *Women in the Middle Ages*, p. 65.

30. Ibid., p. 64.

31. Ibid.

32. Dolgoff and Feldstein, *Understanding Social Welfare*, p. 43.

33. Merchant, *Death of Nature*, pp. 47–48.

34. Gies and Gies, *Women in the Middle Ages*, pp. 168–169, 181.

35. Ibid., pp. 157–161.

36. Ibid.

37. Robert S. Lopez, *Commercial Revolution of the Middle Ages, 950–1350* (Cambridge: Cambridge University Press, 1976), p. 72. Quoted in Gies and Gies, *Cathedral, Forge and Waterwheel*, p. 169.

38. Merchant, *Death of Nature*, p. 48.

39. Joseph Klaits, *Servants of Satan: The Age of the Witch Hunts* (Bloomington: Indiana University Press, 1985), p. 21.

40. Ibid., p. 21.

41. Ibid., p. 37.

42. Ibid., p. 77.

43. Ibid., p. 52.

44. Nider's *Formicarium*, in De Riencourt, *Sex and Power*, pp. 252–263.

45. J. Sprenger, *Malleus Maleficarum*, M. Summers (trans.) (New York: B. Blom, 1970), pp. 112–121. Discussed in De Riencourt, *Sex and Power*, p. 249 ff. Jacob Sprenger's rationale for this state of affairs is interesting and ingenious. After stating the exceptional vulnerability of the "fragile sex" and the eagerness of women for explanations on this topic, he elaborates:

> Now the wickedness of women is spoken of in Ecclesiasticus XXV: All wickedness is but little to the wickedness of a woman.... What else is a woman but a foe to friendship, an unescapable punishment, a necessary evil, a natural temptation, a desirable calamity, a domestic danger, a delectable detriment, an evil of nature, painted with fair colors! Therefore if it be a sin to divorce her when she ought to be kept, it is indeed a necessary torture ... since they are feebler both in mind and body, it is not surprising that they should come more under the spell of witchcraft ... they have slippery tongues, and are unable to conceal from their fellow-women those things which by evil arts they know; and since the natural reason is that she is more carnal than a man ... she is an imperfect animal, she always deceives ... a woman is beautiful to look upon, contaminating to the touch and deadly to keep.

It is significant that in England, where judicial torture was not allowed, witch hunting started much later. According to De Riencourt in *Sex and Power* (p. 254), in 1487 the University of Cologne gave its official seal of approval to the *Malleus Maleficarum* and stated that

whosoever denied the reality of witches and witchcraft should be prosecuted for raising obstacles to the Inquisition's labors. It had the full support of public opinion, and on numerous occasions, the crowds, frightened by natural catastrophes, took matters in their own hands without waiting for official sanction and killed scores of unfortunate women ... the Reformers themselves, Luther and Calvin at their head, entertained exactly the same beliefs regarding witchcraft as did Roman Catholics, and persecuted witches with as much fanaticism as their Catholic antagonists. Persecution started in earnest, however, to reach its climax, not under the relatively lenient Church of England, but under the fanatical Puritans; the number of Englishwomen who were burned without ever having been brought to trial will never be known but must have been considerable. King James VI was not far behind Pope Innocent VIII and Sprenger in his persecuting zeal.

46. Mary Daly, *Gyn/Ecology: The MetaEthics of Feminism* (Boston: Beacon Press, 1978).

47. Klaits, *Servants of Satan*, p. 89.

48. Keith Thomas, *Religion and the Decline of Magic* (London: Weidenfeld and Nicolson, 1971), p. 554; and Alan MacFarlane, *Witchcraft in Tudor and Stuart England* (New York: Harper & Row, 1970), esp. pp. 92–99; also see Klaits, *Servants of Satan*, p. 89.

49. Klaits, *Servants of Satan*, pp. 94–95.

50. Eleanor S. Riemer, "Women, Dowries, and Capital Investment in Thirteenth-Century Siena," in Marion A. Kaplan (ed.), *The Marriage Bargain* (New York: Haworth Press, 1985), pp. 59–79.

51. Dolgoff and Feldstein, *Understanding Social Welfare*, p. 46.

52. Gies and Gies, *Cathedral, Forge and Waterwheel*, p. 172.

53. Beulah Compton, *Introduction to Social Welfare and Social Work: Structure, Function, and Process* (Homewood, IL: The Dorsey Press, 1980), p. 153.

54. Dolgoff and Feldstein, *Understanding Social Welfare*, p. 46.

55. Gerald N. Grob, *State and Public Welfare in Nineteenth-Century America* (New York: Arno Press, 1976), p. 7.

56. Gies and Gies, *Cathedral, Forge and Waterwheel*, p. 235.

57. Klaits, *Servants of Satan*, pp. 90–91.

58. Max Weber, *Protestant Ethic and the Spirit of Capitalism* (New York: Scribner, 1976), p. 3.

59. Ibid., p. 54.

60. De Riencourt, *Sex and Power*, p. 261. Martin Luther as quoted in De Riencourt.

61. E. Lamy, *La Femme de Demain* (Paris, n.d.), p. 100. Quoted in De Riencourt, *Sex and Power*, p. 259.

62. John Knox (ed.), "First Blast of the Trumpet Against the Monstrous Regiment of Women," in Merchant, *Death of Nature*, pp. 146–147.

63. Samuel Mencher, *From Poor Law to Poverty Programs* (Pittsburgh: University of Pittsburgh Press, 1967), p. xvi.

64. Frank Dekker Watson, *The Charity Organization Movement in the United States* (New York: Arno Press and the New York Times, 1971), p. 15, originally printed by Macmillan, 1922.

65. Ibid., p. 23.

66. Handel, *Social Welfare*, p. 63.

67. Ibid., p. 96.

68. Blanche Coll, *Perspectives in Public Welfare: A History* (Washington, D.C.: U.S. Government Printing Office, 1971), p. 7.
69. Ibid.
70. Mencher, *Poor Law to Poverty Programs*, p. 30.
71. Ibid., p. 27.
72. De Schweinitz, *England's Road to Social Welfare* (1943), pp. 65–66. In Compton, *Introduction to Social Welfare*, p. 58.
73. Ibid., p. 73.
74. Grob, *State and Public Welfare*, p. 8.
75. Jeffrey Galper, *Social Work Practice: A Radical Perspective* (Englewood Cliffs, NJ: Prentice Hall, 1980), p. 25.
76. Adam Smith, *The Wealth of Nations* (New York: Modern Library, 1937), p. 14.
77. Adam Smith, *Adam Smith's Moral and Political Philosophy*, Herbert W. Schneider (ed.) (New York: Hafner, 1948), p. 25.
78. Mencher, *Poor Law to Poverty Programs*, pp. 67–68.
79. Ibid., p. 60.
80. De Schweinitz, *England's Road*, p. 24.
81. Handel, *Social Welfare*, p. 121.
82. Friedlander and Apte, *Introduction to Social Welfare*, p. 94.
83. Watson, *Charity Organization Movement*, pp. 13–14.

Chapter 5

1. Eric Williams, *Capitalism and Slavery* (New York: G. P. Putnam's Sons, 1966), pp. 1–10.
2. Ian K. Steele, *Warpaths: Invasions of North America* (New York: Oxford University Press, 1994), p. 3.
3. Colin F. Taylor, Editorial Consultant, *The Native Americans: The Indigenous People of North America* (London: Salamander Books LTD., 1993), p. 6.
4. Marvin Harris, *Patterns of Race* (New York: W. W. Norton and Co., 1964), p. 3.
5. Ibid., pp. 7–10.
6. Ibid., pp. 8–10.
7. Frances Gies and Joseph Gies, *Cathedral, Forge and Waterwheel: Technology and Invention in the Middle Ages* (New York: HarperCollins, 1994), pp. 285–286.
8. Gavin Menzies, *1421: The Year China Discovered America* (New York: HarperCollins, 2003). pp. 47–52, 65–70, 89–106.
9. Steele, *Warpaths*, p. 175. A case in point is the alliance of the Hurons with the French and that of the Five Nations with the English around fur-trading in the middle 1600s. In 1648 the Seneca and Mohawk began recruiting their fellow Iroquoians to destroy the Huron trading network. The Five Nations, in an unprecedented off-season night attack, overwhelmed a camp of nearly six thousand Huron who, because they had not been able to plan and tend crops because of Five Nations incursions, were already starving. Burning their own villages, they abandoned their indefensible fields, dividing into small clan groups. "The dispersal of the Huron was a cultural catastrophe with widespread consequences. . . . Most would support the French against the Five Nations and later, against the English. . . . " Steele, pp. 70–72.
10. Steele, *Warpaths*, p. 69.
11. Paula Gunn Allen, *The Sacred Hoop* (Boston: Beacon Press, 1986), pp. 2–4.
12. Ibid., p. 26.
13. Ted Morgan, *Wilderness at Dawn: The Settling of the North American Continent* (New York: Simon & Schuster, 1993), p. 102.
14. Ibid., p. 104.
15. Ibid., pp. 196–197.
16. Lerone Bennett, Jr., *Before the Mayflower: A History of the Negro in America, 1619–1964* (Chicago: Johnson Publishing Company, 1966), p. 101.
17. Morgan, *Wilderness at Dawn*, p. 48.
18. Ibid., pp. 52, 55–56.
19. Joe R. Feagin, *Racial and Ethnic Relations*, 2nd ed. (Englewood Cliffs, NJ: Prentice Hall, 1984), p. 298.
20. Morgan, *Wilderness at Dawn*, p. 75.
21. Harris, *Patterns of Race*, p. 15.
22. Carl A. Sauer, *Seventeenth Century in North America* (Berkeley, CA: Turtle Island Foundation, 1980), p. 230.
23. Morgan, *Wilderness at Dawn*, pp. 213–214.
24. Sauer, *Seventeenth Century*, p. 60.
25. Stanley Elkins, *Slavery*, 2nd ed. (Chicago: University of Chicago Press, 1968), p. 61.
26. Morgan, *Wilderness at Dawn*, p. 157.
27. Ibid.
28. Steele, *Warpath*, pp. 110–120. Steele says, "In 1624 the Iroquois Confederacy was roughly comparable to the . . . Huron Confederacy. Each was a league of as many as thirty thousand agricultural peoples, living in palisaded towns containing up to two thousand . . . The Iroquois Confederacy . . . had begun in the sixteenth century as a league of peace between five belligerent, though related, nations: The Seneca, Cayuga, Onondaga, Oneida, and Mohawk" (p. 113).
29. Feagin, *Racial and Ethnic Relations*, p. 179.
30. Harris, *Patterns of Race*, pp. 80–82.
31. Morgan, *Wilderness at Dawn*, p. 121.
32. Ibid., pp. 121–122.
33. Williams, *Capitalism and Slavery*, p. 26.
34. Bennett, *Before the Mayflower*, p. 36.
35. Carole Hymowitz and Michaele Weissman, *A History of Women in America* (New York: Bantam Books, 1980), p. 8.
36. Beulah Compton, *Introduction to Social Welfare and Social Work: Structure, Function, and Process* (Homewood, IL: The Dorsey Press, 1980), p. 199.
37. Williams, *Capitalism and Slavery*, pp. 11–12.
38. Compton, *Introduction to Social Welfare*, p. 188.
39. L. F. Strock, ed., *Proceedings and Debates in the British Parliament Respecting North America* (Washington, D.C., 1924–1941), p. 249. Quoted in Williams, *Capitalism and Slavery*, p. 17.
40. From the *Calendar of State Papers*, Colonial Series, v. 229. Report of the Council for Foreign Plantations (August 1664). In Williams, *Capitalism and Slavery*, p. 18.
41. Williams, *Capitalism and Slavery*, p. 18.
42. Compton, *Introduction to Social Welfare*, among others.
43. Gerald Handel, *Social Welfare in Western Society* (New York: Random House, 1982), p. 67.
44. Morgan, *Wilderness at Dawn*, p. 122.
45. William Jay Jacobs, *Women in American History* (Encino, CA: Glencoe Publishing, 1976), p. 7.
46. Ibid., p. 3.
47. Hymowitz and Weissman, *History of Women*, p. 11.
48. Linda E. Spaeth, "More Than Her 'Thirds': Wives and Widows in Colonial Virginia," in Linda Spaeth and

488 Notes

Alison Duncan Hirsch (eds.), *Women, Family, and Community in Colonial America: Two Perspectives* (New York: Haworth Press, 1983), p. 11.

49. Amaury De Riencourt, *Sex and Power in History* (New York: Dell Publishing, 1974), p. 308.

50. Julia Cherry Sprull, "Housewives and Their Helpers," in Linda K. Kerber and Jane de Hart Mathews (eds.), *Women's America* (New York: Oxford University Press, 1982), p. 26.

51. Alice Kessler-Harris, *Out to Work: A History of Wage-Earning Women in the United States* (New York: Oxford University Press, 1982), p. 13.

52. Hymowitz and Weissman, *History of Women*, p. 22.

53. Ibid., p. 23.

54. Spaeth, "More Than Her 'Thirds,' " p. 11.

55. Hymowitz and Weissman, *History of Women*, p. 21.

56. Jacobs, *Women in American History*, p. 14.

57. Kessler-Harris, *Out to Work*, p. 16.

58. Hymowitz and Weissman, *History of Women*, p. 128.

59. Kessler-Harris, *Out to Work*, p. 17.

60. Ibid.

61. Walter A. Friedlander and Robert Z. Apte, *Introduction to Social Welfare*, 9th ed. (Englewood Cliffs, NJ: Prentice-Hall, 1974), p. 62.

62. Compton, *Introduction to Social Welfare*, p. 198.

63. Gerald N. Grob (advisory ed.), "Maryland Report on Almshouses," in *The State and Public Welfare in Nineteenth-Century America* (New York: Arno Press, 1976), pp. 6–7.

64. Ibid.; a note in Senate Document 2, Jan. 1859, historical references taken from the New Colony of Plymouth and Massachusetts Colonial Acts, p. 38.

65. June Axinn and Herman Levin, *Social Welfare: A History of the American Response to Need*, 2nd ed. (New York: Harper & Row, 1982), p. 19.

66. Walter Bremner (ed.), *Children and Youth in America: A Documentary History* (New York: Arno Press, 1969; originally published in 1914), p. 12. Quoted in Kessler-Harris, *Out to Work*, p. 5.

67. Grob, *The State and Public Welfare*, p. 16.

68. Axinn and Levin, *Social Welfare*, p. 20.

69. Compton, *Introduction to Social Welfare*, pp. 201–202.

70. Ibid., p. 198.

71. Ralph Dolgoff and Donald Feldstein, *Understanding Social Welfare*, 2nd ed. (New York: Longman Press, 1984), p. 65.

72. Compton, *Introduction to Social Welfare*, p. 176.

73. Bennett, *Before the Mayflower*, p. 36.

74. A. Leon Higginbotham, Jr., *Shades of Freedom: Racial Politics and Presumptions of the American Legal Process* (New York: Oxford University Press, 1996), pp. 195–196.

Higginbotham says the assumption of inferiority of people of African descent in American Slavery Jurisprudence is based on ten principles:

1. Inferiority: presume, preserve, protest, and defend the ideal of the superiority of whites.
2. Property: define the slave as property, maximize the master's economic interest, disregard the slaves' humanity, and deny slaves the fruits of their labor.
3. Powerlessness: keep them submissive and dependent in every respect, not only to master, but whites in general. Limit access to justice and establish differential punishment for blacks and whites. Utilize violence and government power to ensure submission.
4. Racial purity: preserve white male sexual dominance.
5. Manumission and free blacks: limit manumission and minimize the number of free blacks, confining them as close to slavery as possible.
6. Family: recognize no rights, destroy family unity, deny the right of marriage, demean and degrade, condemn both for conduct and state of mind.
7. Education and culture: denied, do not allow literacy.
8. Religion: recognize no rights to define, practice, choose leaders, or worship with other blacks. Encourage adoption of white masters' religion. Use religion to justify inferior status.
9. Liberty or resistance: rebellion and flight punishable by death, freedom of movement restricted.
10. By any means possible: support all measures that maximize slavery's profitability, legitimize racism, and, by use of violence if necessary, [end any activity] that advocates slavery's abolition or white supremacy's domination (pp. 195–196).

75. A. Leon Higginbotham, Jr., *In the Matter of Color: Race and the American Legal Process: The Colonial Period* (New York: Oxford University Press, 1978), p. 32.

76. Ibid., p. 3.

77. Ibid., p. 34.

78. Ibid., p. 38.

79. Ibid., p. 36.

80. Ibid., pp. 114, 169.

81. Ibid., pp. 8–9.

82. Ibid., p. 44.

83. Ibid., p. 285.

84. Ibid., p. 67.

85. Williams, *Capitalism and Slavery*, pp. 23, 25.

86. Harris, *Patterns of Race*, pp. 13–14.

87. Bennett, *Before the Mayflower*, p. 38.

88. Ibid., p. 30.

89. Jacobs, *Women in American History*, p. 11.

90. Williams, *Capitalism and Slavery*, p. 46.

91. Olaudah Equiano, "The Interesting Narrative of Olaudah Equiano," in Thomas R. Frazier, *Afro-American History: Primary Sources* (New York: Harcourt, Brace, and World, 1970), pp. 18–20.

92. Feagin, *Racial and Ethnic Relations*, p. 213.

93. Joe R. Feagin, *Racist America: Roots, Current Realities, and Future Reparations* (New York: Routledge, 2001), p. 48.

94. Williams, *Capitalism and Slavery*, p. 108.

95. Ibid.

96. Jacobs, *Women in American History*, p. 19, quoting Abigail Adams.

97. Ibid., p. 16.

98. Sally Smith Booth, *The Women of '76* (New York: Hastings House, 1973), p. 144. Quoted in Hymowitz and Weissman, *History of Women*.

99. Thomas R. Dye and L. Harmon Zeigler, *The Irony of Democracy* (Belmont, CA: Wadsworth Publishing, 1970), p. 42.

100. Feagin, *Black Racism*, p. 14.

101. Ibid., p. 6.

102. Ibid., pp. 14–15.

103. Dye and Zeigler, *The Irony of Democracy*, p. 51.

Chapter 6

1. For example, Massachusetts and New York required male voters to have $300, up to $1,000 to run for Congress, $1,500 to $3,000 to run for the Senate, and $5,000 to run for governor. Pennsylvania allowed any man who paid taxes to vote or run for office and in 1812 New York allowed the same, even extending voting rights to some free property-owning African Americans. See Thomas R. Dye and L. Harmon Zeigler, *The Irony of Democracy* (Belmont, CA: Wadsworth Publishing, 1970), pp. 6–14; and Beulah Compton, *Introduction to Social Welfare and Social Work: Structure, Function, and Process* (Homewood, IL: The Dorsey Press, 1980), p. 218.
2. Dye and Zeigler, *The Irony of Democracy*, p. 65.
3. Ibid., p. 67.
4. Michael B. Katz, *Poverty and Policy in American History* (New York: Academic Press, 1983), p. 10.
5. David Macarov, *Work and Welfare: The Unholy Alliance* (Beverly Hills, CA: Sage Publications, 1980), pp. 234–235.
6. Samuel Mencher, *From Poor Law to Poverty Programs* (Pittsburgh: University of Pittsburgh Press, 1967), p. 167.
7. Ibid., p. 136.
8. Blanche Coll, *Perspectives in Public Welfare: A History* (Washington, D.C.: U.S. Government Printing Office, 1971), pp. 22–23.
9. Mencher, *From Poor Law to Poverty Programs*, p. 77.
10. Compton, *Introduction to Social Welfare*, p. 226.
11. Maxine Seller, *Immigrant Women* (Philadelphia: Temple University Press, 1984), p. 50.
12. Coll, *Perspectives in Public Welfare*, p. 24.
13. Carole Hymowitz and Michaele Weissman, *A History of Women in America* (New York: Bantam Books, 1980), p. 195.
14. Ibid.
15. Ibid., p. 198.
16. John A. Drout and Dixon R. Fox, *The Completion of Independence* (New York: Macmillan, 1944), pp. 373–374. In Mencher, *Poor Law to Poverty Programs*, pp. 133–134.
17. Coll, *Perspectives in Public Welfare*, p. 34.
18. Hymowitz and Weissman, *History of Women*, p. 236.
19. Edith Abbott, *Women in Industry: A Study of American Economic History* (New York: Arno Press, 1910, first published by *The New York Times*, 1909), pp. 48–62. Referenced in Compton, *Introduction to Social Welfare*, p. 228.
20. William Jay Jacobs, *Women in American History* (Encino, CA: Glencoe Publishing, 1976), p. 31.
21. Hymowitz and Weissman, *History of Women*, p. 238, quoting Marie Van Vorst, a wealthy woman who took a job posing as a poor woman in a South Carolina mill to investigate working conditions of women and children.
22. Mencher, *From Poor Law to Poverty Programs*, p. 137.
23. Jacobs, *Women in American History*, p. 32.
24. Compton, *Introduction to Social Welfare*, p. 228.
25. Katz, *Poverty and Policy*, p. 12.
26. Compton, *Introduction to Social Welfare*, p. 227.
27. Coll, *Perspectives in Public Welfare*, p. 34.
28. Seller, *Immigrant Women*, p. 162.
29. Katz, *Poverty and Policy*, p. 202.
30. Ibid., p. 115.
31. Ibid., p. 194.
32. 1818 Report of the Society for the Prevention of Pauperism, founded in 1817 by Thomas Eddy and John Griscom. Quoted in John B. McMaster, *A History of the People of the United States* (New York: D. Appleton, 1895), pp. 527–528; and John V. N. Yates, Secretary of the State of New York, 1824; and reported in Mencher, *From Poor Laws to Poverty Programs*, pp. 145–146.
33. David Scheider and Albert Deutsch, *The History of Public Welfare in New York State* (Chicago: University of Chicago Press, 1938), p. 212.
34. J. V. N. Yates, "Report of the Secretary of State in 1824 on the Relief and Settlement of the Poor," reprinted in the *34th Annual Report of the State Board of Charities of the State of New York, 1900*. Vol. 1, pp. 939–963.
35. Frank Dekker Watson, *The Charity Organization Movement in the United States* (New York: Arno Press and *The New York Times*, 1971), p. 690.
36. Compton, *Introduction to Social Welfare*, p. 236.
37. Quoted in Philip S. Foner, *History of the Labor Movement in the United States* (New York: International Publishers, 1947), p. 98. Reported in Mencher, *From Poor Law to Poverty Programs*, p. 144.
38. Watson, *Charity Organization Movement*, p. 73.
39. Ibid., pp. 75–76.
40. Coll, *Perspectives in Public Welfare*, p. 36.
41. Ibid., p. 37.
42. Mencher, *From Poor Law to Poverty Programs*, p. 83.
43. Compton, *Introduction to Social Welfare*, p. 287.
44. Seller, *Immigrant Women*, p. 179.
45. Coll, *Perspectives in Public Welfare*, p. 30.
46. Ibid., p. 22.
47. Katz, *Poverty and Policy*, p. 196.
48. Gerald N. Grob (advisory ed.), *The State and Public Welfare in Nineteenth-Century America* (New York: Arno Press, 1976), p. 3 of Senate Document D.
49. Ibid., pp. 6–7.
50. Coll, *Perspectives in Public Welfare*, p. 25.
51. Grob, *State and Public Welfare*, p. 9 of Senate Document D.
52. Ibid., p. 53 of Senate Document 2: "Massachusetts State Charities Report of the Special Joint Committee Appointed to Investigate Charitable Institutions of the Commonwealth of Massachusetts, 1858" (Boston: William White, printer to the State, 1859).
53. Grob, *State and Public Welfare*, p. 50 of Senate Document 2.
54. Katz, *Poverty and Policy*, discussing the Erie County, New York, poorhouse, pp. 66 and 217.
55. Coll, *Perspectives in Public Welfare*, p. 22.
56. Ibid., p. 31. Also, Philadelphia blamed inadequate almshouses for the growing need for outdoor relief and over ten years (ending in 1824) spent $621,000 for outdoor relief and $470,000 for almshouses. By 1857, Philadelphia preferred outdoor relief, with investigation and supervision by paid staff, as less expensive and more humane than almshouse care.
57. Robert W. Bruere, "The Good Samaritan, Inc.," *Harper's Monthly Magazine*, Vol. 120 (1910), p. 834. Referenced in Watson, *Charity Organization Movement*, p. 79.
58. Barbara Ehrenreich and Deirdre English, *Complaints and Disorders: The Sexual Politics of Sickness* (New York: The Feminist Press, Glass Mountain Pamphlet #2, 1973), p. 19.
59. Ibid., p. 48.
60. Ibid., p. 16.
61. Hymowitz and Weissman, *History of Women*, p. 68.

62. Ehrenreich and English, *Complaints and Disorders*, p. 33.
63. Seller, *Immigrant Women*, pp. 97–98.
64. Grob, *State and Public Welfare*, p. 13: "A Report on the Public Charities, Reformatories, Prisons, and Almshouses of the State of Maryland," by C. W. Chancellor, Maryland Secretary of the State Board of Health, July 1877.
65. Seaton W. Manning, "The Tragedy of the Ten-Million-Acre Bill," *Social Service Review*, Vol. 36 (March 1962), pp. 44–50; and Roy Franklin Nichols, *Franklin Pierce* (Philadelphia: University of Pennsylvania Press, 1958), p. 289.
66. Jacobs, *Women in American History*, p. 17.
67. Ibid., p. 25.
68. Ibid., p. 22.
69. Compton, *Introduction to Social Welfare*, p. 289.
70. Zebulon Brockway, *Fifty Years of Prison Service*, pp. 397–398. Discussed in Anthony M. Platt, *The Child Savers: The Invention of Delinquency*, 2nd ed. (Chicago: University of Chicago Press, 1977), p. 48.
71. Anthony B. Platt, *The Child Savers: The Invention of Delinquency*, 2nd ed. (Chicago: University of Chicago Press, 1977), p. 73.
72. Ibid., pp. 67–68.
73. Compton, *Introduction to Social Welfare*, p. 289.
74. Platt, *The Child Savers*, p. 63.
75. Albert Roberts, in a preliminary review of Day, *A New History of Social Welfare*.
76. Grob, *State and Public Welfare*, p. 100.
77. Jeffrey Galper, *Social Work Practice: A Radical Perspective* (Englewood Cliffs, NJ: Prentice Hall, 1974), p. 51.
78. Ted Morgan, *Wilderness at Dawn: The Settling of the North American Continent* (New York: Simon & Schuster, 1993), p. 438.
79. Joe R. Feagin, *Racial and Ethnic Relations*, 3rd ed. (Englewood Cliffs, NJ: Prentice Hall, 1989), p. 179.
80. Carolyn Merchant, *The Death of Nature: Women, Ecology, and the Scientific Revolution* (San Francisco: Harper & Row, 1980), p. 28.
81. Morgan, *Wilderness at Dawn*, p. 427.
82. Ibid., p. 417.
83. Compton, *Introduction to Social Welfare*, p. 221.
84. Feagin, *Racial and Ethnic Relations*, p. 178.
85. Joseph Hraba, *American Ethnicity* (Itasca, IL: F.E. Peacock Publishers, 1979), p. 222.
86. Feagin, *Racial and Ethnic Relations*, p. 178.
87. Ibid., p. 181.
88. Jack Chen, *The Chinese in America* (San Francisco: Harper & Row, 1980), pp. 1–30.
89. Joe R. Feagin, *Racist America: Roots, Current Realities, and Future Reparations* (New York: Routledge, 2001), p. 6, p. 14.
90. Ibid., p. 213.
91. Ibid., p. 85.
92. Lerone Bennett, Jr., *Before the Mayflower: A History of the Negro in America, 1619–1964* (Chicago: Johnson Publishing Company, 1966), p. 84.
93. Dye and Zeigler, *The Irony of Democracy*, p. 57.
94. Ibid., p. 57.
95. Bennett, *Before the Mayflower*, p. 93.
96. Ibid., p. 75.
97. Hymowitz and Weissman, *History of Women*, p. 62.
98. Jacobs, *Women in American History*, p. 12.

99. Patricia Hill Collins, *Black Feminist Thought*, 2nd ed. (New York: Routledge Press, 2000), p. 51.
100. Feagin, *Racist America*, p. 46.
101. Collins, *Black Feminist Thought*, p. 139. Collins also cites the case of Sarah Bartmann, called the Hottentot Venus, who was exhibited nude in the fine salons of Europe, where women and men could examine her "sexual differences" from the white race. "Upon her death, in 1815, she was dissected, with her genitalia and buttocks placed on display ... " so that she was reduced to her sexual parts (p. 137). Bartmann's remains were returned to Africa in the late 1900s for burial.
102. Hymowitz and Weissman, *History of Women*, p. 48.
103. Michael P. Johnson, "Smothered Slave Infants: Were Slave Mothers at Fault?" in Linda K. Kerber and Jane DeHart Mathews (eds.), *Women's America* (New York: Oxford University Press, 1982), pp. 102–105.
104. Jerome H. Schiele, *Human Services and the Afrocentric Paradigm* (New York: Haworth Press, 2000), pp. 38–39.
105. Collins, *Black Feminist Thought*, p. 49.
106. See, among others, Schiele, *Human Services and the Afrocentric Paradigm*, Chapter 3. "The Evolution of Black Social Work and its Pitfalls," pp. 37–56; Collins, *Black Feminist Thought*; Feagin, *Racist America* Elmer Martin and Joanne Martin, *Spirituality and the Black Helping Tradition* (Washington, D.C.: NASW Press, 2002).
107. Hymowitz and Weissman, *History of Women*, p. 43.
108. Hraba, *American Ethnicity*, p. 43.
109. Angela Davis, *Women, Race, and Class* (New York: Vintage Press, 1983), p. 6.
110. Feagin, *Racist America*, p. 53.
111. Ibid., p. 51.
112. Bennett, *Before the Mayflower*, p. 99.
113. Feagin, *Racial and Ethnic Relations*, p. 218.
114. Dye and Zeigler, *The Irony of Democracy*, p. 71.
115. Feagin, *Racial and Ethnic Relations*, p. 270.
116. Ibid.
117. Ibid., p. 272.
118. A. Sinclair, *The Emancipation of the American Woman*. In Jacobs, *Women in American History*, p. 12.
119. Hymowitz and Weissman, *History of Women*, p. 823.
120. Seller, *Immigrant Women*, p. 256.
121. Jacobs, *Women in American History*, p. 43.
122. Hymowitz and Weissman, *History of Women*, p. 173.

Chapter 7

1. Michael B. Katz, *Poverty and Policy in American History* (New York: Academic Press, 1983), p. 130.
2. Marvin B. Gettleman, "Charity and Social Classes in the U.S., 1874—1900," *American Journal of Economics and Sociology*, Vol. 22 (April–July 1963), pp. 313–329. Reported in Jeffrey Galper, *Social Work Practice: A Radical Perspective* (Englewood Cliffs, NJ: Prentice Hall, 1974), pp. 427 ff.
3. J. Saville, "The Welfare State: An Historical Approach," in E. Butterworth and R. Hobman, *Social Welfare in Modern Britain* (Glasgow: Fontana-Collins, 1975). Referenced in Peter Day, *Social Work and Social Control* (London: Tavistock Publications, 1981), p. 14.
4. Frances Fox Piven and Richard Cloward, *Regulating the Poor* (New York: Random House, 1971).
5. Burton, Orville Vernon. Quoted by Bordewich, Fergus, in *Smithsonian*, April 2011. p. 78.

6. Bordewich, Fergus. "Opening Salvo," *Smithsonian*, April 2011, pp. 76–99. P. 80.

7. Ibid.

8. Thomas R. Dye and L. Harmon Zeigler, *The Irony of Democracy* (Belmont, CA: Wadsworth Publishing, 1970), pp. 69–70.

9. Ibid., p. 79.

10. Carole Hymowitz and Michaele Weissman, *A History of Women in America* (New York: Bantam Books, 1980), pp. 148–149.

11. Lerone Bennett, Jr., *Before the Mayflower: A History of the Negro in America, 1619–1964* (Chicago: Johnson Publishing Co., 1969), p. 67.

12. Joseph Hraba, *American Ethnicity* (Itasca, IL: F.E. Peacock Publishers, 1979), p. 266.

13. Bennett, Before the Mayflower, p. 168.

14. William Jay Jacobs, *Women in American History* (Encino, CA: Glencoe Publishing, 1976), pp. 96–97.

15. Ibid., p. 98.

16. Ibid.

17. June Axinn and Herman Levin, *Social Welfare: A History of the American Response to Need*, 2nd ed. (New York: Harper & Row, 1983), p. 94.

18. Ibid., p. 92.

19. Ibid.

20. V.O. Key. Quoted in Dye and Zeigler, *The Irony of Democracy*, pp. 79–80.

21. Katz, Poverty and Policy, p. 130.

22. Blanche D. Coll, *Perspectives in Public Welfare: A History* (Washington, D.C.: U.S. Government Printing Office, 1971), p. 40.

23. Ibid., p. 41.

24. Axinn and Levin, *Social Welfare*, p. 97.

25. Alice Kessler-Harris, *Out to Work: A History of Wage-Earning Women in the United States* (New York: Oxford University Press, 1982), p. 146.

26. Angela Davis, *Women, Race, and Class* (New York: Vintage Press, 1983), p. 137.

27. Kessler-Harris, *Out to Work*, p. 91

28. Hymowitz and Weissman, *History of Women*, p. 240.

29. A nineteenth-century discussion of pauperism, in Hymowitz and Weissman, *History of Women*, pp. 240–241.

30. Jacobs, Women in American History, p. 107.

31. Kessler-Harris, *Out to Work*, p. 91.

32. Bettina Berch, *The Endless Day: The Political Economy of Women and Work* (New York: Harcourt Brace Jovanovich, 1982), pp. 40–41.

33. Axinn and Levin, *Social Welfare*, p. 131.

34. Coll, Perspectives in Public Welfare, p. 40.

35. Ibid.

36. Hraba, *American Ethnicity*, p. 305.

37. Jack Chen, *The Chinese in America* (San Francisco: Harper & Row, 1980), pp. 136–142.

38. Ibid., pp. 162–164.

39. Hraba, *American Ethnicity*, p. 302.

40. Joe R. Feagin, *Racial and Ethnic Relations*, 2nd ed. (Englewood Cliffs, NJ: Prentice Hall, 1984), pp. 194–195.

41. Ibid., p. 199.

42. Ibid., p. 201.

43. Ibid.

44. Hraba, *American Ethnicity*, p. 216.

45. Bennett, *Before the Mayflower*, pp. 92–93.

46. Ibid., p. 202.

47. Ibid.

48. Ibid., p. 217.

49. Ibid., p. 197.

50. Hraba, *American Ethnicity*, p. 278.

51. Joe R. Feagin, *Racist America: Roots, Current Realities, and Future Reparations* (New York: Routledge, 2001), pp. 61–62.

52. Bennett, *Before the Mayflower*, p. 197.

53. Davis, *Women, Race, and Class*, p. 89.

54. Bennett, *Before the Mayflower*, p. 239.

55. "Jim Crow" was a name made famous in a comedy in the early 1700s. It became synonymous with African Americans.

56. Kessler-Harris, *Out to Work*, p. 185.

57. Hymowitz and Weissman, *History of Women*, p. 205.

58. Kessler-Harris, *Out to Work*, p. 185.

59. Hymowitz and Weissman, *History of Women*, p. 220.

60. Davis, *Women, Race, and Class*, pp. 87–88.

61. Jacobs, *Women in American History*, p. 144.

62. Hymowitz and Weissman, *History of Women*, p. 299.

63. Dr. Clelia Duel Mosher studied the sexual habits of married women as a student at the University of Wisconsin before 1892. The project spanned twenty years, with 70 percent of the women born before 1870. Most were more highly educated than poor, with twenty-seven teachers. They were upper-middle or middle-class women rather than members of a leisure class and, despite a high level of education knew little about sex before marriage.

64. Carl N. Degler, "What Ought to Be and What Was: Women's Sexuality in the 19th Century," in Judith Walzer Leavitt (ed.), *Women and Health in America* (Madison: University of Wisconsin Press, 1984), pp. 40 ff.

65. Ibid.

66. Pamela Johnson Conover and Virginia Gray, *Feminism and the New Right: Conflict over the American Family* (New York: Praeger Publishing, 1983), pp. 4–8.

67. Beulah Compton, *Introduction to Social Welfare and Social Work* (Homewood, IL: The Dorsey Press, 1980), p. 298.

68. James Reed, "Doctors, Birth Control, and Social Values, 1830–1970," in Leavitt, *Women and Health*, p. 127.

69. Ibid., p. 201.

70. Mark Thomas Connelly, "Prostitution, Venereal Disease, and American Medicine," in Leavitt, *Women and Health*, p. 201.

71. Sidney Fine, *Laissez-Faire and the General Welfare State* (Ann Arbor: University of Michigan Press, 1964), p. 173. Referenced in Gerald Handel, *Social Welfare in Western Society* (New York: Random House, 1982), p. 213.

72. Dye and Zeigler, *The Irony of Democracy*, p. 73.

73. Coll, Perspectives in Public Welfare, p. 42.

74. Piven and Cloward, *Regulating the Poor*, pp. 165–166. Paraphrased in Macarov, *Design of Social Welfare*, p. 197.

75. Frank Dekker Watson, *The Charity Organization Movement in the United States* (New York: Arno Press and The New York Times, 1971), p. 281.

76. Mrs. Charles Russell Lowell, "The Economic and Moral Effects of Public Outdoor Relief," *National Conference of Charities and Corrections Proceedings*, 1879, p. 203. Quoted in Coll, *Perspectives in Public Welfare*, pp. 44–45.

77. Watson, *The Charity Organization Movement*.

78. Compton, *Introduction to Social Welfare*, p. 286.
79. Coll, *Perspectives in Public Welfare*, p. 61.
80. Watson, *The Charity Organization Movement*, p. 324.
81. Ibid.
82. Robert McHenry (ed.), *Famous American Women: A Biographical Dictionary from Colonial Times to the Present* (New York: Dover Publications, 1980), p. 44.
83. Ibid. p. 45.
84. Ibid.
85. Handel, *Social Welfare in Western Society*, p. 70.
86. Hymowitz and Weissman, *History of Women*, p. 224.
87. Ibid., p. 232.
88. Ibid., p. 233.
89. Ibid., p. 228.
90. McHenry, *Famous American Women*, p. 234.
91. Ray Ginger, "Women at Hull House," in Linda K. Kerber and Jane DeHart Mathews (eds.), *Women's America* (New York: Oxford University Press), p. 272.
92. McHenry, *Famous American Women*, p. 135.
93. Ibid., p. 1.
94. Ibid.
95. Ginger, "Women at Hull House," p. 272.
96. McHenry, *Famous American Women*, p. 387.
97. Bennett, *Before the Mayflower*, p. 168.
98. Katz, *Poverty and Policy*, p. 193.
99. Gerald N. Grob, *The State and Public Welfare in Nineteenth-Century America* (New York: Arno Press, 1976), p. 145.
100. Compton, *Introduction to Social Welfare*, p. 298.
101. Senate Bill 2 (Boston: William White, printer to the State, 1859). Quoted in Grob, *The State and Public Welfare*, p. 137.
102. Axinn and Levin, *Social Welfare*, p. 146.
103. Dye and Zeigler, *The Irony of Democracy*, p. 79.
104. Coll, *Perspectives in Public Welfare*, p. 64.
105. Katz, *Poverty and Policy*, p. 190.
106. Coll, *Perspectives in Public Welfare*, pp. 43–44.
107. Katz, *Poverty and Policy*, p. 233.
108. Walter A. Friedlander and Robert Z. Apte, *Introduction to Social Welfare* (Englewood Cliffs, NJ: Prentice Hall, 1974), p. 80.
109. Ralph Dolgoff and Donald Feldstein, *Understanding Social Welfare*, 2nd ed. (New York: Longman Press, 1984).
110. Axinn and Levin, *Social Welfare History*, p. 102.
111. McHenry, *Famous American Women*, pp. 346–347.
112. Ibid
113. Elmer P. Martin and Joanne M. Martin, *Spirituality and the Black Helping Tradition in Social Work* (Washington D.C.: NASW Press, 2002), p. 95.
114. Ibid., p. 115.
115. Ibid., p. 116.
116. Ibid., p. 125.

Chapter 8

1. June Axinn and Herman Levin, *Social Welfare: A History of the American Response to Need*, 2nd ed. (New York: Harper & Row, 1982), p. 134.
2. Beulah Compton, *Introduction to Social Welfare and Social Work: Structure, Function, and Process* (Homewood, IL: The Dorsey Press, 1980), pp. 350–352.
3. John Ehrenreich, *The Altruistic Imagination: A History of Social Work and Social Policy in the United States* (Ithaca, NY: Cornell University Press, 1985), p. 37.
4. Axinn and Levin, *Social Welfare*, p. 135.
5. Blanche Coll, *Perspectives in Public Welfare: A History* (Washington, D.C.: U.S. Government Printing Office, 1971), p. 63.
6. Axinn and Levin, *Social Welfare*, p. 129.
7. Ibid., p. 128.
8. Angela Davis, *Women, Race, and Class* (New York: Random House, 1983), p. 212.
9. Joseph Hraba, *American Ethnicity* (Itasca, IL: F.E. Peacock Publishers, 1979), p. 18.
10. Thomas Leonard, "'Who Shall Select the Fittest?' Eugenics, Economics, and the Origins of an American Reform," Paper developed for Duke University Department of Economics, History of Political Economy Seminar, February 25, 2005. Available at www.econ.duke.edu/~staff/wrkshop_papers/2005.
11. Davis, *Women, Race, and Class*, p. 214.
12. Stephen Kern, *The Culture of Time and Space: 1880–1918* (Cambridge: Harvard University Press, 1983), p. 260.
13. Ehrenreich, *Altruistic Imagination*, pp. 45–47.
14. Axinn and Levin, *Social Welfare*, pp. 128–129.
15. Coll, *Perspectives in Public Welfare*, p. 63.
16. Compton, *Introduction to Social Welfare*, pp. 322–323.
17. Coll, *Perspectives in Public Welfare*, p. 66.
18. Compton, *Introduction to Social Welfare*, p. 322.
19. Hraba, *American Ethnicity*, p. 321.
20. Compton, *Introduction to Social Welfare*, p. 349.
21. Axinn and Levin, *Social Welfare*, pp. 128–129.
22. Lerone Bennett, Jr., *Before the Mayflower: A History of the Negro in America, 1919–1964* (Chicago: Johnson Publishing Co., 1966), p. 287.
23. Ibid., pp. 292–293.
24. Ibid., an account by Walter White, p. 294.
25. Ibid., p. 277.
26. Elmer P. Martin and Joanne M. Martin, *Spirituality and the Black Helping Tradition in Social Work* (Washington, D.C.: NASW Press, 2002), p. 132.
27. Ibid., p. 133.
28. Ibid., pp. 139–140.
29. Richard R. Wright, Jr., "Social Service," *The Christian Recorder* (Philadelphia, 1922 [*sic*]), p. 14. Quoted in Martin and Martin, Op. Cit., p. 148.
30. Bennett, *Before the Mayflower*, pp. 296–297.
31. Linda K. Kerber and Jane DeHart Mathews (eds.), *Women's America* (New York: Oxford University Press, 1982), pp. 261–262.
32. Bennett, *Before the Mayflower*, p. 284; and Robert McHenry (ed.), *Famous American Women: A Biographical Dictionary from Colonial Times to the Present* (New York: Dover Publications, 1980), pp. 434–435.
33. Angela Darenkamp, John McClymer, Mary Moynihan, and Arlene Vadum, *Images of Women in American Popular Culture* (New York: Harcourt Brace Jovanovich, 1985), p. 343.
34. Ibid., p. 166.
35. Ibid., pp. 170–173.
36. Ibid., pp. 173–176.
37. Ibid., pp. 177–186.
38. Ibid., p. 151.
39. Samuel Mencher, *From Poor Law to Poverty Programs* (Pittsburgh: University of Pittsburgh Press, 1967), p. 382.
40. Ibid., p. 385.
41. Ehrenreich, *Altruistic Imagination*, p. 45.

42. Alice Kessler-Harris, "Where Are the Organized Women Workers?" in Kerber and Mathews, *Women's America*, pp. 226–241.

43. William Jay Jacobs, *Women in American History* (Encino, CA: Glencoe Publishing, 1976), p. 140.

44. Axinn and Levin, *Social Welfare*, p. 141.

45. Compton, *Introduction to Social Welfare*, p. 337.

46. Alice Kessler-Harris, *Out to Work: A History of Wage-Earning Women in the United States* (New York: Oxford University Press, 1982), p. 238.

47. Ibid.

48. Carole Hymowitz and Michaele Weissman, *A History of Women in America* (New York: Bantam Books, 1980), pp. 254–259.

49. Ibid., p. 259.

50. Pauline Newman, "Triangle Shirt Waist Fire," in Kerber and Mathews, *Women's America*, p. 224.

51. Maxine Seller, *Immigrant Women* (Philadelphia: Temple University Press, 1984).

52. Newman, "Triangle Shirt Waist Fire," p. 224.

53. Robert McHenry, Ed. *Famous American Women: A Biographical Dictionary from Colonial Times to the Present* (New York: Dover Publications, 1980).

54. Michael B. Katz, *Poverty and Policy in American History* (New York: Academic Press, 1983), pp. 226–227.

55. Coll, *Perspectives in Public Welfare*, p. 74.

56. Axinn and Levin, *Social Welfare*, p. 127.

57. Seller, *Immigrant Women*, p. 198.

58. Compton, *Introduction to Social Welfare*, pp. 331–332.

59. Hymowitz and Weissman, *History of Women*, p. 239.

60. Compton, *Introduction to Social Welfare*, p. 332.

61. Mother Jones, *The Autobiography of Mother Jones*, 3d rev. ed. (Chicago: Charles H. Kerr, 1977), pp. 138–139.

62. Jacobs, *Women in American History*, p. 124.

63. Compton, *Introduction to Social Welfare*, p. 332.

64. Ibid., p. 364.

65. Ibid., p. 360.

66. Coll, *Perspectives in Public Welfare*, p. 77.

67. Winifred Bell, *Aid to Dependent Children* (New York: Columbia University Press, 1965), p. 6.

68. Axinn and Levin, *Social Welfare*, p. 160.

69. Coll, *Perspectives in Public Welfare*, p. 79.

70. Bell, *Aid to Dependent Children*, p. 21.

71. Coll, *Perspectives in Public Welfare*, p. 80.

72. Ibid., p. 79.

73. *Social Service Review*, 1951, p. 384. Quoted in Compton, *Introduction to Social Welfare*, p. 364.

74. Nancy Schrom Dye, "Mary Breckinridge, The Frontier Nursing Service, and the Introduction of Nurse-Midwifery in the United States," in Judith Walzer Leavitt (ed.), *Women and Health in America* (Madison: University of Wisconsin Press, 1984), pp. 327–344.

75. Ehrenreich, *Altruistic Imagination*, pp. 65–67.

76. William Sadler, *Theory and Practice of Psychiatry*. Discussed in Mary Shea, "The Ideology of Mental Health and the Emergence of the Therapeutic Liberal State: The American Mental Hygiene Movement, 1900–1930," Ph.D. diss., University of Illinois at Champaign–Urbana, 1980; in Ehrenreich, *Altruistic Imagination*, pp. 65–67.

77. Ehrenreich, *Altruistic Imagination*, p. 67.

78. Axinn and Levin, *Social Welfare*, p. 155.

79. Ibid.

80. Gerald Handel, *Social Welfare in Western Society* (New York: Random House, 1982), p. 131.

81. Frank Dekker Watson, *The Charity Organization Movement in the United States* (New York: Arno Press and *The New York Times*, 1971), p. 369.

82. Handel, *Social Welfare in Western Society*, p. 131.

83. Axinn and Levin, *Social Welfare*, p. 145.

84. Coll, *Perspectives in Public Welfare*, p. 81.

85. Ibid.

86. Katz, *Poverty and Policy*, p. 225.

87. Axinn and Levin, *Social Welfare*, p. 137.

88. Katz, *Poverty and Policy*, p. 222.

89. Watson, *Charity Organization Movement*, p. 372.

90. Jacobs, *Women in American History*, p. 213.

91. Dale Spender, *There's Always Been a Women's Movement This Century* (Boston: Pandora Press, 1983), p. 16.

92. Ibid., p. 22.

93. Doris Stevens, *Jailed for Freedom* (New York: Boni and Liveright, 1920), pp. 187–189. Referenced in Seller, *Immigrant Women*, pp. 269 ff.

94. Seller, *Immigrant Women*, p. 117.

95. Ibid., p. 130.

96. Compton, *Introduction to Social Welfare*, p. 338.

97. Mark Thomas Connelly, "Prostitution, Venereal Disease, and American Medicine," in Leavitt, *Women and Health*, pp. 196–221.

98. Ibid., p. 200.

99. Ibid., p. 201.

100. Ibid., p. 197.

101. Ibid., p. 203.

102. Bettina Berch, *The Endless Day: The Political Economy of Women and Work* (New York: Harcourt Brace Jovanovich, 1982), p. 45.

103. Seller, *Immigrant Women*, pp. 130 ff.

104. James C. Mohr, "Patterns of Abortion and the Response of American Physicians, 1790–1930," in Leavitt, *Women and Health*, pp. 117–123, esp. p. 119.

105. Ibid.

106. Hymowitz and Weissman, *History of Women*, p. 293.

107. Jacobs, *Women in American History*, p. 191.

108. Kerber and Mathews, *Women's America*, p. 312.

109. Ibid., p. 318.

110. Hymowitz and Weissman, *History of Women*, p. 296.

111. James Reed, "Doctors, Birth Control, and Social Values, 1830–1970," in Leavitt, *Women and Health*, p. 131.

112. Ehrenreich, *Altruistic Imagination*, p. 49.

Chapter 9

1. June Axinn and Herman Levin, *Social Welfare: A History of the American Response to Need*, 2nd ed. (New York: Harper & Row, 1982), p. 175.

2. Ibid., p. 176.

3. John Ehrenreich, *The Altruistic Imagination: A History of Social Work and Social Policy in the United States* (Ithaca: Cornell University Press, 1985), p. 86.

4. Thomas R. Dye and L. Harmon Zeigler, *The Irony of Democracy* (Belmont, CA: Wadsworth Publishing, 1970), p. 83.

5. Axinn and Levin, *Social Welfare*, p. 192.

6. Carole Hymowitz and Michaele Weissman, *A History of Women in America* (New York: Bantam Books, 1980), p. 303.

7. Frances Fox Piven and Richard Cloward, *Regulating the Poor* (New York: Random House, 1971).

8. Hymowitz and Weissman, *History of Women*, p. 307.

9. Alice Kessler-Harris, *Out to Work: A History of Wage-Earning Women in the United States* (New York: Oxford University Press), 1982, pp. 257–260.

10. Ibid., p. 264.

11. Axinn and Levin, *Social Welfare*, p. 187.

12. Ibid., p. 202.

13. Kessler-Harris, *Out to Work*, p. 256.

14. Axinn and Levin, *Social Welfare*, p. 181.

15. From Albert U. Romasco, *The Poverty of Abundance—Hoover, the Nation, and Depression* (New York: Oxford University Press, 1965), p. 147. In Gerald Handel, *Social Welfare in Western Society* (New York: Random House, 1982), p. 134.

16. Axinn and Levin, *Social Welfare*, p. 190.

17. Ehrenreich, *Altruistic Imagination*, p. 87.

18. Joe R. Feagin, *Racial and Ethnic Relations*, 3d ed. (Englewood Cliffs, NJ: Prentice Hall, 1989), p. 280.

19. Ehrenreich, *Altruistic Imagination*, p. 88.

20. Axinn and Levin, *Social Welfare*, p. 189.

21. Ehrenreich, *Altruistic Imagination*, p. 89.

22. Ibid., p. 93.

23. Ibid., p. 95.

24. Ibid., p. 97.

25. Dye and Zeigler, *The Irony of Democracy*, p. 83.

26. Joseph Heffernan, *Introduction to Social Welfare Policy* (Itasca, IL: F.E. Peacock Publishers, 1979), p. 194.

27. Axinn and Levin, *Social Welfare*, p. 194.

28. Ehrenreich, *Altruistic Imagination*, p. 96.

29. Axinn and Levin, *Social Welfare*, p. 214.

30. Ibid., p. 204.

31. While Heffernan, *Introduction to Social Welfare Policy*, p. 199, says that all benefits were to be paid in cash, Axinn and Levin, *Social Welfare*, p. 214, say that most often benefits had to be worked off on public property.

32. Axinn and Levin, *Social Welfare*, p. 184.

33. Ibid.

34. Ibid., p. 185.

35. Ehrenreich, *Altruistic Imagination*, p. 93.

36. Axinn and Levin, *Social Welfare*, p. 186.

37. Ibid.

38. Kessler-Harris, *Out to Work*, p. 270.

39. Gerald Handel, *Social Welfare in Western Society*, p. 136.

40. David Macarov, *Work and Welfare: The Unholy Alliance* (Beverly Hills, CA: Sage Publications, 1980), p. 209.

41. Axinn and Levin, *Social Welfare*, p. 181.

42. Beulah R. Compton, *Introduction to Social Welfare and Social Work: Structure, Function, and Process* (Homewood, IL: The Dorsey Press, 1980), p. 414.

43. Axinn and Levin, *Social Welfare*, p. 180.

44. Ibid., p. 182.

45. William Jay Jacobs, *Women in American History* (Encino, CA: Glencoe Publishing, 1976), p. 238.

46. William H. Chafe, "Eleanor Roosevelt," in Linda K. Kerber and Jane DeHart Mathews (eds.), *Women's America* (New York: Oxford University Press, 1982), pp. 344–353; and in Robert McHenry (ed.), *Famous American Women: A Biographical Dictionary from Colonial Times to the Present* (New York: Dover Publications, 1980), p. 354.

47. Winifred Bell, *Contemporary Social Welfare* (New York: Macmillan, 1983), p. 7.

48. Michael B. Katz, *Poverty and Policy in American History* (New York: Academic Press, 1983), p. 221.

49. Samuel Mencher, *From Poor Laws to Poverty Programs* (Pittsburgh: University of Pittsburgh Press, 1967), p. 306.

50. F. D. Roosevelt, "Message to Congress," June 8, 1934, 73rd Congress 2nd Session (Washington, D.C.: United States Government Printing Office, 1934), pp. 10, 770. Quoted in Mencher, *Poor Law to Poverty Programs*, p. 333.

51. *New York Review of Books*, February 28, 1986, p. 7, reviewing Gosta Esping-Anderson, Martin Rein, and Lee Rainwater (eds.), *Stagnation and Renewal in Social Policy* (New York: M.E. Sharpe, 1986).

52. Andrew W. Dobelstein, *Politics, Economics, and Public Welfare* (Englewood Cliffs, NJ: Prentice Hall, 1980), p. 29.

53. Ehrenreich, *Altruistic Imagination*, p. 99.

54. Jeffrey Galper, *Social Work Practice: A Radical Perspective* (Englewood Cliffs, NJ: Prentice Hall, 1980), p. 77.

55. Harry Hopkins, quoted in Robert E. Sherwood, *Roosevelt and Hopkins* (New York: Harper & Row, 1948), p. 297.

56. Axinn and Levin, *Social Welfare*, p. 220.

57. Ralph Dolgoff and Donald Feldstein, *Understanding Social Welfare*, 2nd ed. (New York: Longman Press, 1984), pp. 180–181.

58. Harry L. Hopkins, in Josephine Chapman Brown, *Public Relief, 1929–39* (New York: Henry Holt, 1940), p. 396. Quoted in Handel, *Social Welfare in Western Society*, p. 138.

59. Axinn and Levin, *Social Welfare*, p. 202.

60. Macarov, *Work and Welfare*, p. 52.

61. Ehrenreich, *Altruistic Imagination*, p. 111.

62. Galper, *Social Work Practice*, p. 169.

63. Ehrenreich, *Altruistic Imagination*, p. 118.

64. Ibid., p. 207.

65. Peter Day, *Social Work and Social Control* (London: Tavistock Publications, 1981), p. 86.

66. Feagin, *Racial and Ethnic Relations*, p. 329.

67. "Italians: Acknowledge Our Internment," *Quad-City Times* (Davenport, IA), October 27, 2000, p. 3A.

68. Feagin, *Racial and Ethnic Relations*, pp. 329–330.

69. Axinn and Levin, *Social Welfare*, p. 231.

70. Ibid., p. 135.

71. Norman Cousins, "Will Women Lose Their Jobs?" *Current History and Forum*, Vol. 41 (Sept. 1939), p. 14. Quoted in Kessler-Harris, *Out to Work*, p. 246.

72. Kessler-Harris, *Out to Work*, p. 276.

73. *Fortune* poll, cited in Sheila Tobias and Lisa Anderson, "Rosie the Riveter: Demobilization and the Female Labor Force," in Kerber and Mathews, *Women's America*, p. 299.

74. Ibid., p. 357.

75. Ibid., pp. 354 ff.

76. Kessler-Harris, *Out to Work*, p. 278.

77. Hymowitz and Weissman, *History of Women*, p. 313.

78. Kessler-Harris, *Out to Work*, p. 291.

79. Axinn and Levin, *Social Welfare*, p. 230.

80. Tobias and Anderson, "Rosie the Riveter," p. 369.

81. Ehrenreich, *Altruistic Imagination*, p. 99.

82. Compton, Introduction to Social Welfare, p. 438.

83. Ibid., p. 440.

84. Discussed in Feagin, *Racial and Ethnic Relations*, p. 229, and Lerone Bennett, Jr., *Before the Mayflower: A History of the Negro in America 1619–1964*, rev. ed. (Chicago: Johnson Publishing Co., 1966), p. 304.

85. Axinn and Levin, *Social Welfare*, p. 242.

86. Ibid.

87. Ibid., p. 243.
88. Ibid., p. 244.
89. Tobias and Anderson, "Rosie the Riveter," p. 361.
90. Ibid., p. 364.
91. Hymowitz and Weissman, *History of Women*, p. 313.
92. Tobias and Anderson, "Rosie the Riveter," p. 371.
93. Ibid.
94. Kessler-Harris, *Out to Work*, p. 297.
95. Chafe, "Eleanor Roosevelt," p. 443. Quoted in Compton, *Introduction to Social Welfare*.
96. Ehrenreich, *Altruistic Imagination*, p. 147.
97. Axinn and Levin, *Social Welfare*, p. 233.
98. Ehrenreich, *Altruistic Imagination*, p. 153.
99. Compton, *Introduction to Social Welfare*, p. 143.
100. McHenry, *Famous American Women*, p. 136.
101. Ehrenreich, *Altruistic Imagination*, p. 135.
102. Dobelstein, *Politics and Welfare*, pp. 84–85.

Chapter 10

1. John Ehrenreich, *The Altruistic Imagination: A History of Social Work and Social Policy in the United States* (Ithaca, NY: Cornell University Press, 1985), p. 140.
2. Beulah R. Compton, *Introduction to Social Welfare and Social Work: Structure, Function, and Process* (Homewood, IL: The Dorsey Press, 1980), p. 437.
3. *Social Security Bulletin*, Vol. 46, no. 7 (July 1983), p. 95.
4. June Axinn and Herman Levin, *Social Welfare: A History of the American Response to Need*, 2nd ed. (New York: Harper & Row, 1982), p. 230.
5. The "poverty line" was developed early in the 1960s by Mollie Orshansky. It was the amount of the budget that constituted a short-term emergency diet times a factor of 3, because it was estimated that a family should not have to spend more than one-third of its budget on food.
6. Ehrenreich, *Altruistic Imagination*, pp. 148–149.
7. Axinn and Levin, *Social Welfare*, p. 235.
8. Carole Hymowitz and Michaele Weissman, *A History of Women in America* (New York: Bantam Books, 1980), p. 326.
9. Compton, *Introduction to Social Welfare*, p. 479.
10. Ibid., p. 253.
11. *Social Security Bulletin*, Vol. 49, no. 2 (Feb. 1986), p. 38.
12. Compton, *Introduction to Social Welfare*, p. 446.
13. *Social Security Bulletin*, July 1983, p. 13.
14. Ibid.
15. Gerald Handel, *Social Welfare in Western Society* (New York: Random House, 1982), p. 139.
16. Axinn and Levin, *Social Welfare*, p. 245.
17. Sar Levitan, Martin Rein, and David Marwick, *Work and Welfare Go Together* (Baltimore: Johns Hopkins University Press, 1972), p. 6.
18. Compton, *Introduction to Social Welfare*, p. 454.
19. Martin Rein, "The Welfare Crisis," in Lee Rainwater (ed.), *Social Problems and Public Policy* (Chicago: Aldine de Gruyter, 1974), p. 50.
20. Levitan, Rein, and Marwick, *Work and Welfare*, p. 12.
21. Betty Reid Mandell, "Welfare and Totalitarianism: Part I. Theoretical Issues," *Social Work* (Jan. 1971), p. 24.
22. Axinn and Levin, *Social Welfare*, p. 246.
23. Levitan, Rein, and Marwick, *Work and Welfare*, 1972, p. 9; Rein, in "Welfare Crisis," pp. 89–102.
24. Winifred Bell, *Aid to Dependent Children* (New York: Columbia University Press, 1965), pp. v and 137.

25. Ibid., p. 121.
26. Joel P. Handler, *Reforming the Poor* (New York: Basic Books, 1972), p. 139.
27. Ibid., p. 26.
28. Dorothy C. Miller, "AFDC: Mapping a Strategy for Tomorrow," *Social Service Review* (Dec. 1983), Vol. 57, pp. 599–613, esp. p. 601.
29. Thomas R. Dye and L. Harmon Zeigler, *The Irony of Democracy* (Belmont, CA: Wadsworth Publishing, 1970), p. 297; Axinn and Levin, *Social Welfare*, pp. 231–232.
30. Lerone Bennett, Jr., *Before the Mayflower: A History of the Negro in America, 1619–1964* (Chicago: Johnson Publishing Co., 1966), p. 303.
31. Ibid., p. 313.
32. Compton, *Introduction to Social Welfare*, p. 482.
33. Dye and Zeigler, *The Irony of Democracy*, pp. 296–297.
34. Clayborne Carson, Director of Martin Luther King, Jr., Papers Project, (ed.) *Civil Rights Chronicle: The African American Struggle for Freedom* (Lincolnwood, IL: Legacy Publishing Co., 2002), p. 172.
35. Joe R. Feagin, *Racial and Ethnic Relations*, 2nd ed. (Englewood Cliffs, NJ: Prentice Hall, 1984), p. 515.
36. Ibid., p. 190.
37. Joseph Hraba, *American Ethnicity* (Itasca, IL: F.E. Peacock Publishers, 1979), p. 227.
38. Feagin, *Racial and Ethnic Relations*, p. 274.
39. M. Barrera, C. Munoz, and C. Ornelas, "The Barrio as an Internal Colony," in Harlan Hahn (ed.), *Urban Affairs Annual Review*, Vol. 6. (Beverly Hills, CA: Sage Publications, 1972), pp. 465–498.
40. Feagin, *Racial and Ethnic Relations*, p. 188.
41. Ibid., p. 299.
42. Ibid., p. 303.
43. Ehrenreich, *Altruistic Imagination*, p. 152.
44. Jack Chen, *The Chinese in America* (San Francisco: Harper & Row, 1980), pp. 201–260.
45. Bennett, *Before the Mayflower*, p. 323.
46. Ibid., p. 338.
47. Ibid., p. 344.
48. Dye and Zeigler, *The Irony of Democracy*, p. 299.
49. Bennett, *Before the Mayflower*, p. 327.
50. Miller, "AFDC: Mapping a Strategy," p. 602.
51. Hymowitz and Weissman, *History of Women*, p. 343.
52. Dye and Zeigler, *The Irony of Democracy*, p. 300.
53. James C. Davies, "Toward a Theory of Revolution," *American Sociological Review*, Vol. 27 (Feb. 1962), p. 318. Cited in Dye and Zeigler, *The Irony of Democracy*, p. 309.
54. Feagin, *Racial and Ethnic Relations*, p. 226.
55. Raymond Hall, *Black Separatism and Social Reality: Rhetoric and Reason* (New York: Pergamon Press, 1978), pp. 165–167.
56. Ibid.
57. Leonore J. Wietzman, "Legal Regulation of Marriage: Tradition and Change," *California Law Review*, Vol. 62 (1974), p. 1187. Quoted in Lisa Peattie and Martin Rein, *Women's Claims: A Study in Political Economy* (New York: Oxford University Press, 1983), p. 42.
58. Alice Kessler-Harris, *Out to Work: A History of Wage-Earning Women in the United States* (New York: Oxford University Press, 1982), p. 305.
59. Hymowitz and Weissman, *History of Women*, p. 327.

60. Jane DeHart Mathews, "The New Feminism and the Dynamics of Social Change," in Linda K. Kerber and Jane DeHart Mathews (eds.),*Women's America* (New York: Oxford University Press, 1982), p. 408.
61. Ehrenreich, *Altruistic Imagination*, p. 182.
62. William N. Eskridge, Jr., *Gaylaw: Challenging the Apartheid of the Closet* (Cambridge, MA: Harvard University Press, 1999), p. 1.
63. Ibid., p. 18.
64. Ibid., p. 42.
65. Ibid., p. 63.
66. Ibid., p. 69.
67. Toby Marotta, *The Politics of Homosexuality* (Boston: Houghton Mifflin, 1981). Quoted in Lisa Langenbach, "Modern and Traditionalist Issue Groups in the American Party System: An Examination of the Realigning Potential of Cultural Issues in Changing Cleavage Structures" unpublished doctoral dissertation, Purdue University, West Lafayette, Indiana, Aug. 1986, pp. 75–76.
68. Eskridge, op. cit., p. 45.
69. Compton, *Introduction to Social Welfare*, p. 439.
70. Feagin, *Racial and Ethnic Relations*, p. 238.
71. Ehrenreich, *Altruistic Imagination*, p. 179.
72. Ibid.
73. Compton, *Introduction to Social Welfare*, p. 473.
74. Frances Fox Piven and Richard Cloward, *The New Class War: Reagan's Attack on the Welfare State and Its Consequences* (New York: Pantheon Books, 1982), p. 14.
75. Levitan, Rein, and Marwick, *Work and Welfare*, p. 8.
76. John E. Tropman, Alan Gordon, and Phyllis J. Day, Welfare Codebook, unpublished manuscript developed 1971, based on data from *Statistical Abstracts of the United States 1971* (Washington, D.C.: U.S. Government Printing Office, 1972); and *County and City Data Book 1964* (Washington, D.C.: U.S. Government Printing Office, 1960), p. 4.
77. Levitan, Rein, and Marwick, *Work and Welfare*, p. 46.
78. Axinn and Levin, *Social Welfare*, p. 246.
79. Ehrenreich, *Altruistic Imagination*, p. 178.
80. Ibid.
81. Ibid.
82. Ibid., p. 177.
83. Ibid., p. 179.
84. Ibid., p. 161.
85. Axinn and Levin, *Social Welfare*, p. 261.
86. Compton, *Introduction to Social Welfare*, p. 134.
87. Axinn and Levin, *Social Welfare*, p. 260.
88. Phyllis J. Day, "Sex Role Stereotypes and Public Assistance," *Social Service Review* (March 1979), Vol. 53, pp. 106–115.
89. Robert Morris, *Social Policy of the American Welfare State* (New York: Harper & Row, 1979), p. 101.
90. Ibid., pp. 101–104.
91. Wilma Doyle, Leonard Z. Breen, and Robert Eichhorn, *Synopsis of the Older Americans Act*, Revised (W. Lafayette, Indiana: Department of Sociology and Anthropology, Purdue University, 1976), pp. 4–10.
92. Ehrenreich, *Altruistic Imagination*, p. 198.
93. Michael B. Katz, *Poverty and Policy in American History* (New York: Academic Press, 1983), p. 231.
94. Ehrenreich, *Altruistic Imagination*, p. 195.
95. Hall, *Black Separatism*, p. 164.
96. Jan Mason, John S. Wodarski, and T. M. Jim Parham, "Work and Welfare: A Reevaluation of AFDC," *Social Work* (May–June 1985), pp. 197–202.
97. Dye and Zeigler, *The Irony of Democracy*, p. 304.
98. Ibid., p. 302.
99. Ibid., p. 303.

Chapter 11

1. June Axinn and Herman Levin, *Social Welfare: A History of the American Response to Need*, 2nd ed. (New York: Harper & Row, 1982), p. 236.
2. Ibid., p. 289.
3. John Ehrenreich, *The Altruistic Imagination: A History of Social Work and Social Policy in the United States* (Ithaca, NY: Cornell University Press, 1985), p. 202.
4. Ibid., p. 203.
5. Beulah Compton, *Introduction to Social Welfare and Social Work: Structure, Function, and Process* (Homewood, IL: The Dorsey Press, 1980), p. 496.
6. Ralph Dolgoff and Donald Feldstein, *Understanding Social Welfare*, 2nd ed. (New York: Longman Press, 1984), p. 272.
7. Andrew W. Dobelstein, *Politics, Economics, and Public Welfare* (Englewood Cliffs, NJ: Prentice Hall, 1980), pp. 150–151.
8. Gerald Handel, *Social Welfare in Western Society* (New York: Random House, 1982), pp. 152–153.
9. Axinn and Levin, *Social Welfare*, p. 289.
10. "Current Operating Statistics," *Social Security Bulletin*, Vol. 46, no. 7 (Washington, D.C.: U.S. Government Printing Office, July 1983), p. 20.
11. Ibid.
12. Aaron Wildavsky, *Speaking Truth to Power: The Art and Craft of Policy Analysis* (Boston: Little, Brown, 1979), p. 106.
13. Francis X. Russo and George Willis, *Human Services in America* (Englewood Cliffs, NJ: Prentice Hall, 1986), p. 242.
14. Winifred Bell, *Contemporary Social Welfare* (New York: Macmillan, 1983), pp. 170–171.
15. Russo and Willis, *Human Services*, p. 244.
16. Handel, *Social Welfare*, p. 194.
17. Joseph Heffernan, *Introduction to Social Welfare Policy* (Itasca, IL: F.E. Peacock Publishers, 1979), p. 238.
18. Bell, *Contemporary Welfare*, p. 157.
19. Ibid.
20. Joel P. Handler, *Reforming the Poor* (New York: Basic Books, 1972), p. 58.
21. Robert Morris, *Rethinking Social Welfare* (New York: Longman Press, 1986), p. 246.
22. Bell, *Contemporary Welfare*, p. 130.
23. Sar A. Levitan and Clifford M. Johnson, *Beyond the Safety Net* (Cambridge, MA: Ballinger Publishing, 1984), p. 78.
24. Ibid., pp. 36–37.
25. Senator Russell Long, quoted in Dobelstein, *Politics, Economics, and Public Welfare*, p. 129.
26. Saul Kaplan, "Support from Absent Fathers of Children Receiving ADC," Public Assistance Report #41 (Washington, D.C.: U.S. Government Printing Office, 1969). Quoted in Bell, *Contemporary Welfare*, p. 214 footnote.
27. Handler, *Reforming the Poor*, p. 32.
28. Bell, *Contemporary Welfare*, pp. 133–135.

29. Ibid., p. 22.
30. Ibid., p. 224.
31. Ibid.
32. Rosemary Sarri, *Under Lock and Key* (Ann Arbor, MI: National Assessment of Juvenile Delinquency, 1974).
33. Axinn and Levin, *Social Welfare*, p. 289.
34. Bell, *Contemporary Welfare*, p. 169.
35. Levitan and Johnson, *Beyond the Safety Net*, p. 124.
36. Frances Fox Piven and Richard Cloward, *The New Class War: Reagan's Attack on the Welfare State and Its Consequences* (New York: Pantheon Books, 1982), p. 31.
37. Levitan and Johnson, *Beyond the Safety Net*, p. 118.
38. Ibid.
39. Ibid., p. 125.
40. Joe R. Feagin, *Racial and Ethnic Relations*, 3d ed. (Englewood Cliffs, NJ: Prentice Hall, 1989), p. 303.
41. Dolgoff and Feldstein, *Understanding Social Welfare*, pp. 201–202.
42. Kenneth Wooden, *Crying in the Playtime of Others* (New York: McGraw-Hill, 1976).
43. Russo and Willis, *Human Services*, p. 65.
44. Compton, *Introduction to Social Welfare*, p. 513.
45. Ramsey Clark, *Crime in America: Observations on Its Nature, Causes, Prevention, and Control* (New York: Simon & Schuster, 1970), p. 335.
46. D. Stanley Eitzen, *In Conflict and Order: Understanding Society*, 3d ed. (Needham, MA: Allyn & Bacon, 1985), p. 213.
47. From the Justice Department's Bureau of Justice Statistics, reported in the *Lafayette (Indiana) Journal and Courier*, July 26, 1986, p. A4.
48. From the American Correctional Association, reported in the *Lafayette (Indiana) Journal and Courier*, Sept. 12, 1986, p. A7.
49. Feagin, *Racial and Ethnic Relations*, p. 234.
50. Ibid., p. 195.
51. Ibid., p. 199.
52. Eric Treisman, "The Last Treaty," *Harper's Magazine*, Feb. 1975, pp. 37–39.
53. Ibid., pp. 37–38.
54. Feagin, *Racial and Ethnic Relations*, p. 193.
55. Ibid.
56. Ibid., p. 198.
57. Ibid., p. 205.
58. *Lafayette (Indiana) Journal and Courier*, AP report, Sept. 17, 1986, p. A1.
59. Feagin, *Racial and Ethnic Relations*, pp. 190–193.
60. Ibid., p. 196.
61. Ibid.
62. Ibid., p. 191.
63. Levitan and Johnson, *Beyond the Safety Net*, p. 119.
64. Feagin, *Racial and Ethnic Relations*, p. 333.
65. Ibid., p. 340.
66. Peter Irons, "The Return of the 'Yellow Peril,'" *The Nation*, Oct. 19, 1985, p. 316.
67. Feagin, *Racial and Ethnic Relations*, p. 362.
68. Ibid., p. 275.
69. Ibid., p. 265.
70. Ibid., p. 264.
71. Feagin, *Racial and Ethnic Relations*, p. 303.
72. Carol Giacomo, "Sterilization Count Higher Than Expected," *Hartford (Connecticut) Courant*, Oct. 13, 1980, pp. A10 and A12.

73. Feagin, *Racial and Ethnic Relations*, p. 351.
74. Ibid.
75. Ibid., p. 245.
76. Ibid., p. 243.
77. Ibid., p. 232.
78. Lisa Langenbach, "Modernist and Traditionalist Issue Groups in the American Party System: An Examination of the Realigning Potential of Cultural Issues in Changing Cleavage Structures," unpublished doctoral dissertation, Purdue University, West Lafayette, Indiana, Aug. 1986, p. 128.
79. Ibid., pp. 138–140.
80. Ibid., quoting the Anti-Defamation League report, 1981, p. 66.
81. Kate Kellogg, "The Far-Right Fringe," *Michigan Today*, June 1987, p. 6.
82. Katherine Gruber, *Encyclopedia of Associations* (Detroit: Gale Research, 1981). Cited in Langenbach, "Modern and Traditionalist Issue Groups," p. 164.
83. Bell, *Contemporary Welfare*, p. 124.
84. All figures are Ibid., pp. 123–124.
85. Ibid., p. 123; Axinn and Levin, *Social Welfare*, pp. 287–288.
86. Langenbach, "Modern and Traditionalist Issue Groups," pp. 75–81.
87. Eitzen, *In Conflict and Order*, pp. 222–223.
88. William N. Eskridge, Jr., *Gaylaw: Challenging the Apartheid of the Closet* (Cambridge, MA: Harvard University Press, 1999), p. 104.
89. Ibid., pp. 232–233.
90. Reagan alluded to gays when he jokingly remarked that Muammar Gadhafi should be sent to San Francisco because he wears robes, and an assistant trivialized both gays and AIDS by suggesting that Gadhafi be infected with AIDS.
91. Elizabeth Neus, "Epidemic Now a Part of Mainstream America," New Jersey *Courier–Post* (July 23, 1995), p. A5.
92. Ibid.

Chapter 12

1. James Midgley, "New Christian Right, Social Policy, and the Welfare State," *Journal of Sociology and Social Welfare*, Vol. 17, no. 2 (June 1990), p. 97.
2. Daniel P. Moynihan, *Pandaemonium: Ethnicity in International Politics* (New York: Oxford University Press, 1993), p. 46.
3. Winifred Bell, *Contemporary Social Welfare* (New York: Macmillan, 1983), pp. 42–43.
4. Midgley, "New Christian Right," p. 94.
5. Sar A. Levitan and Clifford M. Johnson, *Beyond the Safety Net* (Cambridge, MA: Ballinger Publishing, 1984), p. 150.
6. Center on Budget and Policy Priorities, "Analysis of Poverty in 1987" (Washington, D.C.: Center on Budget and Policy Priorities, 1988), pp. 3–6.
7. David A. Stockman, *The Triumph of Politics: Why the Reagan Revolution Failed* (New York: Harper & Row, 1986), p. 373. Cited in Moynihan, *Pandaemonium*, p. 17.
8. Ralph Dolgoff and Donald Feldstein, *Understanding Social Welfare*, 2nd ed. (New York: Longman Press, 1984), p. 144; U.S. Bureau of the Census reports. Cited in *Chicago Tribune*, July 19, 1986, pp. 1–2.
9. Levitan and Johnson, *Beyond the Safety Net*, p. 151.

10. Ibid.
11. James M. Fendrich, Mamie Miller, and Tim Nichel, "It's the Budget, Stupid: A Policy Analysis of Clinton's First Budget," *Journal of Sociology and Social Welfare*, Vol. 21, no. 4 (Dec. 1994), p. 7.
12. Frances Fox Piven and Richard Cloward, *The New Class War: Reagan's Attack on the Welfare State and Its Consequences* (New York: Pantheon Books, 1982), p. 7.
13. Diana DiNitto, *Social Welfare: Politics and Public Policy*, 4th ed. (Needham, MA: Allyn & Bacon, 1995), pp. 57, 60.
14. Fendrich, Miller, and Nichel, "It's the Budget, Stupid," p. 18.
15. U.S. Bureau of the Census reports. Cited in *Chicago Tribune*, July 19, 1986, pp. 1–2.
16. Jule M. Sugarman, Gary D. Bass, Nancy Amidei, David Plocher, Shannon Ferguson, and Julie Quiroz, *OMB Watch: A Citizen's Guide to Gramm–Rudman–Hollings* (Washington, D.C.: Focus Project, Inc., 1986); United Way of Indiana, "Capital Steps" (Indianapolis: United Way of Indiana, n.d.).
17. Levitan and Johnson, *Beyond the Safety Net*, p. 150.
18. John L. Palmer and Isabel V. Sawhill (eds.), *Reagan Record: An Assessment of America's Changing Domestic Priorities* (Cambridge, MA: Ballinger Publishing, 1985), p. 222.
19. Mark Robert Rank, *Living on the Edge* (New York: Columbia University Press, 1994), p. 20.
20. Howard J. Karger, "Income Maintenance Programs and the Reagan Domestic Agenda," *Journal of Sociology and Social Welfare*, Vol. 19, no. 1 (March 1992), p. 57.
21. Ibid.
22. Fendrich, Miller, and Nichel, "It's the Budget, Stupid," p. 18.
23. Palmer and Sawhill, *Reagan Record*, p. 217.
24. Ibid., p. 193 and footnote, p. 193.
25. Levitan and Johnson, *Beyond the Safety Net*, p. 152.
26. Children's Defense Fund, "American Children in Poverty" (Washington, D.C.: CDF, 1984), p. 3.
27. Ibid., p. x.
28. Fendrich, Miller, and Nichel, "It's the Budget, Stupid," p. 18.
29. Levitan and Johnson, *Beyond the Safety Net*, p. 151.
30. Palmer and Sawhill, *Reagan Record*, p. 31.
31. From the Democratic Study Group, U.S. House of Representatives, James L. Oberstar, chairman, "Special Report: Gramm–Rudman—the Cutting Begins" (Washington, D.C.: U.S. House of Representatives, Jan. 1986), no. 99–26, p. 20; Children's Defense Fund, "American Children," p. 3.
32. Sugarman, Bass, Amidei, Plocher, Ferguson, and Quiroz, *OMB Watch*, p. 23.
33. Francis X. Russo and George Willis, *Human Services in America* (Englewood Cliffs, NJ: Prentice Hall, 1986), p. 245.
34. "Current Operating Statistics," *Social Security Bulletin* (Washington, D.C.: U.S. Government Printing Office), Sept. 1984, p. 3.
35. DiNitto, *Social Welfare*, p. 111.
36. Ibid., p. 110.
37. Ibid., p. 107.
38. Julie Rovner, "Ending the Greatest Terror of Life," *AARP Bulletin*, Special Report (1995), p. 12.
39. Ibid.
40. Neil Howe and Richard Jackson, "The Most Unfair Noncut of All: Federal Pensions," *Christian Science Monitor* (July 21, 1995), p. 18.
41. "Panel: Welfare Exams Wasted Millions," *Lafayette (Indiana) Journal and Courier* (Oct. 30, 1986), p. 1.
42. John Ehrenreich, *The Altruistic Imagination: A History of Social Work and Social Policy in the United States* (Ithaca, NY: Cornell University Press, 1985), p. 217.
43. Levitan and Johnson, *Beyond the Safety Net*, p. 40.
44. Howard J. Karger, "Income Maintenance Programs," p. 51.
45. Children's Defense Fund, "American Children," pp. 27–28.
46. Levitan and Johnson, *Beyond the Safety Net*, p. 132.
47. Michael Harrington, *The New American Poverty* (New York: Holt, Rinehart, & Winston, 1984), p. 42.
48. Daniel P. Moynihan, "The Case Against Entitlement Cuts," *Modern Maturity* (Nov.–Dec. 1994), pp. 13–14.
49. Howard Stanback, "Attacking Poverty with Economic Policy," in Alan Gartner, Colin Greer, and Frank Reismann (eds.), *Beyond Reagan: Alternatives for the Eighties* (New York: Harper & Row, 1984), pp. 57–73, esp. p. 62.
50. "Change in America," *Chronicle of Higher Education*, Vol. 32, no. 3 (Sept. 17, 1986), p. 1.
51. Mimi Abramovitz, "The Reagan Legacy: Undoing Class, Race, and Gender Accords," *Journal of Sociology and Social Welfare*, Vol. 19, no. 1 (March 1992), p. 102.
52. Joel A. Devine and James D. Wright, *The Greatest of Evils: Urban Poverty and the American Underclass* (New York: Aldine de Gruyter, 1993), p. 63.
53. *Lafayette (Indiana) Journal and Courier*, Oct. 2, 1986, p. 37.
54. U.S. Bureau of the Census, Population Reports, *Social Benefits*, from Internet.
55. Piven and Cloward, *New Class War*, pp. 3–4.
56. Ibid.
57. Nancy Rose, "Gender, Race, and the Welfare State: Government Work Programs from the 1930s to the Present," *Feminist Studies*, Vol. 19, no. 2 (Summer 1993), p. 334.
58. Tom Joe, "The Case for Income Support," in Alan Gartner, Colin Greer, and Frank Reismann (eds.), *Beyond Reagan: Alternatives for the Eighties* (New York: Harper & Row, 1984), pp. 81–90.
59. Deborah K. Zinn and Rosemary Sarri, "Turning Back the Clock on Public Welfare," *Signs: Journal of Women in Culture and Society*, Vol. 10, no. 2. (Winter 1984), pp. 355–370, esp. p. 357.
60. Bell, *Contemporary Social Welfare*, p. 105.
61. DiNitto, *Social Welfare*, p. 212.
62. Robert Lekachman, *Greed Is Not Enough: Reaganomics* (New York: Pantheon Books, 1982), p. 85.
63. Children's Defense Fund, "American Children," p. 33.
64. Loretta Schwartz-Nobel, *Starving in the Shadow of Plenty* (New York: G.P. Putnam's Sons, 1983). A review in *Lafayette (Indiana) Journal and Courier* (Oct. 27, 1983), p. C-3.
65. "Current Operating Statistics" (Feb. 1986), p. 21.
66. DiNitto, *Social Welfare*, p. 258.
67. "Current Operating Statistics," *Social Security Bulletin*, Vol. 46 (April 1983), p. 70.
68. Children's Defense Fund, "American Children," p. viii.
69. Terri Combs-Orme and Bernard Guyer, "American's Health Care System, the Reagan Legacy," *Journal of Sociology and Social Welfare*, Vol. 19, no. 1 (March 1992), pp. 3–88.
70. Children's Defense Fund, "American Children," pp. 1–4.
71. Ibid., p. 6.
72. Wheeler, in Howell and Howell, "Food Stamps," p. 730.

73. "Reducing the Infant Mortality Rate," *Lafayette (Indiana) Journal and Courier* (Feb. 4, 1987), p. C-4.

74. Levitan and Johnson, *Beyond the Safety Net*, p. 115.

75. Children's Defense Fund, "American Children," p. 33.

76. Ibid.

77. Beth Rubin, James D. Wright, and Joel A. Devine, "Unhousing the Urban Poor: The Reagan Legacy," *Journal of Sociology and Social Welfare*, Vol. 19, no. 1 (March 1992), p. 142.

78. Ibid., p. 129.

79. Elizabeth A. Mulroy and Terry S. Love, "Housing Affordability, Stress and Single Mothers: Pathway to Homelessness," *Journal of Sociology and Social Welfare*, Vol. 19, no. 3 (Sept. 1992), pp. 55–56.

80. C. Dolbeare from a paper prepared for the Policy Conference on Assisting the Homeless, U.S. Advisory Commission on Intergovernmental Relations (Nov. 1988), p. 39. Quoted in Rubin, Wright, and Devine, "Unhousing the Urban Poor," p. 136.

81. Ibid.

82. Democratic Study Group, "Gramm Rudman—The Cutting Begins," pp. A18–A19.

83. Mulroy and Love, "Housing Affordability," p. 60.

84. "HUD Defends Accuracy of Count: Group Rebuts Report on Homeless," *Kansas City Times* (Aug. 16, 1984), p. 5.

85. Jack Anderson and Dale van Atta, "Model Shelter or Workhouse?" *Washington Post* (July 21, 1985), p. 2.

86. Rubin, Wright, and Devine, "Unhousing the Urban Poor."

87. Anderson and van Atta, "Model Shelter or Workhouse?" p. 2.

88. Rubin, Wright, and Devine, "Unhousing the Urban Poor," p. 112.

89. Alice K. Johnson and Michael Sherraden, "Asset Based Social Welfare Policy: Homeownership for the Poor," *Journal of Sociology and Social Welfare*, Vol. 19, no. 3 (Sept. 1994), p. 78.

90. Ibid., p. 74.

91. Rubin, Wright, and Devine, "Unhousing the Urban Poor," p. 116.

92. Levitan and Johnson, *Beyond the Safety Net*, p. 128.

93. Bell, *Contemporary Social Welfare*, p. 131.

94. Levitan and Johnson, *Beyond the Safety Net*, p. 128.

95. "Education," *Newsweek on Campus* (Feb. 1987), pp. 10–18.

96. Michael Wines, "At Issue: Civil Rights," *National Journal* (March 27, 1982), p. 539.

97. William N. Eskridge, Jr. *Gaylaw: Challenging the Apartheid of the Closet* (Cambridge, MA: Harvard University Press, 1999), pp. 146–147.

98. Ibid., p. 235.

99. M. V. Lee Badgett, "The Wage Effects of Sexual Orientation Discrimination," *Industrial and Labor Relations Review*, Vol. 48, p. 726. Reported in Eskridge, *Gaylaw*, p. 234.

100. Palmer and Sawhill, *Reagan Record*, p. 208.

101. Lynn C. Burbridge, "The Impact of Changes in Policy on the Federal Equal Employment Opportunity Effort" (Washington, D.C.: The Urban Institute, Nov. 1983), Table 3. From Table 6.5, "OFCCP Enforcement Activities, FY 1980–1983." Cited in Palmer and Sawhill, *Reagan Record*, p. 205.

102. Palmer and Sawhill, *Reagan Record*, p. 539.

103. Joe R. Feagin, *Racial and Ethnic Relations*, 2nd ed. (Englewood Cliffs, NJ: Prentice Hall, 1984), p. 240.

104. Wines, "At Issue," pp. 536–541.

105. Palmer and Sawhill, *Reagan Record*, p. 208.

106. Levitan and Johnson, *Beyond the Safety Net*, p. 128.

107. Ibid., p. 109.

108. Leonard Beeghly, "Illusion and Reality in the Measurement of Poverty," *Social Problems*, Vol. 31, no. 3 (Feb. 1984), pp. 324–333, esp. p. 329.

109. Ehrenreich, *Altruistic Imagination*, p. 222.

110. "Current Operating Statistics" (Feb. 1986), p. 20.

111. Ibid., Table 3, p. 17.

112. United Way of Indiana, "Capital Steps," p. 1.

113. "Current Operating Statistics" (Feb. 1986), p. 18.

114. U.S. Bureau of the Census, *Statistical Abstracts 1994*, Government Expenditures for Health Services and Supplies, millions of dollars, 1990 and 1991, Table 154, p. 113.

115. Ray Mosely, *Chicago Tribune* (May 24, 1992), section 4, page 3. Quoted in Moynihan, *Pandaemonium*, p. 18.

116. Palmer and Sawhill, *Reagan Record*, pp. 214–215.

117. Levitan and Johnson, *Beyond the Safety Net*, p. 157.

118. Ehrenreich, *Altruistic Imagination*, p. 185.

Chapter 13

1. Beth Belton, "National Debt Expected to Hit $5 Trillion," New Jersey *Courier–Post* (Aug. 28, 1995), p. 6D.

2. U.S. Office of Management and Budget 2000, *A Citizen's Guide to the Federal Budget: Budget of the United States Government FY 2000*. Available at http://w3.access.gpo.gov/usbudget/fy2000/guide04.html, p. 1.

3. Children's Defense Fund, *CDF Reports* (Washington, D.C.: CDF, Dec. 1994), pp. 4–5.

4. Diana DiNitto, *Social Welfare: Politics and Public Policy*, 4th ed. (Needham, MA: Allyn & Bacon, 1995), p. 60.

5. David S. Broder, "States Will Only Compound Federal Losses Affecting Poor," New Jersey *Courier–Post* (Oct. 2, 1995), p. 5A.

6. Ibid.

7. Sam Walker, "200 Day Drive by GOP Slices Federal Programs," *Christian Science Monitor* (Aug. 7, 1995), pp. 1, 15.

8. U.S. Department of Health and Human Services Administration, Office of Family Assistance, "AFDC Information Memo," to replace first four pages of "Characteristics and Financial Circumstances of AFDC Recipients FY 92." Mimeographed memo Dec. 12, 1994, no. ACF 1M-94–7.

9. Children's Defense Fund, *CDF Reports* (Jan. 1995), pp. 4–5.

10. Children's Defense Fund, *Welfare Reform Briefing Book* (Washington, D.C.: CDF, Jan. 1995), Table 1, p. 1.

11. Children's Defense Fund, *CDF Reports* (March 1995), p. 8.

12. U.S. Department of Health and Human Services, "Aid to Families with Dependent Children (AFDC) Information Memo no. ACF 1M-94–7" (mimeograph). Dec. 12, 1994, p. 1.

13. Mark Robert Rank, *Living on the Edge: The Realities of Welfare in America* (New York: Columbia University Press, 1994), pp. 116–118.

14. Children's Defense Fund, *CDF Reports* (Jan. 1995), pp. 4–5.

15. Children's Defense Fund "Contract with America Unfair to Children," *CDF Reports* (Washington, D.C.: CDF, Jan. 1995), Vol. 16, no. 2, p. 2.

16. Ron Jackson, NASW Government Relations, Action Network for Social Education and Research, "Child

Welfare and Training Programs (Title IV-E and IV-B)." E-mail transmitted Feb. 12, 1996.

17. Children's Defense Fund, *CDF Reports*, Vol. 16, no. 4 (Washington, D.C.: CDF, March 1995), p. 4.

18. Children's Defense Fund, *CDF Reports*, Vol. 16, no. 10 (Washington, D.C.: CDF, Sept. 1995), p. 2.

19. Steven V. Roberts, Dorian Friedman, and Kalia Hetter, "Reform by 1000 Cuts," *U.S. News and World Report* (July 31, 1995), pp. 22–24.

20. James M. Fendrich, Mamie Miller, and Tim Nichel, "It's the Budget, Stupid: A Policy Analysis of Clinton's First Budget," *Journal of Sociology and Social Welfare*, Vol. 21, no. 4 (Dec. 1994), p. 18.

21. Ed Lazere, "Welfare Balances After Three Years of TANF Block Grants," Center on Budget and Policy Priorities. Available at www.cbpp.org/1-12-2000wel.html, pp. 1, 21.

22. Ruth E. Murphy, e-mail correspondence to welfarem-L@american.edu, March 13, 1998.

23. Administration for Children and Families. Office of Legislative Affairs and Budget, "All-Purpose Table: Fiscal Years 2000–2003." Available at www.acf.dhhs.gov/programs/olab/budget/apt02.htm, p. 5.

24. Sar A. Levitan, Garth L. Mangum, Stephen L. Mangum, and Andrew M. Sum, *Programs in Aid of the Poor*, 8th ed. (Baltimore: Johns Hopkins University Press, 2003), p. 156.

25. Ibid., pp. 157–159.

26. Department of Health and Human Services, Administration for Children and Families Office of Child Support Enforcement, "Child Enforcement: A Clinton Administration Priority." Available at www.acf.dhhs.gov/program/ses/fet/9803117b.html, pp. 3–4.

27. Children's Defense Fund, *State of America's Children: 1998*, pp. 39–40.

28. Ibid., p. 41.

29. Ibid., pp. 30–32.

30. Ibid.

31. U.S. Department of Health and Human Services, Administration for Children and Families, *HHS Fact Sheet*. Available at http://www.acf.dhhs.gov/news/press/1998/cc/fund.html, p. 2.

32. Frederick C. Thayer, "The Holy War on Surplus Americans: Soviet Dogma, Old-Time Religion, and Classical Economics." *Social Policy* (Fall 1997), pp. 8–18.

33. U.S. Department of Health and Human Services, Administration for Children and Families, HHS Fact Sheet.

34. Frederick C. Thayer, "The Holy War on Surplus Americans." Social Policy.

35. 104th Congress, 1st session (January 4, 1995), H.R. 4 (Washington, D.C.: U.S. Government Printing Office, 1995), p. 1.

36. Barbara Ehrenreich, "Real Babies, Illegitimate Debates," *Time* (Aug. 2, 1994), p. 90.

37. Joseph P. Shapiro and Andrea R. Wright, "Sins of the Fathers," *U.S. News and World Report* (Aug. 14, 1995), pp. 51–52.

38. Robert Bryce, "Texas Stamps a New Brand on Job Training Programs," *Christian Science Monitor* (Sept. 19, 1995), p. 3.

39. Jeremy Rifkin, *End of Work*. Cited in William Raspberry, "End of Work," New Jersey *Courier–Post* (June 13, 1995), p. 9A.

40. Sonya Ross, "Poll: Americans Still Want to Fight Poverty," New Jersey *Courier–Post* (Dec. 8, 1994), p. 11A.

41. Sharon Hays, *Flat Broke with Children* (New York: Oxford University Press, 2003).

42. U.S. Department of Health and Human Services, Administration for Children and Families. "Statistics: Change in TANF Caseloads Since Enactment of New Welfare Law." Available at www.acf.dhhs.gov/news/stats/aug-dec.html, p. 1.

43. Ibid.

44. Ibid., and ACF Statistics Chart, "Temporary Assistance for Needy Families October 2000–June 2001." Available at www.acf.dhhs.gov/news/stats/recipients.html, p. 2.

45. Sheldon Danziger, "After Welfare Reform and an Economic Boom: Why Is Child Poverty Still so Much Higher in the U.S. than in Europe?" Paper presented at the 8th International Research Seminar of the Foundation for International Studies on Social Securities, "Support for Children and Their Parents," Sigtuna, Sweden, June 2001, p. 1.

46. Danziger, "After Welfare Reform and an Economic Boom," p. 1.

47. Ibid., p. 18, Table 1-1.

48. Center on Budget and Policy Priorities, "Average Incomes of Very Poor Families Fell During Early Years of the Welfare Reform, Study Finds," Aug. 22, 1999. Available at www.cbpp.org/8-22-99wel.html, pp. 1–2.

49. Ron Haskins, "Welfare Reform: A Mother's Work," *Washington Post* online. Available at www.washingtonpost.com/wp-dyn/articles/A18589-2001N0v.12.html, p.1.

50. Ibid.

51. Center on Budget and Policy Priorities, "Testimony of Ed Lazere Before the House Committee on Education and the Workforce, Oct. 7, 1999." Available at www.cbpp.org/10-7-99wel.html, p. 1.

52. Pamela LoPrest, "How Are Families That Left Welfare Doing? A Comparison of Early and Recent Welfare Leavers," Urban Institute, April 2001. Available at www.newfederalism.urban.org/html/series_b/b36/b36.html, p. 5.

53. Center on Budget and Policy Priorities, "Poverty Rate Among Working Single-Mother Families Remained Stagnant in Late 1990s Despite Strong Economy," Aug. 16, 2001. Available at www.cbpp.org/8-16-01wel-pr.html, pp. 1–2.

54. Danziger, "After Welfare Reform and an Economic Boom," pp. 13–14.

55. Ibid., p. 18, Table 1-1.

56. "TANF Fact Sheet" (1998). Department of Health and Human Services. Available at www.acf.dhhs.gov/news/caseload.htm, p. 1.

57. Daniel Weisman, "Litigation Strategies and 'Welfare Reform'." Paper presented at Baccalaureate Program Directors Meeting, Albuquerque, NM, October 5–9, 1998.

58. DiNitto, *Social Welfare*, p. 137.

59. Levitan et al., *Programs in Aid of the Poor*, pp. 75–76.

60. Social Security Bulletin: Annual Statistical Supplement 2000. SSI Summary. Table 7.A1. "Number of Persons Receiving Federally Administered Payments Total Amount and Average Monthly Amount, by Source of Payment, Category, and Age, December 1999," Couples SSI income from SSI Summary Table 7.A2, p. 263.

61. Office of Management and Budget, "Income Security," Table 14-1. "Federal Resources in Support of Income Security. Available at www.whitehouse.gov/omb/budge/fy2002/bud14.html, p. 3 of 7.

62. Levitan et al., *Programs in Aid of the Poor*, pp. 75–76.

63. Children's Defense Fund, *CDF Reports* (Washington, D.C.: CDF, July 1995), p. 2.

64. Danziger, "After Welfare Reform and an Economic Boom," p. 20, endnote 4.

65. United States Embassy, Japan, "Fact Sheet: President Clinton on Economic Accomplishments," released January 9, 2001. Available at http://usembassy.state.gov/japan/www.je132.htm.

66. Isaac Shapiro, Allen Dupree, and James Sly, "An Estimated 12 Million Low- and Moderate-Income Families—with 24 Million Children—Would Not Benefit from Bush Tax Plan," Center on Budget and Policy Priorities, February 7, 2001. Available at www.treas.gov/tigta/reports/2000401fr.html.

67. Jami Curley and Michael Sherraden, *Policy Report: The History and Status of Children's Allowances: Policy Background for Children's Savings Accounts* (St. Louis, MO: Center for Social Development, Washington University in St. Louis, 1998), p. 13.

68. *AARP Bulletin*, Vol. 36, no. 6 (June 1995), p. 13.

69. Daniel P. Moynihan, "The Case Against Entitlement Cuts," *Modern Maturity* (Nov.–Dec. 1994), pp. 13–14.

70. Ibid.

71. "The Federal Budget Dollar: Where Does It Come From?" *Citizen's Guide to the Federal Budget.* Budget of the United States Government FY 1999. Office of the President (Washington, D.C.: Government Printing Office, 1998).

72. "OASDI Current-Pay Benefits: Summary," *Social Security Bulletin Annual Statistical Supplement 2001.* Table 5.A1, "Number and average monthly benefit, by type of benefit, race, age, and sex" (Washington, D.C., December 2000), p. 159.

73. "The Federal Budget Dollar: Where Does It Come From?" *Citizen's Guide to the Federal Budget.* Budget of the United States Government FY 1999. Office of the President (Washington, D.C.: Government Printing Office, 1999).

74. "OASDI Current-Pay Benefits: Summary," pp. 159–162.

75. Social Security Bulletin: Annual Statistical Supplement 2000, p. 2.

76. David A. Smith, "Later Retirement: A 'Disaster' for Many," *AARP Bulletin* (Nov. 1998), Vol. 39, no. 11, p. 29.

77. Ibid., p. 12.

78. Stan Hinden, "Raw Deal for Women?" *AARP Bulletin*, Vol. 42, no. 8 (September 2001), p. 18.

79. Stan Hinden, ibid., pp. 18–19.

80. Ibid., p. 19.

81. Diana DiNitto, *Social Welfare: Politics and Public Policy*, 4th ed. (Needham, MA: Allyn & Bacon, 1995), pp. 214–216.

82. U.S. Department of Agriculture, Food and Nutrition Services, "FSS Summary, December 2001." Available at www.fns.usda.gov/pd/fssummar.htm, pp. 1–2.

83. U.S. Department of Agriculture, Food and Nutrition Services, "FSS Summary, December, 21, 2001." Available at www.fns.usda.gov/pd/fsmonthly.htm, p. 1.

84. U.S. Department of Agriculture, Food and Nutrition Services, "Overview: December 2001." Available at http://fns.usda.gov/pd/Overview.htm.

85. DiNitto, *Social Welfare*, p. 61.

86. U.S. Department of Agriculture, Food and Nutrition Services, "FSS Summary, December 21, 2001," pp. 1–2.

87. U.S. Department of Agriculture, Food and Nutrition Services, "Cost of Food Distribution Programs December 21, 2001." Available at www.fns.usda.gov/pe/fd$sum.htm, pp. 1–2.

88. Children's Defense Fund, *State of America's Children: 1998*, p. 33.

89. Levitan et al., *Programs in Aid of the Poor*, Footnote 11, p. 29.

90. Children's Defense Fund, *State of America's Children: 1998*, p. 16.

91. Levitan et al., *Programs in Aid of the Poor*, p. 112.

92. U.S. Department of Housing and Urban Development. "Homelessness: Programs and the People they Serve: An Overview of Homeless Clients: Demographic Characteristics." Available at www.huduserorg/publications/homeless/homelessness/ch_2b.htm, p. 5.

93. National Coalition for the Homeless, "How Many People Experience Homelessness?" *NCH Fact Sheet #2* (February 1999). Available at http://nch.ari.net/numbers.htm, pp. 2–3.

94. Levitan et al., *Programs in Aid of the Poor*, p. 113.

95. Barbara Sard and Jennifer Daskal, "Housing and Welfare Reform: Some Background Information," Center on Budget and Policy Priorities, Washington, D.C., February 12, 1998, p. 7.

96. Children's Defense Fund, *State of America's Children: 1998*, p. 17.

97. National Coalition for Homelessness "2001 Budget and Homelessness" (June 30, 2000). Available at http://nch.ari.net/fy2001.htm, p. 2.

98. Edward Scanlon, "Homeownership and Its Impacts: Implications for Housing Policy for Low-Income Families," Working Paper 96–2 (1996), Center for Social Development, Washington University, St. Louis, MO, p. 9.

99. "Mortgages May Be Difficult for Minorities to Obtain," Davenport, IA: *Quad City Times* (Nov. 15, 1998), p. 5B.

100. Children's Defense Fund, *CDF Reports* (Washington, D.C.: CDF, July 1995), p. 2.

101. Jami Curley and Michael Sherraden, *Policy Report: The History and Status of Children's Allowances: Policy Background for Children's Savings Accounts* (St. Louis, MO: Center for Social Development, Washington University in St. Louis, 1998), p. 13.

102. Children's Defense Fund, *The State of America's Children: 1998*, p. 24.

103. Ibid., pp. 26–30.

104. Danziger, "After Welfare Reform and an Economic Boom," p. 3.

105. Levitan et al., *Programs in Aid to the Poor*, p. 90.

106. Norm Brewer, "Several Thorny Issues Still Await Congress," New Jersey *Courier–Post* (Oct. 1, 1995), p. 15A.

107. Johnathan S. Landay, editorial in *Christian Science Monitor* (July 28, 1995), p. 20.

108. *U.S. News and World Report* (July 3, 1995), p. 13. A Report from Health Care Financing Administration, Congressional Research Service, based on *Statistical Abstracts*, 1994.

109. Health Care Financing Administration, "Highlights," p. 1.

110. Children's Defense Fund, *CDF Reports*, Vol. 16, no. 9 (Aug. 1995), p. 7; report from Health Care Financing Administration, Division of Medicaid Statistics, p. 7.

111. Children's Defense Fund, *CDF Reports* (July 1995), p. 1.

112. Health Care Financing Administration, Congressional Research Service, *Statistical Abstracts of the United States: 1994*. Reported in *U.S. News and World Report* (July 3, 1995), p. 13.

113. Children's Defense Fund, *CDF Reports*, Vol. 16, no. 5 (Washington, D.C.: CDF, April 1995), p. 1.

114. Children's Defense Fund, *The State of America's Children: 1998*, pp. 30–32.

115. Fendrich, Miller, and Nichel, "It's the Budget, Stupid," p. 7.

116. Frances Fox Piven and Richard Cloward, *Regulating the Poor* (New York: Random House, 1971).

117. Remember again the James Rule Treatise (*Insight and Social Betterment: Applied Social Science*) on the ways in which social conflicts which have no solutions that will maintain the state of power of the few over the many, are redefined as social problems, implying that the powerful elite are working on solutions to immediate needs. This also reinforces the status of social workers as agents of social control even though they are working at social treatment.

118. David Ho, "U.S. Prison Population Rising: Incarceration Rate May Top Russia as Highest in World," ABCNEWS.com, Washington, D.C., April 20, 2000. Available at http://my.abcnews.go.com/PRINTERFRIENDLY . . . section/us/DailyNews/prisons000420.htm.

119. Ho, "U.S. Prison Population Rising."

120. Alan Eisner, "Analysis: Huge U.S. Prison Population Social Cost Mounts" (Reuters) (Washington, D.C., January 2001). Available at http://www.mapinc.org/drugnews/v01/n136/a02.html.

121. Allen J. Beck and Christopher J. Mumola, "Prisoners in 1998," Substance Abuse and Mental Health Services Administration, "National Household Survey on Drug Abuse: Summary Report 1998" (Rockville, MD, 1999), p. 13; Bureau of Justice Statistics, *Sourcebook of Criminal Justice Statistics 1998* (Washington, D.C.: U.S. Department of Justice, August 1999), p. 343. Available at www.lindesmith.org/news/DailyNews/2million_inmates.html.

122. Amnesty International, "Not Part of My Sentence: Violations of the Human Rights of Women in Custody" (Washington, D.C.: Amnesty International, March 1999), p. 1.

123. P. Thomas, "Study Suggests Black Male Prison Rate Impinges on Political Process," *The Washington Post* (January 30, 1997), p. A3.

124. Children's Defense Fund, *CDF Reports* (Dec. 1994), pp. 4–5.

125. Ibid.

126. United States Embassy, Japan, "Fact Sheet," pp. 7, 8.

127. "Clinton–Gore Administration Accomplishments: Progress by the Numbers," p. 2.

128. Robert Kilborn, Jr., "Seeking New Jobs after the Pink Slip," *Christian Science Monitor* (July 17, 1995), p. 1.

129. Molly Ivins, "Workers', Futures Hang on Result of Race for AFL-CIO Leadership," New Jersey *Courier–Post* (Sept. 4, 1995), p. 7A.

130. U.S. Embassy, Japan, "Fact Sheet," p. 1.

131. Center on Budget and Policy Priorities. "Increase in Number of Unemployed Over Past 12 Months Was Largest in Nearly 20 Years" (Washington, D.C., December 7, 2001), p. 1.

132. "Jobless Rate Reaches 5.7%," *Layfayette Journal and Courier* (December 8, 2001), p. A1.

133. Trish Nicholson, "50-Plus Workers Hit by Cutbacks," *The Nation*, AARP (Washington, D.C., October 2001), pp. 1, 24.

134. Center on Budget and Policy Priorities. "Increase in Number of Unemployed," p. 1.

135. DiNitto, *Social Welfare*, p. 376.

136. Justice Sandra Day O'Connor, writing for the majority, reported by Larry G. Gerber, "H-Net List for 'Putting the State Back in,'" AP story on ADARAND decision "High Court Delivers Strong Blow to Affirmative Action," Internet, July 1995.

137. Barbara Reynolds, "Let's Not Lose This Right," New Jersey *Courier–Post* (June 22, 1995), p. 9A.

138. Clarence Lusane, "Decline in Funding for Civil-Rights Agencies Is Cause for Concern," Progressive Media Project. Available at www.progressive.org/pmpbvc10.htm. The six agencies were: Department of Education Office of Civil Rights; U.S. Equal Employment Opportunity Commission; Department of Labor Office of Federal Contract Compliance Programs; Department of Justice Civil Rights Division; Department of Health and Human Services Office of Civil Rights; and Department of Housing and Urban Development Office of Fair Housing and Equal Opportunity.

139. "Military Discharges of Gays Up in 2000," *Quad City Times* (Davenport, IA), June 2, 2001, p. A1.

140. Partners Task Force for Gay and Lesbian Couples, "Defense of Marriage Act: Description and the Bill's Text." (2000). Available at www.buddybuddy.com/doma.htm.

141. Ibid.

142. William N. Eskridge, Jr., *Gaylaw: Challenging the Apartheid of the Closet* (Cambridge, MA: Harvard University Press, 1999), p. 232.

143. David Wagner, *What's Love Got to Do With It? A Critical Look at American Charity* (New York: The New Press, 2000), p. 131.

144. Ibid., p. 119.

145. "Sweet Charity," *U.S. News and World Report* (June 4, 2001), p. 10.

146. "Most State Welfare Programs Pass on Charitable Choice," *Quad-City Times* (Davenport, IA), March 20, 2001, p. A4.

147. Wagner, *What's Love Got to Do With It*, p. 105.

148. Ibid., p. 112.

149. Guy Halverson, "Giving by Firms Registers Big Jump," *Christian Science Monitor* (December 4, 2000), p. 19.

150. Wagner, *What's Love Got to Do With It*, pp. 112–113.

151. "The 50 Largest U.S. Charities Ranked by Total Income," *Christian Science Monitor* (December 4, 2000), p. 16.

152. Bruce S. Jansson, *The Sixteen-Trillion Dollar Mistake* (New York: Columbia University Press, 2001), pp. 297, 309, 345.

153. John Miller, Citizens for Tax Justice, "Clinton and Congress Feed the Wealthy," Dollars and Sense: What's Left in Economics (Nov.–Dec. 1997). Available at www.dollarsandsense.org/issues/nov97/tax.html.

154. All figures from Dave Skidmore, "Lawmakers Propose $500 Child Credit," New Jersey *Courier–Post* (October 23, 1995), p. 3A.

155. Ibid.

156. Center on Budget and Policy Priorities, "Pathbreaking CBO Study Shows Dramatic Increases in both 1980s and 1990s in Income Gaps Between the Very Wealthy and Other Americans. (May 31, 2001). Available at www.centeronbudget.org/5-31-01tax-pr.htm.

157. Iris J. Lav and Robert Greenstein, "Tax Bill Contains Only Modest Benefits for Middle Class Despite Its High Cost," Center on Budget and Policy Priorities (August 20, 1999). Available at www.cbpp.org/8-20-99tax.htm.

158. "Surprise Goodies from Uncle Sam," *U.S. News and World Report* (June 11, 2001), pp. 44–45.

159. Susan Roth, "Daschle: Tax Cut Hurt the Nation," *Lafayette Journal and Courier* (Lafayette, IN) (January 5, 2002), p. A.3.

160. "Corporate Welfare: A Special Report," *Time* (Nov. 9, 1998), p. 38.

161. David Espo, "Senate Votes Give to the Rich, Then Takes Away from the Poor," New Jersey *Courier–Post* (Oct. 14, 1995), p. 1A.

162. Molly Ivins, "Watt's Back: So Are (Ugh!) His Policies," New Jersey *Courier–Post* (March 27, 1995), p. 5A.

163. David Broder, "Best Way to Cut U.S. Budget: Attack on Corporate Welfare," New Jersey *Courier–Post* (May 24, 1995), p. 9A.

164. Mortimer B. Zuckerman, "The GOP Needs Some Education," *U.S. News and World Report* (Sept. 11, 1995), pp. 62, 74.

165. Karger, "Income Maintenance," pp. 9–11.

166. Ibid., p. 8.

167. Bernard Sanders, "And Now for Some Meaningful Hearings," *Christian Science Monitor* (Aug. 17, 1995), p. 19.

168. Citizens for Tax Justice, "Buy Now, Pay Later: How Generous Corporate Campaign Donors Save Billions in Taxes." Available at www.ctj.org/html/camptax.htm, p. 1.

169. Ibid., p. 2.

170. Ibid.

171. "Fat Cat Campaign Donors: Who They Are; What They Give," *Christian Science Monitor* (October 20, 2000), p. 24.

172. David R. Francis, "More Firms Find Tax Loopholes," *Christian Science Monitor* (October 20, 2000), pp. 1, 4.

173. Curt Anderson, "Senator: Corporate Pricing Schemes Cost U.S. $45 Billion," *Lafayette Journal and Courier* (Lafayette, IN) (November 22, 2001), p. A.3.

174. Johnathan Landay, "Congress, Clinton Battle over Antimissile System," *Christian Science Monitor* (Aug. 3, 1995), p. 3.

175. Johnathan Landay, "Pet Pork Projects Slip into GOP Defense Budget," *Christian Science Monitor* (Aug. 4, 1995), p. 3.

176. Johnathan Landay, "Pentagon Hit for Hiding Spending on 'Star Wars,' " *Christian Science Monitor* (Sept. 5, 1995), p. 3.

177. Johnathan Landay, "Political Futures, Jobs Hang on Defense Budget Choices," *Christian Science Monitor* (Sept. 12, 1995), p. 3.

178. Zuckerman, "The GOP Needs Some Education," p. 74.

179. Landay, "Pet Pork Projects," p. 3.

180. William D. Hartung and Michelle Ciarroca, "Star Wars Revisited: Still Dangerous, Costly, and Unworkable," *Foreign Policy in Focus*, Vol. 4, no. 24 (September 1999, revised April 2000). Available at www.foreignpolicy-infocus.org/briefs/vol4/v4n24star.html.

181. Ibid.

182. Ibid.

183. Ibid.

184. Office of Management and Budget, Budget of the United States Government, FY 2003, "Table 2-3. Total Spending by Function." Available at www.whitehouse.gov/omb/budget/fy2002/guide02/htm, p. 11.

185. Figures for TANF are from Zoe Euberger, "TANF Expenditures Increased in the Last Fiscal Year," Center on Budget and Policy Priorities. Available at www.cbpp.org/11-1-01wel.html.

186. NAFTA Index, "Public Citizen: Global Trade Watch." Available at www.citizen.org/pctrade/naftaindex.htm.

187. Joshua Karliner, *The Corporate Planet* (San Francisco: Sierra Club Books, 1997), p. 5.

188. Ibid., p. 25.

189. Mike Crawley, "Rich Nations Grant Poorest Twenty-Two a Checkbook Reprieve," *Christian Science Monitor* (December 26, 2000), p. 7.

190. Karliner, *Corporate Planet*, p. 17.

191. Ibid., p. 22.

192. Friends of the Earth U.S., "OECD Multilateral Agreement on Investment: Fact Sheet." (Feb. 19, 1997). Available at www.igc.org/trac/feature/planet/maii_foe.html.

193. Karliner, *Corporate Planet*, p. 10.

194. "Central America Joins Mexico," *Quad-City Times* (Davenport, IA) (June 17, 2001), p. A9.

195. Geri Smith, with Elisabeth Malkin, Jonathan Wheatley, Paul Magnusson, Michael Arndt, and bureau reports, "The Free Trade Area of the Americas," *BusinessWeek* (April 23, 2001), p. 62.

196. "Official: Thirty-five Countries Ratify African Pact," *Quad-City Times* (Davenport, IA), (April 8, 2002), p. A3.

197. "Leaders Create Health Fund at Summit to Combat AIDS," *Quad-City Times* (Davenport, IA) (July 21, 2001), p. A1.

198. David Gergen, "Warming to the Task," *U.S. News and World Report* (June 25, 2001), p. 76.

199. Earnest Becker, *The Denial of Death* (New York, The Free Press, 1973), p. 57.

200. David G. Gil, "Work, Violence, Injustice, and War," *Journal of Sociology and Social Welfare*, Vol. 16, no. 1 (March 1989), pp. 41, 43.

201. Thanks to Gladys Robinson, MSW from Temple University.

Chapter 14

1. See Kevin Phillips, *American Dynasty: Aristocracy, Fortune, and the Politics of Deceit in the House of Bush* (New York: Penguin Books, 2004).

2. Kevin Phillips, *American Theocracy: The Peril and Politics of Radical Religion, Oil, and Borrowed Money in the 21st Century* (New York: Viking Press, 2006).

3. Phillips, *American Dynasty*, p. 97.

4. Ibid., p. 72.

5. Ibid., p. 294.

6. Michael Klare, *Blood and Oil: The Dangers and Consequences of America's Growing Dependence on Imported Petroleum* (New York: Henry Holt and Co., 2004). Front matter. Cited in Phillips, *American Theocracy*, pp. 84–85.

7. Albert Gore, *Assault on Reason* (New York: Penguin Press, 2007), p. 195. Classifying documents is another

evidence of secrecy: Immediately upon his assumption of office in 2001, Bush classified all documents concerning his father's administration. In 2006, 231,995 documents were classified, and also classified are his "presidential signing statements," written arguments against bills passed by Congress, numbering at least 151 statements challenging 1,149 provisions.

8. Phillips, *American Dynasty*, p. 272.

9. Julian Barnes, "Bush Says $200 Billion More Needed for Iraq War," *Lafayette Journal and Courier* (Lafayette, IN) (September 22, 2007), p. A3.

10. "Adding Insult to Injury," *The Week* (March 23, 2007), p. 13.

11. Ibid., p. 97.

12. Phillips, *American Dynasty*, pp. 68–69.

13. Center for American Progress, "Wages Not Keeping Up with Inflation," (July 20, 2004). Available at www.americanprogress.org/issues/2004/07/b124737.html.

14. "Report: Most Workers Not Seeing Wages Outpace Prices—Aug. 28, 2006," CNNMoney.com. Available at http://money.cnn.com/2006/08/28/news/economy/real_wages/index.htm.

15. InflationData.com, "2000-Present Current Consumer Price Index-All Urban Consumers," Available at http://inflationdata.com/inflation/Consumer_Price_Index/CurrentCPI.asp.

16. Phillips, *American Dynasty*, p. 128.

17. Treasury Direct, "Interest Expense on the Debt Outstanding." Available at www.treasurydirect.gov/govt/reports/ir/ir_expense.htm.

18. Phillips, *American Dynasty*, p. 125.

19. "The National Debt is $9 Trillion!" Federal Spending and the National Debt. Available at http://federalbudget.com, p. 1.

20. Ibid.

21. U.S. Census Bureau, "USA Statistics in Brief—Income." (December 20, 2006) Available at www.census.gov/copendia/statab/files/govtsoclaw.html, p. 1.

22. Ibid.

23. Joel Handler and Yeshenkel Hasenfeld, *Blame Welfare: Ignore Poverty and Inequality* (New York: Cambridge University Press, 2007), p. 30.

24. Sam Pizzagati, "Congress Eyes Corporate Payday," *Progressive Populist* (October 1, 2007), p. 9.

25. Nicholas Kristof, "The Most Overpaid Man in the Land," *The Week* (November 17, 2006), p. 51.

26. Barbara Ehrenreich, *Bait and Switch: The (Futile) Pursuit of the American Dream* (New York: Henry Holt and Co., 2003), p. 224.

27. Scott W. Allard, "The Changing Face of Welfare During the Bush Administration," *Publius: The Journal of Federalism* (June 2007), p. 315. Available at the National Poverty Center Working Paper Series at www.npc.umich.edu/publications/working_papers/.

28. Department of Health & Human Services (DHHS), Administration for Children and Families (ACF), "Advancing the Health, Safety, and Well-Being of Our People: Substance Abuse and Mental Health Services Administration (SAMHSA)" (U.S. Government Printing Office: Washington, D.C., 2007), pp. 41, 80. Available at www.hhs.gov/budget?docbudget.htm.

29. Hugh Heclo, "The Politics of Welfare Reform." In Rebecca Blank and Ron Haskins, eds., *The New World of Welfare* (Washington, D.C.: Brookings Institute Press, 2001), pp. 169–200.

30. Allard, "The Changing Face of Welfare," p. 317.

31. Ibid., p. 316.

32. U.S. DHHS News Release ACF Press Office "HHS Awards $57.8 million Through Compassion Capital Fund" (October 19, 2007). Available at www.hhs.gov/news/press/2007pres/10/pr20071019a.html.

33. U.S. Census Bureau, *Statistical Abstract of the United States, 2007*. Table 599. "Displaced Workers by Selected Characteristics: 2004," p. 387.

34. John Halpin and Christian Weller, "The $871,000 Job Subsidy," *Center for American Progress* (November 17, 2006). Available at www.americanprogress.org/issues/2006/11/job_subsidy.html, pp. 1–2.

35. Joint Economic Committee Democrats, "Talking Points for Charts: The Bush Economy," (October 17, 2007), pp. 1–7. Available at http://jec.senate.gov.

36. David Smith, "Minimum Wage Bill Signed: Other Issues Await Resolution," *Lafayette Journal and Courier* (Lafayette, IN) (September 2, 2007), p. A6.

37. Wayne O'Leary, "Free Trade Consensus Crumbles," *The Progressive Populist* (October 1, 2007), p. 16.

38. InflationData.com, "2000-Present CPI."

39. Michael A. Fletcher, "Study: Many Blacks Worse Off than Parents," *Lafayette Journal and Courier* (Lafayette, IN) (November 13, 2007), p. A4. Source of figures: The Economic Mobility Project.

40. Ibid.

41. Jason Furman, "Tax Reform and Poverty," Center on Budget and Policy Priorities (April 2006). Available at www.cbpp.org/4-10-06tax.htm, p. 2.

42. Michael O'Connor, "Using the Internet to Make Work Pay for Low-Income Families," Brookings Institution (May 2002). In Center for Policy Alternatives, Ibid. Available at www.stateaction.org/issues/issue/cfm/issue/EITC.xml, p. 1.

43. David K. Shipler, *The Working Poor: Invisible in America* (New York: Vintage Books, 2004), p. 14.

44. Furman, "Tax Reform and Poverty."

45. Center for Policy Alternatives, "Earned Income Tax Credit" (November 27, 2007). Available at www.stateaction.org/issues/issue.cfm/issue/EITC.xml, p. 1.

46. Sar A. Levitan, Garth L. Mangum, Stephen L. Mangum, and Andrew M. Sum, *Programs in Aid of the Poor*, 8th ed. (Baltimore, Johns Hopkins Press, 2003), p. 79.

47. "New Freedom Initiative." Available at www.whitehouse.gov/infocus/newfreedom/.

48. U.S. Census Bureau, *Statistical Abstract of the United States: 2007*. Table 53.3. "Social Security (OASDI)—Benefits by Type of Beneficiary: 1990 to 2005." Available at www.census.gov/parod/2006pubs/07/statab/defense.pdf, p. 351.

49. Levitan et al., *Programs in Aid to the Poor*, pp. 47–48.

50. Ibid., p. 1 of 2.

51. U.S. Census Bureau, "Facts for Features: Americans with Disabilities Act: July 26, 2006." Available at www.census.gov/Press-Release/www/releases/archives/facts-_for_features_special_e...

52. U.S. Census Bureau, American FactFinder. Available at http://factfinder.census.gov/jsp/saff/SAFFinfo.jsp?_page10=tp4_disability

53. "The Line Starts Here," *AARP Bulletin* (October 2007), pp. 31–32.
54. Ehrenreich, *Bait and Switch*, pp. 204–205.
55. U.S. Census Bureau, *Statistical Abstract 2007*. Table 544. "State Unemployment Insurance—Summary: 1990 to 2005," p. 356.
56. Ron Nixon, "OSHA Leaves Worker Safety in Hands of Industry," *The New York Times*, (April 25, 2007), p. 3. Available at www.nytimes.com/2007/04/25/washington/25osha.html, pp. 1–3.
57. Levitan et al., p. 77.
58. Figured from Social Security Administration, Supplemental Security Record, "SSI Federally Administered Programs," Table 1. "Recipients (by type of payments), total payments, and average monthly payments, January 2001–December 2001"; and Table 1. "Recipients (by type of payment), total payments, and average monthly payment October 2006–October 2007." Available at ssi.monthly@ssa.gov.
59. U.S. Census Bureau, *Statistical Abstract 2007*, Table 549. "Supplemental Security Income—Recipients and Payments: 1990 to 2004," p. 359.
60. Center on Budget and Policy Priorities, "Implementing the TANF Changes in the Deficit Reduction Act: Win–Win Solutions for Families and States, 2nd ed.," (February 9, 2007), p. 1. Available at www.cbpp.org/2_-07tanf.htm, p. 1 and www.cbpp.org/pubs/welfare.htm, p. 2.
61. U.S. Department of Health and Human Services, "The Next Phase of Welfare Reform: Implementing the Deficit Reduction Act of 2005." Available at www.hhs.gov/news/press/2002pres/welfare.html, p. 1
62. U.S. Census Bureau, *Statistical Abstracts*, Table 552. "Temporary Assistance for Needy Families—Recipients by state and Other Areas: 2000 to 2005," p. 360.
63. Sharon Parrot and Arloc Sherman, "The 10th anniversary of the Temporary Assistance for Needy Families Program? Results Are More Mixed than Often Understood." *World Hunger Notes*. Available at www.worldhunger.org/articles/o6/us/tanf.htm, pp. 1–2.
64. Robert Greenstein and Jocelyn Guyer, "Supporting Work Through Medicaid and Food Stamps," In Blank and Hoskins, eds., *The New World of Welfare* (Washington, D.C.: Brookings Institute Press, 2001), pp. 335–368. pp. 338–339.
65. Public Agenda, "Poverty and Welfare: Fact File," (February 13, 2007), p. 1. Available at www.publicagenda.org/issues/factfiles_detail.cfm?issue_type=welfare$list=15.
66. Center on Budget and Policy Priorities, p. 2. Available at www.cbpp.org/pubs/welfare.htm.
67. Public Agenda, "Poverty and Welfare." Available at www.publicagenda.org/issues/factfiles_detail.cfm?issue_type=welfare$list=13.
68. Parrot and Sherman, ibid., p. 13.
69. Communications Workers of America, "From the State House to the White House" (March 2, 2006). Available at www.cwa.legislative.org/fact-sheets/page.jsp?itemID=27482970.
70. J. Capizzano, G. Adams, and F. Sonenstein, "Child Care Arrangements for Children Under Five: Variation Across States" (Washington, D.C. The Urban Institute, 2000); Centers for Disease Control and Prevention, "CDC Child Care Health and Safety Action Plan" (Atlanta, GA: (1995); and Children's Defense Fund, "Overview of Child Care, Early Education, and School-Age Care," 1999 Key Facts (Washington, D.C.: 1999). Available at www.answers.com/topic/childcare?cat=biz-fin, p. 4 of 10.
71. "Rapid Growth Seen in Lightly Regulated Child Care Ministries," *Lafayette Journal and Courier*, (Lafayette, IN) (November 25, 2007), p. C11.
72. Department of Health and Human Services, Administration for Children and Families, Available at www.acf.hhs.gov/programs/ofs/data/2006/overview.html.
73. Department of Health and Human Services, Administration for Children and Families, "2005–2007 All-Purpose Table." Available at www.acf.dhhs.gov/programs/olab/budget/2007/fy2007apt.htm, p. 1 of 8.
74. Pat Eaton-Robb, "Homeless Families on Rise," *Lafayette Journal and Courier* (Lafayette, IN) (October 8, 2007), p. A4.
75. Department of Health and Human Services, Administration for Children and Families, "2005–2007 All-Purpose Table."
76. Howard N. Snyder and Melissa Sickmund, *Highlights: Juvenile Offenders and Victims: 2006 National Report*, Washington, D.C.: U.S. Department of Justice, Office of Justice Programs, Office of Juvenile Justice and Delinquency Prevention, pp. 2–3.
77. Stephen Ohlemacher, "U.S. Lags Behind in Life Expectancy," *Lafayette Journal and Courier* (Lafayette, IN) (August 12, 2007), p. A4.
78. Rank, pp. 39–40.
79. Ibid.
80. "Home Searches by Welfare Officers OK'd," *Lafayette Journal & Courier* (Lafayette, IN) (November 27, 2007), p. A5.
81. Nord, M., Andrews, M., and Carlson, S. "Household Food Security in the United States, 2003." Food Assistance and Nutrition Report, Number FANRR42 (Washington, D.C.: Economic Research Service, U.S. Department of Agriculture, 2004). Available at www.ers.usda.gov/publication/fanrr42/
82. Weinman, R. E., Murphy, M., Little, M., Pagano, M., Wehler, C. A., Regal, K., and Jellinek, M. S. "Hunger in Children in the United States: Potential Behavioral and Emotional Correlates," *Pediatrics*, 101 (January 1998). Available at www.pediatrics.org/cgi/content/full/101/1/e3.
83. Levitan et al., *Programs in Aid of the Poor*, p. 115.
84. U.S. Conference of Mayors, *U.S. Conference of Mayors—Sodexho Hunger and Homelessness Survey 2004* (The United States Conference of Mayors, December 2004). Available at www.usmayors.org/uscm/hungersurvey/2004/onlinereport/HungerandHomelessnessReport2004.pdf.
85. Dorothy Rosenbaum, Center on Budget and Policy Priorities, "President's Budget Would Cut Food for 440,000 Low-Income Seniors." Available at www.cbpp.org/2-6-07fa.htm, pp. 1–3.
86. Ibid.
87. Food Stamp Program Annual Summary, "Food Stamp Program Participation and Costs." Available at www.fns.usda.gov/pd/fssummar.htm, (6/28/2007), p. 2.
88. Levitan et al., *Programs in Aid of the Poor*, p. 118.

89. U.S. Department of Agriculture, Food and Nutrition Service, "Characteristics of Food Stamp Households: Fiscal Year 2006—Summary." Available at www.fns. usda.gov/oane/MENU/published/FSP/FSP.htm, pp. 1–2.

90. Ibid., p. 2.

91. U.S. Department of Agriculture, Food and Nutrition Service, "National School Lunch Program" (July 2007). Available at www.fns.usda.gov/cnd.

92. Handler and Hasenfeld, *Blame Welfare*, p. 97.

93. USDA Food and Nutrition Service, "School Breakfast Program Participation and Meals Served" (October 26, 2007). Available at www.fns.usda.gov/pd/sbsummar.htm, pp. 1–2.

94. Levitan et al., *Programs in Aid of the Poor*, p. 121.

95. USDA Food and Nutrition Service, "Child and Adult Care Food Program" (October 26, 2007). Available at www.fns.usda.gov/pd/ccsummar.htm, pp. 1–2.

96. USDA Food and Nutrition Service, "WIC Participant and Program Characteristics 2004: Summary" (March 2006). Available at www.fns.usda.gov/oane/MENU/published/WIC/FILES/PC2004ExecSum.pdf, pp. 1–3.

97. Ibid.

98. Handler and Hasenfeld, *Blame Welfare*, pp. 97–98.

99. Sheila R. Zedlewski and Sandi Nelson, "Many Families Turn to Food Pantries for Help," Urban Institute Publications (November 25, 2003), pp. 1–3. Available at www.urban.org/publications/310895.html.

100. Ibid, p. A2.

101. Eaton-Robb, "Homeless Families on Rise," p. A6.

102. National Coalition for the Homeless, "Who Is Homeless," *NCH Fact Sheet* #3, pp. 1–3. Available at www.nationalhomeless.org.

103. Ibid.

104. U.S. Conference of Mayors, 2005, reported in National Coalition for the Homeless, "How Many People Experience Homelessness?" *NCH Fact Sheet* #2, p. 1.

105. Ibid., p. 1.

106. Stacy Teicher Khadaroo, "Homeless Children Tell Their Stories," *Christian Science Monitor* (May 25, 2007), pp. 14, 16.

107. Kimberly Hefling, "Veterans Are a Fourth of the Homeless," *Lafayette Journal and Courier* (Lafayette, IN) (November 8, 2007), p. A3.

108. Bina Venkataraman, "Help Lags for Homeless Female Veterans," *Christian Science Monitor*, (July 18, 2007), p. 2.

109. Center on Budget and Policy Priorities, "Nearly All Recent Section 8 Growth Results from Rising Housing Costs and Congressional Decisions to Serve More Needy Families," (February 2, 2004). Available at www.cbpp .org/2-2-04hous.htm. Reported in Children's Defense Fund, "Bush Administration Policies Exacerbate Growing Housing Crisis for Families with Children" (January 2005), p. 2.

110. *Meeting Our Nation's Housing Challenges*, Report of the Bipartisan Millennial Housing Commission (May 2002). Reported in Children's Defense Fund, "Bush Administration Policies Exacerbate Growing Housing Crisis for Families with Children," p. 1.

111. Centers for Medicaid Services (CMS), *Medicare and You, 2007* (Washington, D.C.: Government Printing Office, 2007), p. 104.

112. Ibid.

113. "Medicare Advantage: Another Privatization Boondoggle," *United Senior Advocate* (April–May 2007), p. 9.

114. Ibid.

115. "Displacing Enrollees in Medicare Drug Plans," *AARP Bulletin* (November 2007), p. 4.

116. CMS, *Medicare and You*, pp. 63–70.

117. "Michael Moore Refocuses Healthcare Debate," *Christian Science Monitor* (June 18, 2007), p. 15.

118. Barbara Miner, "Labor Offers Business Health Care Cures," *The Progressive* (May 2007), pp. 24–25.

119. Mark Lange, "A Landmark in Corporate Welfare," *Christian Science Monitor* (July 18, 2007), p. 2.

120. Dennis Cauchon, "For First Time, Less Spent on Medicaid," *Lafayette Journal and Courier* (Lafayette, IN) (November 27, 2006), p. A4.

121. Haya El Nasser, "Census: Number of Elderly in Nursing Homes Has Declined," *Lafayette Journal and Courier* (Lafayette, IN) (September 27, 2007), p. A8.

122. Ibid.

123. "House Subcommittee Passes Slim Increase for Older Americans Act," *United Senior Advocate* (June–July 2007), p. 3.

124. Ibid., p. A3.

125. Ohlemacher, "U.S. Lags Behind in Life Expectancy," p. A4.

126. Sam Uretsky, "Compassionate Child Abuse," *Progressive Populist* (October 1, 2007), p. 15.

127. U.S. Census Bureau, *Statistical Abstracts*, Table 140. "State Children's Health Insurance Program (SCHIP)—Enrollment and Expenditures by State: 2003 and 2005," p. 104.

128. James Anderson, "The State Children's Health Insurance Program." From a paper presented to the Unitarian Universalist Forum, November 4, 2007; Uretsky, "Compassionate Child Abuse," p. 15.

129. Jennifer Loven, "Second Child Health Insurance Bill Vetoed," *Lafayette Journal and Courier* (Lafayette, IN) (December 13, 2007), p. A3.

130. "Brain Injuries Abound in U.S. Troops," *Lafayette Journal and Courier* (Lafayette, IN) (November 23, 2007), p. A1.

131. "Adding Insult to Injury," *The Week* (March 23, 2007), p. 13.

132. Arman Keteyian, "Suicide Epidemic Among Veterans: A CBS News Investigation Uncovers A Suicide Rate for Veterans Twice that of Other Americans," CBS News, New York, November 13, 2007.

133. Armen Keteyian, "CBS News Investigates" (November 22, 2007). Available at www.cbsnews.com/stories/2007/11/13/cbsnews_investigates/main349471.shtml, pp. 1–3; and CBS News, "Veteran Suicide: Methodology" (November 13, 2007), pp. 1–2; and www.cbsnews.com/stories/2007/11/13/cbsnews_investigates/printable3498625.shtml, pp. 1–2. CBS News asked all states for their suicide data, based on death records, for veterans and nonveterans. Forty-five states responded. In 2005, in those states reporting, there were at least 6256 suicides among those who served in the armed forces.

134. Lolita C. Baldor, "Army Desertion Rate Highest Since 1980," *Lafayette Journal and Courier* (Lafayette, IN) (November 17, 2007), p. A13.

135. Department of Health and Human Services (DHHS), "Indian Health Service Year 2007 Profile," (Based on 2000–2006 data). Available at http://info.ihs.gov/Files/ProfileSheet-July2007.doc.

136. DHHS, "Indian Health Service 2007 Profile."

137. Charles W. Grim, U.S. Department of Health & Human Services, "Statement of the Indian Health Service" (March 15, 2007), p. 2 of 3. Available at www.dhhs.gov/asl/testify/2007/03/t20070315a.html.

138. Levitan et al., *Programs in Aid of the Poor*, pp. 99–100.

139. Ibid.

140. Department of Health and Human Services, Health Resources and Services Administration, "Hill–Burton Free and Reduced Cost Health Care." Available at www.hrsa.gov/hillburton/default.htm, p. 1.

141. National Alliance on Mental Illness (NAMI), "Policy Topics: The Federal Mental Health Courts Program: Medicaid and Mental Health Care." Available at www.nami.org/Template.cfm"Section=Issue_Spotlights&template=/ContentManagement/html.

142. William G. LeFurgy, "A Reversal of Fortune for Mentally Ill Patients," *Lafayette Journal and Courier* (Lafayette, IN) (August 23, 2007), p. A7.

143. National Alliance on Mental Illness (NAMI).

144. "Bill Signed to Expand Head Start Program," *Lafayette Journal and Courier* (Lafayette, IN) (December 13, 2007), p. A3.

145. Department of Health and Human Services, Administration for Children and Families, "2005–2007 All-Purpose Table," p. 2 of 8.

146. Handler and Hasenfeld, quoting A. Pallas and Y. Nonoyama, "K–12 Education in New York City," p. 6.

147. Diana Jean Schemo, "A Leaner Year is Proposed for Schools," *New York Times* (February 7, 2006). Available at www.nytimes.com/2006/02/07/politics/07educ.html?_r=1&oref=slogin, pp. 1–2.

148. Axinn and Stern, *Social Welfare*, p. 337.

149. "Integration: The Impossible Dream?" *The Week* (July 20, 2007), p. 1.

150. Pearson Education, publishing as Infoplease.com 2000–2007, "A Timeline of Recent Worldwide School Shootings," pp. 1–3.

151. Ibid.

152. Department of Education, "Highlights of the Final Report of the Secretary of Education's Commission on the Future of Higher education: a Test of Leadership—charting the Future of U.S. Higher Education" (September 2006), pp. 1–2. Available at www.ed.gov/print/about/bdscomm/list/hiedfuture/pre-pub-report-highlights.html.

153. Office of Juvenile Justice, *Statistical Briefing Book*, "Law Enforcement and Juvenile Crime." Available at http://ojjdp.ncjrs.org/ojstatbb/crime/qa05101.asp"qaDate=2005, pp. 1–2.

154. Federal Advisory Committee on Juvenile Justice, "Annual Recommendations Report, August 2007." Available at http://facjj.org/annualreports/ccFACJJ%20Report508.pdf, p. 6.

155. Snyder and Sickmund, *Highlights*, pp. 1–8.

156. Department of Health and Human Services, Administration for Children and Families, "All-Purpose Table 2004–2007," p. 2 of 8.

157. Campaign for Justice, "Report March 2007." Available at www.campaign4youthjustice.org/Downloads/NEWS/JP1014Consequence-Summary.pdf, pp. 6–10.

158. Rank, pp. 116–117.

159. Rank, pp. 117–118.

160. Department of Justice, Office of Justice Programs, "Probation and Parole Statistics: Summary Findings." Available at www.ojp.usdoj.gov/bus/pandp.htm, pp. 1–2.

161. Shannon McCaffrey, "Prisons Face Growing Population of Elderly Inmates," *Lafayette Journal and Courier* (Lafayette, IN) (September 30, 2007), p. A11.

162. Ibid.

163. Charles C. Haynes, "Danger Signs from 2007 for Religious Freedom in 2008," *Lafayette Journal and Courier* (Lafayette, IN) (January 9, 2008), p. A7.

164. Greg Palast, "New Orleans Two Years After …," *Progressive Populist* (October 2, 2007), pp. 8–9.

165. Ibid.

166. Steve Neavling, "Blood Trial Done in Minority-Heavy Cities," *Lafayette Journal and Courier* (Lafayette, IN) (December 22, 2007), p. A3.

167. World Hunger Notes. Available at www.worldhunger.org/articles/06/us/tanf.htm.

168. "Walling off the Southern Border," *The Week* (December 7, 2007), p. 13.

169. "The Diddly Awards," *Mother Jones* (November–December 2006), p. 14.

170. June Axinn and Mark J. Stern, *Social Welfare: A History of American Response to Need* 7th ed. (Boston: Allyn and Bacon, 2008), p. 337.

171. United States District Court for the District of Columbia, *Cobell et al. v. Norton*, Civil Action No. 96-1285 (RCL). Available at www.indiantrust.com/_pdfs/20050712/MemorexNoticeyoClass.pdf, pp. 1, 2.

172. Ibid.

173. CNN.com, Law Center, "Justices Uphold Ban on Abortion Procedure." Available at http://cnn.com/2007/LAW/04/18/scotus.abortion/index, p. 1.

174. Eleanor J. Bader, "Glee in the Anti-Abortion Crowd," *The Progressive* (September 2007), pp. 24–26.

175. Jim Hightower and Phillip Frazer, eds. *Hightower Lowdown*, vol. 9, no. 7 (July 2007), p. 3.

176. "Breakthrough Year Seen for Gay Rights Bills," Gay.com. Available at www.gay.com/news/election/article.html?2007/02/26/1html, p. 2 of 2.

177. Axinn and Stern, *Social Welfare*, p. 339.

178. U.S. Department of Health and Human Services, CPS Data 2004, March 2006. "The Supply and Demand of Professional Social Workers: Providing Long-Term Care Services: A Report to Congress." Available at http://aspe.hhs.gov/daltcp/reports/2006/swsupply.htm.

Chapter 15

1. Catherine Rampell. "Great recession: A brief etymology [Blog entry]." *Economix*. New York, NY: The New York Times, 2009. Vol. 2011.

2. Josh Bivens. *Worst economic crisis since the Great Depression? By a long shot*. Washington, U.S.: Economic Policy Institute, 2010.

3. Chris Isidore, "The great recession," *CNNMoney* (Atlanta, GA, March 25, 2009). Available online at http://money.cnn.com/2009/03/25/news/economy/depression_comparisons/index.htm.

4. Michael Ettlinger, and Michael Linden. "Who's to Blame for the Deficit Numbers." (2009). Available online at http://www.americanprogress.org/issues/2009/08/deficit_numbers.html.

5. U.S. Congress, "American Recovery and Reinvestment Act." (Washington, D.C.: U.S. Congress, 2009). Available online at http://www.gpo.gov/fdsys/pkg/PLAW-111publ5/content-detail.html.

6. Office of Community Planning and Development, "The 2009 annual homeless assessment report." (Washington, D.C.: U.S. Department of Housing and Urban Development, 2010). Available online at http://portal.hud.gov/hudportal/HUD?src=/press/press_releases_media_advisories/2010/HUDNo.10-124.

7. Christopher J. O'Leary. "UI in the safety net: Lessons from the Great Depression." *Rethinking the Safety Net after the Great Recession Symposium*. Washington, D.C.: Brookings Institution, 2011.

8. Ibid.

9. Michael Peltier, "Florida to test all welfare recipients for drugs," *Reuters.com* (New York, NY, May 31, 2011). Available online at http://www.reuters.com/article/2011/05/31/us-florida-welfare-drugs-idUSTRE74U6W320110531.

10. CNN Wire Staff, "Florida governor defends measure requiring drug tests for welfare," *CNNPolitics* (Atlanta, GA, June 5, 2011). Available online at http://articles.cnn.com/2011-06-05/politics/florida.welfare.drug.testing_1_drug-testing-tanf-welfare-recipients?_s=PM:POLITICS.

11. Elise Gould, and Heidi Shierholz. *A lost decade: Poverty and income trends paint a bleak picture for working families*. Washington, D.C.: Economic Policy Institute, 2010.

12. Caroline Ratcliffe, and Signe-Mary McKernan. *Child poverty persistence: Facts and consequences*. Washington, D.C.: Urban Institute, 2010.

13. Ibid.

14. Food and Nutrition Service, "Supplemental nutrition assistance program (SNAP) monthly data." (Washington, D.C.: U.S. Department of Agriculture, 2011). Available online at http://www.fns.usda.gov/pd/SNAPmain.htm.

15. Ibid.

16. Mark Nord, et al. *Household food security in the United States, 2009*. Washington, D.C.: Economc Research Service (U.S. Department of Agriculture), 2010.

17. Ibid.

18. Food and Nutrition Service, "WIC program annual summary." (Washington, D.C.: U.S. Department of Agriculture, 2011). Available online at http://www.fns.usda.gov/pd/wicmain.htm.

19. Federal Register, "Supplemental nutrition assistance program, regulation restructuring: Issuance regulation update and reorganization to reflect the end of coupon issuance systems." (Washington, D.C.: U.S. Government Printing Office, 2010). Available online at http://www.gpo.gov/fdsys/pkg/FR-2010-12-29/pdf/2010-32686.pdf.

20. ibid., "Food stamp program: Eligibility and certification provisions of the Farm Security and Rural Investment Act of 2002." (Washington, D.C.: U.S. Government Printing Office, 2010). Available online at http://www.gpo.gov/fdsys/pkg/FR-2010-05-04/pdf/2010-10391.pdf.

21. Larry J. Siegel. *Criminology: The core*. 3rd ed. (Belmont, CA: Thomson/Wadsworth, 2008).

22. Children's Defense Fund. *State of America's children® 2010 report*. Washington, D.C.: Children's Defense Fund, 2010.

23. "White House homepage on education." (Washington, D.C., 2009). U.S. Office of the President. Available online at http://www.whitehouse.gov/issues/education.

24. Henry M. Levin. *Levin, H.M. (2000). A comprehensive framework for evaluating educational vouchers*. New York, NY: National Center for the Study of Privatization in Education (Teachers College, Columbia Universtiy), 2001.

25. Joseph L. Bast. "Why conservatives and libertarians should support school vouchers." *The Independent Review* 7.2 (2002): 265–76.

26. Ibid.

27. Tom Moroney, and Jeffrey Young, "Michelle Rhee resigns as D.C. schools chancellor," *Bloomberg Businessweek* (New York, NY, October 13, 2010). Available online at http://www.businessweek.com/news/2010-10-13/michelle-rhee-resigns-as-d-c-schools-chancellor.html.

28. William G. Howell, and Paul E. Peterson. *The education gap: Vouchers and urban schools*. (Washington, D.C.: Brookings Institution Press, 2002).

29. *Jonathan Kozol. Savage inequalities: Children in America's schools. (New York, NY: Harper Perennial, 1992)*.

30. William G. Howell, and Paul E. Peterson. *The education gap: Vouchers and urban schools*. (Washington, D.C.: Brookings Institution Press, 2002).

31. Ibid.

32. Federal Bureau of Investigation, "Preliminary annual uniform crime report, January–December 2010." (Washington, D.C.: FBI, 2011). Available online at http://www.fbi.gov/about-us/cjis/ucr/crime-in-the-u.s/2010/preliminary-annual-ucr-jan-dec-2010.

33. Ryan S. King. *Disparity by geography: The war on drugs in America's cities*. Washington, D.C.: The Sentencing Project, 2008.

34. Ibid.

35. Ibid.

36. Michelle Alexander. *The new Jim Crow: Mass incarceration in the age of colorblindness*. (New York, NY: New Press, 2010).

37. Ibid.

38. Lauren E. Glaze, "Correctional populations in the United States, 2009," (NCJ 231681). (Washington, D.C.: U.S. Department of Justice, 2010). Available online at http://bjs.ojp.usdoj.gov/index.cfm?ty=pbdetail&iid=2316.

39. James Vicini, "Supreme court orders California prisoner release," *Reuters.com* (New York, NY, May 23, 2011). Available online at http://www.reuters.com/article/2011/05/23/us-california-prisons-court-idUSTRE74M3DQ20110523.

40. Joseph L. Bast. "Why conservatives and libertarians should support school vouchers." *The Independent Review* 7.2 (2002): 265–76.

41. National Association of Drug Court Professionals. "What are drug courts?". (Alexandria, VA, 2011). NADCP. Available online at http://www.nadcp.org/learn/what-are-drug-courts.

42. Ibid.

43. Office of the White House Press Secretary, "President Obama releases national strategy to reduce drug use and its consequences." (Washington, D.C.: Office of the White House Press Secretary, 2010). Available online at http://www.whitehouse.gov/the-press-office/

president-obama-releases-national-strategy-reduce-drug-use-and-its-consequences.

44. R. Kochhar. *In two years of economic recovery, women lost jobs, men found them* (The Pew Research Center, Social and Demographic Trends, 2011).

45. Ibid.

46. Ibid.

47. Bureau of Labor Statistics, "Women in the labor force: A databook," (Report 1026). (Washington, D.C.: U.S. Government Printing Office, 2010). Available online at http://www.bls.gov/cps/wlf-databook-2010.pdf.

48. Edana E. Lewis. "The EEOC and trends for working women: Current and emerging issues." *2007 National Equal Opportunity Professional Development Forum*. U.S. Equal Employment Opportunity Commission, 2007.

49. Ibid.

50. S. G. Stolberg, "Obama signs equal-pay legislation," *The New York Times* (New York, NY, January 30, 2009). Available online at http://www.nytimes.com.

51. Kristin D. Sostowski. "U.S. Supreme Court rules in Ledbetter v. Goodyear Tire and Rubber Co. that title VII pay discrimination claims must be filed within EEOC statute of limitations." Jul. 6 (2007). Available online at http://www.gibbonslaw.com/news_publications/articles.php?action=display_publication&publication_id=2173.

52. Ibid.

53. Ibid.

54. U.S. Census Bureau, "Civilian Population—Employment Status by Sex, Race, and Ethnicity: 1970 to 2009 (Table 586)." (Washington, D.C.: U.S. Government Printing Office, 2011). Available online at http://www.census.gov/compendia/statab/2011edition.html.

55. Ibid.

56. U.S. Bureau of Labor Statistics, "Economic news release, Table A-2, Employment status of the civilian population by race, sex, and age." (Washington, D.C.: U.S. Bureau of Labor Statistics, 2011). Available online at http://data.bls.gov/cgi-bin/print.pl/news.release/empsit.t02.htm.

57. Carmen DeNavas-Walt, Bernadette D. Proctor, and Jessica C. Smith, "Income, poverty, and health insurance coverage in the United States: 2009." (Washington, D.C.: U.S. Census Bureau, 2010). Available online at http://www.census.gov/hhes/www/poverty/data/incpovhlth/2009/index.html.

58. Ibid.

59. Ibid.

60. Debbie Gruenstein Bocian, Wei Li, and Keith S. Ernst. *Foreclosures by race and ethnicity: The demographics of a crisis*. Washington, D.C.: Center for Responsible Lending, 2010.

61. Ibid.

62. Ibid.

63. Barbara Ehrenreich, and Dedrick Muhammad, "The recession's racial divide [Op-ed]," *The New York Times* (New York, NY, September 13, 2009). Available online at http://www.nytimes.com/2009/09/13/opinion/13ehrenreich.html?_r=2.

64. Ibid.

65. Michael Lewis. *The big short: Inside the doomsday machine*. 1st ed. (New York, NY: W.W. Norton, 2010).

66. William J. Wilson. *The truly disadvantaged: The inner city, the underclass, and public policy*. Paperback ed. (Chicago, IL: University of Chicago Press, 1990).

67. 'Lectric Law Library. "Summary and analysis: Defense of Marriage Act, 1996." (Carson City, NV, 2011). 'Lectric Law Library. Available online at http://www.lectlaw.com/files/leg23.htm.

68. *Diana Hess, et al. The 14th amendment and same-sex marriage: Do laws and constitutions that prohibit same-sex marriage violate the 14th amendment? Denver, CO.*

69. Ibid.

70. Ibid.

71. Jonathan Rauch. *Gay marriage: Why it is good for gays, good for straights, and good for America*. (New York, NY: Times Books/Henry Holt and Co., 2004).

72. Ibid.

73. Jonathan Rauch. *Gay marriage: Why it is good for gays, good for straights, and good for America*. (New York, NY: Times Books/Henry Holt and Co., 2004).

74. Ibid.

75. Brian Montopoli, "Obama administration will no longer defend DOMA," *CBSNews.om* (New York, NY, February 23, 2011). Available online at http://www.cbsnews.com/8301-503544_162-20035398-503544.html?tag=mncol;lst;1.

76. "Obama extends benefits for gay federal employees," *Reuters* (New York, NY, June 2, 2010). Available online at http://www.reuters.com/article/2010/06/02/us-usa-gay-rights-idUSTRE6516WD20100602.

77. Ibid.

78. Ibid.

79. William Branigin, Debbi Wilgoren, and Perry Bacon, "Obama signs DADT repeal before big, emotional crowd," *The Washington Post* (Washington, U.S., 2010/12/22). Available online at http://www.washingtonpost.com/wp-dyn/content/article/2010/12/22/AR2010122201888.html.

80. "Gay marriage: Where's Mr. Obama? [Editorial]," *The New York Times* (New York, NY, June 26, 2011). Available online at http://www.nytimes.com/2011/06/27/opinion/27mon2.html.

81. F. Newport. *For the first time, majority of Americans favor legal gay marriage*: Gallup Organization, 2011.

82. Jackie Calmes, "Democrats resisting Obama on social security," *The New York Times* (New York, NY, February 23, 2009, 2009). Available online at http://www.nytimes.com/2009/02/23/us/politics/23social.html.

83. U.S. House of Representatives Budget Committee, "The path to prosperity: Restoring America's promise, Fiscal Year 2012 Budget Resolution." (Washington, U.S.: U.S. Government Printing Office, 2011). Available online at http://budget.house.gov/UploadedFiles/PathToProsperityFY2012.pdf.

84. Michelle Alexander. *The new Jim Crow: Mass incarceration in the age of colorblindness*. (New York, NY: New Press, 2010).

85. P.N. Van de Water, and A. Sherman. *Social security keeps 20 million Americans out of poverty: A state-by-state analysis*: The Center on Budget and Policy Priorities, 2010.

86. A. Cawthorne. *The not-so-golden years: Confronting elderly poverty and improving seniors' economic security*: The Center for American Progress, 2010.

87. Social Security Administration, "One time economic recovery payment, 2009," (SSA Publication No. 05-10519).

(Washington, U.S.: U.S. Government Printing Office, 2009). Available online at http://www.socialsecurity .gov/pubs/10519.pdf.

88. *Ibid.* "Annual Report of the Supplemental Security Income Program." (Washington, U.S., 2010). U.S. Government Printing Office. Available online at http:// www.ssa.gov/oact/ssir/SSI10/index.html.

89. Ibid.

90. Bazelon Center for Mental Health Law. "Letter to President Obama: Letter from various advocacy organizations requesting that President Obama not cut SSI benefits for children with mental disabilities." (2011). Available online at http://www.bazelon.org.

91. Tea Party Patriots. "Tea party patriots mission statement and core values." 2011) http://www.teapartypatriots.org/ Mission.aspx.

92. "Tea party movement," *The New York Times* (New York, NY, March 2, 2011). Available online at http://topics .nytimes.com/top/reference/timestopics/subjects/t/tea_ party_movement/index.html?scp=1-spot&sq=tea%20 party&st=cse.

93. C. Hulse, "Budget deal to cut $38 billion averts shut-down," *The New York Times* (New York, NY, April 8, 2011). Available online at http://www.nytimes.com.

94. Kristin D. Sostowski. "U.S. Supreme Court rules in Ledbetter v. Goodyear Tire and Rubber Co. that title VII pay discrimination claims must be filed within EEOC statute of limitations." Jul. 6 (2007). Available online at http://www .gibbonslaw.com/news_publications/articles .php?action=display_publication&publication_id=2173.

95. S. Wilson, "Obama: U.S. had responsibility to act in Libya," *The Washington Post* March 28, 2011). Available online at www.washingtonpost.com.

96. Robert Burns, and Pauline Jelinek, "Obama rules out 'land invasion' in Libya," *Associated Press* (New York, NY, March 23, 2011). Available online at http://www .ap.org/.

97. M. Donig, "Arab uprisings may pave the way for extremism," *The Jerusalem Post*?? ??, 2011, 2011). Available online at http://www.jpost.com/MiddleEast/ Article.aspx?id=226707.

98. Ibid.

99. Jerome H. Schiele. "Literature search in the journal, *Social Work*, 2009–2011." Athens, GA: University of Georgia, 2011.

100. Harry Specht, and Mark E. Courtney. *Unfaithful angels: How social work has abandoned its mission.* (New York, NY: Free Press, 1994).

101. Howard J. Karger, "Income Maintenance Programs and the Reagan Domestic Agenda," *Journal of Sociology and Social Work*, Vol. 19, no. 1 (March 1992), p. 51.

102. Joel A. Devine and James D. Wright, *The Greatest of Evils: Urban Poverty and the American Underclass* (New York: Aldine de Gruyter, 1993), p. 80.

103. David Macarov, *Work and Welfare: The Unholy Alliance* (Beverly Hills, CA: Sage Publications, 1980), p. 201.

Photo Credits

Chapter 1: p. 1, Roger Viollet/Getty Images; p. 21, Ocean/Corbis.

Chapter 2: p. 29, Courtesy University of Michigan Photo Services; p. 43, Joel Stettenheim/Corbis.

Chapter 3: p. 58, Geoff Brightling/Dorling Kindersley, Ltd; p. 79, Musee d'Histoire de la Medecine, Paris, France/Archives Charmet/ The Bridgeman Art Library.

Chapter 4: p. 83, Private Collection/The Bridgeman Art Library; p. 105, The Gallery Collection/Corbis.

Chapter 5: p. 117, North Wind Picture Archives/Alamy; p. 130, SuperStock/SuperStock.

Chapter 6: p. 151, Select Images/Alamy; p.155, Bettmann/Corbis.

Chapter 7: p. 189, Bettmann/Corbis; p. 213, Underwood & Underwood/Corbis.

Chapter 8: p. 225, Bettmann/Corbis; p. 247, Bettmann/Corbis.

Chapter 9: p. 260, Bettmann/Corbis; p. 266, Corbis.

Chapter 10: p. 295, AP Images; p. 316, AP Images.

Chapter 11: p. 330, Bettmann/Corbis; p. 345, Bettmann/Corbis.

Chapter 12: p. 357, Bettmann/Corbis; p. 376, Robert Brenner/PhotoEdit, Inc.

Chapter 13: p. 387, Denis Paquin/AP Images; p. 408, Ira Wyman/Sygma/Corbis.

Chapter 14: p. 429, Neville Elder/Corbis; p. 432, Manuel Balce Ceneta/AP Images.

Chapter 15: p. 456, STAFF/Reuters/Corbis; p. 473, Kristoffer Tripplaar/Pool/Corbis.

Index

ANSWER KEY TO PRACTICE TEST

Below are the answers to the multiple choice practice tests.

Chapter 1
1.) B   2.) C   3.) A   4.) D   5.) D   6.) B

Chapter 2
1.) C   2.) B   3.) C   4.) B   5.) B   6.) C

Chapter 3
1.) A   2.) A   3.) A   4.) A   5.) D   6.) B

Chapter 4
1.) B   2.) A   3.) A   4.) B   5.) C   6.) A

Chapter 5
1.) A   2.) B   3.) A   4.) A   5.) B   6.) D

Chapter 6
1.) C   2.) B   3.) A   4.) B   5.) B   6.) A

Chapter 7
1.) B   2.) B   3.) C   4.) A   5.) D   6.) B

Chapter 8
1.) D   2.) C   3.) B   4.) D   5.) A   6.) B

Chapter 9
1.) A   2.) B   3.) B   4.) B   5.) A   6.) B

Chapter 10
1.) C   2.) A   3.) D   4.) C   5.) B   6.) A

Chapter 11
1.) B   2.) D   3.) D   4.) C   5.) B   6.) A

Chapter 12
1.) A   2.) B   3.) B   4.) A   5.) C   6.) D

Chapter 13
1.) B   2.) D   3.) C   4.) B   5.) D   6.) A

Chapter 14
1.) A   2.) C   3.) B   4.) A   5.) C   6.) A

Chapter 15
1.) D   2.) C   3.) A   4.) D   5.) C   6.) C

ANSWER KEY TO PRACTICE TEST

Below are the answers to the multiple-choice practice tests.

Chapter 1
1-B 2-C 3-A 4-D 5-D 6-B

Chapter 2
1-C 2-B 3-C 4-B 5-B 6-C

Chapter 3
1-A 2-A 3-A 4-A 5-D 6-B

Chapter 4
1-B 2-A 3-A 4-B 5-C 6-A

Chapter 5
1-A 2-B 3-A 4-A 5-B 6-D

Chapter 6
1-C 2-B 3-A 4-B 5-D 6-A

Chapter 7
1-B 2-C 3-A 4-A 5-D 6-B

Chapter 8
1-D 2-C 3-B 4-D 5-A 6-B

Chapter 9
1-A 2-A 3-D 4-B 5-A 6-D

Chapter 10
1-C 2-A 3-D 4-C 5-B 6-A

Chapter 11
1-B 2-D 3-D 4-C 5-A 6-A

Chapter 12
1-A 2-B 3-B 4-A 5-C 6-D

Chapter 13
1-D 2-D 3-C 4-D 5-D 6-A

Chapter 14
1-A 2-C 3-A 4-A 5-D 6-A

Chapter 15
1-D 2-C 3-A 4-D 5-C 6-C